Excellence in Public Relations and Communication Management

Edited by

James E. Grunig
University of Maryland

with

David M. Dozier
San Diego State University

William P. Ehling
Syracuse University

Larissa A. Grunig
University of Maryland

Fred C. Repper
*Public Relations Consultant,
Ingram, Texas*

Jon White
*Management Consultant,
Bedford, United Kingdom*

 LAWRENCE ERLBAUM ASSOCIATES, PUBLISHERS
1992   **Hillsdale, New Jersey**   **Hove and London**

Lawrence Erlbaum Associates, Inc., Publishers
365 Broadway
Hillsdale, New Jersey 07642

Library of Congress Cataloging-in-Publication Data

Excellence in public relations and communication management / edited
    by James E. Grunig with David M. Dozier . . . [et al.].
        p.   cm. — (Communication textbook series. Public relations)
    Product of a research project of the IABC Research Foundation.
    Includes bibliographical references and indexes.
    ISBN 0-8058-0226-6. — ISBN 0-8058-0227-4 (pbk.)
    1. Public relations.   2. Communication in management.   I. Grunig,
James E.   II. IABC Research Foundation.   III. Series.
HD59.E95   1992
659.2 — dc20   92-8200
                                                                  CIP

Printed in the United States of America
10   9   8   7   6   5   4

This book is dedicated to the 10th anniversary of the International Association of Business Communications (IABC) Research Foundation in 1992. The foundation took a chance on excellence, and the authors express their appreciation to the men and women on the board and staff of the foundation for their support and acceptance of our work.

The IABC Research Foundation was founded in 1982 as the research and education arm of the 11,500-member IABC. The foundation sponsors educational and research projects that advance the professional development of organizational communicators. Its largest project has been the study, Excellence in Public Relations and Communication Management, from which this book has resulted.

Contents

Contributors

Jody Buffington is director of advertising and sales promotion for Blue Cross and Blue Shield of Maryland. She holds a masters degree from the University of Maryland.

David M. Dozier is a professor in the Department of Journalism at San Diego State University and a member of the excellence team. Dozier holds a PhD from Stanford University.

William P. Ehling was professor and head of the public relations department in the S. I. Newhouse School of Public Communication at Syracuse University. He is now retired.

James E. Grunig is a professor in the College of Journalism at the University of Maryland, College Park. He is the director of the IABC excellence project for which this book was produced. Grunig holds a PhD from the University of Wisconsin.

Larissa A. Grunig is an associate professor in the College of Journalism at the University of Maryland, College Park and a member of the excellence team. Grunig holds a PhD from the University of Maryland.

Linda Childers Hon is an assistant professor of communication at the Florida Institute of Technology. She is a doctoral candidate at the University of Maryland and a former research assistant on the excellence project.

Fred C. Repper is the retired vice-president of public relations for Gulf States Utilities, Beaumont, Texas and a member of the excellence team. He now works as a public relations consultant.

K. Sriramesh is an assistant professor of communication at Purdue

University. He holds a PhD from the University of Maryland and is a former research assistant on the excellence project.

Jon White is a consultant for several programs granting degrees in public relations in the United Kingdom. He formerly taught public relations at the Cranfield School of Management in the United Kingdom and at Mount Saint Vincent's University in Halifax, Nova Scotia, Canada.

Preface

In 1982, the International Association of Business Communicators (IABC) made a commitment to research in business communication and public relations when it formed the IABC Research Foundation. In 1985, the foundation committed itself to the largest research project in the history of public relations — a project that has come to be called the excellence project. I was fortunate to be the director of the team chosen to conduct the research. The purpose of the excellence project was to answer two fundamental questions about public relations: What are the characteristics of an excellent communication department? How does excellent public relations make an organization more effective, and how much is that contribution worth economically?

The excellence team began its work with a thorough review of the literature in public relations and related disciplines relevant to these research questions. This book is the product of that first stage of the research. The team then developed a program of survey and qualitative research to test the propositions derived from the literature review. The results of that research will be published in additional books.

Authors or editors almost always are enthusiastic about their product when they send it to the publisher. The "beating your head against the wall theory" may explain the reason: "If you beat your head against the wall long enough and hard enough you will think it was a good experience when you quit because it feels so good not to be hitting yourself any longer." Yet, I cannot help but believe this book will be a seminal book in the history of public relations.

What started out as a routine review of the literature turned out to be a massive effort to build theory. Members of the research team identified the concepts they thought would be relevant to our research, and then assigned chapters related to each of these concepts to different members. In some chapters, we have integrated research that has been available in public relations for some time. In other chapters, we have built new theory from the related disciplines of sociology, psychology, management, marketing, women's studies, philosophy, anthropology, and communication. The results have exceeded my most optimistic hopes for the project.

What started as a literature review has ended in what I believe is a general theory of public relations—a theory that integrates most of the wide range of ideas about and practices of communication management in organizations. The general theory integrates most of the available body of knowledge in public relations and expands it to an even more powerful body of knowledge. That theory has provided guidance for the empirical stages of the excellence research project, and we hope that it will provide guidance for other public relations scholars. In addition, I believe the general theory provides a theoretical explanation for the best current practice of public relations—which our theory says is excellent—that organizations and society do not understand or appreciate.

ACKNOWLEDGMENTS

Lest this preface begin to sound like press agentry, one of the models of public relations that characterize mediocre public relations, I would like to thank the many people who made this project possible. My thanks go first to the members of the excellence team and graduate assistants who produced this book. In addition to the authors of chapters, my thanks go to Jane Ballinger and Jo Nell Mietenin, graduate assistants at San Diego State University. Then my thanks go to the IABC members and staff who made this project possible, especially the chairs of the foundation board (Fred Halperin, Wilma Mathews, Linda Stewart, and Lou Williams) and the foundation managers (Erin Stevenson and Maria Forte) who have worked closely with the team. You admonished the team to underpromise and overproduce. We believe we overproduced when we wrote this book; we hope you consider it worth the wait.

James E. Grunig

1 Communication, Public Relations, and Effective Organizations: An Overview of the Book

James E. Grunig
University of Maryland

Throughout the world, but especially in Western democracies, thousands and perhaps millions of men and women perform communication duties for organizations. They counsel managers, manage communication programs, write, edit, design publications, produce videotapes, do research, communicate interpersonally, and perform many similar tasks. Although these tasks may seem commonplace, three important questions seldom are asked about them:

1. When and why are the efforts of communication practitioners effective?
2. How do organizations benefit from effective public relations?
3. Why do organizations practice public relations in different ways?

Although there is no shortage of opinions on these issues, the opinions differ widely and few of them are based on scientific research or sound theory. In fact, most communication scholars specializing in public relations would place these three questions among the great unresolved problems of social science.

The three questions are of great theoretical interest to researchers, but they may be of even greater practical concern to working public relations professionals. Practitioners must plan and defend public relations programs. Defending a communication program is a difficult task, however, when organizations often expect miracles from public relations and there is little theory to tell practitioners what to do, what effects are possible from organizational communication programs, and why.

The IABC Research Foundation saw the importance of these questions to the future of public relations and organizational communication when it sought research to answer the question: How, why, and to what extent does communication affect the achievement of organizational objectives? This "bottom-line question" is the focus of this book. The book is part of a long-term research project funded by the IABC Research Foundation to find answers to this question. The authors of chapters in the book are members of the research team conducting the IABC project. The project has two major stages – a theoretical and an empirical stage. This book is the product of the theoretical stage. Additional books and publications will report the results of the empirical stage.

Excellence in Public Relations and Communications Management resulted from a comprehensive literature review to support and refine a theory that is being tested empirically in the research phase of the project. Too often social scientists leap into the empirical stage of research without thoroughly studying the research and theorizing that has come before. Seldom, therefore, do those social scientists build a solid theory from the building blocks provided by other scholars.

We have searched the literature in communications, public relations, management, organizational psychology and sociology, social and cognitive psychology, feminist studies, political science, decision making, and culture to produce this book. The result is a theory of excellence and effectiveness in public relations that is based on research reviewed in this book. We believe that we have produced the first general theory of public relations – a theory that integrates the many theories and research results existing in the field. Yet this book is only the first stage in the development of the theory. The research team is testing and revising the theory through an international survey of over 300 organizations in the United States, Canada, and the United Kingdom and through additional qualitative research.

We may have a different theory when the research is completed. Science builds theory piece by piece. Seldom is a theory completely overturned. Rather it is shaped, revised, and improved to make it more useful for solving problems and directing human behavior – in this case directing the behavior of public relations practitioners and solving the problems they face. In this book, therefore, we offer the best answers we have to the three questions posed at the beginning of this chapter. This is what we know now: our hypotheses. After completing the research, we may know more or know it better, but this book represents our interpretation of what social science theory and research tell us today about the nature of effective organizational communication, excellent public relations departments, and the contribution that effective communication makes to successful organizations.

THE BUILDING BLOCKS OF THE THEORY

This book is organized in five major parts. The chapters in Parts I through V describe the building blocks that went into the development of the theory. In searching for these building blocks, we began with the question posed by the IABC Research Foundation: How does communication affect the achievement of organizational objectives? That question is the focus of Part I, which constructs the basic theory of effectiveness that connects the parts of our general theory of public relations. The central chapter of Part I, and perhaps of the book, is chapter 3, which discusses what it means for an organization to be effective and explains theoretically how effective public relations makes organizations more effective.

We learned quickly, however, that the one question posed by the IABC Research Foundation—the *effectiveness* question—was not enough. Thus, we added what we call the *excellence* question: How must public relations be practiced and the communication function be organized for it to contribute the most to organizational effectiveness. To answer the excellence question, we first had to determine how public relations should be managed for it to be effective in meeting public relations objectives. This is what we call the *program* level of analysis in Part I: the strategic management of individual communication programs.

We realized, also, that many organizations do not manage communication programs strategically and that these programs do not make their organizations more effective. Thus, we examined literature related to excellence in public relations management and for the organization as a whole. Peters and Waterman (1982) discovered that excellently managed corporations have characteristics in common that make them more successful than other organizations. The same is true for communication departments in organizations. Not all public relations programs are effective, only the excellent ones. And the excellent programs share characteristics that are suggested in the literature. We discuss these characteristics in Part II, which deals with the departmental level of the theory.

The program level tells us how effective public relations programs should be managed. The departmental level tells us the characteristics of departments that most often manage communication in this way. The problem that remained, however, was to determine the conditions that are associated with organizations that have excellent communication departments. The conditions that bring about excellent public relations are suggested by research on organizations and their environments, the organizational-level variables described in Part III.

The first three parts answer the "how" and "why" parts of the original question posed by the IABC Research Foundation: How and why does public relations affect the achievement of organizational objectives. In Part IV, we address the bottom-line question also posed in the request for proposal: how much effective communication is worth to an organization.

Given this overview of how the four parts of the book are connected to one another in a coherent theory, we turn to definitions of public relations and communication and then to an overview of each part of the theory.

SOME DEFINITIONS

Thus far in this chapter we have used the terms *public relations, communication management,* and *organizational communication* interchangeably. We have done so intentionally, recognizing that many practitioners will disagree with our definitions. Although public relations is probably the oldest concept used to describe the communication activities of organizations, many organizations now use such terms as *business communication* and *public affairs* to describe these activities—in part because of the negative connotations of public relations.

Many practitioners define communication more broadly than public relations. They see communication as the management of the organization's communication functions. They see public relations as one of several more narrow functions, especially as publicity, promotion, media relations, or marketing support.

Others, in contrast, see public relations as the broader term and apply communication narrowly to techniques used to produce such products as press releases, publications, or audiovisual materials. Many in the latter school also see public relations as a policy-making function of organizations, which sometimes but not always uses communication techniques in making or announcing policy decisions. Often these practitioners use the term *public affairs* to broaden public relations to include the interaction with groups and government that leads to public policy.

Following Grunig and Hunt (1984, p. 6), we define *public relations* as the "management of communication between an organization and its publics." This definition equates public relations and communication management. Public relations/communication management is broader than communication technique and broader than specialized public relations programs such as media relations or publicity. Public relations and communication management describe the overall planning, execution, and evaluation of an organization's communication with both external and internal publics—groups that affect the ability of an organization to meet its goals.

In that sense, public relations/communication management is also organizational communication, although we use that term in a broader sense than it has come to be used in the academic world. In the academic world, especially in departments of speech communication, organizational communication largely has been used to describe the communication of individuals inside organizations. That is, organizational communication describes how top managers, subordinates, middle-level managers, and other employees communicate with each other in an organization.

Scholars of organizational communication in that narrow sense often pay some attention to external communication, internal publications, and systems of communication among groups in organizations; but their major interest is in interpersonal communication among individual members of an organization. We define organizational communication/public relations as communication *managed* by an organization, especially as communication managed for the organization by communication specialists. Organizational communication, therefore, may be either internal or external.[1]

Finally, some practitioners argue that our definition of public relations/ organizational communication as managed communication excludes the role of public relations in counseling management and formulating public policy for an organization. They argue that public relations is more than communication.

We respond that public relations managers should be involved in decision making by the group of senior managers who control an organization, which we call the *dominant coalition* throughout this book. Although public relations managers often vote in policy decisions made by the dominant coalition, we argue that their specialized role in the process of making those decisions is as communicators.

Public relations managers who are part of the dominant coalition communicate the views of publics to other senior managers, and they must communicate with publics to be able to do so. They also communicate to other senior managers the likely consequences of policy decisions after communicating with publics affected by the potential policy.

The term public affairs, therefore, applies to fewer communication activities than does public relations/communication management. Public affairs applies to communication with government officials and other

---

[1]Some of the communication behaviors studied by scholars in speech communication can be included in our definition of organizational communication/public relations. Communication behaviors of individuals would be included in our broader definition if communication specialists in a public relations department try to manage interpersonal communication in the organization through training or some other intervention. If, in contrast, individuals communicate without assistance from specialists, then the study of that communication behavior falls outside our definition. Conrad (1985, p. 18) limited the term *organizational communication* in much the same way. He described organizational communication as the study of how individuals communicate strategically in situations they face in organizations.

actors in the public policy arena. Not all public relations programs deal with public affairs—for example, marketing communication or employee communication.

THE BASIC THEORY

Part I develops the overall assumptions about public relations and the theory of organizational effectiveness that provide the glue that integrates the parts of our general theory of public relations discussed in the remaining parts of the book. The question of organizational effectiveness is addressed directly in chapter 3. Chapters 2 and 4, however, are necessary components of the basic theory. Chapter 2 describes the worldview that encompasses our basic theory, and chapter 4 describes public relations as a management function—the type of function it must be to make organizations effective. In chapter 5, the practitioner member of our research team discusses the practical application of our general theory.

We begin the book with a chapter on worldview because we believe readers cannot understand the general theory we present unless they understand that worldview that provides boundaries for that theory. Readers with a different worldview of public relations—which many will have—will find what we say to be irrelevant or idealistic unless they first enlarge their worldview to understand ours, if not to accept it. Our general theory of public relations, then, begins with the glue of philosophical assumptions.

Philosophical Assumptions About Public Relations

Public relations scholars and practitioners not only differ widely in how they define and describe public relations and organizational communication but also in the assumptions they hold about their purpose and effects. Some see the purpose of public relations as manipulation. Others see it as the dissemination of information, resolution of conflict, or promotion of understanding.

In chapter 2, we discuss alternative sets of presuppositions about public relations. We do so for two reasons: to help readers understand the theory of public relations presented in this book and because our literature search suggests that the excellent programs of organizational communication are based on what we call *symmetrical* more often than *asymmetrical* assumptions.

At one time, philosophers of science (as well as most other people) looked at a scientific theory as free of values, a neutral explanation of how a phenomenon such as public relations works that could be proven to be true or false. Theories, however, are used not just by public relations scholars, scientists, and other kinds of researchers. Public relations practitioners have them too, even though their theories may be specific to certain situations and based on intuition or experience rather than research. Practitioners have "working" theories, which — among other things — tell them what to do when an organization faces a communication problem and the strategy that will be most effective.

Like scientists, public relations practitioners would like to have evidence that their theories are "true" or "proven," assurance that a given strategy will produce predictable results in a specific situation. Today, however, philosophers of science realize that theories are not value-free, that they cannot exist independently of the basic worldview of the people who develop or hold them.

A domain of scientific or scholarly inquiry, such as public relations, is held together not so much by agreement on theories as by agreement on the problems that theories used in the domain should solve. Public relations scholars and practitioners, for example, want to solve such problems as defining the contribution that communication makes to an organization, segmenting and targeting publics, isolating the effects of communication programs, gaining support of senior management for the communication function, understanding the roles and behaviors of public relations practitioners, identifying and managing issues, using communication to increase the satisfaction of employees, learning how public relations interacts with marketing, or defining how organizations should participate in the public affairs of a system of government.

Within the domain of public relations, as in any other domain, scholars and practitioners approach and attempt to solve these problems differently. They approach these problems differently because they apply different theories. Not all theories can be compared, though. Philosophers have identified two levels of theories, theories at the level of *presuppositions* and theories at the levels of *laws* or *propositions*.

The second level of theory, the laws or propositions, is familiar to most communication practitioners. Most are in the form of if–then statements. For example:

> If an organization is credible, then it will be more persuasive when it communicates.
>
> If a public is involved with the consequences of what an organization does, then it will communicate more actively with the organization.
>
> If an organization is socially responsible, then it will meet less interference from government.

The first level, that of presuppositions, is less familiar to practitioners and scholars. Yet it is more important in understanding where theories come from and why there is conflict over them. Presuppositions define the worldview of scholars and practitioners. They are a priori assumptions about the nature of truth, of society, of right or wrong, or simply of how things work in the world.

The presuppositions that make up the worldview of scholars or practitioners cannot be measured or tested directly. Still they are extremely powerful. Presuppositions determine the priority that people give to problems in a domain. In addition, practitioners and scholars generally study and use theories only if they fit within the boundaries of their worldview.

Our literature review suggests that much of the practice of public relations has been built on a set of presuppositions that has made it less effective than it could be, has led to unrealistic expectations for organizational communication, and has limited its value to the organization it serves.

Presuppositions about public relations begin with its role in society. The first worldview is that of many practitioners who believe that public relations has no social role other than to help a client meet its objectives. This worldview can be described as the:

Pragmatic Social Role: Public relations is a useful practice, something that adds value to a client by helping to meet its objectives.

Practitioners with a pragmatic view of public relations usually see no need for codes of conduct or ethical standards because they may interfere with "getting results" for a client.

Some social scientists take what they consider to be an objective view of public relations: It is a neutral practice that is to be observed as an object of study:

Neutral Social Role: Public relations, like society itself, is a neutral object of study. Researchers can discover how practitioners view their social role and what their motivations are.

Other practitioners and scholars see public relations as a set of behaviors influenced by worldview. Two contrasting presuppositions see public relations as an instrument for maintaining or gaining power:

Conservative Social Role: Public relations maintains a system of privilege by defending the interests of the economically powerful.
Radical Social Role: Public relations leads to social improvement, reform, and change.

The conservative and radical presuppositions assume that organizational communication can have powerful effects on society. They see public relations as a tool used in a war among opposing social groups. They are asymmetrical presuppositions. They assume that organizations and opposing groups use communication to persuade or manipulate publics, governments, or organizations for the benefit of the organization sponsoring the communication program and not for the benefit of the other group or of both. In the language of game theory, public relations based on asymmetrical presuppositions is a zero-sum game: One organization, group, or public gains and the other loses.

An alternative to this worldview, the idealistic view, is based on a set of symmetrical presuppositions. A symmetrical worldview sees public relations as a non-zero-sum game in which competing organizations or groups can both gain if they play the game right. Public relations is a tool by which organizations and competing groups in a pluralistic system interact to manage conflict for the benefit of all:

Idealistic Social Role: Public relations is a mechanism by which organizations and publics interact in a pluralistic system to manage their interdependence and conflict.

Although these presuppositions about the social role of organizational communication are couched in the language of external communication and the organization's macrolevel role in society, they are equally applicable to internal communication and social relationships within an organization. Asymmetrical communication systems inside an organization generally are found in highly centralized organizations with authoritarian cultures and systems of management. Symmetrical communication systems are found in decentralized organizations with participatory systems of management—a relationship described in chapter 20.

The theory we develop in this book fits within the idealistic framework. We believe that public relations should be practiced to serve the public interest, to develop mutual understanding between organizations and their publics, and to contribute to informed debate about issues in society. In a sense, we also take the neutral view of public relations: It is an object that can be studied relatively objectively. But we also realize, as we point out in chapter 2, that an observer never can be free of his or her presuppositions. That is why we contrast our symmetrical, idealistic presuppositions with the asymmetrical presuppositions of the conservative and radical worldviews.

In studying public relations in this book and in the larger IABC project of which it is a part, then, we also have looked at public relations from the perspective of a final social role:

Critical Social Role: Public relations or a communication system is part of a larger organizational or societal system. These systems are *constructed;* therefore they can be *deconstructed* and *reconstructed.* Public relations scholars and practitioners can and should criticize public relations for poor ethics, negative social consequences, or ineffectiveness; and they should suggest changes to resolve those problems.

In adopting the critical social role, we do not accept public relations as it is currently practiced as "the way public relations is" or the way it must be practiced. If we did, a study of excellence would be meaningless. We look at public relations as a profession and a function in society as something that can be constantly improved.

Practitioners often do not understand or accept theories like ours because they work from a pragmatic or conservative worldview. We argue that practitioners with a pragmatic worldview have a set of asymmetrical presuppositions even though they do not realize it. They take an asymmetrical view, usually a conservative one, because their clients hold that view.

We hope to make the case for our symmetrical presuppositions pragmatically as well as philosophically. Our research suggests that external communication programs and internal communication systems based on symmetrical presuppositions characterize excellent public relations or communication departments. Philosophically, we believe that symmetrical public relations is more ethical and socially responsible than asymmetrical public relations because it manages conflict rather than wages war. But, pragmatically, our literature review shows that symmetrical communication programs also are successful more often than asymmetrical ones and contribute more to organizational effectiveness.

Asymmetrical presuppositions suggest that organizations can achieve powerful effects with communication. These effects seldom occur, however, and thus asymmetrical public relations programs usually fail. Symmetrical presuppositions suggest more realistic programs and effects. Symmetrical communication programs often succeed and make the organizations that sponsor them more effective.

In addition to discussing the symmetry of public relations, chapter 2 discusses the role of gender in affecting worldview. It shows that the feminine worldview approximates the worldview we have developed better than the masculine worldview. We also discuss the common worldview that public relations is a technical function, which we believe must be enlarged to integrate the technical function of public relations into a broader managerial function. We conclude, therefore, that excellent public relations embodies a worldview that defines the communication function in organizations as symmetrical, idealistic and critical, and managerial.

Organizational Effectiveness

Chapter 3 moves down from the level of worldview to develop a theory of why public relations—managed communication—makes organizations more effective—the answer to our effectiveness research question and the second application of glue that holds the rest of our theory together.

Chapter 3 reviews theories of organizational effectiveness and concludes that managed interdependence is the major characteristic of successful organizations. The literature reviewed shows that organizations are effective when they attain their goals. However, goals must be appropriate for the organization's environment, or strategic constituencies (stakeholders and publics) within that environment will constrain the autonomy of the organization to meet its goals and achieve its mission.

Organizations strive for autonomy from the publics in their external or internal environment that limit their ability to pursue their goals. Organizations also try to mobilize publics that support their goals and thus increase their autonomy. Having the autonomy to pursue their goals is important to organizations, because our literature review shows that effective organizations are able to choose appropriate goals for their environmental and cultural context and then achieve those goals.

Autonomy, however, is an idealized goal that no organization ever achieves completely. Thus, organizations work toward this idealized goal by managing their interdependence with publics that interact with the organization as it pursues its goals. Organizations plan public relations programs strategically, therefore, when they identify the publics that are most likely to limit or enhance their autonomy and design communication programs that help the organization manage its interdependence with these strategic publics. Public relations departments help the organization to manage their independence by building stable, open, and trusting relationships with strategic constituencies. Thus, the quality of these relationships is a key indicator of the long-term contribution that public relations makes to organizational effectiveness.

Strategic management, chapter 6 points out, is a primary characteristic of excellent public relations. Strategic management, therefore, provides the integrating link that connects our theory of excellence to level of public relations programs discussed in Part II.

The Management Level of Public Relations

The integrating theory of public relations outlined in Part I, therefore, indicates that public relations must be a management function if it is to make organizations more effective. Chapter 4, therefore, sets forth a theory of levels of decision making in organizations and shows why public relations must be a function that operates at the highest levels in an organization for it to contribute to organizational effectiveness in the ways described in chapter 3.

Chapter 4 argues that excellent public relations departments contribute to decisions made by the dominant coalition of senior managers by providing information to that coalition about the environment of the organization, about the organization itself, and about the relationship between the organization and its environment. This chapter also proposes that excellent departments engage in environmental scanning, have access to the dominant coalition, and present information at an appropriate level of abstraction for different levels of management. The chapter concludes that organizations will be more likely to have excellent communication departments when they face a high level of environmental uncertainty.

Given this basic theory, the book then turns to the program level of communication management in Part II: how the excellent public relations department should manage communication.

THE PROGRAM LEVEL: EFFECTIVE PLANNING OF COMMUNICATION PROGRAMS

Part II of this book sets forth a *normative* theory, a theory that prescribes how to do public relations in an ideal situation, and contrasts that theory with our predictions of how public relations generally is practiced. We argue that excellent public relations departments will practice public relations in a way that is similar to our normative model, in contrast to the way that public relations is practiced in the typical, less excellent department.

Our normative model specifies that organizational communication should be practiced *strategically*—a type of communication management that Part I shows is necessary for public relations to make organizations more effective. An organization that practices public relations strategically develops programs to communicate with publics, both external and internal, that provide the greatest threats to and opportunities for the organization. These strategic publics fit into categories that many theorists have called *stakeholders*.

Chapter 6 begins with a review of theories of strategic management. Organizations use strategic management to define and shape their missions, but they do so through an iterative process of interacting with their environments. Most theories of strategic management do not suggest a formal mechanism in the organization for interacting with the environment and do not acknowledge the presence of public relations. Excellent public relations departments, however, provide the obvious mechanism for organizations to interact with their environments.

When public relations is part of the organization's strategic planning function, it also is more likely to manage communication programs strategically. The senior public relations manager helps to identify the stakeholders of the organization by participating in central strategic management. He or she then develops programs at the functional level of public relations to build long-term relationships with these strategic publics. In this way, public relations communicates with the publics that are most likely to constrain or enhance the effectiveness of the organization.

Chapter 6 then moves on to review theories and techniques that have been used by public relations and marketing practitioners to segment markets and publics. These include demographics, psychographics, values and lifestyles, cultural analysis, geographic/demographic characteristics, and communication situations. We then ask whether these segmentation devices can identify strategic publics as defined by our normative theory. Chapter 7 adds to this discussion by reviewing the kinds of segmentation research, as well as other kinds of research, that practitioners can purchase from commercial firms.

Our review of the literature shows that the ideal segmentation device for strategic public relations places people into groups that have a similar response to an organization's behavior or communication activity. The response of one public should be a differential response from that of other groups. We argue that the publics identified for public relations programs should respond differentially to problems that occur in the relationship between an organization and its internal or external publics.

Conflict occurs when publics move in a different direction from that of the organization, resulting in friction or collisions. Conflict also could occur when a potentially supportive public has not been motivated to move with the organization and, in a sense, "drags its feet" when it could accelerate the movement of the organization toward achieving its goals. When conflict occurs, publics "make an issue" out of the problem. Organizations use the process of *issues management* to anticipate issues and resolve conflict before the public makes it an issue. Organizations that wait for issues to occur before managing their communication with strategic publics usually have crises on their hands and have to resort to short-term *crisis communication*.

Strategic public relations, therefore, begins when communication practitioners identify potential problems in the relationship with the organization's stakeholders and define the categories of stakeholders that are affected by the problem. The second stage in strategic public relations is the segmentation of publics that respond differentially to those problems — publics that arise within stakeholder categories. Chapter 6 maintains that a situational theory of publics provides the best set of concepts and techniques for identifying those publics.

We add, however, that many of the segmentation devices that have been borrowed from marketing—values and lifestyles, demographics, geodemographics, psychographics, and others—can supplement the situational theory by helping to identify the publics that respond differentially to issues. The segmentation techniques from marketing, however, are more useful in defining *markets* than *publics*. Organizations create markets for their products and services by segmenting a population into components most likely to purchase or use a product or service. Publics, however, create themselves when people organize to deal with an organization's consequences on them.

After identifying problems, publics, and issues, strategic public relations identifies objectives for communication programs, uses these objectives to plan communication programs, and evaluates the effects of those communication programs—that is, whether they achieved the objectives set for them and as a result contributed to organizational effectiveness.

Chapter 7 examines studies of the effects of communication programs to provide an understanding of these last three steps in the strategic management of public relations. Strategic practitioners use these objectives to design communication programs and then measure them when they evaluate the effectiveness of those programs. Our conclusions about the effects of communication programs are based on studies of the effects of the mass media and from research on communication effects in cognitive and social psychology.

In our normative theory, we argue that objectives for communication programs should be chosen that maximize the extent to which an organization is able to manage its relationships with strategic publics. We then point out that most practitioners react to that challenge by choosing a powerful effect as an objective, especially a change in the behavior of a public or a change in attitude that they hope will result eventually in a change of behavior.

Our literature review shows, however, that communication programs seldom change behavior in the short term, although they may do so over a longer period. Communication programs change behavior in the short term only under very specific conditions. The behavior to be changed must be a simple one and the program must be aimed at a well-segmented public, supplemented by interpersonal support among members of the public, and executed almost flawlessly. The more significant, the more widespread, and the longer lasting the effect chosen as an objective, the longer it will take a communication program to achieve that effect.

The asymmetrical mind-set about public relations described in the previous section usually leads public relations practitioners to choose powerful effects as short-term objectives for their communication programs. Our literature review explains, therefore, why asymmetrical communication programs usually fail.

In contrast, chapter 7 shows why symmetrical programs usually work better. Practitioners of symmetrical public relations choose short-term cognitive effects rather than long-term behavioral effects. The choice of cognitive effects (changes in the way people think about and understand issues) makes it more feasible for practitioners to measure and evaluate the effects of communication program in the short term when evaluation makes it possible for them to make midcourse changes in the programs.

Yet the literature review also shows that achieving short-term cognitive effects through symmetrical communication programs maximizes the chances for long-term behavioral changes. Publics who are treated as equals of an organization and whose ideas are communicated to the organization—as well as the ideas of the organization being communicated to the publics—more often support or fail to oppose an organization than do publics whose behavior the organization tries to change directly in the short term.

On the basis of this literature review, we predict that excellent public relations departments will practice this strategic approach to organizational communication. The less excellent programs, in contrast, will expect direct and powerful effects on the behavior of vaguely defined publics in the short term. The less excellent departments also will justify communication programs historically rather than strategically. That is, communication programs will reflect what always has been done rather than what should be done to manage the relationships between an organization and its publics.

Excellent public relations programs, in summary, are managed strategically at the program level. We turn then to the departmental level to search for the characteristics of public relations departments whose parent organizations allow them to manage communication strategically.

THE DEPARTMENTAL LEVEL: CHARACTERISTICS OF EXCELLENT PUBLIC RELATIONS/COMMUNICATION DEPARTMENTS

Excellence in management has been the subject of many studies of successful organizations in recent years, studies that have defined successful organizations as profitable, innovative, or growing. Excellent organizations, these studies have found, have characteristics in common that managers can recognize and attempt to install in their organizations to make them more effective.

In Part III, we review management and public relations research in search of the characteristics of excellent public relations departments. Excellent public relations departments are defined as those that are managed strategically in order to maximize the contribution of communication programs to organizational effectiveness.

Chapter 9 opens Part III with a review of the literature on excellence in management. We conducted that search to determine whether organizations identified as excellent overall also will have excellent communication programs. The review isolated 12 characteristics of excellent organizations, some of which suggest characteristics of excellent public relations departments and some of which suggest how communication contributes to excellence in overall management. The characteristics include:

1. *Human Resources.* Excellent organizations empower people by giving employees autonomy and allowing them to make strategic decisions. They also pay attention to the personal growth and quality of work life of employees. They emphasize the interdependence rather than independence of employees. They also emphasize integration rather than segmentation and strike a balance between teamwork and individual effort.

2. *Organic Structure.* People cannot be empowered by fiat. Organizations give people power by eliminating bureaucratic, hierarchical organizational structures. They develop what organizational theorists call an *organic structure.* They decentralize decisions, managing without managers as much as possible. They also avoid stratification of employees, humiliating some by having such symbols of status as executive dining rooms, corner offices, or reserved parking spaces. At the same time, they use leadership, collaboration, and culture to integrate the organization rather than structure.

3. *Intrapreneurship.* Excellent organizations have an innovative, entrepreneurial spirit—frequently called *intrapreneurship.* Intrapreneurship, too, is related to the other characteristics of excellent organizations: A spirit of internal entrepreneurship occurs in organizations that develop organic structures and cultivate human resources.

4. *Symmetrical Communication Systems.* Although studies of organizational excellence do not use the term symmetrical communication, they all describe it—with both internal and external publics. Excellent organizations "stay close" to their customers, employees, and other *strategic constituencies.*

5. *Leadership.* Excellent organizations have leaders who rely on networking and "management-by-walking-around" rather than authoritarian systems. Excellent leaders give people power but minimize power politics. At the same time, excellent leaders provide a vision and direction for the organizations, creating order out of the chaos that empowerment of people can create.

6. *Strong, Participative Cultures.* Employees of excellent organizations share a sense of mission. They are integrated by a strong culture that values human resources, organic structures, innovation, and symmetrical communication.

7. *Strategic Planning.* Excellent organizations strive to maximize the bottom line by identifying the most important opportunities and constraints in their environment.

8. *Social Responsibility.* Excellent organizations manage with an eye on the effects of their decisions on society as well as on the organization.

9. *Support for Women and Minorities.* Excellent organizations recognize the value of diversity by employing female and minority workers and taking steps to foster their careers.

10. *Quality Is a Priority.* Total quality is a priority not only in words or in the company's philosophy statement but a priority when actions are taken, decisions are made, or resources are allocated.

11. *Effective Operational Systems.* Excellent organizations build systems for the day-to-day management of the organization that implement the previous characteristics.

12. *A Collaborative Societal Culture.* Organizations will be excellent more often in societies whose cultures emphasize collaboration, participation, trust, and mutual responsibility.

Of these 12 characteristics, we already have identified strategic planning and the practice of symmetrical communication as characteristics of excellent public relations departments. In addition, chapter 20 identifies the key role that a symmetrical system of internal communication plays in making an organization more effective. Social responsibility is an integral part of the symmetrical worldview of public relations defined in chapter 2. Most of the other characteristics emerge in Parts III or IV as characteristics of excellent public relations departments or of the organizations that foster excellent public relations: support for women and minorities, human resources, organic structures, intrapreneurship, leadership, participative organizational cultures, and collaborative societal cultures. The remaining chapters of Part II, then, describe how excellent public relations departments should be organized to practice strategic planning, effective operational systems, and quality public relations programs.

Chapter 9 concludes that excellent public relations does not exist in isolation. It is a characteristic of an excellent organization. The characteristics of excellence in the organization as a whole provide the conditions that make excellent public relations possible. In addition, excellent communication management can be the catalyst that begins to make organizations excellent and continues to make them more excellent as time passes. With the framework provided by chapter 9, the rest of the book describes the characteristics of excellent public relations departments and of the organizations that house them.

Optimal Decision Making in Public Relations

Chapter 10 reviews normative theories of operations research to show how excellent public relations departments should make strategic choices of communication programs. The chapter demonstrates how communication managers can use the mathematical theories of management science, decision theory, and operations research to make strategic decisions about public relations. It argues that excellent public relations departments plan and choose communication systems to minimize conflict and maximize cooperation between an organization and its strategic publics.

Models of Public Relations

Chapter 11 reviews research on four *models* of public relations, four typical ways of conceptualizing and practicing communication management. The *press agentry* model applies when a communication program strives for favorable publicity, especially in the mass media. A program based on the *public information* model uses "journalists in residence" to disseminate relatively objective information through the mass media and controlled media such as newsletters, brochures, and direct mail.

Both press agentry and public information are one-way models of public relations; they describe communication programs that are not based on research and strategic planning. Excellent public relations departments base their communication programs on more sophisticated and effective models. Press agentry and public information also are asymmetrical models: They try to make the organization look good either through propaganda (press agentry) or by disseminating only favorable information (public information).

The third model, the *two-way asymmetrical* model, is a more sophisticated approach in that it uses research to develop messages that are most likely to persuade strategic publics to behave as the organization wants. Our research suggests, however, that two-way asymmetrical public relations — like press agentry and public information — is less effective than two-way symmetrical public relations.

Two-way symmetrical describes a model of public relations that is based on research and that uses communication to manage conflict and improve understanding with strategic publics. Our research suggests that excellent public relations departments, therefore, model more of their communication programs on the two-way symmetrical than on the other three models.

Most do not practice a pure symmetrical model, however. Excellent public relations departments serve as advocates both for their organizations and for strategic publics. Thus, excellent departments generally practice a mixture of the two-way symmetrical and two-way asymmetrical models—a *mixed-motive* model—although their practice is more symmetrical than asymmetrical.

Public Relations Roles

Whereas models describe the mind-set and overall purpose of communication programs, *roles* describe daily behavior patterns of individual communication practitioners. Extensive research, which is described in chapter 12, has identified two major public relations roles: managers and technicians.

Communication managers conceptualize and direct public relations programs. Communication technicians provide technical services such as writing, editing, photography, media contacts, or production of publications. Technicians are found in all public relations departments, but managers are a necessary component of excellent departments. Less excellent departments consist mostly of technicians whose work is supervised by managers outside the public relations department, managers who usually have less potential for strategic management of public relations than managers trained in communication management.

Research shows that communication managers more often are found in organizations with threatening environments and that they engage in environmental scanning and evaluation research. Managers are found in organizations with an *open-system* mind-set. Managers also are more likely to practice the two-way symmetrical or asymmetrical models of public relations than the press agentry or public information models. Finally, technicians are more likely to see public relations as a creative, artistic endeavor than are managers.

Public Relations and Marketing

Chapter 13 addresses the relationship between public relations and marketing. In it, we argue that marketing and public relations are distinct conceptually. We predict that excellent public relations departments will be separate from marketing departments whereas less excellent ones will be sublimated to marketing.

In the past, marketing theory has been more advanced than public relations theory. Organizations that want to manage public relations strategically, therefore, have turned to marketing practitioners because strategic management has been part of marketing theory for some time. When marketing practitioners manage public relations, however, public relations usually is reduced to technique rather than strategy. Public relations practitioners then are mere technicians working in support of marketing rather than public relations objectives.

We argue that marketing theory is inadequate for public relations for several reasons. First, we argue that the marketing function should communicate with the markets for an organization's good and services. Public relations should be concerned with all of the publics of the organization. The major purpose of marketing is to make money for an organization by increasing the slope of the demand curve. The major purpose of public relations is to save money for the organization by building relationships with publics that constrain or enhance the ability of the organization to meet its mission.

Second, we argue that asymmetrical presuppositions work better in marketing than in public relations, even though marketing theorists often use such symmetrical concepts as *bilateral exchange* or a *customer orientation*. Customer markets, in contrast to publics, usually do not have to buy the products of a given organization. Publics, in contrast, often cannot avoid the consequences of an organization's behavior: consequences such as pollution, discrimination, or chemical waste. Because these other publics are more involved with an organization, persuasive communication seldom will work well enough to keep them from being a threat to an organization's mission.

Finally, the strategies used in marketing—such as product, price, and promotion—seldom are useful in public relations and thus provide a poor normative theory for public relations practitioners. And most of the segmentation techniques of marketing are only marginally useful in public relations; they are useful as supplements to public relations techniques rather than as replacements.

We believe, then, that public relations must emerge as a discipline distinct from marketing and that it must be practiced separately from marketing in organizations. Some organizations may choose to place both functions in the same department. That placement will not harm either function, unless one is sublimated to the other. If sublimation occurs, the organization will lose one of these valuable communication functions. Public relations can use concepts in marketing as analogies in developing its own theory, for example, the analogy of strategic public relations. Strategic public relations is not strategic marketing, however, and a separate theory must be developed—as we are doing in this book.

Organization of the Communication Function

The studies of excellent organizations reviewed in chapter 9 identified an appropriate operational system as a characteristic of outstanding organizations. In chapter 14, we describe how excellent public relations departments should be structured as an operational system for delivering public relations programs.

A normative theory, open-systems theory, shows that organizations should have an excellent public relations department when they:

1. Locate the public relations department in the organizational structure so that the department has ready access to the managerial subsystem.
2. Integrate all public relations functions into a single department rather than subordinate them under other departments such as personnel, marketing, or finance. Only in an integrated department is it possible for public relations to be managed strategically.
3. Develop dynamic horizontal structures within the department, to make it possible to reassign people and resources to new programs as new strategic publics are identified and other publics cease to be strategic.

In contrast to these normative characteristics of excellent departments, however, chapter 14 hypothesizes that the structures of less excellent public departments develop historically rather than strategically. As a result, we predict that public relations structures in less excellent departments will reflect the preferences of senior managers who had the most power in the organization at the time public relations programs first developed and that the structure of the communication department will have changed little since.

Gender Differences

Chapter 15 reviews studies that have documented a trend toward a female majority in the public relations profession. It also reviews studies showing that women more often are found in the technician role and men in the manager role. Women in the communication field hold less prestigious positions and earn lower salaries than men.

Feminization of organizational communication, therefore, could limit the potential of public relations departments if organizations discriminate against women communicators. Chapter 15 documents the existence of discrimination against women, although it concludes that discrimination usually results from subtle processes rather than overt acts. The majority of students studying communication management today are women. Therefore, organizations will lose the opportunity for their communication programs to contribute maximally to organizational effectiveness if they fail to promote women from the technician to the manager role and instead allow men from other fields to encroach upon communication management roles without proper training or experience.

We hypothesize, therefore, that excellent public relations departments will have women in communication management roles and that they will have mechanisms to help women gain the power they need to advance from the technician to the management role — mechanisms that also are described in chapter 15.

Academic Preparation and Professional Experience

Until recently, public relations has been a field without a body of knowledge, a field that has not required specialized training or experience. Chapter 16 maintains that excellent public relations departments will employ professionals who have learned a specialized body of knowledge. Chapter 16 describes the role of education in professionalization. It then describes the curriculum and body of knowledge recommended for public relations education by several professional organizations, which we believe provide a conceptual grounding that will enhance the potential of public relations practitioners to contribute to organizational effectiveness.

THE ORGANIZATIONAL LEVEL: THE CONDITIONS THAT MAKE EXCELLENCE IN PUBLIC RELATIONS POSSIBLE

In Part II, we defined excellent public relations departments as departments that manage communication with strategic publics, publics that threaten or enhance the ability of the organization to pursue its goals. In Part III, we identified the characteristics of public relations departments that most often manage communication strategically. In Part IV, then, we explain why excellent public relations departments make organizations more effective and identify the characteristics of organizations and their environments that lead to excellent programs of communication.

Chapter 17 reviews literature on the relationship between organizations and environments to show how organizations should interact with publics. Early theories of interorganizational relationships predicted that an *environmental imperative* would determine the structure and communication system of an organization. According to this theory, organizations with changing, turbulent environments should be forced to engage in two-way communication with the environment and to develop organic management structures in order to manage their environmental interdependencies successfully. Extensive research, however, has failed to show a strong relationship between the nature of an organization's environment, its structure, and the models of public relations it practices.

Chapter 17 concludes, therefore, that although public relations should make organizations more effective by helping them to interact successfully with their environments, organizations in reality seldom choose the most appropriate models of public relations for their environments. The reason is simple: Environments are not objective reality for the managers of organizations. Instead, managers choose, subjectively, to observe only parts of their environment. The parts they choose to observe are products of their mind-set and organizational culture.

Our research suggests, therefore, that a power-control theory explains why organizations practice public relations in the way they do better than an environmental theory does. A power-control theory states that organizations behave in the way they do—in our case they choose the public relations programs they do—because the people who have power in an organization choose that behavior. Organizations frequently do not choose the most rational type of communication behavior for their environment because the dominant coalition does not make a rational decision.

The flowchart in Fig. 1.1 depicts a power-control model of public relations that we have abstracted from the macrolevel literature on organizational behavior. The model answers three questions important to our quest for the predictors of excellence in communication management:

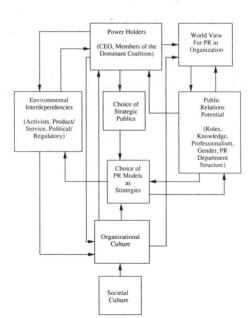

FIGURE 1.1   Factors influencing the choice of a model of public relations.

1. How organizations should use public relations to interact with their environments.
2. Why some organizations use public relations to interact effectively with their environments and others do not.
3. Why organizations with excellent public relations departments are more likely to manage communication strategically and therefore are more effective than organizations that do not have excellent departments.

The focal point of the model in Fig. 1.1 is the box labeled *Choice of Public Relations Models as Strategies.* We believe that the choice of the symmetrical model of public relations is the key choice made by effective organizations. Figure 1.1 shows, however, that the public relations department does not make that choice. The choice is made by the power holders of the organization, the dominant coalition.

The dominant coalition makes the choice of a model of public relations in two stages. It first chooses what it perceives to be the strategic publics in its environment. Top public relations managers contribute to the choice of strategic publics only if they are part of the dominant coalition. Figure 1.1 shows that the top public relations manager will be in the dominant coalition only when public relations potential is high in the organization.

Public relations potential increases when the characteristics of an excellent public relations department identified in Part 3 are present: strategic management, managerial roles, education for the two-way models of public relations, lack of discrimination against women, and an integrated public relations function.

Chapter 18 describes power-control theories of organizations and elaborates on the concepts of power and the dominant coalition. It also reviews research showing that enhancing the potential of the public relations department increases the likelihood that the top public relations manager will be in the dominant coalition. This chapter and chapters 4, 11, and 14 show that the public relations director must be part of the dominant coalition or have ready access to it if public relations is to contribute maximally to organizational success.

The box labeled Worldview for Public Relations describes the mind-set for — the presuppositions about — public relations that are dominant in an organization. As depicted by a downward arrow, the schema limits or enhances the potential of the public relations department to practice sophisticated models of public relations. As depicted by three other arrows, the worldview for public relations is a product of the worldview of the dominant coalition, the potential of the public relations department, and the culture of the organization.

As chapter 18 shows, the arrow from *Environmental Interdependencies* to *Power Holders* indicates that managers who gain power in an organization do so in part because they have knowledge and skills relevant to a crucial problem in the organization's environment. That conclusion also suggests that public relations managers gain power when they have knowledge and skills that help organizations manage crucial environmental interdependencies — such as skills in financial relations when stockholders are a key interdependency or skills in government relations when government is a key public.

As chapters 3 and 20 discuss, the arrow from *Power Holders* to *Environmental Interdependencies* indicates that the environment is in part at least the subjective perception of the dominant coalition. The power holders observe the parts of the environment that they think are crucial and then choose strategic publics for public relations programs from that perceived environment.

The arrow from *Choice of PR Models as Strategies* to the environment depicts the critical relationship between strategic management of public relations and organizational effectiveness that has been discussed several times in this chapter. If organizations choose the most appropriate public relations strategy for communication with strategic publics, then that strategy will help the organization to manage critical environmental interdependencies and make the organization more effective.

Chapter 19 reviews research on a crucial component of that environment for public relations programs: the behavior of activist groups. Chapter 19 argues that activists play the key role in limiting the organization's ability to pursue its mission. But chapter 19 also shows that organizations seldom choose activist groups as strategic publics unless forced to by confrontation or litigation. When organizations do use public relations to respond to activist groups, they seldom choose the most appropriate model of public relations, the symmetrical model, as a way of responding to them.

The final two boxes in Fig. 1.1 depict the relationship among societal culture (chapter 22), organizational culture (chapter 21), and excellence in public relations. As the arrows in Fig. 1.1 show, organizational culture is created by the dominant coalition, especially by the founder of an organization. Yet managers do not gain power if their values and ideology differ substantially from that of the organization. Organizational culture also is affected by the larger societal culture and by the environment.

Organizational culture affects public relations in the long term by molding the worldview for public relations. In the short term, it influences the choice of a model of public relations. If culture is essentially authoritarian, conservative, segmented, and reactive, the dominant coalition generally will choose an asymmetrical model of public relations. If culture is participative, integrative, liberal, and interactive, the dominant coalition will be more likely to choose a symmetrical model of public relations.

Figure 1.1, in summary, pulls together most of the variables that we have identified as essential to excellence in communication management in this book. It describes how organizations should respond strategically to their environments. It shows why power holders often do not make the most appropriate choices of strategic publics and models of public relations. And it shows why organizations more often make correct choices for public relations programs when they have excellent public relations departments.

Part IV ends with chapters on internal communication and on cultural differences in public relations. Chapter 20 develops a model of the relationship between organizational structure, internal communication systems, and employee satisfaction that is similar to the model of external communication in Fig. 1.1.

This chapter argues that a symmetrical system of internal communication helps to increase employee satisfaction and organizational effectiveness. Most systems of internal communication are asymmetrical, however, and they do not increase morale or organizational effectiveness. A symmetrical communication system is one in which employees are provided mechanisms for dialogue with each other and with supervisors and top managers. Interpersonal communication is crucial in a symmetrical system, although employee media can complement it.

In addition, chapter 20 reviews literature showing that a communication system cannot be made symmetrical without concurrent changes in organizational structure, to make it more organic. As we saw in chapter 9, an organic organizational structure also helps the organization to cultivate its human resources. Employee morale, therefore, results from an organic structure, cultivation of human resources, and symmetrical communication.

Symmetrical communication, as a result, contributes to organizational effectiveness in two ways. When communication helps to improve morale, employees are more likely to enhance rather than constrain the organization's ability to achieve its goals. And in a decentralized, organic organization, symmetrical communication is necessary for the organization to coordinate the behavior of its relatively autonomous subsystems. Such coordination is necessary for the organization to be effective.

Chapter 22 explores the possibility that the theory of public relations developed in this book might not apply outside the United States. Studies of public relations practice in Great Britain and Canada suggest that the theory works well in other Western democracies. Research on the effect of culture on management suggests that public relations will be practiced differently in non-Western cultures. Chapter 22, therefore, explores concepts from cultural anthropology that we will use in later stages of the IABC project to develop such comparative research.

THE ECONOMIC LEVEL: HOW PUBLIC
RELATIONS CONTRIBUTES TO THE BOTTOM LINE

In the final chapter of the book, chapter 23, we explore literature that might suggest whether and how a monetary value can be placed on the contribution that public relations makes to organizational effectiveness. Our theory states that communication programs that are managed strategically help organizations to manage relationships with strategic publics that have the power to constrain the ability of the organization to achieve its goals.

When organizations manage these interdependencies poorly, the strategic publics protest, boycott, go to court, or ask for government regulation to constrain the autonomy of the organization. All of these activities cost the organization money. If strategic communication is successful, it should help to save the organization money even though it often may not help it to make money.

Chapter 23 explains a technique, taken from literature on evaluation research, that researchers can use to estimate the value of communication programs in managing interdependencies. Top managers, members of the dominant coalition, can be asked to estimate what it is worth to them to avoid or manage conflict with strategic publics. Through a series of iterations (Would you pay $X? If not, would you pay $Y?), researchers can place a value on the benefits of communication programs that can be compared with their costs in a cost-benefit analysis.

Research must be done, however: first to test the premises of the theory we have outlined and second to place a value on the benefits of public relations.

HOW TO READ THE REST OF THE BOOK

This chapter has presented a general theory of public relations as a theory of communication management. That theory specifies how public relations makes organizations more effective, how it is organized and managed when it contributes most to organizational effectiveness (i.e., when it is excellent), the conditions in organizations and their environments that make organizations more effective, and how the monetary of excellent public relations can be determined. Table 1.1 outlines the major concepts of that theory and identifies the chapters in which each concept is explained.

TABLE 1.1
Characteristics of Excellent Public Relations Programs

I. Program Level
    1. Managed strategically (chapters 6, 7, 8)
II. Departmental Level
    2. A single or integrated public relations department (chapter 14)
    3. Separate function from marketing (chapter 13)
    4. Direct reporting relationship to senior managment (chapter 4)
    5. Two-way symmetrical model (chapter 11)
    6. Senior public relations person in the managerial role (chapters 10, 12)
    7. Potential for excellent public relations, as indicated by:
        a. Knowledge of symmetrical model (chapters 2, 10, 11, 20)
        b. Knowledge of managerial role (chapters 4, 10, 12)
        c. Academic training in public relations (chapter 16)
        d. Professionalism (chapter 16)
    8. Equal opportunity for men and women in public relations (chapter 15)
III. Organizational Level
    9. Worldview for public relations in the organization reflects the two-way symmetrical model (chapter 2)
    10. Public relations director has power in or with the dominant coalition (chapter 18)
    11. Participative rather than authoritarian organizational culture (chapters 21, 22)
    12. Symmetrical system of internal communication (chapter 20)
    13. Organic rather than mechanical organizational structure (chapter 17)
    14. Turbulent, complex environment with pressure from activist groups (chapters 17, 19)
IV. Effects of Excellent Public Relations
    15. Programs meet communication objectives (chapter 7)
    16. Reduces costs of regulation, pressure, and litigation (chapter 19, 23)
    17. Job satisfaction is high among employees (chapter 20)

In addition, each chapter is preceding by a short overview summarizing how that chapter fits into the general theory of public relations. Some readers will want to read all of these chapters. Others will want to work from this overview and read the chapters that elaborate on a particular concept. In either case, Table 1.1 and the chapter overviews should help you in finding your way through the rest of the book.

REFERENCES

Conrad, C. (1985). *Strategic organizational communication*. New York: Holt, Rinehart & Winston.

Grunig, J. E., & Hunt, T. (1984). *Managing public relations*. New York: Holt, Rinehart & Winston.

Peters, T. J., & Waterman, R. H. (1982). *In search of excellence*. New York: Harper & Row.

I THE BASIC THEORY

Part I sets forth the basic components of a general theory of excellence in public relations and the contribution it makes to organizational effectiveness. It begins at the philosophical level of worldview and ends with the practical advice of an experienced public relations professional.

2

The Effect of Worldviews
On Public Relations Theory
and Practice

James E. Grunig
University of Maryland

Jon White
Management Consultant
Bedford, United Kingdom

ABSTRACT

*The general theory of excellence in communication management and its
contribution to organizational effectiveness begins at the level of worldview—
the way that people and organizations think about and define public relations.
To understand the theory developed in this book, we must revise and expand
conventional thinking about science and research and about public relations.
For public relations to be excellent, this chapter maintains, public relations
must be viewed as symmetrical, idealistic and critical, and managerial.*

Thought has a self-reproductive power, and when the mind is held steadily to
one idea it becomes coloured by it, and, as we may say, all the correlates of
that thought arise within the mind. Hence the mystic obtains knowledge about
any object of which he [sic] thinks constantly in fixed contemplation.
— H. P. Blavatsky (1831–1891)

The scientific method has changed the world and the way people think
about the world. In general, the scientific method has improved people's
lives and has forced them to think logically and systematically about the
things they observe and experience. As a result, many professions—
including public relations—have looked to science to ground the practice of
their profession.

Despite the obvious benefits of the scientific method, however, there are
many myths about it that have shaped the thinking of scientists, professionals, and people in general—in ways that have been detrimental to
scientific understanding, professional development, and human progress.

Those myths include the belief that science can be totally objective, that it can be kept neutral of values, and that it can discover "truth."

Many leading communication professionals look to the scientific method to produce a body of theoretical knowledge that will instill order on the chaos that seems to exist in public relations. Communication professionals often seem to flounder without direction in their work. In actual practice, public relations has no consistent definition. Realistically, it can be defined as little more than "what public relations people do." The work of public relations people varies tremendously from one organization to another or from one practitioner to another. To many critics, that work seems unprincipled, unethical, and atheoretical.

Scientific research and the theory it produces can help to bring order to the chaos of public relations. It cannot do that, however, unless we first identify and explore the fundamental beliefs and assumptions that people have about public relations. In the last 30 years, philosophers and historians of science have changed their views dramatically about the nature of science. Once, they believed that the scientific method could remove subjectivity from the thinking and observing of people. Scientists, they believed, could follow systematic methods to identify and understand the truth that lies outside their minds. Now they know that science is a very human undertaking and that humans impose their fundamental beliefs about the world on their thinking and observing.

Public relations, like the social and behavioral sciences, is especially susceptible to human subjectivity because its practitioners try to understand and explain the behavior of people. People, in other words, observe the behavior of people. Most people have theories about why they and others behave as they do. Those theories may seem illogical to others, but they generally make perfect sense to the people who hold them. Thus, it is quite easy for the observer—the communication researcher or practitioner—to use his or her fundamental beliefs about the world to frame and understand the behavior of others. It also is quite easy for the observed—members of publics or public relations practitioners—to reject the explanations of researchers because those explanations do not coincide with their fundamental beliefs.

The practice of public relations and theories about its practice, therefore, are affected by the assumptions that practitioners and theorists have about such things as morality, ethics, human nature, religion, politics, free enterprise, or gender. People not involved in public relations have other assumptions about the profession—assumptions that cause these people to heap scorn and mistrust upon practitioners.

Such assumptions cannot be changed easily because they usually are rooted in the culture of organizations, communities, and societies. Although the assumptions that make up the worldviews of people are subjective and generally rigid, philosophers and social scientists believe that they can be identified and compared and that some worldviews work better than others in solving the problems of organizations and societies.

We introduce the concept of worldview in this chapter because we do not believe that practitioners and scholars of public relations will be able to understand and use our concepts of excellent public relations unless they first understand the worldview that undergirds these concepts and how that worldview differs from others. We begin the chapter, therefore, by explaining the nature of a worldview. We then identify differing worldviews about public relations and select the worldview that we believe—and that research is beginning to show—helps organizations to use public relations most effectively.

THE ROLE OF WORLDVIEW IN THEORY AND RESEARCH

The concept of worldview appears in literature throughout the humanities and social sciences, although with many names. Kearney (1984), an anthropologist, defined *worldview* as "a set of images and assumptions about the world" (p. 10). In describing the term *image,* Kearney used a definition that is more precise than the way the term image is used in public relations practice.[1] He pointed out that image has two meanings. One is the "literal sense of a visual representation in the mind" (p. 47)—which also is the meaning of image in cognitive psychology (Paivio, 1971). The other meaning, which pertains to worldview, is what Kearney called "organizing principles that have variously been called schemata, *Gestalten,* plans, structures, and so on" (p. 47). This also is the meaning of image made famous by the economist Kenneth Boulding (1956).

Kearney (1984) also referred to worldview as "macrothought." Macrothought describes well the concept of schema that now is extremely popular in cognitive and social psychology. Schemas (or schemata) are large, abstract structures of knowledge that people use to organize what they know and to make sense of new information that comes to them.

---

[1] The term used in public relations has so many meanings that it has little use in building theory. Public relations practitioners use the term *image* to refer to many different concepts, such as reputation, perception, attitude, message, attributes, evaluation, cognition, perception, credibility, support, belief, communication, or relationship. The average person sees image as the opposite of reality. In everyday language, images are projected, manipulated, polished, and tarnished. We believe the only escape from this confusion is not to use the term. Instead, we prefer to use one of the more precise terms to which image refers—such as *reputation, perception,* or *evaluation.* We also try to avoid use of the term to refer to worldview, preferring the more precise notion of assumptions about the world.

Psychologists have defined schemas in different ways (Anderson, 1983; J. Grunig & Childers [aka Hon], 1988; J. Grunig, Ramsey, & Schneider [aka L. Grunig], 1985; Schneider [aka L. Grunig], 1985). The essence of schemas can be captured, however, in Craik's (1979) notion of depth of processing — that schemas have "abstract, symbolic properties" (p. 457) — and in Markus and Zajonc's (1985) conclusion that psychologists generally view schemas as "subjective 'theories' about how the social world operates" (p. 145).

Worldview in Philosophy of Science

Once we realize that worldviews — or schemas — are theories of a sort, we can look to recent thinking about theories in the philosophy of science to help understand and evaluate the different worldviews that influence the study and practice of public relations.

In recent years, philosophers have abandoned the ideas of logical positivism that dominated science and the philosophy of science for decades. Logical positivists believed that theories are "true" representations of reality that can be verified by objective observation — the excessively optimistic view of the scientific method described at the beginning of this chapter. Philosophers of science now realize that scientists are human, that humans are subjective, and that subjectivity plays a role in theory building.

Led by Thomas Kuhn (1970), a historian of science, many philosophers abandoned logical positivism for a completely relative view of science. They argued that science is as subjective as any other kind of thinking and that competing theories cannot be compared and evaluated objectively. Most philosophers, however, rejected this relative view, which was as extreme in the opposite direction as was logical positivism. Instead, philosophers now describe science and the theories it produces in ways that we would describe as a quasi-objective way of building knowledge (Laudan, 1977; Shapere, 1984; Suppe, 1977, 1989).[2]

Logical positivists, in general, viewed the relationship between theory and the real world as a relationship between two levels of abstraction. Theories are abstract and general. Their truth cannot be determined unless the concepts in a theory can be "operationalized" — that is, unless concrete measures of the abstract concepts can be observed in the real world. These concrete measures typically were called hypotheses, research questions, or research problems.

Contemporary philosophers of science solved the dilemma of subjectivity by adding a third level of abstraction to their view of theory and reality. This third level corresponds to what we are calling worldview in this

---

[2]See J. Grunig (1989b) for a review of these changes in philosophy of science and their importance for public relations.

chapter. Kuhn (1970) coined the term for worldview that is used most often in science. He described worldview as a "paradigm"—a "disciplinary matrix" that "stands for the entire constellation of beliefs, values, techniques, and so on shared by the members of a given community" (p. 175).

Meehan (1968) referred to worldview as a "conceptual framework through which perceptions are screened" (p. 41). Suppe (1977) used the German term *Weltanschauung,* which refers to a comprehensive mind-set. Laudan (1977) described worldview in terms of a research tradition, such as Darwinism in biology or behavioralism in psychology. Laudan said a research tradition is broader than a theory and that it has presuppositions— or assumptions—that are difficult to test. Brown (1977) also used the term presupposition to refer to worldview—"*a priori* propositions that the scientist sees as necessary truths" (pp. 101–109).[3]

Whatever the term used, philosophers of science generally have agreed that worldview functions as a type of theory at a level more abstract than the levels of theory and observation recognized by logical positivists. In their current thinking, philosophers describe worldview as a gestalt or mind-set that focuses the attention of a scientist primarily upon theories or observations that fit within that mind-set. For example, a free-market economist would be unlikely to see Marxist theory as relevant or to study exploitation of labor as a research problem. Nor would a behavioral psychologist be likely to have an interest in the psychology of the mind and to try to understand the nature of a thought. (A behavioralist, in addition, would not see the relevance of this chapter.)

Philosophers also generally agree that the presuppositions of a worldview cannot be tested directly. The theories and hypotheses that fit within the worldview can be tested. But because the worldview focuses the mind of the scientist only on theories and hypotheses that are relevant to or make sense within his or her worldview, this third and most abstract level of theory introduces subjectivity into the philosopher's explanation of how science works.

Worldview in Other Disciplines

In addition to anthropology, psychology, and philosophy, concepts of worldview appear in other disciplines. Morgan (1986), for example, described eight different images—or metaphors—that theorists have used to describe and explain organizations—organizations as machines, organisms, brains, cultures, political systems, psychic prisons, "flux and transformation," and instruments of domination.

---

[3]Kearney (1984) also identified the concept of presuppositions in Collingwood's (1940) writing on metaphysics.

The introduction of a subjective level of theory into our understanding of science also opens the possibility of a merging of science with religion or with ethics, which generally have been considered to be metaphysical— beyond physics—and therefore untestable. Torrance (1989), a theologian, sounded much like a philosopher of science when he said: ". . . funda- mental ideas . . . actually play a considerable and indeed an essential part in scientific investigation and verification. Hence the more rigorous scien- tific inquiry is, the more it will take care to examine and test these fundamental ideas, if only because they determine the kind of question we ask and the kind of answers we receive" (p. 71).

Vroom (1989) compared the major religions of the world and concluded that although each has a different worldview each of these worldviews has common elements. Kearney (1984) developed a similar theory of culture- based worldviews.

Thus, we begin to see that worldviews can be compared and evaluated even though they are subjective. From the perspective of science, this means that different conceptual frameworks can be compared for their ability to solve important problems (Laudan, 1977). From the perspective of religion, it means that morals and ethics can be introduced into science. According to Torrance (1989), for example, ". . . the moral imperative, the 'ought' that had been banished from the realm of science in the Age of Reason would have to be restored to the conceptual structure of science" (p. 73).

Evaluating Worldviews

> Mind moves matter.
>
> —Vergil (B.C. 70–19)

> Mind is indeed the source of bondage and also the source of liberation. To be bound to things of this world: This is bondage. To be free from them: This is liberation.
>
> —Upanishads (c. B.C. 800)

The subjectivity of the human mind plays an important role in how people think about public relations—and in how they study it and practice it. As a result, we must address this subjective component of theories about public relations—both popular and scientific—if we are to understand and foster excellence in communication practice. To distinguish excellent from less excellent public relations, we must be able to compare and evaluate worldviews.

As Vergil said, "Mind moves matter." In more recent times, Kearney (1984) said the same thing: "In the short run people's actions are best explained by the ideas they have in their heads" (p. 4), and "Specific worldviews result in certain patterns of behavior and not in others" (p. 53). But, as Upanishads added, only the mind can free people of the bondage of their worldview. That is, we can change worldviews only by identifying them and choosing to adopt one or to change to another.

Some philosophers such as Collingwood (1940), Kuhn (1970), Feyerabend (1970), and Bohm (1977) have argued that worldviews are completely subjective. They believe that people, groups, or societies choose one worldview rather than another by arguing, fighting, voting, or mobilizing supporters—a dialectical process—rather than through reason, negotiation, or compromise. Others, however, maintain that there are quasi-rational ways of evaluating worldviews.

Kearney (1984) said, for example, that worldviews can be evaluated on the basis of internal and external criteria. From an internal perspective, he said that some worldviews have assumptions that "are logically and structurally related to each other better than others" (p. 52). Vroom (1989) listed similar internal criteria: "obviousness, coherence, freedom from contradiction, unity, relevance, etc." (p. 96). From an external perspective, Kearney said that some worldviews allow people to relate better to their environments than others. He also said that we can judge worldviews by "some presumably more valid historical perspective" (p. 57).

Philosophers of science also have suggested ways of comparing and evaluating worldviews. Suppe (1977) and Shapere (1984) both said that the theories generated by competing worldviews can be compared by neutral direct observations or through indirect observations that are based on noncontroversial background information or background theories. In other words, these philosophers believe that people can find some criteria or effects on which they agree to compare worldviews.

Laudan (1977) suggested perhaps the most useful criterion—the ability of a worldview (and the theories it generates) to solve important problems. In public relations, we might ask, for example, which worldview generates public relations programs that best resolve conflict in society, resolve national and international issues, make organizations more socially responsible, or—the theme of this book—make organizations more effective. Morgan (1986) elaborated on this view after identifying eight images that theorists have used to understand organizations:

> Our discussion brings us to a very important point: that there is a close relationship between the way we think and the way we act, and that many organizational problems are embedded in our thinking. This has very important consequences. First, it encourages us to take ownership of the part we play in shaping the problems we have to solve. . . . Second, an appreciation of the close relationship between thoughts and actions can help to create new ways of organizing. (p. 335)

Worldviews also can be compared on the basis of ethics. Vroom (1989) reported that writers on religion have mentioned love as a criterion or the ability of a worldview to "help people find a right relationship to themselves, their neighbor, and the universe" (p. 96). Torrance (1989) said that science should look for the "good" as well as the "orderly" and suggested that the "good" is that which produces a "reunified human culture" (p. 82).

From this we can conclude that an excellent worldview for public relations will be one that is logical, coherent, unified, and orderly—the *internal* criteria. It also should be effective in solving organizational and human problems, as judged by relatively neutral research or by history—the *external* criterion. Finally, it should be *ethical* in that it helps organizations build caring—even loving—*relationships* with other individuals and groups they affect in a society or the world.

Given this understanding of the nature and effect of worldviews and means of evaluating them, we now can describe the worldviews that we believe affect the practice of public relations and the management of organizations. We then can use the three criteria just identified to evaluate the contribution of those worldviews to excellence in public relations.

In our opinion, three worldviews have limited the excellence and accompanying effectiveness of public relations—the view that public relations is asymmetrical (something that organizations do to publics), the view that public relations has either a neutral or advocacy role in society, and the view that public relations is a technical function. In contrast, we argue that excellent public relations is symmetrical, idealistic or critical, and managerial.

SYMMETRICAL VERSUS ASYMMETRICAL PUBLIC RELATIONS

For me, public relations boils down to getting people to do what you want them to do.
—James L. Tolley (1988)

If you are communicating effectively, you will get positive recognition from the audiences you are trying to influence, which means people will think what you are doing is right and that you are doing it in the right way. When you get positive recognition your influence grows. You are perceived as competent, effective, worthy of respect—*powerful*.
—Robert L. Dilenschneider (1990, p. 8)

What I'll call the "Department of State" P.R. model is an idealistic goal, but a great deal of P.R. activity fits within a "Department of Defense" analogy. There are vigorous P.R. battalions on both side of many of the divisive issues

our society is confronting, with limited or little hope of negotiation. These battalions seek dominant status for their viewpoints.
—Lawrence R. Tavcar (personal communication, August 16, 1990, p. 1)

Each of these three quotes comes from a practitioner who works or has worked in major public relations firms or for major corporations. Each quote describes what we consider to be the dominant worldview in public relations—the asymmetrical view that public relations is a way of getting what an organization wants without changing its behavior or without compromising. It is an alluring mind-set for most organizations: All one has to do to get what one wants is to hire a public relations person who will make you look "competent, effective, worthy of respect—*powerful,*" even if you are not.

Alluring as this mind-set may be, we contend that research does not support its supposed powerful effects. And, we believe that the mind-set guides organizations in directions that are ineffective and not in their long-term interests. We believe that excellent public relations departments adopt the more realistic view that public relations is a symmetrical process of compromise and negotiation and not a war for power. In the long run, the symmetrical view is more effective: Organizations get more of what they want when they give up some of what they want.

J. Grunig and his colleagues and students launched the discussion of asymmetrical and symmetrical worldviews in public relations when they introduced the concept of four models of public relations (J. Grunig & Hunt, 1984; J. Grunig & L. Grunig, 1989; see also chapter 11 of this book).

Press agentry, public information, and *two-way asymmetrical* are asymmetrical models—that is they attempt to change the behavior of publics without changing the behavior of the organization. Under the press agentry model, public relations strives for publicity in the media in almost any way possible. With the public information model, public relations uses journalists in residence to disseminate objective but only favorable information about the organization. With two-way asymmetrical public relations, the organization uses research to develop messages that are most likely to persuade publics to behave as the organization wants.

An organization that uses the two-way symmetrical model, in contrast, uses research and dialogue to manage conflict, improve understanding, and build relationships with publics. With the symmetrical model, both the organization and publics can be persuaded; both also may change their behavior.

J. Grunig (1989b) first described the worldviews that he believes are inherent in these four models at a conference on public relations theory at Illinois State University. In that paper, he argued that an asymmetrical mind-set has dominated the practice of public relations and, in addition, public perceptions of public relations. Such a mind-set, he said, "defines public relations as the use of communication to manipulate publics for the benefit of organizations" (p. 18).

The difference between the asymmetrical and symmetrical worldviews has a number of implications for the construction of a theory of excellence in public relations. Worldview defines which special theories are relevant for a general theory of public relations and which problems constitute public relations problems. The worldview of a public relations department also relates closely to the worldview of the organization that sponsors it, a relationship that explains the underlying conditions necessary for excellent public relations.

Symmetry and Asymmetry in Communication

The difference between symmetrical and asymmetrical communication was highlighted in papers presented by J. Grunig (1989b) and Miller (1989) and the debate that ensued at the conference on public relations theory at Illinois State University. At that conference, J. Grunig argued that the asymmetrical worldview steers public relations practitioners toward actions that are unethical, socially irresponsible, and ineffective. He argued that practitioners with an asymmetrical worldview presuppose that the organization knows best and that publics benefit from "cooperating" with it. Asymmetrical practitioners with a social conscience, he added, sometimes convince themselves that they are manipulating publics for the benefit of those publics—as Olasky (1984) argued was the case for Edward L. Bernays. J. Grunig argued, however, that the mutual benefits of asymmetrical public relations are self-deceptive:

> Although the asymmetrical perspective may sound like a reasonable position, keep in mind that organizations often expect publics to accept strange things as a result of "cooperation": pollution, toxic waste, drinking, smoking, guns, overthrow of governments, dangerous products, lowered salary and benefits, discrimination against women and minorities, job layoffs, dangerous manufacturing plants, risky transportation of products, higher prices, monopoly power, poor product quality, political favoritism, insider trading, use of poisonous chemicals, exposure to carcinogens, nuclear weapons, and even warfare. The list could on and on. The list is important because few of the organizations advocating these positions believe the practices are detrimental to the publics they ask to adopt the behaviors. (p. 32)

J. Grunig then concluded that—in spite of the good intentions of practitioners—it is difficult, if not impossible, to practice public relations in a way that is ethical and socially responsible using an asymmetrical model.

Miller (1989), in contrast, argued that persuasion and public relations are

"Two 'Ps' in a Pod"—that communication and persuasion are linked inextricably even though they may not be synonymous terms.[4] Miller argued that communication is the way in which human beings attempt to exert control over their symbolic environment:

> From birth to death, people seek warmth rather than chilling cold; full bellies rather than empty ones; and respect, affection, and love rather than contempt, social isolation, and hatred. Thus, the quest for environmental control is a crucial fabric of the tapestry of our lives, a human activity as natural and pervasive as breathing. In this broad sense, then, the concept of seeking control is *amoral,* just as breathing or eating is amoral; it is an inevitable aspect of *being alive.* (p. 46)

Miller then went on to define public relations as "a process that centers on exerting symbolic control over certain aspects of the environment . . . of attempting to exert symbolic control over the evaluative predispositions ("attitudes," "images," etc.) and subsequent behaviors of relevant publics or clienteles. . . . *Whenever control of the environment hinges on the attitudes and behaviors of others, attempts to control these attitudes and behaviors are inevitable*" (p. 47).

Miller (1989, p. 47) admitted that the control of attitudes and behaviors of publics is considerably narrower than the all-inclusive goal of living comfortably in one's environment, which he described as an inevitable aspect of being alive. Thus, we would separate Miller's general and specific goals. We would argue that an organization does not have to control its environment to survive and live comfortably in it. In fact, Miller's argument that it is inevitable for an organization to control its symbolic environment is directly analogous to a view of the relationship between the human race and its physical environment that has led to the despoiling of that environment so familiar to us all.

Lowe (1987) traced the philosophical views of the relations between humans and their environment in the literature on environmental ethics. One view, which is found in the Bible among other places, parallels Miller's (1989) definition of public relations as control. That view argues that humans should conquer the earth and exert dominion over it. The other view argues that people are "plain members and citizens of the biotic community, instead of conquerors of it" (p. 43)—a view popularized by Aldo Leopold (1949). Lowe pointed out that "pollution, loss of habitat and species, and other signs of environmental degradation" cannot be halted

---

[4]A position that Berlo (1960) took in an early and influential book on communication theory.

unless people "change some of our fundamental values and assumptions with which we define our place in nature" (p. 2).

In their symbolic environment, we believe, organizations can wreak havoc on their publics when their fundamental values and assumptions — their worldview — suggest that it is ethical for the organization to "exercise dominion" over that environment. Kruckeberg and Starck (1988) took the same view as Aldo Leopold (1949), in essence, when they argued, symmetrically, that public relations "should be practiced as an active attempt to restore a sense of community" rather than as a "vocation utilizing persuasive communication to obtain a vested goal on behalf of a represented client" (p. xi).

We cannot prove by analogy that the damage that people have done to their natural environment supports the conclusion that organizations have done similar damage to publics in their symbolic environments. The comparison does suggest that we compare the quality of life of organizations and publics and the relationships among them as a means of evaluating the symmetrical and asymmetrical worldviews — an aspect of ethics that we examine at the end of this chapter.

Symmetry and Asymmetry in Organizations

Public relations units do not exist in isolation in organizations, however, and the presuppositions guiding their activities are a part of the social structure and culture that integrates the organization (see chapter 17 on organizational structure and chapter 21 on organizational culture). No one public relations practitioner or even a single public relations department is accountable for the approach that an organization takes to communication. In the words of the prominent sociologist and management theorist, Rosabeth Moss Kanter (1981), "Insuring that organizations conform to societal purposes requires that the desired perspectives are implanted into the core decision processes of the organization. It requires becoming involved with the formulation of the patterns themselves, rather than holding accountable individuals whose acts have largely been shaped by those patterns" (p. 87).

Thus, to develop excellence in public relations, one must look at the cultural presuppositions of the organization as well as the presuppositions of public relations. In his book, *World View,* Kearney (1984) isolated what he considered to be "universals" in the worldviews of all cultures. As we see, scholars both of public relations and of organizations have identified similar characteristics in the cultures of organizations.

Of these universals the most important for our purpose is the relationship between "Self and Other." According to Kearney (1984), people see themselves as distinct from the environment. Some cultures see the relationship as one of interdependence and harmony and others as one of subordinance and dominance. In the first worldview, people see an "ecological relationship," in which they "see themselves as intimately connected with the Other . . . and see their well-being as dependent on its well-being" (p. 74). Other cultures, in contrast, see the relationship as one of individualism or "as a struggle for existence in which the fittest survive" (p. 76).

J. Grunig (1989b) spelled out several presuppositions that he believes explain the asymmetrical and symmetrical worldviews, worldviews that characterize this same difference in assumptions about the relationship between self and other. The asymmetrical worldview, he said, is characterized by the following (pp. 32–33):

Internal Orientation. Members of the organization look out from the organization and do not see the organization as outsiders see it.

Closed System. Information flows out from the organization and not into it.

Efficiency. Efficiency and control of costs are more important than innovation.

Elitism. Leaders of the organization know best. They have more knowledge than members of publics. Wisdom is not the product of a "free marketplace of ideas."

Conservatism. Change is undesirable. Outside efforts to change the organization should be resisted; pressure for change should be considered subversive.

Tradition. Tradition provides an organization with stability and helps it to maintain its culture.

Central Authority. Power should be concentrated in the hands of a few top managers. Employees should have little autonomy. Organizations should be managed as autocracies.

In contrast to these asymmetrical presuppositions, J. Grunig (1989b) said that organizations with a symmetrical worldview typically have the following presuppositions in their culture (pp. 38–39):

Interdependence. Organizations cannot isolate themselves from their environment. Although organizations have boundaries that separate them from their environment, publics and other organizations in that environment "interpenetrate" the organization.

Open System. The organization is open to interpenetrating systems and freely exchanges information with those systems.

Moving Equilibrium. Organizations as systems strive toward an equilibrium with other systems, an equilibrium state that constantly moves as the environment changes. Systems may attempt to establish equilibrium by controlling other systems; by adapting themselves to other systems; or by making mutual, cooperative adjustments. The symmetrical worldview prefers cooperative and mutual adjustment to control and adaptation.

Equity. People should be given equal opportunity and be respected as fellow human beings. Anyone, regardless of education or background may provide valuable input into an organization.[5]

Autonomy. People are more innovative, constructive, and self-fulfilled when they have the autonomy to influence their own behavior, rather than having it controlled by others. Autonomy maximizes employee satisfaction inside the organization and cooperation outside the organization.

Innovation. New ideas and flexible thinking rather than tradition and efficiency should be stressed.

Decentralization of Management. Management should be collective; managers should coordinate rather than dictate. Decentralization increases autonomy, employee satisfaction, and innovation.

Responsibility. People and organizations must be concerned with the consequences of their behaviors on others and attempt to eliminate adverse consequences.

Conflict Resolution. Conflict should be resolved through negotiation, communication, and compromise and not through force, manipulation, coercion, or violence.

Interest-Group Liberalism. Classical liberalism, which typically champions big government, can be as closed-minded as classical conservatism, which typically champions big business. Interest-group liberalism, however, views the political system as a mechanism for open negotiation among interest or issue groups (J. Grunig, 1989a; Lowi, 1979). Interest-group liberalism looks to citizen groups to "champion interests of ordinary people against unresponsive government and corporate structures" (Boyte, 1980, p. 7).

Pauchant and Mitroff (1988) isolated a similar set of presuppositions embedded in the cultures of organizations that respond to crises in what they considered a healthy manner and in those that respond in an unhealthy manner. They called the unhealthy organizations "self-inflated corporations" (p. 56). They are "essentially narcissistic . . . They care only or mainly about themselves. A crisis is something which happens mainly only to them and not to their customers or their environment" (p. 56). The

---

[5]J. Grunig (1989b) called this presupposition "equality" rather than "equity." We now see *equity* as a more appropriate term. People should be treated equitably even though equality seldom results. The change from equality to equity comes from reading Gilligan (1982), which is discussed later in the section on gender.

healthy organizations, which they call "positive self-regard organizations," have "exactly the opposite characteristics" (p. 56).

Pauchant and Mitroff (1988) compared the two kinds of organizations on five presuppositions and found differences that nearly mirror those described by J. Grunig (1989b):

Humanity's Relationship to Nature. Unhealthy organizations see their relationship to the environment as one of dominance or subjugation. Healthy organizations treat the stakeholders in the environment as "fellow human beings" and try to alleviate the impact of a crisis on them as well as on the organization (p. 57).

The Nature of Reality and Truth. Unhealthy organizations use many defense mechanisms to avoid responsibility "when the reality of crises confronts their self-inflated fantasies" (p. 57). Healthy organizations more often assume responsibility.

The Nature of Human Nature. Unhealthy organizations divide stakeholders into "them and us," "good guys and bad guys." They especially are likely to perceive the mass media as "evil" when they focus the attention of outsiders on "the lack of perfection of the particular corporations under crisis" (p. 58). Healthy companies, in contrast, know their "strengths and competencies" but also "point out their deficiencies and need for improvement" (p. 59).

The Nature of Human Activities. Unhealthy organizations are passive and fatalistic. They do something "for the sake of doing something" or because they are used to doing it. The healthy organizations "believe in strategic action. They accept the guilt and anxiety induced by crises in order to be in a position to act against them" (pp. 59–60).

The Nature of Human Relationship. Unhealthy organizations see their relationships with other groups of people as competitive and individualistic. Healthy organizations more often view the relationship as cooperative, although, paradoxically, most look upon the relationship as both competitive and cooperative.

Pauchant and Mitroff's (1988) discovery that organizations can mix competition and cooperation suggests that a symmetrical worldview of public relations does not force practitioners to divorce themselves from the self-interest of their clients. In fact, most practitioners will have *mixed motives* and excellent public relations, as we see next, can blend self-interest with public interest.

Mixed Motives in the Symmetrical Worldview

Some critics of the symmetrical worldview—both practitioners and theorists—claim that the approach is unrealistic or idealistic. They argue that organizations hire public relations people as advocates to advance their interests and not as "do-gooders" who "give in" to outsiders with an agenda different from that of the organization. In short, these critics believe that organizations would not hire a public relations person who does not practice asymmetrically.

Organizations do indeed want public relations people to work in their interest. They do not want to give in to all outside demands on the organization when they believe the organization's position is right. As Tuleja (1985) put it, "no responsible manager completely rejects return on investment . . . Corporations are not charitable organizations" (p. 185). But, he added, people in organizations have "divided loyalties" to the organization and to society. And, he maintained, "good guys can finish first": ". . . there is very good evidence that those who behave ethically toward their various constituencies are also those who make the most money" (p. 199).

Another term for *divided loyalties* is *mixed motives,* a concept from game theory that Murphy (1991) introduced to public relations theory. Public relations people generally are motivated both by their loyalty to the organization that employs them and by the publics affected by the behavior of the organization. These mixed motives do not make the symmetrical worldview unrealistic, however. Tuleja (1985) pointed out that the Golden Rule (Do unto others as you would have them do unto you) works because it is a selfish rule: "The Golden Rule works not in spite of selfishness, but because of it. Jesus, that supreme psychologist, was also a supreme egoist. That is why he understood love" (p. 24). The rule is selfish because it mandates that people should think of how they would like to be treated by others and then treat others in the same way.

Thirty years ago, the functionalist sociologist Alvin Gouldner (1960) wrote that a "norm of reciprocity" is a universal component of moral codes. He pointed out that Aristotle had observed that people are "more ready to receive than to give benefits." People tend toward egoism, he said, "a salient (but not exclusive) concern with the satisfaction of one's own needs" (p. 173). But, he added, "there is an altruism in egoism, made possible through reciprocity"—". . . egoism can motivate one party to satisfy the expectations of the other, since by doing so he [sic] induces the latter to reciprocate and to satisfy his [sic] own" (p. 173).

In short, excellent organizations realize that they can get more of what they want by giving publics some of what they want. Reciprocity means that publics, too, will be willing to give up some of what they want to the organization. The logic of reciprocity breaks down, however, when one actor (such as an organization) has more power than another (such as a public). "Given significant power differences," according to Gouldner

(1960), "egoistic motivations may seek to get benefits without returning them" (p. 174).

Rakow (1989b), for example, criticized the symmetrical approach to public relations as impractical because she believed that organizations in the U.S. social system, at least, have more power than publics and therefore no motivation for reciprocity. Mallinson (1990), similarly, argued that the two-way symmetrical model would work better in the more egalitarian cultures of Europe than it would in the United States. And Pavlik (1989) showed, in game theory terms, that organizations are unlikely to practice public relations symmetrically until publics gain equal power.

Part of the answer to the dilemma of unequal power has been resolved because publics have gained power by organizing into activist groups. But in many relationships with publics, organizations still hold the upper hand. In that case, Gouldner (1960) proposed that a "generalized norm of reciprocity" would solve the dilemma of unequal power. Most moral codes, he said, contain a norm that reciprocity is good or necessary — even if people or organizations can get what they want by exerting their power. Organizations that do not adhere to this general norm lose the trust and credibility of the larger society of which they are a part. Thus, excellent organizations would seem likely to incorporate the norm into their business or organizational ethics and, in turn, into their public relations ethics. The norm of reciprocity is the essence of what generally is called social responsibility. In Gouldner's words:

> The norm of reciprocity, however, engenders motives for returning benefits even when power differences might invite exploitation. The norm thus safeguards powerful people against the temptations of their own status; it motivates and regulates reciprocity as an exchange pattern, serving to inhibit the emergence of exploitative relations which would undermine the social system and the very power arrangements which had made exploitation possible. (p. 174)

As the last sentence of this quote indicates, Gouldner (1960) argued that a norm of reciprocity stabilizes a social system. But he also addressed the most frequently cited failure of functional theory — its inability to explain the origins of social systems as well as the stability of ongoing systems. The norm of reciprocity provides a "starting mechanism" for social relationships, he explained, an assumed type of behavior that allows social actors — including organizations and publics — to deal with each other when they have had no prior relationship.

When we assume that the other party will reciprocate our actions, in other words, we can treat it fairly even though we might have more power.

Reciprocity, Gouldner (1960) added, also can be negative. That is, we can assume that if an organization treats a public poorly, the public will in turn treat the organization poorly. The norm of reciprocity, therefore, is an integral part of the symmetrical worldview that is an essential part of excellent public relations.

The concept of reciprocity—including both selfish reciprocity and the generalized norm when there are differences in power—allows us to accommodate mixed motives into the symmetrical worldview. Chapter 11 describes research and theory building on the four models of public relations that integrates the two-way asymmetrical and two-way symmetrical models into a mixed-motive model. In addition, recent advancements in rhetorical theory by scholars of speech communication allow us to "come to terms with mixed motives," in the words of Cheney and Tompkins (1984, p. 18). Much of this advancement is based on the work of Kenneth Burke and Jurgen Habermas and has produced theories that "counterbalance the sender orientation of traditional rhetoric with stress on a receiver orientation in the (Burke's) rhetoric of identification" (Cheney & Tompkins, 1984, p. 18).

Booth (1981), for example, described four types of rhetoric that parallel the four models of public relations:

Sub-Rhetoric. ". . . words or other symbols are being used to deceive or to obscure issues or evade action" (p. 29). (= press agentry)

Mere Rhetoric. ". . . the whole art of sincere selling of any cause, not just the trickery part of the disguise, but the genuinely persuasive parts too, including the logical arguments" (p. 29). (= public information)

Rhetoric-B. This, essentially, is the rhetoric of Aristotle, in which the rhetorician discovers or invents the "possible means of persuasion in reference to any subject whatsoever" (p. 31):

Rhetoric-B is the art of knowing what you want, and finding the really good arguments to win others to your side, It is the art of the good lawyer, of the effective business leader, of the successful fund raiser, and it is not to be scoffed at or ignored. But it does not itself teach us what ends it should serve; it is still an art without essential restraints other than those provided by the counterrhetoric created by other warriors or competitors. The world it builds, left on its own, is a world of a free market of atomized persons and ideas, each privately seeking victory and hoping that in the melee a public good will be produced by some invisible hand. (pp. 32–33) (= two-way asymmetrical)

Booth's (1981) description of Rhetoric-B, in particular, identifies the shortcomings of the asymmetrical worldview. In that worldview, communication becomes a war of words with no restraints built in to preserve the public good—an ethical difference that is addressed in the last section of this chapter. Contrast Rhetoric-B with a new form of rhetoric:

Rhetoric-A. ". . . a supreme art of inquiry through symbols that is designed, not to win by cheating, as in sub-rhetoric, nor merely to win sincerely, as in mere rhetoric, and not just to marshall all of the good reasons there might be for accepting what one knows already, but rather to discover and refine, in critical exchange, our ends, our purposes, our values" (pp. 34–35). (= two-way symmetrical)

Booth (1981) added that no other society has "committed itself so passionately to the search for rhetoric-A . . . with committee work, with the cumbersomeness of representative government, with the absurdities of our thousands of national conventions, colloquia, conferences, workshops and commissions. . . . Well, that rhetoric-A for you?" (p. 35).

Much argument, debate, persuasion—and compromise—take place in these communication forums. Motives are mixed but when the worldview is symmetrical, in the words of Cheney and Dionisopoulis (1989), "Organizations, specifically their communications officers, should represent interests in such a way that both persuades and allows for others to persuade" (p. 148).

The symmetrical worldview can accommodate mixed motives in public relations. Before leaving the discussion of the difference between asymmetrical and symmetrical worldviews, however, we address an additional correlate of those worldviews: gender differences.

Gender Differences in Worldview

As the events of women's lives and of history intersect with their feelings and thought, a concern with individual survival comes to branded as "selfish" and to be counterposed to the "responsibility" of a life lived in relationships. . . . The truths of relationship, however, return in the rediscovery of connection, in the realization that self and other are interdependent and that life, however valuable in itself can only be sustained by care in relationships.

—Gilligan (1982, p. 127)

In her pioneering book, *In a Different Voice,* Gilligan (1982) articulated a difference in the orientations of men and women that also has been reflected in an extensive literature on women in management (e.g., Moore, 1986; Stead, 1985). Men are more concerned with competition, rights, and fairness; women are more concerned with relationships, responsibility, and equity (Gilligan, 1982, p. 164). The conventional wisdom has been that these differences make men more suitable as managers because of their preference for competition and "toughness." Recently, however, re-searchers have begun to realize that women's preference for nurturance and relationships may be exactly what is needed by managers in the future (e.g., Aburdene, 1990).

In recent years, the gender balance in public relations has moved from being a heavy male majority to being a female majority. Many leaders in the public relations profession have worried that female dominance would limit the salaries in and status of public relations because of traditional discrim-ination toward female-dominated professions (Toth, 1988). Feminists, however, have argued just the opposite, that the feminine viewpoint will be valuable to public relations because of a "commitment to antiauthoritarian, antielitist, participatory, and emancipatory values" (L. Grunig, 1988, p. 53). Rakow (1989a) added:

> The classical liberal ideology of individualism and competition might be thought of as the dominant (i.e., public), masculine one, the alternate ideology of cooperation and community as the suppressed (private) feminine one. . . . feminist research has demonstrated that white women are likely to think of themselves in terms of their relationships rather than in terms of autonomy; to perform unrecognized and unvalued work holding together relationships, families, and communities; to prefer cooperative and collabo-rative styles of interacting and organizing. (pp. 293–294)

Terms such as values, ideology, and truths in the aforementioned quotes make it clear that the differences commonly attributed to men and women are part of their respective worldviews. The feminine worldview seems to be a symmetrical worldview and the masculine worldview an asymmetrical one. Thus, a female majority in public relations could move the field toward excellence as the symmetrical worldview of most women begins to replace the more asymmetrical worldview of most men.

That women could enhance the excellence of public relations does not mean, however, that men cannot practice in an excellent fashion also. Psychologists have demonstrated that both men and women can have feminine worldviews or that their worldview can have both feminine and masculine components (Wetherell, 1989). In public relations, this means that men who want to practice excellent public relations can learn the value of such concepts as interdependence, relationships, and equity from women (L. Grunig, 1989). As we see in the next chapter, these concepts explain how public relations contributes to the effectiveness of an organization.

PRESUPPOSITIONS ABOUT THE SOCIAL ROLE
OF PUBLIC RELATIONS

Throughout our discussion of asymmetrical and symmetrical worldviews about public relations, we have mentioned concepts such as community, the social system, and social responsibility. Public relations has a role in society, and many European scholars such as Ruhl (1990) have devoted more of their theorizing to understanding that role than to understanding the value of public relations to an organization.

Most practitioners and scholars have presuppositions about the social role of public relations, even though they may not articulate them or be aware of them. Some of these extant presuppositions enhance the excellence of public relations and others detract from it. In addition, some are symmetrical and some are asymmetrical. First, we look at some of the worldviews on social role that are less likely to lead to excellence.

The Pragmatic Social Role

This view of social role appears in statements about the contribution of public relations to the bottom line or in public relations as a results-oriented practice. The presupposition here is that public relations is a useful practice, which "adds value" and which can be used to meet the objectives of a client organization in a way that benefits the client. This presupposition underlies the commercial practice of public relations and typically allies it with marketing objectives. It also may underlie arguments against the development of codes of conduct or ethical standards in public relations practice, because these may set unacceptable limits on what can be done to achieve the client's objectives.

When followed to its extreme, this presupposition leads to practices that, if brought to public attention, brings public relations into disrepute or, at least, allows the client to dictate public relations practice. Public relations firms, especially, practice pragmatic public relations when they provide any service to a client in order to make money for the firm. When practiced pragmatically, the pragmatic worldview sees society as composed of competing groups, target audiences, and markets from whom commercial advantage is to be won. Society is a marketplace for ideas, services, and products. Publics are customers, and opposition is to be neutralized in pursuit of commercial objectives.

The pragmatic social view is common in public relations; because of its concern for doing what the client wants, however, it cannot be excellent and seldom makes the organization more effective. Generally, the pragmatic worldview also is asymmetrical because that is how the client organizations perceive public relations. The next two presuppositions about social role, however, are clearly asymmetrical.

The Conservative Social Role

According to the conservative presupposition, public relations defends and maintains the status quo (see, e.g., Tedlow, 1979, who described public relations as a "defensive political device"). Pimlott (1951) suggested that public relations justifies and defends the privileges of the economically powerful and that public relations practitioners, like politicians and teachers, are essentially articulate apologists for a social system based on what are, in some cases, insupportable inequalities. Sussman (1949) described public relations as based on a defensive ideology.

Modern reflections of this view are found in the writings of Philip Lesly (1984) in books such as *Overcoming Opposition,* which explains how public relations can overcome threats to the status quo. In practice, a conservative view of social role leads practitioners to adopt a defensive or protective outlook on their client's interests—that is, an asymmetrical outlook.

Practitioners with this social view also see society in conservative terms. They believe in defending the status quo and an idealized capitalist system from attack. Writers on public relations working from this presupposition talk of public relations' "arsenals," armories or weapons, which can be used to overcome opposition, target audiences, or defeat "intellectual terrorists" (a term recently used in the United Kingdom to describe opponents of some of the activities of tobacco and drug companies [Pielle Newsletter, 1988]). The next worldview, which comes from the opposite side of the political spectrum, is equally asymmetrical.

The Radical Social Role

The radical worldview presupposes that public relations contributes to change, within organizations and in society. It does so by providing an outside perspective to management about the organization and its internal functioning. In the wider society, public relations contributes to social change by providing information for use in public debate, by establishing links between groups in society, and by bringing resources together that can be brought to bear on the solution of social problems.

This worldview sees society as a system in which knowledge and information provide power and influence, which can be used to bring about change. Goldhaber, Dennis, Richetto, and Wiio (1979) argued, for example, that power and influence within organizations now have passed to people such as public relations practitioners who can provide information about the environment to decision makers. Hofstede (1980) argued that practitioners should act as agents of change within organizations, to help them to adjust to changing public expectations.

Both the conservative and radical worldviews assume that organizational communication can have powerful effects on society. They see public relations as a tool to be used in a war among opposing social groups. More excellent public relations programs, we believe, take the next, more symmetrical approach.

The Idealistic Social Role

Idealistic presuppositions about public relations appear in codes of conduct, definitions of the practice, conference speeches, and academic writing about the practice. Indeed, they can be found throughout this book. This worldview presupposes that public relations serves the public interest, develops mutual understanding between organizations and their publics, contributes to informed debate about issues in society, and facilitates a dialogue between organizations and their publics.

This worldview sees society as emerging from compromise—from the peaceful resolution of conflict between groups in society. It assumes a pluralist and progressive society, in which a diversity of views and their reconciliation lead to social progress.

In other terms, the idealistic social view assumes that a norm of reciprocity governs society and that norm makes it possible for public relations to play the role envisioned in the symmetrical worldview, which is closely aligned with this worldview. Excellent public relations practice, therefore, generally will be symmetrical and idealistic. Two, more academic views of the social role of public relations remain, however, which are analogues of these more practice-oriented views.

The Neutral Social Role

Scholars who take this view adopt the view of science that we called logical positivism early in this chapter. They view public relations as a neutral object of study and focus on such questions as the motivations of organization when they initiate public relations activities, the goals and objectives toward which public relations activities are directed, and the effects of public relations. Like sociologists, these scholars view society as an object of study and raise questions about the social role of public relations.

Observation and interpretation are the essence of all scholarship, but philosophers of science now generally reject the idea that observation and interpretation can be neutral. Worldview and values affect both, and both lead to criticisms of the behaviors observed and recommendations for more effective behaviors. As a result, the final social role reflects the approach of this book.

The Critical Social Role

Critical scholars range from radical Marxists to empirical scholars who draw implications from their data for change in public relations practice. Critical scholars view organizations and society as *constructed* systems,

systems that can be *deconstructed* and *reconstructed*. Critical scholars have done research to document the poor ethics, negative social consequences, or ineffectiveness of forms of public relations that differ from normative theories of excellent public relations.

Some critics have evaluated public relations from a political perspective. Olasky (1987, 1989), a conservative, maintained that corporations have used public relations to consort with government — thus restricting competition. Gandy (1982), a Marxist, argued that public relations helps to preserve the dominant power structure in society. Other critical scholars such as Rakow (1989b) have suggested that the two-way symmetrical model of public relations cannot work in the United States without a radical transformation of its culture and political structure.

Rhetorical theorists such as Smilowitz and Pearson (1989), Cheney and Dionisopoulos (1989), or Pearson (1989a, 1989b) have examined public relations against the yardstick provided by rhetorical theories such as Habermas's (1984) ideal communication situation or Burke's theory of "identification" in persuasion — the cocreation by the persuader and persuadee of a state of affairs (Gusfield, 1989).[6] As mentioned earlier, a large and growing community of scholars have begun to use feminist theory to criticize public relations (e.g., Cline, 1985; Creedon, 1991; L. Grunig, 1988, 1989; Rakow, 1989a; Toth, 1988). Finally, quantitative researchers have used the theories they have developed from observing how organizations practice public relations to criticize that practice and to advocate more effective practices (see, e.g., chapters 10, 11, 12, and 14 of this book).

Excellent public relations, in summary, views its role in society from an idealistic worldview. And it is fostered, we believe, by scholars who criticize actual practice against such a standard. Many public relations practitioners reject that worldview, however, as well as the criticism of scholars. Thus, they would not be receptive to the theory developed in this book. One aspect of the dominant — but not excellent — worldview of public relations remains, however, before we examine the normative implications of the excellent worldview.

TECHNICAL AND MANAGERIAL PRESUPPOSITIONS ABOUT PUBLIC RELATIONS

Public relations is a craft, a technique, a discipline; but it's not a profession. . . . Apart from academe, who ever worries about PR's not having a

---

[6]Toth and Heath (1992) have provided a complete volume of research using rhetorical and critical approaches to public relations.

substantial body of knowledge? I'll bet it keeps Hill & Knowlton CEO Robert Dilenschneider awake nights.

— The Ragan Report, March 20, 1989

This opinion, stated in one of the mostly widely read newsletters on public relations and communication, reflects another element in the worldview of many organizations and public relations practitioners — that public relations is technique and not theory. It can be found in popular books on public relations such as *Confessions of a PR Man* (Wood with Gunther, 1988), which was written by a former executive of Carl Byoir and Associates and which describes the day-to-day work of public relations only in terms of technique. The worldview also can be found in the more sophisticated book by Hill and Knowlton's former CEO, Robert Dilenschneider (1990), *Power and Influence,* which Edward L. Bernays (1990) described in a book review as more about tactics than strategy.

The worldview of public relations as technique is associated closely with the press agentry and public information models of public relations. And it underlies the notion that public relations is a marketing function. Kotler and Andreasen (1987), for example, argued that marketing is strategic but public relations is not.

Chapter 12 documents the need for a managerial as well as a technical role in excellent public relations departments. The need for a managerial role falls on deaf ears, however, when the prevailing worldview among practitioners or in an organization is that public relations is a set of techniques and that a theory of management is not necessary to underlie those techniques.

A NORMATIVE THEORY OF ETHICAL PUBLIC RELATIONS

Worldviews are subjective. In addition, most people are not aware of the power that worldviews have over their behavior: "Mind moves matter." Yet the literature cited in this chapter showed that people can become aware of their worldviews and that they can choose an alternative worldview if they want.

In this chapter, we have developed the argument that public relations cannot be excellent if organizations have a culture that is authoritarian, manipulative, and controlling of others — asymmetrical in its worldview of relationships with others. Public relations also cannot be excellent if the schema for public relations in the organization (the component of worldview related to public relations) conceives of public relations as asymmetrical, in a neutral or advocacy role, and solely technical in nature. Instead, we have argued, excellent public relations is based on the worldview that public relations is symmetrical, idealistic in its social role, and managerial.

The literature on worldview cited earlier in this chapter showed that worldviews can be evaluated on three criteria—their internal logic and coherence, their external effectiveness in allowing people and organizations to solve problems originating in their environments, and their ethical ability to promote good or social harmony. On the internal criterion, you as a reader must judge the logic of the worldview we have developed here as a characteristic of excellent public relations. For the external criterion, we present research evidence and supporting theories throughout this book to support the effectiveness of this worldview in solving organizational problems. In addition, the empirical study of excellence in public relations, which will follow this book, should provide evidence in support of the worldview. What remains for this chapter, then, is a discussion of the ethics of the competing worldviews.

The Practicality of Idealism

To some practitioners and scholars, the term *idealistic* suggests that the worldview we have proposed is impractical, abstract, theoretical, and unrealistic—meanings for the term revealed in a thesaurus. Yet the same thesaurus identifies the words *optimistic* (positive, confident, promising) and *utopian* (ideal, model, or exemplary) as alternative meanings for idealistic. The terms *ideal* or *exemplary* capture best what we think is the value of this worldview. It serves as a normative standard for ethical public relations—of how it should be practiced. Pearson (1989b) developed a theory of public relations ethics based on symmetrical principles, like those articulated in this chapter, that he called the "ideal public relations situation." His theory, we believe, supports the view that the worldview of public relations developed in this chapter is more ethical than competing worldviews.

For over a century, philosophers have debated the merits of two types of ethical theories: utilitarian and deontological theories.[7] Utilitarian theories emphasize the practical aspects of behavior—the consequences on others. Deontological theories emphasize formal, universally true principles of what is good or evil.

A utilitarian approach to ethics often runs into trouble because of its relativity. Sometimes behaviors have both positive and negative consequences; and, as Tuleja (1985) put it, ". . . in calculating the net sum of good and bad in a potential action, I am not likely to be dispassionate and impartial but to weight my own happiness more heavily than that of others"

---

[7]For a review of this debate, see Pearson (1989b), Tuleja (1985), or Merrill and Odell (1983).

(p. 20). Relativity presents the greatest difficulty when power is not equal. In that case the consequences desired by the powerful get greater weight than consequences on the less powerful (Tuleja, 1985, p. 21).

Consequences on others are important in public relations. J. Grunig and Hunt (1984), for example, said that an organization does not have a public relations problem unless it has consequences on publics or publics have consequences on it. But as we saw earlier, organizations with great power probably will ignore the consequences of their behaviors on publics unless they react to a moral imperative such as the norm of reciprocity. The norm of reciprocity underlies our symmetrical worldview and, we believe, makes that worldview inherently ethical.[8]

Asymmetrical public relations can be ethical if its practitioners can show that the consequences of their behavior do not harm people. Practitioners frequently disagree, however, about what actions are ethical when they take an asymmetrical approach. Is it ethical to market cigarettes, for example, or to campaign against gun laws? Should a public relations firm promote the position of the Catholic Church on abortion? Many who practice asymmetrical public relations avoid the question, adopting the presuppositions of the neutral social role or those of the conservative or radical advocacy roles. Most, to use the words that Booth (1981) used to describe the practitioners of his Rhetoric-B, ". . . show themselves to be, in effect, available to the highest bidder: they fail to provide, from within themselves, any hint about limits to how and when their techniques are to be used" (p. 33).

We believe, in contrast, that public relations should be based on a worldview that incorporates ethics into the process of public relations rather than on a view that debates the ethics of its outcomes. Such an approach could, for example, set up a dialogue between tobacco companies, smokers, and antismoking groups or between various religious groups and abortion rights groups. The outcome then must be ethical if all parties participate in making decisions and accept the choice of consequences that are to be sought and those that are to be avoided. Both Cheney and Tompkins (1984) and Pearson (1989b) developed such ethical theories that reflect the symmetrical worldview.

Burke on Ethics

Cheney and Tompkins (1984) based their ethical theory on Kenneth Burke's concept of "identification" — a "shorthand description of the process of

---

[8]Pearson (1989a) and Pratt (1990) also argued that symmetrical public relations is inherently ethical.

communication."[9] "An ethic of identification," they added, "must account for both explicit and implicit forms of linking one's interests with those of others" (p. 6). Cheney and Tompkins, then, isolated four deontological rules of rhetoric that constitute ethics of what we have called mixed-motive, symmetrical communication:

> *Guardedness.* Communicators, or organizations, should not capitulate "willy nilly" to the persuasive demands of others.
> *Accessibility.* Communicators should be open to the possibility of being persuaded for their own benefit.
> *Nonviolence.* We should attempt to persuade rather than to coerce others. In doing so, however, we should not "arouse and solidify hostile feelings nor should we present our view of the world as the single, correct one" (pp. 12–13).
> *Empathy.* We should listen to others as much for our sake as for theirs. We should be "genuinely concerned with the arguments, opinions, values and philosophies of others." (p. 14)

Pearson on Habermas

Pearson (1989b) developed a similar, but more extensive theory of public relations ethics based in large part on the theories of the German philosopher and rhetorician Jurgen Habermas.[10] In developing his theory of ethics, however, Pearson also used traditional philosophical theories of ethics and psychological theories of moral development—especially those of Kohlberg (1981) and Gilligan (1982) as well as Habermas.

Habermas's theory of ethics rests on his concept of an ideal communication situation—a situation characterized by dialogue and in which participants agree upon a system of rules to facilitate that dialogue. These rules constitute the formal, deontological aspects of ethics. According to Pearson (1989b), the following rules apply to each of four communication acts:

> *Communicatives* are communication acts that open lines of communication. As such, they should be *intelligible* to the person to whom they are directed. The communicator should "clarify, offer synonyms, make whatever repetitions are necessary so that a hearer understands, and . . . select

---

[9]For an overview of Burke's rhetorical theory, see Gusfield (1989).

[10]This discussion of Habermas is based on Pearson's (1989b) discussion of his work. Readers wanting a more detailed discussion of Habermas's work should consult McCarthy (1978) or the translations of several of Habermas's books.

channels of communication that increase the likelihood of understanding" (p. 235).

Constatives "assert, report, explain, predict, deny, object, or estimate." They "make an implicit claim to truth," and the communicator should support that claim to truth by *providing grounds or reasons* (p. 236).

Representatives are "expressive speech acts that reveal how a speaker feels." In making such statements, a communicator should *be sincere and show trustworthiness* by behavior "that matches his or her expressed intention" (p. 237).

Regulatives "include orders, commands, requests, admonitions, promises, agreements, and refusals." In making them, the communicator claims that they are *based on valid norms* or on his or her authority and responsibility. The communicator, therefore, must justify these claims by explaining the norms that give the speaker the "conviction" that he or she is right. If the hearer disagrees, the claim should be debated (p. 237).

Pearson (1989b) explained that people — or organizations and publics — that follow these rules will not always agree on practical decisions when they have different values or different concepts of what is good. That is, they often will not agree on the utilitarian or practical aspect of ethics. People, to use our terms, will have mixed motives — the conviction that they are right and the conviction that others should be respected. What is needed is an approach to ethics that combines "moral conviction and tolerance" (Pearson, 1989b, p. 315). When people disagree about what is moral, therefore, they debate and attempt to persuade one another.

In doing so, however, they should follow rules like those of Cheney and Tompkins (1984) that leave them open to persuasion at the same time that they try to persuade others. What is right or wrong, true or false can be determined only through dialogue and agreement and not through the evidence or "raw organizational data provided by one party or one organization." Pearson (1989b) said, for example, that the statement that an organization has "advanced minorities into management ranks" can be said to be "true" only when the organization and a representative of a minority public agree that it is true (p. 239).

Political theorist Bruce Ackerman (1980) advanced similar principles of openness and dialogue for resolving disputes over right and wrong and truth. Ackerman said that a power holder (such as an organization or management) cannot suppress the claims of someone else to power (such as a public or employees) without giving reasons for doing so — what Ackerman called "rationality" (p. 372). Ackerman added that the reasons must be consistent from one occasion to another. And, he said, a reason is not a good one if the holder of power asserts that his or her "conception of the good" is better than that of someone else or that he or she is "intrinsically superior to one or more of his [sic] fellow citizens" (p. 11). Pearson (1989a) summarized Ackerman's position by saying, "The upshot of this final rule is that an illegitimate claimant to power over scarce resources will be reduced to silence, because he or she will not be able to provide reasons, only unsupportable claims of superior moral insight" (p. 72).

Psychologists such as Kohlberg (1981) have shown that people must advance through several stages of moral development before developing the ability to take others into account by adopting formal rules like the Golden Rule—that is, before accepting the norm of reciprocity. But Pearson (1989b) added that Habermas and feminist psychologists such as Gilligan (1982) have argued that moral development has one more stage—that of interactive competence or the ability to engage in dialogue. At that stage, people base morality on responsibility rather than on rights and develop a greater sense of interdependence and relationship.

In short, the more ethically developed an individual is—and also an organization—the more he or she uses the concepts of reciprocity and symmetry to decide what is moral (Pearson, 1989b, p. 244)—twin concepts that are crucial components of the worldview developed in this chapter.

Pearson (1989b) then developed an ethical theory for public relations based on the following basic premise and two moral imperatives:

> *Basic premise:* Ethics in public relations is not fundamentally a question of whether it is right or wrong to tell the truth, steal clients from one another, accept free lunches or bribes or provide information for insider trading etc. Rather, ethical public relations practice is more fundamentally a question of implementing and maintaining inter-organizational communication systems which question, discuss and validate these and other substantive ethical claims.

> *Basic moral imperatives:* 1) It is a moral imperative to establish and maintain communication relationships with all publics affected by organizational action. 2) It is a moral imperative to improve the quality of these communi- cation relationships, that is, to make them increasingly dialogical. More precisely and more concretely this means working toward rule identification, rule clarification and rule change such that measures of organization/public understanding of and agreement on communication rules become increasingly positive. (p. 377)

From an Idealistic to a Positive Normative Theory

In this chapter, we believe that we have presented a strong, logical argument supporting the internal validity and ethical superiority of the symmetrical worldview articulated here over the dominant asymmetrical worldview that pervades public relations. Throughout the rest of the book, authors derive theoretical principles of public relations and organizational behavior from our worldview. Our worldview, like all worldviews, is normative — it reflects what we and other theorists cited in this chapter think should be. But, as Massy and Weitz (1977) put it, useful normative theory should provide solutions "under typical conditions encountered in actual practice" (p. 123).

Thus, in reviewing literature in this book and in the field research that will follow, we also intend to show that this worldview works well in real communication situations as well as in ideal situations. Our idealistic worldview, in other words, also is an effective, realistic theory. The next chapter, then, explores the concept of organizational effectiveness and the relationship of public relations to it.

REFERENCES

Aburdene, P. (1990, November). Speech to the Public Relations Society of America, New York.

Anderson, J. R. (1983). *The architecture of cognition*. Cambridge, MA: Harvard University Press.

Ackerman, B. A. (1980). *Social justice in the liberal state*. New Haven, CT: Yale University Press.

Berlo, D. K. (1960). *The process of communication*. New York: Holt, Rinehart & Winston.

Bernays, E. L. (1990). [Review of Robert L. Dilenschneider's *Power and influence*]. *Public Relations Review, 16*(2), 82–83.

Bohm, D. (1977). Science as perception-communication. In F. Suppe (Ed.), *The structure of scientific theories* (pp. 37–391). Urbana: University of Illinois Press.

Booth, W. C. (1981). Mere rhetoric, rhetoric & the search for common learning. In E. I. Boyer (Ed.), *Common learning: A Carnegie colloquium on general education* (pp. 23–55). Washington, DC: Carnegie Foundation for the Advancement of Teaching.

Boulding, K. E. (1956). *The image*. Ann Arbor: University of Michigan Press.

Boyte, H. C. (1980). *The backyard revolution: Understanding the new citizen movement*. Philadelphia: Temple University Press.

Brown, H. I. (1977). *Perception, theory and commitment: The new philosophy of science*. Chicago: University of Chicago Press.

Cheney, G., & Dionisopoulos, G. N. (1989). Public relations? No, relations with publics: A rhetorical-organizational approach to contemporary corporate communication. In C. H. Botan & V. Hazleton, Jr. (Eds.), *Public relations theory* (pp. 135–158). Hillsdale, NJ: Lawrence Erlbaum Associates.

Cheney, G., & Tompkins, P. K. (1984, March). *Toward an ethic of identification*. Paper presented at the Burke Conference, Philadelphia, PA.

Cline, C. G. (1985). Public relations: The $1 million dollar penalty for being a woman. In P. J. Creedon (Ed.), *Women in mass communication: Challenging gender values* (pp. 263–275). Newbury Park, CA: Sage.

Collingwood, R. G. (1940). *An essay on metaphysics*. London: Oxford University Press.

Craik, F. I. M. (1979). Levels of processing: Overview and closing comments. In L. S. Cermak & F. I. M. Craik (Eds.), *Levels of processing in human memory* (pp. 447–461). Hillsdale, NJ: Lawrence Erlbaum Associates.

Creedon, P. J. (1991). Public relations and "women's work": Toward a feminist analysis of public relations roles. *Public Relations Research Annual, 3,* 67–84.

Dilenschneider, R. L. (1990). *Power and influence.* New York: Prentice-Hall.

Feyerabend, P. R. (1970). Consolations for the specialist. In I. Lakatos & A. Musgrave (Eds.), *Criticism and the growth of knowledge* (pp. 197–230). Cambridge, England: Cambridge University Press.

Gandy, O. H., Jr. (1982). *Beyond agenda setting: Information subsidies and public policy.* Norwood, NJ: Ablex.

Gilligan, C. (1982). *In a different voice.* Cambridge, MA: Harvard University Press.

Goldhaber, G. M., Dennis, H. S., Richetto, G. M., & Wiio, O. A. (1979). *Information strategies: New pathways to corporate power.* Englewood Cliffs, NJ: Prentice-Hall.

Gouldner, A. W. (1960). The norm of reciprocity: A preliminary statement. *American Sociological Review, 25,* 161–178.

Grunig, J. E. (1989a). Sierra Club study shows who become activists. *Public Relations Review, 15*(3), 3–24.

Grunig, J. E. (1989b). Symmetrical presuppositions as a framework for public relations theory. In C. H. Botan & V. Hazleton, Jr. (Eds.), *Public relations theory* (pp. 17–44). Hillsdale, NJ: Lawrence Erlbaum Associates.

Grunig, J. E., & Childers (aka Hon), L. (1988, August). *Reconstruction of a situational theory of communication: Internal and external concepts as identifiers of publics for AIDS.* Paper presented at the meeting of the Association for Education in Journalism & Mass Communication, Portland, OR.

Grunig, J. E., & Grunig, L. A. (1989). Toward a theory of the public relations behavior of organizations: Review of a program of research. In J. E. Grunig & L. A. Grunig (Eds.), *Public relations research annual* (Vol. 1, pp. 27–63). Hillsdale, NJ: Lawrence Erlbaum Associates.

Grunig, J. E., & Hunt, T. (1984). *Managing public relations.* New York: Holt, Rinehart & Winston.

Grunig, J. E., Ramsey, S., & Schneider (aka Grunig), L. A. (1985). An axiomatic theory of cognition and writing. *Journal of Technical Writing and Communication, 15,* 95–130.

Grunig, L. A. (1988). A research agenda for women in public relations. *Public Relations Review, 14*(3), 48–57.

Grunig, L. A. (1989, August). *Toward a feminist transformation of public relations education and practice.* Paper presented at the meeting of the Association for Education in Journalism and Mass Communication, Washington, DC.

Gusfield, J. R. (1989). *Kenneth Burke on symbols and society.* Chicago: University of Chicago Press.

Habermas, J. (1984). *The theory of communicative action* (Vol. 1) (T. McCarthy, Trans.). Boston: Beacon.

Hofstede, G. (1980). Angola coffee—Or the confrontation of an organization with changing values in its environment. *Organization Studies, 1,* 21–40.

Kanter, R. M. (1981). Contemporary organizations. In E. I. Boyer (Ed.), *Common learning: A Carnegie colloquium on general education* (pp. 75–93). Washington, DC: Carnegie Foundation for the Advancement of Teaching.

Kearney, M. (1984). *World view.* Novato, CA: Chandler & Sharp.

Kohlberg, L. (1981). *The philosophy of moral development.* San Francisco: Harper & Row.

Kotler, P., & Andreasen, A. R. (1987). *Strategic marketing for nonprofit organizations* (3rd ed.). Englewood Cliffs, NJ: Prentice-Hall.

Kruckeberg, D., & Starck, K. (1988). *Public relations and community: A reconstructed theory.* New York: Praeger.

Kuhn, T. S. (1970). *The structure of scientific revolutions.* Chicago: University of Chicago Press.

Laudan, L. (1977). *Progress and its problems.* Berkeley: University of California Press.

Leopold, A. (1949). *A Sand County almanac.* New York: Ballantine.

Lesly, P. (1984). *Overcoming opposition.* Englewood Cliffs, NJ: Prentice-Hall.

Lowe, J. T. (1987). *Environment themes in the news: A qualitative content analysis of the Baltimore Sun.* Unpublished master's thesis, University of Maryland, College Park.

Lowi, T. J. (1979). The end of liberalism: The second republic of the United States (2nd ed.). New York: W. W. Norton.

Mallinson, B. (1990, June). *Bridging the gap between theory and practice in post-1992 Europe: The changing face of public relations.* Paper presented at the meeting of the International Communication Association, Dublin.

Markus, M., & Zajonc, R. B. (1985). The cognitive perspective in social psychology. In G. Lindsey & E. Anderson (Eds.), *Handbook of social psychology* (Vol. 1, pp. 137–230). New York: Random House.

Massy, W. F., & Weitz, B. A. (1977). A normative theory of market segmentation. In F. M. Nicosia & Y. Wind (Eds.), *Behavioral models for market analysis: Foundations for marketing action* (pp. 121–144). Hinsdale, IL: Dryden.

McCarthy, T. (1978). *The critical theory of Jurgen Habermas.* Cambridge, MA: MIT Press.

Meehan, E. J. (1968). *Explanation in social science.* Homewood, IL: Dorsey.

Merrill, J. C., & Odell, S. J. (1983). *Philosophy and journalism.* New York: Longman.

Miller, G. R. (1989). Persuasion and public relations: Two "Ps" in a pod. In C. H. Botan & V. Hazleton, Jr. (Eds.), *Public relations theory* (pp. 45–66). Hillsdale, NJ: Lawrence Erlbaum Associates.

Moore, L. L. (1986). *Not as far as you think: The Realities of working women.* Lexington, MA: Lexington.

Morgan, G. (1986). *Images of organization.* Newbury Park, CA: Sage.

Murphy, P. (1991). The limits of symmetry: A game theory approach to symmetric and asymmetric public relations. In J. E. Grunig & L. A. Grunig (Eds.), *Public relations research annual* (Vol. 3, pp. 115–132). Hillsdale, NJ: Lawrence Erlbaum Associates.

Olasky, M. N. (1984). Retrospective: Bernays doctrine of public opinion. *Public Relations Review, 10,* 3–11.

Olasky, M. N. (1987). *Corporate public relations: A new historical perspective.* Hillsdale, NJ: Lawrence Erlbaum Associates.

Olasky, M. N. (1989). The aborted debate within public relations: An approach through Kuhn's paradigm. In J. E. Grunig & L. A. Grunig (Eds.), *Public relations research annual* (Vol. 1, pp. 87–96). Hillsdale, NJ: Lawrence Erlbaum Associates.

Paivio, A. (1971). *Imagery and verbal processes.* New York: Holt, Rinehart & Winston.

Pauchant, T. C., & Mitroff, I. I. (1988). Crisis prone versus crisis avoiding organizations: Is your company's culture its own worst enemy in creating crises? *Industrial Crisis Quarterly, 2*(1), 53–63.

Pavlik, J. V. (1989, May). *The concept of symmetry in the education of public relations practitioners.* Paper presented at the meeting of the International Communication Association, San Francisco.

Pearson, R. (1989a). Beyond ethical relativism in public relations: Coorientation, rules, and the idea of communication symmetry. In J. E. Grunig & L. A. Grunig (Eds.), *Public relations research annual* (Vol. 1, pp. 67–86). Hillsdale, NJ: Lawrence Erlbaum Associates.

Pearson, R. (1989b). *A theory of public relations ethics.* Unpublished doctoral dissertation, Ohio University, Athens.

Pielle Public Relations Consultancy Newsletter (1988, January). London.

Pimlott, J. A. R. (1951). *Public relations and American democracy.* Princeton, NJ: Princeton University Press.

Pratt, C. A. (1990, August). *Gender implications in public relations ethics: Kohlberg, Gilligan, and the PRSA code of professional standards.* Paper presented at the meeting of the

Association for Education in Journalism and Mass Communication, Minneapolis.

Rakow, L. F. (1989b). From the feminization of public relations to the promise of feminism. In E. L. Toth & C. G. Cline (Eds.), *Beyond the velvet ghetto* (pp. 287–298). San Francisco: International Association of Business Communicators.

Rakow, L. F. (1989a). Information and power: Toward a critical theory of information campaigns. In C. T. Salmon (Ed.), *Information campaigns: Balancing social values and social change* (pp. 164–184). Newbury Park, CA: Sage.

Ruhl, M. (1990, December). *Public relations: Innenansichten einer emergierenden kommunikationswissenschaft*. Paper presented at the Professional Conference of the Herbert Quandt Stiftung Communication Group, Salzburg, Austria.

Schneider (aka Grunig), L. A. (1985). Implications of the concept of schema for public relations. *Public Relations Research & Education, 2*(1), 36–47.

Shapere, D. (1984). *Reason and the search for knowledge*. Dordrecht, Netherlands: Reidel.

Smilowitz, M., & Pearson, R. (1989). Traditional, enlightened, and interpretive perspectives on corporate annual giving. In C. H. Botan & V. T. Hazleton, Jr. (Eds.), *Public relations theory* (pp. 83–98). Hillsdale, NJ: Lawrence Erlbaum Associates.

Stead, B. A. (1985). *Women in management* (2nd ed.). Englewood Cliffs, NJ: Prentice-Hall.

Suppe, F. (1977). *The structure of scientific theories* (2nd ed.). Urbana: University of Illinois Press.

Suppe, F. (1989). *The semantic concept of theories and scientific realism*. Urbana: University of Illinois Press.

Sussman, L. A. (1949). The personnel and ideology of public relations. *Public Opinion Quarterly, 12*, 697–708.

Tedlow, R. S. (1979). *Keeping the corporate image: Public relations and business 1900–1950*. Greenwich, CT: JAI.

Tolley, J. L. (1988). *Even when you've made it, you haven't got got it made*. Vern Schrantz Lecture, Department of Journalism, Ball State University, Muncie, IN.

Torrance, T. F. (1989). *The Christian frame of mind: Reason, order, and openness in theology and natural science*. Colorado Springs: Helmers & Howard.

Toth, E. L. (1988). Making peace with gender issues in public relations. *Public Relations Review, 14*(3), 36–47.

Toth, E. L., & Heath, R. L. (Eds.). (1992). *Rhetorical and critical approaches to public relations*. Hillsdale, NJ: Lawrence Erlbaum Associates.

Tuleja, T. (1985). *Beyond the bottom line*. New York: Facts on File.

Vroom, H. M. (1989). *Religions and the truth*. Grand Rapids, MI: Eerdmans.

Wetherell, B. J. (1989). *The effect of gender, masculinity, and femininity on the practice of and preference for the models of public relations*. Unpublished master's thesis, University of Maryland, College Park.

Wood, R. J., with Gunther, M. (1988). *Confessions of a PR man*. New York: North American Library.

3 What Is an Effective Organization?

Larissa A. Grunig
James E. Grunig
University of Maryland

William P. Ehling
Syracuse University

ABSTRACT

This chapter addresses one of the central questions that a general theory of public relations must answer: Does managed communication make an organization more effective and, if so, how does it do so? The chapter traces the history of research on organizational effectiveness in sociology and concludes that public relations does make organizations more effective. It does so by using communication programs to build relationships with strategic constituencies of an organization — those constituencies that constrain or enhance the ability of an organization to achieve its goals.

A few years ago, the budget makers of a large government agency told the agency's public relations manager that he would have to show how successful communication programs contribute to organizational effectiveness or his department would suffer "negative budget adjustments."

Several answers immediately came to his mind: Public relations increases profits. Public relations gains support in the community or in government. Public relations increases employee morale and productivity. None of these answers can be supported by research or theory. The contribution of public relations to the bottom line requires a logical, theoretical argument to connect communication objectives to broader organizational goals. No single empirical measure can tell "the" contribution of public relations to meeting organizational goals.

Chapter 1 began by listing three critical questions about public relations that have motivated this book and the larger research project of which it is a part. Two of these questions ask about the effectiveness of public relations and its contribution to organizational effectiveness:

1. When and why are the efforts of communication practitioners effective?
2. How do organizations benefit from public relations?

The first question addresses the problem of how to evaluate the effectiveness of communication programs, which is a part of the microlevel management of public relations addressed in chapter 7. The evaluation of public relations programs has been one of the hottest topics at professional meetings and seminars and in professional publications in the last 15 years. Many organizations now routinely evaluate communication programs and campaigns, and both research firms and public relations firms can do such evaluative research for clients (as described in chapter 8).

As chapter 7 shows, communication programs can be evaluated by identifying the public for which a program is intended, specifying the objectives of the program, and measuring those objectives to determine if the program accomplished them. The second question, however, moves to a higher level of effectiveness to ask whether public relations programs that meet their objectives also make the organizations that sponsor them more effective. That bottom-line question is of great concern to organizations that want to know whether they need public relations departments or counsel. It also concerns communication professionals who must explain why an organization needs their expertise.

Communication practitioners and scholars generally cannot answer the second question except in general, clichéd terms. The answer lies in organizational theory and not in communication theory, research, or practice. In particular, the answer lies in the literature on organizational effectiveness. That literature contains the work of scholars who have defined what an effective organization is and have searched for factors that increase effectiveness once it has been defined. This chapter reviews that literature to determine if public relations is one of the factors and, if it is, to explain the mechanism that allows public relations to increase the success of organizations.

This chapter sets the stage for the remaining elements of a theory of excellence in communication management. From the theoretical relationship between public relations and organizational effectiveness, we can derive the principles of microlevel strategic management of Part I. We also can explain the management structures needed to implement excellent public relations in Part II. Finally, the theory identifies the macrolevel concepts in Part III that help to explain why some organizations develop excellent communication programs and others do not.

AUTONOMY, INTERDEPENDENCE,
AND RELATIONSHIPS

In the next section of this chapter, we review the stages of thinking about the nature and causes of organizational effectiveness. That literature makes more sense, however, if we begin by introducing the three concepts of autonomy, interdependence, and relationships—concepts that reveal the contribution that public relations makes to organizational effectiveness.

The first theories of organizational effectiveness defined effectiveness as the extent to which organizations were able to meet their goals. Those theories assumed, however, that organizations were closed systems—that they could fulfill their missions without support or interference from their environments. In other words, the *closed-system* perspective assumed that organizations had *autonomy* from their environments and that internal management structures would determine the difference between effectiveness and ineffectiveness.

Theorists such as Katz and Kahn (1978) soon turned to an *open-system* perspective. That perspective recognized that organizations are interdependent with other organizations and groups in their environment. It also recognized that these other systems influence both what goals organizations choose and the extent to which they can meet those goals.[1] Pfeffer and Salancik (1978), for example, defined success in meeting internal goals as efficiency. They defined effectiveness as ". . . an *external* standard of how well an organization is meeting the demands of various groups and organizations that are concerned with its activities" (p. 11).

Public relations fits into what organizational sociologists call a *boundary-spanning* role—it helps the organization to manage its relationship with groups in the environment. As a result, public relations contributes to organizational effectiveness, as defined by Pfeffer and Salancik (1978), rather than to efficiency.

Organizations struggle constantly to achieve their mission—the goals selected by internal decision makers—in the face of constraints imposed by outside groups or interests. In the words of Pfeffer and Salancik (1978), "Organizations comply with the demands of others, or they act to manage the dependencies that create constraints on organizational actions" (p. 257).

If given the opportunity, most senior managers would prefer their organizations to remain autonomous from their environment (see, e.g., Hage, 1980; Mintzberg, 1983, pp. 631–663). Autonomy allows organizations to pursue their goals with the least interference from outside.

---

[1] Many public relations theorists have built their theories on an open-systems perspective also. See, for example, Cutlip et al. (1985), J. Grunig and Hunt (1984), and Pavlik (1987).

Organizations do not want to be regulated by government or pressured by activist groups. Loss of autonomy costs money—to comply with regulations or to make changes to accommodate pressure groups. Having willing consumers and employees also increases an organization's autonomy, because fewer changes in behavior are necessary to sell them a product or to get them to work productively.

Organizations, therefore, are ". . . involved in a constant struggle for autonomy and discretion, confronted with constraint and external control" (Pfeffer & Salancik, 1978, p. 257). Organizations in which an asymmetrical worldview, as defined in chapter 2, dominates its culture typically expect public relations to secure autonomy by what Hage (1980) called controlling or dominating outside groups. Public relations generally cannot do so, however, because the organization confronts the reality of interdependence with other organizations and groups. Instead, the organization must adapt to (Katz & Kahn, 1978), cooperate with (Hage, 1980), or interact with (Buchholz, 1989) groups that limit its autonomy.

The concept of interdependence appears throughout the organizational literature. According to Pfeffer and Salancik (1978), ". . . interdependence exists whenever one actor does not entirely control all the conditions necessary for the achievement of an action or for obtaining the outcome desired from the action" (p. 40). Gray (1985, 1989) defined interdependence in terms of multiple stakeholders in an organization. Gollner (1983, 1984), then, defined public relations and public affairs as the management of interdependence.[2]

Defining interdependence in terms of stakeholders and public affairs makes sense because organizational theories also point out that organizations are political in nature and no longer function as the rational machines depicted in the organizational theories of the 1930s and 1940s—if, indeed, they ever functioned in that way. According to Pfeffer and Salancik (1978):

> Books about how to manage or how to succeed are ill-advised because they give the impression that there is some set of rules or procedures that will guarantee success. The essence of the concept of interdependence means that this cannot be the case. In any interdependent situation, outcomes are at least partially in the control of other social actors, and the successful outcomes achieved through performing various managerial roles derive in part from actions take by others outside the manager's control. (pp. 267–268)

---

[2]Gollner (1983, 1984) did not distinguish between public relations and public affairs. He argued that public relations today must be directly involved with an organization's public affairs.

Pfeffer (1981) listed several factors familiar to public relations practitioners as reasons why organizations throughout society have become increasingly politicized:

Scarcity of resources and the conflict and use of power resulting from scarcity.

An increasingly heterogeneous society, because of diverse values, beliefs, attitudes, socialization, and cultures.

Erosion of confidence in most organizations and institutions and in the legitimacy of their power and authority.

A growing movement for *corporate accountability and social responsibility.*

The previous chapter of this book cited critical theorists who have argued that organizations will not communicate symmetrically with publics that have less power than the organization. The politicization of organizations suggests that organizations no longer have a monopoly of power. Stakeholders have attained what Galbraith (1967) called "countervailing power." Politicization also suggests that public relations departments will gain power in the dominant coalitions that manage organizations because of the increasing need to manage relationships with the environment (Pfeffer, 1978, p. 167).

According to Mintzberg (1983), organizations become highly politicized when they cannot develop a "harmonious distribution of power" with groups competing for power inside and outside the organization (p. 450). Politicization of organizations benefits society, he added, because politics kills organizations that are not well suited to their environments.

The reality of interdependence means that organizations have relationships with outside stakeholders—with publics and other organizations—whether they want such relationships or not. Relationships limit autonomy, but good relationships limit it less than bad relationships. Pfeffer and Salancik (1978) expressed the impact of relationships well: "The price for inclusion in any collective structure is the loss of discretion and control over one's activities. Ironically, to gain some control over the activities of another organization, the focal organization must surrender some of its own autonomy" (p. 16).

Building relationships—managing interdependence—is the substance of public relations. Good relationships, in turn, make organizations more effective because they allow organizations more freedom—more autonomy—to achieve their missions than they would with bad relationships. By giving up autonomy by building relationships, ironically, organizations maximize that autonomy.

Having set forth the basic contribution that public relations makes to organizational effectiveness, therefore, we turn to the organizational literature to support it.

THEORIES OF ORGANIZATIONAL EFFECTIVENESS

Just as public relations practitioners play a boundary-spanning role between the organization that employs them and its relevant constituencies, public relations theory spans the two scholarly domains of sociology and business management. Working on parallel tracks, researchers from organizational sociology and management have studied organizational effectiveness, in particular. Most recently, scholars in public relations have tried to determine the contributions—if any—of public relations to effectiveness. This section of the chapter explores the concept of organizational effectiveness from the literature of those three domains—sociology, management, and public relations.

The concept of *effectiveness,* according to Hage (1980), seems to mean all things to all people. He contended that the effectiveness concept has been made to cover too much. As a result, some scholars have suggested we eliminate the concept from the lexicon of organizational research (Hannan & Freeman, 1977b). Others, such as Pfeffer (1977), have countered that the challenge of defining and measuring effectiveness is necessary for understanding any organizational system.

Accepting this challenge, then, we argue that the value of public relations as a contributing factor to organizational effectiveness or even survival cannot be overstated. Farace, Monge, and Russell (1977) pointed up its *Bedeutung:* "The communication system of an organization is an increasingly powerful determinant of the organization's overall effectiveness, and it may have a limiting effect on the ability of the organization to grow, to perform efficiently, or to survive" (p. 7).

At the time Farace et al. (1977) were writing, however, little research or even theorizing had been done by scholars of public relations. The challenge of developing theory in public relations is at least as important to practitioners as to scholars in the field. Because practitioners must plan and defend their programs, they would value the answers to what we consider to be among the great unresolved problems of social science—the central questions of this study. They ask when and why the efforts of communication practitioners are effective and how the public relations function must be organized and managed if it is to make an organization more effective. Questions also center on how organizations benefit from effective public relations and how and to what extent public relations contributes to the bottom line of an organization—to making it more effective.

We reasoned that only excellent public relations departments would contribute to bottom-line organizational effectiveness. Thus, we titled this project "Excellence in Public Relations and Communication Management." However, we continue to believe that practitioners only rarely conceptualize theoretically the process of public relations and its relationship to the effective management of organizations—despite Robbins's (1990) contention that the concept of effectiveness is fundamental to theories of organizations.

Even before the results are in from the IABC Excellence study, we know that integrating the communication subsystem into the stated or implied goals of the organization can go a long way toward organizational success. This level-spanning approach is important from a theoretical as well as an applied standpoint. European scholars, such as Gurevitch and Blumler (1982), have advocated holistic efforts to integrate the mesolevel of the public relations department with the macrolevel of the organization. In so doing, we address the process of communication rather than products per se as the distinctive element of public relations. We also conduct our investigations in a manner consistent with systems theory—a major contribution from researchers in organizational sociology.

The *systems* perspective, then, becomes the first of four major ways of looking at effectiveness discussed in this chapter. It is compared with the *competing-values, strategic-constituencies,* and *goal-attainment* approaches that follow.[3]

The Systems Perspective on Effectiveness

Systems theory emphasizes the interfaces between organizations and their environments, as well as between subsystems within the organizational system and between subsystems and the organizational whole. This systems perspective serves as the basis for the definition of public relations found in a leading U.S. textbook in the field. As Cutlip, Center, and Broom (1985) explained, public relations helps establish and maintain mutually dependent relationships between an organization and the publics with which it interacts.

Thus systems theory, also called the *natural systems model* and the *systems resource* approach, suggests one viable perspective from which to explore the notion of effectiveness in organizations. Miller (1978) was among the first scholars to point out that organizations do not have simple,

---

[3]Although this list is by no means inclusive, it does include the most influential perspectives guiding organizational analysis to date. For a review of additional approaches, see Scott, Flood, Eloy, and Forrest (1978).

measurable goals but instead must be evaluated on the bases of systems characteristics such as growth, equilibrium, or decline.

Similarly, Yuchtman and Seashore (1967) argued that organizations could be judged by their ability to acquire vital inputs and process these inputs in such a way as to maintain their stability within the market environment. They emphasized the process rather than specific ends as a way for the organization to survive and to thrive. To be effective as defined by Yuchtman and Seashore, then, the organization must be aware of environmental publics such as customers, suppliers, governmental agencies, and communities and interact successfully with them. All of these constituencies, of course, have the power to disrupt or at least constrain the operation of the organization.

Because the systems approach implies that the organizational whole is composed of interrelated subparts, the performance of any single subsystem will affect the entire system. Thus the public relations department, as one managerial subsystem, contributes to the success or failure of any organization. Management relies on communication professionals to maintain good relationships with the organization's external publics. In fact, the involvement of boundary spanners—such as public relations professionals—in decision making is predicated to some degree on an unstable and threatening environment. Communication skills also contribute to the coordination of internal operations.

However, contemporary theorists who are concerned about the importance of communication may have oversimplified its nature. As the seminal writers on systems theory Katz and Kahn (1966) pointed out, "The blanket emphasis upon more communication fails to take into account the functioning of an organization into a social system and the specific needs of the subsystem" (p. 225). Still, Thayer (1961) considered the formal communication function to be a prerequisite for organized behavior; he contended that the organization's success is directly related to the success of its communicative efforts. Walton (1969) went even further in describing the importance of organizational communication: *"It is contended here that the most significant factor accounting for the total behavior of the organization is its communicating system, and that the dynamics of the organization can best be understood by understanding its system of communication"* (p. 108).

J. Grunig (1976; J. Grunig & Hunt, 1984) developed the first systems theory of public relations. Perhaps the most ambitious attempt at the development of a systems theory of public relations, however, has been a doctoral dissertation (Schneider, aka L. Grunig, 1985)[4] with three-fold

---

[4]Ehling (1975) considered the lack of a general systems theory in public relations a critical void in the field.

goals: to allow managers to monitor their immediate situation (to know how things are); to help them decide how their department should operate, contingent on their environment; and to guide managers in changing their communication subsystem, to institutionalize reforms that enhance effectiveness. In other words, the theory would allow practitioners not only to understand what traditionally has accounted for public relations programs but to forecast how such programs must change in response to evolving environmental conditions—especially internationalization.

This adaptation to future conditions is significant to scholars as well as to practitioners. Hanken and Reuver (1981) contended that the complexity of problems facing organizations requires developing a theory that encompasses several highly specialized disciplines. What these two systems theorists called the "mixed strategy" of combining the specialized—such as public relations—with the more general—such as management—should lead to a unified viewpoint for the study of organizational communication. The contribution of the dissertation lies in its explication of the role of public relations within the framework of the general organizational system.

More specifically, Schneider (aka L. Grunig, 1985) sought to discover how the practice of public relations varies with the structure and environment of organizations. Within the literature of organizational sociology, much has been written to support the structuralist position that structure and organizational constraints—externally imposed limitations on an organization's openness to innovation (J. Grunig, 1984)—control the flow of information both within the organization and from it to its relevant external publics. As Hall (1972) summarized: "The communications system is vitally affected by other structural factors. Communications do not exist outside the total organizational framework" (p. 291).

Literature on the behavior of organizations, of course, comes from many theoretical perspectives. In this IABC study, for example, we draw primarily from public relations, management, and sociology but also from cognitive and social psychology, marketing, communication, decision making, anthropology, political science, philosophy, and feminism. In that same way, systems theory itself developed from the analogy with the human system in biology to the social sciences, beginning with the work of Pareto in 1916 (cited in Henderson, 1967). Along the way, systems theory has been informed by contributions from the schools of classicalism (Fayol, 1916), human relations (Mayo, 1976), revisionism (Blake & Mouton, 1984), conflict (Crozier, 1964; Cyert & March, 1963), decision making (Simon, 1977), contingency (Woodward, 1965), and structural-functionalism (Parsons, 1951).

Structural-functionalism focuses on how organizations design their internal departments contingent on the environment. This last perspective offered particular promise for understanding how public relations is, or could be, managed strategically. In fact, structural-functionalism has had the greatest impact. Weber's (1947) theory of social and economic organization laid the foundation for the structuralists who followed. His definition of a formal organization has been the basis for numerous, subsequent similar descriptions. He also is remembered primarily for his observations of the rapid growth of rationalization in the large-scale operations of the 1920s that led to the ideal type of organization he called "bureaucracy."

This ideal-type construction, according to Hage (1980), proposed the first structural-functional theory of organizations by exploring the reasons for the most efficient form of organization. Efficiency, of course, is not the same as effectiveness. The failure of the systems perspective to differentiate between these two concepts is a major criticism of Price (1968) in his seminal work on organizational effectiveness.[5]

Further, the results of the dissertation research provided only limited support to the structural-functional approach. That is, Schneider (aka L. Grunig, 1985) concluded that structural-functionalism alone is insufficient as a framework within which to construct such theory.

Achieving maximum effectiveness by matching the organization's structure and function to its environment seems to be more a normative ideal than a reality in most organizations studied. If the environmental imperative were realized, the role of public relations practitioners as boundary spanners, mediators, and participants in managerial decision making would be more highly valued. And, as a result, we can agree that systems theory alone fails to explain public relations and its contribution to effectiveness. So, we turn our attention next to another measure of organizational effectiveness: what Hage (1980) and others have considered the *competing-values* approach.

The Competing-Values Perspective on Effectiveness

Like systems theory, the competing-values approach is an integrative framework. However, it encompasses both means and ends rather than emphasizing the means of acquiring resources from the environment. Hage's (1980, p. 135) typology of kinds of effectiveness, adapted from Perrow (1967), illustrates the juxtaposition inherent in this perspective. That typology contrasted the value of efficiency with innovation and of quality with quantity. From this, Hage developed the following definition

---

[5]Other, related criticisms include the focus on inputs with concomitant damaging effects on outputs (Scott, 1977), the fact that only the organizational director's viewpoint is considered (Scott, 1977), and the inappropriateness of the model for nonprofit organizations (Molnar & Rogers, 1956).

of effectiveness: "The achievement relative to the priorities of innovation versus cost and quality versus quantity" (p. 136).

Hage (1980) suggested only somewhat facetiously that this definition boils down to the notion that "effectiveness is achievement *vis-a-vis* priorities" (p. 136). His conclusions grew out of the work of the factor-analytic studies of scholars such as Yuchtman and Seashore (1967) and Campbell and his colleagues (Campbell, Dunnette, Lawler, & Weick, 1970), whose work resulted in multiple dimensions of effectiveness. In fact, Campbell (1977) denied the viability of discussing effectiveness in general terms when he identified 30 criteria of effectiveness. He further suggested that practitioners need some theoretical framework to help identify the criteria most appropriate for their organizations. In an earlier review of studies of effectiveness, Steers (1975) catalogued 15 measures of effectiveness.

Hage (1980) explained that these and similar inventories make the question of effectiveness seem more complex than it is. He countered that by collapsing categories or factors (such as productivity and efficiency or satisfaction and employee retention), the underlying dimensions of these values become apparent. What remains are the standards used by different organizations to demonstrate their effectiveness. As he explained: "All dominant coalitions attempt to survive . . . Profits can be made by cutting costs or by producing new products. It is this difference we want to capture" (p. 135).

The work of Quinn (Quinn & Hall, 1983) went a long way toward capturing that difference, typically organized into four dimensions. The first, growing out of the human relations school of management, emphasizes the value of human resources and training through cohesion and morale. The second, consistent with open-systems theory, emphasizes growth, resource acquisition, and external support through adaptability and readiness. The third, called the *rational-goal model,* emphasizes productivity and efficiency through planning and goal setting. The fourth, or internal process model, emphasizes stability and control through information management and communication.

Any one of these sets of values will be more or less appropriate for an organization depending on its stage in the life cycle. The concept of *life stage* comes directly from systems theory, which holds that organizations are like people in several important ways. They come to life, they mature, and—eventually—they cease to exist. Along the way, their survival depends on obtaining necessary resources, transforming those resources into products, and releasing those products or services into the greater environment. The competing-values perspective is particularly useful for the organization in transition, when it may be unclear about its own emphases. It acknowledges that multiple criteria for effectiveness and conflicting interests underlie any effort at assessing the success or ineffectiveness of the organization (Robbins, 1990).

The Strategic-Constituencies Perspective on Effectiveness

The strategic-constituencies approach is a more contemporary measure of organizational effectiveness. Like the systems perspective, it focuses on interdependencies. However, it concentrates on the segments within the environment that most threaten the organization rather than on the total environment. The standard becomes how well the organization satisfies the demands of its relevant external publics—the people, groups, and other organizations upon which the organization depends for its survival.

Strategic constituencies represent the groups that are deemed to be most critical to the organization, in terms of their potential for support or for adversarial action. They may be called stakeholders (Freeman, 1984) or simply publics, most common in the literature of public relations. Whatever their designation, these organized bodies with consequences on the organization (or vice versa) represent the raison d'être for public relations. As Ehling (Staff, 1988) said: "Adversarial environments are what make public relations communication distinct. Every pr public is at least a *potential* adversary" (p. 1).

The increasingly common interplay between organizations and their external environments makes this perspective particularly important to public relations practitioners. The concept of specificity within the organization's domain or environmental niche is important to the boundary spanners who must help the dominant coalition determine target audiences or external publics to reach in their programs.

The power elite, of course, typically decides on both the organization's critical publics (be they adversarial or cooperative) and the strategy for dealing with those publics (J. Grunig, in Staff, 1988). The findings of Schneider's (aka L. Grunig, 1985) dissertation, buttressed by a number of other, similar studies (see J. Grunig & L. Grunig, 1989), showed that the model of public relations practiced is determined largely by the dominant coalition. However, the determination of which publics are strategic, or most important to the organization at the time, is a responsibility that also may lie within the public relations department. This seems most likely to happen when the head of public relations is included within the dominant coalition.

Just as important distinctions exist between the notions of mass versus public, actual versus perceived environments are an important consideration. Research has shown that correlations between the organization's actual environment and the dominant coalition's perception of that external setting are at times minimal (Downey, Hellriegel, & Slocum, 1975). Further,

Robbins (1990) contended that managers' perceptions—rather than objective assessments of the environment—are the basis for their decisions regarding organizational design. In other words, the perceived environment dictates the resultant structure as well as attempts at achieving effectiveness through interacting with key publics in that environment.

Other problems typically associated with the strategic-constituency criterion of effectiveness in the literature of organizational sociology and of management will not trouble many practitioners of public relations. Robbins (1990) listed those difficulties as (a) separating key publics from the larger environment, (b) further delineating strategic constituencies from "almost" strategic constituencies, and (c) identifying accurately the expectations that those important groups hold for the organization. The professional public relations manager, of course, should be comfortable with and adept at all three of these processes.

Organizational theorists also talk about the *resource-dependence* perspective on effectiveness—an approach we consider related to strategic constituencies in that it emphasizes the external environment. Pfeffer and Salancik (1978) argued that organizations behave as they do in an attempt to control their environments. The measure of effectiveness in this reactive model becomes securing resources from constituencies that are most critical to the organization's survival or growth.

From the resource-dependence perspective, uncertainty in the environment becomes increasingly decisive when coupled with interdependence between the organization and its strategic publics (Pfeffer, 1978). Most theoreticians (see, e.g., Lawrence & Lorsch, 1967; Roos & Starke, 1981) agree that perceived environmental uncertainty also leads to an increase in boundary spanning, especially environmental scanning (Thompson, 1967). Weick (1969) found, however, that boundary-spanning activity can lead decision makers to perceive even more uncertainty.

A second related but even more reactive perspective, according to Denison (1990), is the *population ecology* approach. This theory of organizational effectiveness proposes that the environment determines which organizations will survive almost irrespective of actions of individuals or organizations. According to Hannan and Freeman (1977a) and McKelvey (1979), certain types of organizations develop to fill niches in the environment. The organization becomes ineffective and declines accordingly when the market demand for that type of organization diminishes. The most problematic aspect of this perspective is its failure to explain the effectiveness or ineffectiveness of any particular firm within a given niche.

The Goal-Attainment Perspective on Effectiveness

Unlike the contemporary criterion of strategic constituencies as the measure of effectiveness, effectiveness most traditionally has been defined in terms of goals. The effective organization, according to Robbins (1990), is one that realizes its goals. And unlike the systems perspective, which focuses on means, or the competing-values perspective with its balance between means and ends, this approach emphasizes ends.

The goal-attainment approach (also called the *rational-systems model*) seems most reasonable among the four major ways of looking at effectiveness, according to Cameron (1984), when goals are clear, time bound, and measurable. It is attractive because of its emphasis on purposeful action. Campbell (1976), for example, saw the organization as controlled by a group of rational decision makers who pursue an agreed-on set of goals.

Defining effectiveness as goal attainment also is consistent with the classic definition first proposed by Parsons (1960) that organizations are social systems with "specific purposes." As such, this definition of effectiveness has been embraced by many prominent organizational theorists— including Gouldner (1959), Parsons (1960), Perrow (1961), Blau and Scott (1962), Etzioni (1964), and Price (1968).

However, the power-control perspective introduces ambiguity into the goal-attainment perspective by questioning whose goals within the organization are being realized. The question becomes, effectiveness for whom?

Just as different managers within an organization may have individual agendas, so too may different scholars embrace diverse criteria for effectiveness. Robbins (1990) listed more than 30 (sometimes contradictory, competing, or mutually exclusive) measures, including efficiency, safety, stability, flexibility or adaptability, productivity, quality, rate of turnover, readiness, and achievement. In pointing out that organizational effectiveness means different things to different people, he argued that the criteria chosen to evaluate an organization reflect more on the scholar than on the organization.

The notion of *self-interest,* of course, is paramount within the framework of power and control in organizations. As Robbins (1990) explained, the interests of decision makers and of their organization rarely are identical. In fact, he argued that at no time would a rational member of the dominant coalition sublimate his or her own interests to the organization. Instead, the typical manager tries to increase the size and scope of his or her domain regardless of the effect on the organizational system. Thus we see that self-interest determines goals to a greater extent than does organizational interest.

Understanding the organization as such a political system has resulted in some theorizing that allows for divergence and conflict among members of the dominant coalition. Certain scholars (Cyert & March, 1963; Hickson, Hinings, Lee, Schneck, & Pennings, 1971; Pfeffer & Salancik, 1974), for example, believed that organizational goals result from negotiations among shifting coalitions of powerful managers. Others, such as March and Olsen

(1976) and Weick (1976), theorized that organizations may accommodate fairly autonomous subsystems capable of pursuing inconsistent objectives.

Pennings and Goodman (1977) were among the first to draw connections between the problems inherent in goal attainment and the diverse, often-competing external and internal constituencies of organizations (see also Pfeffer, 1982, who regarded coalitions within organizations as stakeholders). Their theory held that although each of these groups plays a part in determining what the organization's goals should be, certain constituencies have more power than others. Power is predicted by how central or indispensable the constituency is to the organization. J. Grunig (J. Grunig & Hunt, 1984) extrapolated from this theory to suggest that organizations will include public relations goals in their definition of effectiveness when the public relations department and strategic external constituencies become part of the organization's dominant coalition. He further suggested that when public relations is represented in that power elite, it may promulgate goals such as social responsibility, public understanding, and two-way communication.[6]

Perhaps Robbins (1990) has been the major critic of the goal-attainment approach—for reasons imbedded in the description just offered. In addition to the problems of sorting out whose goals should be accomplished, whether short- or long-term goals are to be considered, the fact that goals change frequently (Kirchhoff, 1977) and what to do about the organization with multiple goals, he explained that goals do not direct behavior. Instead, he echoed Weick's (1969) assertion that actions already completed more often lead to the articulation of a goal to justify those actions than the other way around. Weick called organizational actions "goal interpreted" rather than "goal governed." And like Warriner (1964) even earlier, Robbins considered the articulation of goals "a fiction" constructed by organizations to rationalize their performance to key audiences. He contended that "only the naive would accept the formal statements made by senior management to represent the organization's goals" (p. 56).

Distilling much of this organizational literature, Robbins (1990) concluded that the most representative definition of organizational effectiveness would be *"the degree to which an organization attains its short- (ends) and long-term (means) goals, the selection of which reflects strategic constituencies, the self-interest of the evaluator, and the life stage of the organization"* (p. 77).

The self-interested nature of top managers, in particular, helps explain

---

[6]On the other hand, practitioners may promote behavioral effects. As the head of a communication management firm (Geduldig, 1991) put it recently, "Any public relations function that wants to demonstrate its effectiveness and have a tangible bottom-line benefit must have behavior as its ultimate goal" (p. 8).

many heretofore anomalous facets of public relations practice. This political perspective in organizational decision making makes sense out of seemingly inappropriate responses both to the environment and to the nature of the public relations process. For example, accommodating the varied interests of the power elite even at the expense of the greater organization may lead to the exclusion of women in public relations from top management, to the selection of marginal—rather than key—publics as target audiences, and to the practice of an anachronistic one-way model rather than the two-way symmetrical approach considered most effective in an era of dynamic and vocal opposition among external publics.

Perhaps the most useful of the theories that define effectiveness as the extent to which an organization satisfies the demands of the strategic constituencies in the environment is Pfeffer and Salancik's (1978) theory of resource dependency. Pfeffer and Salancik began with the proposition that organizations need resources. To obtain those resources, however, organizations must interact with organizations and groups in their environment that control the resources. They said, "These actors, which may be other organizations, groups, or individuals, constitute the social environment or context of the organization" (p. 259). The more an organization needs a resource controlled by an outside group, the more control that group has on the goals and mission of the organization.[7]

Organizations dislike external control, however, and try to reduce the uncertainty in their environment. They may try to avoid external control through asymmetrical devices—many of which are typical of public relations departments operating with an asymmetrical worldview: ". . . organizations attempt to avoid influence and constraint by restricting the flow of information about them and their activities, denying the legitimacy of demands made upon them, diversifying their dependencies, and manipulating information to increase their own legitimacy" (Pfeffer & Salancik, 1978, p. 261). Organizations also try to shape their environment through "merger, joint ventures, cooptation, growth, political involvement" (Pfeffer & Salancik, 1978, p. 262).

Pfeffer and Salancik (1978) described four ways in which organizations can be designed to be more effective. One is to diversify to "loosen dependencies." A second is to avoid concentrating too much power in chief executive positions. The other two designs relate directly to the public relations function and suggest the value of a symmetrical approach. One device is to develop mechanisms for "scanning the environment" to identify potent outside groups, to bring information into the organization, and to

---

[7]For example, Pfeffer and Salancik (1978, pp. 56–59) described a study showing that organizations that depended on government contracts were more responsive to government regulations for the hiring of women than were organizations that did not depend on contracts.

help senior managers act on that information. Like Weick (1979), Pfeffer and Salancik believed that environments are "enacted" rather than objective. Thus, units that scan the environment must help the organization enact the environment that truly controls the organization—the strategic aspects of the environment. Second, Pfeffer and Salancik said that organizations can develop mechanisms for "managing conflicting demands and constraints" (p. 273). They explained, for example, that organizations develop consumer affairs departments to deal with consumers, industrial relations departments for employees, and affirmative action departments for minorities.

Pfeffer and Salancik (1978) did not mention public relations as a mechanism for managing the organization's response to external control. Gollner (1984) filled that gap by noting the growth in numbers of organizations with public affairs departments as a response to interdependence.[8] Gollner also said that public relations and public affairs should be a single function. That department, he added, should be involved in public issues and issues management. He said, ". . . if public relations/ public affairs is to grow up to assume its rightful place in the new managerial revolution, it must become a full partner in strategic decision-making processes" (p. 10).

Chapter 6 defines strategic management as a critical component of excellent public relations departments. The strategic-constituencies theories of organizational effectiveness explain why. If public relations can identify the strategic publics in the environment and manage the organization's response to these interdependencies, these theories of effectiveness show, public relations can help the organization reduce uncertainty and reduce conflict by stabilizing relationships with key publics on which the organization depends. Next, then, we explore the nature of relationships.

ORGANIZATIONAL RELATIONSHIPS

The nature of relationships between organizations and stakeholders—which may be publics or other organizations—emerges, then, as a central concept in a theory of public relations and organizational effectiveness. Ferguson (1984) argued that relationsips between organizations and their publics should be the central unit of study for public relations researchers. Few scholars have studied those relationships, however. That lack of interest is strange because organizations must deal with other organizations daily.

---

[8]Zeitz (1975) and Boddewyn (1974) are two organizational sociologists who have recognized that the "external affairs function" has become a unique, important, and growing function in organizations.

They may compete economically with other organizations. Politically, an organization may lobby for or against legislation that other organizations support or oppose. Members of publics form into well-organized activist groups and coalitions that compete and conflict with each other about public policies. The media, which are obviously of great concern in public relations, also are organizations.

The group of organizations with which a given organization interacts is called the "organization set" (Evan, 1976). Evan divided these linked organizations into "input sets" and "output sets." The former include suppliers, labor unions, and even governmental agencies that regulate the organization. Output linkages include dealers, ad agencies, trade associations, and so forth. Esman (1972) would consider trade associations "normative" linkages, or relationships with other organizations that face similar problems or share values. As J. Grunig (J. Grunig & Hunt, 1984) explained, "Associations exist to facilitate communication between member organizations so that the members can jointly attack common problems" (p. 142).

Thus we see that in organizational theory, a body of knowledge does exist on the relationships among organizations, but theorists have not developed an integrated theory of those relationships (Van de Ven, Emmett, & Koenig, 1975). Organizational researchers, too, virtually have ignored the role of communication in organizational relations; although research does suggest that good communication and interaction among organizations are related to the management of conflict. Hall and Clark (1975) concluded that organizations that have "disagreements or disputes" with other organizations rely on communication to resolve that conflict and that efforts to communicate increase the frequency of interaction between the conflicting parties (pp. 119–120).

Theories of organizational relationships, therefore, do support the idea that there is a functional connection between the quality of communication—the excellence of public relations—and the nature of relationships between organizations and their stakeholders. The IABC study of excellence in public relations and its relationship to organizational effectiveness should confirm or modify our conceptualization of that connection. We and other researchers will have to isolate attributes of relationships, however, before we can do such research.

Relationships can be viewed either from the perspective of a focal organization or from the perspective of a community or social system consisting of many organizations (Aldrich, 1975, 1979; Zeitz, 1975). Although most communication managers will look at the relationships of the organization that employs them, they also should think of the broader perspective of a community of organizations. Relationships among organizations other than the focal one may affect the relationships between that organization and one or more of the others.

Aldrich (1975, 1979) identified four dimensions of organizational relationships that could serve as dependent variables affected by public relations:

> *Formalization:* The extent to which the organizations recognize the relationship and assign intermediaries (such as public relations people) to coordinate the relationship.
> *Intensity:* The extent to which organizations commit time and money to the relationship.
> *Reciprocity:* The extent to which all organizations devote resources to the relationship and mutually determine how interaction will take place.
> *Standardization:* The extent to which interaction becomes fixed.

For a theory of public relations, this list suggests that organizations should develop formalized, intense, and standardized relationships with their strategic publics—characteristics of excellent public relations isolated in chapter 6. Reciprocity, as mandated by the symmetrical norm of reciprocity discussed in chapter 2, can be isolated as an effect rather than a component of excellent public relations.

Ferguson (1984) identified similar attributes of relationships that scholars and practitioners can use to define and measure the quality of an organization's relationships with strategic publics: (a) dynamic versus static, (b) open versus closed, (c) the degree to which both organization and public are satisfied with the relationship, (d) distribution of power in the relationship, and (e) the mutuality of understanding, agreement, and consensus. To this list, we would add two concepts that are stalwarts of theories of interpersonal communication: trust and credibility. Finally, Pfeffer (1978) defined another relevant attribute of relationships—the concept of organizational legitimacy or the "congruence between social values and organizational actions" (p. 159). A relationship of legitimacy, therefore, would be one in which both parties accept the legitimacy of the other.

Researchers and practitioners could use any of these concepts to measure the quality of the strategic relationships of organizations, but we suggest that the following are most important: reciprocity, trust, credibility, mutual legitimacy, openness, mutual satisfaction, and mutual understanding. Equality of power may be necessary, but as the authors of chapter 2 argued, a norm of reciprocity may produce a quality relationship even if power is unequal.

Ferguson (1984) pointed out that the coorientation model popular in communication research (see, e.g., Broom, 1977; Grunig & Hunt, 1984, pp.

127–129) provides a convenient set of concepts for translating these attributes of relationships into objectives for public relations programs. Chapter 7, therefore, discusses how communication managers can use coorientation theory and similar theories at the microlevel to plan and evaluate specific programs.

Our theory of the relationship between excellent public relations and organizational effectiveness, therefore, is nearly complete. One relevant concept, however, remains.

DIVERSITY AND REQUISITE VARIETY

Until recently, most public relations practitioners were White men. Today, many practitioners are women, non-White, and from non-Western cultures. The principle of requisite variety (Weick, 1979, pp. 188–195) suggests that diversity in public relations departments enhances organizational effectiveness. The reason can be seen in the theories of external control and organizational relationships described earlier.

Weick (1979) developed the idea that the environments of organizations are enacted rather than objective (p. 177). Enacted means that the environment of an organization will not be perceived as the same environment by different people in the same organization or by people outside the organization. The principle of requisite variety, which Weick took from general systems theory, states that there must be at least as much variety—or diversity—inside the organization as outside for the organization to build effective relationships with all critical or strategic parts of the environment. If, for example, an organization affects or could be affected by minority publics, it probably will not recognize those stakeholders as part of the environment if all the public relations practitioners are White. Or, White practitioners may not recognize that diverse publics do not consider the organization to be legitimate—one of the attributes of relationships.

"Contradictions and ambivalence," in Weick's (1976, p. 231) words, therefore, are good for an organization because they make it possible for the organization to enact critical parts of the environment that it might overlook otherwise. Diversity in public relations, in turn, may enhance the careers of minorities; but it also enhances the effectiveness of organizations that employ them.

THE VALUE OF PUBLIC RELATIONS IN MONETARY TERMS

In this chapter, we have developed the theory that public relations can increase the effectiveness of an organization. First, it helps the organization to enact an environment that includes the stakeholders most likely to constrain or enhance the ability of the organization to carry out its mission — to meet its goals. Second, public relations can increase effectiveness if it develops communication programs that build quality relationships with strategic publics. These relationships help the organization manage interdependencies, simultaneously limiting and enhancing the autonomy of the organization. The better the organization manages its interdependencies, the more likely it is to succeed in meeting its goals — although factors other than public relations contribute to that success as well. In this last section, then, we explore literature that suggests what monetary value can be assigned to quality relationships built by excellent public relations.

Preston (1981) reviewed studies of the relationship between "socially relevant behaviors" of corporations and economic performance and concluded that "there is practically no evidence of any strong association among socially relevant behaviors, whether desirable or undesirable, and any of the usual indicators of economic success" (p. 9). Instead, he concluded that responsible behavior has an indirect effect on performance. Large corporations, he explained, engage in "externally-oriented activity" to maintain the sociopolitical status quo — to preserve an environment in which to work.

Tuleja (1985) argued, likewise, that ethical behavior helps corporations to enhance the bottom line indirectly by developing more productive employees, improving public relations, and "keeping government and nongovernment regulators off the corporation's back" (p. 187). Spending on good works does not necessarily bring profits, he added, but corporations that are socially responsible have done everything they can to secure market advantage. Goodwill of constituencies, Tuleja added, is not the only reason for success, however. He used what he considered "two key terms" to describe the results of ethical behavior: "goodwill" and "long term" (p. 200). These terms, of course, also describe quality relationships with stakeholders.

According to Ermann and Lundman (1982), society sees organizations as deviant when they have bad relationships with stockholders, employees, customers, and the public at large:

> First, some individuals or organizations accuse the corporation of an act that they perceive as deviant. In response, the corporation typically resists these accusations by "stonewalling," attacking the motives or competence of its accusers, or enhancing its identity as a socially responsible entity. Witnessing this process of give-and-take is an audience that includes branches of government, consumers, and potential plaintiffs, and that evaluates the accusations and defenses and occasionally applies negative sanctions to the corporation. As a result of this process, corporations and their actions at some times and in some places come to be defined as deviant. (p. vii)

The penalties for deviance, Ermann and Lundman added, include bad publicity, regulatory and criminal fines, private suits, and penetration of the firm by activist groups and government.

Government regulation can be extremely costly (see Buchholz, 1989, for one review of the costs of regulation). Poor relationships also can produce litigation that "can exact a heavy monetary toll" (Lieberman, 1983, p. 168). Poor relationships, in other words, can cost an organization a great deal although good relationships may not necessarily make money for the organization. At the same time, good relationships can make money through productive employees, satisfied customers, and supportive donors, stockholders, or legislators.

We cannot say that excellent public relations alone can save an organization the costs of activism, regulation, or litigation, that it makes employees more productive, or that it brings in resources from satisfied customers, donors, stockholders, or legislators. But good relationships do contribute to these bottom-line behaviors, and by looking at their value to an organization we believe it is possible to estimate the monetary value of public relations to an organization. Chapter 23 ends this book by developing a methodology for making such estimates. That methodology can be used by practitioners and researchers to estimate the economic value of the contribution of public relations to organizational effectiveness.

We end this chapter, therefore, by stating the major proposition about the relationship between public relations and organizational effectiveness that we have derived from the literature reviewed here:

Proposition: Public relations contributes to organizational effectiveness when it helps reconcile the organization's goals with the expectations of its strategic constituencies. This contribution has monetary value to the organization. Public relations contributes to effectiveness by building quality, long-term relationships with strategic constituencies. Public relations is most likely to contribute to effectiveness when the senior public relations manager is a member of the dominant coalition where he or she is able to shape the organization's goals and to help determine which external publics are most strategic.

REFERENCES

Aldrich, H. E. (1975). An organization-environment perspective on cooperation and conflict between organizations in the manpower training system. In A. R. Negandhi (Ed.), *Interorganizational theory* (pp. 49–70). Kent, OH: Kent State University Press.

Aldrich, H. E. (1979). *Organizations and environments.* Englewood Cliffs, NJ: Prentice-Hall.

Blake, R. R., & Mouton, J. S. (1984). *Solving costly organizational conflicts.* San Francisco: Jossey-Bass.

Blau, P. M., & Scott, W. R. (1962). *Formal organizations.* San Francisco: Chandler.

Boddewyn, J. J. (1974). External affairs: A corporate function in the search of conceptualization and theory. *Organizational and Administrative Science, 5,* 67–112.

Broom, G. M. (1977). Coorientational measurement of public issues. *Public Relations Review, 3*(4), 110–119.

Buchholz, R. A. (1989). *Business environment and public policy* (3rd ed.). Englewood Cliffs, NJ: Prentice-Hall.

Cameron, K. S. (1984). The effectiveness of ineffectiveness. In B. M. Staw & L. L. Cummings (Eds.), *Research in organizational behavior* (Vol. 6, p. 276). Greenwich, CT: JAI.

Campbell, J. P. (1976). Contributions research can make in understanding organizational effectiveness. *Organization and Administrative Science, 7,* 29–48.

Campbell, J. P. (1977). On the nature of organizational effectiveness. In P. S. Goodman & J. M. Pennings (Eds.), *New perspectives on organizational effectiveness* (pp. 13–55). San Francisco: Jossey-Bass.

Campbell, J. P., Dunnette, M. D., Lawler, E. E., III, & Weick, K. E., Jr. (1970). *Managerial behavior, performance, and effectiveness.* New York: McGraw-Hill.

Crozier, M. (1964). *The bureaucratic phenomenon.* Chicago: University of Chicago Press.

Cutlip, S. M., Center, A. H., & Broom, G. M. (1985). *Effective public relations* (6th ed.). Englewood Cliffs, NJ: Prentice-Hall.

Cyert, R. M., & March, J. G. (1963). *A behavioral theory of the firm.* Englewood Cliffs, NJ: Prentice-Hall.

Denison, D. R. (1990). *Corporate culture and organizational effectiveness.* New York: Wiley.

Downey, H. K., Hellriegel, D., & Slocum, J. W., Jr. (1975). Environmental uncertainty: The construct and its application. *Administrative Science Quarterly, 20,* 613–629.

Ehling, W. P. (1975). PR administration, management science, and purposive systems. *Public Relations Review, 1,* 15–42.

Ermann, M. D., & Lundman, R. J. (1982). *Corporate deviance.* New York: Holt, Rinehart & Winston.

Esman, M. J. (1972). The elements of institution building. In J. W. Eaton (Ed.), *Institution building and development* (pp. 19–40). Beverly Hills, CA: Sage.

Etzioni, A. (1964). *Modern organizations.* Englewood Cliffs, NJ: Prentice-Hall.

Evan, W. H. (1976). An organizational-set model of interorganizational relations. In W. M. Evan (Ed.), *Interorganizational relations* (pp. 78–90). New York: Penguin.

Farace, R. V., Monge, P. R., & Russell, H. M. (1977). *Communicating and organizing.* Reading, MA: Addison-Wesley.

Fayol, H. (1916). *Administration industrielle et generale.* Paris: Dunod.

Ferguson, M. A. (1984, August). *Building theory in public relations: Interorganizational relationships.* Paper presented at the meeting of the Association for Education in Journalism and Mass Communication, Gainesville, FL.

Freeman, R. E. (1984). *Strategic management: A stakeholder approach.* Marshfield, MA: Pitman.

Galbraith, J. K. (1967). *The new industrial state.* Boston: Houghton Mifflin.

Geduldig, A. (1991, January). Impacting behavior proves value. *Public Relations Journal,* p. 8.

Gollner, A. B. (1983). *Social change and corporate strategy.* Stamford, CT: Issue Action Publications.

Gollner, A. B. (1984). Public relations/public affairs in the new managerial revolution. *Public Relations Review, 10*(4), 3–10.

Gouldner, A. W. (1959). Organizational analysis. In R. K. Merton, L. Broom, & L. S. Cottrell, Jr. (Eds.), *Sociology today* (pp. 400–428). New York: Basic.

Gray, B. (1985). Conditions facilitating interorganizational collaboration. *Human Relations, 38,* 911–936.

Gray, B. (1989). *Collaborating: Finding common ground for multiparty problems.* San Francisco: Jossey-Bass.

GRUNIG, GRUNIG, EHLING 88

Grunig, J. E. (1976). Organizations and public relations: Testing a communication theory. *Journalism Monographs, 46.*

Grunig, J. E. (1984). Organizations, environments, and models of public relations. *Public Relations Research and Education, 1*(1), 6–29.

Grunig, J. E., & Grunig, L. A. (1989). Toward a theory of the public relations behavior of organizations: Review of a program of research. *Public Relations Research Annual, 1,* 27–63.

Grunig, J. E., & Hunt, T. (1984). *Managing public relations.* New York: Holt, Rinehart & Winston.

Gurevitch, M. M., & Blumler, J. (1982). *An agenda for research in public communication: An overview and some proposals.* Paper presented to the faculty of the College of Journalism, University of Maryland, College Park.

Hage, J. (1980). *Theories of organizations: Form, process, and transformation.* New York: Wiley.

Hall, R. H. (1972). *The formal organization.* New York: Basic.

Hall, R. H., & Clark, J. P. (1975). Problems in the study of interorganizational relationships. In A. R. Negandhi (Ed.), *Interorganizational theory* (pp. 111–127). Kent, OH: Kent State University Press.

Hanken, N. J., & Reuver, D. L. (1981). *Social systems and learning systems.* Boston: Martinus Nijhoff.

Hannan, M., & Freeman, J. (1977a). The population ecology of organizations. *American Journal of Sociology, 82,* 929–964.

Hannan, M., & Freeman, J. (1977b). Obstacles to comparative studies. In P. Goodman & J. Pennings (Eds.), *New perspectives on organizational effectiveness* (pp. 106–131). San Francisco: Jossey-Bass.

Henderson, L. J. (1967). *Pareto's general sociology: A physiologist's interpretation.* New York: Russell & Russell.

Hickson, D. J., Hinings, C. R., Lee, C. A., Schneck, R. E., & Pennings, J. M. (1971). A strategic constituencies theory of intraorganizational power. *Administrative Science Quarterly, 16,* 216–229.

Katz, D., & Kahn, R. L. (1966). The social psychology of organizations. New York: Wiley.

Katz, D., & Kahn, R. L. (1978). *The social psychology of organizations* (2nd ed.). New York: Wiley.

Kirchhoff, B. A. (1977). Organizational effectiveness measurement and policy research. *Academy of Management Review, 2,* 348–355.

Lawrence, P. R., & Lorsch, J. W. (1967). Differentiation and integration in complex organizations. *Administrative Science Quarterly, 12,* 1–47.

Lieberman, J. K. (1983). *The litigious society.* New York: Basic.

March, J. G., & Olsen, J. P. (1976). *Ambiguity and choice in organizations.* Bergen, Norway: Universitetsforlaget.

Mayo, E. (1976). Hawthorne and the Western Electric Company. In D. S. Pugh, (Ed.), *Organization theory* (pp. 215–229). Harmondsworth, Middlesex, England: Penguin Education.

McKelvey, B. (1979). Comment on the biological analog in organizational science, on the occasion of Van de Ven's review of Aldrich. *Administrative Science Quarterly, 21,* 212–226.

Miller, J. (1978). *Living systems.* New York: McGraw-Hill.

Mintzberg, H. (1983). *Power in and around organizations.* Englewood Cliffs, NJ: Prentice-Hall.

Molnar, J. J., & Rogers, D. (1956). Organizational effectiveness: An empirical comparison of the goal and systems resource approaches. *Sociological Quarterly, 1,* 64–67.

Parsons, T. (1951). *The structure of social action.* Glencoe, IL: Free Press.

Parsons, T. (1960). Structure and process in modern societies. Glencoe, IL: Free Press.

Pavlik, J. V. (1987). *Public relations: What research tells us.* Newbury Park, CA: Sage.

Pennings, J. M., & Goodman, P. S. (1977). Toward a workable framework. In P. S. Goodman & J. M. Pennings (Eds.), *New perspectives on organizational effectiveness* (pp. 146–184). San Francisco: Jossey-Bass.

Perrow, C. (1961). The analysis of goals in complex organizations. *American Sociological Review, 26,* 854–865.

Perrow, C. (1967). A framework for the comparative analysis of organizations. *American Sociological Review, 32,* 194–209.

Pfeffer, J. (1977). Usefulness of the concept. In P. S. Goodman & J. M. Pennings (Eds.), *New perspectives on organizational effectiveness* (pp. 132–145). San Francisco: Jossey-Bass.

Pfeffer, J. (1978). *Organizational design.* Arlington Heights, IL: AHM.

Pfeffer, J. (1981). *Power in organizations.* Boston: Pitman.

Pfeffer, J. (1982). *Organizations and organization theory.* Marshfield, MA: Pitman.

Pfeffer, J., & Salancik, G. R. (1974). Organizational decision making as a political process: The case of a university budget. *Administrative Science Quarterly, 19,* 135–151.

Pfeffer, J., & Salancik, G. R. (1978). *The external control of organizations: A resource dependence model.* New York: Harper & Row.

Preston, L. E. (1981). Corporate power and social performance: Approaches to positive analysis. *Research in Corporate Social Performance and Policy: A Research Annual, 3:*1–16.

Price, J. L. (1968). *Organizational effectiveness: An inventory of propositions.* Homewood, IL: Irwin.

Quinn, R. E., & Hall, R. H. (1983). Environments, organizations, and policymakers: Toward an integrative framework. In R. H. Hall & R. E. Quinn (Eds.), *Organizational theory and public policy* (pp. 281–298). Beverly Hills, CA: Sage.

Robbins, S. P. (1990). *Organization theory: Structure, design, and applications* (3rd ed.). Englewood Cliffs, NJ: Prentice-Hall.

Roos, L. L., Jr., & Starke, F. H. (1981). Organizational roles. In P. C. Nystrom & W. H. Starbuck (Eds.), *Handbook of organizational design* (pp. 48–66). New York: Oxford University Press.

Schneider (aka Grunig), L. A. (1985). *Organizational structure, environmental niches, and public relations: The Hage-Hull typology of organizations as predictor of communication behavior.* Unpublished doctoral dissertation, University of Maryland, College Park.

Scott, W. R. (1977). Effectiveness of organizational effectiveness studies. In J. M. Pennings & P. S. Goodman (Eds.), *New perspectives on organizational effectiveness* (pp. 63–95). San Francisco: Jossey-Bass.

Scott, W. R., Flood, A. B., Ewy, W., & Forrest, W. H., Jr. (1978). Organizational effectiveness and the quality of surgical care in hospitals. In M. W. Meyer & Associates (Eds.), *Environments and organizations* (pp. 290–305). San Francisco: Jossey-Bass.

Simon, H. A. (1977). *The new science of management* (rev. ed.). Englewood Cliffs, NJ: Prentice-Hall.

Staff, (1988, January 11). The state of public relations 1988: Part II. *pr reporter,* pp. 1–4.

Steers, R. (1975). Problems in the measurement of organizational effectiveness. *Administrative Science Quarterly, 20,* 546–558.

Thayer, L. O. (1961). *Administrative communication.* Homewood, IL: Irwin.

Thompson, J. D. (1967). *Organizations in action.* New York: McGraw-Hill.

Tuleja, T. (1985). *Beyond the bottom line.* New York: Facts on File.

Van de Ven, A. H., Emmett, D. C., & Koenig, R., Jr. (1975). Frameworks of interorganizational analysis. In A. R. Negandhi (Ed.), *Interorganizational theory* (pp. 19–38). Kent, OH: Kent State University Press.

Walton, R. (1969). *Interpersonal peacemaking.* Reading, MA: Addison-Wesley.

Warriner, C. K. (1964, Spring). The problem of organizational purpose. *Sociological Quarterly,* pp. 139–146.

Weber, M. (1947). *The theory of social and economic organization.* New York: Oxford University Press.

Weick, K. E. (1969). *The social psychology of organizing.* Reading, MA: Addison-Wesley.

Weick, K. E. (1976). Educational organizations as loosely coupled systems. *Administrative Science Quarterly, 21,* 1–19.

Weick, K. E. (1979). *The social psychology of organizing* (2nd ed.). Reading, MA: Addison-Wesley.

Woodward, J. (1965). *Industrial organizations: Theory and practice.* Oxford, England: Oxford University Press.

Yuchtman, E., & Seashore, S. E. (1967). A systems resource approach to organizational effectiveness. *American Sociological Review, 3,* 891–903.

Zeitz, G. (1975). Interorganizational relationships and social structure: A critique of some aspects of literature. In A. R. Negandhi (Ed.), *Interorganizational theory* (pp. 39–48). Kent, OH: Kent State University Press.

4 Public Relations and Management Decision Making

Jon White
*Management Consultant,
Bedford, United Kingdom*

David M. Dozier
San Diego State University

ABSTRACT

*Communication departments cannot make organizations more effective un-
less public relations functions as an integral part of management. The
previous chapter showed that organizations must communicate with strategic
constituencies in their environment to be effective. This chapter explains that
members of organizations identify — enact — their environments and that they
need trained boundary-spanning personnel to do so effectively. Excellent
public relations departments do environmental scanning for their organizations. This chapter also introduces the key concepts of the dominant coalition
(the group of managers who hold the most power in an organization), levels
of decision making, and strategic management. The general theory of public
relations maintains that the senior public relations practitioner must be part of
the dominant coalition, function at a high level of decision making, and
participate in strategic management if public relations is to be excellent and is
to make the organization more effective.*

Excellent public relations requires that the top practitioner in an organization participate in management decision making. This assertion is derived
from the normative theory posed in chapter 1: Strategic public relations
requires practitioner access to decision-making authority in an organization. In chapter 12, the organizational role of the practitioner is linked to
participation in management decision making. In chapter 14, the vertical
location of the public relations unit in the organizational structure is posed
as an enhancing or limiting factor in strategic management of the function.

What role do communication managers and public relations practitioners play in strategic decision making? This chapter develops the concept of strategic decision making and indicates the ways in which practitioners make useful contributions to decision making.

REPRESENTATIONS OF THE ORGANIZATIONAL ENVIRONMENT

When organizations make decisions, they do so based on a representation of both the organization itself and the organization's environment. A *representation* is the set of shared perceptions of the organization and its environment that organization members use to make decisions. Members of the organization have shared perceptions of what is "out there," but those perceptions are frequently difficult to specify (Leifer & Delbecq, 1978; Millikin, 1987). Starbuck (1976) suggested that it is difficult to determine where the organization stops and the organization's environment begins. Organizations decide where the boundary lies: "an organization's environment is an arbitrary invention of the organization itself" (Starbuck, 1976, p. 1078). Practitioners routinely seek to influence the malleable perceptions of publics of their organization (improving the corporate image). Less obvious is that the organization's perceptions of itself and of its environment are also malleable. Public relations practitioners play an important role in shaping perceptions of the environment — and the organization itself — among decision makers.

Weick (1969, 1979) saw organizations as psychological creations of their members; an *organization* is an idea or perception in the minds of people who make it up or who are in contact with its members. Organizations are not responsive to all the social, political, and economic events (inputs) occurring in the world. The *environment* can be thought of as a construction built from the flow of information into the organization (Duncan, 1972). The organization cannot be responsive to the tidal wave of information potentially available to it. Rather, parts of the information flow from the environment are marked off and saved for further scrutiny, a process Weick (1969, 1979) called *enactment*. Thus, organizations create their own environments by paying attention to some information from out there while ignoring other information. This subset of information from outside the organization's boundary becomes the environment, the perception of the external world upon which all subsequent decisions are based.

Scholars differ as to how systematic organizations are when they construct environments. Starbuck (1976) regarded this process as largely unreflective, disorderly, incremental, and strongly influenced by social norms and customs. However, Millikin (1987) suggested such disorganized constructions of environmental perceptions occur largely when decision makers are uncertain about the environment.

DOMINANT COALITIONS

Who are the decision makers in organizations? Organizational charts provide a ready answer, but anyone who has worked in an organization knows that decision makers and decision making are considerably more complex than what organizational charts suggest. Organizations are not of a common mind. Rather, organizations are coalitions of varying interests, made up of participants whose preferences and goals may be incompatible (Pfeffer & Salancik, 1979; Hickson, Butler, Mallory, & Wilson, 1986).

Child (1972) argued that a group forms in organizations with the power to make and enforce decisions about the direction of the organization, its tasks, its objectives, and functions. Such groups are called *dominant coalitions,* groups with the power to set organizational structures and strategies over a sustained period of time. The dominant coalition's power becomes recognized as legitimate in time by those over whom such power is exercised. That power may be institutionalized through binding legal documents, charters of incorporation, and so forth (Holmes, 1965; Weber, 1947).

BOUNDARY SPANNING

The dominant coalition needs information to help make decisions. That information frequently is provided by *boundary spanners,* individuals within the organization who frequently interact with the organization's environment and who gather, select, and relay information from the environment to decision makers in the dominant coalition. Communication managers and public relations practitioners are among an organization's designated boundary spanners (see Aldrich & Herker, 1977).

Boundary-spanning activities can be formalized through management information systems (MIS). Such systems provide decision makers with information needed to make decisions (Ackoff, 1967). Such systems must organize information in suitable forms and at appropriate points and levels in the decision-making process (Humphreys, 1985). To be useful to decision making, information gathered by boundary-spanning practitioners must be organized in a manner that fits the decision-making structure and process.

Organizations and dominant coalitions construct environments from a subset of the information that flows into the organization. As Wohlstetter (1962) reported, ignoring seemingly irrelevant information from the environment can have disastrous consequences for organizations, as when the American armed forces ignored information forewarning of an imminent attack on Pearl Harbor by Japanese forces in 1941. Dominant coalitions pay greater attention to information from boundary spanners under conditions of environmental turbulence (Emery & Trist, 1965), because decision makers are less certain as to which information to attend to and which information to ignore as they manage the organization's response to rapid environmental change (Kiesler & Sproull, 1982).

DECISIONS AND DECISION MAKING

Mintzberg, Raisinghani, and Theoret (1976) defined a decision as a specific commitment to action. Berkeley and Humphreys (1982) defined *decision making* as the moment of choice among alternative immediate acts. The act chosen is seen as public and irreversible. Decision making cannot be stripped of the social setting in which decisions are made and the social consequences of such decisions. The decision-making process is both social (Radford, 1977) and political (Eden & Sims, 1979; Pfeffer, 1981).

The process begins with the identification of a stimulus to action and ends with a specific action (Mintzberg et al., 1976). The stimulus to action may be described as a *decision problem,* one that gives rise to the need for a decision. Decision problems are likely to be unstructured or ill-defined (Eden, Jones, & Sims, 1983).

Some decision problems are especially ill-defined. Humphreys (1984) described such problems as those that, from the outset, involve considerable uncertainty as to what precisely the problem involves and how that problem can be represented (modeled or perceived) as the focus of decision making. The detection of decision problems by organizations involves a "cognitive process of noticing and constructing meaning about environmental change so that organizations can take action." The initial construction of meaning or representation of the decision problem constrains and limits the range of responses or decision of the organization.

Detection of decision problems is the first step in the structuring the problem for resolution. Radford (1977, p. 149) identified three steps in structuring a decision problem. The first step involves problem perception and the gathering of information about the problem itself, possible courses of action, and possible future consequences of actions. Such future consequences are expressed in the form of scenarios. In the second step, participants in the decision-making process evaluate—by intuition or formal analysis—the strategic structure of the problem (in the form of alternative scenarios) to assess preferences among outcomes. In the third step, decision-making participants communicate, negotiate, and bargain among each other to select a resolution.

For example, a high-tech corporation pays high salaries and provides substantial employee benefits to senior systems specialists, who are essential to designing the expanding line of products the company manufactures. The employee communication manager notes that, in recent years, this former all-male occupation has attracted a growing minority of women. The manager does further information gathering by contacting the 15 universities around the United States that provide training in this specialized field.

The manager finds that the majority of students currently enrolled in the major are women. A survey of male and female senior system specialists at the company reveal that women have different needs and interests than their male counterparts. Whereas male employees value the company's on-site weight-lifting room, women would prefer an on-site child-care center. Women express a strong interest in flex schedules; men do not.

The employee communication manager has detected a potential decision problem and has gathered information relevant to the problem: The needs and interests of a valued set of employees will shift in the future, because of a change in employee demographics. The employee communication manager works with other members of the dominant coalition to construct alternative scenarios that respond to the problem. In the second step, alternative scenarios are analyzed. One scenario—hire only male employees—has several undesirable consequences. Such discrimination is illegal and, in the future, such discrimination would limit the company to a shrinking pool of acceptable (male) prospects to select from. A second scenario—provide scholarships to male students to major in the specialty—also has undesirable consequences. The scenario again involves discrimination, would take too long to implement, and would again reduce the number of acceptable candidates. A third scenario—alter company policies to accommodate the needs and interests of women employees—has both positive and negative consequences. Positive consequences include full opportunity (and perhaps some attractive incentives) to hire the best candidate, because gender would not be an issue. Negative consequences involve initial capital expenditures and significant restructuring of personnel policies. In the third step, members of the dominant coalition discuss the various scenarios, negotiate details, and bargain organizational resources that each member controls in order to reach a decision and a course of action.

Levels of Decision Making

Some decisions are relatively low level, involving *concrete operational* decisions related to tasks concretely and physically at hand (Humphreys, 1984, p. 19). As first posited by Jaques (1982), such decisions include many of the activities of practitioners playing the technician role in organizations (see chapter 12). Examples include decisions about the cover of the employee magazine (color or black-and-white?), handling technical aspects of producing public relations materials (use printer A or printer B?), and editing for grammar and spelling the writing of others in the organization (compound sentence or two sentences?). Such technical decisions are made in relatively short order, frequently involve a single decision maker, and are made within a highly structured "goal-closed small world" (Humphreys, 1984, p. 19).

Table 4.1 displays the levels of decisions made in organizations. As one

Table 4.1

Comparison of Demand Characteristics of Tasks Facing Personnel Having Responsibilities at Given Organizational Level with Structuring Capabilities Required in Representing Decision Problems at That Level (Characteristics of Levels 8–10 Can, in Theory, Be Ascertained by Extrapolation form Levels 3–5, Respectively)

Level Number	Organisational Level in Employment Hierarchy	Time Span Inherent in Problem Representation at Given Level	Demand Characteristics of Tasks Facing Personnel with Responsibility at Given Level	Structuring Capabilities Required in Representing Decision Problems at Given Level (Decision Support Must Also Include Capabilities at All Low Levels)	Number of Existing DSS Incorporating Support Formalised at Given Level
7	Chairman M/D of corporate group; head of large government department.	20–50 years	Anticipation of changes in sociological, technilogical, demographic and political developments; leading corporate strategic development to meet them.	Isomorphic with Level 2, except can conduct sensitivity analysis, simulating changes in Level 5 representations; assessing their impact within cultural structure.	None
6	Corporate group/sector executive.	10–20 years	Coordination of social and theoretical systems; translation of corporate strategic development into business direction.	Isomorphic with Level 1, except each node is now a Level 5 problem representation within fixed cultural structure.	None

Sociocultural decision making: goal-closed small worlds structured within cultures (in theory, up to Level 10).

Individual decision making under uncertainty: uncertainties and preferences structured within goal-closed small worlds.

5	Corporate subsidiary/enterprise managing director	5–10 years	Problem not dealt with in context set wholly from above; can modify boundaries within policy, i.e. define work system.	Articulation of principles for conditional (goal) closing of an open system, and/or reopening of a conditionally closed system (e.g., through scenario generation).	None
4	General management, (of, e.g., development, production *or* sales, within work system).	2–5 years	Detachment from specific cases, seeing them representative examples of issues calling for development of a system.	Selecting/interfacing capability between structural types (requires use of problem structuring language).	Very few (prototypes)
3	Department Managerial/principal specialist.	1–2 years	Control of trend of tasks and problems arising. Extrapolation from trend to ways of formulating problems.	Restructuring capability within single fixed structural type (e.g., attribute generation in multiattribute model).	A few
2	Front-line managerial/professional.	3 months to 1 year	*Formal operational*, can anticipate changes in tasks due to any *one* of: demand, object, production resource, pathway, or pathway resource.	Manipulation of data on one variable at a time within fixed structure (e.g., sensitivity analysis).	Many
1	Shop and office floor.	less than 3 months	*Concrete operational* limited to tasks concretely and physically at hand.	Estimation of values at nodes within fixed structure (e.g., information retrieval system).	Many

Note. Reproduced with permission from P. C. Humphreys (1984). Levels of Representation in Structuring Decision Problems. *Journal of Applied Systems Analysis*, 3–22.

moves from the lower level concrete operational decisions to higher levels, decisions become more social and more abstract (more removed from concrete specifics). Relevant information needed to make higher level decisions becomes more ambiguous; decision support systems frequently do not exist at higher levels of decision making. Higher level decisions are more open from a systems perspective. At the same time, such decisions are frequently more important.

Strategic decisions are those that profoundly affect the future success and destiny of the organization (Jemison, 1984). Mintzberg et al. (1976) specified strategic decisions as important ones, in terms of actions to be taken, resources to be committed, and consequences for the organization and those who make such decisions. Strategic decisions typically involve a significant change of direction for the organization, such as the decision by a manufacturing company to enter into a new market. Keller (1983) suggested that strategic decisions are those that contribute to effective use of organizational resources to deal with environmental competition. Strategic decisions affect the survival and growth of organizations. Such decisions require adequate representations (perceptions) of the organization's environment upon which to base actions. Such representations become more ambiguous and difficult to construct as decision levels increase.

Radford (1977) described such problems as "complex" or "wicked." *Wicked problems* have several characteristics:

1. Inadequate information is available to decision makers.
2. Multiple and conflicting objectives are involved.
3. Several decision makers are involved.
4. The problem environment is dynamic and turbulent.
5. Several such problems are linked together.
6. Resolution may involve costly, irreversible commitments.

Despite these complications, wicked problems must be structured for resolution. Such structuring becomes more difficult as the level of abstraction, both cognitive and organizational, increases. High-level strategic decision problems require abstract thinking and, because they are strategic, such decision problems are dealt with by those high in the organizational structure. The challenge for communicators and public relations practitioners is to understand and respect the qualitative differences between concrete operational decisions that they routinely make as technicians and abstract strategic decisions they must make as managers.

Strategic decisions of relevance to communication managers occur at Level 5 in Table 4.1. Unlike the technical production decisions that practitioners individually make at Level 1, strategic decisions at Level 5 involve many decision makers. Further, decision problems at Level 5 involve substantial communication, negotiation, and bargaining simply to define or construct the problem (Kiesler & Sproull, 1982). Decisionmakers struggle with inventing adequate language with which to define or structure the problem. (See March & Simon, 1958; Pondy & Mitroff, 1979; Silverman, 1971.)

BOUNDARY SPANNING AND CONSTRUCTING MEANING

Some decisions require construction of new meanings about the organization in relation to its environment. Such construction of meaning typically involves action to change existing meanings. In such situations, boundary spanners such as communication managers have an important role to play. Decision problems requiring changes in organizational meanings also require an understanding of the organization from the outside. Organizations have *cultures* with implicit, unstated, and often invisible assumptions about the organization and its relation to its environment. Only when one leaves one's native land does one confront the somewhat arbitrary constructions of one's own culture. When viewed from the outside, *meaning* is seen as a cultural artifact because it is juxtaposed against an alternative construction. Within organizations, boundary spanners are uniquely equipped to structure new meanings regarding organization and environment.

For example, an industry association of logging companies perceives timber (trees) as a renewable resource, a crop to be harvested like wheat or corn. (The association's mission is to educate the public about logging and to protect logging industry interests with regulators and legislators.) Timber association members construct a meaning of timber consistent with their purposes (logging), making arguments that timber is preferable to nonrenewable building materials such as plaster, concrete, steel, and plastics. Information from the environment inconsistent with such perceptions is likely to be ignored.

But timber is also home to species of animals that would cease to exist without trees. Trees also convert carbon dioxide to oxygen, playing a critical role in maintaining the planet as habitat for humans and other animals. Standing virgin or old-growth trees also hold special aesthetic meaning of great importance to many city dwellers.

In order to respond intelligently to environmental activists, the timber industry association must supplement or even change the meaning its decision makers construct with regard to timber. Who among the decision makers can act as such a change agent? Perhaps the association's communication manager, who is a member of the Sierra Club (an environmental activist group) as well as a staff member of the timber association. Spanning the gap between the timber industry association and the Sierra Club, the practitioner is uniquely qualified to construct new meanings to concepts or ideas such as timber.

REQUISITE SCENARIOS

When abstract decision problems are detected, decision makers must resort to their imaginations to construct scenarios so that decision making can proceed. Such scenarios are not precisely defined. At best, they are simplified models of possible futures that help focus attention on crucial variables and decision points (Phillips, 1982). Such scenarios are *requisite* when they provide a sufficient basis for solving particular problems through an appropriate decision. Requisite scenarios are social constructions; they are fashioned through communication among decision makers and are developed in an iterative manner.

For example, a school district is under fire from environmental activists for using styrofoam containers in district high school cafeterias. Top district administrators and powerful members of the school board (the dominant coalition) hold a series of meetings to fashion an organizational response to the decision problem detected in the district's environment. Decision makers imagine a series of scenarios of possible actions and reactions by the district and the environmentalists. The decision-making process is iterative: An action by the district (or the environmental activists) sets the stage for a number of possible responses in reaction to the initial action. Each such action or reaction generates a series of options or branches. The possibilities are bounded only by the imagination of the decision makers and the perceptions/meanings they bring to the decision-making process.

A requisite scenario in this example is one that permits the school district and environmental activists to resolve the conflict in a mutually beneficial manner. Any public relations decision problem permits many requisite scenarios. Organizations, however, need only the imagination and perceptions/ meanings to come up with one requisite scenario, one that "satisfices." Given the ambiguity and uncertainty of most higher level decision problems, finding even one such requisite scenario taxes the decision makers' "sense-making" capacity.

THE COMMUNICATION FUNCTION
AND MEANING

Much of the behavior of the dominant coalition, the management group giving direction to the organization, is directed toward managing boundary conditions of the organization. This task includes managing exchanges across the organizational boundary to ensure that the organization responds to environmental demands and opportunities (Katz & Kahn, 1966; Levine & White, 1961).

Organizational boundaries can be associated with, if not defined by, communication boundaries or impedance (Tushman & Scanlan, 1981). That is, one aspect of an organizational boundary is that communication and shared meaning are easier and more frequent within the boundaries and more difficult and less frequent across organizational boundaries. Given this, communication managers and public relations practitioners would seem natural counsel to decision makers and integral members of the dominant coalition. Research on roles and environmental scanning, however, indicates that such a counseling role and decision-making participation is not automatic (Dozier, 1990).

One reason why boundary-spanning practitioners are not included in decision making is related to the manager-technician distinction. *Environmental scanning,* especially informal environmental scanning, can be viewed as a largely technical activity. For example, a public relations practitioner might define environmental scanning as reading the popular and industry press and clipping articles about the organization and issues important to the organization. This technical approach to scanning-as-clipping typically is subcontracted to clipping services.

Such technical monitoring of the media is only a first step, however, in the management function of environmental scanning. The communication boundaries that help define the organization's boundaries are created by the interaction of idiosyncratic language/coding schemes and by the development of local conceptual frameworks. Returning to the aforementioned example of the timber industry association, members of the association will develop language/coding schemes wherein entire eco-subsystems, forests, are described as timber stands. The very language used within the association carries with it an entire set of presuppositions (see chapter 3). A timber stand is like a field of corn, an agricultural product that is grown for the purpose of harvesting and sale. Timber stands, however, are also habitats, complex ecosystems, and aesthetic experiences. The local conceptual framework (trees as timber) is embedded in the specialized language of the association.

The boundary-spanning practitioner plays a useful technical role when he or she reads the Sierra Club newsletter. The practitioner plays an even more important role by changing the language/coding schemes and local conceptual frameworks to include *habitat, ecosystem,* and *aesthetic experiences.* Without such expanded language/coding schemes, the association's internal perceptual, sense-making tools are inadequate for decision making.

As the local (within organization) conceptual framework and language/

coding schemes become more insulated from the environment, external communication from the organization becomes increasingly bizarre and nonsensical to those outside the organization. For example, American armed forces fighting in Vietnam from 1963 to 1975 developed idiosyncratic language to describe their behavior to the outside world. Bombing a village became a "protective reactive strike." As the American military became more insulated from an increasingly hostile environment (both in Vietnam and in the United States), the local conceptual framework within the American military became more idiosyncratic. For example, an American officer commented on the aerial destruction of a Vietnam village: "We had to destroy the village in order to save it."

In summary, boundary spanning by communication managers has both managerial and technical components. Putting newspaper and magazine clips about the organization in a folder for decision makers to review is a technical function. Public relations managers, however, fail to perform their role when their contribution to decision making is limited to such technical support. More important and valuable to the decision-making process is the change of idiosyncratic language/coding systems and local conceptual frameworks. When boundary-spanning communication managers overtly change local, idiosyncratic language/coding schemes, they provide other members of the dominant coalition with the perceptual tools required for developing requisite scenarios and making decisions that satisfice.

Although such contributions by boundary-spanning practitioners improve the decision-making process, such behavior of change agents is not without risk. Paradoxically, a boundary spanner may be denied full access to information about organizational concerns regarding the environment. Aldrich and Herker (1977) pointed out that boundary-spanning individuals, although exerting some influence within the organization because of their control of external information, may be denied greater influence because their loyalty is suspect. (Consider the timber association communicator who is a member of the Sierra Club!) Suspicion may follow as a consequence of relatively frequent contact between the boundary spanner and outsiders. Those inside the organization, locked into idiosyncratic language/coding systems and local conceptual frameworks, will become suspicious of boundary spanners who introduce "foreign" language/coding schemes, for such behavior undermines local conceptualizations and sense-making representations constructed by the organization. Boundary spanners violate the demarcation between organization and environment, a demarcation that protects organization members from "extra systemic influences" (Leifer & Delbecq, 1978, p. 4). The demarcation is largely psychological; violation of the demarcation and local conceptual frameworks threatens a member's sense of belonging. Boundary spanners are viewed as identifying with external rather than internal interests. The messenger, it seems, may well be blamed for unwelcome messages, regardless of their value to decision making.

The communication manager must walk a fine line. On the one hand, practitioners must challenge partial representations of the organizational environment that lead to poor management decisions. On the other hand, the practitioner must be keenly sensitive to the fact that such behavior may lead to suspicion by other decision makers and possible exclusion from decision making. In the long run, practitioners who help organizations make better decisions will earn enduring participation in strategic decision making. In the short run, practitioners must maintain the trust of the dominant coalition, even while communicating disturbing and unwelcome input from the organizational environment.

THE COMMUNICATION MANAGER'S ROLE

Communication managers and public relations practitioners span organizational boundaries to perform two functions (Aldrich & Herker, 1977): information processing and external representation. Practitioners most frequently act to represent the organization to the external environment. Indeed, journalistic training and the public information model of public relations (see chapter 11) emphasize the external representation function of public relations practitioners. Environmental scanning and program research are relatively innovative practices in public relations (Dozier, 1990). Yet the role of information gatherer and processor is key to the communication manager's participation in management decision making. Keegan (1974) found that public relations practitioners are regarded as good sources of information about the environments of large multinational organizations. Goldhaber, Dennis, Richetto, and Wiio (1979) suggested that considerable control in organizations has passed to staff groups from line groups. This is due to the role that staff play in gathering, organizing, and interpreting information about the environment to decision makers.

Many practitioners are not included in management decision making, in part because they play the technical role predominantly (see chapter 12) and because they do not engage in environmental scanning (Dozier, 1990). Environmental turbulence and uncertainty create opportunities for practitioners to participate in strategic decision making. Lack of information, ambiguity in information, or uncertainty regarding the likelihood of outcomes in given situations make decision makers uncertain. Under such conditions, boundary spanners play important roles in providing information about environmental contingencies to decisionmakers (Adams, 1976; Aldrich & Herker, 1977; Jemison, 1984; Leifer & Delbecq, 1978; Leifer &

Huber, 1977; Miles & Perreault, 1976). Turbulence and uncertainty increase the frequency of boundary-spanning activities and the influence of boundary spanners in decision making (Lebleci & Salancik, 1981; Leifer, 1975).

Decision-making groups are established over time and are formally recognized as such (boards of directors, senior management groups, etc.). In times of turbulence and uncertainty, however, decision-making groups are hurriedly reconfigured to deal with crises or to work on particularly demanding special projects.

The decision-making process itself was perhaps best described by Eden and Sims (1979) as: "A complicated drama which involves power, influence, negotiation, game playing, organizational politics, complex social relationships with real people, not merely officer holders" (p. 120). Regarding the decision-making process as a drama, communication managers ought to carefully consider the roles they play in it. Vari and Vecsenyi (1984) suggested that, in group decision making, five distinct participant roles are identifiable:

1. *Decision Makers*: these participants have executive power to define the use of outputs from the phases of the decision-making process.

2. *Proposers*: participants who only have the power to make recommendations.

3. *Experts*: participants who primarily supply input to the currently modeled problem structure.

4. *Consultants or Decision Analysts*: participants who advise on methods of problem representation.

5. *Facilitators*: participants who do not have a direct role in the decision-making process but who facilitate collaboration of experts and the transmission of results within and between rounds of decision making.

As detailed in chapter 12, these five participant roles in the decision-making process are reflected in Broom's early theory development regarding public relations practitioner roles in organizations (see Broom & Smith, 1979). The public relations manager role originally was conceptualized as three separate roles: expert prescription (Role 3), problem-solving process facilitation (Role 5), and communication facilitation. Subsequent empirical studies indicate, however, that public relations managers (in their day-to-day work) shift easily from expert prescription, process facilitation, and communication facilitation. The conceptually discrete types of practitioner organizational roles are empirically indistinguishable.

Regarding the Vari and Vecsenyi (1984) participant roles in decision making, communication managers are (with rare exception) not formally empowered as decision makers (Role 1). The other roles (Roles 2–5) are forms of participation within the range of roles practitioners can play. Regarding communication and the media, practitioners can draw upon their specialized experience and expertise to play the expert role. Even without formal decision-making authority, practitioners can play the proposer role. Practitioners also can develop skills as facilitators or experts. Regarding high-level, strategic decisions, however, boundary-spanning practitioners perhaps play their most important role when they serve as consultants who advise on methods of problem representation. As environmental scanners, practitioners make important decisions when they decide to present some information (but not other information) to the decision-making session. Other decision makers will tend toward constructing partial representations of the organizational environment, giving importance to only that information that affects their area of specialization (Dearborn & Simon, 1958). As generalists, practitioners must strive to provide fuller representations of the environment to decision makers. Communication managers are uniquely positioned to ensure that decision makers have adequate (rather than idiosyncratic) language/code systems and appropriate (rather than local) conceptual frameworks for representing the decision problem in a form that permits a solution that satisfices.

For example, Nestlé's marketing executives used a partial representation of the organizational environment in the 1970s when the multinational conglomerate decided to market infant milk formula in third-world nations. The conceptual framework used was one of aspiring third-world families switching from breast feeding to more "modern" bottle feeding.

Left out of the conceptual framework were unintended consequences of mixing inadequate qualities of the infant formula with contaminated water available in many third-world nations. The consequences: many infant deaths from malnutrition and disease. Activists organized international boycotts of dozens of Nestlé's products, sold throughout the industrial world, to protest Nestlé's actions.

Using Nestlé's partial, marketing-based representation of the environment, the campaign to market formula in the third world seemed to satisfice. A fuller representation of the environment, provided by a public relations practitioner scanning and interpreting the larger organizational environment, might have led to a more appropriate decision not to launch an infant milk formula marketing campaign in the third world.

PROPOSITIONS

The previous theoretical discussion suggests a series of propositions regarding public relations practitioner participation in management decision making:

Proposition 1: The more environmental scanning that practitioners conduct, the greater their participation in management decision making.

Proposition 2: The more turbulent and uncertain the organizational environment, the more environmental scanning practitioners will be expected to conduct.

Proposition 3: The more turbulent and uncertain the organizational environment, the greater the participation of practitioners in management decision making.

Proposition 4: The greater the conflict between practitioner-provided input and existing language/codes/frameworks, the greater the mistrust of practitioner loyalty to the organization.

Proposition 5: The greater the conflict between practitioner-provided input and existing language/codes/frameworks, the better the quality of the decisions reached.

These propositions serve as the basis for further research on public relations practitioners and participation in management decision making.

REFERENCES

Ackoff, R. L. (1967). Management misinformation systems. *Management Science, 14,* 147–156.

Adams, J. S. (1976). The structure and dynamics of behavior in organizational boundary roles. In M. D. Dunnette (Ed.), *Handbook of industrial and organizational psychology* (pp. 1175–1199). Chicago: Rand McNally.

Aldrich, H., & Herker, D. (1977). Boundary spanning roles and organization structure. *Academy of Management Review, 2,* 217–230.

Berkeley, D., & Humphreys, P. (1982). Structuring decision problems and the bias heuristic. *Acta Psychologica, 50,* 201–252.

Broom, G., & Smith, G. D. (1979). Testing the practitioner's impact on clients. *Public Relations Review, 5*(3), 47–59.

Child, J. (1972). Organizational structure, environment and performance: The role of strategic choice. *Sociology, 6,* 1–22.

Dearborn, D. C., & Simon, H. A. (1958). Selective perception: A note on departmental identification of executives. *Sociometry, 21,* 140–144.

Dozier, D. M. (1990). The innovation of research in public relations practice: Review of a program of studies. In L. A. Grunig & J. E. Grunig (Eds.), *Public relations research annual* (Vol. 2, pp. 3–28). Hillsdale, NJ: Lawrence Erlbaum Associates.

Duncan, R. B. (1972). Characteristics of organizational environment and perceived environmental uncertainty. *Administrative Science Quarterly, 17,* 313–327.

Eden, C., & Sims, D. (1979). On the nature of problems in consulting practice. *Omega, 7,* 119–127.

Eden, C., S. Jones, & D. Sims (1983). *Messing about in problems: An informal structured approach to their identification and management.* Pergamon, Oxford.

Emery, F. E., & Trist, E. L. (1965). The causal texture of organizational environments. *Human Relations, 18,* 21–32.

Goldhaber, G., Dennis, H. S., Richetto, G. M., & Wiio, O. A. (1979). *Information strategies: New pathways to corporate power.* Englewood Cliffs, NJ: Prentice-Hall.

Hickson, D. J., Butler, R. J., Mallory, G. R., & Wilson, D. C. (1986). *Top decisions: Strategic decision-making in organizations.* Oxford, England: Basil Blackwell.

Holmes, R. (1965). *Legitimacy and the politics of the knowable.* London: Routledge & Kegan Paul.

Humphreys, P. C. (1984). Levels of representation in structuring decision problems. *Journal of Applied Systems Analysis, 11,* 3–22.

Humphreys, P. C. (1985). *Intelligence in decision support.* Paper presented at the 10th research conference on subjective probability, utility, and decision-making, Helsinki.

Jaques, E. (1982). *Free enterprise, fair employment.* London: Heineman.

Jemison, D. B. (1984). The importance of boundary spanning roles in strategic decision making. *Journal of Management Studies, 21,* 132–152.

Katz, D., & Kahn, R. L. (1966). *The social psychology of organizations.* New York: Wiley.

Keegan, W. J. (1974). Multinational scanning: A study of the information sources utilized by headquarters executives in multinational companies. *Administrative Science Quarterly, 19,* 411–421.

Keller, G. (1983). *Academic strategy: The management revolution in American higher education.* Baltimore & London: Johns Hopkins University Press.

Kiesler, S., & Sproull, L. (1982). Managerial response to changing environments: Perspectives on problem sensing from social cognition. *Administrative Science Quarterly, 27,* 548–570.

Lebleci, H., & Salancik, G. R. (1981). Effects on environmental uncertainty of information and decision processes in banks. *Administrative Science Quarterly, 26,* 578–596.

Leifer, R. P. (1975). *An analysis of the characteristics and functioning of boundary spanning personnel.* Unpublished doctoral dissertation, University of Wisconsin, Madison.

Leifer, R. P., & Delbecq, A. (1978). Organizational/environmental interchange: A model of boundary spanning activity. *Academy of Management Review, 3,* 40–50.

Leifer, R. P., & Huber, G. P. (1977). Relations among perceived environmental uncertainty, organization structure and boundary spanning behavior. *Administrative Science Quarterly, 22,* 235–247.

Levine, S., & White, P. E. (1961). Exchange as a conceptual framework for the study of interorganizational relationships. *Administrative Science Quarterly, 5,* 583–601.

March, J. G., & Simon, H. A. (1958). *Organizations.* New York: Wiley.

Miles, R. H., & Perreault, W. (1976). Organizational role conflict: Its antecedents and consequences. *Organizational Behavior and Human Performance, 17,* 19–44.

Millikin, F. J. (1987). Three types of perceived uncertainty about the environment: State, effect and response uncertainty. *Academy of Management Review, 12,* 133–143.

Mintzberg, H., Raisinghani, D., & Theoret, A. (1976). The structure of unstructured decision processes. *Administrative Science Quarterly, 21,* 246–275.

Pfeffer, J. (1981). *Power in organizations.* Marshfield, MA: Pitman.

Pfeffer, J., & Salancik, G. (1979). *The external control of organizations.* New York: Harper & Row.

Phillips, L. D. (1982). Requisite decision modelling: A case study. *Journal of the Operational Research Society, 33,* 303–311.

Pondy, L. R., & I. I. Mitroff (1979). Beyond open system models of organization. *Research in Organizational Behaviour, 1,* 3–39.

Radford, K. J. (1977). *Complex decision problems: An integrated strategy for resolution.* Reston, VA: Reston Publishing.

Silverman, D. (1971). *The theory of organization.* New York: Basic.

Starbuck, W. H. (1976). Organizations and their environments. In M. D. Dunnette (Ed.), *Handbook of industrial and organizational psychology* (pp. 1069–1124). Chicago: Rand McNally.

Tushman, M., & Scanlan, T. J. (1981). Boundary spanning individuals: Their role in information transfer and their antecedents. *Academy of Management Journal, 24,* 289–305.

Vari, A., & Vecsenyi, J. V. (1984). Selecting decision support methods in organizations. *Journal of Applied Systems Analysis, 11,* 23–36.

Weber, M. (1947). *The theory of social and economic organizations.* New York: Free Press.

Weick, K. (1969). *The social psychology of organizing.* Reading, MA: Addison-Wesley.

Weick, K. (1979). Cognitive processes in organizations. *Research in Organizational Behavior, 1,* 41–74.

Wohlstetter, R. (1962). *Pearl Harbor: Warning and decision.* Stanford, CA: Stanford University Press.

How Communication Managers Can Apply the Theories of Excellence and Effectiveness

5

Fred C. Repper
Public Relations Consultant
Ingram, Texas

ABSTRACT

The major purpose of this book is to construct a theory of public relations that will be of practical use to communication managers. Professionals, however, often recoil at the word theory, *equating the term with* impractical. *Everyone has a theory to guide almost every behavior, although most people could not articulate their working theories. Few people also have time to build and improve their theories. In this chapter, a veteran practitioner points out that the purpose of scholarly research is to think and analyze and to uncover "the reasons why" things work as they do. He adds that he would have been more effective as a practitioner had he known of the theory presented in this book. He argues that the concepts of symmetrical communication and the power of the dominant coalition have special value for the management of communication.*

My role as part of the research team looking for excellence in public relations and communication management is to interpret the nature and needs of professional communication practitioners and their organizations to the academic team members. As an experienced business public relations practitioner, I counsel them on the practical applications of their ideas, concepts, and theories.

But even given my experience as a practitioner, you might question whether I can represent the interests of the thousands of professional communicators or the thousands of different businesses, government agencies, and private institutions. I cannot. That would be impossible. I have yet to find two public relations practitioners who agree on much of anything — much less the definition of public relations.

Fortunately, representing all communication practitioners is not my function on the team. My purpose is to act as a sounding board off which the academic team members can bounce their ideas. In that regard, I submit that I qualify. During my 33 years as a public relations practitioner, I have been shot, stomped on, thrown at, and "bounced off" enough times that I can respectively say, "I've been there — at least once."

You also might question whether university professors can contribute anything of real value to our front line, down-in-the-trenches, everyday rough and tumble world. Some professors are somewhat copious of hand and mouth, and some have a tendency to categorize ideas into hard-to-understand word descriptions and phrases. Academics often appear tenured and cloistered within ivy-clad walls seemingly sheltered from capitalistic reality.

Scholars, however, are paid to think and analyze — activities that precious few of us ever have the time or inclination to do. We spend most of our waking hours planning and administering the how, what, and when of our activities. The reason why is often forgotten in our rush to put out the fires. The contribution of academics, therefore, lies in their ability to conceptualize ideas and form them into theories that can be tested and evaluated. Scholars are searchers for the reason why, the foundation blocks that are needed so vitally and of such great concern to the practitioner.

I have found that in the time I have served with the research team, I have become less of a critic and more of an enthusiastic cheerleader urging team members on with frequent exclaimers such as, "Boy, I wish I had known that 30 years ago," or "That's exactly what we need," or "This will do more for the professional than anything that has been done in the last 100 years!" In fact, all of the researchers agree that the results of the literature review are of such immediate value to communicators that the results should be published now instead of at the end of the project.

The literature review is the first and most comprehensive survey of almost everything that has been written about communicators, regardless of their type of business, government agency, or other institution. This book, based on the literature review, is the first that gives communicators a ruler by which we can measure the effectiveness of ourselves, our organizations, and our communication programs. In effect, we now have a road map to excellence in public relations and communication management.

After reading the first chapter of the book, you may be thinking that this book is not necessarily going to be easy to read. You are right. A lot of thought, study, and rereading are required. You will not find solutions to the problems of your next communication program laid out for you in table form. Nor does the book provide you with case histories of excellent communication programs that you can easily copy. "The answer" in one 25-words-or-less statement is simply not there.

You also may find, as I have, that the communication model under which you practice is one of the least effective and carries with it asymmetrical presuppositions that are part of a pragmatic or conservative worldview. Thinking back about the communication model I used, I know it was my responsibility as a public relations manager to attempt to bring public opinion in agreement with what my company wanted. I do not recall that this asymmetrical communication goal was ever explicitly written or said in exactly those words, but this goal was the accepted purpose of public relations, understood and expected by management and me. For example, I might be told to convince the public of the need for higher utility rates or the need for a nuclear power plant. Regardless of the communication task, the inference was clear. Reduce or eliminate customer complaints and conflict with the company. Change public opinion and behavior to agree with company desires using advertising, speeches, direct mail, and all the tricks of the trade.

Reading about the presuppositions of the different communication models therefore may challenge your preconceived beliefs and experiences. At the same time, though, your reading may make you more aware and help you to analyze and explain — even question — your beliefs and experiences. For example, it came as a shock to me to read that direct, persuasive communication (part of an asymmetrical communication model) is seldom effective at changing customer opinions and behavior. I thought this type of communication is what public relations is all about!

I say this revelation came as a shock. Maybe that is too strong a statement. It might be more appropriate to say learning about asymmetrical communication was an eye-opener because I must admit that my communication programs were seldom successful at gaining the powerful behavioral changes expected, no matter how skillful the planning or execution of the program.

While conducting my communication programs, I never found the public particularly ecstatic over higher electrical bills, and no one was exactly breaking down the door demanding more nuclear power plants. In fact, I found it increasingly difficult to defend proposed communication programs and the expenditure of thousands and even millions of dollars.

It seemed that every officer and manager had a different — and they thought — better idea of what message would be the most persuasive. Furthermore, calling in outside experts and consultants helped to establish credibility with management but seldom ensured better results. This book, however, gives us theories that explain why asymmetrical communication programs often fall short of achieving desired effects.

Prior to reading several preliminary chapters of the book, I had not thought of or heard of the presuppositions tied to the communication models or the different worldviews to which management might subscribe. Further, I did not realize that I had been using an asymmetrical model of communication. Nor was I aware of other models that are more effective.

But, bringing realizations like these to light is exactly the book's purpose. And for the first time, a methodology is given to practitioners by which we can compare, analyze, and evaluate our experience, our organizations, and our programs. However, we should not accept without question every statement, concept, or theory presented in the book. As J. Grunig stated in chapter 1, the theories presented here are hypothetical, not yet confirmed by empirical data.

The nature of these theories suggests to me how practitioners can apply the theories of excellence and effectiveness. We can try the shoe on and see how it fits. Each of us can become a part of the research project. Each of us can evaluate the presuppositions, concepts, and theories within the context of our individual experiences and our own organizations.

We can start to do this by asking questions. Do any of the philosophical presuppositions correspond to your organization's worldview? Does this worldview help to explain why your organization practices public relations the way it does? Are the communication effects you try to achieve tied to asymmetrical presuppositions? How does your organization's management style (centralized vs. decentralized) equate with its philosophy of external communication? Do the theories agree with your experiences on the effectiveness of the various communication models? Undoubtedly, these questions and more will occur to you as you read each chapter.

One thing communicators never have been able to do is to compare our communication programs with a program that is considered the best and most effective. However, the *normative* theory provided in the book gives us an opportunity to measure the effectiveness of our communication programs against that of an ideal program. This comparison is the how to part of the book that each practitioner can use in planning his or her next communication program.

You will feel at home with the normative theory because it involves activities you are probably familiar with—strategic planning, segmentation, issue management, research, choosing goals and objectives, and evaluation of results. This theory is your outline for excellence that you have been waiting for.

The normative theory, together with the models of public relations, are the design tools you can use to carve your niche in communication history— high on the totem pole. However, you cannot carve this niche alone. No practitioner can without the full understanding and support of the head of the organization.

This last point brings to light what I think is the most important part of the literature review — the recognition of the role that top management plays in determining the way an organization practices its public relations. This revelation involves recognizing the power the dominant coalition, the group of key decision makers, has in determining the culture, communication philosophy, public relations schema, recognition of publics, choice of interdependencies, selection of public relations models, and the organization and hierarchical placement of the communication function. Scholars call this consideration of politics as an important determinant of organizational functioning the *power-control* perspective of organizations.

To me, the power-control perspective simply says that the big boss sets the public relations tone for the organization. How true! In my career, I have worked for eight CEOs. Each had a very different idea of what public relations was all about. You might say one or two were "public relations wise," whereas the rest were otherwise. One CEO was scared to death of the media (Don't tell anyone anything about anything.). Another thought activists were a bunch of weirdo-kooks whom the organization should ignore (Don't acknowledge them and maybe they'll go away.). And, one CEO's idea of public relations was for the employees to be active in Rotary, Little League, and United Way (Nothing else really matters.). You can imagine what the role and programs of the communication function were under each regime.

It goes without saying that each of the CEOs I worked for was a brilliant person. Each had a very keen desire to see the company succeed. Some were engineers, one was an accountant, one was a lawyer, and another was a salesman. None of them had any formal training in public relations or communication, and for that reason, I think each would have welcomed reading this book.

I do not think, however, that reading this book necessarily would have changed the way the one CEO felt about activists or would have made the other CEO less scared of the media. But I do think all of them would have had a new and more profound understanding of communication and the reason why some organizations are more successful than others at achieving their goals.

At least for the first time the boss and I would have had a common language denominator when discussing public relations and communication instead of reflecting individual biases, hunches, and seat-of-the-pants ideas. In fact, I am confident that in the CEO, I would have found an understanding and supportive ally when presenting and defending a communication program before staff officers. I know that the role and programs of communication under each regime would have been measurably improved.

After all, no has a greater desire than the CEO to find out what public relations contributes to the organization. The CEO also needs a yardstick to measure how well communication employees are doing their jobs. The CEO, therefore, will have a vested interest in the results of this study because we are trying to determine what public relations contributes to organizational effectiveness and also provide the yardstick for measuring excellence in communication. Thus, I believe this book will be as interesting and valuable to the CEO and organizational decision makers as to the professional communication practitioner.

My purpose in this chapter has been to suggest how communication managers can apply the theories of excellence and effectiveness presented in this book. I do not want to belabor this point because reading what the researchers have written is more important. So, I purposely have kept this chapter short.

In closing, however, one important suggestion arises that I want to emphasize. Through IABC, practitioners might become aware of this study and this book before the CEO or head of the organization does. Therefore, I highly recommend that practitioners buy a copy of the book to personally present to him or her.

Better yet, give a copy to each member of your dominant coalition. Together you can discuss the presuppositions, concepts, and theories you have read about. Mutually determine what your communication goals are for your organization. Arrive at strategies. Agree on objectives and the expected results. The rest will come easily. You will be thinking on the same terms. You will have a common language. You will have taken your first step to communication excellence. I wish I could have done that eight CEOs ago!

II

THE PROGRAM LEVEL: EFFECTIVE PLANNING OF COMMUNICATION PROGRAMS

Part II moves from the basic theory of Part I to the practical level of public relations designed to communicate with the strategic publics of the organization. It discusses how strategic public relations coordinates with the organization's strategic planning and discusses theory and research techniques that can be used to plan and evaluate individual communication programs.

6 Strategic Management, Publics, and Issues

James E. Grunig
University of Maryland

Fred C. Repper
Public Relations Consultant
Ingram, Texas

ABSTRACT

If public relations makes organizations more effective by building long-term relationships with strategic constituencies, it is only a small logical jump to deduce that public relations must participate in the organization's strategic planning and that communication programs must be managed strategically to have that effect. This chapter reviews theories of strategic management and identifies the strategic role of public relations as defining and understanding the organization's environment. It then reviews theories of publics and of issues management and their accompanying research methods that practitioners can use to manage communication programs strategically.

To be strategic, public relations must pass one basic test: At a minimum, everything done must be aligned with the corporate vision or mission—the company's reason for being—and must substantially contribute to achieving the organization's objectives. Ideally, public relations should be part of the team helping to *create* the corporate mission and set the objectives.
—Philip J. Webster (1990, p. 18)

Strategic communications is just a short-hand way of saying: make good policy and make it stick with consistent, intelligent communications.
—Edward W. Block (1987, p. 6)

. . . if you don't know where you are going, any road will take you there.
—Uyterhoeven, Ackerman, and Rosenblum (1977, p. 7)

In many organizations, public relations departments are little more than a neutral entity in the organizational structure. Practitioners, and the senior managers to whom they report, assume that favorable publicity, good media relations, slick employee publications, or the like are ends in themselves. If pressed for why organizations need such communication activities, practitioners frequently respond that they produce "goodwill," a "good image," or a "favorable climate of public opinion." Few can explain why these vague effects have value for an organization.

Many organizations seem to have no public in mind for their communication programs. They develop programs for a *general public* or a *mass audience,* for example. Yet Broom (1986) pointed out that in most cases there is an historical reason for communication programs that have become entrenched in organizational structure. At some point, for example, the organization probably got unfavorable media coverage. Thus, the general public or the mass audience developed as convenient terms for people who use the mass media. For that organization, public relations means no more than media relations. Similarly, most organizations have employee communication programs because they once had an influx of new employees, labor unrest, or a shortage of employees.

At one point in their history, in other words, organizations developed public relations programs for strategic purposes—but over time inertia caused them to stop planning them strategically.[1] Chapter 3, however, set forth a basic theory of how public relations contributes to organizational effectiveness. According to that theory, public relations makes organizations more effective by developing relations with stakeholders in the internal or external environment that constrain or enhance the ability of an organization to accomplish its mission. Public relations programs for general publics or the public at large might build relationships accidentally with stakeholders, but more often than not they communicate with no one important to the organization. And, in the process of doing nothing, they cost the organization a great deal of money.

In this chapter, we show that excellent public relations—communication programs that enhance organizational effectiveness—fits squarely into the concept of strategic management that pervades modern theories of management. We show that public relations must be managed strategically before it contributes to organizational effectiveness. Therefore, we conclude that strategic management of public relations is the key characteristic of excellent public relations at the micro- or programmatic level of public relations.

---

[1]Chapter 14 develops this historicist theory in more detail to explain why organizations organize their public relations departments as they do.

STRATEGIC MANAGEMENT

Traditional theories of management set forth principles for developing an internal structure to supervise internal processes. *Strategic management,* in contrast, balances these internal activities with strategies for dealing with external factors (Pearce & Robinson, 1982; Uyterhoeven et al., 1977). Two words, *mission* and *environment,* pervade the literature on strategic management.

Higgins (1979), for example, defined strategic management as "the process of managing the pursuit of the accomplishment of organizational mission coincident with managing the relationship of the organization to its environment" (p. 1). Greene, Adam, and Ebert (1985), similarly, defined it as "a process of thinking through the current mission of the organization, thinking through the current environmental conditions, and then combining these elements by setting forth a guide for tomorrow's decisions and results" (p. 536).

According to Steiner, Miner, and Gray (1982), "strategic management" can be distinguished from "operational management" by "the growing significance of environmental impacts on organizations and the need for top managers to react appropriately to them" (p. 6). Managers who manage strategically do so by balancing the mission of the organization—what it is, what it wants to be, and what it wants to do—with what the environment will allow or encourage it to do. Pearce and Robinson (1982) described this internal–external balancing act as "interactive opportunity analysis" (p. 65)—"Its purpose is to provide the combination of long-term objectives and grand strategy which will optimally position the total firm in the external environment as the means to achieving the company mission" (p. 65).[2]

A Model of Strategic Management

Most writers on strategic management have developed models of the steps in the process—for example, Uyterhoeven et al. (1977, p. 9), Higgins (1979, pp. 9–10), Steiner et al. (1982, p. 18), Greene et al. (1985, p. 544), Holt (1987, p. 161), and Massie and Douglas (1985, p. 113). Pearce and Robinson's (1982) model incorporates the steps in most of the others:

1. Determination of the *mission* of the company, including broad statements about its purpose, philosophy, and goals.

---

[2]An empirical study by Prescott (1986) confirmed the value of balancing mission and environment. He found that environments changed the strength of the relationship between strategy and performance but not the form of the relationship. That is, the same strategy may work in different environments, but it works better in some than in others.

2. Development of a company *profile* that reflects its internal condition and capability.
3. Assessment of the company's *external environment,* both in terms of competitive and general contextual factors.
4. *Interactive opportunity analysis* of possible options uncovered in the matching of the company profile with the external environment.
5. *Identification of desired options* uncovered when the set of possibilities is considered in light of the company mission.
6. Strategic choice of a set of long-term objectives and *grand strategies* needed to achieve the desired options.
7. Development of annual *objectives* and short-term strategies that are compatible with the long-term objectives and grand strategies.
8. *Implementation* of strategic choice decisions using budgeted resources and matching tasks, people, structures, technologies, and reward systems.
9. Review and *evaluation* of the success of the strategic process to serve as a basis of control and as an input for future decision making.

The emphasis that theories of strategic management place on monitoring the external environment and adjusting the organization's mission to it suggests a crucial role for public relations in the process. And the emphasis on organizational mission provides the connection to organizational goals that public relations must have to contribute to organizational effectiveness. Public relations must be involved in the process in two ways for it to contribute to organizational effectiveness. First, it must be a part of the strategic management of the total organization — in surveying the environment and in helping to define the mission, goals, and objectives of the organization. Involvement in the total process provides direction to public relations from the corporate/organizational level. Without corporate direction, according to Webster (1990), trying to establish a strategic public relations program "is a little like driving cross country without a road map" (p. 19).

In addition to contributing to overall strategic management, public relations also should manage its own programs strategically, a step in the process that is consistent with principles of strategic management.

Levels of Strategic Management

According to Pearce and Robinson (1982, pp. 6–7), strategic management takes place at three levels:

At the *corporate or organizational level,* where the board of directors, chief executive officer, and chief administrative officers set grand strategies and reflect the interests of stockholders and society.

At *business or specialty levels,* which deal with market segments or provide specialized services.

At *functional levels,* composed of managers of products, geographic areas, or functions such as marketing or public relations.

Brody (1987, p. 9) pointed out that public relations traditionally has been relegated to the functional level, where it has been assigned responsibility for implementing organizational objectives but not for helping to develop them. Kotler and Andreasen (1987), for example, concluded that marketing is strategic but that public relations is not. When public relations is restricted to the functional level, it usually implements the strategies of other departments such as marketing or human resources and is restricted to the application of technique rather than the formulation of policy.

A survey of public relations counselors reported in Nager and Truitt (1987), however, showed that respondents rated strategic planning and in-depth counseling of senior executives as the most important contributions that their firms make to clients. Only half as many counselors responding rated implementation of communication programs as their most important contribution. Public relations managers and counselors aspire to be a part of total strategic management, in other words, even if organizations do not assign them to that task. The theory of organizational effectiveness presented in chapter 3, however, explains why public relations should be part of the overall process if organizations are to be most effective.

Pearce and Robinson (1982, p. 10) explained that a team from all three levels should develop and govern the strategic management process. Since the 1960s, they added, organizations have developed planning departments or staffs to coordinate the strategic process. Often, we can add, planning departments have taken over public relations functions, just as have marketing departments, legal departments, or human resources departments — an encroachment problem discussed in chapter 14. Encroachment, however, damages the ability of the organization to manage external relationships because most of the encroaching departments have the expertise to work only with parts of the environment or lack the knowledge needed to manage public relationships.

Ideally, then, public relations should be an integral part of strategic management, providing input to the planning department and senior managers about stakeholders in the environment.

The Concept of Environment

Like mission, the concept of environment pervades the literature on strategic management. Pearce and Robinson (1982) defined environment as "the sum total of all conditions and forces that affect the strategic options of a business but that are typically beyond its ability to control" (p. 62). These writers mention many components of the environment such as customers, suppliers, creditors, and competitors. They also mention economic and cultural conditions. Most also mention the traditional stakeholders with whom public relations manages relationships: governments, communities, stockholders, and employees (e.g., Holt, 1987, pp. 149–151; Steiner et al., 1982, p. 18). Pearce and Robinson explained that executives must pay attention to "economic conditions, social change, political priorities, and technological developments" (p. 3). They added: "However, the attention to all of these influences is often subordinated to the fourth major consideration in executive decision making—the multiple and often mutually inconsistent objectives of the stakeholders of the business: its owners, top managers, employees, communities, customers, and country" (p. 3).

Wheelen and Hunger (1987) distinguished between the task environment and the societal environment. In accomplishing its mission, an organization works in its task environment, but the societal environment may divert its attention from the task environment:

> . . . strategic managers must examine both the societal and task environments for those strategic factors that are likely to strongly influence their corporation's success—factors that are, in other words, opportunities and threats. Long-run developments in the economic, technological, political-legal, and sociocultural aspects of the societal environment tend to affect strongly a corporation's activities by asserting more immediate pressures on the corporation's task environment. Such societal issues as consumerism, governmental regulations, environmental pollution, energy costs and availability, inflation-fed wage demands, and heavy foreign competition tend to emerge from stakeholders in the firm's task environment. (p. 148)

In this quote, Wheelen and Hunger, in addition to mentioning the importance of stakeholders, mentioned issues that affect organizations and that public relations usually addresses. Uyterhoeven et al. (1977, pp. 19–20) and Higgins (1979, pp. 63–64) also mentioned the issues of environmentalism, consumerism, discrimination, and equal employment.

Although writers on strategic management discuss the environment and make lists of its components, they seldom describe how the organization should diagnose the environment[3] or who in the organization should observe the environment. Few, if any, of these writers recognize or describe the role of public relations in helping the organization to identify—to

---

[3]One exception is Harrison (1987), whose book, *Diagnosing Organizations,* includes a chapter on how to diagnose the environment.

"enact" (Weick, 1979)[4]—the most important components of its environment. A few public relations writers such as Brody (1987), Nager and Truitt (1987), Block (1987), and Webster (1990) have filled that gap, but the contributions of public relations scholars generally have not penetrated the thinking of management scholars.

We believe that excellent public relations will fill the environmental void in theories of strategic management. And, we believe that theories of strategic management will fill the void in public relations theory of how public relations can contribute to effective organizations. We develop a strategic theory of public relations after a brief note about the ethical connotations of the term *strategic*.

Strategic as a Symmetrical Term

The term *strategic* like the term *manage,* has negative connotations for many people. To them, manage means to control or to manipulate. Strategic means to do only what will enhance the interests of an organization. For example, Pearson (1990) described "two faces of systems theory." One of these faces looks at the relationship of an organization and its environment strategically—emphasizing "system maintenance and environmental control." The other face looks at organizations and their environments in terms of "interdependence" (p. 227).

We define the term manage as thinking ahead or planning rather than as manipulation and control. And we define strategic symmetrically rather than asymmetrically (see chapter 2 for additional discussion of these terms). We believe that it is in the strategic interest of organizations to change their behavior when they provoke opposition from the environment as well as to try to change the behavior of environmental stakeholders.

Several synonyms for strategic found in a thesaurus suggest more positive connotations. Strategic publics, according to these synonyms, are the stakeholders that are critical, crucial, essential, important, or vital for an organization. Important publics can be those that threaten the organization. They also can be publics on which the organization has negative consequences but that do not yet have the power to constrain the organization. Because of a norm of reciprocity (see chapter 2), organizations should feel a moral obligation to modify the behavior that produces these negative consequences. A strategy, then, is an approach, design, scheme, or system. Strategically managed public relations, therefore, is designed to build relationships with the most important stakeholders of an organization.

---

[4]See chapter 3 for a discussion of Weick's (1979) concept of the environment as enacted rather than objective.

A MODEL FOR THE STRATEGIC MANAGEMENT
OF PUBLIC RELATIONS

Table 6.1 describes a model of strategic management in public relations that incorporates the dual role of public relations in strategic management — in both the overall strategic management of the organization and in the strategic management of public relations itself. The first three components of the model are described as stages rather than steps because they describe the evolution of publics and issues. Public relations practitioners cannot control these stages. On the other hand, public relations makes its contribution to overall strategic management by diagnosing the environment to make the overall organization aware of stakeholders, publics, and issues as they evolve.

Organizations need different kinds of public relations programs for each

TABLE 6.1
The Strategic Management of Public Relations

1. *Stakeholder Stage.* An organization has a relationship with stakeholders when the behavior of the organization or of a stakeholder has consequences on the other. Public Relations should do formative research to scan the environment and the behavior of the organization to identify these consequences. Ongoing communication with these stakeholders helps to build a stable, long-term relationship that manages conflict that may occur in the relationship.
2. *Public Stage.* Public form when stakeholders recognize one or more of the consequences as a problem and organize to do something about it or them. Public relations should do research to identify and segment these publics. At this stage focus groups are particularly helpful. Communication to involve publics in the decision process of the organization helps to manage conflict before communication campaigns become necessary.
3. *Issue Stage.* Publics organize and create "issues" out of the problems they perceive. Public relations should anticipate these issues and manage the organization's response to them. This is known as "issues management." The media play a major role in the creation and expansion of issues. In particular, media coverage of issues may produce publics other than activist ones — especially "hot-issue" publics. At this stage, research should segment publics. Communication programs should use the mass media as well as interpersonal communication with activists to try to resolve the issue through negotiation.

Public relations should plan communication programs with different stakeholders or publics at each of the above three stages. In doing so, it should follow Steps 4-7.

4. Public relations should develop formal objectives such as communication, accuracy, understanding, agreement, and complementary behavior for its communication programs.
5. Public relations should plan formal programs and campaigns to accomplish the objectives.
6. Public relations, especially the technicians, should implement the programs and campaigns.
7. Public relations should evaluate the effectiveness of programs in meeting their objectives and in reducing the conflict produced by the problems and issues that brought about the programs.

of these stages at the functional level—the level of the public relations department. Thus, Steps 4–7 define the traditional steps of strategic management that the public relations department should apply to each program it implements at these different stages. Chapter 7 discusses Steps 4–7—objectives, planning, implementation, and evaluation—in detail. The rest of this chapter is organized around the first three stages, which essentially are stages in the development of publics.

J. Grunig and Hunt (1984) pointed out that a crucial distinction for segmenting a population of people into publics is the extent to which they passively or actively communicate about an issue and the extent to which they behave in a way that supports or constrains the organization's pursuit of its mission. Publics are more likely to be active when the people who make them up perceive that what an organization does involves them *(level of involvement)*, that the consequences of what an organization does is a problem *(problem recognition)*, and that they are not constrained from doing something about the problem *(constraint recognition)*. (This situational theory is described in greater detail in the section of this chapter on publics.)

If none of these conditions fits a group of people, these people constitute a *nonpublic;* and they are of no concern to an organization. Whenever an organization does something that has consequences on people or people have consequences on the organization, there is a likelihood that the people will perceive an involvement and recognize a problem. Thus, consequences produce, at the minimum, a *latent* public—a public that is passive but has the potential to be active. As level of involvement and problem recognition increase and constraint recognition decreases, however, these publics can become *aware* and then *active*. Publics generally move from the latent to the aware and active stages, therefore, as strategic management of public relations moves through the first three stages of the process.

THE STAKEHOLDER STAGE

Often the terms *stakeholder* and *public* are used synonymously. There is a subtle difference, however, that helps to understand strategic planning of public relations. People are stakeholders because they are in a category affected by decisions of an organization or if their decisions affect the organization. Many people in a category of stakeholders—such as employees or residents of a community—are passive. The stakeholders who are or become more aware and active can be described as publics.

Stakeholders are people who are linked to an organization because they and the organization have consequences on each other—they cause problems for each other.[5] People linked to an organization have a stake in it, which Carroll (1989) defined as "an interest or a share in an undertaking" (p. 56) A stakeholder, therefore, is "any individual or group who can affect or is affected by the actions, decisions, policies, practices, or goals of the organization" (Freeman, 1984, p. 25).[6] Brody (1988) defined stakeholders somewhat more symmetrically as "groups of individuals whose interests coincide in one or more ways with the organization with which the public relations practitioner is dealing" (p. 81).

The first step in strategic management of public relations, therefore, is to make a list of the people who are linked to or have a stake in the organization. Freeman (1984) called this list a stakeholder map of the organization. A typical stakeholder map for a corporation, Freeman added, contains owners, consumer advocates, customers, competitors, the media, employees, special interest groups, environmentalists, suppliers, governments, and local community organizations.

A public relations practitioner can draw a stakeholder map by thinking through the consequences an organization has on people and that they have on the organization. These consequences can be identified through environmental scanning research.[7] Practitioners can scan the environment by conducting or using public opinion polls, studying the mass media and specialized media, reading scholarly or legal journals, conferring with political or community leaders, or calling on experts in the organization to serve on issues management committees.[8]

Pfeffer and Salancik (1978) pointed out that organizations typically do little environmental scanning and that when they do, the "scanning unit frequently attends to only one portion of the environment" (p. 269). Instead, scanning units — such as public relations — need a "variety of interests, backgrounds, and types of expertise" (Pfeffer & Salancik, 1978, p. 269) — the concept of requisite variety discussed in chapter 3.

After thoroughly researching their stakeholders, public relations managers should rank or assign weights to them to indicate their impact on the organization or the extent to which the organization believes it should moderate its consequences on them (J. Grunig & Hunt, 1984, chapter 8; Pfeffer & Salancik, 1978, p. 52). They then should plan ongoing communication programs with the most important — the most strategic — stakeholders — working down the ranked list until the resources available for public relations are used up. Communication at the stakeholder stage —

---

[5]See J. Grunig and Hunt (1984, pp. 139-143) for a discussion of organizational linkages.

[6]Carroll (1989, p. 57) defined a stakeholder in almost the same terms.

[7]Dozier (1990) reviewed research on the extent to which public relations practitioners do research to scan the environment.

[8]See Harrison (1987, chapter 5) for a discussion of how to scan the environment.

ideally before conflict has occurred — is especially important because it helps to develop the stable, long-term relationships that an organization needs to build support from stakeholders and to manage conflict when it occurs.

The stakeholder approach to public relations differs sharply from the conventional wisdom of many practitioners — and CEOs — that public relations is media relations alone. People applying this conventional wisdom seldom think about who attends to a message after it appears in the media. A general public is a contradiction in terms, according to the definitions we see next, because publics form in response to particular problems that seldom affect everyone in the population. Mass media supposedly reach mass audiences; but mass communication theorists such as McQuail (1987), Wright (1986), and Lowery and DeFleur (1983) no longer view the audiences of the media as a mass — large, heterogeneous, disconnected, and anonymous to the communicator.

McQuail (1987) suggested that media audiences are more massive in size than that they have the properties of a mass. Instead, according to McQuail, media audiences include many small, selective, or local audiences — publics. At times, a public relations program might reach publics effectively through the massive media — especially when the problem that produces the public is dispersed widely in the population. For example, public relations officers for the military at time of war must communicate with a public that includes most of the population. More often, however, specialized or local media, controlled publications, or interpersonal communication are more effective ways of reaching publics than are the massive media (J. Grunig, 1990).[9]

We turn, therefore, to a conceptualization of publics — the segments of stakeholder categories that are the most important components of the environment of an organization.

THE PUBLIC STAGE

Stakeholder maps contain broad categories of people or groups who affect or are affected by an organization. Not all people in these categories will be equally likely to communicate with or affect the organization. As public relations practitioners develop communication programs for stakeholders, therefore, they can increase the probability of communicating with the strategic publics by dividing the category into segments.

Few scholars in mass communication have constructed *segmentation* theories, and most of those theories are poorly developed. In public

---

[9]In particular, research shows that specialized media reach environmental publics more effectively than do the mass media (J. Grunig, 1977b, 1983a).

relations, J. Grunig's situational theory of publics (e.g., J. Grunig & Hunt, 1984, chapter 7) is the only segmentation theory that has been researched extensively. On the other hand, marketing theorists have developed numerous segmentation theories, whose applications marketing research firms can provide to clients. As a result, techniques of *market* segmentation are used more widely in public relations than are techniques to segment *publics*.

The distinction between publics and markets is important for understanding the nature of publics and for clarifying the difference between public relations and marketing. Organizations can choose their markets, but publics arise on their own and choose the organization for attention. Levitt (1986) described how organizations select markets: "The purpose of a business is to create and keep a customer" (p. 5). An organization chooses a market to help meet its mission. According to Bonoma and Shapiro (1983), "If segmentation is done well, marketers can make intelligent choices about the fit between their company and products and the needs of each segment. Those segments that fit the company's capabilities are chosen for penetration. Those segments that do not suit the company's capabilities are left for others to serve" (p. 2).

Publics, in contrast, organize around issues and seek out organizations that create those issues—to gain information, seek redress of grievances, pressure the organizations, or ask governments to regulate them. As publics move from being latent to active, organizations have little choice other than to communicate with them; whereas, as Bonoma and Shapiro reminded us, organizations can choose to ignore markets if they wish.

Public relations practitioners, therefore, communicate with publics that threaten the organization's mission or provide opportunities to enhance that mission. Marketing practitioners, in contrast, create and seek out markets that can use their company's product's or services. Consumers provide an example of the difference. They constitute a market segment for marketing communicators, but they become a public of concern to public relations practitioners when a faulty product becomes an issue that turns a market into a public.[10] Publics usually are more active than are markets.[11]

---

[10]A study of consumers of electricity conducted by Cambridge Reports (1985, 1986) for the Edison Electric Institute provides an illustration of the interaction of public relations and marketing in customer satisfaction. The study found that electric utilities interact with customers both as a "product provider"and as a "service institution that is concerned and cares about its customers' needs" (Cambridge Reports, 1986, p. ii). The reports showed that customers, as markets, will tolerate negative perceptions of a product and its price if, as publics, the organization has a caring relationship with them as people. In fact, a statistical model showed "that the negative impact of a $35-a-month rate increase for a family of four is essentially offset by the customer perceptions of increased company concern and availability of cost-control options" (Cambridge Reports, 1985, p. xi).

[11]A difference also recognized by McQuail (1987, pp. 221–222).

As a result, communication with publics must be symmetrical more often.

Although there is a difference between publics and markets, the principles of segmentation used to identify them are similar. Most of these principles have come from marketing researchers.

Principles of Segmentation

A public, a market, or any other segment of a population exists only because a researcher or practitioner uses a particular theoretical concept to identify it. To identify publics or markets, therefore, we must develop criteria to define what constitutes a useful segment.

Smith (1978) introduced segmentation to marketing by contrasting market segmentation with product differentiation. Product differentiation, he said, attempts to bend demand to the will of supply. It uses advertising and promotion to distinguish a product from competing products and, as a result, to increase demand and reduce competition for that product. Market segmentation, in contrast, works from the demand side of the market — the consumer. Segmentation bends supply to demand by identifying lucrative segments of the market and developing products specifically to fit those segments.

Segmentation became "one of the most influential and fashionable concepts in marketing," a concept that has "permeated the thinking of managers and researchers . . . more than any marketing concept since the turn of the century" (Lunn, 1986, p. 387). Green, Carroll, and Goldberg (1981) used almost the same words: "If one were to ask what phrases seem to have captured the fancy of most marketers over the past decade or so, clearly the terms product positioning and market segmentation would be high on most pollsters' lists" (p. 17).

The basic idea of segmentation is simple: Divide a population, market, or audience into groups whose members are more like each other than members of other segments. Michman (1983), for example, defined market segmentation as "the process of taking the mass market for consumer or industrial goods and breaking it up into small, more homogeneous submarkets based on relevant distinguishing characteristics" (p. 127). Bonoma and Shapiro (1983) added the idea that segmentation can be viewed "either as a process of aggregating individual customers, prospects, and buying situations into groups or as a process of disaggregating a total market into pieces" (p. 1).

Kotler and Andreasen (1987, p. 119) contrasted "target marketing" with "mass marketing." Cravens (1982, p. 167) described segmentation as a "niche" market strategy rather than a "mass" strategy. Lovelock and Wineberg (1984, pp. 109–111) called segmentation "segregation" as opposed to "aggregation." Both Cunningham and Cunningham (1981, p. 203) and

Luck and Ferrell (1985, p. 191) contrasted market segmentation with "undifferentiated marketing."

Marketing textbooks (e.g., Assael, 1987, pp. 501–513; Cravens, 1982, p. 174; Cunningham & Cunningham, 1981, pp. 191–203; Kotler & Andreasen,1987, pp. 117–155; Lovelock & Weinberg, 1984, p. 119; Luck & Ferrell, 1985, p. 194; Lunn, 1986, pp. 392–398; Taylor, 1986, p. 34) and articles in public relations trade journals (e.g., Winkleman, 1987) contain lists of segmentation concepts. These concepts include demographics, psychographics, values and lifestyles, geodemographic clusters of postal zip codes, geographic regions, consumer behaviors, elasticities of consumer responses to products, product benefits, amount of consumption, and purchase/use situations.

Marketing theorists such as Kotler and Andreasen (1987, pp. 123–124), Taylor (1986, p. 33), and Lovelock and Weinberg (1984, p. 111) have provided criteria for segmentation. Segments must be definable, mutually exclusive, measurable, accessible, pertinent to an organization's mission, reachable with communications in an affordable way, and large enough to be substantial and to service economically. Kotler and Andreasen pointed out, however, that "differential responsiveness" is "perhaps the most crucial criterion" for choosing segments (p. 124). Two or more market segments may meet all of the other criteria, they explained, but still respond exactly alike to a product or communication strategy.

When marketing theorists use the term *differential response,* they generally mean a behavioral response: a purchase, adoption, use, or similar desired behavior. To isolate these differences in behavior, they look for variables that predict them, such as demographics, attitudes, or geographic location. Public relations managers also are concerned about the behavior of publics because these behaviors—such as donating money, approving appropriations, demonstrating, petitioning government, or refusing to work—interfere with or enhance the ability of the organization to achieve its goals. Thus, a segmentation scheme must identify the people most likely to behave in a way that affects the organization or whose behavior is affected by behaviors of the organization.

In addition to these behaviors, both marketing and public relations practitioners are concerned with the effects of communicating with members of the segments they isolate. As chapter 7 shows, however, public relations programs cannot always be evaluated by monitoring direct effects on behaviors. Behaviors usually are less sensitive to public relations programs than are variables that occur earlier in the chain that begins with seeking of or exposure to a message and continues through cognition, attitude, and behavior (Flay & Cook, 1989).

For public relations programs, the differential effect sought may be communication behavior alone. In that situation, planners should choose a segment of the population with which they will be able to communicate about the problem or issue that affects the organization or a public. For other programs, planners may choose an additional objective of achieving an effect from communicating with a segment of the population. Not always, however, will that effect be on behavior. Campaigns also may strive for effects on cognitions and attitudes—sometimes as an intermediary effect on the path to behavioral change but sometimes as ends in themselves. In addition, public relations planners may attempt to affect collective behavior by creating and mobilizing activist, issue groups.[12]

Behaviors of people in segments and effects of communication on these behaviors can be predicted better with what Frank, Massy, and Wind (1972) and Kotler and Andreasen (1987, p. 126) called *inferred* variables rather than *objective* variables. Researchers measure inferred variables by questioning members of a population directly. Examples are measures of perceptions, cognitions, or attitudes. Objective variables can be measured from secondary sources. Examples are demographics, geographic location, or use of media.

Inferred variables are more effective in segmentation because they indentify segments in which nearly all of the people in them exhibit the desired differential response. However, managers of marketing and public relations more often use objective measures because they are more available and less expensive to gather (Massy & Weitz, 1977, pp. 133–136). Kotler and Andreasen (1987) explained further:

> . . . field research to determine responsiveness and information source behavior is costly and time-consuming and not every organization has the funds and the patience to make the necessary investment. Second, the sheer *number* of segmentation decisions a manager must make precludes such care and attention except in rare, very important situations.
>
> As a result, managers typically use *surrogates* for what they *ideally* would like to measure. Segmentation is often based on demographics, for example, because managers assume that such characteristics will be related to likely responses and reachability. (p. 125)

For public relations programs, segmentation theories based on inferred variables predict desired behaviors and effects more accurately than those based on objective variables. As a result, segmentation research based on inferred variables reduces the costs of media and interpersonal communication needed to reach targeted segments. Public relations managers should weigh the additional cost of measuring inferred variables against the cost of

---

[12]See J. Grunig and Hunt, 1984, chapter 6, for further discussion of these objectives for public relations programs.

a communication program for a segment that is imprecise and contains many people who do not interact with the organization (Massy & Weitz, 1977, pp. 135–136). J. Grunig (1989a) grouped the segmentation variables commonly used in public relations into a *nested* model to explain this tradeoff, a model that should help public relations managers decide when to conduct new segmentation research and when to use secondary research from other sources.

A Nested Model of Segmentation

J. Grunig (1989a) got the idea for a nested model for public relations from Bonoma and Shapiro's (1983) nested approach to classifying industrial markets. By nested, Bonoma and Shapiro meant that "subtle, hard-to-assess" or "inferred" variables are located within general, more easily observed "objective" variables (p. 8). A variable in an inner nest can pinpoint a public or a market segment precisely. A variable in an outer nest can locate the segments in the inner nests also, although it will not be able to discriminate among several segments that could be identified by variables in the inner nest. Massy and Weitz (1977, p. 134) called the inner nest *microsegments* that can be aggregated into *macrosegments* in the outer nests.

Bonoma and Shapiro (1983, p. 8) suggested that decision makers should begin with variables in the outer nest and work inward until they reach the point where the additional costs of segmentation no longer justify the expected differential responses. J. Grunig (1989a) said, however, that the variables in the inner nest are more effective in communication planning and that decision makers should begin with the inner nest and work outward only when resources are not available for the research and time needed to work with the inner nests.

Figure 6.1, therefore, depicts concepts developed by scholars and practitioners in marketing and public relations, organized into nests that become more general but less powerful concepts as one moves from the center to the outside. In addition, the inner nests generally segment with inferred variables and the outer nests with objective variables. Some of the nests overlap and are not pure, but the analogy of nests helps to explain why mass audiences or segmentation categories produced by demographics contain many people who are not in a public that develops in a strategic stakeholder category.

J. Grunig (1989a) said that the best segmentation concepts lie in the second nest, that of publics, but that the behavior of publics can be understood only by understanding the individual behaviors in the innermost

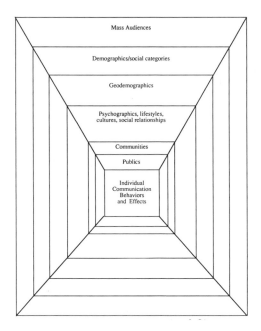

FIGURE 6.1 Nested segmentation concepts.

nest.[13] The groupings in the outer nests, in turn, can help to locate the inner groups. They also can serve as surrogates for the inner nests when budget constraints prohibit identification of segments in inner nests. Finally, the inner nests correspond most closely to publics — useful in public relations — and the outer nests to markets — useful in marketing.

Individual Behaviors and Effects of Communication

Theories that fit in the first nest are concerned with the fundamental question of all the social and behavioral sciences (Why do people behave as they do?) and the fundamental questions of communication science (Why do people communicate when they do? How does communication affect people?). Behavioral scientists have used such concepts as needs, motiva-

---

[13]According to Kotler and Andreasen (1987, p. 121) and Massy and Weitz (1977, p. 133), the perfect segmentation concept would make it possible for a communication planner to study each member of a market or public and to develop a personalized communication strategy for that person. Such a strategy is impractical. In addition, organizations usually need not be concerned with consequences unless several people are affected. There are exceptions, of course, such as when a single government official can stop the appropriation for an organization or when a corporation wants to build a plant on the property of a single individual.

tions, attitudes, perceptions, cognitions, feelings, and problems to explain behavior. Communication scientists have related many of these concepts to communication behavior—to explain why people communicate and to explain the effects of communication.[14]

Two of the most popular individual concepts used for segmentation are attitudes and cognitions. Researchers have aggregated individuals with similar attitudes toward a product (e.g., Cunningham & Crissy, 1972) or toward a company (Cambridge Reports, 1985, 1986) into segments. Others have grouped people who say they would be most likely to buy a product or to rate an organization favorably if it had certain attributes—using the procedure called *conjoint analysis* (e.g., Cambridge Reports, 1985, 1986; Green et al., 1981; Moore, 1980). Generally, however, aggregating people who have similar attitudes and cognitions provides useful information only for an asymmetrical approach to communication. It provides a map of how to describe or position a product or organization so that people will accept it, rather than a map of the people affected by an organization and the problems they face.[15]

According to J. Grunig (1989a), the concept of a situation allows the aggregation of individuals into publics in a way that is more useful for symmetrical communication programs than do the concepts of attitudes and cognitions. Several marketing researchers have used situations as a segmention concept (e.g., Assael, 1987, chapter 18; Bonoma & Shapiro, 1983, pp. 67–74; Dickson, 1982; Lehmann, Moore, & Elrod, 1982; Lunn, 1986, p. 395; Srivastava, Alpert, & Shocker, 1984). Situational variables have included physical and social surroundings, time, the specific task for which a product is used, personal state of mind at purchase, social or financial pressure, uncertainty, or a situation served inadequately by existing products. Communication researchers such as Dervin (1981, 1984, 1989; Dervin, Jacobson, & Nilan, 1982) and J. Grunig (1989a) have defined situations as a somewhat more general type of recurring situation: for example, dealing with a heart problem, AIDS, or environmental pollution.

A final concept similar to problems and situations is that of issue. An issue can be defined as a political or social problem—a problem whose resolution creates conflict in political or social systems (Cobb & Elder, 1972, p. 82). These three concepts make up the basic components of J. Grunig's (e.g., J. Grunig & Hunt, 1984, chapter 7) situational theory of individual communication behavior and, in the next nest, of publics.

---

[14]See J. Grunig (1989a) for a discussion of the value of variables such as needs and attitudes for segmentation.

[15]Cambridge Reports (1985, 1986), however, used conjoint analysis to determine which communication programs respondents would most like to have their electrical utility provide. Conjoint analysis also could be used to determine which organizational problems are most important to different segments of people.

J. Grunig (1978, 1983a, 1989b; J. Grunig & Childers, 1988; J. Grunig & Hunt, 1984) theorized that three variables explain why people engage in a behavior and communicate in the process of planning that behavior: problem recognition, level of involvement, and constraint recognition. In particular, Grunig and colleagues used these three variables to explain communication behavior and the likelihood that communicating has an effect on cognitions, attitudes, and other behaviors.

Problem Recognition. J. Grunig took the concept of problem recognition from Dewey (1910, 1938, 1939). Dewey defined problem recognition as the perception that something is lacking in a situation; he theorized that people inquire (seek information) and think when they recognize an indeterminate or problematic situation. According to J. Grunig (1989a), problems may arise from the situation, environment, or social system. Or they may arise internally from curiosity or lack of understanding (J. Grunig & Childers, 1988, pp. 12–15).[16]

The concept of problem recognition is tied to the concept of a situation. Dewey (1910, 1938, 1939) argued that problems arise in life situations or as Dervin (1981) called them, "specific moments in time-space when information is used" (p. 80). Because people communicate about problematic situations, analysis of how they perceive different types of life situations shows when and about what people will communicate.

Constraint Recognition. J. Grunig's (1971, 1983a; J. Grunig & Hunt, 1984, pp. 151–152) second variable, constraint recognition, discourages communication behavior: People do not communicate about problems or issues about which they believe they can do little or about behaviors they do not believe they have the personal efficacy to execute.

Concepts similar to constraint recognition appear in several social science theories. A constraint is a major concept in linear programming, a statistical concept used in economics and management science (e.g., Greene et al., 1985, pp. 715–720). Linear programming can be used—among other things—to maximize profits within the constraints of available resources

---

[16]Theorists of consumer behavior such as Engel, Blackwell, and Kollat (1978), Lovelock and Weinberg (1984), Assael (1987), and Walters and Bergiel (1989) also use the concept of problem recognition to explain what initiates consumer behavior. However, consumer theorists typically say that problems arise in needs. We believe that the concept of need is inherently tautological with the behavior it is supposed to explain. That is, the name given to a need generally is the same name for the behavior it is supposed to explain. For example, people who seek power supposedly do so because of a need for power. Thus, J. Grunig's situational theorist posits instead that problems arise from the involvement of people in situations and their perceptions of situations and not from hidden, internal needs. See J. Grunig (1989a, pp. 209–211) for a more complete explanation.

available to a decision maker. In psychology, Brehm and Cohen (1962, pp. 201–220) found that individual volition (the absence of constraints) was a necessary condition for cognitive dissonance. Constraint recognition also can be seen as "personal efficacy" in Bandura's (1977) social learning theory, a theory that has been used to explain the results of several studies of communication campaigns (e.g., Anderson, 1989; Maccoby & Solomon, 1981).

Level of Involvement.   J. Grunig's third concept, level of involvement, has been used extensively in marketing and communication research (for a review, see Salmon, 1986). Although definitions of involvement vary widely, Lovelock and Weinberg (1984) provided the "common-sense interpretation" that involvement is the "degree of importance or concern" that a product or behavior generates in different individuals (p. 73). Because involvement varies with individuals as well as products and behaviors, it can be used as a concept for segmentation (Assael, 1987, pp. 100–107; Kassarjian, 1981; Slama & Tashchian, 1985). Measures of involvement can be used to separate populations into active and passive segments, which are characterized by complex as opposed to passive purchase and communication behaviors (Assael, 1987, chapters 2 & 4; Lovelock & Weinberg, 1984, p. 75; Ray, 1973). Active segments—active publics—are especially important in public relations because they are the strategic publics of an organization.[17]

One must be careful in comparing involvement studies, however, because Salmon (1986) and Chaffee and Roser (1986) found that definitions and measures of the concept differ widely in the literature. Involvement has been defined variously as a personality trait, a state of ego involvement, a characteristic of a situational stimulus that varies among individuals, and a characteristic of a product or issue that is the same for most people. J. Grunig has defined involvement as an individual's cognitive perception of a situation: It is a person's perception that he or she has a connection with a situation.[18] Recently, J. Grunig and Childers (1988) isolated two types of involvement: *internal* (ego involvement, as defined by Sherif, Sherif, & Nebergall, 1965), and *external* (situational connections, as defined by Krugman, 1965, and more recently by Petty & Cacioppo, 1986). Both internal and external involvement generate active communication behavior,

---

[17]A study by Heath and Douglas (1990) provides an example of research in public relations using the concept of involvement. They used involvement to explain the reaction of people to public policy issues.

[18]The idea that involvement is cognitive comes from Krugman (1965) and the idea that it is situational comes from Preston (1970), Ray (1973), and Rothschild and Ray (1974). Cameron (1989) also conceptualized involvement as a cognitive process.

although individuals may not perceive both types of involvement for all situations.

Although most marketing and communication researchers have used the concept of involvement separately from problem recognition and constraint recognition, J. Grunig's research shows that the three variables together explain communication behavior better than any one alone (e.g., J. Grunig, 1983a; J. Grunig & Childers, 1988). In particular, the three variables identify publics, which occupy the second nest of segmentation—the nest most useful for planners of public relations programs.

The three concepts together predict not only when people will communicate; they also predict that active communication behavior more often results in effects of communication—cognitions, attitudes, individual and collective behaviors—than does passive communication behavior (J. Grunig, 1982b, 1983a, 1989b; J. Grunig & Ipes, 1983; J. Grunig & Stamm, 1979; Stamm & J. Grunig, 1977). Because these differential responses include most objectives for a public relations program, the three concepts provide an especially effective theory of segmentation.

Thus far, however, we have used the situational theory only to explain the communication behavior of individuals. The theory is most useful in public relations when it is used to aggregate people into publics—the second nest in Fig. 6.1.

Publics

The second nest in Fig. 6.1, labeled as *publics,* fits the concept of publics described in the second stage of the strategic management model in Table 6.1. At this second stage, public relations managers should determine which segments of their stakeholder categories are active publics and which are passive. Members of active publics affect organizations more than passive ones because they engage in individual behaviors to do something about the consequence of organizational actions. They may boycott a product, support government regulation, or oppose a rate increase. Other active publics support the mission of the organization by buying its stock or its products, supporting its policies, giving it money, or adopting a health or other behavior advocated by the organization. They also join activist groups—engage in collective behavior—to pressure the organization or to resolve the problem in other ways.

Organizations can communicate more easily with active than passive publics because they seek out information rather than passively receive it. On the other hand, active publics are not easy to persuade because they seek information from many sources and persuade themselves more than they are persuaded by others. Of course, passive stakeholders can become active, and the organization should not ignore them. Public relations managers should pay attention to all members of a stakeholder category but should devote most of their resources for communication programs aimed at the active publics.

At this stage of the strategic management process, public relations managers should do formative research on publics—research to plan a program. Focus groups provide an especially useful technique. With this technique, several small groups of people affected by an organization are brought together to focus on and to discuss the issue that affects them.[19] Focus groups will be most useful, however, if researchers focus them on concepts that identify publics and explain their communication behaviors. The concepts in J. Grunig's situational theory are especially useful. J. Grunig also has developed a quantitative method of identifying publics from survey research that can be applied at this stage. Several examples of research using the situational theory are described later in this section.

Once active publics have been identified, public relations managers should develop programs to involve them in the decision-making processes of the organization—such as committees of employees or community residents or open hearings before decisions are made. If active publics are involved early in the process, their concerns can be addressed before conflict occurs and before they feel they have no recourse other than to pressure the organization to change a decision, oppose the organization, or refuse to adopt a behavior advocated in a communication campaign.

Let us examine, then, how J. Grunig has used the situational concepts to segment publics. J. Grunig based his concept of public on the ideas of Dewey (1927) and Blumer (1966), who were among the first social scientists to develop a theory of publics. They observed that publics arise around problems that have consequences on them. Problems, therefore, define publics more than publics define problems (J. Grunig & Hunt, 1984, pp. 143–147; Price, 1987, p. 6). Cobb and Elder (1972) added that "a rather important implication that follows . . . is that there is not a single, undifferentiated public; a public is always specific to a particular situation or issue" (p. 102).

Dewey (1927) also acknowledged the crucial role that publics play in American democracy: After recognizing that problems affect them, publics organize into issue groups to pressure organizations that cause problems or that are supposed to help resolve problems. Publics, therefore, begin as disconnected systems of individuals experiencing common problems, but they can evolve into organized and powerful activist groups engaging in collective behavior.

Dewey's (1927) theory and the other classic theories of publics fit logically with the concepts of individual communication behavior and effects

---

[19]See L. Grunig (1990) for a more complete discussion of this technique.

identified in the previous section: Publics consist of people with similar levels of problem recognition, constraint recognition, and involvement for the same issues or problems. In several studies done to develop public relations theory, J. Grunig (1975, 1977a, 1978, 1979b, 1982a, 1982b, 1983a, 1983b; J. Grunig, Nelson, Richburg, & White, 1988) developed a methodology to identify publics arising around situational issues — publics that are optimal targets for communication campaigns.

A typical study has begun by identifying related problems that the organization believes may create publics. For example, J. Grunig (1983a) used eight problems (such as air pollution, extinction of whales, and strip mining) in two studies of environmental publics. He then used canonical correlation to correlate the independent variables (problem recognition, involvement, constraint recognition) simultaneously with the dependent variables (active and passive communication behavior) for all of the situations. The canonical variates provided profiles of the active and passive publics arising from the set of situations studied.

The canonical variates produced by this research have identified four kinds of publics consistently enough to assume they have theoretical regularity:

All-issue Publics. Publics active on all of the issues.

Apathetic Publics. Publics inattentive to all of the issues.

Single-Issue Publics. Publics active on one or a small subset of the issues that concerns only a small part of the population. Such issues have included the slaughter of whales or the controversy over the sale of infant formula in third-world countries.

Hot-Issue Publics. Publics active only on a single issue that involves nearly everyone in the population and that has received extensive media coverage (such as the gasoline shortage, drunken driving, or toxic waste disposal).

The situational theory has been applied widely in academic research on public relations. It has been used to identify employee publics of an electric utility and a telephone company (J. Grunig, 1975), scientific organizations (J. Grunig, 1977a; L. Grunig, 1985; Pelham, 1977; Schneider [aka Grunig], 1978), educational systems (J. Grunig, 1985, 1987; J. Grunig & Theus, 1986), and a community college (Waddell, 1979); members of an association (J. Grunig, 1979a); consumer publics of a supermarket chain (J. Grunig, 1974); community publics of a hospital (J. Grunig, 1978; J. Grunig & Disbrow, 1977), a local government (Conley, 1977), and a prison (Jenkins, 1976); environmental publics (Essich, 1984; J. Grunig, 1983a, 1989b; J. Grunig & Disbrow, 1977); agricultural publics (J. Grunig et al., 1988; Myers, 1985; Turner, 1981); student publics for an economic education program (J. Grunig, 1982a); reporter publics for business issues (J. Grunig, 1983b); corporate publics for social responsibility issues (J. Grunig, 1979b, 1982b); publics for campaigns on drunk driving (J. Grunig & Ipes, 1983), AIDS (J. Grunig & Childers, 1988), and fire safety (Spicer, 1985); users of an information service for the disabled (Al-Doory, 1974); publics of the Federal Reserve System (Baldwin, 1989); readers of science news (Bishop, 1983), an issues newsletter (Davis-Belcher, 1990), and a university magazine (Gibbs, 1986); and donor publics of a fund-raising program (Kelly, 1979).

Most applications of the theory, therefore, have been by academic researchers or by graduate students doing thesis research on particular organizations. The theory is cited frequently in the newsletter *pr reporter*. Commercial research firms have not used the theory, however, probably because research instruments have not been developed for commercial use as have instruments for the techniques in the outer nests of Fig. 6.1 (see chapter 8 for a discussion of techniques available from commercial firms). Most of these research firms have greater knowledge of market research techniques than of techniques applicable to public relations. Thus, public relations managers more often buy research to identify markets than to identify publics.

Communities

The community nest may overlap both the public nest within it and the lifestyles nest above it, in that members of publics may be found in several communities and several lifestyles may be found in the same community. We place communities at this level, however, because they are close to the concept of public and vary in the number and diversity of publics in them. Communities also are important segments because many organizations have community relations programs.

Tichenor, Donohue, and Olien (1977, 1980) provided the most useful concept for segmenting communities: the extent to which communities vary in pluralism (see also Aiken & Mott, 1970, for related studies). Pluralistic communities consist of more than one public, and these publics become more diverse as the community increases in pluralism. Thus, communication campaigns aimed at the community level should differ depending on the pluralism of the community. J. Grunig and Hunt (1984, chapter 13) provided advice on how to segment communities in this way, and Lindenmann (1980) described how a commercial research firm used community case studies to plan public relations programs. Two prominent studies of health campaigns, the Stanford and Minnesota heart health campaigns, have been based at the community level, although differences in the communities themselves have not been variables in the studies (e.g., Flora,

Maccoby, & Farquhar, 1989; Mittelmark et al., 1986; Nash & Farquhar, 1980).

Psychographics, Lifestyles, Subcultures, Social Relationships

These four concepts represent population segments grouped by psychological or social characteristics or both. These concepts are broader than publics because the segments they produce may house several publics. The concepts should be locators of publics because people with similar activities, values, and lifestyles usually are involved in similar situations and experience similar problems and constraints.[20]

Although the segments produced by these variables may be used alone by communication planners, they are most valuable when used in conjunction with measures that isolate publics — such as those provided by J. Grunig's situational theory. Because segmentation data are available readily from commercial firms, however, public relations managers often use them rather than doing original research to identify their own publics.

Social Relationships. Several mass communication researchers have used the concept of social relationships to explain how people use media and how the media affect them — as Lazarsfeld, Berelson, and Gaudet (1948) and Katz and Lazarsfeld (1955) did early in the history of communication research. In marketing, Assael (1987) devoted separate chapters in his book on consumer behavior to social classes, reference groups, families, opinion leaders, and the diffusion process.

This last sociological concept, the diffusion of innovations, is familiar to most public relations practitioners, although few apparently use the concept in research. Diffusion researchers (Lionberger & Gwin, 1982; Rogers, 1983) have segmented populations of users of an innovation by the amount of time that has passed before adoption of the innovation — essentially segmentation by behavior. Segments have included five "adopter types," each of which occupies a different role in a social system: innovators, early adopters, early majority, late majority, and laggards (Rogers, 1983, pp. 248–251).

The diffusion model has been used for segmentation in marketing (e.g., Assael, 1987, chapter 17; Robertson, 1971). Myers (1985) showed that the adopter categories can be explained by J. Grunig's situational theory of publics in that segments move from active to passive communication behavior (because of lower problem recognition or involvement or higher

---

[20]Marketing researchers call these characteristics from outer nests descriptors of segments (Frank et al., 1972, p. 18; Massy & Weitz, 1977, p. 125).

constraint recognition) as they move from innovators to laggards. Diffusion theory can be useful in segmentation because the adopter categories provide one way to operationalize the concept of social relationships (Rogers, 1983, pp. 260-261). The concepts that follow—psychographics, lifestyles, and subcultures—provide additional variables and measures that convert the idea of social relationships into measured segments.

Psychographics and Lifestyles.   Wells and Tigert (1971) introduced what they called AIO items—for activities, interests, and opinions—to research in marketing and advertising. These items, they said, "focus on . . . activities, interests, prejudices, and opinions" to "draw recognizably human portraits of consumers" (p. 28). Researchers developed the term *psychograpics* as an analogue to *demographics*. Demographics are based on the descriptive categories used by demographers. Psychographics are based on the psychological characteristics of people. Analysis of lifestyles goes beyond psychological characteristics to examine how people live their lives. In current practice, most of the widely used methods incorporate both psychographics and lifestyles in the same research instrument.

The measurement instrument used most by marketing and public relations practitioners is VALS (for values and lifestyles)—a system developed by SRI International (1985). SRI International markets VALS at a cost to corporate and other users. About 150 users pay from $20,000 to $150,000 per year to use VALS (Rice, 1988, p. 49). Although the VALS instrument is not in the public domain, other researchers have developed similar systems that could be used by communication planners (see, e.g., Assael, 1987, chapter 10; Blackwell & Talarzyk, 1983; Hanan, 1980). Mitchell (1983)—who developed VALS—included some of its items in an appendix.

The VALS typology was developed from combinations of Abraham Maslow's psychological hierarchy of needs and David Riesman's sociological concepts of people who are inner and outer directed (Mitchell, 1983; Rice, 1988). The VALS typology contains nine lifestyles, whose names provide some indication of the nature of the segments: sustainers, survivors, belongers, emulators, achievers, the I-Am-Me's, experientials, socially conscious, and integrateds.

Nager and Truitt (1987, pp. 105-109) described how two public relations firms—Ketchum and Hill and Knowlton—have used VALS in planning public relations and marketing communication programs. Although lifestyle concepts such as VALS are used widely, the concepts have not been rigorously tested or validated (Lastovicka, 1982). The technique also has been criticized frequently, essentially because the profiles do not come close enough to the concepts of individual communication and consumer behavior in the innermost nest of Fig. 6.1 (Lesser & Hughes, 1986). An advertising executive (Rice, 1988), for example, criticized VALS for not being situational: "People don't always think and behave consistently in every context. Some individuals may vote as Belongers but think like Achievers when they walk into the automobile showroom" (p. 50). Or as John Paluszek, president of Ketchum Public Affairs, put it in describing a campaign for the Beef Industry Council (Winkleman, 1987): "The health issue is intrinsic to beef . . . Whom do we really want to talk to about beef? We want to go to the people active on the issues" (p. 23).

In 1989, SRI International introduced a new version of VALS, VALS 2, which Staff (1989) said has moved "toward making the system particularly useful in marketing—vs. broader relationships." That move, *pr reporter* added, "undoubtedly reflects SRI's own market, large consumer product companies" (p. 1). The new typology is more subject to Paluszek's (Winkleman, 1987) criticism than the original because it steers away from issue questions (such as "How do you feel about abortion?") and uses consumption questions (such as "My idea of fun at a national park would be to stay at an expensive lodge and dress for dinner.") (Staff, 1989, p. 1). The new categories in VALS 2 are strugglers, makers, experiencers, strivers, achievers, believers, fulfilleds, and actualizers.

Subcultures. This last concept in the third nest refers more to what Assael (1987, chapter 12) called "subcultures" than to broad national cultures—groups with similar values, customs, norms, beliefs, and behaviors. Cultural groups are much like psychographic and lifestyle groups, and some researchers working in public relations (especially Steve Barnett, who formerly worked with the Planmetrics firm and with Research & Forecasts, Inc.) use anthropological techniques to study cultures and lifestyles (Miller, 1986).

Geodemographics

The next nest contains a segmentation technique that consists partly of lifestyles and partly of geographic demographics—a technique widely used in marketing, politics, and public relations. Several commercial firms such as Claritas, Donnelly, CACI, and National Decision System take data from the US Census, correlate them with data from market and political surveys, and use cluster analysis to group postal zip codes into similar categories (Winkleman, 1987). These surveys include "the list of new-car buyers from R. L. Polk, the TV viewing diaries of A. C. Neilsen, and the consumer buying polls of Mediamark Research, Inc. and Simmons Market Research Bureau" (Weiss, 1988, p. 14).

The best known system is PRIZM (Potential Rating Index for Zip Markets), marketed by the Claritas Corp. of Alexandria, VA (Claritas,

1985).[21] PRIZM was developed in the early 1970s by Jonathan Robbin, whom Weiss (1988) described as a "57-year-old social scientist turned entrepreneur" and "a Harvard-educated computer whiz" (p. 10). Weiss explained how Robbin developed PRIZM:

> He began with the 1930s theories of University of Chicago sociologists who described city neighborhoods as prime examples of "social clustering," where people tend to congregate among people like themselves. Then he programmed Claritas computers to analyze each zip code according to hundreds of characteristics in five groups: social rank, mobility, ethnicity, family life cycle and housing style. From the morass of census results—which included such data as the number of Samoans with indoor plumbing—Robbin identified thirty-four key factors that account, statistically speaking, for 87 percent of the variation among US neighborhoods. Finally, he instructed a computer to rate each zip code on the thirty-four factors simultaneously in order to assign it to one of forty clusters.
>
> Why forty? In fact, Claritas analysts tested more than three dozen experimental models, some involving one hundred neighborhood types. But the forty-cluster system proved the ideal compromise between manageability and discriminating power. (pp. 11–12)

The 40 clusters of neighborhoods have descriptive names such as Blue Blood Estates ("America's wealthiest neighborhoods . . . includes suburban homes and one in ten millionaires"), Furs and Station Wagons ("New money in metropolitan bedroom suburbs"), Shotguns & Pickups ("Crossroads villages serving the nation's lumber and breadbasket needs"), and Coalburg & Corntown ("Small towns based on light industry and farming") (Weiss, 1988, pp. 4–5). Although PRIZM data, like VALS data, are proprietary, Weiss provided a great deal of information about them in *The Clustering of America*. Weiss obtained a large amount of propriety data from Claritas. In addition, he chose one zip code for each neighborhood type, visited that neighborhood, and wrote profiles of each.

Geodemographics is obviously a powerful tool for marketing. According to Weiss (1988):

> Those five digits can indicate the types of magazines you read, the meals you serve at dinner, whether you're a liberal Republican or an apathetic Democrat. Retailers use zips to decide everything from where to locate a designed boutique to what kind of actor to use in their TV commercials—be it Mean Joe Green, Morris the Cat or Spuds McKenzie. College and military recruiters even rely on a city's zip codes to target their efforts to attract promising high school graduates. (p. xi)

---

[21]The name Claritas is Latin for "clarity" (Weiss, 1988, p. 11).

For public relations, geodemographics can be important when it is used to relate people's positions on issues to the clusters. In politics, for example, strategists have targeted the clusters must likely to be concerned about a particular issue or to take a particular stand on an issue (Weiss, 1988, pp. 21-25). Because the clusters also contain data on media use and other communication activities, they obviously have great value for strategic communication. Most uses in public relations, however, have been asymmetrical — that is, communication managers target clusters most likely to agree with their position and then direct messages to mobilize support.

Geodemographic segmentation, like lifestyle segmentation, falls in an outer nest of Fig. 6.2 and does not predict communication behavior and the existence of publics directly. If public relations planners can correlate concepts used to identify publics, such as problem recognition and level of involvement, with the clusters, however, they would have a powerful tool to locate publics and direct messages to them. Thus, a public relations planner who works with one of the commercial firms doing geodemographic research should look in the firm's data base for questions similar to those used in the situational theory. Issues data, as we see in the last section of this chapter, offer special promise — as long as the planner looks at those issues symmetrically to identify and communicate with publics who disagree with the organization as well as those who agree.

Demographics and Social Categories

Communication researchers and planners long have used demographic crosstabulations to avoid unfocused dissemination of information to a mass audience. Demographics are better than no segmentation. They also serve as useful locators of publics and other segments in inner nests. When time or money does not permit other research, demographics may be the only segmentation tool available to the communication planner.

Mass Audiences

A major premise of this chapter has been that public relations programs seldom will be effective if they are directed to a mass audience. Mass audiences do have segments embedded in them that communicate actively, and messages directed at an unsegmented population may reach the active segments. Although there will be fewer research costs if a campaign is directed at a mass, the costs of the campaign itself will be much greater because messages are directed to passive or nonpublics as well as to active publics. As Cobb and Elder (1972) pointed out, mass audiences (general publics) consist primarily of the most passive and unresponsive publics.

At times, communication planners may have no alternative to appealing to a mass audience. Marketing theorists such as Assael (1987, chapter 4), Lovelock and Weinberg (1984, pp. 73–74), and Ray (1973) have developed strategies for low-involvement consumer segments. In addition, Biocca (1988, pp. 62–66) provided evidence from cognitive psychology that messages processed passively can—through preconscious processes—produce cognitive effects. As a result, communication planners should not write off massive audiences. However, they should expect communication programs for masses to be considerably less effective than those planned for segments such as publics.

Organizations should construct communication programs with publics rather than segments in the outside nests because they have greater chance that those programs will be effective. More importantly, publics are more strategic than other segments—they create issues for organizations. We turn, then, to this third stage of the model.

THE ISSUES STAGE

If an organization has had effective public relations at each of the previous two stages of the process of strategic management, it will have resolved most of the problems with publics before they become issues. A public perceives a problem when something is missing that it would like to occur—such as clean air, a good community, or a successful organization. Publics make issues out of problems that have not been resolved. An issue, according to Heath and Nelson (1986), is "a contestable question of fact, value, or policy" (p. 37). At this stage of the strategic management of public relations, communication managers cross paths with the function that has come to be called *issues management*. Issues management, in practice, essentially is another name for the external component of strategic management.

Most discussions of issues management credit Howard Chase, a veteran public relations practitioner, with inventing the term and discussing it in Chase (1977). Jones and Chase (1979) published their first model in *Public Relations Review*. Chase (1984) followed with a book that elaborated the model. He maintained that issues management is a new science, which has evolved in a historical process beginning with press relations and moving through public relations and public affairs to issues management. Jones and Chase reasoned that without issues management, business would be the captive of activist groups. In language similar to that used in chapter 3 describing the cost of poor public relations, they explained: "And when business loses its trial before the court of public opinion, it is usually forced to accept costly legislative, regulatory, administrative, or judicial verdicts that severely inhibit the entrepreneurial decision-making function at the cost of loss of productivity" (p. 7).

Ehling and Hesse (1983) questioned whether issues management represented a new concept and concluded that Jones and Chase (1979) had done little more than redefine public relations as issues management. They also reported the results of a survey of public relations practitioners that showed that "the overwhelming majority of respondents did not consider 'issue management' anything new; rather they merely view 'issue management' as being a new term for an everyday type of activity that has been going on for a long time" (p. 29). However, Ehling and Hesse found that 78% of their respondents knew little or nothing about issues management and that 85% of those who were aware of it reported that their organization did not use issues management.

Heath and Nelson (1986, pp. 21–22) cited surveys showing that Ehling and Hesse (1983) were right about the contribution of public relations practitioners to issues management but wrong about the adoption of the practice by corporations. They reported that 91% of Fortune 500 companies had established issues management programs but that there was little evidence that public relations practitioners are involved in them. They explained, "While in theory, public relations, public affairs, and issues management overlap, the reality is that public relations/public affairs experts often are not meaningfully involved in corporate planning" (p. 22).

Issues Management = Strategic Public Relations

Throughout the literature on issues management, writers make frequent reference to issues management as the external component of strategic management (e.g., Ewing, 1980; Heath 1990; Heath & Cousino, 1990; Heath & Nelson, 1986, p. 24). Heath (1990) concluded, for example, that: ". . . issues management evolved from public affairs and public relations to help organizations integrate public policy planning and strategic planning. This development helped strategic planning mature from budgeting to long-range planning" (p. 32).

Organizations place the issues management function in several places in the organizational structure—most frequently, according to Heath (1990) in "public affairs, corporate planning, corporate communication, government affairs, or policy analysis" (p. 32). In short, issues management typically is a joint function of a planning department and a department carrying out one or more public relations functions. As chapter 14 maintains, an excellent public relations function should be integrated into a single department. Too often, though, organizations name the media relations aspect of public relations "public relations," the policy and issue portion "public affairs," and the planning and counseling function "corporate communication" or "external relations." Schwartz and Glynn (1990) also reported that a survey of members of the Issues Management Association showed that issues management may be moving away from public relations departments into planning departments.

Thus we see that most organizations seem to realize the need to incorporate external planning into strategic planning, but many assign that function to a newly created department carrying out a public relations function but not named public relations or to the planning department rather than to public relations. When a public relations department is excellent, however, we believe it will handle the issues management function as part of the strategic planning of public relations. That is the issues stage of the strategic planning function.

Making an Issue Out of It

Crable and Vibbert (1985; Vibbert, 1987, 1988) developed a rhetorical theory that maintains that issues enter the public agenda because someone makes an issue out of a problem: "An issue is created when one or more human agents attaches significance to a situation or perceived problem" (Crable & Vibbert, 1985, p. 5). Crable and Vibbert seemed to conceptualize organizations as the major initiators of issues—by choosing areas of potential policy that they would like to control. Many other writers, however, recognize that activist groups—the most active publics—make issues out of problems (Chase, 1984; Hainsworth, 1990; Heath & Nelson, 1986, p. 195; Jones & Chase, 1979). Jones and Chase and Chase, however, decried this abdication of power to outside groups and suggested strategies for a process by which organizations could wrest control from them.

Most theories of issues management, then, suggest alternative strategies for managing issues or, for some, managing the organization's response to issues. Chase (1984) described three strategies: reactive (in which the organization always opposes change), adaptive (in which the organization attempts to satisfy the demands of outside groups), and dynamic (in which the organization "creates and directs policy rather than merely reacts to policy trends established by other forces" [p. 7]. Chase obviously took an asymmetrical approach to issues, even though Heath and Nelson (1986) maintained that Chase noted the importance of issues managers "in helping corporate decision makers modify those institutional policies needing reevaluation once public expectations and involvement are identified" (p. 20).

Chase's (1984) worldview, however, is probusiness and antigovernment: "Evidence grows that corporate governance is far more flexible and adaptable than state or national governance" (p. 28). His dynamic strategy also is clearly asymmetrical: "This strategy anticipates and attempts to shape the direction of public policy decisions by determining the theater of war, the weapons to be used, and the timing of the battle itself" (p. 59).

Other theorists suggest a third strategy that more nearly resembles the symmetrical and mixed-motive worldview of public relations (chapters 2 and 11). Buchholz, Evans, and Wagley (1989, p. 63) named four such approaches: reactive (fighting change), accommodative (adapting to change), proactive (influencing change), and interactive (adjusting to and influencing change). Crable and Vibbert (1985) described a "catalytic" strategy in which the organization balances its mission with external demands (pp. 9–10). These interactive, catalytic strategies are the types of strategies that chapters 2 and 11 have described as characteristics of excellent public relations.

The Role of the Media

Despite the preoccupation of most public relations practitioners with media coverage, this model of the strategic management of public relations shows that excellent publics relations needs the media less than poor public relations does because the organization solves external problems before publics make issues out of them (J. Grunig, 1990). When publics make issues out of problems, they typically use the mass media to bring attention to their cause (VanLeuven & Slater, 1991). They do this by staging events such as protests, marches, strikes, and sometimes even hunger fasts and violent demonstrations. When publicity mounts, stakeholders and even members of nonpublics hear about the issue—they become hot-issue publics.

Vibbert (1987) described four stages through which issues progress— definition, legitimation, polarization, and identification. The media play active roles in the last two stages, polarizing two sides of the issue so that people seem forced to identify with one side or another. When organizations delay public relations programs until the issue stage rather than beginning at the stakeholder or public stage, they usually are forced to develop programs of crisis communication—especially when polarization occurs. In addition, they begin to campaign against the activists asymmetrically, the activists do likewise, and the conflict degenerates into a shouting match and campaigns to convince passive publics to support each position. Sometimes, one side can declare a short-term victory—by defeating legislation or winning a lawsuit, for example—but seldom does the other side give up. The only means of resolving issues at this stage is though negotiation and "horsetrading" with the activist group.[22]

Ideally, however, organizations do not wait until the issues stage to deal

---

[22]See, for example, Dilenschneider's (1990) chapter on special interest groups.

with problems. Instead, they try to identify issues while they are still problems and to manage the organization's response to the problems and issues (Ewing, 1990, p. 20).[23] Issues management programs should be managed by the public relations department in cooperation with a corporate or organizational planning department. When such coordination takes place, strategic management of public relations can be integrated into the overall strategic management of the organization (Heath, 1990, p. 32).

TWO PROPOSITIONS

The theories and research on strategic management, publics, and issues can be reduced to two major propositions:

Proposition 1: Public relations is most likely to be excellent—to contribute to organizational effectiveness—when it is an integral part of an organization's strategic management process and when public relations itself is managed strategically.

Proposition 2: Public relations is managed strategically when it identifies stakeholders, segments active publics from stakeholder categories, and resolves issues created by the interaction of organization and publics through symmetrical communication programs (interactive or catalytic strategies) early in the development of issues.

REFERENCES

Aiken, M., & Mott, P. E. (Eds.). (1970). *The structure of community power.* New York: Random House.

Al-Doory, S. A. (1974). *An analysis of information seeking parameters of the blind and physically handicapped.* Unpublished master's thesis, University of Maryland, College Park.

Anderson, R. B. (1989). Reassessing the odds against finding meaningful behavioral change in mass media health promotion campaigns. In C. H. Botan & V. Hazleton, Jr. (Eds.), *Public relations theory* (pp. 309–322). Hillsdale, NJ: Lawrence Erlbaum Associates.

Assael, H. (1987). *Consumer behavior and marketing action* (3rd ed.). Boston: Kent.

Baldwin, W. R. (1989). *Situational publics of the Federal Reserve System.* Unpublished master's thesis, University of Maryland, College Park.

Bandura, A. (1977). *Social learning theory.* Englewood Cliffs, NJ: Prentice-Hall.

Biocca, F. A. (1988). Opposing conceptions of the audience: The active and passive hemispheres of mass communication theory. In J. A. Anderson (Ed.), *Communication yearbook 11* (pp. 51–80). Newbury Park, CA: Sage.

---

[23]Some writers advocate a broad look at issues. Ewing (1990) described how Allstate Insurance set up an issues forum on AIDS, a macro issue with an indirect effect on the insurance industry. Wilson (1990) maintained that organizations should think of issues globally.

Bishop, W. B. (1983). *Communication from a scientific meeting.* Unpublished master's thesis, University of Maryland, College Park.

Blackwell, R. D., & Talarzyk, W. W. (1983). Life-style retailing: Competitive strategies for the 1980s. *Journal of Retailing, 59*(Winter), 7–27.

Block, E. W. (1987). Practicing what we preach: Strategic communications. *Public Relations Review, 13*(4), 3–10.

Blumer, H. (1966). The mass, the public, and public opinion. In B. Berelson & M. Janowitz (Eds.), *Reader in public opinion and communication* (2nd ed., pp. 43–50). New York: Free Press.

Bonoma, T. V., & Shapiro, B. P. (1983). *Segmenting the industrial market.* Lexington, MA: Lexington.

Brehm, J. W., & Cohen, A. R. (1962). *Explorations in cognitive dissonance.* New York: Wiley.

Brody, E. W. (1987). *The business of public relations.* New York: Praeger.

Brody, E. W. (1988). *Public relations programming and production.* New York: Praeger.

Broom, G. M. (1986, May). *Public relations roles and systems theory: Functional and historicist causal models.* Paper presented at the meeting of the International Communication Association, Chicago.

Buchholz, R. A., Evans, W. D., & Wagley, R. A. (1989). *Management response to public issues.* Englewood Cliffs, NJ: Prentice-Hall.

Cambridge Reports, Inc. (1985). *Residential customer market segmentation study* (Vol. 2). Washington, DC: Edison Electric Institute.

Cambridge Reports, Inc. (1986). *Residential customer program segmentation study.* Washington, DC: Edison Electric Institute.

Cameron, G. T. (1989). *The effects of involvement and prior knowledge on recall and recognition of persuasive statements.* Unpublished doctoral dissertation, University of Texas, Austin.

Carroll, A. B. (1989). *Business & society: Ethics and stakeholder management.* Cincinnati: South-Western.

Chaffee, S. H., & Roser, C. (1986). Involvement and the consistency of knowledge, attitudes, and behaviors. *Communication Research, 13,* 373–399.

Chase, W. H. (1977). Public issue management: The new science. *Public Relations Journal, 33,* 25–26.

Chase, W. H. (1984). *Issue management: Origins of the future.* Stamford, CT: Issue Action Press.

Claritas (1985). *PRIZM: The integration marketing solution.* Alexandria, VA.

Cobb, R. W., & Elder, C. D. (1972). *Participation in American politics: The dynamics of agenda building.* Baltimore: Johns Hopkins University Press.

Conley, J. L. (1977). *Government communication: A study of the communication behavior of citizen publics with their local government.* Unpublished master's thesis, University of Maryland, College Park.

Crable, R. E., & Vibbert, S. L. (1985). Managing issues and influencing public policy. *Public Relations Review, 11*(2), 3–16.

Cravens, D. W. (1982). *Strategic marketing.* Homewood, IL: Irwin.

Cunningham, W. H., & Crissy, W. J. E. (1972). Market segmentation by motivation and attitude. *Journal of Marketing Research, 9,* 100–102.

Cunningham, W. H., & Cunningham, I. C. M. (1981). *Marketing: A managerial approach.* Cincinnati: South-Western.

Davis-Belcher, P. O. (1990). *Communication behaviors and the management of public policy issues.* Unpublished masters' thesis, University of Maryland, College Park.

Dervin, B. (1981). Mass communicating: Changing conceptions of the audience. In R. E. Rice & W. J. Paisley (Eds.), *Public communication campaigns* (pp. 71–87). Newbury Park, CA: Sage.

Dervin, B. (1984). A theoretical perspective and research approach for generating research helpful to communication practice. *Public Relations Research & Education, 1*(1), 30–45.

Dervin, B. (1989). Audience as listener and learner, teacher and confidante. In R. E. Rice & C. K. Atkin (Eds.), *Public communication campaigns* (2nd ed., pp. 71–87). Newbury Park, CA: Sage.

Dervin, B., Jacobson, T. L., & Nilan, M. S. (1982). Measuring aspects of information seeking: A test of a quantitative/qualitative methodology. In M. Burgoon (Ed.), *Communication yearbook 6* (pp. 419–444). Newbury Park, CA: Sage.

Dewey, J. (1910). *How we think.* New York: Heath.

Dewey, J. (1927). *The public and its problems.* Chicago: Swallow.

Dewey, J. (1938). *Logic: The theory of inquiry.* New York: Henry Holt.

Dewey, J. (1939). *Theory of valuation.* Chicago: University of Chicago Press.

Dickson, P. R. (1982). Person-situation: Segmentation's missing link. *Journal of Marketing 46*(Fall), 56–64.

Dilenschneider, R. L. (1990). *Power and influence.* New York: Prentice-Hall.

Dozier, D. M. (1990). The innovation of research in public relations practice. In L. A. Grunig & J. E. Grunig (Eds.), *Public relations research annual* (Vol. 2 pp. 9–28). Hillsdale, NJ: Lawrence Erlbaum Associates.

Ehling, W. P., & Hesse, M. B. (1983). Use of 'issue management' in public relations. *Public Relations Review, 9*(2), 18–35.

Engel, J. G., Blackwell, R. D., & Kollat, D. T. (1978). *Consumer behavior* (3rd ed.). Hinsdale, IL: Dryden.

Essich, T. (1984). *Environmental communication behavior of industry managers.* Unpublished master's thesis, University of Maryland, College Park.

Ewing, R. P. (1980). Evaluating issues management. *Public Relations Journal, 36*(6), 14–16.

Ewing, R. P. (1990). Moving from micro to macro issues management. *Public Relations Review, 16*(1), 19–24.

Flay, B. R., & Cook, T. D. (1989). Three models for summative evaluation of prevention campaigns with a mass media component. In R. E. Rice & C. K. Atkin (Eds.), *Public communication campaigns* (2nd ed., pp. 175–196). Newbury Park, CA: Sage.

Flora, J. A., Maccoby, N., & Farquhar, J. W. (1989). Communication campaigns to prevent cardiovascular disease: The Stanford community studies. In R. E. Rice & C. K. Atkin (Eds.), *Public communication campaigns* (2nd ed., pp. 233–252). Newbury Park, CA: Sage.

Frank, R. E., Massy, W. F., & Wind, Y. (1972). *Market segmentation.* Englewood Cliffs, NJ: Prentice-Hall.

Freeman, R. E. (1984). *Strategic management: A stakeholder approach.* Boston: Pitman.

Gibbs, J. D. (1986). *An evaluation of Grunig's decision-situation theory of communication.* Unpublished master's thesis, University of Florida, Gainesville.

Green, P. E., Carroll, J. D., & Goldberg, S. M. (1981). A general approach to product design optimization via conjoint analysis. *Journal of Marketing, 45*(Summer), 17–37.

Greene, C. N., Adam, E. A., Jr., & Ebert, R. J. (1985). *Management for effective performance.* Englewood Cliffs, NJ: Prentice-Hall.

Grunig, J. E. (1971). Communication and the economic decisionmaking processes of Columbian peasants. *Economic Development and Cultural Change, 19,* 580–597.

Grunig, J. E. (1974, August). *A case study of organizational information seeking and consumer information needs.* Paper presented at the meeting of the Association for Education in Journalism and Mass Communication, San Diego.

Grunig, J. E. (1975). Some consistent types of employee publics. *Public Relations Review, 1*(4), 17–36.

Grunig, J. E. (1977a). Evaluating employee communication in a research operation. *Public Relations Review, 3*(4), 61–82.

Grunig, J. E. (1977b). Review of research on environmental public relations. *Public Relations Review, 3*(3), 36–58.

Grunig, J. E. (1978). Defining publics in public relations: The case of a suburban hospital. *Journalism Quarterly, 55,* 109–118.

Grunig, J. E. (1979a). *Membership survey and communication audit.* Washington, DC: American Alliance for Health, Physical Education, Recreation, and Dance.

Grunig, J. E. (1979b). A new measure of public opinions on corporate social responsibility. *Academy of Management Journal, 22,* 738–764.

Grunig, J. E. (1979c). Time budgets, level of involvement and use of the mass media. *Journalism Quarterly, 56,* 248–261.

Grunig, J. E. (1982a). Developing economic education programs for the press. *Public Relations Review, 8*(3), 43–62.

Grunig, J. E. (1982b). The message-attitude-behavior relationship: Communication behaviors of organizations. *Communication Research, 9,* 163–200.

Grunig, J. E. (1983a). Communication behaviors and attitudes of environmental publics: Two studies. *Journalism Monographs, 81.*

Grunig, J. E. (1983b). Washington reporter publics of corporate public affairs programs. *Journalism Quarterly, 60,* 603–615.

Grunig, J. E. (1985, May). *A structural reconcepualization of the organizational communication audit, with application to a state department of education.* Paper presented at the meeting of the International Communication Association, Honolulu.

Grunig, J. E. (1987, July). *An audit of organizational structure, job satisfaction, and the communication system in the Allegany County School System.* Cumberland, MD: Allegany County School System.

Grunig, J. E., (1989a). Publics, audiences and market segments: Models of receivers of campaign messages. In C. T. Salmon (Ed.), *Information campaigns: Managing the process of social change* (pp. 197–226). Newbury Park, CA: Sage.

Grunig, J. E. (1989b). Sierra club study shows who become activists. *Public Relations Review, 15*(3), 3–24.

Grunig, J. E. (1990). Theory and practice of interactive media relations. *Public Relations Quarterly, 35*(3), 18–23.

Grunig, J. E., & Childers, L. (1988). *Reconstruction of a situational theory of communication: Internal and external concepts as identifiers of publics for AIDS.* Paper presented at the meeting of the Association for Education in Journalism & Mass Communication, Portland, OR.

Grunig, J. E., & Disbrow, J. B. (1977). Developing a probabilistic model for communications decision making. *Communication Research, 4,* 145–168.

Grunig, J. E., & Hunt, T. (1984). *Managing public relations.* New York: Holt, Rinehart & Winston.

Grunig, J. E., & Ipes, D. A. (1983). The anatomy of a campaign against drunk driving. *Public Relations Review, 9*(3), 36–53.

Grunig, J. E., Nelson, C. L., Richburg, S. J., & White, T. J. (1988). Communication by agricultural publics: Internal and external orientations. *Journalism Quarterly, 65,* 26–38.

Grunig, J. E., & Stamm, K. R. (1979). Cognitive strategies and the resolution of environmental issues: a second study. *Journalism Quarterly, 56,* 715–726.

Grunig, J. E., & Theus, K. T. (1986, August). *Internal communication systems and employee satisfaction.* Paper presented at the meeting of the Association for Education in Journalism and Mass Communication, Norman, OK.

Grunig, L. A. (1985). Meeting the information needs of employees. *Public Relations Review, 11*(2), 43–53.

Grunig, L. A. (1990). Using focus group research in public relations. *Public Relations Review, 16*(2). 36–49.

Hainsworth, B. E. (1990). The distribution of advantages and disadvantages. *Public Relations Review, 16*(1), 33–39.

Hanan, M. (1980). *Life-styled marketing* (rev. ed.). New York: Amacom.

Harrison, M. I. (1987). *Diagnosing organizations: Methods, models, and processes.* Newbury Park, CA: Sage.

Heath, R. L. (1990). Corporate issues management: Theoretical underpinnings and research foundations. In L. A. Grunig & J. E. Grunig (Eds.), *Public relations research annual* (Vol. 2, pp. 29–66). Hillsdale, NJ: Lawrence Erlbaum Associates.

Heath, R. L., & Cousino, K. R. (1990). Issues management: End of first decade progress report. *Public Relations Review, 16*(1), 6–18.

Heath, R. L., & Douglas, W. (1990). Involvement: A key variable in people's reaction to public policy issues. In L. A. Grunig & J. E. Grunig (Eds.), *Public relations research annual* (Vol. 2, pp. 193–204). Hillsdale, NJ: Lawrence Erlbaum Associates.

Heath, R. L., & Nelson, R. A. (1986). *Issues management.* Newbury Park, CA: Sage.

Higgins, H. M. (1979). *Organizational policy and strategic management: Texts and cases.* Hinsdale, IL: Dryden.

Holt, D. H. (1987). *Management: Principles and practices.* Englewood Cliffs, NJ: Prentice-Hall.

Jenkins, L. (1976). *Prison communication: A study of the public perception of Lorton Prison.* Unpublished master's thesis, University of Maryland, College Park.

Jones, B. L., & Chase, W. H. (1979). Managing public policy issues. *Public Relations Review,* (2), 3–23.

Kassarjian, H. H. (1981). Low involvement — A second look. In K. B. Monroe (Ed.), *Advances in consumer research* (Vol. 8, pp. 31–34). Ann Arbor: Association for Consumer Research.

Katz, E., & Lazarsfeld, P. F. (1955). *Personal influence.* Glencoe, IL: Free Press.

Kelly, K. S. (1979). *Predicting alumni giving: An analysis of alumni donors and non-donors of the College of Journalism at the University of Maryland.* Unpublished master's thesis, University of Maryland, College Park.

Kotler, P., & Andreasen, A. R. (1987). *Strategic marketing for nonprofit organizations* (3rd ed.). Englwood Cliffs, NJ: Prentice-Hall.

Krugman, H. E. (1965). The impact of television advertising: Learning without involvement. *Public Opinion Quarterly, 29,* 349–356.

Lastovicka, J. L. (1982). On the validation of lifestyle traits: A review and illustration. *Journal of Marketing Research, 19*(February), 126–138.

Lazarsfeld, P. F., Berelson, B., & Gaudet, H. (1948). *The people's choice.* New York: Columbia University Press.

Lehmann, D. R., Moore, W. L., & Elrod, T. (1982). The development of distinct choice process segments over time: A stochastic modeling approach. *Journal of Marketing, 46*(Spring), 48–59.

Lesser, J. A., & Hughes, M. A. (1986). The generalizability of psychographic market segments across geographic locations. *Journal of Marketing, 50*(January), 18–27.

Levitt, T. (1986). *The marketing imagination* (exp. ed.). New York: Free Press.

Lindenmann, W. K. (1980). Use of community case studies in opinion research. *Public Relations Review, 6*(1), 40–50.

Lionberger, H. F., & Gwin, P. H. (1982). *Communication strategies: A guide for agricultural change agents.* Danville, IL: Interstate Printers & Publishers.

Lovelock, C. H., & Weinberg, C. B. (1984). *Marketing for public and nonprofit managers.* New York: Wiley.

Lowery, S., & DeFleur, M. L. (1983). *Milestones in mass communication research.* New York: Longman.

Luck, D. J., & Ferrell, O. C. (1985). *Marketing strategy and plans* (2nd ed.). Englewood Cliffs, NJ: Prentice-Hall.

Lunn, T. (1986). Segmenting and constructing markets. In R. M. Worcester & J. Downham (Eds.), *Consumer market research handbook* (3rd ed.)(pp. 387–423). Amsterdam: North Holland.

Maccoby, N., & Solomon, D. S. (1981). Heart disease prevention: Community studies. In R. E. Rice & W. J. Paisley (Eds.), *Public communication campaigns* (pp. 105-126). Newbury Park, CA: Sage.

Massie, J. L., & Douglas, J. (1985). *Managing: A contemporary introduction* (4th ed.). Englewood Cliffs, NJ: Prentice-Hall.

Massy, W. F., & Weitz. B. A. (1977). A normative theory of market segmentation. In F. M. Nicosia & Y. Wind (Eds.), *Behavioral models for market analysis: Foundations for marketing action* (pp. 121-144). Hinsdale, IL: Dryden.

McQuail, D. (1987). *Mass communication theory* (2nd ed.). Newbury Park, CA: Sage.

Michman, R. C. (1983). *Marketing to changing consumer markets.* New York: Praeger.

Miller, D. A. (1986). *Psychographics . . . a study in diversity.* Unpublished manuscript, University of Maryland, College Park.

Mitchell, A. (1983). *The nine American lifestyles.* New York: Macmillan.

Mittelmark, M. B., Luepker, M. D., Jacobs, D. R., Bracht, N. F., Carlaw, R. W., Crow, R. S., Finnegan, J., Grimm, R. H., Jeffery, R. W., Kline, G. F., Mullis, R. M., Murray, D. M., Pechacek, T. F., Perry, C. L., Pirie, P. L., & Blackburn, H. (1986). Community-wide prevention of cardiovascular disease: Education strategies of the Minnesota heart health program. *Preventive Medicine, 15,* 661-672.

Moore, W. L. (1980). Levels of aggregation in conjoint analysis: An empirical comparison. *Journal of Marketing Research, 17*(November), 516-523.

Myers, R. E., Jr. (1985). *Communication behaviors of Maryland farmers: An analysis of adopters and nonadopters of innovations to reduce agricultural pollution of the Chesapeake Bay.* Unpublished master's thesis, University of Maryland, College Park.

Nager, N. R., & Truitt, R. H. (1987). *Strategic public relations counseling.* New York: Longman.

Nash, J. D., & Farquhar, J. W. (1980). Applications of behavioral medicine to disease prevention in a total community setting: A review of the three community study. In J. M. Ferguson & C. B. Taylor (Eds.), *The comprehensive handbook of behaviorial medicine* (pp. 313-335). New York: Spectrum.

Pearce, J. A., II, & Robinson, R. B., Jr. (1982). *Strategic management: Strategy formulation and implementation.* Homewood, IL: Irwin.

Pearson, R. (1990). Ethical values or strategic values? The two faces of systems theory in public relations. In L. A. Grunig & J. E. Grunig (Eds.), *Public relations research annual* (Vol. 2, pp. 219-234). Hillsdale, NJ: Lawrence Erlbaum Associates.

Pelham, K. L. (1977). *Using communication at the Naval Surface Weapons Center: An analysis using Grunig's multi-system theory.* Unpublished master's thesis, University of Maryland, College Park.

Petty, R. E., & Cacioppo, J. T. (1986). *Communication and persuasion: Central and peripheral routes to attitude change.* New York: Springer-Verlag.

Pfeffer, J., & Salancik, G. R. (1978). *The external control of organizations.* New York: Harper & Row.

Prescott, J. E. (1986). Environments as moderators of the relationship between strategy and performance. *Academy of Management Journal, 29,* 329-346.

Preston, I. L. (1970). A reinterpretation of the meaning of involvement in Krugman's models of advertising communication. *Journalism Quarterly, 47,* 287-295.

Price, V. (1987). *Effects of communicating group conflicts of opinion: An experimental investigation.* Unpublished doctoral dissertation, Stanford University, Stanford, CA.

Ray, M. L. (1973). Marketing communication and the hierarchy of effects. In P. Clarke (Ed.), *New models for mass communication research* (pp. 147-176). Beverly Hills, CA: Sage.

Rice, B. (1988, March). The selling of lifestyles. *Psychology Today,* pp. 46-50.

Robertson, T. S. (1971). *Innovative behavior and communication.* New York: Holt, Rinehart & Winston.

Rogers, E. M. (1983). *Diffusion of innovations* (3rd ed.). New York: Free Press.

Rothschild, M. L., & Ray, M. L. (1974). Involvement and political advertising effect: An exploratory experiment. *Communication Research, 1,* 264–285.

Salmon, C. T. (1986). Perspectives on involvement in consumer and communication research. In B. Dervin & M. J. Voigt (Eds.), *Progress in communication sciences* (Vol. 7, pp. 243–269). Norwood, NJ: Ablex.

Schneider (aka Grunig), L. A. (1978). *Employee communication at a university-based R & D center: An analysis using Grunig's theory of communication behavior.* Unpublished master's thesis, University of Maryland, College Park.

Schwartz, D. F., & Glynn, C. J. (1990, June). *Issues management and corporate public relations: Perceptions of corporate planners and public relations professionals.* Paper presented at the meeting of the International Communication Association, Dublin.

Sherif, C. W., Sherif, M., & Nebergall, R. E. (1965). *Attitude and attitude change: The social judgment-involvement approach.* Westport, CT: Greenwood.

Slama, M. E., & Tashchian, A. (1985). Selected socioeconomic and demographic characteristics associated with purchasing involvement. *Journal of Marketing, 49*(Winter), 72–82.

Smith, W. R. (1978). Product differentiation and market segmentation as alternative marketing strategies. In C. G. Walters & D. P. Robin (Eds.), *Classics in marketing* (pp. 433–439). Santa Monica, CA: Goodyear.

Spicer, S. R. (1985). *Effectiveness of a fire department public information campaign.* Unpublished master's thesis, University of Maryland, College Park.

SRI International (1985). *VALS—Values and lifestyles of Americans.* Menlo Park, CA.

Srivastava, R. K., Alpert, M. I., & Shocker, A. D. (1984). A customer-oriented approach for determining market structures. *Journal of Marketing, 48*(Spring), 32–45.

Staff. (1989, July 31). Revamped VALS typology reflects a blending of societal values as psychographics turns toward purchasing behavior. *pr reporter,* pp. 1–2.

Stamm, K. R., & Grunig, J. E. (1977). Communication situations and cognitive strategies for the resolution of environmental issues. *Journalism Quarterly, 54,* 713–720.

Steiner, G. A., Miner, J. B., & Gray, E. R. (1982). *Management policy and strategy* (2nd ed.). New York: Macmillan.

Taylor, J. W. (1986). *Competitive marketing strategies.* Radnor, PA: Chilton.

Tichenor, P. J., Donohue, G. A., & Olien, C. N. (1977). Community research and evaluating community relations. *Public Relations Review, 3*(4), 96–109.

Tichenor, P. J., Donohue, G. A., & Olien, C. N. (1980). *Community conflict and the press.* Newbury Park, CA: Sage.

Turner, D. (1981). *Communication behavior of linking agents in the Maryland Cooperative Extension Service.* Unpublished master's thesis, University of Maryland, College Park.

Uyterhoeven, H. E. R., Ackerman, R. W., & Rosenblum, J. W. (1977). *Strategy and organization.* Homewood, IL: Irwin.

VanLeuven, J. K., & Slater, M. D. (1991). How publics, public relations, and the media shape the public opinion process. In L. A. Grunig & J. E. Grunig (Eds.), *Public relations research annual* (Vol. 3, pp. 165–178). Hillsdale, NJ: Lawrence Erlbaum Associates.

Vibbert, S. L. (1987, May). *Corporate communication and the management of issues.* Paper presented at the meeting of International Communication Association, Montreal.

Vibbert, S. L. (1988, September). *Managing issues and influencing public communication.* Paper presented at the meeting of the Herbert Quandt Foundation Transatlantic Forum, Philadelphia.

Waddell, D. G. (1979). *Employee communication at a multi-campus community college: An analysis using Grunig's communication behavior theory.* Unpublished master's thesis, University of Maryland, College Park.

Walters, C. G., & Bergiel, B. J. (1989). *Consumer behavior: A decision making approach.* Cincinnati: South-Western.

Webster, P. J. (1990). Strategic corporate public relations: What's the bottom line? *Public Relations Journal, 46*(2), 18–21.

Weick, K. E. (1979). *The social psychology of organizing* (2nd ed.). Reading, MA: Addison-Wesley.

Weiss, M. J. (1988). *The clustering of America*. New York: Harper & Row.

Wells, W. D., & Tigert, D. J. (1971). Activities, interests, and opinions. *Journal of Advertising Research, 11*(August), 27–35.

Wheelen, T., & Hunger, J. (1987). *Strategic management* (2nd ed.). Reading, MA: Addison-Wesley.

Wilson, L. J. (1990). Corporate issues management: An international view. *Public Relations Review, 16*(1), 40–51.

Winkleman, M. (1987). Their aim is true. *Public Relations Journal, 43*(August), 18–19, 22–23, 39.

Wright, C. R. (1986). *Mass communication: A sociological perspective* (3rd ed.). New York: Random House.

7 Evaluation of Public Relations Programs: What the Literature Tells Us About Their Effects

David M. Dozier
San Diego State University

William P. Ehling
Syracuse University

ABSTRACT

Once a public relations practitioner identifies the strategic publics for which communication programs are necessary, he or she should practice public relations by objectives *to maximize the success of those programs and their contribution to the long-term effectiveness of the organization. Communication managers should use realistic objectives to plan communication programs. Then, they should measure these objectives through research to determine the success of programs. Too often, however, both senior managers of the organization and public relations managers expect the equivalent of magical effects from those programs—getting publics to behave the way the organization wants them to behave. This chapter reviews research on communication effects and concludes that strong behavioral effects are unlikely in the short term. Cognitive effects are more likely in the short term; and symmetrical, strategic communication programs increase the likelihood that they will occur. Over the long term, then, short-term cognitive effects of symmetrical programs enhance the possibility of behavioral change—thus producing a relationship with strategic publics that is relatively free of conflict.*

The purpose of this chapter is to review two interrelated issues of great importance to public relations practitioners and communication managers. These issues can be posed as questions. First, what kinds of effects are possible consequences of public relations programs? To answer this question, the research literature from mass communication effects, cognitions, attitude formation and change, and persuasion are briefly reviewed. The second question is: How can communication program managers measure or evaluate the effectiveness of public relations programs?

These questions are important only if one accepts at least one presupposition. Made explicit, public relations and communication management are purposive activities. The news release, the employee newsletter, and the special event are all tools used to impact publics and management of organizations. Managed communication by an organization is not an end itself, but rather a means to an end. Conceptually, the effects achieved by public relations programs include awareness, knowledge, opinions, attitudes, and behavior of those affected by the program.

Although the presupposition of purpose seems imminently reasonable, many public relations practitioners and communication managers engage in communication and public relations activities as an end in themselves. They pursue public relations without goals and objectives, without purpose.

PUBLIC RELATIONS WITHOUT PURPOSE

Bell and Bell (1976) introduced the imagery of functional and functionary public relations to delineate what they saw as the growing schism between two approaches to the practice. *Functionary* public relations, they argued, simply is selling a favorable image of the organization, free of any environmental scanning, interpretation, and management counseling. The imagery of public relations as functionary can liken it to a hood ornament on an automobile. Highly visible and perhaps pleasing aesthetically, functionary public relations departments are regarded by the dominant coalition—and so regard themselves—as symbolic of a corporation or organization that has achieved sufficient size and resources to afford the "luxury" of public relations. As with hood ornaments, hard times (downsizing) often mean that functionary public relations departments are the first nonessentials to go.

Grunig and Hunt (1984) noted that top managers in organizations "just assumed their organizations needed a public relations department" but "seldom asked why" (p. 115). Noting the importance of program goals and objectives, they observed that communication managers frequently do not share that view: "They think in terms of process—how many press releases must they get out, when must the annual report be done, how can the latest media crisis be handled?—and not in terms of effects—why was the press release needed, what should the annual report communicate, how should the media ideally behave in a crisis?" (Grunig & Hunt, 1984, p. 115).

Broom (1986) used open-systems theory to explain activities of public relations programs without purpose. Using Stinchcombe's (1968, pp.

118–125) *historicist causal imagery* Broom conceptualized dynamics of functionary public relations:

> As the boundary between the organization and its environment becomes impermeable to environmental inputs, public relations structure and process increasingly reflect historical, routine and institutionalized behaviors. Explanations of public relations under these conditions call to mind the imagery of a perpetual motion machine—infinite, self-replicating causal loops with the original causes or motivations lost in history. The behaviors observed represent routine patterns of responses insensitive to changes in the environment. (p. 7)

According to Broom (1986), public relations departments first were organized perhaps in response to an environmental threat, such as extensive media criticism, a strike, or a factory explosion. On the other hand, as suggested by Grunig and Hunt (1984), a public relations department may be established by the dominant coalition because of the desire or preference to have one.

Once established, the department operates without regard to environmental change, replicating on an annual cycle the activities and programs of the previous year. A company hosts an annual retirement dinner or "adopts" an inner-city high school because "that's what we did last year." Endless recycling of past program activities is reinforced through selective hiring and training of new staff, through the authority of senior practitioners who direct and restrict organizational behavior of new staffers, and through records kept of past activities. Budgetary commitment to public relations departments become institutionalized and routine. Next year's communication budget is an incremental adjustment of last year's budget.

Institutional routine is reinforced by "sunk costs" associated with the status quo (Broom, 1986). To reconfigure public relations programs in response to changing environments requires more resources than simple replication of activities deemed adequate previously. Budgeting is easier if past experience serves as a guide, whereas budgeting in anticipation of future demands is more problematic. As Broom argued, "public relations units and activities become survivors of routine decision making" (p. 9).

Hermetically sealed in closed-system decision making—organizational boundaries impervious to environmental inputs—historically driven public relations programs suggest images of organizational *ritual,* of largely symbolic activities, the meanings of which have been lost in organizational antiquity. Such communication and public relations programs have little use for environmental scanning or program impact evaluation, because they are not conceived as effects oriented in the first place. Rather, the communication technician produces communication products as ends in themselves.

In a 1988 survey of International Association of Business Communicators members, the IABC Research Foundation (1989) found that 35% of college-educated communicators in the United States majored in journalism, dwarfing the second most popular major category of English and/or speech. In Canada, 26% of college-educated communicators majored in journalism. This fact is related significantly to viewing communication as an end in itself. Schooled in the objective news style, many journalists adopt a mixed libertarian/social responsibility ethical framework. Since the advent of wire services, journalists carefully have distinguished objective news from commentary and opinion. The prevailing ethic is that journalists "objectively" select and write news, leaving readers to decide for themselves what sense to make of the "facts." Journalists, then, are taught not to think about maintenance or change of attitudes and behavior of audiences. Editors and colleagues reward this behavior in the workplace. Small wonder that communicators in organizations, often reporters before they were practitioners, find satisfaction in communication activities as ends in themselves.

Broom and Dozier (1983) argued that when the communication function in organizations is not concerned with effects or measuring them, communication "is relegated to the status of an output function that executives systematically exclude from decision making and strategic planning" (p. 5). In this role (see chapter 12 for an extensive review of roles), "practitioners operate as 'journalists-in-residence,' hired on the basis of their journalistic skills, experience and contacts" (p. 5). They noted that journalistic training does not provide communicators with strategic planning, environmental scanning, and impact evaluation skills required to operate in organizational settings driven by a management-by-objectives (MBO) philosophy.

In developing their typology of research applications in public relations and communication management, Broom and Dozier (1990) used a continuum conceptualized by Robinson (1966, p. 48). At one end of the continuum is the individualistic stage of the practice, wherein public relations and communication management are practiced as a creative art. The practice is subjective, intuitive, and personal, with little use for social or behavioral research. Practitioners make decisions by the "seat of their pants." At the other end of Robinson's continuum is the scientifically derived knowledge state, where decisions are based on the "best available evidence." The practice is objective and rigorous, based on application of empirical knowledge and social/behavioral theory.

At the seat-of-the-pants end of the continuum, Broom and Dozier (1990) identified the functionary, historicist, closed-system approach to communication and public relations as the *no-research* approach. They stated that job descriptions "indicate prescribed activities to be carried out and call for a minimum of management-level decision making. The 'goal' under this approach is to generate a steady flow of public relations output, usually in the form of communication from management to internal and external publics" (p. 14). Under this approach, the goals and objectives of communication activities are simply to communicate. Process is outcome. Program impact is measured by pounds of news clippings.

PUBLIC RELATIONS BY OBJECTIVES

Once communication is properly regarded as a means to an end, a tool for achieving some desired end state, communication managers and public relations practitioners must consider the effects of public relations programs. In organizations where an MBO philosophy prevails, communication managers must set goals and objectives for public relations programs.

Goals are generalized end states that programs are designed to achieve, typically too abstract to be directly measured. Program objectives are more specific, and success or failure in achieving objectives can be measured. By achieving program objectives that are linked logically to a goal, attainment of a goal can be inferred by achieving objectives (Grunig & Hunt, 1984, pp. 116–117).

Cutlip, Center, and Broom (1985, p. 232) provided a 10-step outline for preparing public relations plans. In their scheme, program goals are abstract, generalized end states. Objectives are specific to publics delineated in the plan. Broom and Dozier (1990, p. 44) stated that an objective, in order to be used in measuring program impact, must specify (a) the target public to be affected, (b) the nature of the intended change, (c) the specific knowledge, attitude, or behavior to be achieved, (d) the amount of change desired, and (e) a target date for achieving the objective.

As practitioners move away from seat-of-the-pants practices, as they abandon the notion that communication is an end in itself, they must consider realistically the kinds of effects programs can achieve. What kind of impact can public relations programs exert on awareness, cognitions, attitudes, and behavior of publics and dominant coalitions of their organizations? In this regard, practitioners often invoke a "strong effects" view of communication, especially mass communication.

Grunig and Hunt (1984, p. 124) graphically illustrated the strong effects assumptions of many communicators. The domino model illustrated in Fig. 7.1 implies strong causal linkage between communication (or messages) from an organization and direct, immediate impact on the knowledge, attitudes, and behavior of publics. The domino model of program impact is most consistent with a communicator's self-image, for it implies communication activities automatically impact knowledge, attitudes, and behavior of publics and management. This model also reduces the dissonance many

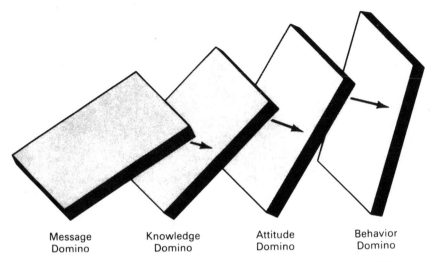

| Message | Knowledge | Attitude | Behavior |
| Domino | Domino | Domino | Domino |

FIGURE 7.1 Domino model of communication effects. From Grunig and Hunt (1984). Reprinted by permission.

practitioners associate with research or evaluation. Research and evaluation skills are not widely disseminated among practitioners (Dozier, 1990) and many practitioners find quantitative methods that such research requires unattractive and forbidding (Dozier, 1984).

THE LITERATURE ON COMMUNICATION EFFECTS

The problem with the domino effects model is that the last 50 years of communication research indicates that the model is wrong. Communication, especially mass communication, does not exert strong, direct, and powerful effects on publics. At one point, one scholar argued that media exert only limited effects, principally to reinforce existing perceptions, opinions, and attitudes of audiences (Klapper, 1961). Since Klapper's seminal work, which designates the low point in posited effects of mass communication, several communication researchers have developed theories of indirect and change-specific communication effects of relevance to public relations practitioners.

Agenda setting is a mass communication effect posited since Klapper (1961). Both administrative and critical scholars have posited that media messages about issues set the public's agenda regarding what is important and what is not (Larson, 1986; McCombs & Shaw, 1972). Public relations practitioners, in turn, help set the media agenda — help determine the issues attended to by the media and the manner in which issues are framed — by subsidizing the collection and organization of information journalists need to create news (Gandy, 1982). Public relations practitioners provide, on a selective basis, the raw material journalists need to construct news. Practitioners thus play a role in framing and shaping media coverage of an organization and issues important to an organization. Media coverage, in turn, shapes public perceptions of the relative importance of some issues over others. Some issues never are addressed in the media, critical scholars assert. Media coverage exerts power through silence, by telling us what not to think about (Katz, 1987).

A second post-Klapper (1961) development in mass communication research is emergence of the uses and gratifications perspective (Blumler & Katz, 1974; Katz, 1987; Rosengren, Wenner & Palmgren, 1986). This perspective is useful to communication managers and public relations practitioners because it reverses direction of Lasswell's source-message-channel-audience chain. Audiences are conceived as active participants, selecting media channels and content to satisfy their own empirically measurable gratifications. Katz (1987), an early researcher in uses and gratifications of media, indicated that such research since the 1970s has been "too mentalistic, too empiricistic, too functionalistic, too psychologistic" (p. S37). Nevertheless, the notion of an active audience "entering into 'negotiation' with a text" is useful to communicators, because outcomes of such negotiations are uncertain. Although audiences are constrained by messages sent, decoding mediated messages is "conceptualized as a process of interpersonal interaction in 'interpretive communities' which, in turn, act as gatekeepers" (Katz, 1987, p. S38). The concept of negotiation, rather than domination or persuasion, is key to understanding effects of communication and public relations programs.

Research to date suggests that claims of communication effects must be circumspect. Wallack (1989) derided what he labeled "mass media fantasy," a belief that any problem "can be adequately addressed if the right message could be communicated to the right people in just the right way at the right time" (p. 354). This is the modern communicator's updated version of the "magic bullet" or "hypodermic needle" theory of powerful mass media effects (Wimmer & Dominick, 1987, p. 6). In fact, communication managers and public relations practitioners do not possess powerful tools for impacting publics, especially if mass-mediated messages are primary to the communication program.

Three factors mitigate the despair some communication managers may experience when they learn the mass media fantasy is false. The first mitigating factor is *choice over effects sought* from public relations and communication management. Behavioral effects are relatively difficult to achieve, but cognitive effects have been achieved in many communication programs (Rice & Atkins, 1989). The second mitigating factor is the *activism of relevant publics*. Targeting public relations programs at the general public, as traditional practitioners of a journalistic orientation have done, makes little sense as that public grows to over 5 billion people globally. Indeed, organizations need to direct communication programs at only relatively small numbers of people who are in some way linked to or affected by the organization. The third mitigating factor is the *opportunity for symmetry* in planning, implementing, and evaluating public relations programs. Each factor is considered next.

Choice Over Effects Sought

Figure 7.1 illustrates the domino model of communication and public relations program effects. As Grunig and Hunt (1984) indicated, the model is flawed because it assumes each domino affects subsequent dominos in the chain of program effects. The model is also flawed because effects need not occur in the sequence suggested by the model (Grunig & Hunt, 1984). Suppose, however, we take certainty out of the domino model. Suppose there is only a 40% chance that the public targeted by a communication program actually is exposed to (reached by) messages communicated through the program. There are only two chances in five that the Message Domino will fall. Suppose that there is only a 50% chance that the public reached by messages actually will learn (know) the key message points communicated. There is only one chance in two that the Knowledge Domino will fall. Further, this effect occurs only among those reached by the message. Further suppose there is only a 20% chance that those who learn the key message points of the communication program actually will adopt opinions or attitudes consistent with program objectives. Finally, suppose only 10% of those holding the desired opinion behave in a manner consistent with those opinions.

What is the chance, then, of public relations messages being successfully communicated to the target public, resulting in knowledge change, attitude change, and—finally—behavior change? The answer can be computed by multiplying all probabilities together, as indicated in the following box:

Message >>> Knowledge >>> Attitude >>> Behavior			
.40 $\times$ .50 $\times$ .20 $\times$ .10 $=$ 0.0004			

The chance of achieving behavior specified as a program objective with any particular member of the target public is 0.04 percent, or only 4 chances in 10,000! A practitioner might find better odds for success in Las Vegas or Atlantic City.

Broom and Dozier (1990) underscored this same point in their discussion of program objectives and levels of program impact criteria. The levels are displayed graphically in Fig. 7.2 In their diagram, program dissemination and impact criteria can be conceptualized at no less than 10 different levels. These range from a count of the number of messages sent or activities executed (lower level dissemination criteria) to such sweeping impact as social or cultural change (higher level impact criteria). The higher the criterion level, the more difficult that criterion is to achieve. But higher level criteria are those of greatest value to organizations.

Although it is easy to count messages sent or public relations activities executed, these actions in themselves are of no particular value to organizations. Marker (1977) described his experience at the Armstrong Cork

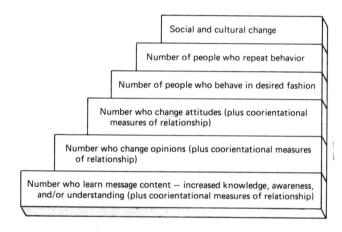

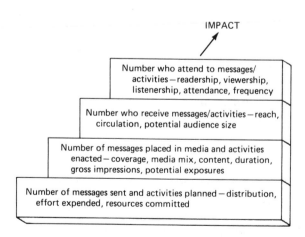

FIGURE 7.2   Levels of implementation and impact criteria for communication and public relations programs. From Broom and Dozier (1990). Adapted by permission.

Company when he laid an impressive clip file on his boss's desk to justify the company's public relations efforts. If clips were laid end to end, Marker told his boss, the trail of favorable publicity would stretch from one end of the building to the other. Marker reported: "I leaned back in my chair, feeling confident that the day was won. And then it came, the question no one had ever asked before: 'But what's all this worth to us?' " (p. 52). Marker's boss sought higher level criteria for measuring the impact of Armstrong's communication and public relations programs. Marker's boss was concerned with higher level strategic benefit of communication to the organization, its bottom-line import. What Marker provided was lower order criteria measuring program dissemination.

If management accepted Marker's (1977) lower level criteria for measuring program success or failure, communication practitioners could release a collective sigh of relief. Pragmatically, lower level criteria are easier to achieve than such higher level criteria as getting publics to engage in and repeat desired behavior. Further, lower level criteria can be met in a shorter period of time whereas higher level criteria can be met only through much effort and over long periods of time. Lower level criteria (Fig. 7.2) are like the initial domino in the communication effects model (Fig. 7.1); this domino is relatively easy to impact, to knock over.

The tension between what is doable and what is beneficial increases when communication managers must assess the value of organizational and corporate communication to society as a whole. As indicated in Fig. 7.2, impact criteria at the highest level involve social and cultural change. These criteria are difficult to achieve, requiring considerable resources and time to occur. The professional imperative of public service and social responsibility (Cutlip et al., 1985, p. 72) may be at odds sometimes with short-term organizational objectives. Broom and Dozier (1990) asked "what are the consequences on public health, the health care system, the insurance industry, etc., of Tobacco Institute programs designed to contradict reported research findings of the effects of smoking?" (p. 86). Not only are social and cultural change hard to achieve (or block, as the Tobacco Institute is discovering), organizational goals may be at odds with the larger public interest and social responsibility. This conflict, however, is reduced when organizations pursue symmetrical communication and public relations goals and objectives. This issue is considered further in the Opportunities for Symmetry section later.

In designing communication programs, practitioners must consider the tension between the two meanings of effectiveness. To be effective, a program must be doable. Communication managers must have some confidence both in their ability to implement the program as planned and that the planned activities—the action and communication strategies of the program—are likely to achieve goals and objectives specified. To be effective, a program must result in maintenance or change in relationships with target publics. The art of strategic communication management is determining what level of impact criteria (see Fig. 7.2) provides the best balance between what is doable and what is beneficial. Important to such decision making is increased sophistication about publics, made possible by recent research on communication and segmentation.

The Activism of Relevant Publics

As noted earlier, the general public is of no relevance to organizations. Nor do organizations have resources to establish and maintain relationships with all peoples and all other organizations. An essential first step in planning communication and public relations programs is to determine who is involved or affected by the problem situation that motivates the program. Conceptually, publics are defined by their connection to an organization in a particular situation. However, a conceptual understanding of linkage between an organization and relevant publics does not provide the operational measures of publics. Broom and Dozier (1990, pp. 32–36) identified nine characteristics or referents that can be used to operationalize publics for communication programs. These include geographics, demographics, psychographics, covert power, position, reputation, membership, role in decision making, and communication behavior based on situational theory.

Geographic boundaries of publics are often useful gross indicators, essentially by eliminating people and organizations outside a geographic area not relevant to the program. Demographic characteristics—age, sex, income, education, and so forth—provide another gross indicator of publics. Used alone, as frequently is done in practice, demographic characteristics are too crude to provide much guidance in program planning and evaluation. Psychographics, the psychological and lifestyle characteristics of individuals, provide additional cross-situational indicators of publics. Some individuals exert covert power to influence decisions in a community; identifying those at the top of the power pyramid (through depth interviews and analyzing how past decisions have been made) provides another indication of relevant publics. Individuals who hold overt positions of influence—doctors, lawyers, teachers, financial analysts, business reporters, and so forth—also can be identified as relevant publics through positions they hold in organizations or professions. The reputations of individuals described by others as knowledgeable or influential concerning organizations or issues can be used to identify relevant publics. Membership in organizations often provides a convenient mechanism for identifying relevant publics. Studying the role of individuals in decision-making processes (through observation, document studies, interviews, and so forth) also can be used to identify relevant publics.

The eight classification or segmentation techniques above tend to be cross-situational. These classifications exist largely independent of time or situation. When communication and public relations programs become institutionalized, when they are perpetuated by historical causes, cross-situational segmentation strategies make decisions about publics routine and simple. Unfortunately, they also make decisions about publics largely irrelevant to specific problems and situations.

Grunig's situational theory of publics (Grunig & Hunt, 1984) provides an approach to defining publics that captures dynamics of changing linkages between organizations and those involved or affected by them. "Publics come and go," Grunig and Hunt asserted, depending on "what an organization does and how people and organizations in the environment react to that organizational behavior" (p. 138). Organizations *create* publics when organizational actions have consequences for other organizations or groupings of people. These become potential interpenetrating systems which may conflict with organizations, limiting their ability to pursue organizational goals. Ideally, organizations seek autonomy, the ability to pursue goals unfettered by interpenetrating systems. In actuality, organizations are linked to organizational environments in four ways (Esman, 1972). *Enabling* linkages to government, regulatory agencies, and the like legitimize organizations, providing them the right to exist and pursue their goals. *Functional* linkages provide organizations needed inputs, such as raw materials and labor, and outputs, or customers or clients. *Normative* linkages, such as to professional or industry associations, provide connections to similar organizations to assist collective efforts to solve shared problems. *Diffused* linkages are organizational connections to groupings of individuals who are not themselves part of an organization. Minority relations, community relations, and environmental relations are attempts to manage linkages with diffused groupings.

Briefly, organizations must manage enabling and functional linkages, because organizations cannot pursue their goals without them. Governments, regulatory agencies, suppliers, labor, and customers all create consequences for organizations. Organizations selectively manage diffuse linkages when organizations create consequences for them. Sometimes diffused publics organize to create consequences for organizations. The more turbulent an organization's environment, the more linkages the organization must manage with its environment and the more rapidly those environmental linkages change.

Publics are formed when people face a similar problem, recognize that a problem exists, and organize to do something about that problem. If there is no common problem that connect people together in some way, such people are a *nonpublic*. When people face a common problem, but fail to recognize it, they are a *latent* public, a potential public relations problem waiting to happen. Once people recognize they have a common problem, they become an *aware* public. When they organize to do something about the problem, they become *active* publics.

Active publics are the only ones that generate consequences for organizations. Because communication managers selectively must use scarce resources to build and maintain relationships with publics, active publics would seem the only ones of concern to organizations. Such a viewpoint is reactive, however. Communication with active publics is extremely difficult. Active publics may well discount any communication from organizations, for they often use alternative information sources to reinforce attitudes already constructed. When an active public circles corporate headquarters with picket lines or boycotts an organization's products, practitioners often only can react.

Proactive communication management and public relations requires information gathering from—and possible communication with—aware and latent publics. Communication is more likely to be effective with aware publics than with active publics. With latent publics, on the other hand, communication is difficult because people in this category do not recognize a problem. They are unlikely to either process information or seek information about a problem they do not recognize.

Information *processing* is passive communication behavior wherein new information is processed more or less at random whenever the individual can receive it with little or no personal effort. Information *seeking* is active communication behavior wherein people seek out information and work to make sense of it. Information actively sought has greater impact than information processed or ignored altogether (Grunig & Hunt, 1984, pp. 146–151).

Problem recognition increases the likelihood of processing or seeking information, as well as the probability that communication effects will occur. *Constraint recognition,* on the other hand, decreases the probability of information processing, information seeking, and communication effects. Constraint recognition is the "extent to which people perceive there are constraints—or obstacles—in a situation that limits their freedom to plan their own behavior" (Grunig & Hunt, 1984, p. 151). When people feel they have little effective freedom, when the situation seems highly constrained, they are unlikely to process or seek out information about a problem. Communication about a problem, under this condition, is likely to be relatively ineffective.

Level of involvement is the extent to which people connect themselves to a situation (Grunig & Hunt, 1984, p. 152). Level of involvement increases information-seeking behavior and reduces passive information processing. Highly involved individuals typically have high problem recognition and low constraint recognition (Grunig, 1979). In a systemic manner, these variables contribute to increasing activism of individuals around a recognized common problem to which they feel connected and which they believe they can do something about. These individuals communicate with each other and organize activities to attack the problem. At a meso level of analysis, a public evolves from an unaware, latent status to aware status to active status as a function of these variables.

High and low levels of involvement, problem recognition, and constraint recognition can be combined together to create eight different types of publics. Although eight publics can be defined in this manner, only some occur with sufficient frequency to warrant attention. In a study of communication and activism of Maryland residents regarding four controversial issues, Grunig (1982) was able to assign 200 respondents to each of the eight publics for each of the four issues. In addition, he was able to measure information processing, information seeking, and whether members of each public had acted regarding each issue (letter writing, product boycotts, attending rallies, etc.). The study, although limited to a single state and four controversial issues, provides an empirical basis for assessing the relative frequency of each type of public, as well as a test of the situational theory's predictions.

Table 7.1 displays four situational publics with the largest percentage of respondents. The largest number of Maryland residents (about one third) fell into what Grunig (1982) labeled the low-involvement, fatalistic public. These individuals do not recognize a problem nor do they see themselves connected to consequences of an organization's behavior. In addition, they do not feel there is anything they could do about the situation anyway. They have low problem recognition, low levels of involvement, and high con-

TABLE 7.1
Types of Situational Publics, Communication, and Likelihood of Behavior

Name of Public	% of Resp.	% Info. Process	% Info. Seeking	% Level of Active Behavior*
Low-involvement, fatalistic	34	62	18	7
High-involvement, constrained	19	92	58	25
High-involvement, Problem-facing	15	96	74	48
High-involvement, fatalistic	12	76	33	13
TOTAL:	80			

*Individuals engage in active behavior when they write a letter, boycott products, attend meetings, and so forth. If individuals engaged in any such activity, they were counted in this column.

straint recognition. As predicted by theory, this public processes and seeks little information about the focal issue and is highly unlikely to act.

Next frequent was the high-involvement, constrained public. These individuals, about 19% of the sample, recognize a problem and feel personally connected to it. But they feel they cannot make a difference in how the issue is handled. High-involvement, constrained publics are more likely than low-involvement, fatalistic publics to process and seek information about the issue. Despite constraint recognition, these individuals are over three times more likely to have acted (wrote letters, boycott products, etc.) than the low-involvement, fatalistic public.

Third frequent was the high-involvement, problem-facing public, constituting 15% of the sample. This public recognizes the problem and feels personally connected to it. In addition, these individuals feel that their efforts can make a difference. These individuals process information at about the same level as the high-involvement, constrained public but actively seek information about the issue much more frequently. These individuals are nearly twice as likely to have acted toward the issue than the aforementioned high-involvement, constrained public.

Fourth frequent was the high-involvement, fatalistic public. These individuals, about 12% of the sample, feel personally connected to the problem. At the same time, they feel there is little they can do about the situation and they do not stop to think about it. Despite recognized personal connections, these individuals have, in essence, detached from what they regard as a hopeless situation. They exhibit low levels of information processing and seeking and are unlikely to have acted. The remaining combinations of involvement, problem recognition, and constraint recognition constitute only 20% of the sample. They are excluded from this analysis.

In addition, Grunig (1982) measured message retention and cognitions by each public. Message retention for the four publics previously discussed was inconsistent with theory. Grunig and Hunt (1984, p. 158) explained that message retention was measured inadequately with a single indicator. Regarding cognitions about issues (either favorable or unfavorable to business), the three high-involvement publics were more likely to have formed cognitions than the low-involvement, fatalistic public. Relatively high incidences of cognition (as operationalized in the study) for all high-involvement publics, however, made discrimination between these highly constrained publics impossible.

Situational variables, then, affect ways individuals use communication about an issue and predict levels of activism toward an issue. What patterns emerge when an individual's activism is aggregated over several issues? In the Maryland survey, Grunig and Hunt (1984) said that some individuals make up the *activist* public. They are highly involved and problem facing for all four issues studied, meaning they perceive many issues as involving recognized problems that they feel they can do something about. The *apathetic* public is made up of individuals not involved and fatalistic about all four issues. The *universal salience* public consists of individuals generally apathetic about issues except those that directly affect nearly everyone in the population, such as a gasoline shortage. The *single-issue* public consists of individuals highly involved and problem facing about only one issue, whereas apathetic about other issues.

Grunig's situational theory of publics has evolved over the last 20 years. Specifically, Grunig and Childers (1988) posited both internal and external dimensions of level of involvement, problem recognition, and constraint recognition. Internal level of involvement is essentially ego involvement (Sherif, Sherif, & Nebergall, 1965) and such involvement makes individuals resistant to attitude change. Regarding communication behavior, individuals with high internal involvement with an issue are likely to actively communicate in order to form cognitions supportive of existing attitudes (Grunig & Childers, 1988, p. 11).

External involvement, in contrast, is an individual's expectation that an issue has significant personal consequences in the world (Petty & Cacioppo, 1986, p. 82). Individuals with high external involvement with an issue are likely to develop reasoned and well-founded attitudes. Petty and Cacioppo's *elaboration likelihood model* predicts that high external involvement leads individuals to follow the *central route* to attitudes, objectively evaluating incoming communication to elaborate on information already received. People with lower external involvement follow a *peripheral route* to constructing attitudes. Less concerned with the quality of persuasive arguments, they think less about the issue and depend on such quick peripheral cues as source credibility to develop attitudes. These concepts are similar to Grunig's (Grunig & Hunt, 1984) information seeking (central route) and information processing (peripheral route).

Grunig and Childers (1988) distinguished internal and external problem recognition. Internal problem recognition is an intellectual awareness of a problem that piques curiosity and stimulates understanding as an end in itself. External problem recognition is a pragmatic recognition of a real-world problem requiring a real-world solution. In a similar manner, Grunig and Childers distinguished internal and external constraint recognition. Internal constraint recognition is the inverse of Bandura's (1977) *efficacy expectation,* the "conviction that one can successfully execute the behavior required to produce the outcomes" (p. 79). External constraint recognition reverses the direction of Bandura's *outcome expectations,* an individual's "estimate that a given behavior will lead to certain outcomes" (p. 79).

Situational variables of problem recognition, constraint recognition, and level of involvement (both internal and external) are posited to affect the construction of cognitions about issues. Acts of cognitive construction affect the way people use communication about issues. When a situation is highly involving, communication that stimulates thinking is most likely to result in the individual forming or changing attitudes. Lasting behavioral effects can occur when attitudes are formed through elaborated cognitions, highly developed constructions about an issue. Cognitive changes stimulated through communication can cause short-term behavioral changes when "such behaviors are specific and easy to implement" (Grunig & Childers, 1988, p. 17).

Cognitions about issues can be decomposed into depth and breadth of processing. Related to long-term memory, *depth of processing* is thinking about an issue through construction of complex schema where cognitive units are related and interconnected in many ways. *Breadth of processing* means the "number of elaborations" (Anderson & Reder, 1979, p. 391), the accumulation of many cognitive units in memory. "Breadth represented *quantity* of elaborations, depth *quality* of elaborations" (Grunig & Childers, 1988, p. 18). Grunig and Childers concluded that communication programs can alter the individual's cognitive breadth about an issue in a limited way, but communication programs alone are posited to be ineffective in changing cognitive depth.

Rich theoretical development in cognitive effects of communication under different situational characteristics provides fertile soil for empirical studies. Studies of cognitive effects of communication depart from past studies in communication and public relations. Much early research in communication and public relations studied persuasion. According to Grunig (1990), "many of the researchers studying the effects of individual messages, campaigns, or the mass media still cling to the idea that communication must persuade (change attitudes or behaviors) to be effective" (p. 8). Waning interest in persuasion among public relations scholars is not just reflective of limited effects of persuasion in empirical media studies. Persuasion is less relevant than other processes (such as negotiation) when a symmetrical model of public relations is practiced. This issue is considered in the next section of this chapter.

Grunig's situational theory of publics, which explains both communication behavior and activism, is enriched by theories of cognition. What practical use can communication managers make of situational and cognitive theory? Grunig's measures of problem recognition, constraint recognition, and level of involvement (see, e.g., Grunig & Hunt, 1984, pp. 150–151) provide powerful early-warning indications of emerging publics. Situational variables suggest whether the organization should respond programmatically to them. As such, situational variables should be measured routinely whenever communication managers scan the organizational environment.

Environmental scanning (Dozier, 1990) is the "detection of environmental turbulence or change likely to affect the homeostasis of the system" (p. 5). In practical terms, environmental scanning is remaining sensitive to "what's going on out there." Practitioners use both formal and informal information-gathering techniques to scan organizational environments. Once the practitioner detects a situation that involves or affects other organizations or groupings of individuals, measures of problem recognition, constraint recognition, and level of involvement should be made of publics affected.

Despite important theoretical developments in academic research, program research by communication practitioners remains innovative and largely under-utilized (Dozier, 1990). In the final analysis, whether public relations programs have demonstrable impact must be determined on a case-by-case basis. To do so, public relations practitioners must incorporate pretest and posttest measures of impact into every public relations program (Broom & Dozier, 1990). Public relations by objectives, including systematic evaluation of program impact, remains in its infancy. Dozier (pp. 18–19) provided evidence that, when program research is done at all, informal information-gathering techniques are favored over more rigorous scientific research. Broom and Dozier (pp. 74–75) argued that every public relations program is a field experiment. The communication program is the treatment; knowledge, attitudes, and/or behavior are the outcomes. Few communication and public relations programs are executed with that perspective in mind (Dozier, 1990). Core questions at the operational level about communication and public relations effects remain largely unanswered. Until professional communicators integrate evaluation research into the routine operation of programs, such linkage between managed communication and program impact will remain elusive.

The Opportunity for Symmetry

This chapter is concerned with the effects of communication and public relations programs—and how to measure them. Typically, effects are conceived as program effects on publics. This presupposition is asymmetrical, however, for it conceives of communication and public relations as something organizations do to—rather than with—people. The presumed objective is to get publics to do what organizations want them to. This presupposition assumes that communication programs are essentially persuasive and that public relations is essentially manipulative. As indicated earlier, the literature on communication effects provides sound pragmatic reasons for reevaluating the asymmetrical presupposition. Asymmetrical public relations programs are very likely to fail. The practitioner's arsenal of persuasive, manipulative tools are for the most part inadequate for the task.

The bleak outlook for successful communication programs improves considerably when symmetrical public relations is practiced. Chapter 11 provides a detailed discussion of the three asymmetrical models of public relations (press agentry, public information, and two-way asymmetrical) and the single symmetrical model. Discussion here is restricted to the significance of symmetry to program effectiveness. Based on what is known about communication effects, symmetrical programs are inherently more likely to achieve symmetrical goals and objectives than are asymmetrical programs. This is because symmetrical programs seek different kinds of effects and direct program efforts in directions typically ignored in asymmetrical programs.

As defined by Grunig and Hunt (1984), the symmetrical model views public relations as dialogue, both in terms of communication and in terms of effect. In two-way communication between publics and top management, "the public should be just as likely to persuade the organization's management to change attitudes or behavior as the organization is likely to change the publics' attitudes or behavior" (p. 23). Communicators who view public relations as symmetrical look to research on conflict resolution and negotiation — rather than persuasion and media effects — to guide program planning. In some respects, top management is as much a target of program efforts as are internal and external publics.

Cutlip et al. (1985) contributed two concepts important to symmetrical public relations: *action strategies* and *coorientation*. In the 10-step public relations planning process, action strategies are the first steps implemented. Action strategies are "steps taken to change the organization's policies, procedures, products, services, and behavior to better serve the mutual interests of the organization and its publics" (p. 258). Action strategies are program responses to "a deep look inside," an internal situation analysis that examines "perceptions and actions of key actors in the organization, the structure and process of organizational units somehow related to the problem, and history of the organization's involvement" (p. 205).

Action strategies are operational manifestations of symmetrical communication and public relations. Building action strategies into every communication program presupposes that mutually beneficial relationships with publics involve adaption and adjustment of both parties. Dominant coalitions of organizations may not, in fact, share symmetrical presuppositions. Chapter 18 discusses the concept of power in communication and public relations. To advocate the public interest in organizations dominated by asymmetrical thinking requires that the top communication manager be part of the dominant coalition. In addition, the emerging standards of the public relations profession, which incorporate symmetrical thinking, help clarify the appropriateness of such advocacy and legitimize such behavior.

Regarding *effectiveness* of communication management, the symmetrical model is inherently more efficacious because it assumes that the knowledge, attitudes, and behavior of both top management and publics are subject to change. Communication managers are more successful moving two parties closer together than converting one party (publics) over wholly to the other party's (dominant coalition) perspective. Application of game theory to communication management suggests that public relations is a mixed-motive game when played by rules of symmetry. Asymmetrical public relations is a zero-sum game where one party wins only when the other party loses. Gossen and Sharp (1987) provided an example of program effectiveness based on what they termed *dispute resolution:*

> An industrial manufacturer begins to build a new plant, only to find the neighborhood organizing to stop the project. Immediately, the manufacturer structures and implements a "win-win" process to resolve the dispute involving themselves, the neighbors, an area economic development group, and the ultimate decision makers: city officials. As a result of the negotiation, the manufacturer gets the okay for construction; the neighbors get job guarantees, an attractive greenbelt encircling the plant, and an agreement for heavy equipment to be operated in the daytime only. The economic development group is credited with another job-attracting success. (p. 35)

Dispute resolution is a process of identifying needs and interests of stakeholders and managing a step-by-step process of negotiation that leads to a win-win solution to a problem. Gossen and Sharp argued that zero-sum solutions to problems are short-lived, because key stakeholders remain dissatisfied. In terms of situational theory, dissatisfied stakeholders remain an aware public that may spring to activism as situations change and constraints are reduced. The two-way symmetrical model (see chapter 11) is similar to Gossen and Sharp's "unbiased self interest" where "the corporation puts the total community interest ahead of its own, in hopes of getting short-term and long-term benefits" (p. 35).

Setting goals and measurable objectives for communication and public relations programs constitutes an innovation in the practice of public relations and communication management. However, the asymmetrical presupposition permeates goals and objectives that specify how communication programs will change (or maintain) awareness, cognitions, attitudes, and behavior of target publics. The parallel innovation of using research to plan, monitor, and evaluate the impact of communication programs frequently is rooted in the two-way asymmetrical model (see chapter 11).

Jones (1975) defined public relations audits (a loose research technique) as asymmetrical when she said audits involve (a) doing interviews with top management to determine the organization's position on key issues, (b) surveying publics to learn their views on the same issues, (c) determining the gap between the two, and (d) recommending communication programs to close the gap. Jones's recommendations, however, all focus on changing knowledge and perceptions of publics.

Dozier (1990) found that practitioners use three research approaches (clusters of activities) to scan environments and to plan, monitor, and evaluate communication programs. They include informal research, mixed research, and scientific research. In a 1987 study of IABC members in the United States, Canada, and the United Kingdom (Dozier, 1990, pp. 22–23), all three research approaches were used frequently in organizations using the two-way asymmetrical model. Research is less frequently used in organizations practicing the two-way symmetrical model, and such research follows the mixed approach. Scientific research is not correlated with the two-way symmetrical model.

Broom and Dozier (1990) utilized the coorientation model to suggest ways that symmetrical goals and objectives can be set for communication programs and how the impact of such programs can be evaluated. The coorientation model is illustrated in Fig. 7.3. The coorientation model directs communication managers and public relations practitioners to examine perceptions that dominant coalitions and publics hold about issues—and about each other. The coorientation model suggests three relationships between the views or perceptions of the dominant coalition and publics. The first relationship is the level of agreement between *Corporate Views of Issue* (see Fig. 7.3) and *A Public's Views of Issue*. This is the relationship researched when practitioners use Jones's (1975) approach to public relations audits. This relationship is also frequently the focus of symmetrical communication programs, wherein both management and publics adjust and adapt to the other party.

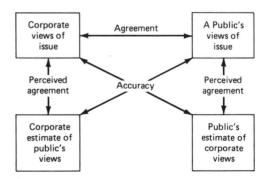

FIGURE 7.3 The coorientation model of relationships between organizations and publics. From Broom and Dozier (1990). Reprinted by permission.

The dominant coalition and publics act and react to each other based on perceptions of the other party. Often perceptions are misperceptions and public relations problems result. How accurate is the public's perception of the organization's views on an issue? How accurate is the dominant coalition's perceptions of the publics' views on an issue? The international boycott of Nestlé's products in the 1970s and 1980s — in response to Nestlé's aggressive marketing of infant milk formula in developing nations — culminated in condemnation of the practice by the World Health Organization in 1981 (Grunig & Hunt, 1984, p. 51). Arguably, the Nestlé company made a marketing decision based on an inaccurate perception of public views on the issue in industrial nations. Public relations programs can set goals and objectives that focus on improving perceptual accuracy of publics and the dominant coalition. This does not necessarily mean that disagreements about issues are resolved as a result of the program. Such communication programs, however, would reduce conflict based on misperceptions of the other party's views.

The model suggests that four coorientation states are created by varying degrees of agreement, accuracy, and perceived agreement (Broom & Dozier, 1990). A state of *true consensus* exists when organizations and publics share the same views or evaluations of an issue, and both parties know that such agreement exists. In such situations, communication programs seek to maintain consensus through two-way communication.

A state of *dissensus* exists when dominant coalitions and publics hold conflicting views about an issue, and both parties are aware of the disagreement. In dissensus, techniques of dispute resolution, involving adaptation and adjustment by both dominant coalitions and publics, should be used — and quickly! Gossen and Sharp (1987) pointed out that dispute resolution works best when stakeholders still retain some flexibility. Indeed, the process is "designed to prevent stakeholders' interests from becoming hardened, irreconcilable positions" (p. 35). Premature communication through the mass media is actually counterproductive in early stages of resolving dissensus. According to Gossen and Sharp, "everyone should agree at what stages, and by whom, media responses or initiatives will be addressed. Once enunciated in the media, a position tends to become irrevocable without loss of face, therefore creating problems in the dispute-resolution process" (p. 36). Communication managers use environmental scanning research to provide the dominant coalition with early warning of emergent dissensus coorientation states and potential activism by latent or aware publics affected or involved with issues important to the organization.

Two other coorientation states exist that are of great importance to communication managers and public relations practitioners. These are false states based on inaccurate perceptions of the other party's views. If the

dominant coalition thinks a target public agrees with the organization about
an issue, policy, or organizational action—but the dominant coalition is
mistaken—then a state of *false consensus* exists. The same state of false
consensus exists when publics are mistaken in their belief that the organization and the public agree on an issue. On the other hand, the dominant
coalition may believe that they and a target public disagree about an issue
when, in fact, both parties actually agree with each other. This state is called
false conflict. False conflict also exists when the target public misperceives
a disagreement between an organization and the public about an issue.

False states offer unique opportunities for communication managers to
avoid a communication crisis or PR crisis resulting from misunderstand-
ings. Environmental scanning (Broom & Dozier, 1990; Dozier, 1990) is a
form of communication from publics to organizations that provides the
dominant coalition with accurate information about what is going on out
there. The dominant coalition, after all, will make strategic and tactical
decisions for the organization based on its perceptions of how other
stakeholders feel and how they will react. Misperceptions can lead to
catastrophic actions, whenever the dominant coalition sees agreement or
disagreement when none actually exists. When target publics misunderstand
the organization's true position on issues, truthful communication about
the organization's views can alleviate potentially damaging coorientation
states. In short, the two false states specify conditions under which
managed communication (including environmental scanning) is optimally
effective.

Broom and Dozier (1990) suggested methods for evaluating symmetrical
communication programs that seek to reduce gaps in agreement and
accuracy through action and communication strategies. Instead of restricting the benchmark survey (in a pretest–posttest design) to target
publics, the organization's dominant coalition also is surveyed. Based on
these data, communication managers can compute *agreement difference
scores,* quantitative measures of the gap in agreement between management
and publics. In addition, the benchmark survey can ask both the dominant
coalition and the target public how they think the other party views or
evaluates key issues. These data can be used to compute difference scores
between perceptions of the other party's views and the other party's actual
views. These are called *accuracy difference scores,* quantitative measures of
how much one party misperceives the views of the other party.

Using benchmark data on agreement and accuracy, program goals can be
developed that seek to increase agreement and accuracy. Objectives can be
specified that seek to reduce agreement difference scores and accuracy
difference scores between the dominant coalition and target publics. As a
symmetrical program, much program effort is directed inward; the dominant coalition is the target of action strategies spelled out in the plan.

Accuracy difference scores are relatively easy to reduce among members of the dominant coalition, because they are few in number and easily available to the communication manager. Communicating results of a benchmark study to top management reduces the dominant coalition's inaccurate perceptions of how publics view the organization or issues important to the organization. Modifying the policies, procedures, products, services, and behavior of the organization are integral to reducing agreement difference scores. At program's end, the success or failure of the program is determined as much by changes in the dominant coalition as by changes in target publics.

Symmetrical public relations programs constitute significant departures from the historically accepted asymmetrical models of press agentry, public information, and—more recently—two-way asymmetrical public relations (Dozier, 1989). Dozier concluded from a study of IABC members in 1987 that symmetrical public relations has not emerged as an observable, operating model in contemporary practice. He argued that the model remains largely normative, a prescription as to how public relations should be practiced, rather than descriptive of existing practices. Nevertheless, two-way symmetrical public relations programs, if implemented, are posited to be generally more effective than asymmetrical approaches to public relations.

CONCLUSIONS

This chapter considers the effects that communication and public relations programs can achieve and how they can be evaluated. In reviewing research and theory on communication, and especially mass communication, effects are limited. Significant changes in the knowledge, attitudes, and behavior of publics are not likely to be achieved in the short term. The conclusion that effects are limited, however, is based on the presupposition that communication and public relations programs seek to dominate organizational environments and manipulate publics. Communication and public relations professionals need not accept that model of practice.

The two-way symmetrical model of public relations suggests that communication, including mediated communication, is indeed effective at achieving symmetrical goals and objectives. The coorientation model suggests that increases in accuracy as well as agreement are worthwhile objectives for communication programs to pursue. The concept of symmetry suggests that the organization itself—and especially the dominant coalition—should adjust and adapt to publics upon whom survival and growth depends. In the process, the organization itself changes. Differences in agreement between organizations and publics are reduced; such reductions are key indicators of communication program effectiveness.

REFERENCES

Anderson, J. R., & Reder, L. M. (1979). An elaborative processing explanation of depth of processing. In L. S. Cermak & F. I. M. Craik (Eds.), *Levels of processing in human memory* (pp. 385–403). Hillsdale, NJ: Lawrence Erlbaum Associates.

Bandura, A. (1977). Self-efficacy: Toward a unifying theory of behavioral change. *Psychological Review, 84,* 191–215.

Bell, S. H., & Bell, E. C. (1976). Public relations: Functional or functionary? *Public Relations Review, 2*(2), 51.

Blumler, J. G., & Katz, E. (1974). *The uses of mass communication.* Newbury Park, CA: Sage.

Broom, G. M. (1986, August). *Public relations roles and systems theory: Functional and historicist causal models.* Paper presented at the meeting of the Public Relations Interest Group, International Communication Association, Chicago.

Broom, G. M., & Dozier, D. M. (1983). An overview: Evaluation research in public relations. *Public Relations Quarterly, 28*(3), 5–8.

Broom, G. M., & Dozier, D. M. (1990). *Using research in public relations: Applications to program management.* Englewood Cliffs, NJ: Prentice-Hall.

Cutlip, S. M., Center, A. H., & Broom, G. M. (1985). *Effective public relations* (6th ed.). Englewood Cliffs, NJ: Prentice-Hall.

Dozier, D. M. (1984). Program evaluation and the roles of practitioners. *Public Relations Review, 10*(3), 13–21.

Dozier, D. M. (1989, May). *Importance of the concept of symmetry and its presence in public relations practice.* Paper presented at the meeting of the Public Relations Interest Group, International Communication Association, San Francisco.

Dozier, D. M. (1990). The innovation of research in public relations practice: Review of a program of studies. *Public Relations Research Annual, 2,* 3–28.

Esman, M. J. (1972). The elements of institution building. In J. W. Eaton (Ed.), *Institution building and development* (pp. 19–40) Newbury Park, CA: Sage.

Gandy, O. H., Jr. (1982). *Beyond agenda-setting: Information subsidies and public policy.* Norwood, NJ: Ablex.

Gossen, R., & Sharp, K. (1987). Workshop: How to manage the dispute resolution. *Public Relations Journal, 43*(12), 35–37.

Grunig, J. E. (1979, August). *A simultaneous equation model for intervention in communication behavior.* Paper presented at the meeting of the Theory and Methodology Division, Association for Education in Journalism, Houston.

Grunig, J. E. (1982). The message-attitude-behavior relationship: Communication behaviors of organizations. *Communication Research, 9,* 163–200.

Grunig, J. E. (1990, December). *The development of public relations research in the United States and its status in communication science.* Paper presented at the meeting of the Professional Conference of the Herbert Quandt Foundation Communication Group, Salzburg, Austria.

Grunig, J. E., & Childers, L. (1988, July). *Reconstruction of a situational theory of communication: Internal and external concepts as identifiers of publics for AIDS.* Paper presented at the meeting of the Communication Theory and Methodology Division, Association for Education in Journalism and Mass Communication, Portland, OR.

Grunig, J. E., & Hunt, T. (1984). *Managing public relations.* New York: Holt, Rinehart & Winston.

IABC Research Foundation. (1989). *Profile '89.* San Francisco: Author.

Jones, J. F. (1975). Audit: A new tool for public relations, *Public Relations Journal, 31*(7), 6–8.

Katz, E. (1987). Communication research since Lazarsfeld. *Public Opinion Quarterly, 51*(4), S25–S45.

Klapper, J. T. (1961). *The effects of mass communication.* Glencoe, IL: Free Press.

Larson, C. U. (1986). *Persuasion* (4th ed.). Belmont, CA: Wadsworth.

Marker, R. K. (1977). The Armstrong/pr data measurement system. *Public Relations Review, 3*(4), 51–59.

McCombs, M., & Shaw, D. (1972). The agenda-setting function of the mass media. *Public Opinion Quarterly, 36*(2), 176–187.

Petty, R. E., & Cacioppo, J. T. (1986). *Communication and persuasion: Central and peripheral routes to attitude change.* New York: Springer-Verlag.

Rice, R. E., & Atkins, C. K. (1989). *Public communication campaigns* (2nd. ed.). Newbury Park, CA: Sage.

Robinson, E. J. (1966). *Communication and public relations.* Columbus, OH: Charles E. Merrill.

Rosengren, K. E., Wenner, L., & Palmgren, P. (1986). *Media gratifications research.* Newbury Park, CA: Sage.

Sherif, C. W., Sherif, M., & Nebergall, R. E. (1965). *Attitude and attitude change: the social judgment-involvement approach.* Westport, CT: Greenwood Press.

Stinchcombe, A. L. (1968). *Constructing social theory.* New York: Harcourt, Brace & World.

Wallack, L. (1989). Mass communication and health promotion: A critical perspective. In R. E. Rice & C. K. Atkin (Eds.) *Public communication campaigns* (2nd ed., pp. 353–368). Newbury Park, CA: Sage.

Wimmer, R. D., & Dominick, J. R. (1987). *Mass media research* (2nd ed.). Belmont, CA: Wadsworth.

8 Research Firms and Public Relations Practices

David M. Dozier
San Diego State University

Fred C. Repper
Public Relations Consultant
Ingram, Texas

ABSTRACT

Research is an essential component of strategic public relations, but few communication managers are trained as researchers. Most practitioners, therefore, buy much of their research from commercial firms. Communication managers should not buy research "off the shelf" from these firms, however, unless that research provides the information needed at a particular stage of strategic public relations. This chapter provides a conceptual framework for public relations research and identifies the stages at which formative and evaluative research is necessary. It then reviews the research techniques available from commercial firms: focus groups, analysis of clippings, survey research, and segmentation techniques. The chapter concludes with tips on how to locate and evaluate research services.

The purpose of this chapter is to outline the different types of research services available to public relations practitioners, to suggest strategies for using such services, and to provide access to research firms either directly or through specialized directories. Although a number of research services are used in public relations practice, this chapter deals with three basic services available commercially and through university-based research units.

The three basic services relate to three types of environmental scanning and evaluative research in public relations. These services include focus-group studies, clipping services and analysis, and survey research. As an adjunct to survey research, the VALS (Values and Lifestyles) psychographic program and the PRIZM geodemographic program are reviewed.

Although these activities do not cover all the research tools available to practitioners, they tend to be services most frequently used. These research services are methodological approaches; they are specific strategies for gathering information about publics. Their strengths and limitations make them appropriate for different stages in scanning and in the evaluation of public relations programs. Before discussing these specific research techniques and services, a conceptual framework for public relations research is useful.

A CONCEPTUAL FRAMEWORK FOR PUBLIC RELATIONS RESEARCH

A key distinction first must be drawn between research conducted to detect problems and assess the status quo, on the one hand, and research designed to evaluate the planning, implementation, and impact of public relations programs on the other. The first kind of public relations research, called *environmental monitoring* or *environmental scanning,* is part of the problem-defining stage of public relations planning (Dozier, 1986). Broom and Dozier (1990) said that environmental scanning moves through the three phases of problem detection, exploration, and description. The second kind of research, evaluation research, is designed to determine how well public relations programs work. This kind of research picks up the research function when scanning is complete, using problem description from the scanning phase as baseline for program evaluation (Dozier, 1984a, 1984b).

Environmental Scanning

According to Broom's (1986) open-systems model of public relations, scanning research is a form of system inputs. Organizations gather intelligence about publics and environmental forces. When these inputs are collected systematically by an organization, the activities are forms of environmental scanning. These activities are conceptually distinct from performance control feedback, program adjustment feedback, and organizational adaption feedback (Broom & Dozier, 1990). These feedback loops are conceptual representations in an open-systems model of the three types of program evaluation that practitioners use to measure the preparation, implementation, and impact of public relations programs. Scanning research is different.

Dozier (1986) argued that scanning research is methodologically distinct from evaluation research. Scanning research is inherently open ended. Such research is exploratory in nature and vulnerable to premature closure. That is, scanning research is vulnerable to examining problems already known to either the practitioner or management. This is a weakness, because the strategic function of scanning is early detection of emerging problems as well as quantification of existing or known problems in the environment.

For these reasons, scanning research is ideally suited for a number of qualitative research techniques, including focus-group studies. In addition, questionnaires of specific publics or a broad cross section of many publics are also useful. These types of surveys, however, differ in many important respects from the highly structured field experimental designs of evaluation research.

Evaluation Research

According to Cutlip, Center, and Broom (1985), public relations evaluation can be divided into three levels, reflecting different points in the public relations process. The first level of evaluation involves preparation criteria and methods.

Preparation Evaluation.   Cutlip et al. (1985, p. 296) subdivided preparation evaluation into three components: adequacy of background information, appropriateness of message content and organization, and quality of message presentations (style, format, and presentation) — see Fig. 8.1. The activities that make up this level of evaluation can be accomplished through internal staff efforts. Further, a number of research firms provide services related to preparation evaluation. The most common services are message testing and focus-group studies.

Focus-group studies are considered in detail later in this chapter. Message testing may take the form of qualitative formative evaluation. Focus groups provide a useful mechanism for testing messages at the concept stage. More structured experimental designs, involving larger numbers of subjects from the target public and quantified measures of reactions to alternative message and media strategies, provide powerful mechanisms for follow-up on concepts tested through qualitative techniques. Another specialized area of implementation evaluation is the use of readability tests and formulas to determine the difficulty of reading written material (Broom & Dozier, 1990). Characteristics such as word length and sentence length are used to determine how difficult a sample of writing is to read. The formulas assign scores to writing samples, scores that can be compared against established standards of readability.

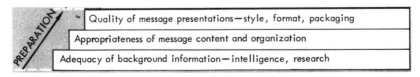

FIGURE 8.1   A model of public relations preparation evaluation. From Cutlip, Center, and Broom (1985). Reprinted by permission.

Implementation Evaluation.   Implementation evaluation includes measures of messages sent (distribution), messages placed (coverage), messages received (circulation, reach), and number of messages attended to by target publics (Cutlip et al. 1985). Public relations firms provide figures on distribution. When messages are sent by internal public relations staff, effective managers systematically track the productivity of their writers. The most common form of implementation or dissemination evaluation is placement tracking. Either through commercial clipping services or through an internal placement tracking system, most practitioners engage in some form of clip file studies. These studies may be as crude as circulating print media clippings to interested parties within the organization to sophisticated analysis of content and audiences reached, as determined through secondary research—see Fig. 8.2.

Impact Evaluation.   The final form of program evaluation is impact evaluation. This is the step of greatest relevance to determining program impact. Effective preparation and implementation, as determined by the various evaluation techniques described previously, are only steps on the path to program impact.

Impact of public relations programs involves the maintenance or change—among clearly defined target publics and management of the practitioner's organization—of awareness or knowledge levels, attitudes and opinions, and behavior and behavioral predispositions. As Grunig and Hunt (1984) argued, the domino metaphor succinctly describes the impact of public relations programs. The effects of a public relations program can be viewed as a line of upright dominos, as in Fig. 8.3. In effect, according to the simplified communication effects model implicit in Fig. 8.3, a message is communicated to a target public that causes a knowledge-level change. This, in turn, causes an attitude or opinion change. This opinion change, in turn, causes a change in behavior or behavioral predispositions. The upright dominos represent the implicit causal chain that many assume connects mediated messages to behavioral changes among target publics.

As Grunig and Hunt (1984, pp. 124–126) indicated, there are a number of

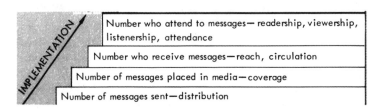

FIGURE 8.2   A model of public relations implementation evaluation. From Cutlip, Center, and Broom (1985). Reprinted by permission.

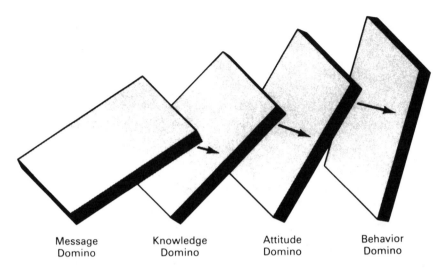

| Message
Domino | Knowledge
Domino | Attitude
Domino | Behavior
Domino |

FIGURE 8.3   Grunig and Hunt's domino model of public relations effects. From Grunig and Hunt (1984). Reprinted by permission.

assumptions in the model that research on communication effects tends to refute. First, move the dominos farther apart. Knocking down the Message domino will not result in a knowledge-level change in the target public. The gap between any pair of dominos may be too large, halting the causal chain that links message and media activities to behavioral change. Further, take some of the dominos out of the causal chain. Or put them in different order. For example, under certain circumstances, behavior may change first, resulting in attitude changes after the fact. In essence, the linkage between messages and behavior is not direct, straightforward, uniformly consistent, or powerful.

In assessing the impact of public relations programs, Cutlip et al. (1985, p. 296) constructed a step model that divides program impact into seven categories. These include measures of the number who learn message content (measures of awareness, knowledge, and understanding), the number who change opinions, the number who change attitudes, the number who behave consistent with message intent, the number who repeat desired behavior, goal achievement and/or problem solution, and social/cultural change. See Fig. 8.4. Like the Grunig and Hunt (1984) domino model, each step in this model of program impact is increasingly difficult to achieve.

The basic tool of impact evaluation is sampling surveys organized according to some form of experimental or quasi-experimental design. As Webb and others (1966) advocated, there are many ingenious ways to measure social behavior besides the standardized questionnaire. An exam-

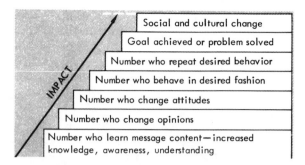

FIGURE 8.4   A model of public relations impact evaluation. From Cutlip, Center, and Broom (1985). Reprinted by permission.

ple, adapted from Webb and others (1966), of such an unobtrusive evaluation measure would be the wear and tear on carpeting in an art museum. A public relations program might seek to increase visitor interest in some underappreciated section of the museum. Measuring the amount of wear and tear on the carpeting before and after the program is implemented provides an indicator of program success, especially if compared to another heavy traffic section of the museum.

Other unobtrusive measures include routine organizational records that track activities of key publics and can be used as measures to evaluate the impact of some programs. These unobtrusive measures have the added advantage of being nonreactive. The measurement activity, in such instances, is not perceived as such by the target public. An example would be the logging of phone complaints which might be routed routinely to the public relations department. The measurement activity itself is not likely to affect the knowledge, attitude, or behavior of publics it seeks to measure.

Despite these other measurement strategies, surveys of publics are standard tools of program evaluation. Unfortunately, surveys—even if properly designed, pretested, and implemented—are of little value as evaluation tools unless they are embedded in an experimental or quasi-experimental design that can isolate program effects from other factors that may affect awareness, knowledge, attitudes, and behavior of publics. When conducting program evaluation, either internally or through a research firm, both questionnaire content/design and overall research design must be carefully considered.

INTERNAL OR EXTERNAL RESEARCH SERVICES?

If research and evaluation are fundamental to the practice of public relations, then internal research capabilities seem essential. As a matter of fact, however, research — especially social scientific research — often requires the services of outside consultants and research firms. As Grunig and Hunt (1984) stated:

> Eventually, we hope, most public relations departments will have their own personnel to do evaluations. Today, few have trained researchers on their staffs, or managers with enough research courses in their background, to do their own research. If a public relations department has the personnel to do its own evaluation, it probably will do more evaluation . . . It is simply easier to keep evaluation going when it is a daily component of a public relations manager's job. (p. 184)

In order to integrate scanning and evaluation research into the function, public relations units internal to organizations need to bring practitioners into the organization with specialized research training. However, not all research activities are best handled internally. As Grunig and Hunt put it:

> We suggest that public relations managers hire personnel capable of doing research, so that they can make evaluation internal, continuous, and part of the management process. But we suggest they call in consultants when new and detached ideas become important, and when the objectivity of an outsider is needed to satisfy top management, rate commissions, or Congress that your program is meeting its objectives. (p. 184)

The purpose of this chapter is to provide techniques for making effective use of outside consultants and research firms. These external services are no substitute for internal research competence. Indeed, the effective contracting of research services from a research firm or consultant requires some research capabilities.

With this framework of public relations research in mind, let us consider some major forms of public relations research. For each type of research considered, we also examine ways in which such research can be purchased from research firms and properly managed by public relations practitioners.

FOCUS-GROUP RESEARCH

Focus-group research is a qualitative research technique that enjoys increasing popularity among marketing, advertising, and public relations practitioners. Like most qualitative research techniques, the conduct of a focus-group study is deceptively simple. In fact, a truly competent focus-group moderator must make sense out of "thousands upon thousands of relevant observations — observations of nuance and feeling, of depth of feeling and conviction, of facial expression and body movement, of conflict, ambivalence, and paradox, and of attitudes, beliefs, and needs" (Mariampolski, 1984, p. 21).

Research facilities commonly involve a focus-group room, with a central table that seats from 7 to 10 participants. Frequently, a two-way mirror permits observers in a darkened adjacent room to observe the focus-group discussion. Frequently the sessions are recorded by audio- or videotape.

Participants in a focus-group discussion are selected from the target public of interest to the researcher. Generally, participation is obtained by paying participants an incentive or "co-op." Recruitment is frequently by phone. A series of qualifier questions are used to identify participants who meet specified criteria for inclusion in the target public. The sample frame may be a phone directory, a list of random digit phone numbers, or even a listing of people previously contacted who expressed an interest in partici-pating in focus-group studies. Because the technique is highly qualitative, samples are generally nonprobabilistic. Thus, generalizations cannot be made from the focus-group sample to the target population using inferen-tial statistics.

The focus-group moderator is key to successful focus-group research. The moderator leads the focus-group discussion using active listening techniques. Frequently, a stimulus is used to initiate the discussion. The stimulus might be an object, a drawing, a slide or transparency, a story board, or a complete communication product such as a public service announcement. The purpose of the stimulus is to focus the discussion on an idea, issue, product, or message of interest to the researcher. The moderator then nurtures the comments of various participants, steering them back on topic if they stray, and elicits rich information from participants.

Mariampolski (1984) divided the focus-group discussion into six compo-nents, guided by the moderator. The *rapport-building* phase is used to establish good communication with participants and moderator and to clarify the task of the group. The *exploratory* phase of the discussion allows participants to define the nature of the dialogue through their responses to very broad questions. Participants might be asked: "What comes to mind when I say 'ecology'?" This is followed by the *probing* phase, where dialogue is guided to more narrow topic areas of interest to the researcher. Participants might write a slogan or use other projective techniques during the *task* phase of the discussion. The task phase may provide creative products from participants that they design to reach people like themselves. Stimuli often are used during the *evaluation* phase of the discussion. Participants evaluate a slogan, story line, message strategy, or some other tangible stimulus. During the *closing* phase, the participants are asked if there is anything they would like to add to the dialogue, allowing the moderator to gather any remaining, untapped information.

Results can be transcribed from tapes or simply listened to by the moderator and condensed in a written report. The report frequently will follow a topic-based format. The narrative generally is laced liberally with direct quotes to capture the texture or quality of the information.

Although focus-group research sometimes is criticized by quantitative, "number-cruncher" researchers as too qualitative, marketing focus-group research is criticized by others as too structured and forced. The Cultural Analysis Group at Planmetrics, Inc., used techniques they labeled *intensive cultural interviews* or *unfocus groups* to gather qualitative data (Planmetrics, 1985). The concern is that traditional focus-group moderators overdirect participants, not permitting the participants to define the nature of the discourse or deal with the issue of focus in their own language and on their own terms. This is a manifestation of *premature closure,* the very "closed endedness" that qualitative research seeks to avoid.

Intensive cultural interviews involve group participants in the completion of a task with minimum interference from the moderator. Planmetrics researchers used anthropological methods of intense observation to discover *mind-sets*—clusters of beliefs, attitudes, and knowledge—that are culturally defined. An example of an unfocus group study was the Gulf States Project. Participants worked together to construct a model of a nuclear power plant from household objects. Each group used a cake cover to enclose the reactor. Planmetrics analysts concluded that enclosure signified safety. Subsequent advertising in support of constructing a nuclear power plant by Gulf States included a visual of a dome on the plant clicking shut (Miller, 1986). Little resistance to nuclear plant construction was encountered from activist publics, according to Gulf State practitioners. More information about the Cultural Analysis Group can be obtained from the Cultural Analysis Group, 110 E. 59th Street, New York, NY 10022.

Focus groups, including the task-based intensive cultural interviews, have applications in several areas of public relations research. They are a useful scanning tool. Focus groups drawn from key publics can comment on their current perceptions of the organization or react to actions being contemplated by the organization. Issues important to the organization can be discussed by participants from key publics. Focus groups can be part of an organization's early warning system, an environmental scanning tool that helps practitioners identify emerging problems or opportunities.

Focus groups are powerful formative evaluation tools during the preparation phase of evaluation. Unlike structured, closed-ended quantitative research, serendipity—the making of fortunate discoveries accidentally—is possible in the open-ended inquiry that focus groups serve. The researcher may make discoveries of things unexpected. As indicated earlier, various message strategies or products can be used as stimuli in focus-group discussions. Because focus groups are relatively inexpensive (from $1,000 to $3,500 per group) and quick (24-hr turnaround is not unreasonable if planned for that time frame), various iterations can be examined and reexamined.

Focus groups are limited by the qualitative nature of data and by the nonprobabilistic character of sample sizes and sampling strategies. Therefore, generalizations from focus-group samples to larger publics from which they are drawn are inappropriate. Focus groups are not useful as inferential tools, in the statistical sense of inference. The findings of focus-group studies are best thought of as indications worthy of more precise quantitative follow-up research.

Qualitative researchers like focus-group moderators have formed an association which can provide membership lists for practitioners seeking qualitative research consultants. The not-for-profit trade group is: Qualitative Research Consultants Association (QRCA), P.O. Box 6767, New York, New York 10022.

Qualitative research like focus-group moderation can be done both by professionals and amateurs, by competent researchers and marginal operators. The best method for identifying competent moderators is through their former clients. Talk to former clients; ask to see any nonproprietary reports provided by the moderator. Practitioners should directly observe the focus-group sessions. No written report can capture the richness of the focus-group dialogue itself. For step-by-step instructions to conduct focus-group studies in a public relations setting, see Broom and Dozier (1990).

Clipping Services and Analysis

As indicated in the section A Conceptual Framework for Public Relations Research, clipping services are an important component of implementation evaluation research. Placement of messages in media that reach target publics is essential to program impact, when public media are part or all of the media strategy. In the parlance of the social sciences, placements are a necessary but not a sufficient condition for program impact to occur. When a program does not work, an examination of placements may help detect what went wrong. When a program does work, as indicated by impact evaluation, the analysis of placements is an integral aspect of understanding why it worked.

According to Lesly (1983, p. 446), there are four national bureaus that attempt to track print media placements and coverage on a national basis. They are:

Bacon's Clipping Bureau
14 E. Jackson Blvd.
Chicago, IL 60604

Burrelle's Press Clipping Bureau
75 E. Northfield Ave.
Livingston, NJ 07039

Luce Press Clipping Bureau
420 Lexington Ave.
New York, NY 10017

also located at:

42 S. Center St.	407 S. Dearborn St.	912 Kansas Ave.
Mesa, AZ 85202	Chicago, IL 60605	Topeka, KS 66612

Press Intelligence, Inc.
734 15th St., N.W.
Washington, DC 20005

Lesly also listed the American Press Clipping Service, 5 Beekman St., New York, NY 10038, as providing a specialized clipping service for trade publications. In addition, Lesly (pp. 446–449) provided a listing of services operating on a state or regional basis, as well as foreign clipping services.

Simple Evaluations Using Clips

What are the uses of clipping services? As with most research activities in public relations, the uses of clipping services depend on the research question to be answered. A simple research question is: How much has been said about our organization (or issues important to our organization) in the mass or specialized media? A raw count of column inches or number of stories provides a rough indicator of the volume of coverage.

Other measures using clip files involve tracking messages sent versus messages placed. How many news releases generated by our staff were used? By which media? Did the news release content remain intact? How much coverage was initiated by our staff? By the mass media? By tracking placements, by recording who (PR staff or media) generated coverage, and by categorizing placements and coverage by media, the practitioner establishes systematic feedback mechanisms for dissemination evaluation. By systematically examining "what works" and "what doesn't work" in placements and coverage, the practitioner becomes increasingly sophisticated in the craft of placements.

Analyzing Audiences Through Clips

By categorizing media placements and coverage by publication, the practitioner can begin evaluating the circulation, reach, and impressions generated by placements and coverage. This is accomplished by merging data from clipping analysis with data from secondary research sources. For print media, the Audit Bureau of Circulation provides circulation figures for member newspapers and magazines. The Arbitron Company and A. C. Nielson Company provide audience measures for television stations. The advertising departments of newspapers and broadcast media generally provide detailed breakdowns of audience characteristics, as well as advertising rates. This information, obtained directly from publications and broadcast media, can be used to generate useful measures. One useful analysis is to convert placements (on a column-inch basis) into market value estimates, using advertising rates for the same amount of space. Advertising and publicity are not directly comparable, because advertising provides controlled access whereas publicity is largely uncontrolled. On the other hand, advertising may exhibit lower source credibility among some target publics precisely because it *is controlled.*

This type of audience analysis is carried to a high level of sophistication in the Publicity Tracking Model developed by Ketchum Communications. An example is provided in Fig. 8.5. Basically, the model takes audience data for media in the 120 top U.S. markets and provides a computerized audience analysis for placements generated by a publicity campaign. The model tracks gross impressions by target audience, as well as key messages placed.

This linkage of audience data with placement and coverage measures helps extend the dissemination evaluation function from the messages sent toward the messages received domain. However, such analysis is no substitute for direct measures of target publics. As Cutlip et al. (1985, p. 301) noted, *delivered* audience and *effective* audience are different. Rarely does the audience reached by a particular medium (delivered) correspond with target publics. As illustrated in Fig. 8.6, the circulation of a publication includes many people who are not members of the target public; further, many members of the target public are not reached by the particular media where messages are placed.

Neither delivered nor effective audience estimates speak to the issue of actual exposure to messages by target publics. Just because a member of a target public subscribes to a magazine where a message has been placed is no guarantee that the target public member actually read the message, understood the message, or retained the message. These latter concerns fall into the domain of readership, viewership, and listenership surveys.

Content Analysis

The measures of clips just described deal simply with the quantity of messages sent and possibly received by target publics. What about the

PLACEMENT TYPE	DMA TARGET AUDIENCE*	AVG. SIZE/ LENGTH	AVG. MEDIA UNITS	PUBLICITY EXPOSURE UNITS	AVG. IMPACT FACTOR	PUBLICITY VALUE UNITS
NEWSPAPERS	4,552,000	1/9 page	.93	4,233,000	1.26	5,334,000
MAGAZINES	268,000	1/2 page	1.66	455,000	1.47	656,000
TELEVISION, network	95,000	5:10 min	1.93	183,000	.81	149,000
TELEVISION, local	504,000	6:05 min	2.13	1,073,000	1.81	1,946,000
RADIO, local	200,000	10:00 min	2.60	520,000	1.40	728,000
TOTALS	5,619,000		1.15	6,454,000	1.37	8,813,000

Publicity Exposure Norm*—Orlando DMA 5,960,000
Publicity Exposure Index—6,454/5,960   1.08
Publicity Value Index—8,813/5,960   1.48—

The Publicity Exposure Index suggests that the campaign's exposure was 1.08 as good as expected on a Normal* (= 1.00) basis.

The Publicity Value Index suggests that the impact value of the campaign was 1.48 times as good as expected on a Normal* (= 1.00) basis.

The Publicity Exposure Norms are established by estimating the target audiences (adults 18–49, weighted 60% male, 40% female) exposure of a "good" hypothetical placement schedule.

FIGURE 8.5 A sample of Ketchum's publicity-tracking model. From Cutlip, Center, and Broom (1985). Reprinted by permission.

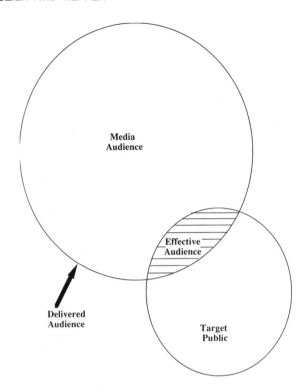

FIGURE 8.6   A model displaying delivered and effective audience.

quality of those messages? To quantify what is said about an organization, techniques of content analysis are useful.

Sophisticated public relations operations, such as American Telephone and Telegraph, have used content analysis for over a decade to track the quality of coverage in the mass media. In content analysis, a particular unit of analysis (a sentence, paragraph, or story) is examined according to objective criteria. Is the unit of analysis saying something positive, negative, or neutral about XYZ? A set of formal rules are used to categorize each unit. The rules are sufficiently specific and objective so that any two evaluators (called coders) would reach the same conclusion about a particular unit examined. In fact, a sample of units content analyzed are subjected routinely to a second analysis by a second coder to determine the reliability of the formal classification rules and of the coders using those rules.

Pro or con classification of content is only one way to classify content. Lindenmann (1983) suggested that public relations practitioners might choose to classify any number of attributes of coverage, based on the research question. For example, content units can be classified as the to presence or absence of particular themes. Adjectives used to describe an organization can be grouped together in clusters and coded for each reference to the company by name. The only requirement for classification is that the attribute classified has meaning or use within the context of the evaluation question and that reliable classifications of that content be achieved through application of a formal set of rules. Stempel (1989) suggested that a useful way to ensure reliability is to provide a small, manageable number of categories for analyzing content.

Rules for sampling content and for analyzing content analysis data are the same as those that apply to survey research. In this case, content units are sampled from a universe of all units, using random or systematic sampling techniques. For purposes of data analysis, the content unit, rather than people, constitute the case. Data can be organized by cases for computer analysis or hand tabulation. The variables for each case are the various classifications made of the content unit. Typically, the content unit is classified as to publication or publication type, date of publication, section of publication (news, editorial columns, letters to editor, etc.), and item length, as well as attributes specific to the content unit itself (favorable, unfavorable, etc.).

By conducting content analysis over time, trends in media coverage can be detected. These trends in media content are indicators of possible trends in the perceived importance of issues, changes in corporate image, and so forth among target publics.

As Lindenmann (1983) warned, however, media content is not the same thing as program impact. When Hill and Knowlton linked content analysis with a survey of the target public, the findings were disquieting. It seemed that the target public responded negatively to an issue important to the client organization, whether media content was positive or negative. Media attention of any sort was correlated with negative reactions to the issue among members of the target public. As Lindenmann noted, sending a favorable message is not the same thing as creating a favorable opinion.

Content analysis can be conducted in-house. A useful reference with a strong mass communication orientation is provided by Stempel (1989). The explanation of statistical procedures for analyzing content is especially useful. Berelson (1952) and Holsti (1969) authored classical treatments of content analysis in the social sciences.

Various research firms will conduct content analysis for practitioners. As with all contracted research, the practitioner should have a clear understanding of the purposes to be served by the content analysis, the relevant publications to be studied, the relevant time frame, and an initial pass at specifying the content categories of interest to the practitioner. Accessing research firms that offer such services is discussed in the Locating Research Firms section.

SURVEY RESEARCH USING PROBABILISTIC
SAMPLING

Perhaps the most powerful tool in the practitioner's arsenal of scanning and evaluation tools is the survey of target publics using probabilistic sampling techniques. There are many types of surveys that practitioners do. Surveys sometimes are conducted of target publics or the general population as special events that generate publicity or serve as a platform for corporate advertising (Pollock, 1981). Finn (1984) classified such probabilistic sampling surveys as *public issues studies*. Finn also identified *needs and perceptions assessments* as another form of survey research used by practitioners. These surveys of probabilistic samples of key publics (employees, financial leaders, potential customers) seek to scan the organizational environment "as a starting point to design a new public relations campaign or to update an existing program" (Finn, 1984, p. 20). Such scanning type surveys are distinguished from *program evaluation* surveys. Finn included both implementation evaluation (such as Ketchum's Publicity Tracking Model) and impact evaluation, surveys that seek to measure awareness, opinions, attitudes, and behavior of target publics. These surveys are embedded in a longitudinal design, such that attributes of publics can be measured at several points in time — before, during, and after program implementation. Finn also identified *issues-tracking/intelligence-gathering* research as using probabilistic sampling techniques and surveys of publics. This is another form of scanning involving elite publics of experts and opinion leaders. Because of the elite nature of these publics, qualitative techniques such as depth interviews and content analysis of key publications complement the surveys of elite publics.

Types of Survey Research

Finn's (1984) list is not exhaustive. In fact, every probabilistic sample survey conducted in public relations could be provided its own label as a type of public relations research. The proliferation of labels for types of research is dysfunctional, because they clutter and confuse the dialogue about public relations research. Here we prefer to use systems theory to make a basic distinction between scanning research and evaluation research.

Scanning research involves the detection and quantification of emerging problems and opportunities facing an organization, as a method of organizing inputs from the environment, a way of answering the question: "What's going on out there?" Probabilistic sampling surveys are useful scanning tools, especially if coupled with qualitative research (such as focus groups) conducted prior to design of the questionnaire.

Evaluation research answers a different question: "Did the program work?" As Broom and Dozier (1990) indicated in their systems model of public relations, evaluation research is systematic feedback involving the outcomes of various stages of implementation. Such research can be classified as preparation, implementation, and impact evaluation. Surveys serve a useful role in preparation of the *situation analysis,* as a means of quantifying the public relations problem or opportunity that drives the public relations program. Probabilistic sampling surveys are an indispensable tool of impact evaluation. If public relations programs identify awareness, knowledge, opinions, attitudes, or behavior as objectives, then measurement of those attributes before and after program implementation is essential. Although measures other than surveys are possible, surveys are the modal impact evaluation measure.

When evaluating a public relations program, surveys must meet at least two criteria. First, if the entire public is not measured before and after program implementation, probabilistic sampling techniques should be used. Second, more than one survey is required to measure program impact.

Probability Sampling

Surveys based on nonprobability sampling techniques are worse than useless; they are dangerous. They deceive practitioners into thinking they know something about the target publics when they do not. The sins of nonprobability sampling perhaps are rooted in the journalistic tradition of treating "man on the street" interviews as somehow representative of public or community opinion.

Prior to the emergence of "precision journalism," journalists commonly would equate five interviews with a convenience sample in front of the city courthouse as somehow "representing" public opinion on an issue. In fact, such a sample size ($N = 5$) and sampling strategy (convenience) precludes any statistical inference from sample to population. Although four out of five people so interviewed might want the mayor impeached, even journalists would be reluctant to conclude that "80% of the city voters want the mayor impeached."

Although such an abuse of inference would strike most people as intuitively inappropriate, public relations practitioners make equally serious inferential errors. An example is Beyer's (1986) survey of readers of *Public Relations Journal (PRJ),* which sought to examine salary patterns. In the introduction, Beyer noted that respondents "were self-selected readers who chose to fill in the [PRJ] Questionnaire [included in an earlier issue] and mail it back"(p. 26). Although discounting the representativeness of the sample, Beyer added that the survey offers "insights into trends in the field and, in many cases, correlate well with data drawn from other formal studies" (p. 26).

A problem occurs, however, when the reader forgets that the convenience sample of *PRJ* readers is not representative of public relations practitioners or even all readers of *PRJ*. The percentage of women practitioners in marketing and median salaries of practitioners in the Midwest, when measured through a probabilistic sample of practitioners, are actual estimates of the values we would obtain if we surveyed all practitioners. When a convenience sample is analyzed as if it were a probability sample, the natural inferences that the reader makes are inappropriate, misleading, and confusing.

It is better to not know something and know you do not than to know nothing and think you do!

Research Design and Survey Research

The issue of research design is critical in all surveys. But an exploratory, cross-sectional survey at one point in time involves fewer design issues than those required in evaluation research.

At the very least, evaluation research requires a before–after measure. This at least permits some measure of change in awareness, knowledge, opinions, attitudes, and/or behavior among target publics. Isolating program effects from other factors in the environment that might affect outcome measures requires the use of control or comparison groups. In making evaluation design decisions, the practitioner should be familiar with the plausible threats to the internal validity of the design. That is, can we isolate program effects from other effects that are giving us indications of positive (or negative!) program impact?

These design issues are dealt with effectively in many research methods books, including Babbie (1985), Bailey (1987), and Stempel and Wesley (1981). The seminal source for research design models and discussion is Campbell and Stanley (1963). The Sage Evaluation Series also provides useful information for designing program evaluations, though the context is programs other than public relations. Broom and Dozier (1990) provided design methods specific for public relations program evaluation.

New Interest in Psychographic Typologies

Public relations practitioners, like their marketing colleagues, increasingly are using audience segmentation services based on geography, lifestyles, and psychographic characteristics of audience clusters. Originally designed for marketing purposes, such audience segmentation strategies have some utility in the management of public relations. Two such systems are considered here: PRIZM and VALS. Both segmentation systems are commercially available from research and public relations firms.

What is psychographic and geodemographic segmentation? The two commercial services considered here are basically techniques for developing typologies of U.S. residents. Marketing and public relations practitioners are faced with a population of several hundred million Americans with diverse lifestyles, beliefs, and purchasing behavior. Segmentation is organizing this population into functional groupings, based on important characteristics that to some degree determine how they will react to an organization, its image, its products, and issues important to that organization. These groupings allow researchers to organize a heterogeneous population into groupings that are relatively homogeneous in terms of important and influential characteristics. Once grouped, these segments can tracked through subsequent research and detailed characteristics of the segment can be fleshed out.

Practitioners generally engage in segmentation when target publics are defined. In issues management, the political orientations and degree of activism play an important role in defining publics or segmenting audiences. A review of public relations textbooks (Cutlip et al., 1985; Grunig & Hunt, 1984) indicates that historically organizations have segmented publics according to shared characteristics: the community, women, youth, minorities, the media, employees, shareholders.

Segmentation is of little value if it fails to generate groupings that are generally more homogeneous internally. However, the traditional publics listed previously are generally quite heterogeneous internally. Thus, practitioners are driven to defining additional subpublics within the heterogeneous publics. Additional attributes are introduced to distinguish one subpublic from another. Although such additional segmentation results in smaller, more homogeneous groupings (which facilitate message and media strategies), the hierarchy of publics and subpublics becomes increasingly unwieldy. Implementing action, message, and media strategies for scores of subpublics becomes cost prohibitive. Further, as subpublics proliferate, the basis for generating such groupings becomes increasingly fuzzy.

The purpose of VALS and PRIZM segmentation is to group publics and subpublics into meaningful and functional groupings and subgroupings. These groupings, in turn, can be used by practitioners as a way of understanding target publics. When publics are defined dynamically, in response to emerging or manifest problems or opportunities in the environment, the practitioner seeks to understand key publics by fleshing out what is known about the people making up that public. Psychographic researchers argue that their typologies or clusters of people humanize social scientific research on audiences.

For example, people opposed to the expansion of a new factory may be made up mostly of two psychographic types. Based on what is already known about these two types from prior psychographic research, the practitioner can develop two separate action, message, and media strategies targeted specifically to each of the relevant psychographic types. Action, including organizational change, can be undertaken to reduce conflict with the values and lifestyles of relevant types. For example, landscaping and stringent environmental protection could be added to the proposed factory expansion in the aforementioned example. Messages can be constructed that take into account the values and lifestyles of each psychographic type. Media can be selected based on known patterns of media usage among each type.

Note that the change here is symmetrical. The organization changes policies, practices, and actions based on an understanding of the cost of alternative actions to relations with key publics. At the same time, target publics change in that they see, through communication from the organization, that the factory expansion does not conflict with their values and lifestyles.

Psychographics also can be used in an asymmetric fashion. Practitioners can use that information about publics to dominate, to gain appropriate compliance from key publics without adapting the organization in any way to the values and lifestyles of those key publics. In each case, however, action, message, and media strategies are based on a clearer understanding of the publics involved.

VALS (VALUES AND LIFESTYLES)

The VALS (Values and Lifestyles) system is a proprietary psychographic segmentation program owned by SRI International, Menlo Park, California. VALS was developed in 1980 as a comprehensive psychographic typology from a series of earlier systems that attempted to cluster lifestyles and values of the American population (SRI International, 1984, 1985). The VALS program has its roots in theory. Grounded in developmental psychology, and borrowing from Riesman's (1961) concepts of "tradition-directed," "inner directed," and "other directed" character types, the VALS model posits four fundamental orientations that cluster American values and lifestyles: need driven, outer-directed, inner-directed, and integrated. The four fundamental orientations are superordinate to nine lifestyle/value clusters or types.

The typology was developed through extensive use of U.S. Census and Department of Labor data. The first empirical validation of the model was conducted in 1980. A probability sample of U.S. households (with telephones) was contacted by phone and sent a lengthy mailed questionnaire, probing respondents' values, lifestyles, media usage, and consumer behavior. A sample of 1,635 completed the 85-page interview. Subsequent surveys have added to the profile of each cluster. The long item set originally used to classify respondents into clusters has been abbreviated in the VALS Lifestyle Classification System. A 30-item set made up of Likert-type scales, the VALS Lifestyle Classification System is adaptable to most interview and self-administered techniques of data collection.

The VALS Typology.   The nine clusters include two types of Americans defined as need driven. They are the *Survivors* and the *Sustainers.* Survivors (some 6 million Americans) are poor, often elderly, and poorly educated. They are unhappy, sometimes bedridden, and see no hope of escaping their lot in life. Sustainers (some 11 million Americans) are generally younger than survivors, but are almost as poor. Described as streetwise and angry at the system, many young minority Americans make up this cluster.

Three clusters are outer directed: *Belongers, Emulators,* and *Achievers.* The values and lifestyles of these clusters are responses to perceptions of how others — how society — expects them to live and the values that others expect them to hold. The Belongers (some 57 million Americans) are "middle Americans." Conservative, ethnocentric, conforming, resistant to change, these Americans want to belong, to be part of the mainstream. Integrated into communities and voluntary associations, they adhere to a strict puritanical code. Emulators (some 16 million Americans) are striving to make it big, to be rich. They are competitive, upwardly mobile, status conscious. With many minority group members in this cluster, Emulators are distrustful of the system. Achievers (some 37 million Americans) are high-income materialists who lead American businesses and professions. Disproportionately male, white, and Republican, Achievers are hard working, successful, and comfortable.

The inner-directed clusters are people whose lifestyles and values come from within, rather than in response to their perception of the expectations of others. The three inner-directed clusters are: *I-Am-Mes, Experientials,* and *Societally Conscious.* The I-Am-Me cluster (some 8 million Americans) is viewed as transitional, a step from the outer-directed clusters to the Experiential or Societally Conscious clusters. Young, individualistic, self-absorbed, exhibitionistic, the I-Am-Me cluster is typified by insecurity, impulsiveness, and inventiveness. They tend to be young, female, and single, sustained by parental support. They tend to be liberal but do not vote. The Experientials (some 11 million Americans) are theorized as a maturation of the I-am-me orientation. Less egocentric, these Americans are concerned about others. Adventuresome, direct, and involved, the Experientials are attracted to natural foods, fitness, and the exotic. Politically liberal, political involvement creeps into their lives, usually through the women's movement and environmentalism. The Societally Conscious (some 14 million Americans) are affluent, but unlike the

Achievers, they see the need for social change. They typically are leaders of activist publics and single-issue campaigns. Not as materialistic as Achievers, these Americans value the quality of life in less material ways. Educated and reformist, the Societally Conscious hold intellectual jobs in the professions. Like Achievers, they see America playing an active global role. Unlike Achievers, they favor cooperation rather than domination. They are supportive of peace movements and environmentalism.

The *Integrateds* blend elements of outer-directed and inner-directed orientations in their values and lifestyles. A small minority (only 3 million Americans make up this cluster), the Integrateds tend to be self-assured, self-actualized, and self-expressive. According to the implicit developmental psychological model of human personality, the Integrateds are fully mature. They "have it all" and are "above it all." They are the special leaders.

Applications. Of what use are the VALS clusters? As indicated earlier, the clusters permit segmentation of target publics. Although a public may be defined dynamically by practitioners in anticipation of — or in reaction to — specific problems and opportunities, the VALS clusters are relatively enduring. Further, the VALS clusters are carefully if not exhaustively profiled: We know a great deal about the values, lifestyles, media usage, and consumptive behavior of the different clusters. We understand what people in the different clusters are like.

For this reason, the VALS Lifestyle Classification System is a useful addition to any probabilistic survey of target publics. By examining publics in terms of the VALS clusters that make them up, the practitioner can humanize publics that might otherwise seem mere statistical aggregates. Because the VALS clusters are extensively detailed in terms of media usage, the VALS Lifestyle Classification System can help practitioners make informed message and media decisions. In short, VALS clusters help practitioners know their publics. A detailed analysis of the VALS typology, its history, and usage is provided in Mitchell's book, *The Nine American Lifestyles* (1983).

New VALS Typology. The original VALS typology was modified in 1989 to reflect what SRI International described as shifts in the orientations of consumers. Called VALS 2, the modified typology divides consumers into three broad groupings: consumers who are principle oriented, status oriented, and action oriented. Eight subcategories are identified under the three major categories: Fulfillers, Believers, Actualizers, Achievers, thrivers, Strugglers, Experiencers, and Makers.

The shift in the VALS typology underscores the dynamic nature of psychographic classification system. Basically, any psychographic classification system can be expected to evolve and change as practitioners match the usefulness of the classification system against experiences in the marketplace and in the social-political arena. The VALS typology likely will go through similar evolution and change in the future.

PRIZM

PRIZM is a proprietary audience segmentation system owned by Claritas, Inc., Alexandria, VA. PRIZM is described as a geodemographic segmentation strategy, based on a hierarchical clustering system that groups people together according to where they live as well as by demographic, psychographic, and purchasing characteristics. Of great value in direct marketing, PRIZM divides the United States geographically into 300 markets, 3,000 counties, 30,000 zip code zones, and 300,000 block groups. The PRIZM model is based on the 1980 U.S. Census, using census block groups and tracks, postal carrier routes, and zip code zones as the smallest unit of analysis. These units are aggregated upward based on shared demographic, psychographic, and purchasing characteristics. At the highest level of analysis, the model consists of 12 *social groups* and 40 *lifestyle clusters* (Claritas, Inc., 1985).

Claritas, Inc., which developed prototypes of the current PRIZM model in the 1970s, used a combination of factor analysis and cluster analysis to group block units together to form *geo-clusters*. Because the U.S. Census approaches a census rather than a sampling survey, PRIZM might best be regarded as a data base. The United States is segmented into 80,000 census-based neighborhoods or geo-units, each consisting of about 1,000 households.

The basic data for each block are the 1,600 variables collected by the U.S. Census in 1980. These variables were factor analyzed to develop factor scales measuring underlying constructs inherent in the measures. Hierarchical cluster analysis was used to group together neighborhoods that shared common characteristics. The objective was to increase the homogeneity within groups along important lifestyle and purchasing dimensions, while at the same time making meaningful distinctions between clusters. The resulting "best fit" solution was judged by Claritas, Inc., to provide optimum discrimination between clusters in terms of a range of consumer behavior.

The outcome is a 40-cluster model of all 80,000 neighborhoods in the United States. Although census data serves as the core of the data base, these data are augmented by data collected through such surveys such as those by Simmons Research Bureau and Market Research, as well as purchase behavior data from National Family Opinion and AccountLine. Data bases such as the Polk New Car Sales Registrations also are merged.

Customer records are linked to the system through PRIZM coding. In essence, large data bases are linked to geo-areas, fleshing out what researchers know about each neighborhood.

The 12 social groupings are given detailed descriptive labels such as *Pre & Post-Child Families and Singles in Upscale, White-Collar Suburbs.* Within each social grouping, three or four clusters are identified with such labels as *God's Country, New Homesteaders,* and *Towns and Gowns.* Although VALS is driven by a theory-based clustering of values and lifestyles, PRIZM is organized primarily by geographic areas, supplemented by data on demographics and consumer behavior of people living in those geographic units. PRIZM is most likely to be useful to public relations programs in support of marketing. However, public relations programs focusing on a wide range of issues may find value in using PRIZM.

HIRING RESEARCH FIRMS

Pollock (1981, pp. 17–20) provided useful guidelines for practitioners seeking to hire a research firm to conduct a survey or other research service. Pollock emphasized organizational "readiness" for research when he cautioned that "research is not automatically valuable to decision makers." He urged practitioners to gain top management support before contracting for research services. This is best done, he suggested, through management participation at all stages of the research process. This point is underscored by Broom and Dozier (1990), who provided a "how-to" appendix on hiring research consultants.

Pollock (1981) also provided some key quality control points that practitioners must consider when contracting research services. These include: *sampling procedures, response rates,* and *interview and reporting quality.*

Sampling Procedures

As indicated previously, probability sampling procedures are essential for making probabilistic inferences about publics from which samples are drawn. With phone interviews, telephone directories are biased sample frames. A better technique is random digit dialing. A four-digit suffix, made up of random numbers, is assigned to a known prefix in the target area. Using this technique, both listed and unlisted numbers are included in the sample frame. With 95% + of households having a telephone, this technique provides a near-universal sample frame for the target area. A good guide for conducting phone surveys is provided by Frey (1983).

Pollock (1981) also suggested a sampling strategy for selecting respondents from within the household. Otherwise, the survey will be random among households but will be biased within the household. For example, women are more likely to answer the phone (within households with multiple residents) than men. This bias can be corrected through random or systematic sampling within the household.

Once survey data collection is complete, biases produced by uneven refusal rates and noncontact rates can be corrected through *weighting* procedures. Weighting procedures are statistical techniques provided by the data analysis software (e.g., SPSS-X, SAS) to bring the sample into harmony with known population characteristics. For example, people over the age of 60 years may constitute only 10% of the population of a community. However, because senior citizens are at home more often than other age groups, and because they like to talk to interviewers, the final survey may include 20% of sample over the age of 60 years. Weighting procedures reduce the number of senior citizens to 10% without removing those cases from the file. Other age groups under represented in the sample are mathematically increased in the sample. This brings the sample into balance with known population characteristics. The biasing effects of the older sample, relative to the population, thus are corrected.

Controlling Quality.   Ryan (1983) provided a checklist of quality control issues that practitioners hiring research firms should consider. Ryan derived his list from similar guidelines developed by the American Association for Public Opinion Research.

Practitioners hiring research firms to do probabilistic sampling surveys should have the research firm specify the sampling frame. The sampling frame is the list or set of sample elements from which the actual sample is drawn. The sample frame should correspond as much as possible to the universe or population you wish to study. Does the sampling frame include the relevant publics? Are qualifiers used at the beginning of the questionnaire to weed out people in the sample frame that are not members of the target public? Is sampling from the sample frame random? If not, is the technique probabilistic? (Although random sampling generally is desired, systematic sampling is often an adequate substitute.) What is the final sample size?

What is the margin of error? Margin of error is the degree to which percentages and medians from the sample accurately estimate the true value in the population. Margin of error usually is described in terms of the *95% confidence interval*. The 95% confidence interval is a range of numbers above and below the sample value that we are 95% sure includes the true population value.

For example, a survey of 400 respondents (randomly drawn from a large population) shows that 40% have a positive image of XYZ Corp. The 95%

confidence interval (derived from probability theory) is plus or minus 5 percentage points. This means that we are 95% sure (based on probability theory) that the true population percentage falls somewhere between 35% and 45%. Increasing the sample size to 1,500 respondents reduces the 95% confidence interval to 3 percentage points. That means if 40% in the sample of 1,500 have a positive image of XYZ Corp., then we are 95% sure that the true population value falls somewhere between 37% and 43%.

Generally, increasing the sample size reduces the margin of error. Margin of error is not the same for all questions in a questionnaire. Often, some questions are asked of only a subsample of the total respondents. When this happens, the margin of error needs to be computed for the subsample answering the question. Practitioners hiring research firms should insist that the margin of error (the 95% confidence interval) is specified for the overall sample and for important subsamples within the questionnaire.

Response Rates

Techniques such as random digit dialing generate random samples of the population (with telephones). However, randomness only holds if all 100% of respondents in the sample frame are successfully interviewed. This is rarely the case however. Some numbers in the sample frame (disconnected numbers, business and government phones) are not really part of the population of study and are not considered part of the final sample frame. Among respondents in the final sample frame, some never will answer the phone, some will refuse to be interviewed, and some will complete the interview. The *response rate* is the percent of households completing interviews among the total households in the final or valid sample.

Pollock (1981) stated that certain industry standards apply to response rates. According to Pollock, a response rate from 55% to 65% is adequate for long phone surveys (30–40 min). Rates as high as 85% can be achieved for surveys lasting only a few minutes. When elite groups such as medical doctors or CEOs are interviewed, a 30%-40% response rate is usually all that is obtained. For mail surveys, professional researchers consider 30% acceptable, although Babbie (1986) considered 50% a more appropriate minimum adequate standard.

Controlling Quality. Response rates are a function of questionnaire length and effort. Although long questionnaires may be unavoidable, any reduction in questionnaire size is desirable. This reduces interview costs and improves response rates. Effort is measured by the number of callbacks made to each number in the sample frame. How many times is each number called? Pollock (1981) suggested that four callbacks represent a "serious effort" to generate an acceptable response rate. Are separate days and times tried? These factors should be discussed with the research firm and procedures specified in the contract or memo of understanding.

Pollock (1981) also suggested strategies for improving response rates for mailed surveys. Follow-up mailings are, of course, key. According to Bailey (1987), two follow-up letters should be sent, the last including a second copy of the questionnaire. Other factors that improve response rates are personalized letters and envelopes, the use of stamps instead of meters, and cover letter on sponsoring organization's letterhead (Pollock, 1981). Bailey provided detailed suggestions for improving response rates for mailed questionnaires.

Interview and Reporting Quality

Sample size and response rate specifications are relatively objective criteria. Although quality interviewing procedures, professional supervision, and adequate reporting procedures are equally important, these factors are not as easy to analyze. Are samples of refusals and completed interviews called back by supervisors to check interviewer quality? How are interviewers supervised during data collection? How are they trained? Pollock (1981) suggested that visiting the research firm while a survey is in progress is a good way to assess the quality of service provided.

Research firms increasingly are using video display terminals (CRTs) rather than paper questionnaires. The interviewer operates from questionnaire items on the terminal screen, then types in responses directly into the computer. This permits more complex branching within the questionnaire and allows for instant data entry of questionnaire results into the computerized data base.

In addition, the computer-assisted data collection procedure allows for quality checks of answers to questions that are out of range. For example, the gender question has only three responses: (1) female (2) male (9) don't know. Any value other than 1, 2, or 9 is out of range. The same kind of quality control can be achieved with well-trained and well-supervised interviewers and paper questionnaires. The real benefit of CRT-assisted interviewing is in reduced costs.

Questionnaire Design Issues.   Related to interview quality is the questionnaire itself. Questionnaire design is too broad a topic for consideration here. Bailey (1987), Babbie (1986), and Broom and Dozier (1990) provided detailed discussion of questionnaire design. However, here are a few quick quality control measures that the practitioner can use.

First, be involved in questionnaire design. Provide the research firm with a set of research questions or information objectives that you hope to satisfy through the survey. Specify what the information will be used for and the time frame of those applications.

Insist on a pilot test of the questionnaire. Some research firms insist that their questionnaire design skills are such that pilot testing is unnecessary. They are wrong. Once the pilot is completed, meet with the individual who supervised the pilot survey. Go through the questionnaire with that individual on an item-by-item basis. This step is ensured when you insist on signing off on the final version of the questionnaire.

Reporting the Results. Specify how the information will be reported to your organization. If the research firm offers only "field and tab" services, realize that the results will be something akin to a computer printout with frequency distributions and cross-tabulations of key variables. If you will require further analysis, specify that analysis in the contract or memo of understanding.

In addition, reserve access to the data base for ad hoc analysis after the final report is accepted. Specify a fee structure for such services. If you have internal computing capability, investigate the possibility of receiving the data base in a computer-readable form for internal ad hoc analysis. Have your computer people talk to their computer people to ensure that glitches do not frustrate this effort. Attempt a transfer of a dummy data file before contracting for services; the research firm will work harder to correct any glitches if securing the contract is at risk.

The research firm also should be prepared to make oral presentations to key managers in your organization. Ask the research firm what types of support media they use for such presentations. Ask to see examples of slides, transparencies, or videos that they have used for such presentations in the past. Assess the communication skills of the presenter, including the ability to answer questions from the floor.

LOCATING RESEARCH FIRMS

When locating research firms for conducting public relations research, the practitioner should consider both commercial and academic research operations.

Academic Research Services. Many universities offer research services on par with commercial research firms. To locate university-based research firms, the *Research Centers Directory* (Wadkins, 1987) is a good source of information. The directory is available in public and university libraries in the reference section. The directory lists 9,200 university-related and nonprofit research organizations. Index headings in the directory of use to practitioners include: Marketing, Public Relations, Public Opinion, and Survey Research. The Survey Research category is perhaps most relevant. Indexing is organized by state. Descriptions of research organizations include a listing of services offered and contact information.

The Center for Organizational Communication Research and Services at the University of South Florida has compiled an abbreviated directory of academic survey research organizations, broken down by states and foreign countries. Copies can be requested from the Department of Communication, University of South Florida, Tampa, FL 33620-5550.

Commercial Research Services. A good reference for locating commercial research firms is the 550-page *Research Service Directory* (MRA, 1987b), an official annual publication of the Marketing Research Association (MRA). In addition, the MRA publishes the *Marketing Research Association Membership Roster* (MRA, 1987b), listing contact information for over 2,200 members. Both directories are $85 each to nonmembers (effective March 1987) and can be purchased through the Marketing Research Association, 111 East Wacker Drive, Suite 600, Chicago, IL 60601. The phone number is (312) 644-6610.

Another directory of use in locating research firms and services is the *Directory of U.S. & Canadian Marketing Surveys & Services* (1986). This directory lists 4,500 multiclient marketing reports and continuing services from 300 consulting firms in the United States, Europe, and Canada. Company specialty index headings of use to practitioners include: Advertising, Readership & Media Auditing, and Attitude, Behavior & Opinion Surveys. The main index lists Surveys, including Consumer, Corporate Image & Corporate Reputation Surveys, as well as Opinion Surveys. The index also breaks down services by industry types. The citations include contact information, a brief description of company services, continuing services such as caravan surveys and periodicals. Also listed are individual service clients and reports over $1,000 and under $1,000.

Practitioners seeking to use the VALS system have a number of choices, according to Stephen Mills, a VALS consultant with SRI International. If the practitioner wants to use the VALS system in-house, the practitioner organization must become members of the VALS program. The initial membership fee is $9,500, which includes training conferences at SRI headquarters in Menlo Park, CA, and reference materials. Annual subsequent membership is $5,000. Membership in the VALS program provides access to research data bases, consulting services from SRI International's VALS program, and use of the VALS classification system. Members can obtain full research firm services from the VALS consultants or simply can use the VALS classification system as part of the organization's own internal research activities. Practitioners can write the VALS Program directly at SRI International, 333 Ravenswood Avenue, Menlo Park, CA 94025.

The hefty price tag, however, may make another strategy more attractive. A number of public relations and advertising firms, such as Ketchum Communications, have become members of the VALS program at a higher rate so that they can provide VALS services to their clients. The directories often will mention whether a firm offers VALS services to clients.

The Claritas PRIZM services can be obtained through two offices. On the West Coast, information about PRIZM can be obtained from Claritas at 520 Broadway, Suite 520, Santa Monica, CA 90401. On the East Coast, information about PRIZM can be obtained from Claritas at 201 N. Union, Alexandria, VA 22314.

If the practitioner is looking for published research reports, *Findex: The Directory of Market Research Reports, Studies and Surveys* is a good reference (DeGrange, 1986). The directory contains references for 11,000 research reports from 520 U.S. and foreign research publishers.

REFERENCES

Babbie, E. (1986). *The practice of social research* (3rd ed.). Belmont, CA: Wadsworth.
Bailey, K. D. (1982). *Methods of social research* (2nd ed.). New York: Free Press.
Bailey, K. D. (1987). *Methods of social research* (3rd ed.). New York: Free Press.
Berelson, B. (1952). *Content analysis in communication research.* New York: Free Press.
Beyer, C. (1986). Salary survey. *Public Relations Journal, 42*(6), 26–30.
Broom, G. M. (1986, May). *Public relations roles and systems theory: Functional and historicist causal models.* Paper presented at the meeting of the Public Relations Interest Group, International Communication Association, Chicago.
Broom, G. M., & Dozier, D. M. (1990). *Using research in public relations: Applications to program management.* Englewood Cliffs, NJ: Prentice-Hall.
Campbell, D. T., & Stanley, J. C. (1963). *Experimental and quasi-experimental designs for research.* Chicago: Rand-McNally.
Claritas, Inc. (1985). *PRIZM: The integrated marketing Solution.* Alexandria, VA: Author.
Cutlip, S. M., Center, A. H., & Broom, G. M. (1985). *Effective public relations* (6th ed.). Englewood Cliffs, NJ: Prentice-Hall.
DeGrange, S. F. (1986). *Findex: The directory of market research reports, studies and surveys* (8th ed.). New York: FIND/SVP.
Directory of U.S. & Canadian marketing surveys and services (6th ed.). (1986). Bridgewater, NJ: Rauch Associates.
Dozier, D. M. (1984a, June). *The evolution of evaluation methods among public relations practitioners.* Paper presented at the Educator Academy meeting of the International Association of Business Communicators, Montreal.
Dozier, D. M. (1984b). Program evaluation and roles of practitioners. *Public Relations Review, 10*(2), 13–21.
Dozier, D. M. (1986, August). *The environmental scanning function of public relations practitioners and participation in management decision making.* Paper presented at the meeting of the Public Relations Division, Association for Education in Journalism and Mass Communication, Norman, OK.

Finn, P. (1984). In-house research becomes a factor. *Public Relations Journal, 40*(7), 18–20.

Frey, J. H. (1983). *Survey research by telephone.* Beverly Hills, CA: Sage.

Grunig, J. E., & Hunt, T. (1984). *Managing public relations.* New York: Holt, Rinehart & Winston.

Holsti, O. R. (1969). *Content analysis for the social sciences and humanities.* Reading, MA: Addison-Wesley.

Lesly, P. (Ed.). (1983). *Lesly's public relations handbook* (3rd. ed.). Englewood Cliffs, NJ: Prentice-Hall.

Lindenmann, W. K. (1983). Content analysis. *Public Relations Review, 39*(7), 24–26.

Mariampolski, H. The resurgence of qualitative research. *Public Relations Journal, 40*(7), 21–23.

Marketing Research Association. (1987a). *MRA membership roster.* Chicago: Author.

Marketing Research Association. (1987b). *Research service directory.* Chicago: Author.

Miller, D. A. (1986). *Psychographics: A study in diversity.* Unpublished manuscript, University of Maryland, College of Journalism, College Park.

Mitchell, A. (1983). *The nine American lifestyles.* New York: Warner.

Planmetrics, Inc. (1985). *The cultural analysis group at Planmetrics.* New York: Author.

Pollock, J. C. (1981). The role of survey research. *Public Relations Journal, 37*(11), 18–21.

Riesman, D. (1961). *The lonely crowd.* New Haven, CT: Yale University Press.

Ryan, M. (1983). Guidelines for proper polling. *Public Relations Journal, 39*(7), 18–20.

SRI, International. (1984). *VALS typology.* Menlo Park, CA: Author.

SRI, International. (1985). *VALS—Values and lifestyles of Americans.* Menlo Park, CA: Author.

Stempel, G. H. (1989). Content analysis. In G. H. Stempel & B. H. Wesley (Eds.), *Research methods in mass communication* (2nd ed., pp. 124–136). Englewood Cliffs, NJ: Prentice-Hall.

Stempel, G. H., III, & Wesley, B. H. (Eds.). (1981). *Research methods in mass communication.* Englewood Cliffs, NJ: Prentice-Hall.

Wadkins, M. M. (Ed.). (1987). *Research centers directory* (11th ed.). Detroit: Gale Research.

Webb, E., et al. (1966). *Unobtrusive measures.* Chicago: Rand-McNally.

III THE DEPARTMENTAL LEVEL: CHARACTERISTICS OF EXCELLENT PUBLIC RELATIONS DEPARTMENTS

Part I determined how public relations must be practiced to contribute to organizational effectiveness. Part II sets forth a normative theory describing how communication programs must be practiced for them to contribute to organizational goals. Part III moves to positive—descriptive—elements of the general theory of public relations. It identifies the characteristics of communication departments that are most likely to practice Part II's normative theory. Each chapter, therefore, identifies an attribute of an excellent public relations department.

9 What is Excellence in Management?

James E. Grunig
University of Maryland

ABSTRACT

This chapter begins the search for excellence in public relations by reviewing the many books that have searched for excellence in the overall management of organizations. Beginning with Peters and Waterman's (1982) book, In Search of Excellence, *management researchers and writers have studied organizations they previously defined as excellent to determine the attributes that made them excellent. The chapter reviews the many studies of excellence and identifies 12 characteristics that appear repeatedly in the literature. It then derives implications for public relations from each of the attributes. Many of the attributes define characteristics of excellence in communication management that appear in the remaining chapters of Part III or are underlying characteristics of organizations that make excellent public relations possible— which are identified in Part IV. The chapter concludes that excellence in communication is a characteristic of excellent organizations. But it also concludes that excellent communication can help to make organizations excellent.*

Perfection: An imaginary state . . . distinguished from the actual by an element known as excellence.

— Ambrose Bierce (1842–1914)

The function of perfection—to make one know one's imperfection.
— Augustine (354–430 A.D.)

There are two perfect men: one dead and the other unborn.
— Chinese Proverb

For the past half dozen years, business leaders have been saturated with tales
of excellence and demonstrations of how the best companies and the best
leaders do it. I have sensed growing weariness with hearing one more heroic
story that simply does not match the mundane issues managers struggle with
every day, the hard choices they must make.

—Rosabeth Moss Kanter (1989, p. 21)

Ten years ago, Peters and Waterman (1982) published the best selling book,
In Search of Excellence, which has sold at least 5 million copies in 16
languages.[1] In the book, Peters and Waterman reported the results of a
study in which they selected 43 excellent companies and identified eight
attributes that made those companies excellent. As Augustine's words state,
they were looking for perfection in management so that other companies
could compare themselves with the excellent companies in order to discover
their own imperfections and what to do about them. As predicted by the
Chinese proverb, however, none of these companies turned out to be
perfect. Within 2 years, *Businessweek* ("Who's Excellent," 1984) reported
that "at least 14 of the 43 excellent companies . . . had lost their luster
. . . —significant earnings declines that stem from serious business problems, management problems, or both" (p. 76).

Since that time, as Kanter (1989) pointed out, managers have been
flooded with books by experts telling them how to reach an imaginary state
of excellence. These books are filled with stories of heroes and heroic
organizations, which many others have hoped to emulate. Most heroes are
not perfect, however, and most fail at some time and at some things.
Therefore, readers of books on excellence who look for a perfect model in
one organization are sure to be disappointed. *Businessweek* ("Who's
Excellent," 1984) reported, for example, that Peters and Waterman (1982)
did not claim that their excellent companies were perfect—that each had all
of the attributes of excellence or that they would stay excellent forever.

On the other hand, if one looks at enough partial heroes, he or she should
be able to isolate enough attributes of each of them to construct a model of
the perfect hero—a model that can be used as a standard of comparison for
self-improvement. A search for excellence, therefore, consists less of a
search for excellent management or excellent companies than of a search for
the attributes of excellence that can be isolated from a study of good
companies.

When we began the IABC excellence study, we took Peters and Waterman's (1982) study as an example of what we wanted to do. Peters and
Waterman isolated the attributes of excellent management in general; we

---

[1]As reported in Peters and Austin (1985, p. ix).

wanted to isolate the attributes of excellent communication management. Because excellence in general management should be related to excellent communication management, we begin Part III of this book—which is devoted to the managerial (or meso) level of our theory of excellence in public relations—with a review of the theories of excellence in management. We do so, first, to determine whether the principles of excellence in general management also apply to the management of communication. If they do apply, they should help us to isolate the principles of excellent communication management. Second, however, this chapter identifies some of the general conditions that must be present in organizations before they can have excellent public relations. As we see, several of these conditions are discussed in Part IV, which explores the macroconditions that make excellent public relations possible.

The attributes of excellence identified in this chapter came from four streams of literature. The first is the Peters and Waterman stream, the original book by Peters and Waterman (1982); follow-up books by Peters and Austin (1985), Peters (1987), and Waterman (1987); and similar studies by Hobbs (1987) and Wholey (1987). The second stream consists of books about innovative and entrepreneurial organizations, including the trilogy by Kanter (1977, 1983, 1989) and Pinchot's (1985) book on intrapreneurship. The third stream consists of books on Japanese management, including Pascale and Athos (1981) and Ouchi (1981, 1984). The final stream consists of literature on Total Quality Management (TQM). Although much of the literature on TQM goes into technical detail beyond the scope of this chapter, some of that literature embraces attributes of management related to the quality movement that are useful here. A review of these attributes by Tuttle (1989) and the guidelines for the Malcolm Baldridge National Quality Award (National Institute of Standards and Technology, 1990) made it possible to isolate those attributes for this chapter. In addition to these four streams of literature, the chapter cites other books on management and on organizational performance that support the choice of attributes of excellence.

As a result of this search for excellence in the literature on excellence, this chapter identifies 12 characteristics that appear repeatedly. This chapter describes each of those characteristics and cites examples of them in the literature. Then it discusses the relevance of each to our search for excellence in public relations and communication management. The term *public relations* seldom appears in any of these books, although the term *communication* appears frequently. Nevertheless, each of the attributes suggests important implications for excellence in public relations and for the conditions that bring it about. Before examining these 12 characteristics, however, it is necessary to describe how scholars of managerial excellence have defined and identified excellence.

HOW IS EXCELLENCE DEFINED?

Although most of the studies of and books on excellence reviewed in this chapter have searched for attributes of management, they have defined excellence and identified it in different ways. Peters and Waterman (1982) used six financial criteria to identify excellent companies for analysis: compound asset growth, compound equity growth, average ratio of market value to book value, average return on total capital, average return on equity, and average return on sales. Hobbs (1987) identified his excellent companies by measuring return on sales and return on owner's investment. Paul and Taylor (1986) used similar financial measures to identify the 101 best performing companies in America.

Carroll (1983), in a review of Peters and Waterman (1982), criticized the use of financial measures for identifying excellence in management. He pointed out that "such factors as proprietary technology, market dominance, control of critical raw materials, and national culture and policy also affect financial performance, regardless of the excellence of management" (p. 79).

Other writers have defined excellence more subjectively. Kanter (1983, 1989) and Pinchot (1985) defined excellence as innovativeness. *Fortune* magazine annually lists the most admired corporations based on quality of management, quality of products and services, innovation, value as a long-term investment, financial soundness, ability to attract, develop, and keep talented people, community and environmental responsibility, and use of corporate assets. Similarly, Lydenberg, Martin, Strub, and the Council on Economic Priorities (1986) rated corporations on their social conscience; Levering, Moskowitz, and Katz (1985) on human resources benefits for employees; and Zeitz and Dusky (1988) on benefits for women.

Hickman and Silva (1984) suggested that each organization create its unique criteria for excellence and then suggested how leadership can help the organization meet those criteria. Finally, Nash and Zullo (1988) named a "Misfortune 500" on the basis of such criteria as "badvertising" campaigns, unjustified promotions, mismanagement, and poorly conceived products. In addition, *Public Relations Journal* ("Business Editors," 1986) and *Communication World* (Arndt, 1988) constructed lists of companies with excellent public relations. Although all of these lists are of corporations, the Public Broadcasting System (PBS) also aired a program in 1990 in which it named and featured several excellent governmental and nonprofit organizations.

In short, lists abound of both excellent and poor organizations. In preparing for our IABC study, we cross-referenced a number of these lists to identify organizations to include in the study. We were only mildly surprised to find that some organizations appeared both on best and worst lists. The problem with such best and worst lists is that they are not really related to criteria for organizational effectiveness, as effectiveness was defined and explained in chapter 3. That chapter explained that organizations are effective when they manage their relationships with strategic constituencies well, making it possible for them to choose and attain realistic goals. Effectiveness may translate into financial success, if the organization chooses that goal. An effective organization also should have a good reputation if it builds good relationships with its constituencies. However, no one set of criteria can be used to identify every effective organization, because some organizations may have more difficult problems, more troublesome constituencies, or different goals.

As a result, excellence in management may produce different results for each organization, which is not too far from Hickman and Silva's (1984) suggestion of setting one's own criteria for excellence. Excellence in general management — and in communication management — should make most organizations more effective, as we have defined effectiveness. But one set of measures cannot be used to measure effectiveness for every organization.

Our task in this chapter, therefore, is to isolate the attributes of excellent management. Excellent management contributes to organizational effectiveness, although other factors also will contribute to effectiveness. We turn, then, to the attributes of excellence in management and examine their implications for the management of communication.

HUMAN RESOURCES

Excellent organizations empower people by giving employees autonomy and allowing them to make strategic decisions. They also pay attention to the personal growth and quality of work life of employees. They emphasize the interdependence rather than independence of employees. They also emphasize integration rather than segmentation and strike a balance between teamwork and individual effort.

It should be no surprise that most books on excellence in management mention human resources as an attribute of excellent organizations and even as the focal point of their description of excellence. Empowering of people through job autonomy and participation in decision making long has been a critical variable in theories of job satisfaction, morale, and communication in organizations.

Utilization of human resources is one of the key criteria for the Malcom Baldridge National Quality Award (National Institute of Standards and Technology, 1990). Chung (1987) listed the management of human resources as the second of three critical success factors in management.

Naisbitt and Aburdene (1985) stressed its importance in their book, *Re-inventing the Corporation*. They pointed out that "in the information society, we are shifting from infrastructure to quality of life" (p. 53) and predicted that "the companies that create the most nourishing environments for personal growth will attract the most talented people" (p. 53). Drucker (1980) added that "managers need to realize that they are being paid for enabling people to do the work for which those people are being paid" (p. 24).

Human resources appeared as a key variable throughout the series of books by Peters and Waterman. Peters and Waterman (1982) included "productivity through people" (p. 233) as one of the eight attributes of their excellent companies. They discussed "trust" (p. 236) and "respect for people" (pp. 238–239) as two characteristics of a people orientation. A people orientation, they added, pervades the structure, culture, and processes of an excellent organization: "What makes it live at these companies is a plethora of structural devices, systems, styles, and values, all reinforcing one another so that the companies are truly unusual in their ability to achieve extraordinary results through ordinary people" (pp. 238–239).

Peters and Austin (1985) retained "People, People, People" (p. 235) as the third of four characteristics of excellence. Peters (1987) made "achieve flexibility by empowering people" his third of five prescriptions for "Thriving on Chaos." People are empowered, he explained, by "high involvement, minimal hierarchy, and increased rewards based upon new performance parameters (quality responsiveness)" (p. 39). Waterman (1987) named "Teamwork, trust, politics, and power" as the fifth of eight characteristics of renewing organizations: "Renewers constantly use words such as teamwork and trust. They are relentless in fighting office politics and power contests, and in breaking down the we/they barriers that paralyze action" (p. 10).

Martin (1983) wrote that excellent organizations allow employees to do more than participate in decision making. He maintained that most employees can be managed without managers and that managers in such a system will have to rely more on human relations skills in dealing with subordinates than on command and control (p. 145).

Kanter (1989) discussed in detail the conditions under which people must work in large corporations to allow these "giants to learn to dance." In what she called the "post-entrepreneurial world," Kanter said that pay will be based on an employee's contribution to projects rather than position or status. She added: "Thus, the post-entrepreneurial age is engendering a variety of balancing acts centering on personal responsibilities and relations. Help in achieving balance can come from better personal time management, better organizational systems, and better institutional supports" (p. 297).

Reich (1987) described the need for a collaborative culture, both in society and in organizations: ". . . the central problem of economic policy becomes less how to discipline drones or tease the last ounce of genius out of lone entrepreneurs, but rather how to create the kinds of organizations in which people can pool their efforts, insights, and enthusiasm without fear of exploitation" (p. 246).

The cultivation of human resources is closely entwined with organizational structure and culture, the next two attributes. We turn to them after discussing the implications of human resources for communication management.

Implications for Public Relations

Good use of human resources in organizations contributes indirectly to excellent public relations by fostering the kind of organization in which excellent public relations can function. Chapter 17, on the structure of organizations, chapter 20, on internal communication, and chapter 21, on organizational culture, show that people have more autonomy, that morale is better, and that people are more innovative in organizations with decentralized, organic structures and with participative cultures. These also are the conditions in which excellent public relations can occur. Excellent public relations, in other words, is entwined with other characteristics of excellent organizations.

In addition, communication contributes greatly to good human relationships in organizations. Therefore, internal public relations — as chapter 20 shows — helps organizations to make quality use of human resources.

ORGANIC STRUCTURE

People cannot be empowered by fiat. Organizations give people power by eliminating bureaucratic, hierarchical organizational structures. They develop what organizational theorists call an "organic structure." They decentralize decisions, managing without managers as much as possible. They also avoid stratification of employees, humiliating some by having such symbols of status as executive dining rooms, corner offices, or reserved parking spaces. At the same time, they use leadership, collaboration, and culture to integrate the organization rather than structure.

Several generations of organizational sociologists have recognized and studied the effects of organizational structure on organizational effectiveness and employee morale, so it is not surprising that writers on managerial excellence should have recognized its importance also. Robbins (1990) defined structure as "how tasks are to be allocated, who reports to whom, and the formal coordinating mechanisms and interaction patterns that will be followed" (p. 5). Katz and Kahn (1966) defined structure as the "interrelated set of events which return upon themselves to complete and renew a cycle of activities" (pp. 20–21). J. Grunig (1976), in a study of the effect of structure on public relations, integrated several of these definitions by saying that "structure is a role relationship or cycle of role relationships between individuals that is not under the control of any one of those individuals acting alone" (p. 15).

Although sociologists have identified several structural characteristics of organizations, the four cited most often are centralization (the extent to which decision making is concentrated at the top of the organization), formalization (the number of formal rules and regulations and the extent to which an organization follows them), stratification (the extent to which rewards and recognition are concentrated on a few people), and complexity (the extent of specialization or differentiation).[2] These four characteristics are correlated with each other in most organizations: One type of organization is centralized, formalized, stratified, and less complex. The most common term for such an organization is *mechanical,* using the terminology of Burns and Stalker (1961). The other type of organization, generally called *organic,* is decentralized, less formalized, less stratified, and complex.[3]

The essential difference between the two organizations is the amount of autonomy given employees and the extent to which all employees participate in the management of an organization. Although mechanical organizations are more efficient than organic organizations, organic organizations are more innovative; and employees in organic organizations have greater job satisfaction and morale (Hage, 1980). Most of the writers on excellence, therefore, have rediscovered these same principles; although they also have recognized that organic organizations require strong leadership and strong cultures to provide the teamwork and collaboration necessary to integrate the organization.

Peters and Waterman (1982) pointed out that excellent companies encourage an entrepreneurial spirit, "because they push autonomy remarkably far down the line" (p. 200). Of Peters and Waterman's eight characteristics of excellent companies, three can be described as structural. One of

---

[2]For reviews of organizational characteristics, see Hage and Aiken (1970), Hage (1980), or Robbins (1990).

[3]Hull and Hage (1982) showed that the mechanical and organic types oversimplify many organizations. In particular large organizations can be a mixture of these two types. In reality, then, the two types of organizations could instead be two structural dimensions that characterize most organizations to varying degrees. To understand the impact of structure, however, we can treat organic and mechanical structures as though they are mutually exclusive.

these principles is "autonomy and entrepreneurship." A second, "simple form, lean staff," describes decentralization—"few administrative layers, few people at upper levels" (p. i). Peters and Waterman described the third, "simultaneous loose-tight properties," as "the coexistence of firm central direction and maximum individual autonomy" (p. 318). Peters and Waterman, however, also found that although excellent companies have loose (organic) structures, they provide discipline through a tight culture—which substitutes for the formal rules and regulations of formalized, mechanical organizations.[4]

Peters and Austin (1985) described what they called "ownership of the job" in excellent organizations: "Does the average person view himself or herself as in command, as listened to, as a vital part of the business (city, staff, school) or not?" (p. 235). Peters (1987) said that the successful firm in the 1990s will be flatter (have fewer layers of organizational structure), populated by more autonomous units, and oriented toward differentiation and the creation of market niches.

In discussing leadership, Peters (1987) advised managers to delegate, "to really let go" (p. 451). He added, "The autonomy granted is real and significant, but it is matched by the psychological pressure to perform up to one's limits and to the highest standards" (p. 453). In addition, as part of his recommendation to empower people, Peters suggested "involving everyone in everything" (p. 285) and using "self-managing teams" (p. 297).

Kanter (1983) coined the terms *integrated* and *segmented* to describe the structures and cultures of innovative and noninnovative organizations. Integrated organizations see problems as wholes:

> Such organizations reduce rancorous conflict and isolation between organizational units; create mechanisms for exchange of information and new ideas across organizational boundaries; ensure that multiple perspectives will be taken into account in decisions; and provide coherence and direction to the whole organization. In these team-oriented cooperative environments, innovation flourishes. . . . Segmentalist approaches see problems as narrowly as possible, independently of the context, independently of their connections to any other problems. Companies with segmentalist cultures are likely to have segmented structures: a large number of compartments walled off from one another—department level above from level below, field office from headquarters, labor from management, or men from women. (p. 28)

Kanter added that integrated organizations encourage participation through "task forces, quality circles, problem-solving groups, or shared responsibility teams" (p. 241). As Peters and Waterman (1982) did in discussing "loose-tight properties," Kanter pointed out that integrated organizations

---

[4]A function that Robbins (1990) also ascribed to culture.

use leadership rather than structure to "keep everyone's mind on the shared vision," put constraints on decisions, and watch for uneven participation (p. 275).

In her later book, Kanter (1989) used the term *newstreams,* or "channels for speeding the flow of ideas and innovations" to describe organic structures: "Newstream people have a quest for autonomy whereas mainstream people have a quest for control" (p. 349).

The school of writers on Japanese management also identified organic structures. Pascale and Athos (1981) contrasted the interdependent, divisional structure of the Matsushita Electric Company with the more hierarchical structure of the American company, ITT. They pointed out that the Japanese value interdependence — "the best of independence without getting the worst of both" (p. 125).

Ouchi (1981) identified seven key concepts of Japanese management, most of which are related to organic structures: lifetime employment, slow evaluation and promotion, nonspecialized career paths, implicit control mechanisms, collective decision making, collective responsibility, and wholistic concern for people. Ouchi added that egalitarianism is a central feature of the Type Z, Japanese, style of management: "Egalitarianism implies that each person can apply discretion and can work autonomously without close supervision, because they are to be trusted." In addition, he said: "In Type Z organizations, the decision-making process is typically a consensual, participative one. Social scientists have described this as a democratic (as opposed to autocratic or apathetic) process in which many people are drawn into the shaping of important decisions" (p. 66).

In a later book, Ouchi (1984) described the "M-Form" of management, which is like the structure of the Matsushita Electric Company described by Pascale and Athos (1981). Like Peters and Waterman's (1982) "loose-tight properties," the M-Form falls between a highly centralized and decentralized organization. Managers of a division must function as though they were solo competitors in the marketplace. They also must function as though they were members of a team. The divisions are interdependent, thus requiring collaboration for the organization to function.

The literature on Total Quality Management calls for essentially the same type of interdependent units. Tuttle (1989) called this "cross-functional management": "Total quality requires that boundary issues be removed. Cross functional committees and associated project teams help to break down the walls. They focus on major organizational issues . . . Committee representatives not only represent their narrow vertical perspective of maintenance, engineering, or human resources, but also the company-wide perspective" (p. 5).

Pinchot (1985), in writing on entrepreneurial organizations, also described "cross-functional teams" as one of 10 "freedom factors" that make innovation possible. Another was, "The doer decides: people are permitted to do the job in their own way without having to stop constantly to explain their actions and ask for permission" (pp. 198–199). Naisbitt and Aburdene (1985) also alluded to smaller, interdependent units when they reported that large companies have found that they must adopt the values of small business to compete in a changing marketplace.

Martin (1983) described the autonomy of organic structures as "managing without managers." He maintained that participative management is not enough. Employees must be allowed to do more than participate in management or serve in advisory groups. Martin added that it is a myth that managers serve an important function. Instead, he maintained that workers should be allowed to manage themselves to free managers for leadership rather than supervision.

Implications for Public Relations

Organic structure is so closely entwined with the use of human resources in organizations that the conclusions for the previous attribute of excellent management apply here also. As chapter 17 discusses, researchers have studied the effect of organizational structure on public relations extensively. This research shows that organic structure alone does not predict the presence of excellent public relations, but it also shows that excellent public relations probably cannot exist within mechanical structures. In addition, chapter 20 shows that excellent internal communication is so entwined with organic structures that the communication system is actually a structural characteristic of organizations.

INTRAPRENEURSHIP

Excellent organizations have an innovative, entrepreneurial spirit — frequently called "intrapreneurship." Intrapreneurship, too, is related to the other characteristics of excellent organizations: a spirit of internal entrepreneurship occurs in organizations that develop organic structures and cultivate human resources.

The introduction to this chapter pointed out that many writers on organizational excellence have defined an excellent organization as one that is entrepreneurial and that cultivates innovation. Pinchot (1985) coined the term *intrapreneur* to describe entrepreneurs who work inside an organization — "those who take hands-on responsibility for creating innovation of any kind within an organization" (p. ix). He defined an entrepreneur as "someone who fills the role of an intrepreneur outside the organization" (p.

ix). Pinchot, as well as other writers, pointed out that the entrepreneurial spirit of small companies dissipates when organizations become large and bureaucratic. As a result, large organizations must learn to foster and use entrepreneurial talent.

Peters and Waterman (1982) described intrapreneurship through two of their eight characteristics of excellence. First, "autonomy and entrepreneurship" characterize excellent organizations—"an ability to be big and yet to act small at the same time" (p. 200). The second intrapreneurial characteristic is "a bias for action"—the willingness "to try things out, to experiment" (p. 134). Peters and Austin (1985) included innovation as the second of four characteristics of excellence—"paying attention to innovation, talking it up, wandering the design spaces, and celebrating the emergence (and even some of the failures) of champions" (p. 133). Innovation, according to Peters and Austin, takes place in "skunkworks"—"those small off-line bands of mavericks that are the hallmark of innovative organizations" (p. 136). Peters (1987) continued to list "fast paced innovation" as one of five characteristics of organizations that "thrive on chaos" (p. 39), and Waterman (1987) included "stability in motion" as the sixth of eight characteristics of renewing companies (p. 11).

Kanter (1983, 1989) defined excellent organizations as those that are innovative—"change masters" and "giants that learn to dance." Kanter (1983) used the term *entrepreneurial organization.* Kanter (1989) added that entrepreneurial organizations fall between "corpocrats"—large bureaucratic firms such as Eastman Kodak—and "cowboys"—small entrepreneurial firms such as Apple Computer.

Naisbitt and Aburdene (1985) also wrote that "Many companies are re-inventing themselves as confederations of entrepreneurs, operating under the main tent of the corporation" (p. 74). Drucker (1980) wrote that managers need a strategy to make large companies capable of innovation (p. 48). Hobbs (1987) found that innovation and R&D activity played a critical role in 14 superior organizations he identified (p. 106). Reich (1987) added that innovation must be collective: "In advanced nations, wealth flows from the collective abilities of groups of people to piece things together in new ways, to conceive of new possibilities, and to make continual improvements in what has come before" (p. 47).

Implications for Public Relations

The discussion of the first three attributes of excellence makes clear that human resources, organic structure, and intrapreneurship occur together. As we see next, excellent systems of communication are essential for entrepreneurial organizations to work. Thus, excellent public relations and communication management are most likely to be found in entrepreneurial organizations, and they are necessary for entrepreneurial organizations to exist.

SYMMETRICAL COMMUNICATION SYSTEMS

Although studies of organizational excellence do not use the term "symmetrical communication," they all describe it — with both internal and external publics. Excellent organizations "stay close" to their customers, employees, and other "strategic constituencies."

Writers on excellence almost never mention the term public relations, but almost all of them describe communication and communications systems of organizations. Almost always, they describe these systems in ways that seem to characterize a two-way symmetrical system of communication, as that type of communication was described in chapters 2, 11, and 20. Symmetrical communication takes place through dialogue, negotiation, listening, and conflict management rather than through persuasion, manipulation, and the giving of orders. Writers on excellence most often describe symmetrical communication when they discuss communication with customers and employees or when they describe how the CEO or leaders of an excellent organization communicate with these and other publics of the organization.

"Staying close to the customer," for example, was one of Peters and Waterman's (1982) eight attributes of excellent companies. Customer satisfaction is a criterion for the Malcolm Baldrige award; it also is a component of most programs of Total Quality Management (Feigenbaum, 1983, p. 7; Tuttle, 1989, p. 4). In the later books by Peters and Waterman, Peters and Austin (1985) and Peters (1987) retained customers and customer responsiveness as one of their characteristics of excellence. This attribute, perhaps, has more to do with marketing than with public relations; but its implications apply to all forms of organizational communication.

These writers suggested that organizations stick close to the customer through symmetrical communication: "Listening to the users: The excellent companies are better listeners. They get a benefit from market closeness that for us was truly unexpected. . . . Most of their real innovation comes from the market" (Peters & Waterman, 1982, p. 159). Peters and Austin (1985) added: "We've developed a term, after careful thought: *smell.* Does your company smell of customers? Do you listen to them directly (via MBWA), act on what you hear, listen naively (i.e., consider their perceptions more important than your superior technical knowledge of service or product)? . . . So the key words in our lexicon are simple ones, such as courtesy, listening, perception" (p. 45). Peters (1987) described the organization that communicates symmetrically with consumers as a porous one: "The customer responsiveness prescriptions add up to a view of a 'porous' organization listening intently to its customers and adjusting rapidly" (p. 39).

Internal communication in excellent organizations also is symmetrical. Peters and Waterman (1982) said, for example: "The excellent companies are a vast network of informal communications. The patterns and intensity cultivate the right people's getting into contact with each other, regularly" (pp. 121–122). Peters and Austin (1985) described symmetrical communication when they talked about MBWA (managing by walking around): "To listen is just that: to listen" (p. 10). Peters (1987) said that organizations that thrive on chaos, "Share virtually all information with everyone" (p. 504).

Chung (1987) included a chapter on communicating with employees as part of his discussion of human resources. "From a managerial perspective," he said, "communication is important because it is a means by which organizational members collect and disseminate the information that they need, and it is also a means by which they achieve coordination and cooperation" (p. 397). Ouchi (1981) described symmetrical communication with employees as "subtlety": "A foreman [sic] who knows his [sic] workers well can pinpoint personalities, decide who works with whom, and thus put together work teams of maximal effectiveness" (p. 6). In describing the M-form of management, Ouchi (1984) also described symmetrical communication: "If the managers meet together and confront one another, if they engage in sustained dialogue and work out their problems, then they can make effective recommendations to the top management of the corporation" (p. 6). Kanter (1983), similarly, described symmetrical communication in entrepreneurial organizations as "open communication, interdependent responsibilities, and frequent team efforts" (p. 241).

In addition to discussing symmetrical communication with customers and employees, writers on excellence also have described symmetrical communication behaviors of leaders and senior managers. Peters (1987) described symmetrical communication as a part of leadership, for which one of his prescriptions was: Pay attention! (More Listening). — "If talking and giving orders was the administrative model of the last fifty years, listening (to lots of people near the action) is the model of the 1980s and beyond" (p. 434). Waterman (1987) added that renewing organizations "get their passport to reality stamped regularly. Their leaders listen. They are open, curious, and inquisitive. They get ideas from customers, suppliers, front-line employees, competitors, politicians — almost anyone outside the hierarchy" (p. 9).

Hickman and Silva (1984) wrote that "new age executives" are sensitive to others, in part because of face-to-face communication. "Sensitivity," they said, "helps you to look inside another person in order to understand that person's expectations and needs. Such understanding helps you act to meet those needs and expectations as if they were your own" (p. 147). Steiner (1983) described "new CEOs" essentially as leaders who are good at symmetrical public relations: "They believe that they must respond as best they can to legitimate public demands. They accept the view that the worst possible strategy would be one that is perceived by the public generally as being nonresponsive, if not in opposition, to important interests of society" (p. 41). Steiner further explained: "Managers must exchange ideas, facts, and opinions with other managers, staff, the board of directors, shareholders, government agencies, etc. Communication is a means of leading, administering, informing, persuading. It can be a unifying force in an organization. . . . More than ever before, top executives are finding it necessary to communicate effectively with the media" (p. 56).

Implications for Public Relations

Although these writers on excellence do not mention public relations, they do describe symmetrical communication with customers and employees and by senior managers. It is only a small leap in logic to conclude that excellent organizations should have an excellent public relations function to manage this symmetrical communication.

LEADERSHIP

Excellent organizations have leaders who rely on networking and "management-by-walking-around" rather than authoritarian systems. Excellent leaders give people power but minimize "power politics." At the same time, excellent leaders provide a vision and direction for the organizations, creating order out of the chaos that empowerment of people can create.

The first three characteristics of excellence describe an organization that empowers people, imposes few structural controls, and relies on communication for collaboration and cooperation. An autocratic skeptic might say that such an organization could not function, that it could not have a clear mission, unless senior managers impose control and discipline. Writers on excellence, however, fill this gap in their theories with the concept of leadership—but not the autocratic concept of leadership found in early management theories. Peters (1987) asked, for example, "how do you lead/guide/control what looks like anarchy by normal standards?" His answer: "New notions of 'control,' such as creating an inspiring vision and being out and about, replace traditional controls by means of written policy directives filtering down from a remote headquarters" (p. 39).

Leadership is one of the criteria for the Malcolm Baldridge quality awards. Hickman and Silva (1984) made leadership the central attribute of their theory of excellence; they maintained that individual leaders and not organizations create excellence. They explained, "Great business, government, and nonprofit organizations owe their greatness to a few individuals who mastered leadership skills and passed those skills on to succeeding generations of executives and managers" (p. 23). Most other writers, however, see leadership as the element that integrates the loose–tight properties of excellent organizations. Leaders are leaders, that is, because they set a vision and then empower everyone in the organization to participate in shaping and implementing that vision.

Peters and Waterman (1982) said that excellent organizations have a bias for action—the first of their eight characteristics of excellence. Excellent organizations, they explained, have transforming rather than transactional leaders: "An effective leader must be the master of two ends of the spectrum: ideas at the highest level of abstraction and actions at the most mundane level of detail" (p. 287). They explained that the leader must be both a "value-shaping manager" and an "implementer *par excellence*" (p. 287). The following quote summarizes Peters and Waterman's ideas and the themes that run throughout the literature on excellence:

> Leadership is many things. It is patient, usually boring, coalition building. It is the purposeful seeding of cabals that one hopes will result in the appropriate ferment in the bowels of the organization. It is meticulously shifting the attention of the institution through the mundane language of management systems. It is altering agendas so that new priorities get enough attention. It is being visible when things are going awry, and invisible when they are working well. It's building a loyal team at the top that speaks more or less with one voice. It's listening carefully much of the time, frequently speaking with encouragement, and reinforcing words with believable action. It's being tough when necessary, and it's the occasional naked use of power—or the "subtle accumulation of nuances, a hundred things done a little better," as Henry Kissinger once put it. (p. 82)

Peters and Austin (1985) continued to list leadership as one of four characteristics of excellence, Peters (1987) included it as one of five principles, and Waterman (1987) included "direction and empowerment" as one of his eight principles. The theme of direction and empowerment also runs throughout the literature. Leaders are not always autocratic or democratic; they find a way to combine the ability to give people autonomy and direction. Vroom and Jago (1988) maintained that participatory leadership is not always best, as most theorists from the human resources school of management maintain (e.g., Lawler, 1986). According to Vroom and Jago, effective leaders vary in style from autocratic to participatory depending on the characteristics of the situation. Waterman stated essentially the same idea: "The renewing companies treat everyone as a source of creative input. What's most interesting is that they cannot be described as either democratically or autocratically managed. Their managers define the boundaries, and their people figure out the best way to do the job within those boundaries. [The management style is] an astonishing combination of direction and empowerment" (p. 7).

Hobbs (1987) also found that whether an organization was centralized or decentralized, managed by an autocratic or participatory-type CEO, "may be far less critical than that each entity has a clear idea of its central task, that the decisions that are made at the top are respected (even if not loved), that managerial succession occurs in a relatively methodical manner, and that the vast majority of promotions occur from within the organization" (p. 81).

Other writers, however, have concluded that leaders cannot be autocratic entirely. Peters and Austin (1985) explained: ". . . for the last twenty-five years we have carried around with us the model of *manager* as cop, referee, devil's advocate, dispassionate analyst, professional, decision-maker, naysayer, pronouncer. The alternative we now propose is *leader* (not manager) as cheerleader, enthusiast, nurturer of champions, hero finder, wanderer, dramatist, coach, facilitator, builder" (p. 311). Naisbitt and Aburdene (1985) added that, "the manager's new role will be to cultivate and maintain a nourishing environment for personal growth" (p. 60). Chung (1987) said that leaders in general have little direct impact on profit, market share, and stock prices but that "they certainly have an influence on labor relations, group behavior, and social climate within a group or organization, which will have some bearing on employee satisfaction and job performance" (pp. 362–363).

Finally, the writers on entreneurial organizations stress the importance of combining loose–tight properties. According to Pinchot (1985), "The age of domineering leaders and subservient team members is over." Successful intrapreneurial leaders, he added, breed "a hybrid of monarchical entrepreneurship and participatory management" (p. 175). Kanter (1983) echoed that idea:

> "Leadership" consists in part of keeping everyone's mind on the shared vision, being explicit about "fixed" areas not up for discussion and the constraints on decisions, watching for uneven participation or group pressure, and keeping time bounded and managed. Then as events move toward accomplishments, leaders can provide rewards and feedback, tangible signs that the participation matters.

> It is clear that managing participation is a balancing act: between management control and team opportunity; between getting the work done quickly and

giving people a chance to learn; between seeking volunteers and pushing people into it; between too little team spirit and too much. (p. 275)

Implications for Public Relations

Chapter 18, on power in the public relations department, shows the crucial role that the CEO and the dominant coalition of an organization play in producing a climate for public relations. Steiner (1983) pointed out that CEOs now spend from 20% to 75% of their time on external affairs. He maintained that leadership extends to external affairs, to leading employees to be more "sensitive to the social and political factors affecting them and the enterprise, and in participating in community and political processes" (p. 49). The conclusion that effective leaders combine direction and empowerment also suggests that excellent leaders probably foster a climate for a combination of asymmetrical and symmetrical public relations—the mixed-motive, professional model described in chapters 2 and 11.

STRONG, PARTICIPATIVE CULTURES

Employees of excellent organizations share a sense of mission. They are integrated by a strong culture that values human resources, organic structures, innovation, and symmetrical communication.

Leadership is necessary to create and instill a vision and direction on the organic structures that characterize excellent organizations, but writers on excellence also maintain that leaders instill that vision through the culture of the organization. Peters and Waterman (1982) were among the first writers to identify the importance of organizational culture, and since publication of *In Search of Excellence* both management and communication researchers have devoted extensive attention to organizational culture.

Peters and Waterman (1982) included "hands-on, value-driven" among their eight characteristics of excellence. Those values come from culture: "Without exception, the dominance and coherence of culture proved to be an essential quality of the excellent companies. Moreover, the stronger the culture and the more it was directed toward the marketplace, the less need was there for policy manuals, organization charts, or detailed procedures and rules" (p. 75). Peters and Waterman added that they were struck by the rich tapestries of anecdote, myth, and fairy tale in the excellent companies: ". . . the excellent companies are unashamed collectors and tellers of stories, of legends, and myths in support of the basic beliefs" (p. 282).

In later Peters and Waterman books, Peters (1985) continued to talk about the need to "develop and live an enabling and empowering vision" (p.

398); and Waterman (1987) listed "causes and commitment" as the last of eight characteristics of renewing organizations. Likewise, Hobbs (1987) included culture as the 3rd of 14 characteristics of his outstanding companies, and Hickman and Silva (1984) stated the premise that "strategic thinking and culture building are the essence of excellence" (p. 25). Pascale and Athos (1981) said, similarly, that "great companies make meaning"— the title of a chapter. Great companies, they said, develop "superordinate goals," "significant meanings," "spiritual values," and "shared values" (p. 178).

In addition to emphasizing the importance of a strong culture, writers on excellence also have maintained that the cultures should stress integration, participation, and collaboration as central values of the organization. Kanter (1983), for example, applied the concepts of integrated and segmented both to structures and cultures. Pinchot (1985) did not mention culture per se, but he did allude to a collaborative culture in organizations when he said, "But the history of humanity is a rocky climb toward ways of working together that produce simultaneously more cooperation and more freedom" (p. 9).

Ouchi (1981) said that his Theory Z organizations have developed a consistency in their internal culture through clans rather than hierarchies. Clans are "intimate associations of people engaged in economic activity but tied together through a variety of bonds" (p. 70). He added that "egalitarianism is a central feature of Type Z organizations" (p. 68) and that in Type Z organizations "the decision-making process is typically a consensual, participative one" (p. 66).

Implications for Public Relations

Chapter 21 reviews the literature on organizational culture and describes the central role of culture in determining a worldview for and a model of public relations in organizations. It concludes that excellent public relations most often occurs in organizations with strong, participative cultures. Culture, like structure, is one of most important underlying conditions that facilitate excellent public relations.

STRATEGIC PLANNING

Excellent organizations strive to maximize the bottom line by identifying the most important opportunities and constraints in their environment.

Strategic planning occupies a chapter or section in almost every basic book on management. For example, Chung (1987) named strategic planning as one of three critical success factors in management. Most MBA programs include a course on strategic management, for which many textbooks and casebooks have been written. In addition, many writers of books on excellence either mention strategic management or allude to it using other terms.

Strategic planning is a central theme in the literature on total quality management because of the origins of that movement in quantitative, engineering theories of quality control. The criteria for the Malcolm Baldridge award include "information and analysis" and "strategic quality planning." Tuttle (1989) added that managing by data is a critical element of TQM: "The systematic use of facts and data to guide decision making is a cornerstone of total quality. . . . Data should be used to identify problems and to help determine when and if action should be taken" (p. 45). Feigenbaum (1983) also said that TQM means "strategic planning that makes quality an integral factor in business planning" (p. xxiv). Wholey (1987), similarly, edited a book on excellence in government agencies in which the principal theme of the authors was how to measure performance goals to evaluate the organization.

As we saw in the last section, Hickman and Silva (1984) posited that strategic thinking and culture building are the basis of excellence: "To unite strategy with culture you first need to develop a vision of the firm's future and then in order to implement strategy for making that vision a reality, you need to nurture a corporate culture that is motivated by and dedicated to the vision" (p. 25). Peters and Austin (1985) reported that "a regular criticism" of *In Search of Excellence* was an alleged internal focus — that it did not take into account changes and discontinuities foisted upon the organization by the outside world. "It was a bum rap," they added, "the management practices we describe are aimed at ensuring that the organization is always externally focused, always sensing change and nascent change before it sneaks up" (p. 6).

Peters (1987) then included decentralization of strategic planning as one of his prescriptions for effective organizational systems. He explained that traditional, centralized strategic planning can damage an organization because it constrains it too much. According to Peters, everyone in the organization should be involved in strategic planning. He added that strategic planning should not be constrained by corporate assumptions, it should be perpetually fresh, it should not be left to planners, and it should include vigorous debate (p. 510).

Waterman (1987) also included "informed opportunism" as one of eight characteristics of renewing organizations. He added that the process of strategic planning is more important than the plan that results. Renewing companies "think strategic planning is great — as long as no one takes the plans too seriously" (p. 6). "The renewing organizations treat information as their main strategic advantage, and flexibility as their main strategic weapon," he added (p. 7).

Drucker (1980) did not use the term strategic management, but he did advocate "concentrating resources on results" (p. 41). He explained: "Organized, continuous, disciplined efforts are needed to commit these resources to actual and potential results. 'Feed the opportunities and starve the problems' is the rule" (p. 42). Hobbs (1987), likewise, found that his 14 organizations with a consistently strong economic performance had "a crystal-clear mission and focused central thrust" (p. 21), which was the first characteristic he identified. Kanter (1989) did not mention strategic management, but she did say that entrepreneurial organizations develop a mechanism for strategic collaboration with the environment—a suggestion that has direct implications for public relations.

Implications for Public Relations

Although Kanter (1989) did not mention public relations, she did talk about "strategic partnerships" with the stakeholders of the organization—a perspective that suggests the symmetrical worldview of public relations described in chapter 2 and the concept of strategic management of public relations described in chapter 6. According to Kanter, strategic partners are "welcome allies, not manipulated adversaries" (p. 142).

Steiner (1983) also discussed strategic management in a way that conforms to our theory of excellence in public relations. He contrasted what he considered to be the new public affairs function of organizations with what he called the older public relations function. That older function, he said, "covered two subjects, namely publicizing the products of the company and building its image" (p. 84). His "public affairs" function is essentially identical to the strategic management process for public relations described in chapter 6. Steiner's model of public affairs consists of scanning the environment, coordinating the analysis of environmental forces, identifying the forces most likely to influence the company, selecting issues, including social and political projections in the strategic management process, developing communication programs for the publics of the enterprise, and developing programs to advance the interest of the company in federal, state, and local governments. When he discussed strategic management, Steiner seemed to have a model like the one in chapter 6 in mind: "A decade or so ago strategic planning decisions were made primarily on the basis of economic and technical considerations. In more recent years, social and political forces—particularly for the large corporation—have come to stand on equal footing in the development of strategic plans" (p. 101).

Clearly, then, excellent organizations plan strategically and excellent public relations departments are those that are integrated into the process of strategic planning.

SOCIAL RESPONSIBILITY

Excellent organizations manage with an eye on the effects of their decisions on society as well as on the organization.

The first seven characteristics of excellence appear almost universally in books on excellence in management. Although the next five characteristics appear in only a few of the books, they appear often enough to suggest that they are important in completing the profile of an excellent organization. Of these five, we discuss social responsibility first because of its connection with strategic planning and its importance in public relations. For example, J. Grunig and Hunt (1984) devoted a chapter to social responsibility — which they called "public responsibility." At the end of that chapter, they concluded that public relations is the practice of social responsibility.

Chung (1987) discussed social responsibility as part of strategic management. "Business firms operate in a society that offers them opportunities to make profits," he explained. "In return, they have the obligation to serve societal needs. This obligation is called social responsibility" (p. 125). Steiner (1983) pointed out that corporations today have the responsibility of being a positive force in the social and political arena: "This is not solely a matter of defending the corporation but involves a deep interest in resolving major social problems, injecting more economic rationality into the political processes, helping to assure that our sociopolitical system works in the interests of everyone, and preserving political and economic freedom" (p. 29). Drucker (1980) saw the manager as a political activist who creates issues. But, he added, "The manager of any institution (but particularly of business) has to think through what the policy should be in the general interest and to provide social cohesion" (p. 218).

Lydenberg et al. (1986) devoted a book to *Rating America's Corporate Conscience.* They pointed out that "social considerations are slowly but surely becoming one of the many aspects of running a company well" (p. 12). "Within the past twenty years," they added, "the concept of social responsibility has earned a place in the practice of corporate management" (p. 14). Lydenberg et al. then rated 130 corporations on seven issues: charitable contributions, representation of women on boards of directors and among top corporate officers, representation of minorities on boards of directors and among top corporate officers, disclosure of social information, involvement in South Africa, conventional weapons-related contracting, and nuclear weapons-related contracting.

Implications for Public Relations

One of the major purposes of excellent public relations is to balance the private interests of the organization with the interests of publics and of society. Excellent public relations does so through strategic planning and symmetrical communication programs. If excellent organizations are to be socially responsible, they need excellent publics relations to help make them that way.

SUPPORT FOR WOMEN AND MINORITIES

Excellent organizations recognize the value of diversity by employing female and minority workers and taking steps to foster their careers.

On the one hand, organizations should foster the careers of women and minorities simply for the sake of women and minorities, as Lydenberg et al. (1986) maintained when they included representation of women and minorities among their criteria for social responsibility. Zeitz and Dusky (1988), similarly, identified 53 companies that are good places for women to work. They based their ratings on the percentage of female employees, promotion of women, number of women in upper management, how the company addresses sex discrimination, flexibility of the company on pregnancy and parenting, and multiple employment centers.

Other writers, however, have maintained that organizations should foster careers of women and minorities not only to be socially responsible but because it will make organizations more effective. As part of his discussion of human resources as a critical success factor, for example, Chung (1987) pointed out that the number of women in management will increase, that evidence shows that women are effective managers, and that many companies such as Citicorp, Control Data, Hallmark Cards, IBM, Mary Kay Cosmetics, J. C. Penney, and Time are actively promoting women in management.

Naisbitt and Aburdene (1985) devoted a chapter to women in the workplace. In it, they pointed out that women are gaining respect and power in the workplace, "forcing companies to recognize their legitimate needs" (p. 238). "As companies acknowledge the key role women are playing in the extraordinary economic vitality of the United States today," they said, [companies] "must increasingly seek to become great places for women to work" (p. 240): "A company does not earn such a reputation by paying women less than they are worth, by letting women fend for themselves about day care, by forcing young mothers to choose between a full-time career or none at all, or by keeping women out of the male managerial club—a club which can learn so much from women about the manager's new role as coach, teacher, facilitator" (p. 240).

The most extensive treatment of women and minorities in organizations can be found, however, in Kanter's (1977) book, *Men and Women of the Corporation*. According to Kanter, the attention that government pays to equal employment opportunity means that "public policy does not consider corporations to be merely money machines that turn out shareholder profits." Rather, "the public interest requires a scrutiny of organizations as producers of jobs as well as products—jobs that have important organizational and individual consequences" (p. 9).

Kanter (1977) theorized that the behavior of people in organizations, including women and minorities, can be explained by organizational structure. She identified three structural variables: opportunity (expectations and future prospects), power (the ability to mobilize resources), and proportions (a quantitative measure of how many people of different types there are in the work place) (pp. 246-249). In general, women and minorities have had little opportunity and power. Most important, however, they have been found in low proportions—often as tokens: "This position as 'tokens' (representatives of their category rather than independent individuals) accounts for many of the difficulties such numerically scarce people face in fitting in, gaining peer acceptance, and behaving 'naturally' " (p. 6).

The common assumption that women and minorities are not qualified to be managers, Kanter (1977) explained, simply reflects their low proportion. They do not appear to be qualified simply because they are different from the majority of managers. The implication, then, is that organizations will come to value the contributions of women and minorities more by increasing their proportion. When organizations do so, they also will become more effective because they have incorporated diverse values and talents into their structure and culture.

Implications for Public Relations

Chapter 15 develops essentially the same argument for incorporating women and their values into public relations as these writers have done for the organization as a whole. Chapter 3 contains a section that shows how the "requisite variety" provided by women and minorities increases the effectiveness of organizations. Organizations that value the contributions of women and minorities are more likely to have excellent public relations departments than those that do not. At the same time, empowering women and minorities in public relations also will provide requisite variety for organizations. Because excellent public relations programs foster their female and minority members, excellent public relations also makes organizations more effective by providing requisite variety.

QUALITY IS A PRIORITY

> Total quality is a priority not only in words or in the company's philosophy statement but a priority when actions are taken, decisions are made, or resources are allocated.

The extent to which an organization pays attention to quality is a characteristic of excellence provided by the total quality movement (TQM). The Malcolm Baldridge award includes "quality assurance of products and services" and "quality results" in its criteria. Many books have been written on TQM, including Juran (1989), Deming (1986), Crosby (1984), Feigenbaum (1983), Ishikawa (1985), and Imai (1986).

TQM originated with engineering theories of quality control, but recent versions of the concept have concentrated on the role of management as well as on quality control. Imai's (1986) book on KAIZEN provides an example of this new management emphasis. KAIZEN is a Japanese word that means "continuous improvement." According to Imai: "KAIZEN means ongoing improvement involving everyone, including both managers and workers. The KAIZEN philosophy assumes that our way of life — be it our working life, our social life, or our home life — deserves to be constantly improved" (p. 3).

Imai (1986) explained that KAIZEN can be contrasted with innovation. KAIZEN emphasizes improvement in processes rather than the development of new processes: "KAIZEN signifies small improvements made in the *status quo* as a result of ongoing efforts. Innovation involves a drastic improvement in the *status quo* as a result of a large investment in new technology and/or equipment" (p. 6).

Implementation of KAIZEN in an organization, however, requires a change in corporate culture. According to Imai (1986), every KAIZEN program implemented in Japan has created a cooperative atmosphere and a cooperative corporate culture. Organizations with KAIZEN programs use quality circles, develop informal leaders among workers, bring social life into the workplace, make the workplace a place where workers can achieve life goals, bring discipline into the workplace, and "train supervisors so that they can communicate better with workers and can create a more positive personal involvement with workers" (p. 218).

Although quality as a criterion of excellence comes primarily from the literature on TQM, it also can be found in other books on excellence. Throughout the literature on excellence as well as TQM, writers define quality in terms of customer satisfaction. Peters and Waterman (1982), for example, emphasized quality in discussing their recommendation to "stick close to the customer." In addition, Peters and Waterman's characteristic of "sticking to the knitting" can be interpreted as striving for quality. By sticking to the knitting, Peters and Waterman meant that excellent companies stick with the business they know well and do not diversify into unfamiliar fields.

Peters and Austin (1985), likewise, recommended that organizations should "live quality in every action" when they discussed recommendations for dealing with customers. Peters (1987) recommended that excellent organizations should "provide top quality, as perceived by the customer" (p. 65). Like Imai (1986), Peters emphasized process. A passion for quality, he said, "must be matched with a detailed process" (p. 64). Waterman (1987) listed "attitudes and attention" as one of eight characteristics of renewing organizations — including the attitude that quality is important. Naisbitt and Aburdene (1985) noted, "In the re-invented corporation, quality will be paramount" (p. 80). And Hobbs (1987) found that his 14 superior organizations had "an obsession with providing top quality, superior performance, and outstanding service" (p. 103).

Implications for Public Relations

The total quality movement can be applied to public relations as well as to other organizational functions. Every public relations process, especially the technical ones, should be improved constantly in an excellent department. At the organizational level, the literature on quality again would suggest that organizations that stress quality through culture and structure will be most likely to have excellent public relations. In addition, communication plays an essential role in cultivating a climate of continuous improvement and in monitoring customer perceptions of quality. Excellent public relations departments should develop internal communication programs in conjunction with managers of programs on quality and should work with marketing departments in monitoring customer perceptions of quality.

EFFECTIVE OPERATIONAL SYSTEMS

Excellent organizations build systems for the day-to-day management of the organization that implement the previous characteristics.

To be able to function, organizations must develop systems and procedures to implement plans and to utilize human resources. Chung (1987), for example, listed effective operational systems as his third critical success factor—"to transform the organizational resources as efficiently as possible" (pp. 24–25). Effective operational systems also are close to the continuous improvement in processes called for by the total quality movement. According to Tuttle (1989), for example, "True quality involves reforming designs, modifying policies or procedures, training people in correct practices, and insuring that customer requirements are known and built into every process step" (pp. 4–5). Likewise, Hobbs's (1987) second principle of excellence was "internal operating procedures: planning and monitoring activities."

Peters and Waterman (1982), Peters (1987), and Waterman (1987) also mentioned or alluded to operating procedures. In doing so, they called for simple structures and flexible systems. Peters and Waterman listed "simple form, lean staff" as one of their characteristics of excellence. The excellent organizations they studied had forms that people could understand and that were flexible in responding to changing conditions in the environment. With the simple organizational form, they explained, "fewer staff are required to make things tick?. . . The bottom line is fewer administrators, more operators" (p. 311).

Peters (1987) advised managers to "build systems for a world turned upside down. He added that these systems should measure the "right stuff (quality, flexibility, innovation) . . . and share information, heretofore considered confidential, with everyone in order to engender fast action on the line" (p. 39). Waterman (1987) likewise called for "friendly facts, congenial controls" as the third of eight characteristics of renewing organizations. He explained, "Their people don't regard financial controls as an imposition of autocracy, but as the benign checks and balances that allow them to be creative and free" (p. 8).

Implications for Public Relations

Public relations departments, like other organizational units, must develop internal systems for implementing and monitoring their activities. Planning, monitoring, and evaluating are as important for public relations as for any organizational function. In addition, public relations, through its internal communication function, should do research to determine when employees believe operational systems and controls inhibit their productivity, their ability to innovate, and the quality of their work.

A COLLABORATIVE SOCIETAL CULTURE

Organizations will be excellent more often in societies whose cultures emphasize collaboration, participation, trust, and mutual responsibility.

In a critical review of Peters and Waterman's (1982) book, *In Search of Excellence,* Carroll (1983) pointed out that management alone cannot make an organization successful. He said that organizations could be successful or unsuccessful for reasons outside management's control. In particular, he listed proprietary technology, market dominance, control of critical raw materials, and national policy and culture. Of these factors, societal culture appears several times in the excellence literature. It also is one of the factors we have considered as an underlying condition necessary for excellent public relations (chapter 22).

Several writers had Japanese culture in mind when they pointed out that a collaborative culture is necessary for organizational effectiveness. The most extensive book on this subject is Reich's (1987) book, *Tales of a New America.* In the book, he criticized both liberal and conservative ideologies: "Liberal conciliation has often degenerated into an indulgence that invites exploitation. Conservative assertiveness has often hardened the resistance of the intended objects of discipline, sparked resentment, and undermined trust" (p. 237). The solution, Reich maintained, is collaboration, which must come from what he called political culture: "All human organization depends on reciprocal obligation and mutual trust that others' obligations will be fulfilled? . . . we tend to forget that civilization, so defined, is not natural but an accomplishment of culture" (p. 238).

Reich (1987) added that political culture must "engender an ongoing search for possibilities of joint gain and continued vigilance against the likelihood of mutual loss" (p. 242). He then pointed out the importance of stories and myths in culture. The stories in a collaborative culture, he said, will feature a subtle assumption of interdependence:

> These new stories will speak less of triumph, conquest, or magnaminity, and more of the intricate tasks of forging mutual responsibility and enforcing mutual obligation. There will be fewer triumphant loners among the heroes, and more talented teammates and dedicated stewards. The villains will be found not in broad categories of malevolent others, but in the cynical betrayers of trust found even close by. (p. 253)

Ouchi (1984) also emphasized collaboration in his M-Form society, which parallels the M-Form of management described earlier in the section Organic Structures. The M-Form combines teamwork and competition. Thus, Ouchi said:

> It would not be at all surprising to discover that a society must also have that combination of teamwork and competition to succeed. If there is a society that has developed a high level of teamwork across sectors of the society, it is Japan. If there is a modern society that has succeeded through healthy

internal competition, it is the United States. We do not seek to relinquish what we have, but rather to improve upon it and grow by learning more about ourselves. (p. 29)

Pascale and Athos (1981) also described the importance of interdependence in Japanese culture. Interdependence, they said, "permits us to preserve the best of independence and dependence without getting the worst of both" (p. 125). "The Japanese accomplish this," they added, "through the concept of *wa*. Technically, *wa* means group harmony. But its full meaning encompasses a range of English words—unity, cohesiveness, team spirit" (p. 125).

Imai (1986) also stressed the importance of Japanese culture in making KAIZEN work: "In the West, cross-functional problems are often seen in terms of conflict-resolution, while KAIZEN strategy has enabled Japanese management to take a systematic and collaborative approach to cross-functional problem solving. Herein lies one of the secrets of Japanese management's competitive edge" (p. xxxii).

Implications for Public Relations

Chapter 21, on corporate culture, and chapter 22, on societal culture, conceptualize the effect of societal culture on organizational culture and of organizational culture on public relations. Excellent management and excellent public relations, in essence, can flourish only in collaborative, participative cultures. This conclusion supports the position of Rakow (1989), who maintained that symmetrical public relations cannot function without a major change in US culture and political structures (see chapter 2).

There is an optimistic side, however. Chapter 2, on worldviews, described how a mixed-motive model of public relations—one that combines symmetrical and asymmetrical purposes—can help to change organizational cultures. Collaborative organizations, in turn, could influence societal cultures—in large part because they are effective. But the task is a difficult and long-term one. Again, public relations cannot be excellent easily in organizations and societies that are not excellent. But public relations could be the catalyst that slowly begins to change them.

CONCLUSIONS

This chapter has identified 12 characteristics of excellent organizations from the literature on excellence. The first six of these attributes—human resources, organic structure, intrapreneurship, symmetrical communication systems, leadership, and culture — are linked logically to each other. That is, organizations would have a difficult time instilling one of the attributes in an organization without simultaneously instilling the others. Thus, symmetrical communication seems to be an integral part of organizational excellence. Often, however, individuals and departments other than public relations manage communication. Because communication is such an important part of an excellent organization, it seems only logical to center the management of communication in a single department. The logical department is public relations — or a department with a synonomous name such as corporate communication or public affairs.

Excellent public relations, in short, seems to be the glue that holds excellent organizations together, because of the importance of symmetrical communication and collaboration in organizations that are organic, value human resources, are innovative, have leaders who inspire rather than dictate, and have strong, participative cultures. In addition, excellent organizations can develop most easily in a societal culture that values collaboration — the last characteristic. Public relations is the organizational function that could bring such a culture into the organization, or that could export a participative organizational culture to the broader society.

The remaining characteristics suggest attributes of excellence for public relations as well as for the rest of the organization: strategic planning, social responsibility, programs to foster careers of women and minorities, an emphasis on quality in all processes, and effective operating systems.

In summary, we can derive the following propositions from this literature:

Proposition 1: Excellent public relations is an integral part of an excellent organization: Organizational excellence provides a hospitable climate for excellent public relations.

Proposition 2: Excellent public relations can help the rest of the organization be excellent.

REFERENCES

Arndt, E. (1988, May). Nobody does it better. *Communication World,* pp. 26–29.

Burns, T., & Stalker, G. M. (1961). *The management of innovation.* London: Tavistock.

Carroll, D. T. (1983, November-December). A disappointing search for excellence. *Harvard Business Review,* pp. 61, 78–79, 82–88.

Business editors rate corporate public relations. (1986, December). *Public Relations Journal,* p. 34.

Chung, K. H. (1987). *Management: Critical success factors.* Boston: Allyn & Bacon.

Crosby, P. (1984). *Quality without tears.* New York: McGraw-Hill.

Deming, W. E. (1986). *Out of the crisis.* Cambridge, MA: MIT Press.

Drucker, P. F. (1980). *Managing in turbulent times.* New York: Harper & Row.

Feigenbaum, A. (1983). *Total quality control.* New York: McGraw-Hill.

Grunig, J. E. (1976). Organizations and public relations: Testing a communication theory. *Journalism Monographs, 46.*

Grunig, J. E., & Hunt, T. (1984). *Managing public relations.* Fort Worth, TX: Holt, Rinehart & Winston.

Hage, J. (1980). *Theories of organizations: Form, process, & transformation.* New York: Wiley.

Hage, J., & Aiken, M. (1970). *Social change in complex organizations.* New York: Random House.

Hickman, C. R., & Silva, M. A. (1984). *Creating excellence.* New York: Plume.

Hobbs, J. B. (1987). *Corporate staying power.* Lexington, MA: Lexington.

Hull, F., & Hage, J. (1982). Organizing for innovation: Beyond Burns and Stalker's organic type. *Sociology, 16,* 564–577.

Imai, M. (1986). KAIZEN: The key to Japan's competitive success. New York: Random House.

Ishikawa, K. (1985). *What is total quality control?: The Japanese way.* Englewood Cliffs, NJ: Prentice-Hall.

Juran, J. M. (1989). *Juran on leadership for quality: An executive handbook.* New York: Free Press.

Kanter, R. M. (1977). *Men and women of the corporation.* New York: Basic.

Kanter, R. M. (1983). *The change masters.* New York: Simon & Schuster.

Kanter, R. M. (1989). *When giants learn to dance.* New York: Simon & Schuster.

Katz, D., & Kahn, R. L. (1966). *The social psychology of organizations.* New York: Wiley.

Lawler, E. E., III (1986). *High involvement management.* San Francisco: Jossey-Bass.

Levering, R., Moskowitz, M., & Katz, M. (1985). *The 100 best companies to work for in America.* New York: Signet.

Lydenberg, S. D., Marlin, A. T., Strub, S. O., & the Council on Economic Priorities (1986). *Rating America's corporate conscience.* Reading, MA: Addison-Wesley.

Martin, S. (1983). *Managing without managers.* Newbury Park, CA: Sage.

Naisbitt, J., & Aburdene, P. (1985). *Re-inventing the corporation.* New York: Warner.

Nash, B., & Zullo, A. (1988). *The misfortune 500.* New York: Pocket.

National Institute of Standards and Technology. (1990). *1990 application guidelines: Malcolm Baldrige National Quality Award.* Gaithersburg, MD: Author.

Ouchi, W. G. (1981). *Theory Z.* New York: Avon.

Ouchi, W. G. (1984). *The M-Form society.* New York: Avon.

Pascale, R. T., & Athos, A. G. (1981). *The art of Japanese management.* New York: Penguin.

Paul, R. N., & Taylor, J. W. (1986). *The 101 best-performing companies in America.* Chicago: Probus.

Peters, T. (1987). *Thriving on chaos.* New York: Knopf.

Peters, T., & Austin, N. (1985). *A passion for excellence.* New York: Warner.

Peters, T. J., & Waterman, R. H., Jr. (1982). *In search of excellence.* New York: Warner.

Pinchot, G., III (1985). *Intrapreneuring.* New York: Harper & Row.

Rakow, L. F. (1989). Information and power: Toward a critical theory of information campaigns. In C. T. Salmon (Ed.), *Information campaigns: Balancing social values and social change* (pp. 164–184). Newbury Park, CA: Sage.

Reich, R. B. (1987). *Tales of a new America.* New York: Times Books.

Robbins, S. P. (1990). *Organization theory: Structure, design, and applications* (3rd ed.). Englewood Cliffs, NJ: Prentice-Hall.

Steiner, G. A. (1983). *The new CEO.* New York: Macmillan.

Tuttle, T. C. (1989). What is total quality? *The Maryland Workplace: Newsletter of the Maryland Center for Quality and Productivity, 11*(1), 1, 4–5, 7.

Vroom, V. H., & Jago, A. G. (1988). *The new leadership: Managing participation in organizations.* Englewood Cliffs, NJ: Prentice-Hall.

Waterman, R. H., Jr. (1987). *The renewal factor.* New York: Bantam.

Wholey, J. S. (1987). *Organizational excellence: Stimulating quality and communicating value.* Lexington, MA: Lexington.

Who's excellent now? (1984, November 5). *Businessweek,* pp. 76–87.

Zeitz, B., & Dusky, L. (1988, June). The 53 best companies for women. *New Woman,* p. 134.

10 Public Relations Management and Operations Research

William P. Ehling
Syracuse University

David M. Dozier
San Diego State University

ABSTRACT

To be excellent, public relations departments must be managed according to the same principles as are other departments of the organization. Managers of most of those departments either have been trained in operations research — management science — or seek counsel from operations researchers in making decisions. This chapter, then, uses the theoretical framework of operations research as a model for the management process that communication managers could use to enhance the status of public relations as a management field. It uses the managerial presuppositions of operations research to define public relations essentially as the management of symmetrical communication. It then examines several techniques from operations research for possible use in communication management.

The purpose of this chapter is to demonstrate the relevance of operations research (OR) to the decisions that communication and public relations managers make. This chapter does not provide a "how to" guide for using operations research in public relations. References cited throughout the chapter provide more detailed, procedural explanations for that purpose. Rather, the goal is to provide instances where operations research could apply in principle to public relations problems and decisions. Perhaps as important, this chapter attacks several of the "technician presuppositions" that seem to make operations research irrelevant to the communication and public relations function.

A recurring problem in communication and public relations practice is the relationship of the function to other organizational functions and participation in management decision making. Other organizational units such as marketing, personnel, and production have used or experimented with operations research techniques for years. The communications and public relations function, on the other hand, has been slow to adopt operations research techniques, as well as other forms of management rigor and discipline. Jack Koten, Senior Vice President—Corporate Communications at Ameritech in Chicago, argued that communicators and public relations practitioners hurt themselves when they fail to speak the facts and figures vocabulary of other members of the senior management team: "If you work in a corporation, you can't be totally different to be successful" (Broom & Dozier, 1990, p. 71). Operations research, then, is seen as one of several managerial innovations (e.g., management by objectives) that practitioners ignore to their peril. At the same time, quantifying much of the information needed for programmable decisions requires further research.

This chapter consists of three major sections. First, a brief history of operations research is provided. Then, the managerial presuppositions of operations research are linked to the communication and public relations function. Last, different techniques of operations research are sketched and applied to public relations problems and decisions.

THE EMERGENCE OF OPERATIONS RESEARCH

The methods and analytic tools associated with scientific decision making in organizational management are called by several different names—*operations research, operational research,* and *management science.* This field emerged during World War II, driven by field problems that occurred during the installation of Allied radar equipment used to detect attacking German aircraft. A team of scientists gathered to solve the problem; their work was forerunner of the operations research movement. Ackoff and Sasieni (1968) noted that:

> During this period military technology was being developed more rapidly than it could be absorbed into military tactics and strategy. Little wonder, then, that the British military executives and managers turned to scientists for aid when the German air attack on Britain began. Specifically, they sought aid in incorporating the then new radar into the tactics and strategies of air defense. Small teams of scientists, drawn from any discipline from which they were willing to come, worked on such problems with considerable success in 1939 and 1940. Their success bred further demands for such services, and the use of scientific teams spread to the Western Allies—the United States, Canada,

and France. These teams of scientists were usually assigned to the executive in charge of operations — to the "line"; hence their work came to be known as operational research in the United Kingdom and by a variety of names in the United States: operational analysis, operations evaluation, operations research, systems analysis, systems evaluation, systems research, and management science. (pp. 4–5)

In the United States, operations research and management science became widely used, with operations research eventually dominating usage. Although drawn from many different disciplines in the past, the primary disciplines of these new researchers were economics and engineering. During and immediately after World War II, these disparate disciplines found they appealed to the same theoretical foundations and mathematical techniques in seeking solutions to problems. Economists came to employ the name *management science* to refer to management decision making, especially when related to product-pricing problems. Engineers, on the other hand, used the term *operational research* in Great Britain and *operations research* in the United States to describe this new field.

Underlying operations research is the imperative to maximize some desired outcome (usually valued in money terms) while minimizing the cost of attaining an outcome. This model has been applied to a variety of research settings, ranging from resource allocation and equipment replacement to waiting line situations and search activity.

After World War II, operations research methods quickly spread to business and industry, followed in time by adoption in government, education, health, and nearly every sector in which operational decision making takes place, including advertising agencies and the mass media. This imperative has been incorporated into the thinking of political science and law (Nagel & Neef, 1976) and in the social sciences in general (Lawrence, 1966).

OPERATIONS RESEARCH AND COMMUNICATION TECHNICIANS

In business management, operations research techniques have been used in such functional sectors of commercial organizations as production, finance, marketing, and personnel (Ackoff & Sasieni, 1968; Miller & Starr, 1961; Radford, 1981). The public relations function is a glaring exception. Public relations practitioners, as well as public relations textbook writers, recognize little relevance of operations research for public relations practice. Some public relations textbook writers have stressed the importance of management theories and management by objectives (MBO) for public relations practitioners (see Nager & Allen, 1984, for employing MBO in public relations). Others treat, in some detail, techniques usually associated with operations research, such as Program Evaluation and Review Techniques (PERT), Critical Path Analysis (CPM), cost-benefit analysis, and expected-value analysis (Grunig & Hunt, 1984). Other than a few notable exceptions, however, textbook authors have ignored operations research.

Why then is operations research—which seeks to solve practical problems facing managers and executives—ignored in communication and public relations activities? Part of the answer can be found in other functional areas. Miller and Starr (1961) noted situations (in marketing, e.g.) involving enormous expenditures of money where executives rely on intuition rather than formal methods to make decisions about how to handle major, controllable strategic variables. Why are such intuitive methods used in problem solving and decision making? Miller and Starr (1961) suggested that the reason may be that "Either the problems . . . are simple enough so that formal methods are unnecessary or else they are so difficult that formal methods cannot easily be devised" (p. 190). In the latter case, operations research techniques are not yet sophisticated enough to solve unusually complex problems. In short, operations research proves most useful in solving institutionally focused problems falling between these two extremes.

Operations research is ignored for two other reasons. First, some managers or executives face problems falling between these extremes but have no awareness or understanding of operations research techniques that could be used to solve such problems. Second, the potential problem solver or decision maker may define the problem so inaccurately, inadequately, or inappropriately that use of operations research is impossible.

All of the aforementioned reasons for ignoring operations research apply to many public relations practitioners or their immediate superiors. The preparation of news releases, for example, is viewed as a simple communication task easily accomplished without need for operations research. Indeed, that may be the case. A similar attitude may be taken to copy placement, a task generally entailing mass mailing of releases to lengthy media lists. Such routine media selection appears simple. But routines ignore the complexity of the media selection problem. The problem of media selection has two parts: (a) to determine precisely the set of desired outcomes to be attained through the media, and (b) to find the best or optimal combination of media outlets to accomplish to desired outcomes. As Miller and Starr (1961) demonstrated, the media selection problem is extremely difficult:

We recognize that media are the instruments by means of which communication or advertising strategies can be fulfilled. The decision problem here is to choose the best alternative from a number of possible strategies. What are the different kinds of strategies that are available? We have magazines, newspapers, radio, television, direct mail, billboards, and others. This is a major classification. Within each class there are large differences but at least the method of communication is the same. For this reason it is easier to compare two magazines than to compare a magazine with television. In order to make a comparison between two dissimilar channels of communication it is necessary to find outcomes or suboutcomes that result from each and that can be compared along the same dimension. Ideally, we would like to be able to discriminate between two media in terms of the different short- and long-range profit outcomes that result from each. We cannot do this even when the type of medium is the same. (pp. 190–209)

To make matters worse, media evaluation usually takes place in the absence of the message. One cannot feasibly produce art and copy for a magazine and programs for TV in order to make a comparative analysis. Even if that were feasible, one could not obtain measures of profit outcomes. Indeed, one can find out how many people noticed the message in various media and how they liked the message. Such data, however, do not tell us what people will do as a result of their awareness or attitude. Only such behavior is transferable into profit outcomes. When one attempts to choose the best media combination without the message, the decision maker does not even have the advantage of these kinds of preliminary data.

The problem is compounded, because the choice of a media combination interacts with a message. Ideally, the communicator would evaluate the message and media together. Such evaluation quickly stalls, however. There are far too many possible combinations of different media and messages to allow a decision maker to evaluate and choose the optimal combination. Although Miller and Starr (1961) showed that such complex problems can be solved through operations research, an optimal solution to the media selection problem in most difficult to find.

Many troublesome situations facing decision makers, including public relations practitioners, contain a host of interacting variables, making analysis difficult and costly. Several authors distinguish between two general classes of problems, simple ones and complex ones. Radford (1981) spoke of "well-structured" and "ill-structured" decisions situations. The former usually are handled at the lower management level where operations are routine and simple, where the information needed (input data) is complete and clear. Procedures used to solve such routine problems are well known and widely accepted as the best. In contrast, top management usually confronts ill-structured decisions situations. Constraining features of such decisions are not easily assessed. No complete, well-established procedures exist for dealing with such problems, and data about such problems are incomplete and poorly defined. As Radford (1981) noted:

Decision situations are classified as ill-structured when conditions in their environment preclude the possibility of resolution using a routine procedure as described above. There are four main characteristics of ill-structured situations, some or all of which may be present in practical circumstances. These characteristics are: (1) lack of complete information regarding the decision situation and its environment, (2) lack of quantitative measures that truly and completely describe the cost and benefits of the available alternatives, (3) the evidence of multiple objectives on the part of organization, individual, or group concerned, and (4) the existence of more than one participant in the decision situation with power to influence the outcome. (pp. 15–16)

Efforts to change and control large segments of society's social structure and cultural patterns provide examples of such decisions. Racial integration of urban schools to foster racial harmony poses many ill-structured problems. Many practitioners frequently argue that the public relations function typically involves ill-structured decisions in a complex world. Such arguments are undercut, however, when the practitioner resorts to simplistic responses, such as producing and placing news releases in a handful of mass media outlets. Implicit in such execution is the belief that a brief flurry of publicity easily can change deeply rooted and complex patterns of mass behavior.

Such responses to complex, ill-structured decision situations distort environmental reality by oversimplification to fit a narrow specialty of copy production. Under such circumstances, practitioners see little need for operations research techniques. When practitioners insist on treating complex, turbulent environments as if they were simple and well structured, they come to believe that virtually all organizationally related problems somehow are solved by communication. "Communication," in this framework, is reduced to copy preparation and mass media placement. Unfortunately, viewing public relations solely as a technical copy production role is widely shared in and out of the ranks of public relations practitioners.

Schramm (1988), for example, wrote that the "external duties" of public relations "involves great variety of communication tasks," including "preparing news releases, writing speeches, issuing publications, planning special events of public interest, answering correspondence, maintaining friendly relations with the media, arranging publicity for persons or products—in fact, anything that has to do with the image presented by the employing organization to persons whose opinions it cares about" (p. 309).

In a similar vein, many public relations texts focus heavily on such activities as public relations writing, public relations advertising, publicity techniques, and the frequent use of various kinds of "support systems" such as photography, graphic and audiovisual materials, radio and television, speakers bureau, and company publications (Cutlip, Center, & Broom, 1985; Lovell, 1982; Marston, 1979; Reilly, 1981; Seitel, 1984). This means public relations is viewed as an assortment of message-producing techniques (Cutlip et al., 1985; Marston, 1979) used to reach and somehow influence various publics rather than the disciplined use of decision-making techniques for resolving problems growing out of conflict, disputes, or controversies. In this context, scant attention is given to managerial responsibilities of public relations practitioners, and little attempt is made to regard practitioners as problem solvers rather than copy producers, as critical decision makers rather than as shrill-voiced attention getters, as communication system designers rather than message conveyers, or as resolvers of conflict rather than peddlers of images. Knee-jerk publicity in response to complex, ill-structured problems reduces the practitioner to simply a publicity technician operating at the low end of the management hierarchy, where, as Krajewski and Thompson (1981), noted, "low-level decisions" are made—decisions that are "usually technical in nature, have little carry-over into or interaction with other decision-making situations and are contained in a limited time frame" (p. 26).

OPERATIONS RESEARCH AND COMMUNICATION MANAGEMENT

As indicated in chapter 12, communication and public relations practitioners do not always enact the role of publicity technician. Public relations managers participate in, and sometimes even assume leadership of, decision-making and problem-solving activities at the top management level. There are those, usually at the rank of vice president, who oversee some or all the planning, directing, and management of activities grouped under the rubric of public relations. Indeed, someone must determine the amount of the public relations budget, the size of working staff, and the types of activities to be performed in the name of public relations. Such decisions are essentially public relations management decisions. What benefits can operations research bestow on public relations managers or those who supervise public relations practitioners? To answer this question, an earlier question first must be answered: What is the nature and purpose of operations research?

Nature of Operations Research.   Kendal (1958) saw operations research as "a body of methods for solution of problems which arise" in the relationship "between men and their environment" (p. 265). Beer (1959) regarded operations research as "a subset of scientific methods" (p. 2) which are appropriate to the analysis of management activity. Ackoff and Sasieni (1968), in turn, spoke of operations research as entailing "(1) the application of scientific method, (2) by interdisciplinary teams to problems involving control of organized (man-machine) systems so as to (3) provide solutions which best serve the purposes of the organization as a whole" (p. 6).

French scholar and author Arnold Kaufmann (1963) stated that operations research constitutes:

> ... the body of methods which makes possible a rational determination of the most efficient or economical solution in policy-decision problems concerning the management of an economic or human phenomenon, drawing upon statistical-mathematical procedures which sometimes require the use of high-speed computers. These methods are based upon a prior analysis of the relationship among technical and psychological factors in the phenomenon's structure, which is achieved by recourse to the various appropriate scientific disciplines. (pp. 3–4)

Englishman W. E. Duckworth (1965), managing director of the Fulmer Research Institute in England, said operations research "is concerned with systems" and is used for "optimization" of the planning effort:

> Clearly the definition of the system is important because all systems in industry are part of a larger system and not all systems are appropriate ones for the study of O.R. One of the first duties of an O.R. worker in an investigation is to make clear the boundaries of the system in which he is working, to ensure that it is appropriate for O.R. and to point out that the optimal solution is only being found for that particular system. If the optimal solution in a particular system has harmful repercussions on the larger system then the O.R. worker must not blind himself to this, but should endeavor to discover it and point out the need for investigation of the wider system. (pp. 14–15)

Elsewhere, Duckworth, Gear, and Lockett (1977) noted that the purpose of operational research (using the English expression) "is to help managers to make decisions." But they were quick to note that this does not mean that the manager's decision-making role is somehow diminished or eliminated. In their words, "The resolution of this impasse is a major conceptual contribution of O.R. . . . The first . . . is that O.R. does not deprive managers of discretion; it frees them for higher levels of judgment. The second is that O.R. does not experiment with the system itself; it experiments with a model of the system" (p. 6). With respect to the manner in which operations research works, they pointed out that "It studies the situation, constructs a model of the system (usually mathematical or of similar abstraction), experiments on it to find the optimum performance, and recommends this to the manager" (p. 7).

Richmond (1968), in turn, commented on the use of mathematical techniques frequently employed in operations research:

> To be sure, there is a group or set of mathematical techniques which have become associated with and identified with operations research. Many of

these are discussed in this book, and most of them have been either developed by operation researchers or used by operations researchers. But these techniques do not constitute operations research. *Operations research is an approach to problem-solving* that makes it possible to use these techniques in social science, in military operations and — most important to us — in management. (italics added).

Richmond (1968) went on to point out that operations research "is the approach to problem-solving that examines the system (a set of interacting entities) in which the decision problem is contained" and then asked and attempted to answer a set of key questions:

1. What are the *controllable variables?*
2. What is the *objective* of the decision?
3. What are the *uncontrollable variables?*
4. What is the *relationship* between the inputs and outputs?

The answers to these questions form a model of the system about which management is concerned. The purpose of constructing such a model is to be informed about all the characteristics — no more and no less — of the system so that a decision can be made. In short, a model is a representative but simplified version of the reality that the manager is attempting to regulate.

Operations research is closely bound to other areas and the theories associated with them. These include the decision-making process (decision theory), organizations in which decisions are made and that provide the purpose of such decisions (organizational and interorganizational theories), management, its structure and function in organizations (management theory), and information upon which decisions rest (management information systems theory).

As Siemens, Marting, and Greenwood (1973) pointed out:

Management of a business firm or government agency involves a large complex of activities consisting of analysis, decision, communications, leadership, motivation, measurement, and control. Operations research (OR) focuses on the fundamentals of analysis and decision-making. The objective of operations research is to implement and enhance the task of analysis and decision-making inherent in controlling complex systems. Naturally, this should be augmented by appropriate information flows in order to achieve rational — if not optimal — decisions.

The field of operations research has demonstrated dynamic expansion and development on two fronts: (1) It has gained universal acceptance by industry and government as an invaluable managerial decision-making tool; (2) By the extension of existing techniques and the introduction and refinement of new techniques for solving a broad spectrum of problems in government, industry, health, urban planning, etc. As the frontiers of OR were diligently and successfully explored, it became increasingly evident that the enlarged scope and complexity of problems now open to OR solutions was inextricably associated with accurate and timely information flows. Without the required problem input information, no practical solution is possible; without *accurate* and *timely* information, the problem solution is meaningless. (p. ix)

Sasieni, Yaspan, and Friedman (1959) pointed out that, from the operations research perspective, a decision is a recommendation that a particular course of action, affecting the system, be carried out. In other words, "The decision-maker attempts to choose that course of action which is expected to yield the 'best' results in terms of the larger goal of the organization of which the system is a part. Another way of putting this is to say that the decision-maker attempts to render the system more *effective* in furthering the goals of the organization" (p. 1).

There is an important interplay between organizational theory (Etzioni, 1964; Etzioni & Lehman, 1980; Hall, 1972; Miner, 1980; Robbins, 1983), interorganizational theory or theory of the manner in which organizations interact with their environments (Brinkerhoff & Kuntz, 1972; Evan, 1978; Meyer & Scott, 1983; Negandhi, 1975), management theory (Atchison & Hill, 1978; Glueck, 1980; Hodgetts, 1982; Ivancevich, Donnelly, & Gibson, 1980; Misshauk, 1979; Newman & Warren, 1977; Robbins, 1974, 1976), decision theory (Bross, 1953; Chernoff & Moses, 1959; Churchman, 1961; Radford, 1981), and operations research (Ackoff, 1961; Ackoff & Sasieni, 1968; Krajewski, 1981; Miller & Starr, 1961; Siemens et al., 1973).

Because management is characterized by decision making, decision making is regarded as central to management theory. Management theory is most concerned with developing and applying techniques that can improve decision making in operations research. Many have made major contributions to what Robbins (1976) called the "decision-science movement" (p. 39), including economists, mathematicians, engineers, and systems theorists, as well as such operations researchers as Martin Starr and Russell Ackoff.

These contributions include the application of statistics, simulation techniques, information models, and optimization models. More specific contributions related to critical-path scheduling, inventory models, replacement models, resource allocation models, and linear and dynamic programming, to mention the better known techniques.

If public relations contains a management component, then there is a place—even a necessity—for operations research in public relations management. If communicators and public relations practitioners are decision makers, then operations research can contribute to public relations management by helping to provide decisions that produce efficient and/or effective courses of action in a rigorous and demonstrable manner.

In the words of Nagel and Neef (1976), operations research methods may be applied wherever and whenever decisions are made by management personnel: "Today it is unrealistic to attempt to pinpoint the applications of operations research. It has become a basic component of most industrial, military, and academic organizations. It can best be defined by its three inherent characteristics: its system, its use of interdisciplinary teams, and its methodology—linear programming, inventory modeling, and decision theory" (p. 5).

Benefits and Operations Research.   What benefits or advantages does operations research hold for public relations decision makers? First, the adoption of operations research methods will introduce rigor, precision, and clarity into communication and public relations thinking when charged with the task of identifying public relations problems, specifying the problem's boundaries (parameters), defining the appropriate alternatives, and selecting an optimal solution. Although conventional public relations practice emphasizes communication production rather than decision making, this emphasis does not mean that practitioners never make decisions. Indeed, practitioners do make complex decisions. Communicators, however, rarely are called upon to exhibit expertise or competence in making scientifically based decisions or to demonstrate that such decisions are "best" (the most efficient, effective, or both).

Thus, communicating program benefits derived from operations research are evolutionary. Operations research thinking forces people to distinguish between performing a technical function and designing or selecting the most efficient function—between what Miller and Starr (1961) called the "doers" and "deciders." Such thinking forces communicators to distinguish people who engage in short-term tactical operations from those who shape long-term strategic options.

Miller and Starr (1961, pp. 105–110) showed that operations research methods can be used in many critical problem-solving and decision-making areas. Specifically, operations research can be used to (a) help develop well-formulated objectives, that is, assist in goal setting; (b) discover "states of nature" (situation analysis); (c) identify possible strategies, including competitive strategies; (d) handle excessive numbers of strategies and states of nature; (e) determine outcomes; (f) valuate outcomes, that is, quantifying the outcome's desirability; and (g) select a specific strategy that is the best, that is, one that is the most efficient or effective or both.

Operations Research and Goal Setting.   Full exploration of the various techniques an operations researcher can use in each of these decision-making areas is not warranted here. Instead, let us consider one of these areas—goal setting.

Miller and Starr (1961) pointed out that "Basically, the identification and choice of objective is an executive function. Operations research can provide some stimulation and guidance, but there is no way of replacing the executive responsibility for objectives" (p. 106). Unfortunately, some top executives cast the communication and public relations function into inappropriate operational roles, such as publicity of the copy-writing-and-placement variety. Sometimes, top management requires public relations personnel to pursue goals lying outside the public relations domain, such as increasing sales via product publicity (a means and end belonging to the domain of marketing).

Under such circumstances, what can operations research do? Although OR cannot dictate to top management what objectives should be accomplished, it can specify conditions for attaining goals. That is, goals must be socially legitimate, functionally appropriate, clearly specified, operationally attainable, quantitatively measurable, and economically worthwhile (i.e., such that the benefits exceed the cost). The effort to apply OR to communication goals helps clarify the domain.

Operations research can show that these criteria rarely are met in traditional public relations, including activities that frequently are approved, if not mandated, by top managers. Not surprisingly, marketing-oriented top executives care little about sharp distinction between public relations management (which should be concerned with dispute resolution) and marketing management (which legitimately is committed to increasing sales). If public relations personnel are available, top executives in many organizations use such personnel to expand the corporation's sales promotion effort.

In periods of "downsizing," communicators and public relations practitioners may find temporary comfort providing technical support for the marketing function as product publicists. However, as Broom, Lauzen, and Tucker (1991) noted, the blurring of the distinction between marketing and public relations is counter productive for marketing, public relations, and organizations served by both functions. Public relations and marketing constitute two conceptually distinct organizational functions and operate on separate but complementary "turfs" (Broom et al., 1991). Operations research can play a valuable role in helping top management understand the conceptual distinction between marketing and public relations. This understanding, in turn, guides senior management to make appropriate administrative use of marketing and public relations personnel.

In short, operations research makes clear to users and nonusers alike that one cannot have fuzzy, vague, or ill-defined goals and still engage in efficient or effective behavior. The determination of what constitutes efficiency or effectiveness requires several basic ingredients: well-defined means (concrete, measurable courses of action or strategies), attainable and verifiable ends (valuated, measurable outcomes), and an appropriate and meaningful standard or norm that can be used to determine which means is the most efficient or effective or both.

Even when public relations is reduced to publicity, selecting the criterion or criteria to set goals is problematic, even for such one-way message dissemination activities. This problem, as Montgomery and Urban (1969) showed, usually is resolved through some form of compromise between the ability to use simple measurements and the relevance of the criterion being measured and evaluated (see Fig. 10.1).

Public relations firms such as Ketchum Public Relations make use of publicity-tracking systems such as the "Ketchum Publicity Planning Discipline" (KPPD) to "aid the publicity professional in achieving" the goal of selecting the "appropriate media vehicles for directing the message to the prime prospects" (see the Public Relations Society of America's Counselors Academy publication, October 1987). This methodology, however, provides only an artificially contrived measure of potential exposure, an intermediate step in the process of achieving program impact. Publicity tracking does not provide an empirically based measure of actual exposure and certainly not one of actual behavioral effects. Potential exposure does not provide a usable model for evaluating an overall objective of maximizing profit as a result of an investment in product publicity. In the words of Ketchum's vice president and director of analytical systems, H. Stuart Hayes (Public Relations Society of America's Counselor's Academy publication, October 1987), "It is important to bear in mind that all aspects of the discipline which have been discussed to this point deal with evaluation of the *presentation* of publicity. The subject of actually measuring the

Sub-goals	Decision Relevance	Ease of Measurement
Potential Exposure	Low	High
Actual Exposure		
Awareness		
Comprehension		
Attitude Change		
Acceptance		
Retention		
Behavior or Action	High	Low

FIGURE 10.1 Decision relevance and ease of measuring sub-goal state.

prospects' awareness of, or attitude toward, the message presented has not been addressed" (p. 5; italics added).

In other words, Ketchum's KPPD provides a relatively easy method of measuring message presentation in potential exposure terms, but cannot measure collective awareness, cognitive states, attitudes, or motivation, and certainly nothing about potential or actual behavior (e.g., sales). The criteria selected by Ketchum to measure some attainable goal set are inappropriate proxy measures of what should be the overall objective of product publicity, namely, to increase sales. The criteria are irrelevant, as well, to the primary mission of public relations management, defined as an activity that is more demanding and more inclusive than publicity, especially product publicity.

The same critique fits the Newlin Company's "Publicity Value Tracking System," which equates public relations (product publicity) with advertising value. This value is measured in potential exposure terms rather than in actual sales or profit terms. (For an account of this methodology by Patricia E. Newlin, president of the Newlin Co., see *PR Week,* Issue 3, 1988, p. 10.)

In trying to introduce research and quantitative methods into the public relations endeavors, public relations firms especially have pushed to reduce the public relations function to publicity production. Publicity, in turn, is reduced to copy preparation and mass media placement. What is measured, then, is potential (not actual) exposure that such placement might provide. However, the faulty rationale of such publicity measurement has not gone unnoticed within the ranks of public relations practitioners (see criticisms by Dr. Sharun Sutton of "two major faults of today's publicity evaluation system," *PR Week,* Issue 4, 1988).

Public relations goal setting, then, strives for ways to measure impact through publicity tracking, because such tracking is simple to execute. The result, however, is that public relations' primary mission is redefined as a simple technical, tactical enterprise. In the process, redefined public relations becomes irrelevant as a function capable of making its own unique contribution to an organization's overall behavior. Tom Harris, president of Golin-Harris, succinctly described the status of redefined public relations when he explained his company's purchase of a Los Angeles public relations firm. For Harris, public relations (using the military-oriented jargon of marketing) is regarded as "a weapon in the marketing arsenal." Public relations, according to Harris, is product publicity. Its sole function is to supplement an advertising campaign with free copy placements in the mass media.

The drawback of such goal reductionism is that intermediate placement and potential exposure, although relatively easy to measure in simple terms, do not relate, as Montgomery and Urban (1969) noted, in any direct and simple fashion to increased sales or profit maximization. Even when potential exposure measures, such as *frequency* and *reach,* are used infrequently by public relations firms, such effort begs the question, because such measures do not answer questions about the eventual impact of exposure on activity states.

These attempts at measurement ignore the complex and variable chain that links copy presentation to actual exposure, exposure to cognitive and attitude change, and such changes in the psychological system to socially and culturally mediated behavior (such as buying behavior). Even more questionable is the popular but erroneous assumption that exposure triggers this chain of activities in a linear, deterministic fashion. Potential exposure levels, viewed as attainable, are not credible proxy measures of behavior. More fundamentally, such measures are inappropriate for the management function of public relations, because they confuse legitimate goals of marketing's product publicity (i.e., sales enhancement) with the fundamentally different function of public relations management.

In short, operations research, when related to public relations activities, requires clarity in specifying the primary mission (goal identification) of public relations management and the social benefits it bestows on an organization of which it is a part. Operations research requires precision in the verifiability of both the goals (ends) to be sought and the means (courses of action) to be employed. Such research imposes rigor on the decision-making process, requiring appropriateness of public relations' goal-seeking activities, compatibility of the ends and means, and the measurability of criteria employed to define goal states.

One, of course, can identify several subgoals, treated as linkage points in the long chain running from potential exposure to the manifestation of overt behavior or action. Such subgoals might include potential exposure, actual exposure, awareness, comprehension (i.e., gaining understanding or knowledge), attitude change (i.e., being positively motivated), acceptance, retention (remembering), and, finally, overt behavior or action of the desired kind. As Montgomery and Urban (1969, p. 96) pointed out (see Fig. 10.1), the case of measurement and the decision relevance are inversely related. The easier variables are to measure, the less relevant the measures are for decision making. Conversely, the greater the relevance of measurements, the more difficult and the more costly they become. You get what you pay for; if it is cheap, it is usually not worth much for making sound decisions.

A number of questions and problems about subgoals confront public relations planners. What subgoal should be selected and justified? How should one trade off between the relevance of measurement and ease of measurement? How should one determine the optimal point in such trade-off situations? These are manager concerns, not concerns of the technician. Avoiding or ignoring these problems reduces the public relations head to the status of a technician. Conversely, the more the public relations head deals with and adequately solves these problems, the more that person assumes the role of a manager. (See chapter 12.)

To use operations research methodology to determine what public relations strategies to execute, the public relations goal or goal set must be well formulated, attainable, and measurable. Public relations practitioners as well as higher executives must see public relations goals not only as legitimate, attainable, and measurable, but as functionally appropriate. They must be *sui generis* or operationally distinct from other organizational objectives, such as marketing, personnel, finance, or production objectives. If this distinction cannot be made, no managerial slot logically can be allocated for public relations. There may be room in an organization for copy producers, publication editors, technical writers, and speechwriters, but these technical chores have little to contribute to the nature and purpose of an organization's public relations management function.

As Koontz, O'Donnell, and Weirich (1982), noted in their comment about the importance of objectives: "Without clear objectives, management is haphazard, and no individual and no group can expect to perform effectively or efficiently unless a clear goal is known and sought. To be meaningful, objectives must be verifiable. The easy way to get verifiability is to put goals in quantitative terms" (p. 96). Not all goals can be or need to be quantifiable, but operations research shows what kinds of goals can be and need to be quantifiable. Such research shows how to handle the defining characteristics of qualitative goals so as to make them precise, enumerable, and, hence, verifiable as well.

Elsewhere, Ehling (1981, 1984, 1985, 1987) argued that public relations management can be justified as an organizational function only to the extent that it can be conceptually, administratively, and operationally separated from other organizational function. If such a separation is not made, jurisdictional conflict, duplication of effort, lack of direction, and wasted resources will result. To avoid such a state of affairs, it has been argued (Ehling, 1981) that public relations endeavors ought to be aligned with and directed to efforts designed to attain cooperation between an organization and other organizations or social groupings under conditions where primacy can be given to institutional communication. Such two-way communication must be thought of as a broad, complex information-exchanging system going well beyond the narrow limits of one-way publicity.

In short, public relations management must be viewed as engaging in problem-solving and decision-making activities as these relate to the resolution of actual or potential disputes or conflicts. Public relations activities seek to bring about necessary and legitimate collective action. The mission of communication management is to create a joint, cooperative win-win arrangement out of a risky, conflictual win-lose situation. (For a review of this approach, see Gossen & Sharp, 1987). Given such a desired end-state—with institutional, two-way communication as the appropriate means—operations research helps determine, among other things, which combination of communication strategies best suits varying circumstances.

From an operations research perspective, Ackoff and Emery (1972) showed that both communication and conflict (or cooperation) can be associated with probability theory. This means that the existence and degree of communication or conflict (cooperation) can be measured in probabilistic terms. The degree to which communication can resolve conflict (or attain cooperation) also can be stated in probabilistic terms. Both communication and conflict (cooperation) can be valuated quantitatively in terms of dollars lost or gained. Hence, public relations endeavors can be evaluated in terms of the probability and cost of communication treated as a means for the attainment of cooperation (or reduction of conflict), where the state of cooperation is assessed in terms of maximizing (monetary) gain or minimizing (monetary) loss.

Moreover, because potential decision makers in public relations management roles can use many different kinds of communication means (systems), operations research techniques allow communication managers to determine which communicative system is the most efficient, most effective, or both.

Operations Research Techniques.   What, then, are some of the specific operations research techniques applicable to communication management and public relations? Some fairly commonplace techniques have been brought over from statistics. Others are unique to operations research, developed by operations researchers to solve specific problems found in such areas as inventory control or service stations. Duckworth, Gear, and Lockett (1977), for example, included in his list of usable techniques those of multiple regression, Delphi analysis, morphological analysis, simulation and Monte Carlo methods, network analysis, operational gaming, discounted cash flow methods, cost-benefit analysis, quality control, and break-even analysis.

Sasieni et al. (1959), using a problem-oriented classification system, spoke of inventory problems, replacement problems, waiting line problems, allocation problems, sequencing problems, competitive problems, and dynamic problems. Miller and Starr (1961) employed a similar nomenclature but preferred the use of the term *models* to produce a listing of inventory models, waiting line models, allocation models, competitive models, replacement models, and search models. A similar listing is found in Ackoff and Sasieni (1968), Richmond (1968), Krajewski and Thompson (1981), and Siemens et al. (1973). Nagel and Neef (1976) explored three commonly used techniques in the social situations—linear programming, inventory modeling, and decision theory. As they pointed out linear programming is the most accessible and comprehensive of the three methods, requiring only elementary facility with mathematics. Several of these techniques applicable to communication management are considered next.

Inventory Modeling and Optimum Level Analysis. This modeling method can be used in a variety of policy situations. These situations, in turn, can be divided into two classes. Linear situations are those in which a straightforward linear (straight-line) relationship occurs. Nonlinear situations are those in which relationships behave in the form of an increasing or decreasing rate of change which looks like a curved line. In both situations, a decision maker or planner seeks (a) an optimum quantity or level of an input variable (e.g., the cost level of a communication program) in the light of (b) a given goal (e.g., the benefits of cooperation) subject (c) to various constraints (e.g., time, money, people, etc.). Generally, this perspective involves one variable input; hence, it deals with what is frequently called an *optimum level problem.*

The simplest type of optimum level problem in communication management and public relations is one in which one can reasonably assume that the input variable (e.g., a communication program) bears a linear relation with a goal variable, such as cooperation enhancement or conflict reduction. More interesting is the situation in which the goal variable (e.g., the cost of attaining or maintaining cooperation) eventually curves downward as the input variable (e.g., cost of communication) increases. The optimum level of the input variable is the point at which the goal variable reaches its peak on a hill-shaped benefit curve. Closely related is the situation in which the total cost variable—which a communication decision maker is trying to minimize—goes down as the input cost variable is increased, but then eventually begins to climb again. The optimum level of the input variable in this situation is the point at which the negative goal variable reaches its bottom on a *u*-shaped or valley-shaped cost curve (see Fig. 10.2).

The most generalized version of this inventory model, in many instances, is also the most useful. Decision makers, including public relations managers, have to work with intuitive notions or formal models of activities around them. These notions or models take the form of assertions in the form of hypotheses, beliefs, propositions, assumptions, or presuppositions. In such situations, the manager must give careful attention to statements he or she makes or others make about the world around them. However, there is always the dilemma of accepting an assertion or hypothesis (a) as true when in fact it is false or (b) of rejecting it as false when in fact it is true.

A number of such assertions or hypotheses suggest themselves. They may

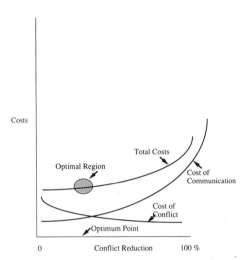

FIGURE 10.2 Location of optimal region of conflict reducation and communication costs on the total cost line.

include belief statements that a certain percentage of a group's members is hostile or noncooperative, that a specific program of action (e.g., a communication strategy) will increase friendliness (cooperativeness) among groups or organizations, or that Program A is more efficient (or effective) than Program B. In all such cases, a decision maker can choose to accept these hypotheses or belief statements as true—or reject them as false. The problem is that the truth condition (or false condition) may not hold in fact.

Accepting a false hypothesis involves Type 2 error cost. Rejecting a true hypothesis involves Type 1 error cost. These two types of costs and their components cover all possible costs directly, and indirectly the complementary benefits to be derived in one's willingness to accept a hypothesis. The cost can include nonmonetary as well as monetary costs. However, in the former case, some common unit of measurement must be employed in order to sum them into a total cost curve and to locate the point or region where the curve reaches a minimum (see Fig. 10.3).

This technique can be called the "nonlinear summation optimization model" (see Nagel & Neef, 1976, p. 55). It is nonlinear to the degree it involves policy problems in which total cost or total benefit produced by varying degrees of policy run down (valley-shaped curve) or run up (hill-shaped curve). It is a summation model in that total costs are determined by summing a falling cost (or benefit) curve and rising cost (or benefit) curve. The model is used primarily to arrive at an optimum policy position.

Mathematical techniques for dealing with inventory problems depend principally on calculus, probability theory, matrix algebra (as in linear programming), and the calculus of variation (as in dynamic programming). Mathematical techniques used in inventory problems also have been applied

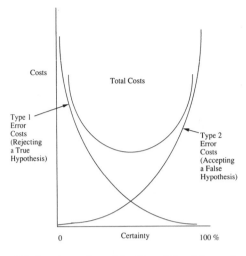

Costs

Total Costs

Type 1
Error
Costs
(Rejecting
a True
Hypothesis)

Type 2
Error
Costs
(Accepting
a False
Hypothesis)

0   Certainty   100 %

FIGURE 10.3 Generalized model of a nonlinear situation involving the acceptance or rejection of hypotheses.

to "defensive advertising" and "pulsing advertising." This model applies to the situation where mass media advertising is conducted for a certain period of time to bring response (e.g., sales in marketing, gifts in fund raising) to a certain level and then stopped. Once advertising stops, responses decline until some predetermined level is reached. At that point, advertising again starts. The challenge is to determine the shape of the decay function over time.

This advertising problem, of course, is shared by any communications or information-dissemination system. Instead of increasing consumer purchases as in the aforementioned case, the goal may be to increase or maintain certain levels of attitude, knowledge, readiness to act, or memory. The goal may be to impact specific behavior such as giving money, casting votes, using seat belts, eating or not eating certain foods, attending certain events, reducing acts of hostility or increasing instances of cooperation, and the like.

The decay curve may be represented as in Fig. 10.4. In Fig. 10.4, the decay of communication impact on some specific state of the message receiver is depicted. This state may be operationalized as change in attitude, knowledge, motivation, or overt behavior (e.g., more instances of cooperation or fewer instances of conflict). This decreasing curve is called a *half-life* decrease. The shape of this half-life curve, however, can vary over time from one situation to the next. Hence, depending on the shape of the curve, a decision maker may adopt different policies with regard to frequency of communication.

If the slope of the curve is steep, as in Fig. 10.5(a), frequent message repetition may be required to retain the desired level of the message receiver's state (e.g., awareness, attitude, or behavior). On the other hand,

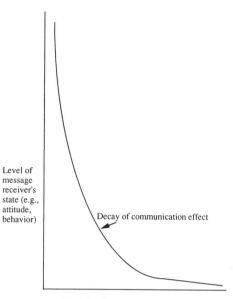

Level of
message
receiver's
state (e.g.,
attitude,
behavior)

Decay of communication effect

FIGURE 10.4   Decay of communication effects.

Time since last communication impact

the slope of the decay may be more gradual, as shown in Fig. 10.5(b). A sequence (or "pulse") of relatively infrequent communication can maintain the level of desired effects.

Allocation Problems.   One widespread and common set of problems confronting managers involves the relationship between available or needed resources, on the one hand, and various kinds of jobs, activities, assignments, or tasks to be done on the other. The resources, of course, may be operationalized in terms of money (e.g., budget allocations), time, number of people, or some combination of such resources. In public relations, two or more programs of action provide an example. The communication manager must allocate resources to one program or the other—or some combination of the two. One program may be based on mediated communication whereas the second program uses interpersonal communication conducted through face-to-face encounters, meetings, conferences, and the like. Of course, communication programs can be designed that use both modes of communication and embrace more than two options.

Allocation problems fall into three categories. One kind of problem is to fit activities (tasks or jobs) to limited (or fixed) resources. As every working practitioner knows, the problem arises because there are more activities than the available resources can support. Therefore, the solution is to determine which tasks should be performed with fixed resources. This kind of problem manifests itself in public relations management under two sets

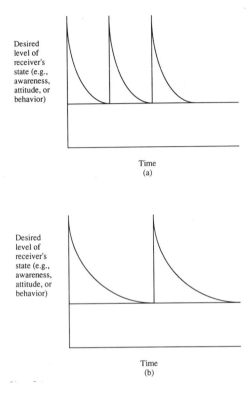

Desired
level of
receiver's
state (e.g.,
awareness,
attitude, or
behavior)

Time
(a)

Desired
level of
receiver's
state (e.g.,
awareness,
attitude, or
behavior)

Time
(b)

FIGURE 10.5 Shape of slope
and message retention.

of circumstances: (a) time allocation, that is, determining how to divide limited time among a long list of accounts or clients to be served, and (b) budget allocation, that is, determining how the budget of a public relations department is to be divided to cover the various activities to be performed over, say, a fiscal year.

The second kind of allocation problem is posed when the manager controls resource amounts and, hence, can increase or decrease the resources at will. The problem, however, is to determine the size of work force (number of people employed in the public relations department) to attain some fixed end (i.e., maximizing efficiency, or optimizing cost-benefit ratio). Instances of this problem emerge in public relations management when the size of the public relations budget or staff must be determined. The same problem occurs when communication managers decide the kinds of tasks the staff people ought to perform, the number of communication channels to use in an information campaign, and the type of communication function that such channels are to perform.

The third kind of problem—perhaps most familiar to working practitioners—occurs when both the number of assigned jobs or activities are fixed and the available resources are fixed. Unfortunately, there are not enough resources to perform each of the jobs or activities in the best possible way. Different jobs, however, can be done in different ways, using different combinations of resources. The problem is to determine how to allocate resources to the jobs or activities so that the overall performance or efficiency of the communication is maximized (i.e., total cost is minimized or total benefits are maximized), even though the individual assigned jobs cannot be performed at optimum levels. Such problems are also assignment problems because certain resources are assigned to each job or activity. Because people are resources, the problem may be to assign one or more available workers to the jobs. The simplest technique to solve such resource allocation problems is linear programming.

Queuing and Sequencing Problems.   Queuing (or waiting line) problems occur when customers arrive at some facility (e.g., banks, theaters) to obtain service. Customers may arrive randomly at a restaurant or counter to be served; automobiles may arrive at a service station or garage to be repaired. Jobs or assignment orders may arrive at a department within a large organization. Job orders are treated as customers, the department is the servicing facility, and serviced customers are the jobs completed or activities performed.

Public relations and communication departments may be analyzed using queuing theory. For the communication department, the problem is to determine the optimal size of the servicing facility (i.e., the right number of people) to handle random arrival of customers (clients, accounts, job requests) such that no one stands idle (too large a work force) but the size of the waiting line is kept to prescribed limits (not too long). The problem is to minimize loss (losing customers when the line is too long) while, at the same time, minimizing cost (keeping down the size of the work force).

As noted previously, this example is somewhat idealized, because the typical situation in communication and public relations departments is long lines (demands for communication and public relations services from the department) and fixed, inadequate resources (i.e., budgets, personnel). However, the inability of communication or public relations departments to resolve such problems may be indicative of unsophisticated management of the department. In many instances, communication managers only wring their hands and complain that "management doesn't understand us." In reality, the communication manager may be the one who does not understand, especially the principles and techniques of scientific management and operations research. In this context, learning operations research and applying queuing theory to communication department problems provides a powerful foundation for rectifying the situation. The strategic thrust of this chapter for working practitioners is not that operations research will solve all problems of public relations and communication management in organizations. Many situations defy cost-effective quantification typically desired for such decision making. Rather, learning principles and techniques of operations research provides communication managers with tools that other managers use to solve problems. When requesting the additional resources needed to optimally perform the communication/public relations function, the manager speaks the common language of management. This increases the confidence of decision makers in the manager's ability to identify and solve managerial problems.

Queuing theory manifests itself in public relations management in many different ways. People involved or affected by an organization may be regarded as stakeholder—a collection of people (the size of which varies over time) who have a stake in the policies and operations of an organization. Such stakeholders may arise when they believe and feel (accurately or inaccurately, rightly or wrongly) that they will gain something from or lose something to the organization. Such problem recognition and involvement puts stakeholders in a search mode, both seeking information and receptive to relevant information provided by the organization's communication or public relations department.

Such stakeholders may be treated as customers arriving at a service facility (an organization's communications or public relations department) with questions to be answered. Such queuing problems include forecasting the queue size at any given time, the length of time spent servicing the customers (providing the needed or requested information), and the staff size required to provide service under varying conditions.

Communication managers also must solve sequencing problems. They must select a queue discipline or procedure so as to minimize an appropriate measure of performance. Many construction and production activities, as well as research and development programs, involve sequencing problems. In such situations, some steps in the process must precede others whereas other steps may be done simultaneously. Such problems are formulated in terms of establishing starting dates and due dates and, then, determining how to sequence the operating steps in such a way as to minimize cost.

For example, a large high-tech corporation seeks to initiate a new employee communication program involving the company's extensive computer and terminal system. Some steps—obtaining or developing a software system to deliver the electronic "publication"—must be completed before other steps—designing the format of the publication. Other steps—focus—group research among employees to determine the niche for the electronic publication among the array of internal communication vehicles—may be completed simultaneous to the software acquisition steps. The goal is to have all the steps in the development of the new electronic publication completed within a reasonably short time period.

Techniques used to deal with such problems include Program Evaluation and Review Technique PERT and Critical Path Methods (CPM). In communication and public relations departments, such techniques may be employed in budget planning and in strategic and tactical public relations planning.

Replacement Problems.   We all are faced with replacing machines, appliances, and even our favorite automobile. Items such as tools, trucks, home appliances, and electric generators wear out, but degeneration typically occurs over time. If parts of the whole unit are replaced as they degenerate, the unit will wear out completely or cease to function only after an extended time period. A second type of replacement problem occurs when an item operates efficiently most of its life and then abruptly ceases to function. Such items include light bulbs, inner tubes, rubber bands, and the like.

In the first case, the longer an item is operated without proper maintenance, the more inefficient becomes its operation, with a corresponding increase in the production cost. Items also may become obsolete as new technological advances bring more efficient items on the market. The problem, then, is to determine when such items should be replaced. If items, machines, or equipment are replaced too frequently, investment costs rise. The problem is to find a replacement pattern that minimizes the sum of both operating and investment costs.

In the second case, the problem is to determine whether nonfunctioning items ought to be replaced only when they suddenly "die" (increasing the cost of piecemeal replacement) or whether replacement ought to occur as lot or group replacement (reducing replacement cost). The former approach is cheaper in that only one part is replaced, whereas the latter is more expensive because the cost of the lot is higher than a single piece. On the other hand, operation costs and per-unit replacement costs soar when units are allowed to fail before they are replaced. In such a situation, the problem is one of establishing a group replacement policy that minimizes the sum of the costs of the items, failures, and replacement operations.

In a similar vein, an organization may have an information program that has remained unchanged for a long time. For example, a nonprofit organization may have used the same "hotline" public service announcement (PSA) of many, many years. Such a long-term program reduces the cost of changing, updating, revamping, or completely replacing it. However, over time, effectiveness of the message begins to decline. This type of problem, of course, is a variation of an advertising/communication pulsing problem discussed earlier. In the replacement situation, the problem is to determine when, for example, the copy of an advertisement should be changed (so as to bring new or different needed information into play). The exact time of reaching a critical level of ineffectiveness is not known but must be determined through research. Obviously, running an advertisement after passing this critical level increases cost or loss, because little is now gained through the advertising message.

On the other hand, an organization may have a number of different information or communication programs in place. Rather than test each one for effectiveness and possible replacement, a policy may be adopted to change the content of all programs at the same time (thereby reducing individualized setup and production costs). The problem, then, is to determine how to optimize reduced production costs without losing those messages that are still effective.

Search Problems.   Search theory in the most general sense includes the procedures of formal research and, hence, incorporates tested procedures used in data gathering and data analysis as well as those used to determine the confidence limit (margin of error) of information produced for decision-making purposes. In this regard, search procedures seek to optimize the trade-off between minimizing errors that result from faulty observations and errors that results from improperly designed samples. For example, a focus-group study provides intense observation of a few participants, but the number of individuals observed reduces confidence in generalizations about the entire population. As efforts are made to reduce observational errors by making closer and more detailed observations, as in the focus-group study mentioned earlier, sampling errors tend to increase under conditions where resources used in search are fixed. For the same money, we might do a survey of many people, but be limited to just a few questions. If resources are fixed at a certain level, then more resources (time, money, personnel, equipment) can be spent on close and precise observations, but fewer resources are available for improving the type and size of the sample. The problem is to find the optimal trade-off point to minimize these two types of errors.

This problem particularly plagues communication and public relations managers held responsible for obtaining information about members of various "publics": what they believe, how they feel, their level of motivation or readiness to act, and/or the kind of behavior they manifest. To the extent managers expend restricted resources on talking to a few people in-depth interviews or focus-group studies, the less able they are to generalize to the entire population making up a sizeable public. The smaller the sample size, the greater the probability error in generalizing. When resources are spent to design and use an adequate sample to scientifically represent the population making up the public, few of these limited resources remain available for detailed probing of individuals making up the sample. The result is incomplete or inadequate information upon which the manager still must make a decision.

When resources are fixed but search techniques are variable, the problem is to select the best combination of techniques to minimize both observational and sampling errors in an optimal way. Broom and Dozier (1990) detailed how to combine intensive and extensive observation to accomplish this in public relations research. The second type of search problem allows resources to vary but fixes the search techniques to be used. By fixing the observational techniques, sample type, sample size, and the level of confidence, the problem is to determine the cost of the search endeavor, that is, to determine the resources needed to carry out the search. In both cases, the search procedures and/or resources are under the control of the individual seeking information or other knowledge (attitude of group members, group cooperativeness, behavior of group majority, and the like).

In the third case, search procedures are not controlled by the decision maker. The decision maker only decides on the thing being sought. Such search problems occur for managers in retail stores. The problem is to efficiently and effectively locate items so they can be found easily by customers. Customers control the search procedures used to find the items. This third case extends to public relations, when communication managers select placement of information in the form of news stories, advertisements, general announcements, and the like. In such cases, the information sought (or processed) by publics is under the control of an organization. Such control includes placement of information in a wide range of media, the resources to be expended, the length of placement, the repetition of placement, and the like. The practitioner cannot control the procedures individuals employ when using media to seek information, knowledge, entertainment, and the like. The problem is to determine how to maximize exposure and utilization of such messages while minimizing placement costs.

Competitive/Conflict Problems.   The units of analysis in the aforementioned cases—the things from which problems arose and about which decisions were made—could be treated as entities not themselves engaged in decision making. In this section, we confront problems in situations where decisions made by decision-maker A are affected by decisions that have been made, are being made, or will be made by decision-maker B. *Game theory* includes concepts that help us understand the formal properties, structure, and mathematical relationship between two or more decision makers where decisions of each affect decisions of the other. The contributors to game theory have been many, for example, Burger (1959), Davis

(1970), Dresher (1961), Luce and Raiffa (1957), Raiffa (1982), Rapoport (1974), Rapoport and Chammah (1965), Schelling (1963), to mention but a few. However, the game theory originated through the pioneering work of John von Neumann and Oskar Morgenstern, which is presented in their book *The Theory of Games and Economic Behavior* (1947). Games may be thought of as decision-making situations in which two or more decision makers (parties that can be individuals, groups, organizations, or whole social systems) take each other's decisions into account to maximize some gain or minimize some loss, where the gains or losses may be their own or someone else's.

The formal properties of games lead to several ways of classifying them. The first distinction is that between *zero-sum games* and *non-zero-sum games*. In zero-sum games, the winning party gains or wins the full amount of what the losing party has lost. The "wins" cancel the "losses," giving rise to the term zero-sum. Suppose that A and B are playing a coin-tossing game in which heads wins; suppose further that A and B bet (or invest) 5 dollars on the outcome. If A flips and heads comes up, A wins (recovers) 5 dollars and B loses 5 dollars, summing to a zero outcome: $5 + (-5) = 0$. In nonzero games, all the parties "win" something or they all may "lose" something. The payoff outcome (P) will be different from zero; the value of the payoff may be positively or negatively valued. The general form of zero-sum games is associated with *competitive* or *conflict* situations. Non-zero-sum games involve *cooperation* or *nonconflict* situations. In addition, games also may be distinguished in terms of the number (called *n*). This gives rise, then, to *two-party* games and *n*-party games. Much work done in game theory has been confined to simple games involving two or three parties. The complexity of trying to deal with large-*n* games—and the resultant difficulty of trying to determine how many coalitions can be formed from *n* parties—pushes such large real-world problems beyond capabilities of contemporary mathematical manipulations. Despite such limits, Davis (1970) presented ways in which *n*-game situations can be conceptualized.

Decisions also are made under different information conditions. Luce and Raiffa (1957) provided an early account of these conditions. The three general information conditions are:

1. Decision making under *certainty* (having complete or perfect information).
2. Decision making under *risk* (having incomplete or not perfect information).
3. Decision making under *uncertainty* (having no information at all).

In the first information situation, quantities or qualities used in decision making are taken as fixed and nonvarying. In the second situation, quantities used in decision making are specified or probabilities are assigned to qualities. In the last situation, constraints are even more severe, because probability values are not known and, therefore, are not "allowable" in such situations.

By combining information conditions with formal properties of games, a matrix can be constructed. See Fig. 10.6. The 12 cells in the Fig. 10.6 matrix may be regarded as well-structured game situations that do not show finer distinctions. Finer distinctions, of course, can be made by including further division of *n*-person games into three-, four-, and five-person games. The matrix also ignores situations in which games start as zero-sum, change to non-zero-sum, and then revert to zero-sum. Games also can convert from non-zero-sum to zero-sum and back to non-zero-sum. Such switching patterns may be complex and long.

Nonetheless, the theory of games gives researchers and managers a conceptual framework in which most competitive and conflict situations can be treated. Frequently, the empirical data needed to formulate game situations are missing or cannot be obtained through experimentation or direct observations. In such circumstances, researchers resort to procedures called gaming or *operational gaming*. A sample of real decision makers is asked to "play" some well-specified competitive or conflict game against each other. The armed forces long have used such military gaming procedures as "maneuvers," peace-time simulation of war used to train military personnel. Combining game theory and gaming and simulation techniques permits managers to deal realistically with practical problems.

In communication and public relations management, executives must face problems that confront their organizations and can use game theory and techniques to help solve them. These problems include formulating communication strategies in labor-management negotiations, as well as negotiations with various interest or pressure groups under adversarial conditions. Game theory suggests ways to provide information to actual or potential support groups. Competitive (conflict) theory may apply the proper timing of the introduction of new information into diffusion systems, such as those described in Rogers (1983).

When the primary mission of public relations management is conflict resolution (or accord maintenance) through two-way communication, game theory has direct relevance. Game theory allows formal specifications of the

	Two-person game		N-person game	
	Zero-sum	Non-zero-sum	Zero-sum	Non-zero-sum
Certainty	1	2	3	4
Risk	5	6	7	8
Uncertainty	9	10	11	12

FIGURE 10.6 Matrix of game types under varying information conditions.

types and conditions of game playing. Game theory gives direction to the solution of various problems arising in games. Game theory provides both the concepts and a formal method for combining these concepts which public relations managers can apply directly to problem solving. Ehling (1984, 1985, 1987) argued that a game theoretic schema can be used to distinguish between the primary mission of marketing management and public relations management. Marketing, committed to the goal of attaining or maintaining a positive slope of the demand (sales) curve, engages in conflictual (competitive) games with competitors. Under these circumstances, organizations seek to enlarge their share of market (at the expense of all other competitors) through the marketing function. Marketing is a clear case of a zero-sum (or win–lose) game.

Public relations management, on the other hand, seeks mutually acceptable resolutions in interorganizational disputes or conflict (such as disagreement in labor-management relations, discord in minority/ethnic relations, or, more generally, controversy in interest/pressure group relations). Such conflict resolution, where primacy is given to communication as the principal and appropriate means, uses concepts of a non-zero-sum game. Emphasis is on maintaining or achieving a win-win (rather than a win-lose) arrangement. This is done by maximizing the difference between conflict (C') and cooperation (C), that is, $max(C - C')$, by manifesting more cooperation than conflict. According to game theory, public relations management and marketing management not only have functionally distinctive missions but also use essentially different concepts and methodologies.

Such conceptualization, in turn, serves the goal-setting function described previously. Operations research cannot tell a policy planner or executive what goals to pursue. Such research, however, can tell managers which goals are jurisdictionally appropriate, attainable, and economically worthwhile. Game theory, as used in operations research, allows communicators and top managers to clarify the nature of public relations management goals and the formal methods to be used in defining and measuring such goals. Game theory clearly distinguished the underlying assumptions employed in the function and administration of public relations management and marketing management. Such distinction is a critical contribution to the professionalization of public relations practice.

SUMMARY AND CONCLUSION

In this chapter an effort was made to identify some of the many analytical and evalutative techniques and methods employed in operations research activities and show their application to many of the practical problems confronting those engaged in public relations practices. Space limitation of this chapter obviously prohibited the spelling out in full technical detail the "how to" application of operations research; those interested in such detail are invited to consult the many references on operations research found at the end of this chapter. Instead of providing a lot of technical detail, it was felt that it was more important to show which of the many operations research techniques have specific relevance to an identifiable public relations and communications problem.

The point of this chapter is not to suggest that every strategic communication or public relations decision must be made fully operationalized as a mathematically designed decision-making model; rather, the point is that operations research thinking can be applied to many situations in which practitioners find themselves; it is the kind of thinking that is more rigorous, more demanding, and more benefit oriented than the questionable "by-guess-and-by-gosh" methods so frequently employed by those who manage by "the seat of their pants."

In contrast, operations research thinking calls for careful planning and designing of public relations and communications programs of action and constant evaluation of program performance. Operations research thinking requires a manager to be mindful that the goals or end-states of public relations and communication activities must be

socially warranted,
ethically acceptable,
conceptually well-specified,
organizationally relevant,
structurally distinguishable,
administratively feasible,
operationally attainable,
empirically measurable, and
economically optimal.

By the same token, the criteria to be used for evaluating the strategies or courses of action to be employed in achieving acceptable goals or end-states include the following:

socially warranted,
ethically acceptable,
conceptually well-specified,
operationally appropriate,
organizationally supportable,
administratively implementable,
empirically connectable to goal(s),
applicably effective, and
economically efficient.

Operations research presupposes that the standards of "socially warranted" and "ethically acceptable" have been met in selecting the ends and means or courses of action. Thereafter, however, operations research methodologies have direct relevance and application in fulfilling the other criteria or standards in the design and evaluation of goals (end-states) and strategies (courses of action) of any public relations and communication activity. Hence, operations research thinking as applied to public relations and communication decisions clearly elevates the sophistication and professionalization of the practice. At the same time, such use of operations research brings the communication function in step with other organizational units that use operations research to solve problems and make decisions.

REFERENCES

Ackoff, R. L. (Ed.). (1961). *Progress in operations research* (Vol. 1). New York: Wiley.

Ackoff, R. L., & Emery, F. E. (1972). *On purposeful systems.* Chicago: Aldine Atherton.

Ackoff, R. L., & Sasieni, M. (1968). *Fundamentals of operations research.* New York: Wiley.

Atchison, T. J., & Hill, W. W. (1978). *Management today.* New York: Harcourt Brace Jovanovich.

Beer, S. (1959). Cybernetics and operations research. *Operational Research Quarterly, 19,* 1–21.

Brinkerhoff, M. B., & Kuntz, P. R. (1972). *Complex organizations and their environments.* Dubuque, IA: Brown.

Broom, G. M., & Dozier, D. M. (1990). *Using research in public relations: Applications to program management.* Englewood Cliffs, NJ: Prentice-Hall.

Broom, G. M., Lauzen, M. M., & Tucker, K. (1991). *Public relations and marketing: Dividing the conceptual domain and operational turf.* Manuscript submitted for publication.

Bross, I. D. J. (1953). *Design for decision: An introduction to statistical decision-making.* New York: Free Press.

Burger, E. (1959). *Introduction to the theory of games.* Englewood Cliffs, NJ: Prentice-Hall.

Chernoff, H., & Moses, L. E. (1959). *Elementary decision theory.* New York: Wiley.

Churchman, W. C. (1961). *Predication and optimal decision.* Englewood Cliffs, NJ: Prentice-Hall.

Cutlip, S. M., Center, A. H., & Broom, G. M. (1985). *Effective public relations* (6th ed.). Englewood Cliffs, NJ: Prentice-Hall.

Davis, M. D. (1970). *Game theory,* New York: Basic.

Dresher, M. (1961). *Games of strategy: Theory and application.* Englewood Cliffs, NJ: Prentice-Hall.

Duckworth, W. E. (1965). *A guide to operational research.* London: Methuen.

Duckworth, W. E., Gear A. E., & Lockett, A. G. (1977). *A guide to operational research* (3rd ed.). London: Chapman & Hall.

Ehling, W. P. (1981, August). *Toward a theory of public relations management: Application of purposive and conflict of communication.* Paper presented at the annual convention of the Association for Education in Journalism, East Lansing, MI.

Ehling, W. P. (1984). Application of decision theory in the construction of a theory of public relations management, I. *Public Relations Research and Education, 1*(Summer), 15–38.

Ehling, W. P. (1985). Application of decision theory in the construction of a theory of public relations management, II. *Public Relations Research and Education, 2*(Summer), 4–22.

Ehling, W. P. (1987, May). *Public relations function and adversarial environments.* Paper presented at the annual conference of the International Communication Association, Montreal.

Etzioni, A. (1964). *Modern Organizations.* Englewood Cliffs, NJ: Prentice-Hall.

Etzioni, A., & Lehman, E. W. (1980). *A sociological reader on complex organization.* New York: Holt, Rinehart & Winston.

Evan, W. M. (Ed.). (1978). *Inter-organizational relations.* Philadelphia: University of Pennsylvania Press.

Glueck, W. F. (1980). *Management* (2nd ed.). Insdale, IL: Dryden.

Gossen, R., & Sharp, K. (1987). How to manage the dispute resolution. *Public Relations Journal, 43,* 35–38.

Grunig, J. E., & Hunt, T. (1984). *Managing public relations.* New York: Holt, Rinehart & Winston.

Hall, R. (Ed.). (1972). *The formal organization.* New York: Basic.

Hodgetts, R. M. (1982). *Management theory, process and practice* (3rd ed.).

Ivancevich, J. J., Donnelly, J. H. Jr., & Gibson, J. L. (1980). *Managing for performance.* Dallas, TX: Business Publications.

Kaufmann, A. (1963). *Methods and models of operations research.* Englewood Cliffs, NJ: Prentice-Hall.

Kendal, M. G. (1958). The teaching of operational research. *Operational Research Quarterly, 9,* 265–278.

Koontz, H., O'Donnell, C., & Weihrich, H. (1982). *Essential of management* (3rd ed.). New York: McGraw-Hill.

Krajewski, L. J., & Thompson, E. (1981). *Management science.* New York: Wiley.

Lawrence, J. R. (Ed.). (1966). *Operational research and the social sciences.* London: Tavistock.

Lovell, R. P. (1982). *Inside public relations.* Boston: Allyn & Bacon.

Luce, R. D., & Raiffa, H. (1957). *Games and decisions: Introduction and critical survey.* New York: Wiley.

Marston, J. E. (1979). *Modern public relations.* New York: McGraw-Hill.

Meyer, J. W., & Scott, W. R. (1983). *Organizational environments.* Beverly Hills, CA: Sage.

Miller, D. W., & Starr, M. K. (1961). *Executive decisions and operations research.* Englewood Cliffs, NJ: Prentice-Hall.

Miner, J. B. (1980). *Theories of organizational behavior.* Hinsdale, IL: Dryden.

Misshauk, M. J. (1979). *Management theory and practice.* Boston: Little, Brown.

Montgomery, D. B., & Urban, G. L. (1969). *Management science in marketing.* Englewood Cliffs, NJ: Prentice-Hall.

Nagel, S. S., & Neef, M. (1976). *Operations research methods.* Beverly Hills, CA: Sage.

Nager, N. R. & Allen, T. H. (1984). *Public Relations Management by Objectives.* New York, Longman.

Negandhi, A. R. (Ed.). (1975). *Interorganizational theory.* Kent, OH: Kent State University Press.

Newman, W. H., & Warren, E. K. (1977). *The process of management* (4th ed.). Englewood Cliffs, NJ: Prentice-Hall.

Radford, K. L. (1981). *Modern managerial decision-making.* Reston, VA: Reston Publishing.

Raiffa, H. (1982). *The art and science of negotiation.* Cambridge, MA: Harvard University Press.

Rapoport, A. (1974). *Conflict in man-made environment.* Hammondsworth, England: Penguin.

Rapoport, A., & Chammah, A. M. (1965). *Prisoner dilemma.* Ann Arbor, MI: University of Michigan Press.

Reilly, R. T. (1981). *Public relations in action.* Englewood Cliffs, NJ: Prentice-Hall.

Richmond, S. B. (1968). *Operations research for management decisions*. New York: Ronald Press.

Robbins, S. P. (1974). *Managing organizational conflict*. Englewood Cliffs, NJ: Prentice-Hall.

Robbins, S. P. (1976). *The administrative process*. Englewood Cliffs, NJ: Prentice-Hall.

Robbins, S. P. (1983). *Organizational behavior* (2nd ed.). Englewood Cliffs, NJ: Prentice-Hall.

Rogers, E. M. (1983). *Diffusion of innovations* (3rd ed.). New York: Free Press.

Sasieni, M., Yaspan, A., & Friedman, L. (1959). *Operations research*. New York: Wiley.

Schelling, T. C. (1963). *The strategy of conflict*. New York: Galaxy.

Schramm, W. (1988). *The story of human communication*. New York: Harper & Row.

Siemens, N., Marting, C. H., & Greenwood, F. (1973). *Operations research*. New York: Free Press.

Seitel, F. P. (1984). *The practice of public relations*. Columbus, OH: Merrill.

Von Neumann, J., & Morgenstern, O. (1947). *The theory of games and economic behavior* (2nd ed.). Princeton, NJ: Princeton University Press.

11 Models of Public Relations and Communication

James E. Grunig
University of Maryland

Larissa A. Grunig
University of Maryland

ABSTRACT

J. Grunig and Hunt (1984) were the first to define four typical ways in which public relations is practiced—four models of public relations. Since that time, the models of press agentry, public information, two-way asymmetrical, and two-way symmetrical public relations have been the objects of intense research by public relations scholars. This chapter reviews this research, including the history of the models, the extent to which the models are valid and reliable descriptions of how public relations actually is practiced, and the conditions in and around organizations that explain why the models are practiced. The chapter argues that the two-way symmetrical model provides a normative theory of how public relations should be practiced to be ethical and effective—a characteristic of excellent communication management. In the actual practice of public relations, the chapter points out, excellent public relations deviates from pure symmetrical public relations and can be described as a combination of the two-way asymmetrical and symmetrical models— mixed-motive public relations.

In 1975, J. Grunig had just completed his first study of the behavior of public relations practitioners and submitted it for publication in *Journalism Monographs*. One of the anonymous referees of the manuscript criticized the basic idea behind the research. The reviewer argued that the activities of public relations practitioners are so diverse that any attempt to classify those activities and to explain why they occur is a futile exercise.

Fortunately, the editor accepted J. Grunig's contention that he had successfully developed categories to describe public relations behavior; and the results of the study were published (J. Grunig, 1976). That study was the first in a program of research that has brought researchers close to an understanding of the different ways in which public relations practitioners and public relations departments of organizations perform communication functions and close to an explanation of why these behaviors differ.

If the anonymous reviewer were correct in saying that public relations behaviors cannot be classified and the reasons why these behaviors occur cannot be explained, then the search for excellence in public relations that we are pursuing in this book also would be fruitless. To achieve our research purpose, we must be able to provide a *model* of excellent public relations and must be able to distinguish that model from other typical ways in which public relations is practiced. We use the term *model* here in the way that it is used in the sciences—as a simplified representation of reality. Although all models are "false" in the sense that no representation can capture reality perfectly, we would have no understanding of reality at all if we had no model with which to work.

We use the term *model* to describe a set of values and a pattern of behavior that characterize the approach taken by a public relations department or individual practitioner to all programs or, in some cases, to specific programs or campaigns. Thus, *model* describes a broader pattern of behavior than does the concept of roles that Dozier describes in the next chapter.

In this chapter, we describe four models of public relations that we have used in our research to capture the enormous variation in public relations practice and to reduce that variation to these four simplified representations. We also explain why we believe one of these models will characterize the behavior of excellent public relations departments, discuss research that has identified the conditions that make the practice of this model possible, and discuss theoretical developments that clarify how to practice the excellent model of public relations.

A HISTORY OF THE CONCEPT OF PUBLIC RELATIONS MODELS

Historians of public relations and authors of textbooks have used crude terms to describe different kinds of public relations. Historian Eric Goldman (1948), for example, contrasted two eras in the history of public relations, the era of "the public be fooled"—his name for press agentry—and the era of the "public be informed"—his name for public information. Similarly, the simple distinction between one-way and two-way communication can be traced to many early textbooks, such as Cutlip and Center's (1952) first edition.

In his first study of public relations behavior, J. Grunig (1976) took the idea of one-way and two-way models of communication but elaborated the idea to include the purpose of the communication as well as the direction. He used Thayer's (1968) concepts of *synchronic* and *diachronic* communication to describe two approaches to public relations. The purpose of synchronic communication, as Thayer explained it, is to "synchronize" the behavior of a public with that of the organization so that the organization can continue to behave in the way it wants without interference. The purpose of diachronic communication is to negotiate a state of affairs that benefits both the organization and the public.

In this 1976 study, J. Grunig measured the extent to which 216 organizations in the Baltimore-Washington area practiced 16 public relations activities, such as the writing of press releases, research to plan a program, research to evaluate a program, or counseling of management. He used factor analysis to reduce these 16 activities to two dimensions that approximated the synchronic and diachronic models of public relations. Later Schneider [aka L. Grunig] (1985b) correlated these 16 activities with four types of organizations described by Hage and Hull (1981).

In these two studies, we had limited success in explaining these two types of public relations behavior. A major reason for this lack of success, we believed, was that the two models were too gross and oversimplified to capture the reality of public relations practice. As a result, it was difficult to predict who would practice the models and in what situations they would be practiced. Later, J. Grunig (1984) also concluded that the terms *synchronic* and *diachronic,* which mean literally "at one time" and "at two times," did not describe accurately the difference in purpose he had in mind for the two kinds of public relations. He replaced these terms with the terms *asymmetrical* and *symmetrical* to describe the purpose of public relations as striving for balanced rather than unbalanced communication and effects.

The philosophical differences between asymmetrical and symmetrical public relations were described in detail in chapter 3. This chapter, then, shows how the presuppositions underlying asymmetrical and symmetrical communication are manifested in models of actual public relations practice.

J. Grunig and Hunt (1984) first identified the four models in the history of public relations. Although J. Grunig and Hunt acknowledged that there had been "public-relations-like" activities throughout history, they claimed that the press agents of the mid-19th century were the first full-time specialists to practice public relations. These press agents practiced the *press agentry/publicity* model of public relations for such heroes as Andrew Jackson, Daniel Boone, Buffalo Bill Cody, and Calamity Jane. The most prominent of these practitioners was P. T. Barnum, who skillfully promoted his circus performers using the axiom, "There is a sucker born every minute."

At the beginning of the 20th century, according to J. Grunig and Hunt (1984), a second model of public relations, the *public information model,* developed as a reaction to attacks on large corporations and government agencies by muckraking journalists. Leaders of these organizations realized they needed more than the propaganda of press agents to counter the attacks on them in the media. Instead, they hired their own journalists as public relations practitioners to write press "handouts" explaining their actions. Although practitioners of the public information model generally chose to write only good things about their organizations, the information they did report generally was truthful and accurate.

J. Grunig and Hunt (1984) identified Ivy Lee as the primary historical figure whose work characterized the public information model. Lee began his career as a newspaper reporter who did his best work writing about banking and business. When he moved to the employ of the businesses he reported, he was able to use his talent for "explaining complicated and misunderstood facts to a popular audience" (Hiebert, 1966, p. 39) to help business explain and defend itself.

Both the press agentry and the public information models represent one-way approaches to public relations—the dissemination of information from organizations to publics, usually through the media. Beginning with the Creel Committee during World War I, however, some public relations practitioners began to base their work on the behavioral and social sciences. Foremost among these practitioners was Edward L. Bernays. As a nephew of Sigmund Freud, he took an interest in psychology and based his practice on it.

Behavioral and social sciences, of course, would not be sciences if they were not based on research. Thus, the introduction of a scientific approach made the practice of public relations two-way: Practitioners both sought information from and gave information to publics. Sciences also are based on theories; and the theories introduced by Bernays were those of propaganda, persuasion, and the "engineering of consent." J. Grunig and Hunt (1984), therefore, described the first two-way model of public relations as the *two-way asymmetrical model.*

According to Olasky (1987, 1989) historical research shows that Bernays believed that humans are manipulable, as evidenced by the success of Nazi propagandists at the time of World War II. Bernays reasoned, however, that if humans could be manipulated for evil purposes, they also could be manipulated for good. The secret of successful manipulation was in understanding the motivations of people and in using research to identify the messages most likely to produce the attitudes and behaviors desired by an organization. The asymmetrical position taken by Bernays may sound reasonable, but, as J. Grunig (1989) pointed out, organizations often believe that publics benefit from "a lot of strange things":

. . . pollution, toxic waste, drinking, smoking, guns, overthrow of governments, dangerous products, lowered salary and benefits, discrimination
against women and minorities, job layoffs, dangerous manufacturing plants,
risky transportation of products, higher prices, monopoly power, poor
product quality, political favoritism, insider trading, use of poisonous
chemicals, exposure to carcinogens, nuclear weapons, and even warfare. (p.
32)

J. Grunig and Hunt (1984) identified many of the assumptions of the
fourth model of public relations, the *two-way symmetrical model,* in the
writings of practitioners such as Lee, Bernays, and John Hill. These
assumptions (p. 42) included "telling the truth," "interpreting the client and
public to one another," and "management understanding the viewpoints of
employees and neighbors as well as employees and neighbors understanding
the viewpoints of management." They added, however, that few of these
practitioners put such assumptions into practice and that it was public
relations scholars and educators who took the practitioners at their word
and made the model the basis of their teaching and research.

The two-way symmetrical model makes use of research and other forms
of two-way communication. Unlike the two-way asymmetrical model,
however, it uses research to facilitate understanding and communication
rather than to identify messages most likely to motivate or persuade publics.
In the symmetrical model, understanding is the principal objective of public
relations rather than persuasion.

Although J. Grunig and Hunt (1984) identified these four models as
stages in the history of public relations, they said they believed that all of
the models are practiced today. Thus J. Grunig (1984) developed measures
of the models and began a program of research to determine if the
theoretical models do indeed describe the practice of public relations and to
identify conditions that explain why organizations practice the models they
do. He began this research by identifying two variables underlying the four
models: direction and purpose. Direction describes the extent to which the
model is one-way or two-way. One-way communication disseminates
information; it is a monologue. Two-way communication exchanges information; it is a dialogue. Purpose describes whether the model is asymmetrical or symmetrical. Asymmetrical communication is imbalanced; it leaves
the organization as is and tries to change the public. Symmetrical communication is balanced; it adjusts the relationship between the organization
and public.

J. Grunig and L. Grunig (1989), therefore, conceptualized the press
agentry model as a one-way asymmetrical model, the public information
model as a one-way symmetrical model, and the two-way asymmetrical and
two-way symmetrical models as their names indicate. Later, J. Grunig
(1989) changed his mind about this two-by-two typology and also described

the public information model as an asymmetrical model. Because practitioners of the public information model selectively disseminate information about their organization—all of which is "true" or "accurate"—J. Grunig reasoned that they do not truly engage in a dialogue.

Thus, he characterized (J. Grunig, 1989, p. 30) the press agentry and two-way asymmetrical models as "craft" and "scientific" versions of asymmetrical public relations and the public information model as "*de facto* asymmetrical public relations.*" Only the two-way symmetrical model, he argued, represented a break from the predominant worldview that public relations is a way of manipulating publics for the benefit of the organization.

Recently, J. Grunig and Hunt's (1984) assertion that the history of public relations can be interpreted as four developmental stages described by the models has come under attack. Olasky (1987) argued that public relations did not originate with press agentry. Instead, he argued, organizations practiced what he called "private relations" before they practiced public relations. With private relations, organizations either did not feel obligated to communicate with publics, or organizational executives communicated directly with publics without the intervention of manipulative public relations practitioners. Although Olasky did not use the term symmetrical, his discussion suggests that private relations were symmetrical before press agents made public relations asymmetrical.

In addition, feminist scholars recently have criticized histories of public relations for ignoring the contributions of women practitioners. L. Grunig (1989), in addition, suggested that preliminary historical evidence suggests that women were practicing public relations early in the history of the United States and that they appear to have practiced the symmetrical model.

Whatever their historical origins, however, the four models of public relations do provide us with a way of describing and explaining how and why contemporary public relations is practiced as it is. The primary proposition of this chapter, therefore, is that excellent public relations departments practice the two-way symmetrical model of public relations. We provide support for that proposition from the research literature. First, however, we turn to research that has established the reliability and validity of the models and has identified the conditions that explain why organizations practice them.

DO THE MODELS EXIST IN THE REAL WORLD?

Many practitioners of public relations, in particular those with anti-intellectual tendencies, often react to theories such as the four models with the well-worn cliché that "it may be true in theory but it doesn't work in practice." Although that statement usually reveals that the person who made it does not understand the nature of a theory, it does focus attention on two questions that are important to an evaluation of the concept of public relations models: whether the models provide a *normative* or a *positive* theory of public relations and, if they provide a positive theory, whether the models describe accurately what practitioners actually do.

A normative theory defines how things should be or how some activity should be carried out. According to Massy and Weitz (1977, p. 122), positive theories are used to understand problems whereas normative theories are used to solve problems. In developing a normative theory, theorists have no obligation to show that an activity actually is conducted in the way the theory describes. They must show only that if an activity were to be conducted as the theory prescribes, it would be effective. Normative theories are common in fields such as management science, operations research, the economics of decision making, and—to a lesser extent—marketing and organizational communication. Ehling in chapters 10 and 23 of this book, in addition, constructs normative theories of public relations.

The "good in theory but not in practice" cliché is relevant to a normative theory. When applied to a normative theory, the cliché would mean that although the theory is logical it is not practical—realistically, it could not be implemented in an actual situation. Theorists construct a normative theory to provide a model that, if followed, would improve the practice of the activity that it models. If that normative theory, in fact, cannot be implemented then it would not be a good theory.

Each of the four models of public relations could serve as a normative theory of public relations. They could tell a practitioner how to be a press agent or public information specialist, for example. We believe, however, that the two-way symmetrical model should be the normative model for public relations—that it describes how excellent public relations should be practiced.

In addition, we believe that the four models describe how public relations actually is practiced—that they are a positive (descriptive) theory of public relations. Positive theories describe phenomena, events, or activities as they actually occur. Most theories in the physical sciences are positive. They describe the rotation of the earth, the nature of the atom, and the origin of the universe. They do not tell the earth how to rotate, how the atom should be structured, or how a new universe could be initiated.

Positive theories can be evaluated in part by whether they correspond to reality. If public relations is not practiced as described by the models, the models would not be a good positive theory. In that case, the "good in theory but not in practice" criticism would not apply. If the theory is not good in describing practice, it could not be good in theory. The evidence from research supports the conclusion that the four models provide a good positive theory: Public relations practitioners do indeed practice all of them. Later we show, however, that practitioners generally do not practice the model that would be best for their organizations. Thus, we have concluded that the relationship of the models to the environment of the organization functions more as a normative than a positive theory. We introduce positive theories, however, that explain why organizations do not practice the theory that normatively would be best for them.

In the social and behavioral sciences, normative and positive theories can overlap in ways that they could not in the physical sciences. They can overlap because humans invent normative theories and apply them in practice. Once practiced, they become positive theories because they then describe practice in the real world. For example, each of the four models of public relations was developed normatively by a theorist such as Ivy Lee, Edward L. Bernays, or Scott Cutlip, who constructed them in the abstract and then implemented them in the real world or taught others how to implement them. Indeed, research should be able to show that a good normative theory functions in practice in the way the normative theory says it should. As Massy and Weitz (1977) put it, useful normative theory should provide solutions "under typical conditions encountered in actual practice" (p. 123).

We believe, therefore, that—normatively—the two-way symmetrical model defines the most excellent way of practicing public relations and that—positively—research will show that model does the most to make organizations effective. To test that model positively against the other models we must be able to show that the concept of the models can be measured and that it has reliability, validity, and accuracy—that the models can be identified and measured accurately in the real world.

Measurement

If the concept of the four models is to be part of a positive theory of public relations, a researcher must be able to measure the extent to which organizations or individual practitioners practice each model. These measures can be either quantitative or qualitative. With quantitative measures, researchers construct a series of items for a questionnaire to which a practitioner or some other observer of an organization would be asked to provide a numerical score to indicate how well each item describes public relations in that organization. With qualitative measures, researchers would, for example, examine publications of an organization, interview a practitioner or other observer, or personally observe public relations activities or descriptions of them. They then could make reasoned judgments about whether one or more of the models describe the public relations activities of an organization.

To date, most researchers have measured the four models quantitatively, although in at least five studies (Buffington, 1988; Hardwick, 1980; Maymi, 1987; Nanni, 1980; Schneider [aka L. Grunig], 1985a) they have used quantitative measures to identify the model practiced and then have supplemented those data with qualitative observations to describe in more detail how organizations practice the models.

J. Grunig (1976) first developed quantitative measures for the concepts of synchronic and diachronic public relations, the concepts that led to the development of the four models. He measured these two concepts with a question asking how often organizations practiced 16 public relations activities. He then used factor analysis to group these procedures into indices of diachronic and synchronic practices.

Because some of these practices, such as the use of press releases or research to plan a project, could be used in all of the models, researchers subsequently moved toward somewhat more subjective measures of the models. Hardwick (1980) and Nanni (1980), for example, asked practitioners both whether they used research and whether their objective was to change attitudes and behavior or to facilitate communication and understanding.

J. Grunig (1984) began the work that has resulted in our current measure of the models by writing eight questionnaire items for each model based on six dimensions described in J. Grunig and Hunt (1984). These dimensions were the purpose of public relations; control versus adaptation as a goal; the role of public relations as advocacy, dissemination, or mediation; one-way versus two-way communication; media relations as an application of the models; and the use of research. Public relations practitioners responded to the items by indicating on a 5-point scale how well each item described the way their organization practiced public relations. These eight items then were averaged to provide an index of each of the models.

Reliability

For these quantitative measures to be good ones, they first must be reliable. That is, they should yield the same results each time they are used — "yield the same results on repeated trials," in the words of Carmines and Zeller (1979, p. 11). To measure reliability, J. Grunig and several other researchers calculated Cronbach's Alpha, one of the standard measures of reliability. Cronbach's Alpha can be interpreted as a correlation of the index with another index that could be constructed to measure the same activities. There is no standard for how high Cronbach's Alpha should be. Carmines and Zeller (1979, p. 51) said they believe it should be .80 or higher for "widely used scales." Alphas of .50 to .65 frequently are reported in communication research, however, and most researchers consider indices with such Alphas to be adequate.

J. Grunig and L. Grunig (1989) reported Cronbach's Alpha for seven studies conducted at the University of Maryland using the models (Fabiszak, 1985; J. Grunig, 1984; Lauzen, 1986; McMillan, 1984, E. Pollack, 1984; R. Pollack, 1986; Schneider [aka L. Grunig], 1985a). In some of these studies, some items were dropped to increase reliability; and several items were rewritten as the research progressed to make them more reliable. After these adjustments, the average Cronbach's Alpha in the seven studies was .62 for the press agentry index, .53 for public information, .57 for two-way asymmetrical, and .59 for two-way symmetrical. (For the two-way asymmetrical index, one study reported an abnormally low alpha, which was not included in this average.)

Ossareh (1987) simplified the instrument by selecting the three items from each index that were most reliable and obtained comparable alphas of .48, .57, .76, and .51 for the press agentry, public information, two-way asymmetrical, and two-way symmetrical models, respectively. In developing the IABC excellence project we took the three items selected by Ossareh and added one more item that also had been reliable in the previous studies. Wetherell (1989) used those four items and an improved scaling technique also used in the excellence project—an open-end "fractionation" scale—and found reliabilities of .78, .60, .81, and .76 for the models in the same order.

In short, we have improved the reliability scores for the four models to the point where they are at or near the standard of .80 with the exception of the public information model. Reliability for that model consistently has been lower than for the other models because many of the items are related to the dissemination of information, which to some extent is practiced in all of the models.

Validity

In addition to being reliable, a theoretical concept must be valid if it is to be part of a good positive theory—that is, researchers must be able to measure what the theory says they should measure. J. Grunig and L. Grunig (1989) consolidated data from four studies (Fabiszak, 1985; McMillan, 1984, 1987; R. Pollack, 1986) that reported two tests of the *concurrent validity* of the four models. Concurrent validity indicates the extent to which measures of a concept correlate with other, criterion, variables with which they logically should correlate (Carmines & Zeller, 1979; Stamm, 1981; Wimmer & Dominick, 1983).

First, J. Grunig and L. Grunig (1989) examined correlations of the models with the 16 public relations practices that J. Grunig (1976) had used to measure diachronic and synchronic public relations and additional practices added to the list in one or more of these four studies. In general, the models did not correlate strongly with any of the journalistic techniques of public relations, such as writing press releases, preparing publications, or holding press conferences. These techniques, the authors concluded, are tools used in all of the models. Some correlations with techniques fit the logic of the models, however, and supported their validity:

> . . . the public information model correlated positively with preparing house organs, magazines, publications, and newsletters and negatively with making informal contact with the public. Tours, events, and open houses correlated positively with the two-way symmetrical model in the federal government and negatively with the public information and press agentry models. Marketing in hospitals correlated positively with the two-way asymmetrical and two-way symmetrical models and negatively with the public information model. Fundraising correlated with two-way asymmetrical public relations in hospitals. In associations, press agentry correlated positively with promoting trade shows and exhibits, building membership, and furnishing advertising materials to members. (p. 37)

Correlations with research activities, however, provided the strongest evidence of the validity of the models. In general, conducting formative and evaluative research correlated positively with the two-way models and negatively with press agentry and public information. The two-way models also correlated positively with the extent to which practitioners reported that they counsel management, and the correlation was highest for the two-way symmetrical model. In addition, contacting government officials and thought leaders correlated positively with the two-way symmetrical model. All of these relationships reflect the logic of the models.

Martinson and Ryan (1989) and Ossareh (1987) reported similar evidence of concurrent validity. Martinson and Ryan found that practitioners with high scores on the two-way models also believed in the value of research in public relations—including theoretical research—whereas those scoring highly on the one-way models did not. Ossareh found that practitioners of the two-way models—especially the two-way symmetrical model—more often used computers in their work than did practitioners of the one-way models.

As a second test of the concurrent validity of the models, J. Grunig and L. Grunig (1989) reported the results of four studies that correlated the indices with the four public relations roles developed by Broom and Dozier and discussed in chapter 12 of this book. Logically, the two-way models cannot be implemented without a communication manager to plan public relations programs. Communication technicians alone can practice the press agentry and public information models, however. As expected, results showed that when the top person in a public relations department was a communication manager, the organization was more likely to practice the two-way asymmetrical or symmetrical model. When the top person was a technician, the organization was more likely to practice press agentry or public information.[1]

Accuracy

We do have evidence, therefore, that the four models of public relations fit the two standard criteria for a positive theory. We also have evidence related to a third standard, which we call *theoretical accuracy*—the extent to which the four models accurately represent the most common ways in which public relations is practiced in the real world. The theoretical models would not be accurate if there actually are more models of public relations being practiced or if these four could be consolidated into fewer models.

J. Grunig and Hunt (1984) developed the models by analyzing the history of public relations. Neither is an historian, however, and research by historians might reveal other models — for example, Olasky's (1987) concept of private relations could constitute another model. In addition, the models are based on the history and practice of public relations in the United States. Research in other cultures (e.g., Sriramesh & J. Grunig, 1988) also may reveal other models.

Several researchers have conducted factor analyses of the items J. Grunig developed to measure the four items. Factor analysis clusters items empirically — that is, it groups the items to which people tend to give the same responses. These empirical clusters can be compared with the theoretical clusters of items to see if reality fits the theory. J. Grunig (1984) and Lauzen (1986) found that factor analysis fragmented the items into dimensions of the models, such as research activities, media relations, or purpose of communication. Thus, they concluded that factor analysis did not produce a better set of models than did J. Grunig's (1984) original theoretical models.

Dozier (1989) and Reagan, Anderson, Sumner, and Hill (1989) found two-factor solutions for the items. A one-way factor combined the press agentry and public information models, and a two-way factor combined the two-way asymmetrical and symmetrical models. Likewise, Turk (1986) had difficulty separating the two-way asymmetrical and symmetrical models for state government agencies. J. Grunig and L. Grunig (1989, p. 40) also

---

[1] Judd (1987) also reported that managers more often practiced the two-way models and technicians the one-way models.

reported consistent positive correlations in six studies between the press agentry and public information and the two-way asymmetrical and two-way symmetrical models.

The two-factor solutions, however, may have been an artifact of the type of factor analysis conducted—exploratory rather than confirmatory factor analysis. Exploratory factor analysis allows the computer to define the factors with no guidance from a theory. Confirmatory factor analysis attempts to confirm the predictions of the theory (Fink & Monge, 1985). To date, all factor analyses of the four models have been exploratory. Although some of the researchers have suggested that there may be only two models of public relations, we believe that confirmatory factor analysis would support the presence of four models. We believe, however, that confirmatory factors representing the press agentry and public information models and those representing the two two-way models would be correlated with each other.

The reliability analyses reported earlier and the correlations among the models reported by J. Grunig and L. Grunig (1989) suggest instead that organizations may mix the models rather than that there are only two models. In addition to the correlations between the one-way and the two-way models, for example, J. Grunig and L. Grunig (p. 40) also reported correlations among press agentry and public information and one or both of the two-way models in some organizations.

J. Grunig and L. Grunig (1989, pp. 56–57) reported evidence from Cupp (1985) and Nelson (1986) that organizations change models of public relations as situations and issues change or that they use different models for different programs. Cupp, for example, found that chemical companies that practiced the public information model in normal times turned to the two-way symmetrical model in a crisis. Similarly, L. Grunig (1986) found that the organizations she studied shifted from one model to another as they dealt with activist groups.

What, then, can we conclude about the four models as a positive theory? They can be reliably measured, they are valid, and they do exist in real organizations. Organizations often do not practice the models purely, however. Many use different models for different situations and different programs. And, in addition, there may be theoretical reasons yet unexplored for why organizations combine the models—which we explore in the last section of this chapter.

WHY DO ORGANIZATIONS PRACTICE THE FOUR MODELS?

In much of our research on the models of public relations, we have predicted that there will be a logical relationship between the structure and environment of an organization and the model or models of public relations it practices. This research began with J. Grunig (1976) and continued through 14 studies reviewed in J. Grunig and L. Grunig (1989). (L. Grunig reviews the literature on the structure and environment of organizations and their effect on the practice of public relations in chapter 17.)

The research on why organizations practice the four models has followed trends in organizational sociology (described, e.g., in Robbins, 1990). Until recently, most organizational sociologists believed that organizations develop structures that are appropriate for their environments and their technology. As chapter 17 shows, however, research has provided only minimal support for these structural and environmental theories—both in sociology and in our research on models of public relations. The least support for a relationship between environments and the models of public relations has come from studies that have used strictly empirical measures of environmental variables (Fabiszak, 1985; McMillan, 1984, 1987; E. Pollack, 1984; R. Pollack, 1986). Studies that have used qualitative observations of the environment of the organizations sampled (J. Grunig, 1984; Hardwick, 1980; Schneider [aka L. Grunig], 1985a; Turk, 1985) have found a stronger relationship with the models, although that relationship still is relatively weak.

Although we think that organizations should practice two-way and symmetrical communication when their environments are complex and turbulent, many—if not most—organizations with such environments do not practice public relations in the way our theory predicted. We have concluded, therefore, that the theoretical relationship between the models of public relations and an organization's environment and structure is more normative than positive.

To develop a positive theory, we have turned to the power-control approach of explaining the behavior of organizations, which has become the dominant theory in organizational sociology (see chapter 18 on power). According to the power-control theory, organizations do what they do because a coalition of the most powerful people in that organization—the *dominant coalition*—chooses to do so. Following this perspective, we have tried to explain why the dominant coalition chooses to practice public relations as it does. Three concepts seem to be important: the culture of the organization, the potential of the public relations department, and the *schema* for public relations in the organization (variables included in the model of the process presented in chapter 1).

Organizational Culture

Organizational culture has a strong influence both on who holds power and on how the organization practices public relations. The relationship between culture and power seems to be circular: People in power develop the culture of an organization and organizational culture influences who gains power.

In a study of 10 Blue Cross-Blue Shield organizations, Buffington (1988) conceptualized organizational culture according to a typology developed by Ernest (1985). Ernest defined four cultures by the interaction of two dimensions: authoritarian versus democratic and reactive versus proactive. *Systematized* cultures are authoritarian and reactive. *Entrepreneurial* cultures are authoritarian and proactive. *Interactive* cultures are democratic and reactive. *Integrated* cultures are democratic and proactive.

Nine of the 10 Blue Cross-Blue Shield organizations studied either had integrated or entrepreneurial cultures. Six of the nine had entrepreneurial (authoritarian/proactive) cultures. As one would expect, five of these six organizations had their highest scores on the press agentry model of public relations. In the three organizations with integrated cultures (democratic/ proactive), the two-way symmetrical model was used in combination with the two-way asymmetrical and press agentry models.

In chapter 20, Sriramesh, J. Grunig, and Buffington reduce this and other typologies of organizational culture to a continuum between authoritarian and participative cultures. Authoritarian cultures generally use a closed-system approach to management and participative cultures an open-system approach. Evidence of the importance of these cultures came from R. Pollack's (1986) study of scientific organizations. R. Pollack developed several questionnaire items to measure Donohue, Tichenor, and Olien's (1973) concepts of "knowledge of" and "knowledge about" science — concepts that can be associated with closed- and open-system styles of management.

Knowledge of science comes from within the science system and reinforces that system. Knowledge about science comes from outside the system and is more critical of it. Authoritarian cultures should be more likely to value knowledge of the organization and participative cultures knowledge about the organization. R. Pollack (1986) found such correlations among these two types of knowledge and the four models of public relations. Valuing knowledge of science correlated with press agentry (.31) and public information (.28). Knowledge about science correlated with the two-way symmetrical model (.20) and the two-way asymmetrical model (.13), but the latter correlation was not statistically significant.

Differences in culture manifest themselves in the ways in which the dominant coalition in an organization exercises power. Although an open-system style of management should work best for most organizations, normatively, most do not use that system because the dominant coalition believes that it can maintain its power more easily through a closed-system approach (Robbins, 1990) — an approach that includes asymmetrical communication. Concurrently, the dominant coalition typically believes that an open, symmetrical system threatens its power.

Potential of the Public Relations Department

According to our definition, public relations departments have more potential if they are headed by a manager rather than a technician, if practitioners in the department—especially the senior person—have training and knowledge of the two-way symmetrical model, and if men and women have equal opportunity in the department. The research reported in J. Grunig and L. Grunig (1989) supports the proposition that the greater the potential of the public relations department, the more likely it will be that the senior person in the department will be in the dominant coalition and the more likely that the organization will practice the two-way symmetrical model.

Earlier in this chapter, we reported strong correlations between the managerial role and the two-way models. In addition, several studies have found positive correlations between the extent to which the top public relations person has formal education in public relations and the extent to which the organization practices the two-way models, especially the two-way symmetrical model, and negative correlations with the other models (Fabiszak, 1985; Nanni, 1980; E. Pollack, 1984; Wetherell, 1989). J. Grunig (1976), Nanni (1980), Buffington (1988), and Wetherell (1989) also found relationships between professionalism and the two-way models of public relations—especially the symmetrical model. Indices of professionalism include, for example, membership and participation in professional societies and readership of professional publications.

In addition, Wetherell (1989) developed indices of the extent to which respondents had specific knowledge needed to practice each model. The indices produced the strongest correlations to date between knowledge and the four models of public relations. Those with knowledge needed for the two-way models were most likely to practice them. Those practicing the two-way models also had the requisite knowledge for the one-way models. Those practicing the one-way models, however, did not have the knowledge needed for the two-way models.

Schema for Public Relations

Several studies (Fabiszak, 1985; McMillan, 1984, 1987; Nanni, 1980; E. Pollack, 1984) have reported positive correlations between the two-way symmetrical model and the extent to which senior management supports and understands public relations or has formal training in public relations. These same variables correlate negatively with press agentry and public information and insignificantly with the two-way asymmetrical model. These results suggest that the way in which senior managers define and understand public relations produces what we call a schema for public relations in the organization.

Cognitive psychologists define a schema as a large, integrated block of knowledge that people develop to make sense of their world (see chapter 6 on effects of public relations programs for more information on schemas). Markus and Zajonc (1985, p. 145) captured the essence of the meaning of schema as we use it here when they defined a schema as a subjective "theory" about how the world operates.

People in general have many different — and usually confused — schemas for public relations, and members of dominant coalitions seldom provide exceptions to this generalization. The way in which members of the dominant coalition conceptualize public relations, in turn, essentially dictates how an organization practices it. Often the schema for public relations allows for the practice of only one of the models. Maymi (1987) found, for example, that managers in the three sports organizations she studied could not conceive of public relations as anything other than press agentry.[2] Nelson (1986) found that the dominant coalition of a telecommunication company defined public relations only as media relations and as a combination of the two-way asymmetrical and press agentry models. The bank she studied identified community publics as most strategic, however, and had a schema for public relations that included the two-way symmetrical model.

The confusion between public relations and marketing also imposes a limited schema on the public relations function in many organizations. Maymi (1987), for example, found that the sports organizations she studied, with a schema of public relations as press agentry, subsumed public relations under marketing. Fabiszak (1985) found that emphasis on marketing in hospitals correlated most strongly with the two-way asymmetrical model.

Research suggests that the schema for public relations can be enlarged in one of two ways. The first way already has been articulated: Organizations with senior public relations managers trained and knowledgeable in two-way symmetrical public relations often become members of the dominant coalition where they can deepen the organization's schema for public relations.[3] The second way is suggested by Nanni's (1980) and McMillan's

---

[2]Moreland (1989), however, provided evidence that the two-way symmetrical model is practiced by the Washington Bullets in the National Basketball Association.

[3]Bissland and Rentner (1988) also found, however, that practitioners who understand two-way symmetrical public relations can be demoralized by an organizational schema that does not include that model. They found that two thirds of a national sample of practitioners preferred the two-way symmetrical model but that two thirds also believed that management

(1984) finding of a relationship between senior managers having taken courses or having other training in public relations and the practice of the two-way models: Educate members of the dominant coalition in a model of public relations other than press agentry or public information.

Gender of the Practitioner

Several feminist scholars of public relations have pointed out the similarity between the presuppositions of the two-way symmetrical model—such as cooperation, negotiation, and compromise—and the characteristics of women (see chapter 15 on gender differences in public relations). Wetherell (1989) conducted an extensive review of research on gender in the psychological and management literature, which supported the likelihood of a link between femininity and the two-way symmetrical model. Data from a national sample of practitioners did not at first confirm that relationship. Instead, Wetherell found that people with feminine characteristics—which includes both men and women—were more likely to practice and to prefer to practice the press agentry and public information models.

Further analysis of the data revealed, however, that femininity correlated with the practice of and preference for the two-way symmetrical model when the effect of the managerial role was controlled. The managerial role correlated with the practice of both two-way models and with masculinity. Although feminine characteristics enhance the ability of a practitioner to practice the two-way symmetrical model, women—and perhaps men with feminine characteristics—often do not get into the managerial role where they can practice that model. Thus, Wetherell's (1989) study suggests that it is crucial for women to develop strategies for overcoming the discrimination and socialization that keeps them out of the managerial role if organizations are to use their feminine characteristics to enhance the excellence of their public relations programs.

When Does the Dominant Coalition Choose Excellent Public Relations?

The research reported here and in J. Grunig and L. Grunig (1989) shows, then, that the dominant coalition of an organization influences public relations first when it identifies strategic publics in the environment as the target for public relations—publics such as employees, the financial community, activist groups, or consumers. The dominant coalition then turns

---

preferred one of the other models. A discrepancy between the model preferred by the practitioner and by management correlated positively with job dissatisfaction.

the problem over to the public relations department and dictates which model would be an appropriate strategy for communicating with the strategic public.

Which model the dominant coalition chooses depends on whether the dominant coalition feels threatened by that model and whether it fits with organizational culture, the schema for public relations in the organization, and whether the public relations department has the potential to carry out the preferred model. Potential is enhanced by having communication managers, people with knowledge of symmetrical public relations, and people with feminine characteristics in the department. Public relations directors who have knowledge or training in either the two-way symmetrical or asymmetrical model and in the managerial role more often will be members of the dominant coalition. In the dominant coalition, public relations directors can influence organizational culture, the strategic public chosen, and the model of public relations to be used for each public.

Previously, we described the two-way symmetrical model as characteristic of excellent public relations. An organization with a turbulent, complex environment and an organic structure should find the symmetrical model to be a rational choice for its public relations programs. Rationality alone, however, is not a sufficient explanation for the practice of public relations. To practice symmetrical public relations, the organization also must have a public relations director who is knowledgeable in that model of public relations and who is a member of the dominant coalition in an organization with an open, participative culture.

WHAT ORGANIZATIONS PRACTICE THE FOUR MODELS?

When J. Grunig and Hunt (1984, p. 22) formulated the four models of public relations they speculated about the extent to which organizations practice each of the models and about the kinds of organizations most likely to practice them. They estimated that 50% of organizations practice public information, 20% two-way asymmetrical public relations, and 15% each press agentry and two-way symmetrical public relations.

J. Grunig and Hunt (1984) also said they believed that press agentry most often is practiced in sports, theater, and product promotion. They thought that public information would be most common in government organizations but that it also would be practiced by nonprofit organizations, associations, and many businesses. They thought that competitive businesses and public relations firms would practice the two-way asymmetrical model and that regulated businesses and public relations firms would practice the two-way symmetrical model.

Since J. Grunig and Hunt (1984) made their initial speculations, 13
studies have been conducted that have produced mean scores on the indices
of the four models for different kinds of organizations. We have consolidated these data in Table 11.1. Several patterns can be identified in that
table, most of which show that J. Grunig and Hunt sometimes were
accurate in their predictions but frequently totally inaccurate. They were

TABLE 11.1

Mean Scores on Indices of Four Models of Public Relations in Different
Types of Organizations from 13 Studies

	N	Press Agentry	Public Information	Two-Way Asymmetrical	Two-Way Symmetrical
General Samples of Practitioners					
J. Grunig (1984)[a]	52	3.23	2.77	3.16	2.90
Schneider [aka L. Grunig] (1985a)[a]	75	3.12	2.92	2.95	2.81
Ossareh (1987)[a]	421	3.18	2.81	3.11	2.95
Wetherell (1989)[b]	378				
Actually Practiced		9.76	9.18	7.65	7.89
Prefer to Practice		8.65	8.16	11.82	11.70
Knowledge to Practice		11.35	13.32	8.39	9.07
Sports Organizations					
Maymi (1987)[b]	3	18.65	13.61	5.85	5.23
Hospitals					
Fabiszak (1985)[a]	180	3.30	3.05	3.04	3.06
Blue Cross/Blue Shield Plans					
Buffington (1988)[a]	10	3.39	2.88	3.23	3.21
Associations					
McMillan (1984)[a]	116	3.21	2.89	2.90	2.88
Federal Government Agencies					
E. Pollack (1984)[a]	310	2.95	3.01	2.65	2.73
State Government Agencies					
Turk (1985)[a]	12	2.80	3.13	2.82	2.92
Scientific Organizations					
R. Pollack (1986)[a]					
Total	178	2.90	3.22	2.89	3.02
Government	34	2.98	3.50	2.77	3.04
Nonprofit	62	2.91	3.28	2.76	3.04
Corporations	77	2.87	3.06	3.03	2.99
Reporter Ratings of Goverment Science Agencies					
Habbersett (1983)[a]	249	3.69	4.00	3.40	2.66
Nelson (1986) Case Studies[a]					
Bank	1	3.26	2.87	3.13	3.76
Telecommunications Co.	1	3.85	2.85	2.85	3.13

[a]Based on a Likert-type 5-point scale.
[b]Based on an open-end fractionation scale with a square-root transformation. A score of 10
represents an average model for an average organization.

quite accurate, for example, in predicting that press agentry would be most common in sports public relations, as supported by Maymi's (1987) case studies of three sports organizations.

J. Grunig and Hunt (1984) were quite inaccurate, however, when they predicted that public information would be the most common model practiced. Studies based on samples of respondents from all types of organizations (J. Grunig, 1984; Ossareh, 1987; Schneider [aka L. Grunig], 1985a; Wetherell, 1989) consistently show press agentry to be the most common form of public relations. The means for the other three models tend to be similar, although public information generally is the lowest of the three. In studies of specific types of organizations, this pattern also was true in associations (McMillan, 1984, 1987), hospitals (Fabiszak, 1985), and Blue Cross and Blue Shield medical plans (Buffington, 1988).

The pattern differed substantially in government agencies, however, where J. Grunig and Hunt's (1984) predictions were quite accurate. In government, public information consistently was the most common model, although press agentry was not far behind (Habbersett, 1983; E. Pollack, 1984; R. Pollack, 1986; Turk, 1985). The public information model especially was strong in scientific organizations (Habbersett, 1983; R. Pollack, 1986).

Although the two-way asymmetrical and two-way symmetrical models did not show up as the dominant form of public relations in any of the studies, the mean scores generally fell at about the middle of the scales used to measure them. This indicates that many organizations within the samples did indeed practice these models. When these models were practiced, the two-way symmetrical model was more common than the asymmetrical in governmental organizations. The two-way asymmetrical was most common in corporations (see especially R. Pollack, 1986).

When Turk (1985) classified 12 agencies in the Louisiana state government by the predominant model practiced, she found that 5 practiced the two-way symmetrical model, 4 the public information model, 2 the two-way asymmetrical model, and 1 the press agentry model. In short, individual government agencies did practice the symmetrical model even though the public information model had the highest mean score across all of the government agencies.

Van Dyke (1989) found a similar pattern for 45 U.S. Navy public affairs officers (PAOs). He used a single item to measure each model of public relations and asked the PAOs to select the item that best described Navy public affairs offices. Forty-nine percent selected the two-way symmetrical model, 29% the public information model, 16% the two-way asymmetrical model, and 7% the press agentry model. Van Dyke also looked at data about the way Navy PAOs performed, however, and concluded that their work corresponded more to the public information model than the two-way symmetrical model, "disseminating truthful information . . . but lacking efforts to evaluate communication effect or efficiency" (p. 52).

Wetherell's (1989) study, however, may have produced the most accurate estimates of the practice of the four models—using methods now being used in the IABC excellence study. She used a fractionation scale to measure the models, an open-end scale that allowed organizations to provide any number from zero to as high as the respondents wanted to go to estimate how well items described their public relations. With the fractionation scale, respondents are told that 100 is the average score for a typical item for a typical organization. Researchers then take the square root of the response to reduce the skew of the data. Thus, Table 11.1 provides respondents' estimates of the extent to which their organizations practice the models in comparison to an average of 10. The mean for press agentry is right at this average, suggesting that it is the typical model in practice. Public information is just below, two-way symmetrical and two-way asymmetrical score at 7.89 and 7.65, respectively—high enough to show they are practiced but below what respondents consider to be average for all organizations.

Wetherell (1989) also developed an index to measure the extent to which practitioners said they would like to practice each of the four models and to measure the extent to which they possessed the knowledge needed to practice each model. These results, too, reveal what seem to be meaningful generalizations about typical public relations practitioners. When respondents reported their preferred model, the two-way symmetrical and asymmetrical models jumped into a virtual tie for first place with scores just below 12 whereas press agentry and public information dropped to 8.65 and 8.16 respectively. Bissland and Rentner (1988) corroborated this finding, when they found that two thirds of the practitioners in their sample preferred the symmetrical model. In Wetherell's study, however, practitioners reported that they had the most knowledge about how to practice the public information (13.32) and press agentry (11.35) models—reflecting, no doubt, their journalistic backgrounds. Practitioners reported that they possess less of the knowledge needed to practice the two-way models.

Gaudino, Fritch, and Haynes (1989) tested J. Grunig and Hunt's (1984) contention that regulated businesses would be most likely to practice the two-way symmetrical model in a study of 27 utilities. They concluded that the utilities did indeed practice public relations in a way similar to the two-way symmetrical model. However, even though the utilities perceived mutual understanding with publics as their goal and had set up mechanisms for dialogue, they generally had asymmetrical results in mind. They believed that if publics were "educated," they would agree with the organization. "If you knew what I knew, you'd make the same decision" was the assumption underlying what on the surface was symmetrical public relations.

Although most of these studies have looked for patterns in the types of organizations that practice the models, two studies suggest that individual public relations programs within an overall public relations function may be a more meaningful place to look for differences in the models. Earlier, we reported that Cupp (1985) had found that chemical companies practiced a different model during a crisis than in precrisis public relations programs. Nelson (1986) conducted two case studies, one of a bank and another of a telecommunication company. The bank had identified community publics as most strategic and used the two-way symmetrical model to communicate with them (see Table 11.1). The telecommunication company had identified consumers as most strategic and used two-way asymmetrical public relations and press agentry for its marketing communication program.

In conclusion, research supports the idea that models of public relations vary among types of organizations and that they vary among programs within organizations. The variation among organizations probably occurs for historical reasons. For example, public information is most common in government because of historical restrictions placed on its practice there. The variation by programs probably is strategic: For some programs (such as communication with activists, during a crisis, or with government) symmetrical communication may be the only choice.

The research reported here also is sobering for the pursuit of excellence in public relations. Organizations practice the least excellent models, press agentry and public information, more than the excellent model, two-way symmetrical public relations. It also is encouraging: Many organizations do practice the excellent model, and most practitioners would like to practice it if they had the knowledge necessary to do so and conditions in their organizations were favorable for its practice.

IS THE TWO-WAY SYMMETRICAL MODEL THE EXCELLENT APPROACH TO PUBLIC RELATIONS?

Throughout this chapter, we have argued that the two-way symmetrical model will be a characteristic of excellent public relations programs — even though there are situations and environments for which organizations can make do with the other models of public relations. Excellent public relations does not exist in a vacuum, however. Throughout this book, we have maintained that the characteristics we have identified of excellent departments make them excellent because these characteristics make their organizations more effective.

Research to date provides evidence that the two-way symmetrical model makes organizations more effective. Two types of research have been done:

on the ethics of public relations and on the effectiveness of the models in achieving public relations objectives. Essentially, this research shows that the two-way symmetrical model is the most ethical approach to public relations and that ethical public relations also is the model most effective in meeting organizational goals.

Ethics of the Models

Discussions of the ethics of public relations frequently hinge on the relativism of an issue, an ideology, or a behavior. Is it ethical, for example, to promote guns, smoking, abortion, or alcohol? J. Grunig (1989) argued that the models other than the symmetrical one can be used to justify almost any cause. Based on the apparent assumption that all public relations is asymmetrical, Olasky (1987) and Gandy (1982) did critical research to support the argument that all public relations is unethical. Dozier (1989), likewise, argued that the symmetrical model of public relations is the only model "*inherently* consistent with the concept of social responsibility" (p. 5).

The two-way symmetrical model avoids the problem of ethical relativism because it defines ethics as a process of public relations rather than an outcome. Symmetrical public relations provides a forum for dialogue, discussion, and discourse on issues for which people with different values generally come to different conclusions. As long as the dialogue is structured according to ethical rules, the outcome should be ethical — although not usually one that fits the value system of any competing party perfectly.

Pearson (1989a, 1989b, 1989c) produced the best developed ethical rationale for the symmetrical model, based primarily on Habermas's (1984) concept of the ideal communication system. Pearson (1989a), for example, developed a set of rules for ethical, symmetrical public relations and provided practical advice for evaluating a public relations program by the extent to which those rules have been followed.

Effectiveness of the Models

Although research supports the idea that the two-way symmetrical model makes public relations more ethical, senior managers of organizations who are oriented to the bottom line also want to know whether it pays for their organizations to be ethical. Research to date suggests that it does. Several studies have shown the ineffectiveness of the press agentry, public information, and two-way asymmetrical models. Although L. Grunig (1986) found that none of the 31 organizations she studied had used the two-way symmetrical model to deal with activist groups, she also found that none of the other models reduced conflict with these groups. Lauzen (1986) found that franchising organizations that used the two-way symmetrical model in combination with the press agentry and two-way asymmetrical models reduced their conflict with franchise holders. Because the franchises combined the three models, however, we cannot conclude whether the symmetrical model alone would have been more effective.

In critical studies of the Nuclear Regulatory Commission and of fund-raising programs in higher education, Childers (1989) and Kelly (1989) documented the failure of asymmetrical models to contribute to organizational goals or to the public interest. Studies of media relations also have demonstrated the superiority of the symmetrical model or the failure of other models. Turk (1986) concluded that public information officers using that model in state agencies had little effect in influencing the "agency picture portrayed by the news media" (pp. 24–25). Habbersett (1983) found that science reporters strongly supported a set of symmetrical procedures for media relations. Theus (1988) measured the extent to which news reports on a sample of organizations were discrepant from the way the organizations thought the stories should have been reported. The more open and symmetrical an organization's communication system, she found, the less the discrepancy in news coverage.

Pavlik (1989) used game theory to compare the benefits of asymmetrical and symmetrical public relations to organizations. In situations in which organizations have greater power than their publics, he concluded, they can get the greatest payoff from asymmetrical public relations. He added, however, that publics now have greater power than they had in the past. In a situation of roughly equal power, game theory showed, organizations get the greatest payoff from symmetrical public relations.

With growing evidence in hand that the two-way symmetrical model is both more ethical and more effective than the other models, therefore, we turn finally to recent theoretical developments that are relevant to that model.

THEORETICAL DEVELOPMENT
OF THE SYMMETRICAL MODEL

To know all your neighbors on the global level does not mean that you will automatically love them all; it does not, in and of itself, introduce a reign of peace and brotherhood. But to be potentially in touch with everybody at least makes fighting more uncomfortable. It becomes easier to argue instead. (Isaac Asimov, *The Fourth Revolution*)

Mixed Motives in the Two-Way Symmetrical Model

Although we have systematically built a case for the superiority of the two-way symmetrical model in this chapter, many practitioners and scholars of public relations counterargue that the persuasion inherent in the asymmetrical models is not unethical or ineffective. Miller (1989), for example, described persuasion as a natural way in which people attempt to control their symbolic environment. Many, if not most, practitioners consider themselves to be advocates for or defenders of their organizations and cite the advocacy system in law as an analogy.

In contrast, Ehling (1984, 1985) developed a theory of public relations as conflict management (see also chapter 10) that states, in essence, that only symmetrical communication management can be considered to be public relations. Others add, however, that persuasion is not inherently asymmetrical. Cheney and Dionisopoulos (1989), for example, argued that organizations can encourage understanding through a process in which they and their publics simultaneously attempt to persuade each other: "Organizations, specifically their communications officers, should represent interests in such a way that both persuades and allows for others to persuade. Here we echo Henry Johnstone's, 1981, dictum to maximize persuasiveness and persuasibility for all parties to communication. That is, corporate communications should not *limit* possibilities for understanding, but rather *encourage* them" (p. 148).

J. Grunig (1989) also argued that symmetrical communication can include what Petty and Cacioppo (1981) called the central route to persuasion (persuasion based on reasoned argument): "The central route to persuasion usually is the first move that people make when using the symmetrical model to resolve conflict. However, conflicting persons or systems must be willing to switch their strategy from persuasion to negotiation or compromise when the central route does not bring about the direct change in attitude and behavior they want, as it seldom does" (p. 13, fn. 13).

Hellweg (1989) reviewed theories of organizational communication in light of the four models of public relations. She found evidence of the asymmetrical models in what has been called the "managerial bias" in organizational communication—a bias in support of the goals of management rather than employees. She added that "interpretive" theorists have begun to examine organizations from the perspective of employees. Even if organizational consultants use that approach, she went on, they still cannot avoid some bias in favor of management because management hires them and works with them to formulate solutions to communication problems.

Thus, Hellweg (1989) pointed out that even symmetrical techniques such as quality circles and team building may produce asymmetrical results through what Tompkins and Cheney (1985) called "concertive" or "unobtrusive" control.[4] This means that by allowing participation in decision making or by facilitating teamwork, organizations coopt employees to accept control in a much more subtle way than they do when they use coercive or overtly persuasive means.

Hellweg (1989) thus explained that what is symmetrical or asymmetrical depends on one's perspective. What an organization considers to be "active listening" or responding to the concerns of publics might be considered advocacy or unobtrusive control by a third party. Thus, she suggested that "The issue of whether two-way symmetrical organizations exist may be resolved by developing a continuum between the two-way asymmetric practice and a true two-way symmetric practice, such that organizations both internally and externally can be measured more by an infinite number of points than an 'either–or' picture might suggest" (p. 22).

Murphy (1991) examined symmetrical public relations from the perspective of game theory by contrasting "games of pure cooperation" with "mixed motive games." In pure cooperation, an organization would try to adapt to what the public wants and vice versa. The result usually is unsatisfactory to both sides, Murphy said, because by bending over backward to do what the other side wants neither side ends up with a satisfactory solution. Instead, organizations have mixed motives: They want both to forward their own interests but also to reach a solution acceptable to the other side.[5]

Conrad (1985) defined a mixed-motive approach to conflict management as one in which both parties "perceive the issue from both their own and the other parties' perspectives" (p. 242). Likewise, Wilson and Putnam (1990) concluded that bargaining involves mixed motives, motives that simultaneously are cooperative and competitive. As a result, they said, bargaining incorporates "compliance gaining tactics with problem-solving and conflict management activities" (p. 375). *Compliance-gaining tactics* is a term popular among researchers to describe attempts to persuade (Reardon, Sussman, & Flay, 1989).

Murphy (1991) thus suggested that the two-way symmetrical model might

---

[4]For a recent study of unobtrusive control in the U.S. Forest Service, see Bullis and Tompkins (1989).

[5]Murphy's (1991) description of pure cooperation is similar to what Buchholz (1989, pp. 507–510) described as an accommodative approach to issues management: adapting to what the public wants as best possible and getting on with business as usual. He contrasted the accommodative approach with reactive, proactive, and interactive approaches to issues. A reactive organization fights change; a proactive organization attempts to control the environment so that no change is necessary. An interactive organization tries to resolve an issue through negotiation. Murphy has equated symmetry with accommodation, although we have seen it more as interaction.

be described as the mixed-motive model because it incorporates both asymmetrical and symmetrical tactics. She then argued that a mixed-motive model does a better job of describing the behavior of public relations practitioners in the real world than does a purely symmetrical model.

Hellweg's (1989) suggestion of a continuum of asymmetrical and symmetrical practices also could explain the correlations we and others have found between the two-way symmetrical and asymmetrical models. Thus, we believe the theory of models can be improved if we conceptualize the four models in terms of two continua: one of *craft* and one of *professional* public relations (Fig. 11.1).

Practitioners of craft public relations seem to believe that their job consists solely of the application of communication techniques and as an end in itself. To them, the purpose of public relations simply is to get publicity or information into the media or other channels of communication. Practitioners of professional public relations, in contrast, rely on a body of knowledge as well as technique and see public relations as having a strategic purpose for an organization: to manage conflict and build relationships with strategic publics that limit the autonomy of the organization.

In practice, professional public relations involves both asymmetrical (compliance-gaining) tactics and symmetrical (problem-solving) tactics. However, we hypothesize that the most effective public relations, excellent public relations, will fall more toward the symmetrical end of the continuum than the asymmetrical end. Thus, Fig. 11.1 places excellent public relations at the same point as the two-way symmetrical model. But the figure also shows that that model contains asymmetrical components.

Elaborating a Symmetrical Theory of Public Relations

If this reconceptualized model of symmetrical public relations is a major characteristic of excellence in public relations, a logical next step for public

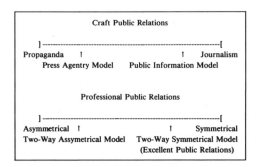

FIGURE 11.1. Four models of public relations placed on two continua.

relations theorists is to develop the model further as a normative theory to guide the practice of public relations. To begin that process, we review theories of dispute resolution, negotiation, mediation, and conflict management in this final section because of the similarities in the presuppositions of these theories and those of the symmetrical model. These theories have been developed in law, speech communication, psychology, and sociology. Few public relations theorists have examined these theories, although Gossen and Sharp (1987) wrote a practical article on how "dispute resolution" can be used in public relations.

We have identified the following seven conceptual themes in the literature that have relevance to a theory of public relations.

Interdependence and Relationships.   Chapters 3 and 6 developed the central proposition of this book—that public relations increases the effectiveness of organizations by managing the interdependence of the organization with publics that restrict its autonomy. Organizations manage interdependence by building long-term, stable relationships with those publics. These same themes of interdependence and relationships also can be found throughout the literature on conflict and negotiation (e.g., Conrad, 1985, p. 241; Fisher & Brown, 1988, p. 166; Gray, 1989, p. 11; Jandt, 1985, p. 135; Keltner, 1987, p. v; Wilson & Putnam, 1990, p. 375).

Conrad (1985), for example, stated that "grounds for conflict arise whenever people are involved in interdependent and interactive relationships" (p. 241). Keltner (1987) said that the goal of negotiation is a settlement that enhances future relationships between parties, whereas Jandt (1985) said "the relationship is more important than the conflict" (p. 135). Fisher and Brown (1988) followed up the best selling *Getting to Yes* (Fisher & Ury, 1981) with *Getting Together,* a book with the subtitle, *Building a Relationship that Gets to Yes.* Whereas *Getting to Yes* addressed "particular transactions," Fisher and Brown emphasized building "working relationships."

Conflict, Struggle, and Shared Mission.   Interdependence produces relationships and the need for public relations. Interdependence produces a need for public relations because it also produces conflict and struggle or, in some cases, a shared mission. Unless relationships are developed that help to manage conflict, conflict can "degenerate into power struggles or escalate into intense moral confrontations" (Conrad, 1985, p. 243).

Keltner (1987, p. 4) described this degenerative process as a "struggle spectrum," which proceeds through six stages: mild difference, disagreement, dispute, campaign, litigation, and fight or war. In the first three stages, communication takes the form of discussion, negotiation, arguing, and bargaining. In the campaign stage, communication moves to persuasion and pressure. It becomes advocacy and debate in the litigation stage. In the final stage, communication gives way to violent conflict. When these stages are applied to public relations, we can see that the two-way symmetrical model can work at all stages—especially the early ones—whereas organizations using the asymmetrical models usually wait until the campaign stage to practice public relations.[6]

In her studies of activist groups, L. Grunig (1986) (see chapter 19) found that conflict between organizations and activists did not always proceed from beginning to end of this spectrum. Many activist groups began by campaigning against an organization or seeking litigation or regulation but then moved to negotiation at the first sign that the organization was willing to seek a mutually acceptable solution.

Communication is not a magical solution to conflict, however, for as Jandt (1985) pointed out, "failure to communicate is a popular explanation for a variety of human maladies" and "conflict could not occur without communication" (p. 71). What is important, he added, is the effectiveness of the communication.

Just as communication can both cause and reduce conflict, so Fisher and Brown (1988) pointed out that a relationship can be a good one without being friendly: "The Bible tells us, 'Love thine enemy,' but does not suggest that we should approve of his *(sic)* conduct. We should care, show concern, be willing to listen, and be willing to work with him *(sic)* in a problem-solving relationship" (p. 153). Fisher and Brown also pointed out that good communication can take place without friendship: "Communicating effectively with those with whom we have fundamental disagreements is more difficult but often more important than communicating with those we like" (p. 85).

Gray (1989) developed the premise that competition no longer is effective in an interdependent world. Instead, she proposed a political and social order based on collaboration. Collaboration differs from cooperation and coordination, which would be on the far-right end of the asymmetrical–symmetrical continuum developed in the previous section. Collaboration is not an "idealistic panacea," according to Gray (1989, p. 24). Collaboration would fall near the point on the continuum of professional

---

[6]Public relations can be ludicrous when both sides of a dispute engage in asymmetrical campaigns, based generally on the press agentry or two-way asymmetrical models—but sometimes on the public information model. One side may "win," but such campaigns rarely resolve conflict. In an "expose" of asymmetrical public relations practices, the *Washington Post Magazine* (Carlson, 1990) described a large number of asymmetrical campaigns with the following teaser on the cover: "Teddy bears lobby Congress. The Senate's filled with caskets. Meryl Streep takes on the apple growers. A congresswoman sledgehammers Japan. And the DEA scores a bag of crack so President Bush can hold it up on TV. Wait a minute—is *everything* in Washington public relations?"

public relations where we placed the two-way symmetrical model: It is the "unfolding of a negotiated order" (p. 233).

Gray (1989) also introduced the concept of shared mission, which seems to increase the relevance of the symmetrical model to public relations. Many public relations programs, such as fund raising or health campaigns, are motivated more by the need for support from a public than from conflict. Gray included both in her theory when she pointed out that the motivation to collaborate may be "induced by conflict or by a shared vision concerning the problem" (p. 7).

In summary, then, the collaborative model could be another name for the two-way symmetrical model, just as Murphy (1991) suggested naming it the mixed-motive model.

Openness, Trust, and Understanding. Openness, trust, and understanding are concepts cited frequently in the literature on negotiation and conflict; clearly they are crucial symmetrical concepts. Hance, Chess, and Sandman (1988), for example, devoted a chapter of their manual on risk communication to "earning trust and credibility." Wilson and Putnam (1990, p. 386) pointed out that a minimal level of trust is needed in negotiation but that trust always is problematic when motives are mixed. Fisher and Brown (1988) added that trust is a "question of assessing risk, not morality" (p. 128). Gray (1989, p. 266) added that disputants must negotiate in good faith.

The need for openness can be found in many references to listening in the literature (e.g., Fisher & Ury, 1981, p. 35; Hance et al., 1988, p. 16; Keltner, 1987, p. 386). Fisher and Brown (1988) put it this way: "But the simplest and most powerful rule of thumb is to consult the relationship partner. Really consult. Ask advice before making a decision—and listen carefully" (p. 106).

Fisher and Brown (1988) also summarized the value of understanding as an objective for a relationship when they stated that "other things being equal, the better the mutual understanding, the better the working relationship" (p. 64).

Key Concepts: Negotiation, Collaboration, and Mediation. Although we generally have equated these concepts, theorists have distinguished among them in a way that shows two-way symmetrical public relations to be a process of collaboration. Conrad (1985) listed collaboration among five strategies for dealing with conflict: avoidance, accommodation, compromise, competition, and collaboration. He defined collaboration as: "All parties believing that they should actively and assertively seek a mutually acceptable solution and being willing to spend large amounts of time and energy to reach such an outcome" (p. 243).

Wilson and Putnam (1990) defined negotiation similarly, as a "process whereby two or more parties who hold or believe they hold incompatible goals engage in a give-and-take interaction to reach a mutually accepted solution" (p. 375). Gray (1989) tied collaboration to negotiation by defining it as "the unfolding of a negotiated order" (p. 233). As mentioned earlier, however, Gray's definition went beyond that of Wilson and Putnam when she pointed out that collaboration can be used to pursue common goals as well as to resolve conflicting ones. These definitions add up to a definition of collaboration as the process of negotiation.

Whereas collaboration involves mixed motives, mediation occurs when a neutral third party enters the process of negotiation (Keltner, 1987). Keltner (p. 8) and Jandt (1985, p. 70) agreed, however, that a third party who is perceived as a party to a conflict cannot function as a mediator. Keltner mentioned lawyers and counselors as such nonneutral third parties; we would include public relations practitioners. Thus, two-way symmetrical public relations cannot be described as mediation, although the literature does suggest that public relations people could bring in mediators when they cannot collaborate successfully with publics of an organization to reach a negotiated order.

Process and Strategies.   When we turn to the processes and strategies for collaboration that have been articulated in the literature, we arrive at normative theories that public relations practitioners can use to guide symmetrical programs.

These theories suggest first that organizations must set up structured systems, processes, and rules for two-way symmetrical public relations activities. In the words of Fisher and Brown (1988), "A relationship is more like a garden; it is constantly changing. It needs regular attention or it will go to seed" (p. 169). Keltner (1987) called the process "the management of struggle by rules" (p. 6). Several theorists set up principles from which processes and rules can be derived. Fisher and Ury (1981) had a theory of principled negotiation with four elements: Separate the people from the problem; focus on interests, not positions; generate a variety of possibilities before deciding what to do; and insist that the result be based on some objective standard.

Fisher and Brown (1988) developed a normative strategy they summarized as "Be unconditionally constructive": "This means that in a relationship with you, I should do those things only that are both good for the relationship and good for me—whether or not you reciprocate" (p. xiv). This principle has six elements: rationality (balancing emotions with reason); understanding (learn how they see things); communication (always consult before deciding—and listen); reliability (be wholly trustworthy, but not wholly trusting); persuasion, not coercion (negotiate side by side); and acceptance (deal seriously with those with whom we differ).

Gray (1989, p. 57) organized the collaborative process into the three phases of problem setting (defining the problem and identifying stakeholders and resources), direction setting (making rules, exploring options, and making decisions), and implementation (building support among constituencies and monitoring the agreement).

Jandt's (1985) theory of "win-win negotiating" is similar to Fisher and Ury's (1981) principles. He, too, suggested bargaining over interests rather than positions: "In positional bargaining, negotiations are seen as a contest from which one side will emerge victorious and the other will be defeated. In interest bargaining, each side strives to help the other achieve its goals" (p. 197). Jandt (pp. 266–267) also set forth a strategy for dealing with the "true scoundrel," the "hardball negotiator." He suggested complaining to a government agency, complaining to a professional society or other association, making the matter public through the media, and making a pest of yourself in other ways. These strategies generally are those that publics, especially activist groups, use against an organization that uses asymmetrical public relations and that can be characterized as a hardball negotiator.

Perhaps the most extensive set of normative rules for collaborative public relations has come from research on risk communication, especially at the Environmental Communication Research Program at Rutgers University. Chess and Hance (1989) described the general approach developed in this program as follows: "The traditional agency strategy of 'decide, announce, and defend' preempts the ability of communities and other interested constituencies to participate in decisionmaking. It also denies agency officials the opportunity to hear public concerns when they can be addressed more easily" (p. 14).

The U.S. Environmental Protection Agency (1988) set forth "Seven Cardinal Rules of Risk Communication" that are normative, two-way symmetrical principles: Accept and involve the public as a legitimate partner; plan carefully and evaluate your efforts; listen to the public's specific concerns; be honest, frank, and open; coordinate and collaborate with other credible sources; meet the needs of the media; and speak clearly and with compassion.

An extensive set of similar principles has been developed in several publications at the Rutgers center. For example, Hance et al. (1988) spelled out more than 100 principles for earning trust and credibility, deciding when to release information, and interacting with the community. On releasing information, for example, they specified symmetrical principles such as:

If it seems likely that the media or someone else may release the information before you are ready, release it yourself. (p. 24)

If it is likely that the media will "fill in" with information concerning an ongoing story while they are waiting for you to speak, speak first. (pp. 24–25)

> If you have decided that you can't communicate right away about the risk, talk to the public about the process you are going through to get more information. *Don't merely remain silent.* (p. 28)

Sandman (1986) stated the case for public participation when he said: "This sort of genuine public participation is the moral right of the citizenry. It is also likely to yield real improvements in the safety and quality of the facilities that are built. As a practical matter, moreover, public participation that is not mere window-dressing is probably a prerequisite to any community's decision to forgo its veto and accept a facility" (p. 456).

Some typical principles from Hance et al. (1988) for interacting with the community are:

> Recognize that input from the community can help the agency make a better decision. (p. 34)
>
> Find out from communities what type of involvement they would prefer. (p. 36)
>
> When appropriate, develop alternatives to public hearings. In particular, hold smaller, more informal meetings. (p. 37)

The literature on conflict, collaboration, and risk communication, therefore, is rich with practical advice that can be translated into advice for public relations practitioners using the two-way symmetrical model (e.g., Gossen & Sharp, 1987).

Limitations, Obstacles, and Effectiveness. Although Gray (1989) claimed that collaboration is not an idealistic panacea, she did suggest conditions under which it does not work well. Those that seem most relevant to public relations are:

> The conflict is rooted in basic ideological differences.
>
> Substantial power differentials exist or one or more groups of stakeholders cannot establish representation.
>
> The issues are too threatening because of historical antagonisms.
>
> Past interventions have been repeatedly ineffective. (pp. 255–256)

Of these limitations, unequal power emerges frequently in the literature. As Pavlik (1989) pointed out, organizations get the greatest payoff from symmetrical public relations when opposing publics have power equal to that of the organization. Some theorists, however, suggest strategies for empowering the weaker party (Jandt, 1985, pp. 155–178; Keltner, 1987, p.

33). Jandt (p. 171), in particular, said that one party can gain power if it controls something the other party wants. Because most active publics can affect the autonomy of an organization, most can empower themselves and reduce the ability of the organization to lapse into asymmetrical public relations.

Gray (1989, pp. 247–255) also identified several reasons why organizations refuse to collaborate, reasons much like those we have identified as reasons for not practicing the two-way symmetrical model: institutional disincentives (such as environmental groups that do not want to dilute their advocacy of a cause), historical and ideological barriers, disparities in power, societal dynamics (such as individualism in the United States), differing perceptions of risk, technical complexity, and political and institutional cultures.

Gray (1989, pp. 256–257) set up criteria for evaluating the success of collaboration—criteria that can be used to evaluate symmetrical public relations programs: Does the outcome satisfy the real issues in dispute? Do the parties feel they affected the outcome? Are the stakeholders willing and able to implement the decision? Does the agreement produce joint gains for the parties? Was communication between the parties increased and the working relationships improved? Has the agreement held up over time? Was the process efficient in terms of time and resources? Does the solution conform to available objective standards? Did the parties perceive the procedures to be fair? Did the procedures conform to accepted standards of procedural fairness?

Finally, Gray (1989, p. 259) reported the results of a study of the effectiveness of collaboration in environmental disputes—data that add to our review of the effectiveness of the two-way symmetrical model reported previously. In 78% of the disputes, the parties reached agreement; and in 70% of those agreements, the agreement was fully implemented. After examining these results for different kinds of disputes, Gray concluded:

> Clearly, the record of collaborations to date is a checkered one. Many experiences contain aspects of both success and failure. While the evidence is not 100 percent favorable, it is heartening. For example, even when parties do not reach agreement, they frequently applaud the process. Moreover, the numbers of disputes and problems for which collaboration is a possible alternative is growing. Finally, as we learn more about what works and what does not, the number of successes should increase. (p. 260)

Mediated Two-Way Symmetrical Communication.   Much of the literature reviewed in this section describes public relations activities that rely more on interpersonal communication than is common in public relations, where communication through the mass media or small-scale media such as brochures or newsletters prevails. Although two-way symmetrical public relations does use interpersonal communication more than the other models do, other literature suggests how mediated communication can be made symmetrical.

In a book on communication in developing countries, Hedebro (1982) described how media can encourage people to participate in society. Media can give people content that helps them to exert control over their environment, Hedebro said. Media also can use a form of presentation that encourages users to "mentally take part in the communication process" and to discover that they need to know more and "need to discuss the article with others." Media can "provide people with relevant and action-oriented knowledge, and they can also show ways to channel such interest" (p. 109).

In their manual on risk communication, similarly, Hance et al. (1988) recommended that organizations should "provide information that meets people's needs, . . . even if they don't ask for it" (p. 14). Lemert (1981) called the kind of information recommended by Hedebro (1982) and Hance et al. "mobilizing information," information that "allows action by persons willing to do so" (Lemert & Larkin, 1979, p. 504).

Dervin (1984) developed an approach she called "sense-making" that public relations practitioners can use to develop symmetrical information. According to Dervin, most organizations define information as what they think publics need to know. With the sense-making approach, however, practitioners do research to ask people what information they need to understand a situation or to make a decision—an approach that truly makes symmetrical communication two-way.

THE MAJOR PROPOSITION RESTATED

The two-way symmetrical model of communication, as we have seen, is a real as well as a normative model. It is a model that organizations can use but often do not use because an authoritarian dominant coalition sees the approach as a threat to its power. Two-way symmetrical public relations, however, epitomizes professional public relations and reflects the growing body of knowledge in the field. This ethical approach also contributes to organizational effectiveness more than other models of public relations.

Practitioners of the two-way symmetrical model are not completely altruistic; they also want to defend the interests of their employers—they have mixed motives. A substantial body of knowledge exists that provides practitioners with advice both on how to collaborate interpersonally with publics and on how to use media symmetrically to communicate with them.

The two-way symmetrical model, as refined in this chapter, therefore, is a major component of excellence in public relations and communication management.

REFERENCES

Bissland, J. H., & Rentner, T. L. (1988, October). *Goal conflict and its implications for public relations practitioners: A national survey*. Paper presented at the meeting of the Public Relations Society of America, Cincinnati.

Buchholz, R. A. (1989). *Business environment and public policy* (3rd ed.). Englewood Cliffs, NJ: Prentice-Hall.

Buffington, J. (1988). *CEO values and corporate culture: Developing a descriptive theory of public relations*. Unpublished master's thesis, University of Maryland, College Park.

Bullis, C. A., & Tompkins, P. K. (1989). The forest ranger revisited: A study of control practices and identification. *Communication Monographs, 56,* 287–306.

Carlson, P. (1990, February 11). The image makers. *Washington Post Magazine,* pp. 12–17, 30–35.

Carmines, E. G., & Zeller, R. A. (1979). *Reliability and validity assessment.* Newbury Park, CA: Sage.

Cheney, G., & Dionisopoulos, G. N. (1989). Public relations? No, relations with publics: A rhetorical-organizational approach to contemporary corporate communication. In C. H. Botan & V. Hazleton, Jr. (Eds.), *Public relations theory* (pp. 135–158). Hillsdale, NJ: Lawrence Erlbaum Associates.

Chess, C., & Hance, B. J. (1989). Opening doors: Making risk communication agency reality. *Environment, 31*(5), 11–15, 38–39.

Childers, L. (1989). Credibility of public relations at the NRC. In J. E. Grunig & L. A. Grunig (Eds.), *Public relations research annual* (Vol. 1, pp. 97–114). Hillsdale, NJ: Lawrence Erlbaum Associates.

Conrad, C. (1985). *Strategic organizational communication: Cultures, situations, and adaptation.* New York: Holt, Rinehart & Winston.

Cupp, R. L. (1985). *A study of public relations crisis management in West Virginia chemical companies.* Unpublished master's thesis, University of Maryland, College Park.

Cutlip, S. M., & Center, A. H. (1952). *Effective public relations.* Englewood Cliffs, NJ: Prentice-Hall.

Dervin, B. (1984). A theoretic perspective and research approach for generating research helpful to communication practice. *Public Relations Research & Education, 1*(1), 30–45.

Donohue, G. A., Tichenor, P. J., & Olien. C. (1973). Mass media functions, knowledge, and social control. *Journalism Quarterly, 50,* 652–659.

Dozier, D. M. (1989, May). *Importance of the concept of symmetry and its presence in public relations practice.* Paper presented at the meeting of the International Communication Association, San Francisco.

Ehling, W. P. (1984). Application of decision theory in the construction of a theory of public relations management, I. *Public Relations Research & Education, 1*(2), 25–38.

Ehling, W. P. (1985). Application of decision theory in the construction of a theory of public relations management, II. *Public Relations Research & Education,2*(1), 4–22.

Ernest, R. C. (1985). Corporate cultures and effective planning. *Personnel Administrator, 30*(March), 49–60.

Fabiszak, D. L. (1985). *Public relations in hospitals: Testing the Grunig theory of organizations, environments and models of public relations.* Unpublished master's thesis, University of Maryland, College Park.

Fink, E. L., & Monge, P. R. (1985). An exploration of confirmatory factor analysis. In B. Dervin & M. J. Voigt (Eds.), *Progress in communication sciences* (Vol. 6, pp. 167–198). Norwood, NJ: Ablex.

Fisher, R., & Brown, S. (1988). *Getting together: Building a relationship that gets to yes.* Boston: Houghton Mifflin.

Fisher, R., & Ury, W. (1981). *Getting to yes: Negotiating agreement without giving in.* New York: Penguin.

Gandy, O. H., Jr. (1982). *Beyond agenda setting: Information subsidies and public policy.* Norwood, NJ: Ablex.

Gaudino, J. L., Fritch, J., & Haynes, B. (1989). "If you knew what I knew, you'd make the same decision": A common misperception underlying public relations campaigns? In C. H. Botan & V. Hazleton, Jr. (Eds.), *Public relations theory* (pp. 299–308). Hillsdale, NJ: Lawrence Erlbaum Associates.

Goldman, E. F. (1948). *Two-way street: The emergence of the public relations counsel.* Boston: Bellman.

Gossen, R., & Sharp, K. (1987). How to manage the dispute resolution. *Public Relations Journal,*(December), 43, 35–36, 38.

Gray, B. (1989). *Collaborating: Finding common ground for multiparty problems.* San Francisco: Jossey-Bass.

Grunig, J. E. (1976). Organizations and public relations: Testing a communication theory. *Journalism Monographs, 46.*

Grunig, J. E. (1984). Organizations, environments, and models of public relations. *Public Relations Research & Education, 1*(1), 6–29.

Grunig, J. E. (1989). Symmetrical presuppositions as a framework for public relations theory. In C. H. Botan & V. Hazleton, Jr. (Eds.), *Public relations theory* (pp. 17–44). Hillsdale, NJ: Lawrence Erlbaum Associates.

Grunig, J. E., & Grunig, L. A. (1989). Toward a theory of the public relations behavior of organizations: Review of a program of research. In J. E. Grunig & L. A. Grunig (Eds.), *Public relations research annual* (Vol. 1, pp. 27–63). Hillsdale, NJ: Lawrence Erlbaum Associates.

Grunig, J. E., & Hunt T. (1984). *Managing public relations.* New York: Holt, Rinehart & Winston.

Grunig, L. A. (1986, August). *Activism and organizational response: Contemporary cases of collective behavior.* Paper presented at the meeting of the Association for Education in Journalism and Mass Communication, Norman, OK.

Grunig, L. A. (1989, August). *Toward a feminist transformation of public relations education and practice.* Paper presented at the meeting of the Association for Education in Journalism and Mass Communication, Washington, DC.

Habbersett, C. A. (1983). *An exploratory study of media relations: The science journalist and the public relations practitioner.* Unpublished master's thesis, University of Maryland, College Park.

Habermas, J. (1984). *The theory of communication action* (Vol. 1) (T. McCarthy, Trans.). Boston: Beacon.

Hage, J., & Hull, F. (1981). *A typology of environmental niches based on knowledge technology and scale.* Working Paper 1, Center for the Study of Innovation, Entrepreneurship, and Organization Strategy, University of Maryland, College Park.

Hance, B. J., Chess, C., & Sandman, P. M. (1988). *Improving dialogue with communities: A risk communication manual for government.* New Brunswick, NJ: Environmental Communication Research Program, Rutgers University.

Hardwick, C. J. (1980). *Public relations and organizational effectiveness: An open systems approach.* Unpublished master's thesis, University of Maryland, College Park.

Hedebro, G. (1982). *Communication and social change in developing nations: A critical view.* Ames: Iowa State University Press.

Hellweg, S. A. (1989, May). *The application of Grunig's symmetry-asymmetry public relations models to internal communication systems.* Paper presented at the meeting of the International Communication Association, San Francisco.

Hiebert, R. E. (1966). *Courtier to the crowd.* Ames: Iowa State University Press.

Jandt, F. E. (1985). *Win-win negotiating: Turning conflict in agreement.* New York: Wiley.

Judd, L. R. (1987). Role relationships using research and organization types. *Public Relations Review, 13*(2), 52–59.

Kelly, K. S. (1989). *Shifting the public relations paradigm: A theory of donor relations developed through a critical analysis of fund raising and its effect on organizational autonomy.* Unpublished doctoral dissertation, University of Maryland, College Park.

Keltner, J. W. (1987). *Mediation: Toward a civilized system of dispute resolution.* Annandale, VA: Speech Communication Association.

Lauzen, M. (1986). *Public relations and conflict within the franchise system.* Unpublished doctoral dissertation, University of Maryland, College Park.

Lemert, J. B. (1981). *Does mass communication change public opinion after all?* Chicago: Nelson-Hall.

Lemert, J. B., & Larkin, J. P. (1979). Some reasons why mobilizing information fails to be in letters to the editor. *Journalism Quarterly, 56,* 504–512.

Markus, M., & Zajonc, R. B. (1985). The cognitive perspective in social psychology. In G. Lindsey & E. Anderson (Eds.), *Handbook of social psychology* (Vol. 1, pp. 137–230). New York: Random House.

Martinson, D. L., & Ryan, M. (1989, August). *Practitioners' use of research and theory in one-way and two-way environments.* Paper presented at the meeting of the Association for Education in Journalism and Mass Communication, Washington, DC.

Massy, W. F., & Weitz, B. A. (1977). A normative theory of market segmentation. In F. M. Nicosia & Y. Wind (Eds.), *Behavioral models for market analysis: Foundations for marketing action* (pp. 121–144). Hinsdale, IL: Dryden.

Maymi, R. A. (1987). *Public relations in sports firms: Models, roles, dominant coalition, horizontal structure and relationship to marketing.* Unpublished master's thesis, University of Maryland, College Park.

McMillan, S. J. (1984). *Public relations in trade and professional associations: Location, model, structure, environment and values.* Unpublished master's thesis, University of Maryland, College Park.

McMillan, S. J. (1987). Public relations in trade and professional associations: Location, model, structure, environment and values. In M. L. McLaughlin (Ed.), *Communication yearbook 10* (pp. 831–645). Newbury Park, CA: Sage.

Miller, G. R. (1989). Persuasion and public relations: Two "Ps" in a pod. In C. H. Botan & V. Hazleton, Jr. (Eds.), *Public relations theory* (pp. 45–66). Hillsdale, NJ: Lawrence Erlbaum Associates.

Moreland, R. (1989). *Excellence in public relations and communication management: A case study of the Washington Bullets.* Paper presented at the Seminar in Public Relations Management, University of Maryland, College Park.

Murphy, P. (1991). The limits of symmetry: A game theory approach to symmetric and asymmetric public relations. In J. E. Grunig & L. A. Grunig (Eds.), *Public relations research annual* (Vol. 3) (pp. 115–132). Hillsdale, NJ: Lawrence Erlbaum Associates.

Nanni, E. C. (1980). *Case studies of organizational management and public relations practices.* Unpublished master's thesis, University of Maryland, College Park.

Nelson, D. G. (1986). *The effect of management values on the role and practice of public relations within the organization.* Unpublished master's thesis, University of Maryland, College Park.

Olasky, M. N. (1987). *Corporate public relations: A new historical perspective.* Hillsdale, NJ: Lawrence Erlbaum Associates.

Olasky, M. N. (1989). The aborted debate within public relations: An approach through Kuhn's paradigm. In J. E. Grunig & L. A. Grunig (Eds.), *Public relations research annual* (Vol. 1, pp. 87–96). Hillsdale, NJ: Lawrence Erlbaum Associates.

Ossareh, J. C. (1987). *Technology as a public relations tool: Theoretical perspectives, practical applications, and actual use.* Unpublished master's thesis, University of Maryland, College Park.

Pavlik, J. V. (1989, May). *The concept of symmetry in the education of public relations practitioners.* Paper presented at the meeting of the International Communication Association, San Francisco.

Pearson, R. (1989a). Beyond ethical relativism in public relations: Coorientation, rules, and the idea of communication symmetry. In J. E. Grunig & L. A. Grunig (Eds.), *Public relations research annual* (Vol. 1, pp. 67–86). Hillsdale, NJ: Lawrence Erlbaum Associates.

Pearson, R. (1989b). Business ethics as communication ethics: Public relations practice and the idea of dialogue. In C. H. Botan & V. Hazleton, Jr. (Eds.), *Public relations theory* (pp. 111–134). Hillsdale, NJ: Lawrence Erlbaum Associates.

Pearson, R. (1989c). *A theory of public relations ethics.* Unpublished doctoral dissertation, Ohio University, Athens.

Petty, R. E. & Cacioppo, J. T. (1981). *Attitudes and persuasion: Classic and contemporary approaches.* Dubuque, IA: Brown.

Pollack, E. J. (1984). *An organizational analysis of four public relations models in the federal government.* Unpublished master's thesis, University of Maryland, College Park.

Pollack, R. A. (1986). *Testing the Grunig organizational theory in scientific organizations: Public relations and the values of the dominant coalition.* Unpublished master's thesis, University of Maryland, College Park.

Reagan, J., Anderson, R., Summer, J., & Hill, S. (1989, August). *Using Grunig's "indices for models of public relations" to differentiate job functions within organizations.* Paper presented at the meeting of the Association for Education in Journalism and Mass Communication, Washington, DC.

Reardon, K. K., Sussman, S., & Flay, B. (1989). Are we marketing the right message: Can kids "just say 'no' " to smoking? *Communication Monographs, 56,* 307–324.

Robbins, S. P. (1990). *Organization theory: The structure and design of organizations* (3rd. ed.). Englewood Cliffs, NJ: Prentice-Hall.

Sandman, P. M. (1986). Getting to maybe: Some communication aspects of siting hazardous waste facilities. *Seton Hall Legislative Journal, 9,* 437–465.

Schneider [aka Grunig], L. A. (1985a). *Organizational structure, environmental niches, and public relations: The Hage-Hull typology of organizations as predictor of communication behavior.* Unpublished doctoral dissertation, University of Maryland, College Park.

Schneider [aka Grunig], L. A. (1985b). The role of public relations in four organizational types. *Journalism Quarterly, 62,* 567–576, 594.

Sriramesh, K., & Grunig, J. E. (1988, November). *Toward a cross-cultural theory of public relations: Preliminary evidence from India.* Paper presented at the meeting of the Association for the Advancement of Policy, Research and Development in the Third World, Myrtle Beach, SC.

Stamm, K. R. (1981). Measurement decisions. In G. H. Stempel III & B. H. Westley (Eds.), *Research methods in mass communication* (pp. 87–104). Englewood Cliffs, NJ: Prentice-Hall.

Thayer, L. (1968). *Communication and communication systems.* Homewood, IL: Irwin.

Theus, K. T. (1988). *Discrepancy: Organizational response to media reporting.* Unpublished doctoral dissertation, University of Maryland, College Park.

Tompkins, P. K., & Cheney, G. E. (1985). Communication and unobtrusive control. In R. McPhee & P. Tompkins (Eds.), *Organizational communication: Traditional themes and new directions* (pp. 179–210). Newbury Park, CA: Sage.

Turk, J. V. (1985). Public relations in state government: A typology of management styles. *Journalism Quarterly, 62,* 304–315.

Turk, J. V. (1986). Information subsidies and media content: A study of public relations influence on the news. *Journalism Monographs, 100.*

U.S. Environmental Protection Agency (1988). *Seven cardinal rules of risk communication* [Brochure]. Washington, DC.

Van Dyke, M. A. (1989, June). *Military public affairs: Is it PR management or technology? A study of U.S. Navy public affairs officers.* Independent study paper, Syracuse University, Syracuse, NY.

Wetherell, B. J. (1989). *The effect of gender, masculinity, and femininity on the practice of and preference for the models of public relations.* Unpublished master's thesis, University of Maryland, College Park.

Wilson, S. R., & Putnam, L. L. (1990). Interaction goals in negotiation. In J. A. Anderson (Ed.), *Communication yearbook 13* (pp. 374–406). Newbury Park, CA: Sage.

Wimmer, R. D., & Dominick, J. R. (1983). *Mass media research.* Belmont, CA: Wadsworth.

12 The Organizational Roles of Communications and Public Relations Practitioners

David M. Dozier
San Diego State University

ABSTRACT

Broom and Smith (1978, 1979) introduced the concept of roles to public relations. Like the models described in the previous chapter, public relations roles have become the subject of extensive research by public relations scholars. Roles define the everyday activities of public relations practitioners. Most practitioners are communication technicians, and public relations departments and communication programs could not function without them. Unless a department also has a practitioner in the role of communication manager, however, it cannot contribute to the strategic management of the organization and cannot make the organization more effective. This chapter reviews the extent to which four communication roles—manager, technician, communication liaison, and media relations—actually describe the practice of public relations. It then reviews the causes and effects of those roles—effects that show that the senior person in a public relations department must be a manager for it to be excellent.

Roles are abstractions of behavior patterns of individuals in organizations. Roles guide actions of individuals, such that actions mesh with repetitive activities of others to yield predictable outcomes (Katz & Kahn, 1978, p. 189). Through roles, organizations delineate expectations of individuals that make up the organization. *Practitioner roles* are key to understanding the function of public relations and organizational communication. Practitioner roles are at the nexus of a network of concepts affecting professional achievements of practitioners, structures and processes of the function in organizations, and organizational capacities to dominate or cooperate with their environments.

Katz and Kahn (1978) gave the concept of role "a central place in our theory of organizations" (p. 186). At the microlevel of analysis, an individual occupies an *office,* a space in the network of relationships that make up the system called the organization. Others in the organization have *role expectations* of the holders of offices; the aggregate of these role expectations define the role. Role expectations are communicated to the focal office holder through *role sending.* The focal office holder receives such communication from members of the *role set,* others within and external to the organization whose expectations are relevant to the focal person. The focal person's perception of these role-sending messages constitutes the *received role.* The received role is mediated by attributes of the focal person, as well as by relations between focal person and the role set. Roles and professional status are tightly intertwined. Professions expect their members to behave in ways consistent with professional role expectations, expectations that may differ from role expectations of the organizational role set. Public relations and organizational communication, some argue, lack strong professional role expectations. The function seems similar to other "semiprofessions," characterized by bureaucratic control patterns, a lack of personal autonomy, structured hierarchy, routinized tasks, and little supervisory responsibility. Simpson and Simpson (1969) classified nursing, teaching, and social work as semiprofessions. Cline et al. (1986) added public relations and organizational communication to the list of semiprofessions. As indicated later, semiprofessional status characterizes the communication technician role, one of two dominant practitioner roles.

Others argue that organizational communication and public relations is an emerging profession (Cutlip, Center, & Broom, 1985). The practice, they argue, is evolving, acquiring attributes of a profession: a set of professional values, membership in strong professional organizations, adherence to professional norms, an established body of knowledge or theory to guide practice, and technical skills learned through professional training (Grunig & Hunt, 1984, p. 66). Although none of these professional attributes is fully actualized, all are evolving as requirements of the function.

Because of its evolving character, the function is subject to considerable *role ambiguity* (Ahlwandt, 1984). The sent role from within the organization may not be consistent with the practitioner's professional role expectations. Practitioners may draw on emerging professional standards of professional organizations such as the International Association of Business Communicators (IABC) or the Public Relations Society of America (PRSA), abstracting *role norms,* activity sets practitioners consider "appropriate or proper" (Ferguson, 1979, p. 2) for their roles in organizations. As Katz and Kahn (1978) noted, the office holder (such as an organizational communicator) is "not merely the passive recipient of role-sending, but to a greater or lesser degree modifies the role and the expectations of the role-set *by the manner of role enactment*" (p. 208; italics added).

Role ambiguity often is analyzed as a negative factor, leading to role stress. Some role ambiguity, however, permits practitioners some autonomy. A moderate degree of role ambiguity is beneficial, allowing an acceptable range of role expectations (Hollander, 1964; Katz & Kahn, 1978).

This range of acceptable role expectations is key to the evolution of the function in organizations. The key issue is: Who will manage the public relations function? At the beginning of the 1980s, PRSA formed a blue ribbon task force to map future goals for the function. The Task Force on the Stature and Role of Public Relations viewed encroachment, the corporate practice of hiring individuals from outside public relations to manage the public relations function, as a grave threat (Lesly, 1981).

The practitioner literature is replete with exhortations that practitioners change their roles in organizations, to rise above technique and manage the public relations and organizational communication function (Close, 1980; Ehling, 1981; Marshall, 1980). As Broom and Dozier (1983) warned, "practitioners must change the practice or see public relations relegated to a low-level support function reporting to others . . ." (p. 5).

ROLES THEORY AND RESEARCH IN PUBLIC RELATIONS

Glen M. Broom fathered roles research in communication and public relations. His seminal works (Broom, 1982; Broom & Smith, 1978, 1979) serve as foundations for most subsequent studies of practitioner roles. His operationalization of practitioner roles, using a battery of 24 self-reported measures of role activities, is widely used to measure practitioner roles.

Broom conceptualized practitioners as consultants to senior management. Roles that practitioners play are viewed as services provided or processes influenced. Four theoretical roles, first conceptualized by Broom and Smith (1979), dominate practitioner roles studies.

The *expert prescriber* role was identified in the practitioner literature (Cutlip & Center, 1971; Newsom & Scott, 1976) as the informed practitioner. Such practitioners are regarded as experts on public relations, best informed about public relations issues and best qualified to answer public relations questions. Like the doctor–patient relationship, the expert prescribes and management obeys. Management's passive involvement in communication and public relations problems and solutions leads to dependent relationships. Steele (1969) called such dependency "seductive," because the relationship is gratifying to the consultant and reassuring to management. According to Argyris (1961, p. 126), such passivity and dependency leads management to regard the program as "belonging" to the consultant. This role logically can be linked to the two-way asymmetric and the publicity-press agentry models of the practice (Grunig & Hunt, 1984, p. 21).

Drawing on the consulting literature (Kurpius & Brubaker, 1976; Walton, 1969), Broom (Broom & Smith, 1979) conceptualized the *communication facilitator* role as that of a "go-between," facilitating communication. The role concerns process, the quality and quantity of information flow between management and publics. Broom found this role described in the professional literature when practitioners served as interpreters and communication links (Newsom & Scott, 1976, pp. 22–23). This microlevel role is reflected at the meso level in Grunig and Hunt's (1984, pp. 25–26) public information and two-way symmetric models of the practice.

Broom (Broom & Smith, 1979) again drew on literature (Baker & Schaffer, 1969; Schein, 1969) to conceptualize the *problem-solving process facilitator* as practitioners helping management systematically think through organizational communication and relations problems to solutions. Problem-solving process facilitators stand in contrast to expert prescribers. Whereas the expert prescriber role leads to passive management involvement, the problem-solving process facilitator works carefully with management to solve problems in a step-by-step manner. Painstaking efforts to involve all members of the dominant coalition in solving communication and public relations problems is time consuming. In the long run, however, such management-involving solutions work better. Solutions prescribed by experts leave management "unenthusiastic about the results, divided among themselves on key decisions, and unable to develop commitment" (Baker & Schaffer, 1969, p. 68). The problem-solving process facilitator role is essential in organizations practicing the two-way symmetric model (Grunig & Hunt, 1984, pp. 25–26).

Broom (Broom & Smith, 1979) conceptualized the *communication technician* role as that of a technical services provider. The dominant coalition makes strategic decisions, specifying organizational actions and designating the communications directed at publics about such actions. The communication technician then is retained to provide those mandated communication services. Broom viewed practitioners playing this role as "journalists-in-residence," practitioners hired away from newspapers and broadcast media because of "their communication skills and mass media experience" (Broom & Smith, 1978, 1979). Practitioners playing this role are essential players in organizations where the press agentry/publicity and public information models are practiced (Grunig & Hunt, 1984, pp. 21–22). Broom saw the communication technician role as embedded in a "provision model," whereby all essential problem-solving decisions are made by management prior to involving the service provider.

Broom and Smith (1978, 1979) conducted an experiment in a public relations course, providing the four types of consulting services as treatments to students developing public relations plans for a case-study client. At semester's end, recipients of the different consulting services reported no differences in the degree of ownership of their plans or dependency on their consultant.

However, significant differences were found in the way client groups viewed the *adequacy* of their final case-study plans, the *efficacy* of the problem-solving process, and their view of the consultant's *expertise* or helpfulness. Generally, the problem-solving facilitator consultant averaged highest on all three satisfaction measures. Communication technicians averaged second; expert prescribers averaged third. The communication process facilitator averaged fourth.

Next, operational indicators of the four practitioner roles were conceptualized and tested extensively in pilot studies. Using a 7-point, never-to-always scale, Broom (1982) generated 24 statements describing practitioner role behavior. Activities ranged from "I make communication policy decisions" to "I produce brochures, pamphlets, and other publications." Six statements measured each of the four conceptual roles.

Broom (1982) surveyed members nationally of the Public Relations Society of America, finding that his behavioral indicators of role activities were highly reliable. Reliability coefficients (Cronbach alpha) were expert prescriber, .93; communication facilitator, .79; problem-solving process facilitator, .90; and communication technician, .84 (Broom, 1982).

However, Broom (1982) also discovered that three of his conceptual roles were highly intercorrelated (p. 20). Although conceptual distinctions can be drawn of expert prescription, problem-solving process facilitation, and communication facilitation, these activities commonly are performed interchangeably by the same practitioner, as part of a common underlying role. See Table 12.1.

Practitioners who play the communication facilitation role frequently also play the problem-solving process facilitation role and the expert prescription role frequently. These activities, although highly correlated with each other, are uncorrelated with the communication technician role. These intercorrelations permit reduction of the four-way typology to a more parsimonious two-way typology.

Ferguson (1979) conducted parallel roles research, but her approach differed from Broom's (1982) in two important respects. First, Ferguson proceeded inductively rather than deductively to develop measures of practitioner roles. Ferguson first constructed a "universe" of practitioner

TABLE 12.1
Correlation of Practitioner Roles

	Communication Facilitator	Problem-Solving Facilitator	Communication Technician
Expert Prescriber	.73	.84	.18
Communication Facilitator		.78	.24
Problem-Solving Facilitator			.12

Note. N = 458.

activities. The universe was drawn from the public relations literature, as well as from several surveys of practitioners. The surveys asked practitioners what tasks or functions they performed in their public relations work. After eliminating duplications, 45 separate items were included in the final questionnaire.

Second, Ferguson (1979) conceptualized roles not as actual organizational behavior but as role *norms* (p. 3). Ferguson asked "how appropriate or proper" each activity was for practitioner respondents. Conceptually, respondents described their received roles, not actual role behavior practiced within organizations.

Ferguson (1979) sampled PRSA members nationally, subjecting her role norm measures to factor analysis. Eight meaningful factors emerged. (Two others were discarded because there were too few items on the factors to permit interpretation.) Ferguson named her role norm factors problem-solver manager, journalist-technical communicator, researcher, staff manager, good-will ambassador, meeting organizer, personnel-industrial relations, and public community relations. Ferguson's empirically derived role norms and Broom's (Broom & Smith, 1978, 1979) theory-based roles differ in their methodological approaches, reflecting natural tension between deductive classical and inductive grounded theoretic research (Glaser & Strauss, 1967; Stephenson, 1967). Broom and Ferguson also differed in the constructs they sought to measure.

Using factor analysis to construct role typologies generates factor solutions somewhat dependent on the number of practitioner activities measured. Ferguson's (1979) 45 activities yielded 10 factors, 8 with a sufficient number of items to be meaningful. Broom's (1982) 24 items yielded four factors. If a larger item set were used (70 items, e.g.), more factors likely would emerge. When Dozier (1986, 1987) used an abbreviated eight-item subset of Broom's 24-item role measure set, only two factors emerged.

As Grunig and Hunt (1984, pp. 90–91) noted, such factor typologies proliferate, fragmenting rather than integrating our understanding of roles. Parsimony is needed.

Ferguson (1979) strived for parsimony when she drew linkages between her empirically generated role norms and Broom's (Broom & Smith, 1978, 1979) conceptually derived role behaviors. Dozier (1984c) factor analyzed Broom's PRSA role measures and found four factors. However, these factors differed from the conceptual roles Broom initially operationalized.

Dozier (1984c) found a *public relations manager* role that included attributes of problem-solving process facilitation, expert prescription, and communication facilitation as interchangeable conceptual components of the same empirical role. Managers make policy decisions and are held accountable for public relations program outcomes. They view themselves and are viewed by others in the organization as communications and public relations experts. They facilitate communication between management and publics and guide management through what practitioners describe as a "rational problem-solving process."

Dozier (1984c) also found a *public relations technician* role that closely matched Broom's (Broom & Smith, 1978, 1979) conceptualization of the service provider role he called the communication technician. Technicians do not participate in management decision making. Rather, technicians carry out the low-level mechanics of generating communication products that implement policy decisions made by others.

In addition to the two major roles just described, Dozier (1984c) found two minor roles. These roles included the *media relations specialist,* similar to technicians in salary and organizational status, except that they specialize in external media relations rather than internal communication production activities. The second minor role was that of *communication liaison,* similar to managers in salary and status, but excluded from management decision making. Liaisons specialize in linking communications between management and key publics.

Dozier's (1984c) factor analysis used only practitioners working inside organizations; consultants from public relations firms were excluded. Factor analysis of agency consultants yielded a six-factor solution. Dozier argued that external consultants play different roles than do practitioners inside organizations. In subsequent factor analyses, internal practitioners were studied exclusively because their roles were relatively enduring. External consultants likely shift roles for different clients.

To resolve seeming conflict between Broom's (Broom & Smith, 1978, 1979) conceptual typology and the factor-based role typology, Dozier (1983) conducted factor analysis on three separate data bases where Broom's 24 role indicators were responded to by public relations practitioners. Included in the analysis were Broom's 1979 national survey of PRSA members, a 1981 survey of PRSA and IABC members in San Diego, and a 1982 national survey of PRSA members.

The major roles of manager and technician emerged clearly in all three surveys. The minor roles did not. Positive correlations were found between the manager and liaison roles, as well as the technician and media relations roles in both the 1981 and 1982 surveys. Dozier (1983, p. 12) argued that liaisons were simply managers "thwarted by organizational constraints" from participation in management decision making. He further argued that the media relations specialist was another type of technician specializing in external media relations rather than internal communication activities.

Because major and minor roles intercorrelated and because minor roles failed to emerge consistently across studies, Dozier (1983, pp. 12–13) urged reduction of the typology to managers and technicians. The two roles are uncorrelated, indicating that they are empirically as well as conceptually distinct. The manager and technician roles emerge empirically time and again in studies of different practitioners. The manager-technican typology provides a parsimonious way to operationalize roles and test relations with antecedent and consequential constructs. The manager and technician factor analysis are provided in Tables 12.2 and 12.3.

Roles are not only useful as descriptions of what practitioners do in organizations, they are powerful theoretical and empirical links between various concepts in a model of the public relations function. Practitioner

TABLE 12.2
Factor Loadings for the Public Relations Manager Role from Three Studies of Public Relations Practitioners

Avg. Loading	1979 PRSA Survey	1981 San Diego Survey	1982 PRSA Survey	Item Description
.81	.80	.87	.77	I take responsibility for the success or failure of my organization's public relations program.
.79	.85	.78	.74	Because of my experience and training, others consider me the organization's expert in solving public relations problems.
.77	.79	.84	.69	I observe that others in the organization hold me accountable for the success or failure of public relations programs.
.70	.76	.67	.66	I make communication policy decisions.
.70	.79	.66	.66	In meetings with management, I point out the need to follow a systematic public relations planning process.
.69	.77	.66	.64	I operate as a catalyst in management's decision making.
.68	.73	.71	.61	I keep management informed of public reactions to organizational policies, procedures, and/or actions.

TABLE 12.3
Factor Loadings for the Public Relations Technician Role from Three Studies
of Public Relations Practitioners

Avg. Loading	1979 PRSA Survey	1981 San Diego Survey	1982 PRSA Survey	Item Description
.77	.80	.72	.79	I produce brochures, pamphlets, and other publications.
.77	.78	.73	.80	I handle the technical aspects of producing public relations materials.
.55	.58	.51	.57	I do photography and graphics for public relations materials.
.52	.55	.54	.47	I am the person who writes public relations materials presenting information on issues important to the organization.
.43	.53	.42	.35	I edit and/or rewrite for grammar and spelling the materials written by others in the organization.

roles are related to gender (see chapter 15), management decision making, practitioner salaries, program evaluation, environmental scanning, the models of public relations used by organizations, practitioner belief systems about the practice, and job satisfaction. Relations also have been found between practitioner roles and perceived threats in the organization's environment.

Before considering the linkage between roles and other concepts, a proposition can be formed from the empirical generalizations implicit in Tables 12.2 and 12.3:

Proposition 1: Variance in practitioner role activities can be parsimoniously accounted for through two basic organizational roles: managers and technicians.

This posits a stable, consistent underlying structure to the role behavior of practitioners.

ROLES, PROGRAM EVALUATION, AND ENVIRONMENTAL SCANNING

The use of research by public relations and organizational communication practitioners is an important element in the professionalization of the function. Social scientific research—as opposed to basic fact finding and information gathering at the library—is a relatively recent innovation among practitioners (Dozier, 1981). Yet such research is essential to the evolution of the practice (Dozier, 1984a). Robinson (1969) argued that practitioners in public relations and the allied fields of marketing and advertising will be required by management to demonstrate "increasing rigor in their day-to-day work" (p. ix). Robinson stated that practitioners will be expected:

> . . . to support their decisions with evidence while solving day-to-day problems. They will be asked increasingly such questions as "How do you know?" "What are the data to support your decision?" "How do you know that you have solved your problem?" "What will it cost to achieve such a goal?" . . . The old "flying by the seat of your pants" approach to solving public relations problems is over. While there will always be a need for the intuitively based decision under some circumstances, decisions based on hunch, guessing, experience and the rationale that "this is the way we have always done it" are a thing of the past.

Robinson argued that intuitive solutions are sometimes appropriate, but that decisions generally should be supported by reliable research data. He saw the practitioner as an "applied social scientist," drawing upon theory and research in psychology, sociology, and economics to make decisions, plan programs, and evaluate their impact.

Robinson (1969) viewed the demand for research as coming from outside public relations, from managers schooled in the management by objectives philosophy, seeking accountability from communications, public relations, and other staff functions.

Within communications and public relations, others were seeking to fight encroachment and elevate the status of the function by adopting an applied social scientific perspective. The professional literature (Close, 1980; Lewis, 1974; Marker, 1977; Marshall, 1980; McElreath, 1977; Pennington, 1980; Wright, 1979) includes many exhortations to the practitioner community to bring research into public relations and a management philosophy to the practice.

Despite these exhortations, practitioners were slow to adopt evaluation research into their daily practice. As Grunig (1983) lamented:

> Lately I have begun to feel more and more like the fundamentalist minister railing against sin; the difference being that I am *for* evaluation. Just as everyone is against sin, so most public relations people I talk to are for evaluation. People keep on sinning, however, and PR people continue not to do evaluation research. (p. 28)

Broom and Center (1983) provided a possible explanation for this reluctance. They discounted the frequent practitioner justifications for not doing research: lack of time, unsophisticated management, tight budgets. Broom and Center coldly concluded that:

> We suspect from personal experience and observation—and some of the research reported in public relations literature supports our suspicions—that most of the practitioners positioned by age or authority to be influential in these matters simply do not know how to provide the leadership to use research in planning, monitoring and evaluating programs. Not knowing and not having engaged in research that would have established some benchmarks from which to measure, it is simply easier to run out the career string as is— or at least until someone else raises the question. (p. 2)

In a related stream of research, Dozier (1981, 1984a, 1984b, 1984c, 1986, 1987) and Broom and Dozier (1985, 1986) studied the ways practitioners use research in public relations practices.

First, Dozier (1981) established a typology of evaluation research in public relations. There are three types or content areas where evaluation research is used: preparation evaluation, dissemination evaluation, and impact evaluation. After Robinson (1969), Dozier (1981) identified two methodological approaches to evaluation: individualistic (or seat-of-pants) and scientific evaluation. These two dimensions of evaluation generated the six-celled matrix displayed in Fig. 12.1.

Dozier (1981, 1984c) used the conceptual matrix in Fig. 12.1 to generate 12 behavioral indicators of evaluation styles of practitioners. In a study of professionally affiliated practitioners in San Diego (PRSA, IABC, and PR Club members), Dozier factor analyzed the 12 behavioral indicators of evaluation activities to generate an empirically based three-way typology of research evaluation styles. Practitioners following the *scientific impact* style incorporate social scientific indicators to plan programs and measure impact. Practitioners following the *seat-of-pants* style use subjective, informal techniques for evaluating preparation, implementation, and impact of public relations programs. Practitioners following the *scientific dissemination* style, sometimes called "clip file counting," use content analysis and detailed counts of placements to measure dissemination of messages.

Factor scales were constructed to measure practitioners' frequency of scientific impact, seat-of-pants, and scientific dissemination evaluation activities (Dozier, 1981, 1984c). These activities then were correlated with practitioner roles. Analysis indicated that practitioners playing the manager role used both scientific impact and seat-of-pants evaluation. Technician role playing, on the other hand, was unrelated to any evaluation style.

A panel of PRSA members, surveyed in 1979 and 1985, provided evaluation style information in the second wave of data collection (Broom

	Content of Evaluation		
I n d i v i d u a l i s t i c	**Preparation**	**Dissemination**	**Impact**
	Communication activities prepared via application of internalized professional standards of quality.	Dissemination of messages evaluated by reactions of mass media professionals.	Impact of PR activities evaluated via subjective, qualitative "sense" of publics' reactions
S c i e n t i f i c	Communication activities prepared via application of scientifically derived knowledge of publics.	Dissemination of messages evaluated by quantified measures of media usage of messages.	Impact of PR activities evaluated via objective, quantitative measure of publics' reactions.

FIGURE 12.1   Conceptual matrix for the content areas and methodological approaches in public relations evaluations.

& Dozier, 1985, 1986). An index of program evaluation activities (summing frequencies of scientific impact, seat-of-pants, and clip file activities) was positively correlated with increased manager role activities since 1979 (Broom & Dozier, 1985, p. 30).

Evaluation activities also correlated with practitioner success in increased participation in management decision making (Broom & Dozier, 1985, p. 30). Those practitioners who increased their participation in decision making from 1979 to 1985 were practitioners who also engaged in high levels of evaluation activities in 1985.

Although scientific impact evaluation is important for professional growth, such activities were the least common form of evaluations in one study (Dozier, 1984a, p. 16). Mean level of scientific impact activity was 2.47 on a 7-point, never-to-always scale among San Diego practitioners. Most frequent was seat-of-pants evaluation (4.38 on the same 7-point scale), whereas the average level of scientific dissemination evaluation was 3.98.

A year later, however, the same practitioner panel was surveyed again. The only evaluation activities to have increased significantly since 1981 were scientific impact activities. Seat-of-pants activities and scientific dissemination activities were virtually unchanged (Dozier, 1984a, p. 18).

Evaluation research is not the only application of research in public relations. As Broom (1986, p. 15) argued, the content areas of evaluation, identified as columns in Fig. 12.1, are all part of the feedback mechanisms in the open systems that are organizations. Borrowing from Hage (1974), Broom developed a feedback model for public relations functions in organizations. See Fig. 12.2. The model indicates that organizations receive inputs from their environments in the form of intelligence about publics and environmental forces. This is not a feedback loop but a source of environmental inputs. Organizations may react to such inputs or proactively seek out such inputs. When organizations are proactive, they use research to gather intelligence about publics and environmental forces (Broom, 1986).

Figure 12.2 displays feedback loops of performance control and program adjustment. These research activities are conceptually distinct from research directed at organizing inputs about publics and other environmental forces. Such research, often called environmental monitoring or *scanning,* serves to alert the organization to turbulence or change in the environment, changes that may affect the survival and growth of the organization. From an open-systems perspective, research activities related to feedback and evaluation are conceptually distinct from scanning, from system inputs.

Dozier (1986) argued that evaluation and scanning research differ in methodology as well:

> The problem with evaluation research is that such studies are among the most sophisticated research activities that a practitioner can undertake. In program evaluation, clearly-defined, quantified goals must be set in terms of the change or maintenance of knowledge, attitudes, and behavior of publics. A longitudinal design must be established to measure the impact variable before and after program implementation. Experimental or quasi-experimental designs, using control groups and comparison groups respectively, are required to isolate program effects from the confounding influences of various threats to internal validity. In short, as Reeves (1983, p. 17) argued, the "bad news is that evaluation is hard to do well." (pp. 9–10)

Scanning, on the other hand, is more open-ended, more amenable to qualitative research methods, more compatible with cross-sectional surveys and "one-shot case studies." Because the tools of scanning research are more accessible to practitioners, perhaps scanning research is a precursor to evaluation research.

Kraemer (1981) found scanning research correlated with corporate planning activities among PRSA members in corporations. In follow-up research, Dozier (1986) used focus-group studies, depth interviews with practitioners, and a review of the professional literature to isolate 40 behavioral indicators of environmental scanning activities. He then sur-

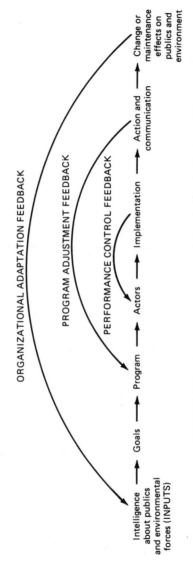

FIGURE 12.2 Broom's open-systems public relations feedback model.

veyed a national sample of IABC and PRSA members and subjected the scanning measures to factor analysis.

Consistent with Kraemer's (1981) findings, factor analysis yielded two major styles or approaches to scanning. The *scientific* style uses social scientific measures of publics to determine "what's going on out there," in the organization's environment. The *informal* style uses individualistic, subjective techniques, nonrepresentative samples of publics, and key contacts to determine what's going on out there.

Factor scales measuring scientific and informal scanning activities were correlated with manager and technician role scores. Both scientific and informal scanning were correlated with the manager role; neither style of scanning was correlated with the technician role. This closely parallels findings (Dozier, 1981, 1984c) that managers use both scientific and seat-of-pants evaluation styles, whereas technician role scores are unrelated with any style of evaluation.

Based on practitioner roles and their use of research, the following propositions are posited:

Proposition 2: Practitioners enacting the public relations manager role will engage in both scientific and informal program evaluation and environmental scanning with greater frequency than practitioners not enacting the manger's role.

Proposition 3: Enactment of the public relations technician role is not related to frequency of scientific and informal program evaluation and environmental scanning activities.

Proposition 4: Practitioner involvement in management decision making is a separate function of manager role enactment and of the practitioner's use of research (scanning and evaluation).

These propositions link practitioner roles to levels of program evaluation and environmental scanning.

ROLES, DECISION MAKING, AND ENVIRONMENTS

Practitioner roles are conceptually and empirically related to participation in management decision making. The involvement of boundary-spanning practitioners in management decision making is influenced, to some degree, by the instability and threatening nature of the organization's environment.

Participation in management decision making is extremely important for practitioners. Many practitioners agree with this view, because such participation enhances their status. Encroachment is blocked if practitioners participate in management decision making. Managers of the function are more likely to be drawn from the ranks of communication and public relations technicians, rather than from other areas such as marketing, personnel management, or operations.

Issues greater than the politics of the organization are involved, however. (See chapter 18 for detailed analysis of power and control in structuring the function.) Broom (1986) and Grunig and Grunig (1986) place participation in management decision making within an open-systems theory framework. If practitioners are to help organizations adapt to changes in the environment, they must participate in the management decision-making process, not simply implement decisions made by others.

However, as Broom (1986, p. 7) noted, some organizations act like closed systems. Their boundaries are relatively impermeable to inputs from the environment. The structure of the communication and public relations unit, and the role of practitioners within that unit, is fixed at some point in the organization's history, replicated every budgetary cycle because "that's the way we've always done it." The dominant coalition decides what the function is. That decision is duplicated each budgeting cycle, because the cost of the function is habitual and decisions about the function routine. As Broom pointed out, "the original motivations for the activities are lost in history and the system is relatively closed to new environmental inputs to the decision-making process" (p. 9).

A closed-systems approach to public relations is consistent with the technician role. Citing Simon (1960), Broom (1986) argued that public relations technicians implement "ritualized" programs based on "programmed decisions." Isolated from management decision making, "public relations is subsumed by another unit and cast in the role of technical support staff to implement programs dictated by others' values and perceptions of the environment" (pp. 16–17).

As decisions about organizational responses to the environment become more novel and nonprogrammed, practitioner roles change. Practitioners in such organizations shift activities from generating communications to making strategic decisions—or helping management to do so. Such managers make communication policy decisions; then are held accountable for program success or failure. They take management through a step-by-step planning and decision-making process.

Empirical links between practitioner roles and participation in management decision making are made in several studies. Broom's national survey of PRSA members in 1979 showed manager role scores were positively correlated with participation in management decision making, whereas public relations technicians scores were not (Johnson & Acharya, 1982). A decision-making participation index measured how frequently practitioners participated in meetings where decisions were made about new policies, major problems, new programs, and implementation, and where results were reviewed.

The expert prescription, communication facilitation, and problem-solving process facilitation components of the manager role are significantly and positively correlated with all five types of decision making. Technician scores, on the other hand, showed only modest correlation with participation in meetings where decisions were made about implementing communication programs. The technician role was negatively correlated with participation in meetings where new policies were decided. For other types of decision making, correlations were insignificant.

The same practitioners were surveyed again in 1985; change scores were used to examine relations between decision-making participation and practitioner roles. Practitioners who increased management role activities from 1979 to 1985 also increased participation in management decision making (Broom & Dozier, 1985, p. 30). Technician change scores were uncorrelated with decision-making participation change scores.

However, technician change scores were correlated with manager change scores. Cross-lag correlations suggested a causal, technician-to-manager chain. That is, practitioners who were active as technicians in 1979 were likely to be active as managers in 1985. Further, increased manager activities were correlated with increased participation in decision making.

Studies of environmental scanning (Dozier, 1986, 1987) provide evidence that participation in management decision making, using Broom's (1982) five-item measure, is correlated with the manager role. Participation is unrelated to the technician role.

Research has linked roles, decision making, and the nature of the organization's environment. Conceptually, Broom (1986) used open-systems theory to argue that public relations is part of an organization's *adaptive* subsystem. The function of public relations includes "gathering, assimilating, interpreting and disseminating intelligence about the environment" (Broom, 1986, p. 2). The structure and process of public relations, Broom postulated, is a function of the organization's sensitivity to its environment (p. 3).

Organizational theorists have conceptualized organizational environments in two-dimensional space, varying along a simple–complex dimension and a static–dynamic dimension (Duncan, 1972; Emery & Trist, 1965; Terreberry, 1968; Thompson, 1967). Acharya (1983) used discriminant analysis to empirically generate indices of the simple–complex and static–dynamic dimensions. Although one discriminant function closely replicated the static–dynamic dimension, the simple–complex dimension was reinterpreted as a threat–nonthreat dimension.

Technicians, Acharya (1983) found, are dominant in organizations with nonthreatening and static environments. Different conceptual components of the managerial role are dominant in organizations with dynamic and/or threatening environments. When the environment is both threatening and dynamic, the role enacted is the public relations manager role, emphasizing expert prescription. When the environment is not threatening but dynamic, the dominant role enacted is the manager role emphasizing communication facilitation. Finally, when the environment is threatening but static, the manager role is enacted, emphasizing problem-solving process facilitation.

Prior research suggests the following postulates, using the more parsimonious manager-technician typology of practitioner roles:

Proposition 5: Practitioners are more likely to enact the manager role in organizations where the environment is unstable, threatening, or both.

Proposition 6: Practitioners are more likely to enact the technician role in organizations where the environment is stable and nonthreatening.

As Broom (1986) argued, roles practitioners play in organizations (managers vs. technicians) are responsive to environmental stability and threats only to the degree that the system is relatively open. When is system is relatively closed, the role of practitioners and the structure of the public relations unit reflects historical preferences of the dominant coalition. The technical role of the practitioner and the technical support function of the public relations unit is frozen, replicated over time through ritualized, programmatic decisions concerning institutionalized commitments and budgets of the public relations unit (Broom, 1986, p. 8). The relative openness of an organization mediates the relation among practitioner role, the communication function, and the organization's environment.

This mediating influence confounded efforts at the University of Maryland to link models of public relations practiced by organizations to environmental characteristics. University of Maryland researchers found that the open or closed mind-set of the dominant coalition strongly mediates the model of public relations followed and the roles that practitioners play (Grunig & Grunig, 1986). The Grunigs' findings, coupled with studies of roles and practitioner research, suggest the following proposition:

Proposition 7: Manager role enactment and research activities are decreased and practitioner involvement in decision making is reduced in organizations where the dominant coalition holds a closed-systems ideology.

These concepts are considered next as they relate to practitioner roles and the models of public relations that an organization practices.

ROLES AND MODELS OF PUBLIC RELATIONS

Roles research operates at the micro (practitioner) level of analysis. The four models of public relations (Grunig & Hunt, 1984) seek to analyze the public relations function at the meso (organizational) level of analysis (Hage, 1980). Although roles research studies individual practitioners and their work activities, Grunig's models of public relations delineate ways the function is performed by the organization as a whole.

Studies at the University of Maryland show clear empirical linkages between practitioner roles and the four models of public relations. These linkages are consistent with theoretical expectations.

University of Maryland researchers studied public relations models in the federal government (Pollack, 1984), hospitals (Fabiszak, 1985), associations (McMillan, 1984), and scientific organizations (Pollack, 1986). Measures of practitioner roles and of the four models of the function were taken. Kendall's Tau correlations between roles and models are displayed in Table 12.4.

Practitioners in organizations practicing the press agentry and public information models of public relations will engage in few activities that define the public relations manager role. Practitioners in organizations practicing the two-way asymmetric and two-way symmetric models of public relations are more likely to play the public relations manager role. This is especially true of associations and scientific organizations.

These correlations are consistent with theory. Problem-solving process facilitation, expert prescription, or communication facilitation are of little value in organizations following a publicity/press agentry or public information model. These one-way models generate messages by organizations for distribution to publics. Publicity/press agentry model organizations spread favorable propaganda about the organization with only moderate regard for information accuracy. Public information model organizations disseminate information with traditional journalistic concerns for objectivity and accuracy. Such low-level staff functions do not require practitioners to enact the manager role.

Organizations that practice the press agentry and public information models need technicians. Communication staff are not involved in strategic planning and problem solving under these models. Once strategic decisions are made and action plans drawn, the technician is brought in to implement outward communication from the organization to target publics. The process is one way; the practitioner is a skilled communicator uninvolved with monitoring the environment. He or she simply provides a technical support service (outward communication) for decisions made and actions taken by others. Consistent with theory, the technician role is positively and significantly correlated with the press agentry and public information

TABLE 12.4
Correlations Between Practitioner Roles and Models of the Public Relations Function

	Press Agentry	Public Info.	Two-Way Asymmetric	Two-Way Symmetric
PR Managers				
Fed. Gov't.	−.17**	−.11*	−.03	+.07
Hospitals	−.25**	−.29**	+.10	+.27**
Associations	−.18*	−.27**	+.20**	+.26**
Science Orgs.	−.18*	−.32**	+.22*	+.14**
PR Technicians				
Fed. Gov't.	+.10*	+.14*	+.06	+.02
Hospitals	+.26**	+.36**	−.11	−.32**
Associations	+.16*	+.28**	−.09	−.06
Science Orgs.	+.13*	+.22**	−.02	−.10
Media Relations Specialists				
Fed. Gov't.	+.06	+.14	−.10	−.06
Hospitals	+.12	+.20**	−.09	−.18**
Associations	+.02	+.10	−.03	−.29**
Science Orgs.	+.10	−.21**	−.28**	−.14*
Communication Liaisons				
Fed. Gov't.	0.00	−.10	0.00	+.04
Hospitals	−.15*	−.32**	+.02	+.24**
Associations	−.02	−.11	−.07	.07
Science Orgs.	−.08	−.16*	+.14*	.15*

Note. Kendall's Tau was used in the study of federal agencies ($N = 310$), as role was measured as a dichotomous variable. In the studies of hospitals ($N = 180$) and associations ($N = 116$), practitioner roles were measured as percentage of time spent by the top practitioner in each role. In the study of scientific organizations ($N = 178$), roles wre measured as percentage of time spent in each role by the entire department. From "Application of Open Systems Theory to Public Relations: Review of a Program of Research" by J. E. Grunig and L. S. Grunig, May 1986, Paper presented at the meeting of the Public Relations Interest Group, International Communication Association, Chicago. Reprinted by permission.
*$p < .05$. **$p < .01$.

models in all four types of organizations. The technician role indicates weak, negative correlations with the two-way models.

The two-way models are concerned with scanning the organization's environment and evaluating implementation and impact of communication programs. The two models differ in goals: Asymmetric model organizations seek environmental domination whereas symmetric model organizations seek cooperation. These models require practitioners to make communication policy decisions and account for program success or failure. They help management solve public relations problems and they facilitate communication between management and publics. The two-way models require practitioners skilled in expert prescription, problem-solving process facilitation, and communication facilitation. Conceptually, the role (manager) and the functions (two-way asymmetric and symmetric models) go hand in hand. Research findings in Table 12.4 support this theory.

Patterns are consistent with theory for the minor roles of media relations specialist and communication facilitator, though the relationships are weaker and not sustained for each type of organization. The media relations specialist role (a technician specializing in external media) is played more frequently in organizations practicing the public information model (though not in scientific organizations). The media relations role is less frequently played in organizations practicing the two-way symmetric model of public relations. The communication liaison role (a high-level communication facilitator who does not make policy decisions) is less likely to be played in organizations practicing the public information model. The liaison role is more frequent in organizations practicing the two-way symmetric model of public relations.

The University of Maryland studies suggest the following three propositions. They are based on consistent empirical generalizations from different organizational settings:

Proposition 8: Manager role enactment is more frequent in organizations practicing the two-way symmetric and asymmetric models of public relations.

Proposition 9: Manager role enactment is less frequent in organizations practicing the press agentry or public information models of public relations.

Proposition 10: Technician role enactment is more frequent in organizations practicing the press agentry and public information models of public relations.

Although relations between practitioner roles and models of practice are generally consistent with theory, relations between public relations models and environmental conditions are not. Grunig and Grunig (1986) found weak and inconsistent relations between organizational environments and models of public relations practiced by organizations.

One explanation for these findings is that organizations have dominant coalitions with different strategic decision-making dynamics and different orientations toward environmental inputs. The process of strategic decision making can be organized by type (Walsh & Fahey, 1986). The process is affected by both underlying beliefs of powerful members of the dominant coalition and the relative concentration of power in such coalitions. Both beliefs and power affect the negotiated belief structures of dominant coalitions. *Belief structures* or schemes are implicit theories and assumptions about desired end states and how to reach those end states. Belief structures help decision makers filter and organize masses of information while simultaneously blinding them to relevant patterns of information external to belief structures.

When power is concentrated and those holding power are in complete agreement and completely certain about means and ends (beliefs are "computational"), the negotiated belief structure is *limited*. When power is dispersed but belief structures are computational, the negotiated belief structure is *contextual*. When power is concentrated but there is disagreement and uncertainty in the dominant coalition regarding belief structures (beliefs are "inspirational"), the negotiated belief structure is *contested*. When power is dispersed and members of the dominant coalition disagree about means and ends, the belief structure is *dialetical*.

Theory suggests that different negotiated belief structures imply certain models of public relations practices. Concentrated power within the dominant coalition suggests preference for environmental domination rather than negotiation. The domineering style of the powerful toward other members of the dominant coalition likely indicates a domineering orientation toward the environment. Uncertainty and disagreement over means and ends within the dominant coalition suggest preference for two-way rather than one-way approaches to the practice. The desire to acquire more information to resolve uncertainty and disagreements about belief structures logically would imply that practitioners would gather as well as disseminate information.

The Maryland studies provide indirect, partial support for these linkages (Grunig & Grunig, 1986). When the dominant coalition excludes public relations practitioners, is politically conservative, favors rigid system codes, and is relatively indifferent to the external environment, the press agentry and public information models dominate. This preference for press agentry and public information is responsive to the ideology of the dominant coalition, not to the environment. Consequently, the public relations technician role is likely to be the role expectation of the role set.

When the dominant coalition includes public relations practitioners, is politically liberal, favors flexible code systems, and is attentive to the organization's environment, the two-way models of public relations are likely to typify the function. Consequently, the public relations manager role is likely to be the role expectation of the role set. This ideology of the dominant coalition, which can be abstracted as how relatively open or closed the organization is structured, mediates the relation between the environment, the model of public relations practiced by the organization, and the role that practitioners play in that organization. These research findings are consistent with the propositions that follow, drawn from open-systems theory (Broom, 1986, p. 3):

> *Proposition 11:* The management role is favored in organizations where the dominant coalition is relatively open to the organization's environment.

> *Proposition 12:* The technician role is favored in organizations where the dominant coalition is relatively closed to the organization's environment.

> *Proposition 13:* The management role is favored where the negotiated belief structure of the dominant coalition is contested or dialetical.

> *Proposition 14:* The technician role is favored where the negotiated belief structure of the dominant coalition is limited or contextual.

ROLES, PRACTITIONER BELIEF SYSTEMS, AND JOB SATISFACTION

Practitioners have subjective belief systems about their work. Practitioner roles are posited to be affected by belief systems about the practice. Roles also are posited to affect the job satisfaction that practitioners derive from their work. Many practitioners are drawn to public relations work because they like to write; writing satisfies a creative need. Wright (1979) noted that practitioners resist measurement of their work because they are "artists rather than managers" (p. 17).

Dozier and Gottesman (1982) conducted a Q-methodological study of practitioner belief systems about public relations practices. Q-statements were obtained through depth interviews with practitioners and public relations educators, as well as through professional literature. Dozier and Gottesman were intrigued with hemispheric research (Springer & Deutsch, 1981) and its relation to the careers people select. Some statements were included in the Q-sort because they reflected either a left-brain (logical, sequential, analytic) dominance or a right-brain (creative, holistic, simultaneous) dominance in attitude statements about public relations. Other statements were included because they reflected the posited values of managers and technicians. A third set of statements reflected cultural attitudes toward public relations (Snow, 1959) grounded in either a literary or scientific cultural perspective. The purpose was to construct a universe of attitude statements about public relations that practitioners could use to construct models of their belief systems through the Q-sort process.

Q-sorts were completed by 28 San Diego practitioners who had participated in a large-sample survey (Dozier, 1981). Using role measures from the survey, subjects were purposively sampled by dominant role. Four factors emerged from the Q-factor analysis: The *upwardly mobile* practitioner, the *creative artistic* practitioner, the *committed proactive* practitioner, and the *literary scientific* practitioner (Dozier & Gottesman, 1982).

Upwardly mobile practitioners hold positive opinions about public relations and practitioners. They equate creativity with challenge but not with artistic spontaneity. They see themselves a sensitive supervisors who practice good public relations (more or less by the book) and who will climb the corporate ladder.

The creative artistic practitioners distrust management's ability to understand public relations, and distrust the price paid for climbing the organizational ladder. They want more say in decisions, but not at the expense of their spontaneity and emotional involvement in the public relations process. The creative artistic practitioner pursues the creative, spontaneous, and humanistic aspects of the practice. A scientific approach to public relations is rejected.

Committed proactive practitioners commit to organizations where they practice public relations. They take an ethical view of the practice. They see management as creative and want the practice to rise about technique. They see public relations as planned and proactive.

The literary scientific practitioners view public relations as an applied social science, but regret the passing of literature from the training of new practitioners. Rooted in the liberal arts, these practitioners see public relations becoming more scientific—and properly so.

Dozier and Gottesman (1982) correlated belief systems of practitioners with roles they played in organizations. Committed proactive practitioner beliefs correlated with manager and communication liaison role scores. Creative artistic practitioner beliefs were highly correlated with technician role scores.

In summary, some practitioners regard public relations as primarily a creative or artistic activity. Management does not understand public relations and such practitioners are suspicious of the creative and artistic cost of advancement. These practitioners self-select the technician role. Practitioners playing the manager role are more likely to be strongly committed to their organization and highly ethical in their view of public relations practices. They see public relations evolving into a management function and they like that trend. They lament the preoccupation of practitioners with technique.

The strong link between creative artistic beliefs about public relations and the technician role helps explain the somewhat unexpected finding that technicians exhibit high levels of job satisfaction. Sullivan found that 46% of the respondents in his national survey of PRSA members picked their actual role (manager, technician, media relations, communication liaison) as their ideal role. These practitioners expressed the highest levels of job satisfaction. Technicians were happy in their actual roles, even as they aspired to roles higher in the role hierarchy. Sullivan, Dozier, and Hellweg (1984, 1985) concluded that most practitioners reported high levels of job satisfaction without regard to their perceived dominant role.

In the panel study of PRSA members, surveyed in 1979 and 1985, Broom and Dozier (1985, pp. 26–27) found that managers exhibited higher levels of job satisfaction in 1979 than did technicians. This was true even after the influence of years of professional experience was controlled. (The 1979 survey indicated that job satisfaction was significantly correlated with professional experience, which was greater among managers.) However, by 1985, differences in job satisfaction between managers and technicians had largely disappeared. Managers were less satisfied, as a group, in 1985 than they were in 1979. Technicians, on the other hand, were more satisfied in 1985 than in 1979.

The findings become more intriguing when changes in practitioner roles are examined. Technicians in 1979 who remained technicians in 1985 posted the largest increase in job satisfaction scores. Despite the lower pay, the isolation from decision making, the lower status of the technician role in the role hierarchy, technicians who stayed technicians exhibited high levels of job satisfaction. This is perhaps because the technician role permits practitioners to do the creative, artistic activities that first attracted them to the practice.

Findings from these studies suggest the following proposition:

Proposition 15: Practitioners who hold creative-artistic beliefs about public relations practices will enact the technician role with greater frequency than practitioners not holding such beliefs.

CONCLUSION

Roles research plays an important part in our understanding of organizational communication and public relations as an emerging profession. The ambiguity that surrounds the public relations role is refected in the array of definitions offered to define the function (Cutlip et al., 1985; Grunig & Hunt, 1984).

Yet systems theory persuasively suggests that the function is essential to the survival and growth of organizations facing increasingly unstable and threatening environments. Definitions of public relations founded on systems theory call for the problem-solving process facilitation, the communication facilitation, and the expert prescription of a manager.

Unfortunately, organizations sometimes look outside the ranks of their own communication and public relations technicians to find managers for this important function. Encroachment is the inevitable by-product of a calling that fails to rise above technique. The career failure of top practitioners to assume the management role within organizations is also a failure to truly emerge as a profession from the communication skill cluster that operationally defines what practitioners do—and what the practice is.

REFERENCES

Acharya, L. (1983, August). *Practitioner representations of environmental uncertainty: An application of discriminant analysis.* Paper presented at the meeting of the Public Relations Division, Association for Education in Journalism and Mass Communication, Corvallis, OR.

Ahlwardt, E. (1984). *Coorientational states as predictors of organizational role ambiguity and conflict: An analysis of U.S. Navy commanding officer and public affairs officer dyads.* Unpublished master's thesis, San Diego State University, San Diego.

Argyris, C. (1961). Explorations in consulting-client relationships. *Human Organization, 20*(3), 126.

Baker, J. K., & Schaffer, R. H. (1969). Making staff consulting more effective. *Harvard Business Review, 47*(1), 68.

Broom, G. M. (1982). A comparison of sex roles in public relations. *Public Relations Review, 8*(3), 17–22.

Broom, G. M. (1986, May). *Public relations roles and systems theory: Functional and historicist causal models.* Paper presented at the meeting of the Public Relations Interest Group, International Communication Association, Chicago.

Broom, G. M., & Center, A. H. (1983). Evaluation research. *Public Relations Quarterly, 28*(3), 2–3.

Broom, G. M. & Dozier, D. M. (1983). An overview: Evaluation research in public relations. *Public Relations Quarterly, 28*(3), 5–8.

Broom, G. M., & Dozier, D. M. (1985, August). *Determinants and consequences of public relations roles.* Paper presented at the meeting of the Public Relations Division, Association for Education in Journalism and Mass Communication, Memphis.

Broom, G. M., & Dozier, D. M. (1986). Advancement for public relations role models. *Public Relations Review, 7*(1), 37–56.

Broom, G. M., & Smith, G. D. (1978, August). *Toward an understanding of public relations roles: An empirical test of five role models' impact on clients.* Paper presented at the meeting of the Public Relations Division, Association for Education in Journalism, Seattle.

Broom, G. M., & Smith, G. D. (1979). Testing the practitioner's impact on clients. *Public Relations Review, 5*(3), 47-59.

Cline, C. G., Toth, E. L., Turk, J. V., Walters, L. M., Johnson, N., & Smith, H. (1986). *The velvet ghetto: The impact of the increasing percentage of women in public relations and business communication.* San Francisco: IABC Research Foundation.

Close, H. W. (1980). Public relations as a management function. *Public Relations Journal, 36*(3), 11-14.

Cutlip, S. M., & Center, A. H. (1971). *Effective public relations* (4th ed.). Englewood Cliffs, NJ: Prentice-Hall.

Cutlip, S. M., Center, A. H., & Broom, G. M. (1985). *Effective public relations* (6th ed.). Englewood Cliffs, NJ: Prentice-Hall.

Dozier, D. M. (1981, August). *The diffusion of evaluation methods among pubic relations practitioners.* Paper presented at the meeting of the Public Relations Division, Association for Education in Journalism, East Lansing, MI.

Dozier, D. M. (1983, November). *Toward a reconciliation of 'role conflict' in public relations research.* Paper presented at the meeting of the Western Communication Educators Conference, Fullerton, CA.

Dozier, D. M. (1984a, June). *The evolution of evaluation methods among public relations practitioners.* Paper presented at the Educator Academy meeting of the International Association of Business Communicators, Montreal.

Dozier, D. M. (1984b, August). *Priority research issues in public relations.* Paper presented at the meeting of the Foundation for Public Relations Research and Education Meeting, Gainesville, FL.

Dozier, D. M. (1984c). Program evaluation and roles of practitioners. *Public Relations Review, 10*(2), 13-21.

Dozier, D. M. (1986, August). *The environmental scanning function of public relations practitioners and participation in management decision making.* Paper presented at the meeting of the Public Relations Division, Association for Education in Journalism and Mass Communication, Norman, OK.

Dozier, D. M. (1987, May). *Gender, environmental scanning, and participation in management decision making.* Paper presented at the meeting of the Public Relations Interest Group, International Communication Association, Montreal.

Dozier, D. M., & Gottesman, M. (1982, July). *Subjective dimensions of organizational roles among public relations practitioners.* Paper presented at the meeting of the Public Relations Division, Association for Education in Journalism, Athens, OH.

Duncan, R. B. (1972). Characteristics of organizational environments and perceived environmental uncertainty. *Administrative Science Quarterly, 17,* 313-327.

Ehling, W. P. (1981, August). *Toward a theory of public relations management: Application of purposive and conflict theories to communication management.* Paper presented at the meeting of the Public Relations Division, Association for Education in Journalism, East Lansing, MI.

Emery, F. E., & Trist, E. (1965). The causal texture of organizational environments. *Human Relations, 18,* 21-31.

Fabiszak, D. L. (1985). *Public relations in hospitals: Testing the Grunig theory of organizations, environments and models of public relations.* Unpublished master's thesis, University of Maryland, College Park.

Ferguson, M. A. (1979). *Role norms, implicit relationship attributions and organizational communication: A study of public relations practitioners.* Unpublished master's thesis, University of Wisconsin, Madison.

Glaser, B., & Strauss, A. (1967). *The discovery of grounded theory.* Chicago: Aldine.

Grunig, J. E. (1983). Basic research provides knowledge that makes evaluation possible. *Public Relations Quarterly, 28*(3), 28–32.

Grunig, J. E., & Grunig, L. S. (1986, May). *Application of open systems theory to public relations: Review of a program of research.* Paper presented at the meeting of the Public Relations Interest Group, International Communication Association, Chicago.

Grunig, J. E., & Hunt, T. (1984). *Managing public relations.* New York: Holt, Rinehart & Winston.

Hage, J. (1974). *Communication and organizational control: Cybernetics in health and welfare settings.* New York: Wiley.

Hage, J. (1980). *Theories of organizations: Form, process, transformation.* New York: Wiley.

Hollander, E. P. (1964). *Leaders, groups and influence.* New York: Oxford University Press.

Johnson, D. J., & Acharya, L. (1982, July). *Organizational decision making and public relations roles.* Paper presented at the meeting of the Public Relations Division, Association for Education in Journalism, Athens, OH.

Katz, D., & Kahn, R. L. (1978). *The social psychology of organizations* (2nd ed.). New York: Wiley.

Kraemer, S. C. (1981). *Public relations practitioner involvement in environmental monitoring research as a predictor of involvement in corporate planning.* Unpublished master's thesis, San Diego State University, San Diego.

Kurpius, D. J., & Brubaker, J. C. (1976). *Psychoeducational consultation: Definition—functions—preparation.* Bloomington: Indiana University Press.

Lesly, P. (1981). The stature and role of public relations. *Public Relations Journal, 37*(1), 14–17.

Lewis, P. M. (1974). Public relations—An applied social science. *Public Relations Journal, 30*(4), 22–24.

Marker, R. K. (1977). The Armstrong/pr data measurement system. *Public Relations Review, 3*(4), 52.

Marshall, L. (1980). The new breed of pr executive. *Public Relations Journal, 36*(4), 9–13.

McElreath, M. P. (1977). Public relations evaluative research: Summary statement. *Public Relations Review, 3*(4), 129–136.

McMillan, S. J. (1984). *Public relations in trade and professional associations: Location, model, structure, environment, and values.* Unpublished master's thesis, University of Maryland, College Park.

Newsom, D. A., & Scott, A. (1976). *This is pr: The realities of public relations.* Belmont, CA: Wadsworth.

Pennington, B. (1980). How public relations fits into the puzzle. *Public Relations Journal, 36*(3), 18–20.

Pollack, E. J. (1984). *An organizational analysis of four public relations models in the federal government.* Unpublished master's thesis, University of Maryland, College Park.

Pollack, R. A. (1986). *Testing the Grunig organizational theory in scientific organizations: Public relations and the values of the dominant coalition.* Unpublished master's thesis, University of Maryland, College Park.

Reeves, B. (1983). Now you see them, now you don't: Demonstrating effects of communications programs. *Public Relations Quarterly, 28*(3), 17–27.

Robinson, E. J. (1969). *Public relations and survey research.* New York: Meredith.

Schein, E. H. (1969). *Process consultation: Its role in organizational development.* Reading, MA: Addison-Wesley.

Simon, H. A. (1960). *The new science of management decision.* New York: Harper & Row.

Simpson, R. L., & Simpson, I. H. (1969). Women and bureaucracy in the semi-professions. In A. Etzioni (Ed.), *The Semi-professions and their organizations: Teachers, nurses, social workers* (pp. 196–197). New York: Free Press.

Snow, C. P. (1959). *The two cultures and a second look.* London: Cambridge University Press.

Springer, S. P., & Deutsch, G. (1981). *Left brain, right brain.* San Francisco: Freeman.

Steele, F. I. (1969). Consultants and detectives. *The Journal of Applied Behavioral Science, 5*(2), 193–194.

Stephenson, W. (1967). *The play theory of mass communication.* Chicago: University of Chicago Press.

Sullivan, B. S., Dozier, D. M., & Hellweg, S. A. (1984, August). *A test of organizational role hierarchy among public relations practitioners.* Paper presented at the meeting of the Public Relations Division, Association for Education in Journalism and Mass Communication, Gainesville, FL.

Sullivan, B. S., Dozier, D. M., & Hellweg, S. A. (1985). Practitioner pursuit of the ideal role. *IPRA Review, 9*(2), 14–18.

Terreberry, S. (1968). The evolution of organizational environments. *Administrative Science Quarterly, 12,* 377–396.

Thompson, J. D. (1967). *Organization in action.* New York: McGraw-Hill

Walsh, J. P., & Fahey, L. (1986). The role of negotiated belief structures in strategy making. *Journal of Management, 12,* 325–338.

Walton, R. E. (1969). *Interpersonal peacemaking: Confrontations and third party consultation.* Reading, MA: Addison-Wesley.

Wright, D. K. (1979). Some ways to measure public relations. *Public Relations Journal, 36*(7), 17.

13 Public Relations and Marketing Practices

William P. Ehling
Syracuse University

Jon White
*Management Consultant,
Bedford, United Kingdom*

James E. Grunig
University of Maryland

ABSTRACT

Public relations and marketing both are essential functions for a modern organization. Marketing managers identify markets *for the products and services of the organization. Then, they supervise marketing communication programs to create and sustain demand for the products and services. Public relations managers, in contrast, supervise programs for communication with* publics — *groups of people who organize themselves when an organization affects them or they affect it. Markets are limited to the consumer segment of an organization's environment. Publics can arise within many stakeholder categories — such as employees, communities, stockholders, governments, members, students, suppliers, and donors, as well as consumers. This chapter maintains that marketing and public relations serve different functions and that public relations cannot be excellent if it is subjugated to the marketing function. When an organization makes public relations a marketing function, practitioners are reduced to the technician role, and the organization loses a valuable mechanism for managing its interdependence with its strategic publics.*

The thesis of this chapter is that public relations activities (especially its managerial activities) can be distinguished from those of marketing and that this distinction can be made on organizational, operational, practical, and theoretical grounds. Let us begin at the organizational level by taking a look, first, internally at efforts to departmentalize public relations management and, second, externally at the kind of social environment in which an organization must function, facing in the process a host of nonmarketing problems that call for solutions that only the methods and communication skills associated with public relations management can provide. The operational and practical perspectives in distinguishing public relations and marketing activities are covered in the second part of the chapter and the theoretical bases for making a distinction are taken up in the third and fourth sections.

The contention of this chapter, then, is that the public relations and marketing functions as structured within an organization have different missions to fulfill and, therefore, appeal to different paradigms or models of the organization's social environment and of the complex communications systems that are constructed and utilized in that environment as the organization relates to a host of interacting institutions, some of whom are friendly but many of which are not.

Corporations in the United States began departmentalizing public relations activities well before World War II, but the big movement in establishing separate public relations departments occurred in the 1950s and 1960s. By the 1980s, virtually all business organizations as well as public service organizations had seen fit to establish public relations departments, usually headed by a senior vice president. Many of these units are clearly identified with the label "public relations"; others, however, operate under a variety of different names ranging from "public affairs" to "corporate communication" (for a sample of terms used, see the latest *Public Relations Journal Register,* which contains a nationwide membership roster of the Public Relations Society of America).

Such departmentalization, of course, implies some kind of division of labor, a clustering of a set of tasks and responsibilities that differs from those associated with other departments; it also implies a certain degree of equality and a certain amount of operational independence such that the public relations department is not made subservient to some other department, say, the marketing department, human resources (formerly, personnel) department, and the like. Hence, in some organizations, the tasks and responsibilities assigned to the public relations department are quite distinct from those of the marketing department. However, that is not always the case. In some organizations, responsibilities assigned to public relations and marketing are murky, often overlapping and frequently conflicting.

This jurisdictional problem is aggravated by several factors. Some of these factors are found in business organizations themselves; others are produced by such support groups as public relations agencies; and still others grow out of the educational system — specifically out of the content of marketing courses and sequences of study in business schools.

THE ORGANIZATIONAL LEVEL

Among an organization's internal factors is the commonsense view that the business enterprise's primary mission is that of profit making where sales exceed production costs. Concomitant with that view is the willingness on the part of top executives on the operational level to invest sizable portions of the company's resources in solving day-to-day marketing problems in an effort to enhance sales.

Given this kind of internal organizational atmosphere, top executives and marketing managers are only too ready to elevate marketing activities to a dominant position whereby marketing is treated as a company's most important commitment around which all other organizational activities revolve in more or less subordinate roles. Within this organizational framework, then, public relations activity is seen not as an equal partner with marketing, but as a low technical function — a set of tasks designed to assist in a direct way the marketing function; the most common of these tasks, if not the only task, is that of product publicity — the preparation and placement of copy about the product (goods or services) in the mass media in the form of free advertising.

The doctrine of marketing dominance and its application gives rise to its own set of problems. First, in cases where the public relations activity is granted departmental status, jurisdictional disputes quickly can emerge between the quest for public relations autonomy and the pressure to subordinate public relations to marketing. Second, marketing rationale and techniques are not equally applicable or even useful to nonbusiness organizations such as educational institutions, not-for-profit hospitals, and public welfare agencies, all of which have primary missions that differ from the profit-making business enterprise. Third, an overemphasis on marketing strategies in a strongly competitive environment easily can lead to abuses or questionable practices in the areas of product production, pricing, and sales promotion; such practices can and do generate opposition, public criticism, and even pressure for punitive legislation from consumer protection groups (for examples of criticisms from health groups and the tightening of regulations by the Food and Drug Administration, see *Time,* July 15, 1991; for opposition to alleged price fixing, see story on class action suit, filed by 50 businesses and individual travelers, against nine airlines, The Associated Press, August 8, 1991).

Drucker (1969), while speaking of the important place of marketing activity in business, criticized some of the marketing practices for giving rise to consumerism, calling it the "shame of marketing." In other words, if marketing genuinely helps organizations adapt to meet the needs and wants of consumers, then consumer interest groups would not need to form to demand more reliable information regarding products or protection from shoddy or faulty products.

Buskirk and Rothe (1970) defined consumerism as the "organized effort of consumers seeking redress, restitution and remedy for dissatisfaction they have accumulated in the acquisition of their standard of living" (p. 62). Drucker (1969), in turn, added additional insight into the emergence of consumerism:

> Consumerism means that the consumer looks upon the manufacturer as someone who is interested in, but who really doesn't know what the consumer's realities are. He regards the manufacturer as somebody who has not made the effort to find out, who does not understand the world in which the consumer lives, and who expects the consumer to be able to make distinctions which the consumer is neither able nor willing to make. (p. 95)

In other words, consumerism emerges at the very points where marketing, whether high-powered or low-keyed, fails. Hence, consumerism is concerned with protecting the consumer from misleading, unethical, or harmful practices; it is a movement that insists that consumers are entitled to expect protection of their health and safety, products that work, clear and understandable warranties, information about products that allow consumers to make intelligent choices, and package labels that do not distort or deceive. Moreover, from the ever growing number of laws, regulations, and guidelines found at state and federal levels that are designed to protect the consumer, it is clear that businesses, through their marketing efforts, are not meeting consumer expectations.

All too often, marketing practices, whether well intentioned or not, are responsible for invigorating or sustaining consumerism. As a result, the views and agendas of consumer protection groups stand in opposition to or in conflict with the ongoing policies, plans, and practices of businesses in general and those of marketing management in particular. Paradoxically, the problems associated with consumerism that grow out of many marketing practices are the very problems that cannot be solved directly by the thinking, methods, and techniques employed by contemporary marketing management. Moreover, the resolution of conflict and the mediation of disputes is essentially a public relations concern and not a concern of marketing; hence, to the extent that marketing activity intensifies consumerism, the more public relations manager must be called upon to undo what marketing so frequently overdoes.

It also may be argued that the centrality and dominance of marketing-oriented activities in an organization are not absolute, but relative — relative to the type and severity of marketing as well as nonmarketing problems confronting an organization at any given time and to the manner by which these problems are evaluated and weighed.

If an organization's environment is benign, then it is reasonable to expect that much of the attention and energy of top executives will be directed toward solving marketing problems—those associated with the four Ps: product planning, product pricing, product placement, and product promotion. On the other hand, if the environment is turbulent and threatening, an organization faces an array of problems, only some of which are related to marketing. These nonmarketing problems (e.g., contract negotiation with labor unions, lobbying for or against pending legislation, handling class action suits directed at a company as a result, say, of oil spills or other contamination of the environment) are problems that also demand attention; not only does the effort to find solutions to such nonmarketing problems compete with an organization's marketing endeavors, but it also may claim an amount of an organization's scarce resources (money, executive's time) that easily can exceed that expended for marketing activities.

These multifacet problems, in turn, have driven large and small organizations to establish and staff departments specializing in handling situations out of which arise nonmarketing problems such as those associated with litigation, investor relations, labor (industry) relations, personnel (now more popularly called human resources) relations, government relations, environmental relations, and the like.

Hence, the uncritical acceptance of the dominance of marketing simply ignores the nature of a volatile and hostile environment in which organizations, especially business enterprises, must function; it also ignores the fact that these nonmarketing problems cannot be dealt with or solved by the conventional techniques and methods employed by marketing management. One does not send a marketing vice president to argue an organization's case in court; nor does one call upon a marketing executive to negotiate a labor contract or deal with striking workers.

Moreover, the overemphasis of marketing concerns easily can jeopardize an organization's viability; such overemphasis tempts top executives to do any number of things that may prove to be liabilities for a firm: downplaying or even ignoring problems and threats arising in sectors other than marketing, subordinating the role of other administrative or departmental units to that of the marketing effort, shifting from long-term strategic planning to short-term (quarterly) sales gains, or even redefining or downgrading public relations problem solving at the strategic level to attention getting and product publicity at the tactical level.

Drucker (1980) made several observations about the nature of turbulent environments in which all organizations, including business corporations, must function. First, he pointed to the emergence, especially since World War II, of what he called the "society of institutions." In a democracy, the political rhetoric is shaped to appeal to the individual—freedom of individual, individual rights, and the like. However, from a societal point of view, ours is a society, not of individuals, but of institutions in which individuals have statuses and occupy roles that are institutionally structured and sustained. In Drucker's words:

> A hundred and fifty years ago, every single social task was either discharged in and through the family or it was not discharged at all. The care of the sick and the care of the old; the upbringing of children and the distribution of income; even getting a job; all was done by the family if they were done at all. Any one of these tasks the family did poorly. The shift to institutional performance thus meant a very great advance in the level of performance. But it also meant that society became pluralist. Today, every single task is being carried out in and through an institution, organized for perpetuity and dependent on leadership and direction given by managers in formal structure. (p. 206)

Drucker (1980) also noted that initially, institutions in modern society were each created for a single purpose. Business corporations exist to produce goods and services; it is an economic institution. Hospitals exist to take care of the sick, whereas universities exist to train tomorrow's educated leaders and professionals, and so on. In short, these institutions were expected to concentrate on one service and to serve one public or constituency. In the business world, the demands of nonconsumer groups for other or additional services were viewed not as obligations to be met, but as restraints to be held down whenever possible. But as Drucker pointed out:

> With the emergence of the society of institutions, all this has changed. Central government has become the more impotent the bigger it has grown. The special-purpose institutions have progressively become carriers of social purposes, social values, social effectiveness. Therefore they have become politicized. They cannot justify themselves any longer in terms of their own contribution areas alone; all of them have to justify themselves now in terms of the impact they have on society overall. All of them have outside "constituencies" they have to satisfy, where formerly they had only restraints that created "problems" for them when disregarded . . . To a large extent this shift expresses the pluralist character of a society in which no one institution is by itself charged with the responsibility for the welfare of the whole. Each institution pursues its own specific goal. But who then takes care of the common weal? This particular problem, which has been central to pluralism at any time, underlies the new demand "to be socially responsible." In a pluralist society every institution becomes a political institution and is defined by its "constituencies." A "constituency" is a group that can impede an institution and can veto its decision. It cannot, as a rule, get an institution to act, but it can stymie and block it. Its support may not be necessary to the

institution; but its opposition is a genuine threat to the institution's capacity to perform and to its survival. (pp. 207–208)

In other words, the change that has occurred since World War II is one in which continual growth and expansion of institutions have forced these institutions to become more or less multipurpose rather than single or special purpose, each with multiconstituencies rather than a single constituency to serve. Again, in Drucker's (1980) words: "In a pluralist society, all institutions are of necessity political institutions. All are multi-constituency institutions. All have to perform in such a way that they will not be rejected and opposed by groups in society that can veto or block them. The managers of all institutions will have to learn to think politically in such a pluralist society" (p. 209).

However, it is precisely this turbulent environment that justifies the existence of public relations endeavors, of their departmentalization, and of the managerial distinction that is made between the rationale, methods, and goals of public relations and those of marketing. Marketing management presupposes a business organization with a single economic purpose, that of producing goods or services for a single constituency (consumers). Public relations management, on the other hand, presupposes an organization (not always a business enterprise) that is multipurpose in its commitment and serves a number of different constituencies, none of which are necessarily friendly and any one of which can come into conflict with the organization or impede or block its performance.

Second, Drucker (1980) argued that because a pluralistic society sustains institutions that are required to be multipurpose to serve multiconstituencies, the tasks and responsibilities of top managers also have been altered to become broader and more inclusive. Drucker noted:

> In all developed countries, top management is already in a process of rapid change. In the United States, top management people in large businesses, such as DuPont, General Electric, or the big banks, spend up to four-fifths of their time on outside relations, and especially on relations with all kinds of government agencies and all kinds of "publics." This is increasingly true for small businesses and for non-business public service institutions as well . . . The burden of outside relationships, the demand that top management become activist and leader, also rules out the traditional American approach in which top management spends practically all its time on managing the business and delegates the outside sphere to subordinates . . . [T]op management can no longer delegate to trade associations. It has to be active in the critical policy and relations areas itself; it has to have time to acquire first-hand knowledge and give leadership. (p. 227)

In other words, the top management of tomorrow will be a team of executives, not just the board chairman and the chief executive officer.

Even today's tasks and responsibilities embrace too much work to be carried out by one or two people. This picture is a far cry from that subscribed to by marketing-oriented specialists and executives. It is a picture that says that dealing with problems arising from a multiconstituency environment is not the kind of work that can be turned over to low-level technicians skilled in writing publicity material, or to trade associations, or to public relations agencies whose only service is one of placing product news in the mass media.

Third, Drucker (1980) also saw change in the nature of environmental turbulence. Turbulence is more than the mere tumult produced by more actors competing for center stage; rather it is a result of a change in the commitment and ideology of various constituencies. According to Drucker's observation, the shift in institutionalized society is from creating consensus so that collective action can be attained to that of generating confrontation and adversarial relations to stall or halt collective action.

Before World War II, the political party system in the United States served as an institution for integrating various factions (interest groups, pressure groups) by forging out of their many different wants a reasonable program of action. Since World War II, however, there has been an increase of single-issue factions (e.g., antiabortion and proabortion groups, Earth First!, Greenpeace, Friends of Animals, and the like); many of these factions are operating outside of the political parties and frequently in opposition to the party structure itself.

As Drucker (1980) pointed out:

> Where parties, by definition, try to create consensus for action, factions try to block action through confrontation . . . They exercise their power not by the support they can muster but by the actions they can block. Their power is not that of assent but that of veto . . . [M]odern politics is increasingly moving from creation of consent to confrontation and adversary proceedings. It is increasingly moving from trying to find the common denominator to identifying the least and most uncommon cause. It is increasingly moving from trying to compromise to trial by combat. (pp. 215–216)

This means, Drucker argued, that traditional ways in which managers operated no longer will work in the turbulent atmosphere of a pluralistic society; instead, today's managers need to understand that what appears obvious to them, such as the specific mission of their organization or the rationale that sustains that mission, are grasped only dimly by members of hostile factions whose commitment is not to understand, but to oppose.

Drucker (1980) went on to say:

> The new manager, whether of a business, hospital or university, will be effective only if he ceases to see himself — and to be seen — as representing a

"special interest." In a political arena overcrowded by "true believers" in "sacred causes," the manager of institutions must establish himself as the representative of the common good, as spokesman for the "general will." He can no longer depend on the political process to be the integrating force; he himself has to become the integrator. He has to establish himself as the spokesman for the interest of society in the producing, in performing, in achieving. And this means that the manager of any institution (but particularly of business) has to think through what the policy should be in the general interest and to provide social cohesion. He has to do this before there is a "problem," before he reacts to somebody else's proposal, before there is an issue. And then he has to become the proponent, the educator, the advocate. The manager, in other words, will have to learn to create the "issues," to identify both the social concern and the solution to it, and to speak for the producer interest in society as a whole rather than for the special interest of "business." (pp. 217–218)

However, to be effective in this new role, top managers must develop and build up support groups or constituencies that accept such managers as representatives of the producer interest and spokesman for the common good. The rationale for this new leadership responsibility rests on several assumptions.

As Drucker (1980) pointed out:

It assumes that management accepts the responsibility for integrating employee ownership into the governance of the corporation, and employee competence into the responsibility of citizenship. It assumes that management stops talking "profit" and accepts the responsibility for earning the cost of society's future, the cost of staying in business. It assumes that management accepts the responsibility also of speaking and acting as representative of the common good rather than continuing to act as representative of one interest, the "business" interest, in which capacity it can only lose . . . Unless executives accept the responsibility of taking leadership in the common interest, they will become more and more powerless in the pluralist environment, and will continue to be the losers in the politics of confrontation . . . No matter whether the business—or the hospital or university—is large or small, management will have to accept that society looks to its institutions to attain ends unrelated to the institution's own purposes, such as preferential employment for "minorities" on the university faculty regardless of scholarship and teaching ability. Managers will have to learn to operate in a political environment, in which the dynamics have shifted to small, single-minded confrontational minorities that can veto, and away from majorities that represent a consensus and can act. Managers will find increasingly that in turbulent times they have to be leaders and integrators in a pluralist society, in addition to managing their institutions for performance. (pp. 219–221)

Here, then, is a rationale for the existence of a public relations function in an organization that cannot be matched by any that are set forth in college-level public relations textbooks. Drucker (1980), without any direct reference to public relations, has provided a clear justification for the establishment and departmentalization of the public relations function and for separating public relations management from marketing management. Drucker not only has presented a challenge to public relations executives but also has mandated that they deal with a host of nonmarketing — or, in Drucker's words, political — problems, which, if not adequately solved, will render modern executives, especially business managers, "powerless" and "losers in the politics of confrontation."

PUBLIC RELATIONS AS PUBLICITY

Drucker's (1980) view, however, is not the view being heralded publicly by public relations agencies, at least not the overwhelming majority of them. These agencies, in the name of public relations, see as their concern that of providing clients with a cheap mode of advertising their product or service by means of free publicity in the guise, or more appropriately, the disguise, of news stories. Their concerns and services are not with the problems and issues that Drucker saw as emerging from the confrontational style increasingly resorted to by single-issue factions in a pluralist society, but rather with copy preparation and the media blitz.

In this mode of operation, public relations agencies, more than any other group, not only have eroded the distinction between public relations management and marketing management, but have vigorously opposed, in practice and in words, any idea that the public relations concern should be anything other than getting media coverage for a company's goods or service.

What we hear and read, then, is a view that sanctions a practice that equates public relations with publicity. In making reference to a survey conducted by Wang Associates, a New York City-based public relations firm specializing in health care, the president of the firm, Julie Wang, said (Drug Executives, 1991): "It's clear from the survey that the use of public relations in promoting pharmaceutical products will continue to increase. Public relations is unique in its ability to reach consumers directly with educational and promotional material" (p. 16).

This is an interesting view for several reasons. First, it comes hard on the heels of the Food and Drug Administration's criticism of the questionable tactics of directly targeting consumers rather than medical professionals, that is, bypassing doctors in an effort to induce consumers to ask for more prescription drugs. Criticism also has come from the media. The *Wall Street Journal* and "60 Minutes" have argued that the use of celebrity spokespersons and video news releases amount to a one-sided presentation that misleads the potential consumers. The second reason Wang's statement is interesting is that it reflects a widespread belief among public relations firms that public relations is nothing more than product publicity, and, hence, a part of marketing's promotional mix. Third, Wang's view of public relations as publicity is precisely what mass media representatives (reporters, editors, and executives) treat with suspicion and contempt by calling those in this business "flacks." As the Associated Press Managing Editors' manual, *APME Guidelines,* put it: "A flack is a person who makes all or part of his income by obtaining space in newspapers without cost to himself or his client . . . A flack is the modern equivalent of the cavalier highwayman of old . . . He will not lie very often, but much of the time he tells less than the whole story" (Cutlip, Center, & Broom, 1985 p. 430).

In the same story just cited, it was pointed out that "providing marketing support is the most popular reason for using outside public relations firms" (for "marketing support" read product publicity), followed by the statement: "Seventy percent of the executives (of public relations firms) said their firms are hired for marketing purposes."

In the same issue of the *Public Relations Journal* there also appears an article about the Food and Drug Administration writing tougher rules for pharmaceutical marketing. Marilyn L. Castaldi (1991) pointed out that companies are now experimenting with more "non-traditional" techniques to help "differentiate themselves and their product" (p. 14). "These activities," wrote Castaldi, "used public relations techniques, not only to target physicians but also to build consumer awareness of prescription drugs" (p. 15). According to Castaldi's view, these so-called "public relations techniques" include the following: "Press conferences, media tours, video news releases, media coverage of scientific symposia and drug research discussions with investment analysis" (p. 15). All these activities, she continued, "helped spur the broad coverage of health science topics throughout the American media" (p. 15).

Hence, it would appear that public relations as publicity has the simple and single mission of getting broad coverage in the American media. As to whether anyone attends to this broad coverage and if they do, whether they take any action or display any kind of behavior (such as buying the product) is left to the imagination and wishful thinking; these matters apparently are of no concern of public relations firms because the overwhelming majority of these firms conduct no "effect" research to provide empirical data about the specific impact such broad media coverage produce; and the few firms that do attempt to get answers do so by conducting research without any kind of scientific rigor that would allow valid generalizations to be made.

Moreover, what we are treated to in these examples of public relations as publicity in a marketing framework, is a view that regards this activity as made up solely of tactics and techniques. Nothing is said of strategies or strategical planning vis-a-vis public relations.

David R. Drobis appears to be mindful of the importance of strategic planning in a company and especially as strategic thinking related to public relations activity. Drobis is president of Ketchum Public Relations in New York City; his firm is a unit of Ketchum Communications, Inc., Pittsburgh, Pa. In an article published in *Public Relations Journal* (Drobis, 1991), he wrote: "We in public relations firms and our counterparts in corporations can significantly increase our contribution to the corporate effort by making strategy part of our repertory of services and by showing corporations how to be more competitive" (pp. 31–32).

As one reads on, however, one finds that for Drobis (1991) there is only one kind of strategy, that which has to do with marketing—or, in Drobis's words, with the "long war against the competition," with the way a company "sees itself in the market," with marketing plans that "concur with the realities of the marketplace." Drobis correctly sensed that strategic thinking should be "the center of every corporate communication program." But for him, corporate communication is an activity that occupies a subordinate position in the company's overreaching marketing strategy. Hence, he equated corporate communication (usually thought of as a public relations activity) with marketing communication (salesmanship, advertising, and product publicity) on the one hand, and marketing communication with publicity on the other. Moreover, he also equated communication strategy with publicity tactics because he wrote that the purpose of a company's "communication strategy" is that of telling the company's "one story and one story only: this is how we serve our customers, this is what makes us different." However, story telling, if you will, is a tactic, not a strategy.

Here, then, we have a case where the author, in an attempt to associate public relations activity with strategic planning, blurred the distinction between public relations strategic planning and marketing strategic planning, and, worse still, between strategy and tactics. In short, for Drobis (1991) corporation communication is really marketing communication, or, even more narrowly, a part of the marketing mix called product promotion. This view, of course, fits the operating philosophy of Ketchum Public Relations because that firm specializes in conducting product publicity campaigns for a large number of business clients, but it is not a view that can address the problems and issues that Drucker wrote about in his books.

Nonetheless, it is a view that, not surprisingly, is shared by Lawrence R. Werner, who also is concerned with strategy planning as it relates to communication and marketing. Werner is executive vice president and director of Ketchum Public Relations in Pittsburgh, PA. He articulated his views of the role of public relations in the article, "Marketing Strategies for the Recession," published in *Management* (Werner, 1991, pp. 29–30).

Werner (1991) wrote, in the opening part of his article, about the need for companies to "enhance their marketing presence," the need for "product exposure," the need "to increase sales" during a recession. He also noted that there is a need to keep expenditures — especially advertising expenses — down during a recession without jeopardizing a company's "marketing position." He then said: "In a sluggish economy, most companies think they can't afford to introduce a new product or enhance its positioning. But heavy marketing often transcends recessionary pressures, and public relations can be a powerful force in generating new excitement for an old, established product."

In a few paragraphs, Werner (1991) made his position clear: (a) the central concern, and presumably that of all businesses, is marketing — marketing position, marketing presence, product exposure, and increased sales; (b) it is these marketing attributes and factors that justify the existence of public relations whose mission is to do something helpful for marketing; and (c) public relations, in the eyes of Werner, is nothing more or less than publicity — efforts directed to obtain as broad a coverage in the mass media as possible. His appeal to the reader, and hopefully some potential clients, is also clear: During a recession, cut back on advertising expenditures and use the money to conduct product publicity campaigns directed by public relations firms, especially his firm.

Werner (1991), to make his case, next turned to what he called "success stories," three publicity endeavors accomplished by his firm for SmithKline Beecham, Digital Equipment Corporation, and American Honda Motor Company. He first reported on a "national survey" — called the N'ICE National Cold Survey — conducted by SmithKline Beecham with the avowed purpose to "generate feature news coverage." There is here the possible question of the misuse or abuse of survey methods for publicity purposes; there also is the question as to whether "300 telephone interviews" constitutes an adequate sample to warrant it being called a national survey. All this, however, does not seem to trouble Werner, who wrote: "The survey was a huge success. It generated media coverage that exceeded a total of 30 million in circulation. Several stories on the survey appeared on the front pages of life-style sections. Through radio interviews and during some of the sample distribution events, SmithKline Beecham representatives spoke directly to consumers."

Media coverage, then, is presented by Werner (1991) as the primary goal or end state of his firm's effort, as the raison d'etre of the so-called public relations effort. However, this raises the question as to the worth of such media coverage. Is one to assume that one stops the marketing effort after media placement has been accomplished? Is media placement an end in itself or, more likely, a means to some higher goals? And if the latter, what are these goals? Werner, almost as if he were stating a foregone conclusion, responded, ". . . the fact that the survey was mentioned on television and in the newspaper not as an ad but as part of the editorial content added credibility. Qualitatively, the N'ICE survey brought the product in closer contact with the consumer and produced benefits that could not have been gained through traditional advertising."

Here, then, we are offered several causal statements in which, presumably, the media coverage is treated as the cause of certain effects or end states such as (a) "added creditability," (b) "the product in closer contact with the consumer," and (c) "benefits that could not have been gained through traditional advertising." No research data are presented to support these statements on the one hand, and, on the other, the reader only can guess what is meant by creditability, in closer contact, and benefits. The reader must accept these publicity accomplishments on good faith or, worse still, accept blindly the notion that these end states flow automatically, irrevocably, and always from a publicity campaign that attains a modicum of media coverage.

Werner's (1991) second case deals with the presumed effect of "The Infinite Voyage," a series of television special programs sponsored by Digital Equipment Corporation. What did this corporation gain from its sponsorship? Werner's answer is that the TV series "generated more than 200 million total circulation" with articles appearing "in *The New York Times, Washington Post, Los Angeles Times, TV Guide,* Associated Press, CNN, and the Mutual Radio Network. All this is offered as proof positive of success; attention is called to 200 million total circulation (an impressive figure, to be sure), but the reader is not told what proportion, if any, of readers of this circulation figure actually were aware of what appeared in the media coverage and what significance, if any, such awareness had for Digital Equipment Corporation.

Apart, then, from counting the number of press clips and TV sound "bites," what additional outcomes emerged from the media coverage? Werner (1991) made an earlier but oblique reference to the need of companies to convey a desired image, promoting their reputation, and attaining good corporate citizenship by doing such things as sponsoring "The Infinite Voyage." No evidence, however, is provided to show that such states actually were set as goals of the media coverage; nor are there any data presented to show unequivocally that these states, whether planned for or not, actually were attained. Instead, the reader is left with hints that there may be some possibility of success; but here Werner is in a realm of wishful thinking, not the world of hard facts about the actual impact.

The case of the American Honda Motor Company presents a similar picture. Werner (1991) reported that Honda was eager to change the "perception held by many car owners that Japanese cars (especially Honda) were merely dependable family cars, not upscale touring vehicles" (such as Honda's new Acura vehicles). He then added:

> Working on the premise that advertising alone could not create the desired consumer mindset, a media strategy was devised to pre-sell Honda's target customers on Acura's special features and to help Acura dealers create showroom traffic. Acura was positioned as much more than a new car introduction—it was touted as a Japanese challenge to an auto market that had been the exclusive domain of European imports.

Werner (1991), then, pointed out that leading auto writers were sent to Japan to preview the Acura, whereas the "public relations team produced a 90-second video news clip that was sent via satellite to more than 1,000 television stations across the country." In addition to all that, Werner reported: "To keep interest alive, when the first shipment of Acuras arrived in the United States, a dockside event heralding the arrival of the 'Japanese Challenge Cars' was staged for TV and printed media."

What is served up next by Werner (1991) is a report of the media coverage of this obvious publicity effort, which he called "the public relations campaign." This endeavor ". . .netted more than nine minutes of network television coverage and more than 50 minutes of local television coverage. In addition, more than 150 newspapers covered the story, including several national publications."

Finally, Werner (1991) added this item to clinch his case of how successful the product publicity activity really was: "Most significantly, the public relations effort helped sell more than 52,000 cars in a year made difficult by the dollar's decline against the yen."

Here, as in the other cases, Werner (1991) appears to be of two minds about what is to be treated as the means and the ends. Given his emphasis on the type and extent of media coverage, it would appear that it is this media coverage that is to be regarded as the end to be attained for Ketchum Public Relations' client, Honda. This media coverage was attained, as Werner carefully detailed, by such means as copy preparation, dissemination of video news releases, staging a "Japanese Challenge Cars" event, and the like. Then, almost as an afterthought, Werner shifted to another level, treating media coverage as a means employed to stimulate car sales.

More troublesome, however, is again Werner's (1991) use of casual language. He asserted that the "public relations effort helped sell more than 52,000 cars." Clearly what is being said is that media coverage (treated as the cause) was responsible in a most helpful way for car sales (the effect). However, it is wholly unclear what is meant by helped sell. What, for example, was the magnitude of this help—the sale of 2 cars, 22 cars, or

2,000 cars. The reader is left to guess—not only about the actual amount of help (if, in fact, there was any help at all), but also about the method, short of clairvoyance, used to find out about the type and extent of this help. Because no mention is made of research as a way of ascertaining the effect (car sales), the reader is left wondering by what evidence Werner had come to know for certain that media coverage was actually responsible for the car sales.

Nonetheless, the logic used to arrive at the causal conclusion of car sales is not hard to discern, because it is a logic widely used to justify publicity efforts devoid of research data. It begins by treating media coverage (whatever its type or extent) in a deterministic way, capable always of producing in a direct, powerful manner a desired outcome (whatever that may be, e.g., product awareness, maintenance of market share, good citizenship, or car sales). Once media coverage actually is attained in some form, the logic leads to the conclusion that the desired effects also have been attained—and (this is the money-saving part) no research-derived empirical evidence is needed to verify the conclusion. It also is a logic that keeps alive the myth of mass media's all-powerful effect, a myth that has been rejected repeatedly by mass communication researchers for the last 40 years, going back to the studies conducted by Lazarsfeld, Berelson, and Gaudet (1948) and the assessment of effect research by Klapper (1960).

Given the prevalence of Werner's (1991) views among those who identify themselves as public relations practitioners, several observations are warranted.

First, it is clear from the way in which Werner (1991) employed the term public relations that he is equating this term with the narrower, technical activity of product publicity—the activity of producing publicity materials and getting these materials used by the mass media. However, this view of public relations as publicity, although a popular notion in or outside of public relations agencies, is not universally accepted.

For example, Dilenschneider (1987), president and chief executive officer of one of the larger public relations firms, Hill and Knowlton, Inc., was highly critical of this kind of public relations as publicity activity. He referred disparagingly to such activity as a "logistic support effort" that does nothing more than trying "to get the message out" to the mass media "whether it's correct or incorrect." Such an activity stands in contrast with what Dilenschneider believed to be public relations' real function, that of engaging in "strategic problem-solving." Further, he chastised public relations as publicity practitioners for succumbing to the lure of media coverage and being so easily taken in "by the color and by the sound and by the light and by the delivery systems and the glitz of the message."

Even within the ranks of public relations agencies, there are those who see public relations activity in strategic decision-making, dispute-resolving terms rather than in copy-preparation and media-placement terms. Ron Gossen and Kay Sharp of Sharp, Gossen and Associates of San Antonio, TX, an affiliate of Hill and Knowlton, Inc., argued in an article published in the *Public Relations Journal* (Gossen & Sharp, 1987) of the need for public relations practitioners to know how to resolve disputes:

> Disputes involving many stakeholders and multiple issues are becoming a way of life in the business and public policy world . . . Designing and implementing processes to prevent or resolve disputes in business/public policy arena are services beginning to be widely demanded of [public relations] practitioners.
>
> "Dispute resolution" processes help enhance the client's ability to function successfully in a volatile environment. Designed to prevent stakeholders' interest from becoming hardened, irreconcilable positions, the process seekers to determine and dissect the interests of divergent groups and ultimately to forge options to satisfy all interests.
>
> This "win-win" negotiation (also known as "integrative negotiation") is the key to lasting success in dispute resolution. (pp. 35–38)

Even more broad ranging have been the efforts of the Public Relations Society of America (PRSA) to disassociate public relations as publicity from the more essential public relations as strategic problem solving. Advocates of this position were successful in 1982 to have PRSA Assembly adopt an "Official Statement on Public Relations," which underscores the problem-solving mission of public management (Cutlip, Center, & Broom, 1985, p. 5).

A similar position has been taken by virtually all authors who write college-level public relations textbooks. Although some see publicity as one of the subfunctions of public relations activity, none equates public relations with publicity. Given this conceptual environment in which public relations management is differentiated from publicity production, Werner (1991), and others who think like him, cannot merely assume that the public relations as publicity view is the only one nor even the preferred one. Instead, it may be argued that public relations should not be used to cover the kind of activities in which Werner's firm is engaged.

Werner's (1991) position, and those of others who agree with him, may be summarized as follows: In the business world, publicity activity should be concerned with a company's products and product sales; hence, product publicity should be associated exclusively with the company's marketing effort and, therefore, should be a support endeavor of sales promotion and one of the subfunctions of marketing communication (the others being advertising and salesmanship). If that be the case, then accuracy and clarity would demand that Werner, and others performing activities similar to those of Werner, should be urged, perhaps even required, to use the perfectly acceptable and unambiguous term *product publicity* to identify the sales promotion service they provide, leaving public relations for higher level management responsible for solving strategic, nonmarketing problems arising out of interinstitutional confrontations of the kind Drucker (1980) spoke about in *Managing in Turbulent Times.*

Second, Werner (1991) blurred the distinction between strategy and tactics. In the several cases he presented, he talked about activities employed to obtain media coverage: sponsorship of television specials, video news releases, a special event, and the like. All these are lumped under what Werner called marketing strategies when, in fact, they are all simple tactics employed to obtain free space in newspapers, and free time on radio and television. It may sound impressive to identify ordinary publicity techniques his firm provides as high-level marketing strategies, but such identification is overblown and misleading.

Third, in the three cases presented by Werner (1991), he seems to be unsure about the distinction between means and ends, and, hence, unsure what endstates really are being pursued. The first impression one has in reading these cases is that the endstates (goals) that were being sought had to do with media coverage; Werner proudly cited a variety of figures to show the extent of such coverage: "generated media coverage that exceeded a total of 30 million circulation" in the SmithKline Beecham case, "generate more than 230 million total circulation" in the Digital Equipment Corporate case, and "more than nine minutes of network television coverage and more than 50 minutes of local television coverage" as well as coverage in "150 newspapers" in the Honda case. But then it appears that media coverage was not the end that had been sought but a means to some other ends: closer contact with consumers, good corporate citizenship, automobile sales. It might be pointed out in passing that it is not at all clear as to the precise nature of the causal connection between, say, 230 million total circulation (which has nothing to do with either readership, i.e., how many people read the item, or behavior) and something vaguely called good corporate citizenship.

Fourth, Werner (1991) appears unable to discern the *functional* difference between public relations management and marketing management, on the one hand, and the *administrative* difference between managerial planning of a strategic kind and technical production on the other. This indifference to these distinctions can be expected from people directing public relations-as-publicity firms. Werner's firm comes to the scene as an outside party, servicing clients in the form of a job-shop, staffed with people skilled in handling copy writing and publicity tasks to attain media coverage. Under such circumstances, these firm executives need not worry about the administrative problems facing corporate executives who maintain separate public relations and marketing departments. For Werner, marketing strategies and public relations strategies are one and the same thing. If this is so, then top corporate executives face the prospect of accepting the conclusion that the public relations and marketing departments are both performing the same functions or that the public relations department, in spite of its departmental status, is a subunit of the marketing department. Neither of these two conclusions are managerially tenable or organizationally acceptable, but this is of little concern to agencies that sell public relations as publicity services as part of marketing strategies.

Fifth, Werner (1991) kept insisting that public relations as publicity is just as cost-effective as advertising, or even more so. He spoke of the success stories about SmithKline Beecham, Digital Equipment Corporation, and Honda as "demonstrating how public relations can cost-effectively keep a company ahead of the competition." He also stated that "a well-orchestrated public relations campaign can cost-effectively raise your company's image and consumer awareness of your product or services." One, however, must take this insistence of cost-effectiveness on blind faith; Werner nowhere showed in his three cases how cost-effectiveness was measured. Werner appeared to proceed on the assumption that the mere use of public relations as publicity tactics makes the publicity campaign cost-effective, and, hence, no measures really are needed.

Sixth, Werner (1991), as noted earlier several times, is given to using causal language in talking about the impact that can be made by media coverage, for example, bringing about a desired image, a good reputation, good corporate citizenship, greater awareness of products, positive recognition, and increased sales. This mode of thinking treats the mass media as a single but powerful factor that alone can bring about the aforementioned effects or outcomes with ease. But it needs to be noted that this powerful effect notion has been rejected as an overly simplistic model of mass media communication, sometime disparagingly called the hypodermic needle model of mass media. If, indeed, mass media have an effect, it is one that is mediated — sometimes amplified, but more often damped or even greatly reduced — by a host of other interacting factors; these factors include scores of social variables that make up the context in which communication takes place, a host of social psychological factors that shape the individual's personal receptivity, and the various attributes of communication itself (the nature of the medium, message length, message form and content, message source, and the like). Only a few of these latter variables are under the control of the publicist; the others, as well as their interaction, are outside of his or her control. Hence, this complex set of interacting variables makes predicting, much less controlling, the types and magnitudes of effects extremely difficult and frequently impossible. To assume otherwise, as Werner did, is to do so without theoretical warranty or scientific sanction.

The aforementioned indictment is not directed at an agency that provides a publicity service; nor is it directed at an activity generally called product publicity. Rather, it is directed at a style of doing business that is predicated on the belief that public relations management with strategic responsibilities can be reduced arbitrarily to product publicity and absorbed into the marketing function as a minor subunit on no stronger grounds than that it is possible to sell clients publicity services in the guise of marketing strategies.

Moreover, in the analysis of Werner's (1991) view of public relations (a view shared by others in and outside of the agency business), an attempt was made to show that (a) the term public relations was being equated with publicity without structural necessity in an organizational sense and without operational justification in a managerial sense; (b) the primary mission or purpose of public relations as publicity never was made clear by Werner, being equated, instead, with a host of opportunistically designated but shifting outcomes that might appeal to an actual or potential client; and (c) the cost-effectiveness of publicity endeavors had been asserted repeatedly but never demonstrated by Werner, leaving one wondering what benefits are attainable that might warrant the existence of public relations as publicity as a purely technical and productive activity.

Hence, we have an article in which a disservice is done to marketing management by reducing the function to a series of product publicity ploys and an injustice to public relations management by divesting it of any significant administrative responsibilities.

MARKETING PRINCIPLES AND PUBLIC RELATIONS

When one turns to the literature of marketing management, especially books that serve as college-level textbooks, one again finds attempts to assign public relations an inferior technical role under the stewardship of marketing. One of the striking features of many of the marketing textbooks is the lack of recognition of the vast literature base found under the rubric of public relations. Instead of making themselves aware of research output and more recent conceptualizations vis-á-vis public relations, many marketing textbook authors proceed as if they are free to define the public relations function in whatever manner they please. The general result, not surprisingly, is a reductionistic one in which public relations activity, usually treated as product publicity or some fuzzy part of sales promotion, is given a subordinate role under marketing.

Within this narrow context, many marketing textbook writers see what frequently has been called "marketing public relations" as playing some kind of role in sales promotion. Shimp and DeLozier (1986) saw public relations and publicity essentially as activities that "serve to supplement media advertising, sales, and sales promotion in creating product awareness, building favorable attitudes toward the company and its products, and encouraging purchase behavior" (pp. 493–494). Stanley (1982) saw public relations, publicity, and institutional advertising as part of a company's sales promotion effort which, in turn, is part of the marketing mix. Schwartz (1982) argued that public relations is but another form of "consumer-oriented sales promotion" with a mission to build or shape the "image" of a business in its support of sales promotion efforts under the control of marketing (p. 8). McDaniel (1979), in turn, asserted that "public relations, like personal selling, advertising, and sales promotion, is a vital link in a progressive company's marketing communication mix," and, further, "public relations complements the role of advertising by building product/service credibility" (p. 455).

However, one is never quite sure of the prime mission of public relations even in this marketing-oriented framework. For McDaniel (1979), public relations is primarily an "information dissemination" activity without any further clarification of the meaning of dissemination. Others see the public relations mission broadened to "foster good will with the organization's various publics" or "to engender a desired corporate image" (Shimp & De Lozier, 1986, pp. 493–94) with no indication of how to evaluate in measurable terms such things as "foster," "good will," "engender," and "image"; unhappily, these latter terms are extremely vague and, in their everyday use, have become little more than overworked clichés without much concrete substance. Still, other authors lump into the public relations mission a hodgepodge collection of means or tactics that are presented as if they were end states or goals to be sought, for example, "preparing publicity," "directing corporate image advertising," "creating product awareness," "encouraging purchase behavior," "humanizing business," "obtaining favorable publicity," and "counteract rumors."

These efforts to bring public relations activity under the jurisdiction of marketing management make no reference to any empirical or conceptual base to support such a move. Moreover, they beg the question about the primary purpose of public relations even within a marketing context to say nothing of its purpose in a nonmarketing context; and, worse still, these efforts assign vaguely stated goals for the public relations activity—goals that, because of their murkiness, fail to fulfill the basic administrative criteria of being attainable, measurable, and economically worthwhile (as determined through benefit-cost analysis).

Paralleling the diminution of the public relations function by emptying it of any worthwhile intellectual content and managerial responsibilities are the efforts to greatly expand the role and operation of marketing.

One of the more prolific and influential writers on marketing is Kotler

(1976, 1982, 1986, 1988). In his various writings, Kotler has made a number of attempts to subsume public relations activity under marketing. For him the "marketing mix" is made up of a set of controllable variables that a firm uses to influence the target market. He proposed that, among these variables, public relations should be conceived as part of marketing in the performance of its communication role.

For Kotler, then, public relations is part of an organization's attempt to package itself and its products to build goodwill. In his book on marketing for nonprofit organizations, Kotler (1982) argued that public relations is most effective when viewed as part of the marketing mix used by an organization to pursue its marketing objectives. He then spelled out his conceptualization of public relations as it relates to marketing:

First, public relations is viewed as primarily a communication tool, whereas marketing includes not only communication but also needs assessment, product development, price setting, and the construction of distribution arrangements.

Second, public relations, in its communication role, attempts only to influence attitudes, whereas marketing directs its efforts at eliciting specific behaviors such as purchasing, voting, or joining.

Third, public relations is not involved in trying to define the goals of an organization, whereas marketing is intricately involved in defining the mission of a business, type of customers being targeted, and kinds of goods or services to be produced.

In this effort to broaden the mission of marketing management, Kotler (1982) appears to be able to apply marketing concepts to nonprofit organization under a guise that has come to be called *social marketing* or megamarketing. Given this more expansive role of marketing, Kotler (1976) wrote that many marketers are of the opinion that public relations should be under the control of marketing, because the function of public relations, they believe, is to make it easier for a company to market its goods.

It is clear from Kotler's perspective that public relations has a minor role to play in the general activities of any organization, and this minor role, if fulfilled at all, is one that must fit into the more inclusive and more important marketing operation. Public relations does not even have a management role in nonprofit organization because, according to Kotler's argument, the concepts and methods of marketing can be, and should be, extended to such organizations.

The diminution and finally the absorption of the public relations function by marketing and, at the same time, the expansion of marketing into not only nonprofit organization but also into virtually all other activity sectors as well are accomplished by Kotler in several ways.

First Kotler shifted the focus of marketing away from the sales effort to that of determining people's wants and needs as spelled out in his work on

Marketing Management (1976). In other words, for Kotler, marketing consists of an organization determining the needs and wants of target markets and adapting itself to delivering satisfactions more effectively and efficiently than its competitors. This conceptualization, then, substitutes for economic exchange in the form of selling and buying that of delivering psychological satisfactions to meet psychologically generated needs and wants. The need, from an economic point of view, to maintain a positive slope of the demand curve by keeping sales steady or advancing still may be useful for accounting purposes, but the main concern of marketing, from Kotler's perspective, is not product sales per se but an understanding of the attributes of wants and needs so that these psychological states can be satisfied; this satisfaction need not be manifested in terms of buying anything.

In the words of Kotler (1976):

> *Marketing* is human activity directed at satisfying needs and wants through exchange processes. The starting point for the discipline of marketing lies in *human needs and wants*. Mankind needs food, air, water, clothing, and shelter to survive. Beyond this, people have strong desire for recreation, education, and other services . . . The existence of human needs and wants give rise to the concept of products. A *product* is something that is viewed as capable of satisfying a want. A want describes a state of felt deprivation in a person. The deprivation produces discomfort and a wish to act to relieve this discomfort. The want energizes the person — puts him into an active state — and gives him direction. The person will perceive certain things outside of himself that would satisfy his want. These things can be called products. They take on value to the individual because of their capacity to satisfy his wants . . . Anything capable of rendering a service, that is, satisfying a need, can be called a product. This includes *persons, places, organizations,* and *ideas.* (p. 18)

From the aforementioned account, one can see something of the breadth of Kotler's view of marketing and product as they are grounded in the psychological concepts of human needs and wants. The function of marketing, then, is to deliver "satisfaction," a psychological state that offsets "felt deprivation" and "discomfort," not necessarily an activity that works for monetary gain (e.g., interests, or a good return on investments) nor even, more broadly, a form of economic consumption in the exchange process.

Such human needs and wants take one well beyond economic exchange whether expressed in monetary terms or not; they also have infinite extension. In following this logic, Kotler had no difficulty in extending marketing thinking and methods to all sectors of human activity. For example, voters have wants (e.g., that government maintains law and order) and needs (e.g., personal security); therefore, politicians, government officials, police officers, and the like are all engaged in marketing activities as they try to satisfy such wants and needs. By the same extension, religious leaders (e.g., ministers, priests, rabbis) really are engaged in marketing when they build places of worship, give homilies or sermons, and provide religious advice and consultation, because all these activities are designed to satisfy needs and wants. Kotler's view of marketing also can be extended to the operations of educational institutions, hospital, welfare agencies, and all kinds of cultural and entertainment activities.

Underlying Kotler's notion of marketing is the concept that sees marketing as a function through which organizations or any group of people adjust their offerings to the ever-changing needs and wants of other people, and, hence, as a link between society's needs and wants and the response by organizations, groups, or individuals to satisfy these needs and wants, whether these organizations are political parties operating during a presidential election year or a lobbyist seeking to influence legislation.

By this extension, Kotler has succeeded in uncoupling marketing from salesmanship and product sales as necessary components of marketing activity. Hence, in the view of Kotler (1976):

> The concept of market also covers exchanges of resources not necessarily involving money. The political candidate offers promises of good government to a *voter market* in exchange of votes. The lobbyist offers services to a *legislative market* in exchange for votes for his cause. A university cultivates the *mass-media market* when it wines and dines editors in exchange for more and better publicity. A museum cultivates the *donor market* when it offers special privileges to contributors in exchange for their financial support. (p. 7)

Kotler (1976), in other words, defined exchange not in economic terms but in social-psychological terms in which at least two parties have something of value for each other, and can find the "terms of exchange that leave them better off (or at least no worse off) then before." A market, then, is a social arena in which the potentiality for such exchanges occur. Moreover, anything can be a product — persons, places, organizations, and ideas. Any clustering of people or just a single party can be a market. And a market can be any social circumstance in which parties exchange something of value, such as two people exchanging information or gossip or a man hunting with his bird dog or a mother nursing her baby. Obviously, with this extension of marketing to all sectors of society and all facets of human activity, there is little need, if any need at all, of public relations, however this term is defined. Even if defined as a product publicity help-maid of marketing, it is simply one of the pieces making up marketing communications and, hence, a working part of the total marketing enterprise.

However, when marketing can be extended to the exchange of gossip, hunting with a dog, or a mother nursing her baby, it would appear that one has reached a point where the term marketing is being used in an unusual and unhelpful way. Here, then, lies the weakness of Kotler's attempt to rework basic ideas about marketing. To the extent marketing can be given unrestricted semantic leeway, to that extent public relations can be defined into a state of unimportance if not out of existence; but by the same token, this semantic freedom also renders the term marketing (and the all-encompassing concepts associated with it) virtually useless in ordinary managerial or scientific usage. If a term can be made to mean everything, then obviously it comes to mean nothing.

The second way Kotler (1976) disfranchises public relations as a management function is by treating the methods of marketing management as if they had universal application in all management activity. He pointed out that "Marketing management is the analysis, planning, implementation, and control of programs designed to bring about desired exchanges with target markets for the purpose of achieving organizational objectives" (p. 7).

In a previous statement, Kotler (1976) said that "marketing management takes place when at least one party to a potential exchange gives thought to his objectives and means to achieving desired responses from other parties" (p. 7). First, it should be kept in mind that exchange, potential or actual, means that there are at least two parties who have something of value for each other and are willing to accept each other's offer; the thing of value need not be money. Second, the term market is not restricted to potential customers who may wish to make a purchase; the notion of market can be expanded to include, in Kotler's words, "voter market" in the political arena, "legislative market" in the sense of lobbying, "mass-media market" in the sense of seeking favorable publicity, and "donor market" in the sense of seeking financial support. Third, within an organization there are a number of managers with different responsibilities (human resources, financing, warehousing, and the like) for programs designed for the "purpose of achieving organizational objectives," for example, hiring workers, doing research development, encouraging investments in a company's operation, and the like.

Putting all this together gives the distinct impression that anyone engaged in the analysis, planning, implementation, and control of programs to achieve organizational objectives, whatever they may be, is using the methodology of marketing management and, hence, is engaged in marketing endeavors. Kotler (1976) did not treat analysis, planning, implementation, and control as generic terms applicable to any kind of managing activity outside of marketing but as terms infused with marketing concerns, namely, with exchanges with target markets.

Kotler (1976) is not unaware of the sweep of this methodological approach, for he wrote:

> The popular image of the marketing manager is that of someone whose task is primarily to stimulate demand for the company's product. However, this is too limited a view of the range of marketing tasks carried out by marketing managers. Marketing management is the task of regulating the level, timing, and character of demand in a way that will help the organization achieve its objectives. (p. 8)

These objectives, it must be remembered, need not be confined to stimulating purchases among members of a customer market; they could include, as Kotler (1976) noted earlier, getting citizens to vote for a certain candidate, legislators to pass or defeat a certain bill, mass media to provide more favorable publicity, and the like. The picture that emerges, then, is one in which all managers in an organization, in spite of their different titles, are really dealing with different markets and, therefore, the "marketing principles apply with equal force" to all these managers. This means, then, that managers of production, finance, personnel, public relations, and the like either are transformed by Kotler's marketing management methodologies into marketing managers, on the one hand, or, on the other, have their different functions subsumed under the management methodologies of marketing.

This would hold especially for public relations, whether conceived as a management function or a technical activity confined to producing publicity materials. In the former case, the business of analysis, planning, implementation, and control would be directed at a market and, therefore, would transform the public relations function into a marketing function, and in the latter case, public relations as publicity would be regarded as a tactic designed to attain some larger marketing goal. In either case, there is little need to distinguish between public relations and marketing.

Not everyone, however, is willing to accept Kotler's view of the centrality of the marketing function in an organization or its dominant role in shaping an organization's policies or action (Smith, 1990). Bennett and Cooper (1981), for example, saw some serious limitations to assign marketing a dominant role. They wrote: "Strict adherence to the marketing concept has damaged American industry . . . It has shifted the strategic focus of the firm away from the product to other elements of the marketing mix, elements that can be manipulated very successfully in the short-run, but leave the business vulnerable in the longer term" (p. 52). Moreover, they argued the heavy emphasis on marketing has obscured some important aspects of the functioning of business organizations. The view of putting the customer first or allowing the customer to dictate the type of products to fulfill his wants and needs has detracted from the quality of the product itself. Hayes and Abernathy (1980), in turn, went further, suggesting that shortcomings in marketing endeavors have detracted from sound corporate strategy and this, in turn, may lead to more serious consequences, such as the loss of competitiveness in the world trading arena. By using various techniques to determine consumer awareness of products, brand images, brand switching, and the like, marketing managers are able to make short-term adjustments in marketing strategies; however, in the longer term, as Drucker and others have observed, difficulties begin to emerge.

Consumers—looking at some of the consequences of poor quality of goods or services, deceptive advertising, the spewing out of hazardous waste during the production process, and the manufacturing of unsafe goods or the marketing of foodstuffs that are dangerous to health—do not feel that their needs or wants really are being met by modern marketing techniques. In addition, as Sethi (1979) pointed out, marketing activities of individual firms have second-order effects that extend far beyond the boundaries of the parties to the immediate exchange; these second-order effects, if ignored, could be serious not only for the individual firm but also for society at large.

But even looking at marketing in the short run, the acceptance of the doctrine that marketers should know and fulfill the needs and wants of consumers raises the specter of marketers being engaged in psychological therapy on a grand scale in their efforts to meet these needs and wants so that consumers can be made more comfortable, psychologically. Even more to the point are the limited number of problems that can be solved by marketing techniques. Marketing principles, whether of the more traditional kind or of those enunciated by Kotler, have no direct application in practice to a score of problems that beset various organizations, especially businesses—litigation, labor contract negotiations, absenteeism, low morale, interdepartment rivalry, dishonest managers or workers, the spread of drugs in the work force, confrontations by activist groups, and strikes, to mention the more obvious ones. Little is gained by trying to bring these kinds of problems under the marketing umbrella in the belief that they are problems in which people manifest needs and wants. They simply are not the problems that traditionally are dealt with or solved by marketing managers.

THE THEORETICAL FOUNDATION

This, then, brings us to the task of clarifying the area of jurisdiction in an organization and the set of responsibilities of public relations management. As conceptualized here, public relations management is an administrative activity directed at a certain class of problems that lie outside the domain of marketing management. In undertaking this task, it first is necessary to identify the theoretical foundation upon which public relations management rests. Hence, the argument presented here holds that such foundation not only exists but that it is derived, at a minimum, from four conceptual systems:

1. *Interorganizational theory* (Aldrich, 1975, 1979; Blau & Scott, 1962; Brinkerhoff & Kuntz, 1972; Evan, 1978; Meyer & Scott, 1983; Negandhi, 1975), which constitutes a set of concepts dealing with the emergence and social interrelationships of constellations and subclusters of institutions and organizations, their patterns of interactions and interdependencies.

2. *Management and decision theory* (Ackoff & Sasieni, 1968; Alderson, 1956; Koontz & O'Donnell, 1976; Longenecker & Pringle, 1981; Massie, 1971; Miller & Star, 1960, 1967; Misshauk, 1979; Newman & Warren, 1977; Radford, 1981; Richmond, 1968; Robbins, 1976; Sasieni, Yaspor, & Friedman, 1959; Siemens, Marting, & Greenwood), which deals with the tasks and responsibilities of management and the nature of decision making under conditions of certainty, risk, and uncertainty.

3. *Communication theory* (DeFleur & Dennis, 1988; Foss, Fuss, and Trapp, 1985; Infante, Rancer, & Womack, 1990; Littlejohn, 1983; McQuail, 1983; Roloff & Miller, 1980; Rice & Paisley, 1981; Rosengren, 1980; Sereno & Mortensen, 1970; Severin & Tankard, 1988; Tan, 1981), which treats concepts dealing with the various components, structure, functions, and processes of various configurations of one-way and two-way symbolic transactions in interpersonal, group, and institutional contexts.

4. *Conflict-resolution theory* (Boulding, 1962; Carpenter & Kennedy, 1988; Kriesberg, 1982; Pneuman & Bruehl, 1982; Raiffa, 1982; Rapoport, 1953, 1974; Schelling, 1963; Thomas & Bennis, 1972; Dahrendroff, 1965; Robbins, 1974), which deals with the nature of disputes, disagreements, controversies, and confrontations, their origins and impacts, and with choice-making behavior and strategies in social situations under conditions where values and conditions are in conflict.

The conceptual framework of public relations management, derived from identifiable theoretical foundations, says in simple terms that social conflict, and its opposite, social cooperation, constitute the units of analysis for public relations executives (Ehling, 1975, 1981, 1984, 1985, 1987). They, in their managerial roles, must calculate the seriousness (and, hence, disruptiveness) and costs of actual or potential conflict (disputes, disagreements, controversies, or confrontations). They must do this by knowing, usually through research, the nature of the social settings and the networks of interacting organizations and institutions in which cooperation and conflict are made manifest. At the same time, they must determine when communication of a negotiational type becomes the appropriate and principal means (course of action, strategy) for mitigating or mediating conflict in the search for common grounds to reach an agreement and cooperation.

This conceptual scheme stands in contrast not only to the primary mission of marketing management, but also to marketing's view of public relations activity. Marketing communication can be understood as not only the main component of the sales promotion effort within the marketing mix, but also as an activity that can be performed without reliance on the conflict-resolution role of public relations. Moreover, marketing communication also can be practiced without being required to reduce public relations to a minor publicity-seeking activity within the marketing operations under conditions where public relations is drained of its intellectual content and administrative responsibilities.

To further clarify the nature of public relations management, there also is a need to point out the different meanings assigned to the term *public relations*. As Cutlip and Center (1978) noted, the term is used in at least three senses: the relationship with an organization's publics or constituents, the means used to achieve favorable relationships, and the quality or status of the relationship. Thus, the one term is used to label both means and ends, to name a condition, and to express the actions taken in relation to that condition.

Moreover, public relations is used as a noun: "How's your public relations?" It also is used as a verb: "They really PRed that situation." And, it is used as a modifier: "It was a public relations triumph."

Many top executives multiply the confusion by allowing the use of other terms to identify departments performing a public relations function, such as "corporate relations," "public affairs," "public communications," "public-sector program," to name a few. In part, some of this confusion can be cleared away when more top executives come to understand the distinction between public relations as an operating concept of administration and public relations as a specialized staff function serving other administrators.

Mass media representatives (reporters, editors, television newscasters) also have contributed to the misuse and abuse of the term *public relations*. Always looking for some "villain" or shifty character to expose, the mass media people have found it convenient to stereotype public relations practitioners who they regard as essentially engaged in deception; they also have found it easy to editorialize under the guise of news reporting by labeling any activity of which they disapprove as a public relations and, hence, a deceptive endeavor. Unhappily, there are just enough people around who employ the term as a cover for bogus operations to lend some credence to the disparaging view held by mass media representatives.

Finally, there are those in the marketing and advertising fields who long have held the belief that public relations is a term to be applied to publicity activities—activities that they believe should be part of a company's sales promotion effort as a supplemental in aiding advertising and personal salesmanship. Hence, they see public relations practitioners performing these activities as low-level technicians who generate and distribute copy, leaving the problem-solving, policy-making functions to higher level executives or, preferably, to the head of the marketing department.

Trying to understand public relations by grasping the meanings of words inevitably leads one into a semantic melee in which everyone makes up his or her own definitional rules. A more promising perspective focuses not on words and definitions but on the social milieu generated by human activity. In this milieu, social units—organizations and social groupings—do things and have things done to them. To speak of the social is to speak of actors—persons in roles and organizations in institutional sets (Blau & Scott, 1962; Emery & Trist, 1965; Evan, 1978; Goffman, 1967), which, in turn, presupposes interaction and transactions among social groupings with interdependencies that lead to social integration.

Cooperation and coordination do not occur easily. They require communication, negotiation, bargaining, and other types of mediating strategies by which differences are resolved, interests are reconciled, conflict and discord minimized, and tentative and workable agreements are reached. These activities make up an ongoing process in which old coalitions are disbanded and new ones formed, old alliances abandoned and new ones struck, old relationships altered and new ones constructed.

It is in this kind of social context that public relations activity has its roots. Thus, appropriate disciplinary approaches to the study of public relations management are social psychology and sociology. They stand in contrast to those of marketing, which rest on microeconomics (the theory of the firm) and on the psychology of consumer behavior (see, e.g., Britt, 1967; Schwartz, 1982, pp. 141–182). Within a sociological framework, organizations and social groupings should be viewed as interdependent social collectivities.

The social focus of public relations can be seen in its use of the term publics in contrast to the use of the term market in marketing. The difference between a public and a market is conceptualized in detail in chapter 6—which discusses a number of segmentation theories used in the two fields. The essential difference is that organizations create markets out of a larger population of potential consumers. They create markets by identifying the most likely consumers for a product or service. Publics, in contrast, are social in nature, and they create themselves. They arise around the consequences that the decisions made by the management of an organization have on people inside or outside the organization who did not make the decision. Once publics develop around these consequences — or problems — they organize to create issues with which organizations must deal through communication and negotiation.

Interdependence of an organization and publics has many dimensions — social, political, economic, legal, cultural, and psychological. An interdependency may be balanced or skewed. *Balanced* means that a relationship occurs between relatively equal units, measured in terms of power, under circumstances in which none of the participants can dictate or issue commands to another. *Skewed* means inequality, measured in terms of a social unit being able to dominate another.

Interdependencies, whether balanced or skewed, always are filled with tensions as the social actors vie with each other to dominate or avoid domination. These manifestations may be as large and complex as the continuous conflict between the Congress and presidency in American politics or the billion-dollar leveraged buyouts and takeovers in the American marketplace. They may be as trivial and commonplace as ordinary business endeavors in which vendors want to sell high and customers want to buy low. Or, they may be unexpected and destructive as when President Reagan, during his first term in office, fired members of the striking airport controllers union and, in the process, destroyed the union.

An organization must monitor the social milieu in which it operates to determine the threats or opportunities that an environment provides. Threats or opportunities occur in social interactions and relationships. Opportunities call for social cooperation and coordination; threats reflect conflict (discord, disagreement, dissensus) and the lack of coordination. The milieu for public relations, therefore, is broader than it is for marketing. Whereas the people who make up a market are concerned only about the characteristics of products and their availability, publics are concerned about one or more aspects of the entire behavior of an organization. Marketing, therefore, is concerned with consumers; public relations also must be concerned with employees, shareholders, government officials, and community members, among others. Marketing and public relations complement each other most often in the consumer component of an organization's environment. Marketing communicates about an available or potential product or service. Public relations, for example, gets involved when an unsafe or unsatisfactory product or the production of that product or service creates a problem — which causes people to form into a public rather than a market (e.g., consumerism).

Social groups (including nation states) deal with actual or potential conflict in many ways. They may resort to police actions or physical violence as in strikebreaking, gang warfare, or wars. Conflict can be resolved or dissolved by mergers, as in unfriendly buyouts and takeovers where differences are resolved in the marketplace. It also can be resolved by political means such as legislative debates or by voting in a referendum. Under certain conditions, however, communication can resolve conflict. To do so, communication must be designed and implemented bilaterally, message exchange must be bidirectional, and the purpose of communication must be to attain or maintain cooperation.

Efforts to use communication to reduce conflict put meaning into such general statements about the mission of public relations as the "fostering of good will between a company and its public," "promotion of good will and understanding between a business and the public," "establishment of a mutually beneficial relationship between an organization and its publics," and "identification of the policies and procedures of an individual or organization with the public interest."

In a complex society, however, communication as a primary means for resolving disagreements cannot be left to chance. If it is, communication seldom will be employed, and other means will be used that are less appropriate. In short, communication to reduce conflict and to induce cooperation must be managed.

The primary purpose of public relations management—the end state it seeks—differs fundamentally, therefore, from that of marketing management. Marketing attempts to maintain a positive slope of the demand curve, a function that has little in common with maximizing cooperation over conflict or with the reconciliation of disputes. Marketing management attempts to attain its primary mission via a marketing mix made up of the four Ps—product planning, pricing, placement, and promotion (Kotler, 1976, 1988).

Public relations management, in contrast, fulfills its mission by creating a special kind of communication system, one that is designed jointly by the parties of an actual or potential conflict situation. This system is based on two-way exchange of messages about issues of concern to the contending parties. It takes the form of what Calhoun (1988) called a dialogue and argument about public issues that goes beyond the revealing of private opinion to the forming of public opinion—the same sense in which Habermas (1962, 1964) referred to public opinion. Therefore, public relations consists of more than simply partaking of a common set of communications, as in hearing the same radio or television broadcasts.

Mass media presentations—whether news, publicity, or product advertising—are designed unilaterally without involving members of the intended audience. Public relations communication, in contrast, is the product of a joint endeavor mutually entered into by the participating parties, best exemplified by the coming together of contending parties in labor-management negotiation. Such communication takes place in two stages, in the sense that contending parties first must determine where they will meet and the items on the agenda before they can communicate and negotiate about their differences.

This approach essentially reflects the symmetrical worldview described in chapter 2 and the two-way symmetrical model of public relations described in chapter 11. It is not a new approach in public relations. Examples of it can be found throughout the history of public relations practice. A good example is the early work done by Ivy L. Lee in resolving conflict between the press and the railroads and the press and coal operators (see, e.g., Hiebert, 1966). More recently, the approach was described in an article in *Public Relations Journal* by Gossen and Sharp (1987) referred to earlier.

For Gossen and Sharp (1987) win-win negotiation (also known as *integrative negotiation*) is the key to lasting success in dispute resolution. It differs radically from the win-lose (zero-sum) mode common in business-to-business transactions. Win-lose bargaining is based on power and persuasion and pays little attention to the wants, needs, or desires of the other parties.

In disputes about public policy, however, zero-sum agreements that favor business interests over public interests often are short-lived or are over-turned by lawsuits initiated by unsatisfied stakeholders (see also the discussion of activists in chapter 19). Win-win communication reaches out to stakeholders seeking to satisfy their underlying interests. As Gossen and Sharp (1987) noted, the philosophies underlying these two bargaining positions differ, therefore, as much as the difference between the process used by a marriage counselor and that used by a used car salesman unloading a lemon. What is unique about dispute resolution in public relations is that it creates and manages communication channels rather than relying on existing channels such as the mass media.

In short, the communication system developed under public relations management is interpersonally focused, bilaterally designed, bidirectionally oriented, and organized in two stages. These attributes set public relations communication apart from, and sometimes in opposition to, marketing communication. In contrast to public relations, marketing communication is characterized by unilateral design, unidirectional message flow, and one-stage operation—with an aim of persuasion to boost sales or increase a company's market share.

From the discussion thus far in this chapter, it should be clear that public relations is a management function engaged in the general activities associated with any management endeavor—conceptualizing, planning, organizing, directly, evaluating, and adapting. Its basic commitment is to assess the environment of the organization of which it is a part to determine the threats and opportunities confronting that organization. To fulfill this commitment, public relations management must focus on problems that can be identified uniquely as belonging to a public relations context.

By using such conceptual schemes as interorganizational theory (see chapter 3), conflict resolution theory (see chapter 11), management/decision theory (see chapters 4 and 10), and communication theory (see chapter 7), one can derive a rationale for public relations management that is in keeping with its historical development, its place in an organization, and its administrative commitment.

Our quarrel with the marketing perspective on public relations is that it does not provide conceptual, organizational, or administrative reasons why public relations should be subsumed under marketing management. The attempts by marketers, in the workplace or in academic settings, to make public relations subservient to marketing management only leads to redefining public relations as product publicity and as strictly a technical function.

Marketing management already possesses product publicity as one of several techniques that it can use for sales promotion, in general, and for marketing communication, in particular. What is to be gained by calling the same activity by two names (marketing communication and marketing public relations)?

The marketing vision of public relations makes that function unsuitable for solving problems that exist independently of those found in the marketplace. If these problems — including social conflict — are not accorded proper regard by the central management of an organization, there might not be an organization around to worry about problems in the marketplace.

Both marketing and public relations are important functions for an organization. Subsuming public relations into marketing, however, deprives the organization of one of those two critical functions. Therefore, we believe that excellent public relations departments exist separately from marketing departments; or, at least, the two functions are conceptually and operationally distinct within the same department. As a result, we can conclude this chapter with the following proposition:

Proposition 1: The public relations function of excellent organizations exists separately from the marketing function, and excellent public relations departments are not subsumed into the marketing function.

REFERENCES

Ackoff, R. L., & Sasieni, M. (1968). *Fundamentals of operations research.* New York: Wiley.

Alderson, W. (1956). *Marketing behavior and executive action.* Homewood, IL: Irwin.

Aldrich, H. E. (1975). An organization-environment perspective on cooperation and conflict between organizations in the manpower training system. In A. R. Negandhi (Ed.), *Interorganizational theory* (pp. 49–70). Kent, OH: Kent State University Press.

Aldrich, H. E. (1979). *Organizations and environments.* Englewood Cliffs, NJ: Prentice-Hall.

Bennett, R. C., & Cooper, R. G. (1981, November-December). The misuse of marketing: An American tragedy. *Business Horizons,* pp. 51–61.

Blau, P. H., & Scott, W. R. (1962). *Formal organizations*. San Francisco: Chandler.

Boulding, K. E. (1962). *Conflict and defense: A general theory*. New York: Harper & Row.

Brinkerhoff, M. B., & Kuntz, P. R. (1972). *Complex organizations and their environments*. Dubuque, IA: Brown.

Britt, S. H. (1967). *Consumer behavior and the behavioral sciences*. New York: Wiley.

Buskirk, H. B., & Rothe, J. T. (1970). Consumerism—An interpretation. *Journal of Marketing, 34*(4), 61–65.

Calhoun, C. (1988). Populist politics, communications media, and large scale societal integration. *Sociological Theory, 6,* 219–241.

Carpenter, S. L., & Kennedy, W. J. D. (1988). *Managing public disputes*. San Francisco: Jossey-Bass.

Castaldi, M. L. (1991). FDA writing tougher prescriptions for pharmaceutical marketing. *Public Relations Journal, 47*(9), 14–16.

Cutlip, S. E., & Center, A. H. (1978). *Effective public relations* (5th ed.). Englewood Cliffs, NJ: Prentice-Hall.

Cutlip, S. E., & Center, A. H. (1985). *Effective public relations* (6th ed.). Englewood Cliffs, NJ: Prentice-Hall.

Dahrendroff, R. (1965). *Class and class conflict in industrial society*. London: Routledge & Kegan Paul.

DeFleur, M. R., & Dennis, E. E. (1988). *Understanding mass communication*. Boston: Houghton Mifflin.

Dilenscheider, R. L. (1987, November). *Corporate accountability with constituent publics*. Paper presented at the annual meeting of the Corporate Section of the Public Relations Society of America, Los Angeles.

Drobis, D. R. (1991). Taking corporate strategy seriously. *Public Relations Journal, 47(8),* 31–32.

Drucker, P. F. (1969, September). Business responds to consumerism. *Business Week*.

Drucker, P. F. (1980). *Managing in turbulent times*. New York: Harper & Row.

Drug executives predict greater role of public relations. (1991, August). *Public Relations Journal*, p. 16.

Ehling, W. P. (1975). PR administration, management science, and purposive systems. *Public Relations Review, 1*(2), 15–42.

Ehling, W. P. (1981, August). *Toward a theory of public relations management: Application of purposive and conflict theory to communication*. Paper presented at the meeting of the Association for Education in Journalism, East Lansing, MI.

Ehling, W. P. (1984). Application of decision theory in the construction of a theory of public relations management I. *Public Relations Research & Education, 1*(2), 25–38.

Ehling, W. P. (1985). Application of decision theory in the construction of a theory of public relations management II. *Public Relations Research & Education, 1*(2), 4–22.

Ehling, W. P. (1987, May). *Public relations functions and adversarial environment*. Paper presented at the meeting of the International Communication Association, Montreal.

Emery, F. E., & Trist, E. L. (1965). The causal texture of organizational environments. *Human Relations, 18,* 21–32.

Evan, W. M. (Ed.). (1978). *Inter-organizational relations*. Philadelphia: University of Pennsylvania Press.

Foss, S. K., Foss, K. A., & Trapp, R. (1985). *Contemporary perspectives on rhetoric*. Prospect Heights, IL: Waveland.

Goffman, I. (1967). *Interaction ritual*. Garden City, NY: Anchor.

Gossen, R., & Sharp, K. (1987). Managing dispute resolution. *Public Relations Journal, 43*(12), 35–38.

Habermas, J. (1962). *The theory of communicative action and lifeworld and reason: rationalization of society* (Vol. 1) (T. McCarthy, Trans.). Boston: Beacon.

Habermas, J. (1964). *The theory of communicative action and lifeworld and system: A critique of functionalist reason* (Vol. 2) (T. McCarthy, Trans.). Boston: Beacon.

Hayes, R. H., & Abernathy, W. J. (1980, July-August). Managing our way to economic decline. *Harvard Business Review,* pp. 67–77.

Hiebert, R. E. (1966). *Courtier to the crowd.* Ames: Iowa State University Press.

Infante, D. A., Rancer, A. S., & Womack, D. E. (1990). *Building communication theory.* Prospect Heights, IL: Waveland Press.

Klapper, J. T. (1960). *The effects of mass communications.* Glencoe, IL: Free Press.

Koontz, H., & O'Donnell, C. (1976). *Management: A systems and contingency analysis of management functions* (6th ed.). New York: McGraw-Hill.

Kotler, P. (1976). *Marketing management* (3rd ed.). Englewood Cliffs, NJ: Prentice-Hall.

Kotler, P. (1982). *Marketing for nonprofit organizations* (2nd ed.). Englewood Cliffs, NJ: Prentice-Hall.

Kotler, P. (1986). Megamarketing. *Harvard Business Review, 64*(2), 30–32.

Kotler, P. (1988). *Marketing management* (5th ed.). Englewood Cliffs, NJ: Prentice-Hall.

Kriesberg, L. (1982). *Social conflicts* (2nd ed.). Englewood Cliffs, NJ: Prentice-Hall.

Lazarsfeld, P. F., Berelson, B., & Gaudet, H. (1948). *The people's choice.* New York: Columbia University Press.

Littlejohn, S. W. (1983). *Theories of human communication* (2nd ed.). Belmont, CA: Wadsworth.

Longenecker, J. G., & Pringle, C. D. (1981). *Management* (5th ed.). Columbus, OH: Merrill.

Massie, J. L. (1971). *Essentials of management* (2nd ed.). Englewood Cliffs, NJ: Prentice-Hall.

McDaniel, C., Jr. (1979). *Marketing: An integrated approach.* New York: Harper & Row.

McQuail, D. (1983). *Mass communication theory.* Newbury Park, CA: Sage.

Meyer, J. W., & Scott, W. R. (1983). *Organizational environments, ritual and rationality.* Beverly Hills, CA: Sage.

Miller, D. W., & Starr, M. K. (1960). *Executive decisions and operations research.* Englewood Cliffs, NJ: Prentice-Hall.

Miller, D. W., & Starr, M. K. (1967). *The structure of human decisions.* Englewood Cliffs, NJ: Prentice-Hall.

Misshauk, M. (1979). *Management: Theory and practice.* Boston: Little, Brown.

Negandhi, A. R. (Ed.). (1975). *Interorganization theory.* Kent, OH: Center for Business & Economic Research.

Newman, W. H., & Warren, E. K. (1977). *The process of management: Concepts, behavior, and practice* (4th ed.). Englewood Cliffs, NJ: Prentice-Hall.

Pneuman, R., & Bruehl, M. E. (1982). *Managing conflict.* Englewood Cliffs, NJ: Prentice-Hall.

Radford, K. J. (1981). *Modern management decision making.* Reston, VA: Reston Publishing.

Raiffa, H. (1982). *The art and science of negotiation.* Cambridge, MA: Harvard University Press.

Rapoport, A. (1953). *Operational philosophy.* New York: Wiley.

Rapoport, A. (1974). *Conflict in man-made environment.* Harmondsworth, England: Penguin Books.

Rice, R. E., & Paisley, W. J. (Eds.). (1981). *Public communication campaigns.* Newbury Park, CA: Sage.

Richmond, S. B. (1968). *Operations research in management decisions.* New York: Ronald.

Robbins, S. P. (1974). *Managing organizational conflict.* Englewood Cliffs, NJ: Prentice-Hall.

Robbins, S. P. (1976). *The administrative process.* Englewood Cliffs, NJ: Prentice-Hall.

Roloff, M. E., & Miller, G. R. (Eds.). (1980). *Persuasion: New directions in theory and research*. Newbury Park, CA: Sage.

Rosengren, K. E. (1980). Mass media and social change: Some current approaches. In E. Inkatz & T. Szecsko (Eds.), *Mass media and social change*. Beverly Hills, CA: Sage.

Sasieni, M., Yaspor, A., & Friedman, L. (1959). *Operations research*. New York: Wiley.

Schnelling, T. C. (1963). *The strategy of conflict*. New York: Oxford University Press.

Schwartz, G. (1982, October 15). Public relations gets short shrift from new managers. *Marketing News*.

Sereno, K. K., & Mortensen, C. D. (1970). *Foundations of communication theory*. New York: Harper & Row.

Sethi, P. (1979). *Promises of good life: Social consequences of private marketing decisions*. Homewood, IL: Irwin.

Severin, W. J., & Tankard, J. W., Jr. (1988). *Communication theories* (2nd ed.). New York: Longman.

Siemens, N., Marting, C. H., & Greenwood, F. (1973). *Operations research*. New York: Free Press.

Shimp, T. A., & DeLozier, M. W. (1986). *Promotion management and marketing communications*. New York: Dryden.

Smith, N. C. (1990). *Morality and the market: Consumer pressure for corporate accountability*. London: Routledge.

Stanley, R. E. (1982). *Promotion: Advertising, publicity, personal selling, sales promotion* (2nd ed.). Englewood Cliffs, NJ: Prentice-Hall.

Tan, A. S. (1981). *Mass communication theories and research*. Columbus, OH: Grid.

Thomas, J. M., & Bennis, W. G. (Eds.). (1972). *Management of change and conflict*. Baltimore: Penguin.

Werner, L. R. (1991, August). Marketing strategies for the recession. *Management,* pp. 29–30.

14

The Organization of the Public Relations Function

David M. Dozier
San Diego State University

Larissa A. Grunig
University of Maryland

ABSTRACT

Previous chapters have maintained that public relations must be placed high in the organizational hierarchy and that it must be practiced strategically if it is to make the organization more effective — and, thus, to be excellent. This chapter builds on this logic to show that the public relations function should be consolidated in a single department rather than distributed as a technical support function among a number of departments. Logically, public relations cannot be placed high in the organization and its senior manager cannot be part of the dominant coalition if the function is distributed throughout the organization. The chapter continues that logic to show that public relations departments should be organized flexibly enough to adapt to changing strategic publics. It adds, however, that organizations often do not organize public relations in this way because historical inertia keeps the function organized in the way it always has been in the past.

This chapter considers the structure of public relations units (departments) within organizations. We first pose a theoretical framework for explaining and predicting various structures of public relations units, based on linkage between organizational environment, overall organizational structure, and structure of the public relations unit. Using that theory, we analyze empirical data that provide only modest support for that theory. Finally, we reassess our theory, borrowing heavily from the power-control perspectives in organizational theory to suggest new strategies for studying the structure of public relations in organizations.

OPEN-SYSTEMS THEORY

At the highest level of abstraction, public relations can be understood using concepts of open-systems theory. In this chapter, we start with systems theory and then derive middle-level theory specific to organizations. Cutlip, Center, and Broom (1985) stated that there is "disagreement even among practitioners as to what would be the 'right' structural setup" (p. 80) for the public relations function within organizations. Although this may be true, open-systems theory provides a basis for locating the function within an organization's structure, suggests how publics ought to be defined, and how the function helps the organization adapt to or control its environment.

Organizations differ in the *vertical* location of the function. Some organizations locate the function high in the organizational hierarchy, reporting directly to the chief executive officer or administrator. Other organizations subordinate the function to a lower hierarchical position, reporting to marketing, personnel, legal, or other executives at a higher level. Some organizations consolidate the function in a single unit; others spread the function among a number of departments and organizational units. Some organizations use outside consultants exclusively to perform the function; others depend entirely on an internal public relations unit. Many use a combination of both internal practitioners and outside consultants.

As J. Grunig and Hunt (1984) indicated, public relations units differ in their *horizontal* structure. These include structure by publics, communication technique, management process, geographic region, account executive system, and organizational subsystem. Whatever approach is followed, including combinations of these, open-systems theory suggests that emphasis should be placed on decentralization and flexibility within the public relations unit. Tasks forces or work groups are pulled together from various subunits of the public relations department (and other departments as well) to solve specific problems. Once the problem is solved, the task force is dissolved. The human and other organizational resources are reassigned to other problems or opportunities; new task forces or work groups are formed.

Normative Issues

Using open-systems concepts, where in the organization chart does the public relations unit belong? To which office should the function report? How should the offices and roles within the public relations unit be organized? How should publics be defined? Although no single organizational structure can be determined to be "ideal" for all organizations and all environments, open-systems theory suggests that certain attributes are desirable for structuring the function, contingent upon the environment and the organization's overall structure.

When an organization is viewed as an open system, the public relations function takes on special significance. As J. Grunig and Hunt (1984) argued, organizations must contend with interpenetrating systems. These interpenetrating systems affect the survival and growth of organizations by allowing them (or not allowing them) to exist and operate, by providing (or not providing) needed system inputs, and by utilizing (or not utilizing) system outputs (p. 141).

Organizational Autonomy. If organizations were wholly autonomous—able to pursue organizational goals and objectives unfettered by their environments—they could operate like closed systems. However, environments change and all environments are to some degree threatening to the organization's survival and growth. Like a perfect vacuum, the fully autonomous organization is an idealization that has no real-world manifestation. Organizations, however, differ in the degree to which their environments are turbulent and threatening.

The function of public relations in an open-systems framework is to help the managerial subsystem of the organization adapt to interpenetrating systems (Cutlip et al., 1985, p. 187). The public relations function is part of the *adaptive* subsystem. This subsystem must be closely linked to the *managerial* subsystem, which controls and directs the other subsystems of production, supportive/disposal, and maintenance (Argyris, 1964; Cutlip et al., 1985; Katz & Kahn, 1978).

Open Versus Closed Systems. Organizations vary in the degree to which they function as open systems. Therefore, organizations vary in the degree to which the public relations function, as part of the adaptive subsystem, is linked to the managerial subsystem. If relatively closed, an organization will devote few organizational resources to operations of its adaptive subsystem. Further, the adaptive subsystem will not be closely linked to the managerial subsystem.

If relatively open, on the other hand, an organization devotes relatively high levels of organizational resources to its adaptive subsystem. The managerial subsystem is closely linked to the adaptive subsystem into many of its control and adjudication decisions. The open organization requires much information from its adaptive subsystem to maintain *homeostasis,* a relatively enduring but changeable goal state. The open organization is more likely to change its internal structures and processes, an operation called *morphogenesis.* To do this, considerable input is required from the adaptive subsystem. The exchange of information between the managerial subsystem and the adaptive subsystem is of increased importance in an open-systems organization.

Functionalism.   Without doubt, the application of open-systems theory to the structuring and functioning of public relations units in organizations has strong normative connotations. Bell and Bell (1976) articulated this when they contrasted *functional* and *functionary* public relations. They defined functionary public relations as the supply of information outward from the organization to interpenetrating systems in the environment. This activity is functionary because it is relatively uninformed about the effectiveness of such communication efforts. Functionary public relations is not concerned with organizing inputs and providing feedback to the organization about its environment. Functionary practitioners do not monitor or scan the organization's environment, nor do they evaluate the impact of their programs. In short, the function is emersed in the "how" of outward communication but isolated from the "why" and "with what effect" dimensions of such activities. The strategic planning that dictates communication outward from the organization to publics is done by other subsystems in the organization.

Functional public relations, on the other hand, participates in management decision making (Bell & Bell, 1976). This is because practitioners organize inputs from the environment and provide feedback on the success or failure of organizational efforts to adapt to interpenetrating systems in the environment. That is, public relations is a clear component of the adaptive subsystem and closely linked to the managerial subsystem.

When public relations is functional, it is proactive. The function anticipates problems and opportunities in the environment and works closely with the managerial subsystem to control or dominate those interpenetrating systems in order to maintain homeostasis. More important, functional public relations helps the managerial subsystem adapt to interpenetrating systems by facilitating morphogenesis, the change of internal structures and processes to adapt to changes in the environment.

Making Norms Explicit.   The normative component of this analysis, then, is that practitioners and public relations units should be functional rather than functionary. Further, there is an implicit argument that practitioners can change their practices from functionary to functional by reconceptualizing their work as part of the adaptive subsystem. As is detailed later, this assumes that the organization has an adaptive subsystem closely linked to the managerial subsystem.

Many organizations operate like closed systems, however; such organizations only react to strong inputs from interpenetrating systems on an ad hoc, reactionary, and nonprogrammed basis. The public relations unit remains functionary and only loosely linked with the managerial subsystem because the managerial subsystem operates the organization like a closed system ensconced in a static environment. These closed organizations regard publics as static and relatively nonthreatening.

Defining Publics Dynamically

Open-systems theory suggests that the public relations function, as part of an organization's adaptive subsystem, would define publics *dynamically*. That is, the organization's turbulent and threatening environment does not permit the delineation of static publics. The adaptive subsystem detects changes and threats to organizational survival and growth in the environment. Public relations, as part of that subsystem, engages in a rational and systematic planning process to respond to or anticipate such changes and threats. As part of that planning process, the publics of public relations programs are defined dynamically. They are specific to the problems or opportunities that motivate the program.

Publics as Decisions. Cutlip et al. (1985) put dynamism in systems terms when they stated that "publics included in the system boundary are abstractions *defined by the public relations manager* applying the open systems approach" (p. 184 emphasis added). Further, "different publics, and therefore a different system boundary, must be defined for each situation or problem" (p. 184). Defining publics is a strategic *decision* of public relations managers.

Conventional public relations thinking suggests that certain types of organizations have certain types of fixed publics, or that all organizations have generic publics that transcend time and circumstances. This is antithetical to an open-systems approach to the practice of public relations.

Linkage Types. J. Grunig and Hunt (1984) provided a powerful model for defining publics dynamically. Based on organizational theories of Esman (1972), J. Grunig and Hunt specified four linkages that organizations have with interpenetrating systems. These include *functional* linkages, *enabling* linkages, *normative* linkages, and *diffused* linkages. Functional linkages are those directly involving organizational inputs (e.g., suppliers, employees) and outputs (e.g., consumers). Enabling linkages involve interpenetrating systems that provide authority and control resources that permit the organization to exist (e.g., stockholders, regulators). Normative linkages are with interpenetrating systems that share common values or face similar threats in their environments (e.g., trade associations, professional societies). Diffused linkages are with loosely structured interpenetrating systems that are not clearly formal organizations (e.g., activist publics). Linkages are not static; linkages couple and uncouple as the organization's environment changes.

When viewed as open systems, organizations define and "undefine" publics, based on the changing conditions and threats in the environment. The definition of new publics can be based on a series of conditions that indicate the likelihood of active behavior by publics. The classification of publics according to their likelihood to act is rooted in the dynamic definition of publics in an open-systems framework.

Publics and Masses. Drawing on the theoretical work of Blumer (1948, 1966), Dewey (1927), and others, J. Grunig (1978) developed a theory for determining situations under which publics emerge and take actions that affect the survival and growth of organizations. With over 5 billion people on the planet, no organization can treat all people as having equal influence on an organization's survival and growth. Therefore, organizations need to be efficient in differentiating *publics* from *masses*. After Dewey and Blumer, masses are aggregates of individuals who do not detect a problem regarding the organization and are unlikely to act. Publics, on the other hand, are people who detect a problem, communicate about that problem, and behave as a loosely structured but unified collective in a manner that affects the organization.

Consequences. How are emerging publics detected among the masses? J. Grunig (1978) argued that consequences create publics. Publics emerge from those sectors of the mass that are affected by the organization. By determining which people are affected by consequences of organizational activities, practitioners can establish linkages between the organization and potential publics. People for whom the organization has no consequences are, by definition and logic, nonpublics. However, because the environment is constantly changing, and because the organization also changes, nonpublics can emerge as publics at a later point in time. Such publics are created from nonpublics by changing consequences.

Types of Publics. Not all potential publics become active publics. J. Grunig and Hunt (1984) identified three types of publics: *latent* publics, *aware* publics, and *active* publics. Active publics have detected a problem regarding the organization or an issue important to the organization. Members of an active public have communicated about the problem or issue and are organizing to do something about it. Aware publics have detected a problem, but have not communicated with each other nor have they organized for action. Latent publics are people affected by consequences of organizational actions, and therefore are linked to the organization.

However, latent publics are unaware of these consequences; such publics have not detected a problem.

J. Grunig's (1978) theory of publics underscores the dynamic nature of defining publics according to concepts of open-systems theory. Following J. Grunig's theory, one sees the open-systems practitioner monitoring the organizational environment, ever vigilant for emergent changes or threats that may affect the organization's survival and growth. Publics are not viewed as fixed or constant. Rather, publics are defined by emergent consequences of organizational actions and issues. They are monitored as they pass from nonpublics status to latent, aware, and active publics. Action and communication strategies are implemented to change publics and adapt the organization to those publics.

Ideology and the Adaptive Subsystem

Open-systems public relations requires an organizational setting that is itself open. Specifically, the managerial subsystem first must recognize that the organizational environment is turbulent and potentially threatening. Sufficient organizational resources must be assigned to the adaptive subsystem. The ideology of the management core must be open.

Public Relations and the Adaptive Subsystem.   Organizations may have an adaptive subsystem that plays a key role in the control and adjudication decisions of the managerial subsystem. However, if the public relations function is scattered as a support activity throughout various subsystems of the organization, public relations may not be an integral part of the adaptive subsystem.

As a consequence, the function may be functionary. The organization operates like a relatively open system but the scattered public relations units do not. Access to management decision making may occur through repositioning public relations activities through environmental scanning, program evaluation, and strategic public relations planning that links public relations goals to the organizational bottom line (Dozier, 1984, 1986).

This is not the case when the public relations unit is part of the adaptive subsystem. With close ties to the managerial subsystem, practitioners define publics and media strategies dynamically. The practitioner is a problem solver, assigning communication resources where they are needed and taking them away once the problem is solved.

No Adaptive Subsystem.   On the other hand, the organization may operate like a closed system, with little or no formal adaptive subsystem. In such an organizational setting, the problem of public relations access to management decision making is severe. The public relations practitioner, if so inclined, must create an adaptive subsystem, not just become part of an existing one. Such a change may require a fundamental reorientation of the dominant coalition ideology regarding the organization's environment.

Dozier (1988, pp. 25–28) argued that a closed-systems approach to public relations results in static publics and frozen media strategies. Publics are static in that communication directed at that public is an ongoing, institutionalized activity of the public relations unit. Communication is directed toward such publics, regardless of the status of the public relations problem that initially defined that public. Further, media strategies are frozen because communication channels can become routinized for static publics. Established channels of communication are used to carry messages to unchanging publics.

The Ideal Structure

There is no organizational structure for the public relations function that will be ideal for all organizations and all environments. However, open-systems theory suggests that the public relations function as a component of the adaptive subsystem has several requirements.

Access to Management Decision Making.   The consequences that J. Grunig (1978) argued create publics are the products of organizational actions. Organizational actions are, to some degree, the product of decisions made by chief executive officers and other members of the dominant coalition. As an organization's autonomy is reduced by proliferating interpenetrating systems, the managerial subsystem must spend more resources adapting to these interpenetrating systems. The managerial subsystem needs input from the adaptive subsystem on a continuing basis, as more decisions have implications or consequences for interpenetrating systems. Linkages between the managerial and adaptive subsystems need to be closer, information exchanges more frequent.

The public relations unit needs access to management decision making. The adaptive subsystem requires up-to-date information on organization decisions and actions under consideration. Only through such information can public relations practitioners initiate proactive programs designed to prevent problems – and active publics – from emerging. Prevention is more cost-effective than repair.

Integrated Unit.   The public relations function must be integrated within a single department. Only within such a structure does the practitioner have the autonomy and mandate to define publics and channels of communication dynamically. Only in such a setting can the practitioner focus on genuine strategic problem solving, rather than routinized communicating.

Dynamic Horizontal Structures.   Dynamic public relations planning and programming suggests that the horizontal structure—the internal organization of functions and tasks within the public relations unit—is flexible, configured to meet the special demands of focal public relations problems. As the situation changes, as new problems are identified and new publics defined, the horizontal structure also changes. A dynamic public relations function requires a dynamic horizontal structure.

THE HAGE-HULL TYPOLOGY

To link open-systems theory to the structure of public relations units, constructs of middle-level organizational theory are helpful. Hage and Hull (1981) developed a typology that links overall organizational structure to the environmental niche in which the organization fits.

The typology is generated from combinations of two organizational factors that subsume a larger set of constructs. *Scale* represents the size and repetitiveness of events that characterize an organization's operations. *Complexity* refers to the technical sophistication or knowledge base inherent in those operations.

Types of Organizations

Juxtaposing the two variables of scale and complexity generates four normative organizational types that occupy four environmental niches. *Traditional* or craft organizations have small scale and a low knowledge base. *Mechanical* organizations are large-scale and low-complexity structures. *Organic* organizations are small in scale but high in complexity. *Mixed* mechanical/organic organizations are large-scale, high-complexity operations.

Traditional and mechanical organizations are normatively appropriate responses to static or stable environments. Organic and mixed organizations are normatively appropriate responses to turbulent environments. Schneider aka L. Grunig (1985a, 1985b) sought to link organizational types to the models of public relations practiced by those organizations.

Models of Public Relations

J. Grunig and Hunt (1984) identified four models of public relations that describe the evolution of the practice as a professional activity. The *press agentry/publicity* model describes propagandistic public relations that seeks media attention in (almost) any way possible. The *public information* model describes those programs employing "journalists-in-residence" to provide truthful and accurate information about an organization but not to volunteer negative information. The *two-way asymmetric* model uses research and scientific persuasion to identify messages most likely to produce the support of publics without having to change organizational behavior. The *two-way symmetric* model uses bargaining, negotiating, and conflict-resolution strategies to bring symbiotic changes in the knowledge, attitudes, and behavior of both publics and the organization.

Models and Systems Theory.   The press agentry/publicity and the public information models both reflect a closed-systems orientation. Communication is one-way—outward from the organization to traditionally defined publics or to an amorphous "general public." Both two-way asymmetric and symmetric public relations involve an open-systems orientation, in that practitioners collect as well as disseminate information. Information brought into the organization by practitioners is used to make strategic and tactical decisions. However, only the two-way symmetric model incorporates the concept of morphogenesis, the alteration of the organization's internal operations and structures in response to the environment.

Models and Organization Types.   Schneider (aka L. Grunig, 1985a, 1985b) studied 48 organizations from the Washington, DC, area in detail to determine if the Hage–Hull (1981) typology correlated with the four models of public relations. J. Grunig (1984) earlier had theorized that craft organizations would practice press agentry, the mechanical organization would practice public information, the organic organization would practice two-way symmetric, and the mixed organization would practice both two-way models. However, four studies that tested these relationships (Fabiszak, 1985; McMillan, 1984; E. Pollack, 1984; R. Pollack, 1986) found consistently small and statistically insignificant relationships.

Schneider's (aka L. Grunig, 1985) study, which examined these same relationships, was different. She studied her organizations intensively, collecting both qualitative and quantitative data, rather than depending on single-source questionnaire data to measure key variables. (Such single-source data were used in the other four studies.) The relationships between organization types and models of public relations are presented in Table 14.1.

Empirical Findings.   As indicated in Table 14.1, hypothesized relationships along the diagonal were confirmed for all but the organic organizations. In addition, the mixed organizations did not correlate with the two-way asymmetric model of public relations, as J. Grunig (1984) predicted. Schneider concluded (J. Grunig & L. Grunig, 1986) that the Hage–Hull (1981) typology could account for some of the variance in the

TABLE 14.1
Kendall's Tau Correlations of Hage–Hull's Four Types of Organizations with
the Four Models of Public Relations

Type of Organization (& Predicted Model)	Press Agentry	Public Information	Two-Way Asymmetric	Two-Way Symmetric
Traditional (Press Agentry)	.13*	.01	− .01	.04
Mechanical (Public Information)	.21**	.22**	.02	− .18**
Organic (2-way Symmetrical)	.03	− .08	− .02	− .01
Mixed Mech./Organic (2-way Symmetrical & 2-way Asymmetrical)	− .36	− .14	.00	.16**

Note. N = 75. From Schneider (aka L. Grunig, 1985a),
*p < .05. **p < .01.

model of public relations practiced in organizations, but that the theory was insufficient to adequately describe why public relations is practiced as it is in most organizations. Indeed, the Hage–Hull typology accounted for less then 10% of the variance in the models of public relations that organizations follow.

Organizational Types and Horizontal Structure

L. Grunig (1987) further analyzed the data from her Washington, DC, study to describe relations between horizontal structure and Hage–Hull (1981) type. This research phase was exploratory; no formal hypotheses were tested. Rather, the purpose was to see if the horizontal structure of public relations units varied across the different Hage–Hull organizational types. Practitioners in the 48 organizations studied were asked to describe the structure of the public relations unit, choosing from the seven structures explicated by J. Grunig and Hunt (1984), some combination of Grunig–Hunt structures, or some unique structure not explicated by J. Grunig and Hunt.

Findings. L. Grunig (1987) found that 53% of the organizations studied combined horizonal structures. The most common combination is by public and by communication technique. The second most common technique was by public and by internal client. Also tied for second was the combination of technique and client. Twelve percent of the organizations were organized horizontally by publics, followed by technique (5%), internal client (5%) and region of the country (4%). Sixteen percent of the organizations organized public relations along lines other than the seven identified by J. Grunig and Hunt (1984).

Implications.   The findings of this analysis are somewhat ambiguous. Does horizontal structure vary by Hage–Hull (1981) type? No, L. Grunig (1987) found no pattern in the horizontal structure by Hage–Hull type and environmental niche. According to open-systems theory, we expect organizations dealing with turbulent and threatening environments to favor flexible horizontal structures. Although the data indicate that environmental niche is not related to horizontal structure, a plurality of organizations (16%) use multiple structures. Because open-systems theory suggests that multiple structures are appropriate organizational responses to complex, threatening, and turbulent environments, does this support open-systems theory as a positive theory? Perhaps.

L. Grunig's (J. Grunig & L. Grunig, 1986; L. Grunig, 1987; Schneider [aka L. Grunig], 1985a, 1985b) stream of research indicates that open-systems theory, as incorporated in the Hage–Hull (1981) typology of environmental niches, is at best a weak positive theory. Indeed, the horizontal structures of public relations units seem idiosyncratic. Although the environmental imperative provides some explanation and prediction of the structure of public relations units, clearly other factors are also influential. Our search for additional explanatory factors has led us to a promising theoretical domain, the power-control perspective in organizational theory.

THE POWER-CONTROL PERSPECTIVE
AND PUBLIC RELATIONS

The seeming idiosyncratic character of public relations units in organizations—unresponsive to environmental pressures—provides a specific instance of the larger problem with the environmental imperative. Some organization theorists have questioned the general notion that environment (along with strategy, technology, and size) determines organizational structure. These theorists offer the power-control perspective as an alternative explanation for the generally weak relationship between environment and structure (Child, 1972; Pfeffer, 1978, 1979, 1981; Simon, 1976).

Structures That Optimize Versus Satisfice

Open-systems theory suggests that organizations select organizational structures that optimize the organization's ability to adapt or control environments. Especially when the environment is complex, turbulent, and threatening, organizations should develop optimum structures that allow the organization to cope with interpenetraing systems. Those structures should be decentralized, organic, and flexible. However, even when environmental factors are coupled with measures of strategy, technology, and size, they together account for no more than 60% of the variance in organizational structure (Ford & Slocum, 1977).

Power-control theorists argue that organizations cannot seek optimum structures because there is no consensus as to what is being optimized (Robbins, 1987, pp. 183–184). Dominant coalitions are made up of different individuals and organizational subunits with divergent interests. Although managers pay homage to optimum structure, they in actuality seek structures that *satisfice,* that are "good enough" to meet the organization's minimum needs. Environmental conditions, along with the other three factors, set broad parameters within which managers make strategic choices that optimize their own self-interests in power and control.

Structural Implications.   Dominant coalitions determine organizational structure in a manner that satisfices overall organizational needs as well as the divergent interests of members of the dominant coalition. It may be in the overall best interest of the organization — from a systems perspective — to design decentralized, informal, and organic structures. But members of the dominant coalition seek to maintain their dominant position through centralization, formalization, and simplicity (Bourgeois, McAllister, & Mitchell, 1978; Pfeffer, 1978).

Mechanistic Versus Organic Structures.   Unlike systems theory, the power-control perspective suggests that mechanistic rather than organic structures will predominate, even in the face of an uncertain environment (Bourgeois et al., 1978). This is because the self-serving structural preferences of members of the dominant coalition are not necessarily optimum from an overall organizational perspective. But these structural decisions do satisfice overall organizational needs while permitting the coalition to retain power and control through a relatively stable, unchanging organizational structure.

Historical Causal Model.   Major structural change requires something akin to a revolution, wherein the dominant coalition is reformed and new power relationships established (Pfeffer, 1978). Short of that, organizations follow an historicist causal model, where structure replicates itself over time. Broom (1986) argued that as the "boundary between the organization and its environment becomes impermeable to environmental inputs, public relations structure and process increasingly reflect historical, routine and institutionalized behaviors" (p. 7).

When the dominant coalition of an organization is relatively closed in its ideology regarding system codes concerning the environment, the public relations function is likely to reflect self-replicating patterns unrelated to conditions in the organization's environment. Consistent with J. Grunig and L. Grunig's (1986) suggestions about closed management ideology, Broom (1986) asserted that, in closed organizations, "observed public relations responses reflect the historical preferences of those with decision-making power" (p. 7).

The Infinite Loop.   Stinchcombe (1968) argued that "one set of causes *once* determined a social pattern . . . then ever since, what existed in one year produced the same thing the next year" (p. 102). An event that was once an effect—a response to an environmental condition—at one point in time becomes the cause of that same effect at later points in time. This, Stinchcomb argued, establishes an "infinite loop," where social forces act to ensure that an activity is maintained perpetually. Through this historicist model, traditions are born.

The historicist model is consistent with what the power-control perspective argues the dominant coalition will do to routinize its power relationships. Broom (1986) argued that the practice of closed-system public relations has all the earmarks of traditional, institutionalized behavior, replicating the power and control relationships of the dominant coalition. Public relations students are trained for the practice through "war stories" and "what-we-did-when-it-hit-the-fan" case studies. Public relations education, then, is among the forces of "activity preservation" that perpetuate functionary public relations.

Socializing Successors.   Stinchcombe (1968) asserted that powerholders shape their successors through control in selecting and socializing their successors. A practitioner in a closed-system organization uses similar mechanisms to groom novice practitioners to perpetuate the practice as it always has been done in that organization. Although this may not be optimum from an overall systems perspective, such replication satisfices those overall organizational needs while perpetuating the power-control relationships of the dominant coalition.

The Significant Historical Event.   Consistent with both the historicist causal model and the power-control perspective, the structure of public relations is defined by some significant event in the organization's history. Perhaps a crisis led to formation of a public relations unit to deal with a specific problem. Perhaps a CEO, a marketing VP, or some other member of the dominant coalition once decided that the organization needed public relations—and implemented a public relations department.

Routinization.   Once initiated, the public relations department "takes on a life of its own." Allied with the dominant coalition that formed it, the public relations unit seeks to replicate itself over time. Members of the dominant coalition that brought the public relations unit into existence seek to replicate it as well, because the public relations unit is part of a structure the perpetuates the dominant coalition. Through training and mechanisms of social control, the structure, plans, and programs of the public relations department are replicated in a perpetual cycle. The organization's public relations budget and commitment to the function "become survivors of routine decision making" (Broom, 1986, p. 9). The original reasons for undertaking these activities, according to the historicist causal model, "are lost in history and the system is relatively closed to new environmental inputs to the decision-making process" (Broom, 1986, p. 9). The public relations unit becomes functionary, as its original mission is lost in history.

Although functionary from an overall organizational perspective, the unit remains useful to members of the dominant coalition. The public relations unit enhances the power and stature of those to whom the unit reports. Public relations constitutes a slack resource at the disposal of the dominant coalition members who control the unit (Bourgeois, 1981).

Sunk Costs.   Part of the organization's ongoing support of the function rests on perceptions of public relations as a *sunk cost.* Stinchcombe (1968) argued that the cost of creating a new resource (like a public relations department) is not recoverable. The cost is sunk. The traditional pattern of public relations practice is maintained by the view that new practices are not "enough *more* profitable to justify throwing away the (old) resource" Innovative practices have start-up costs that traditional practices have "retired"; the effect is that "sunk costs tend to preserve a pattern of action from one year to the next" (p. 121).

Stinchcombe (1968) noted that people involved in routinized, traditional behavior often provide "a variety of unconvincing explanations" (p. 107) for their behavior. Broom (1986) argued that the "ritualized" activities of many practitioners likewise defy convincing explanation. Although practitioners may not be able to provide convincing explanations for why they do what they do in a closed organization, the behavior is maintained through the infinite loop of an institutional-historicist causal structure.

Change and the Historicist Model

Stinchcombe (1968) noted that changes in the historicist model can occur when a group of power holders are "converted to a new set of values" (p. 119). This is similar to the "quasi-revolutions" required from a power-control perspective to change organizational structure (Pfeffer, 1978). This view is useful when interpreting the spread of the management by objectives (MBO) philosophy among corporate and institutional managers. Practitioners who justify next year's budget by arguing that "that's what we did last year" are rudely awakened to a new value set. Some view with horror the demand that they show linkage between public relations activities and measureable benefit to the organization.

Reactive Change.   Although the interpenetration of systems in the environment drive the organization to an open-systems orientation, the model is not simple cause-effect, as J. Grunig and L. Grunig (1986) discovered. Rather, the interpenetration of environmental systems can be dealt with proactively or reactively by the organization. The power-control perspective suggests that such change is generally reactive (Robbins, 1987, p. 197).

The choice of organizational response is driven by the "openness" or "closedness" of management ideology. That ideology of the management core is reflected in the structure and process of the adaptive subsystem, including public relations. Nor is it sufficient to simply understand the ideology of the dominant coalition. Rather, formation of the overall organizational structure and of the public relations unit must be understood in the context of the divergent interests of the dominant coalition at the time the structure was formed. Changes in organizational structure must be understood in terms of the specific power relations within the dominant coalition and the forces at play that led to structural change.

The Usefulness of Open-Systems Theory.   Where does all this leave open-systems theory? Regarding the actual behavior of organizations, dominant coalitions are unlikely to alter the structure of public relations to achieve some optimum form suggested by systems theory. The present structure satisfices; it meets the minimum needs of the overall organization. Within that latitude, the dominant coalition will seek to reduce complexity, as well as increase formalization and centralization. These actions run counter to the flexible and decentralized structure suggested by open-systems theory for the public relations department.

Researchers studying the structure of public relations units—and practitioners working in them—are advised to reconsider open-systems theory from the power-control perspective. In the final section of this chapter, we consider the structure of public relations units within organizations from a new perspective. We treat open systems as normative theory and the power-control perspective as positive theory.

IMPLICATIONS FOR RESEARCH AND PRACTICE

To summarize, open-systems theory suggests that the public relations unit should be unified within a single department rather than fragmented and distributed as a technical support function among several organizational units. Further, the public relations unit should be placed high in the organizational hierarchy. That is because public relations, as part of the adaptive subsystem, must exchange information with the managerial subsystem, must participate in strategic decision making that affects the organization's relations with internal and external publics. Regarding horizontal structure, the unit should be flexible and decentralized. As a boundary-spanning function within organizations, the public relations unit should change its structure and processes in response to environmental pressures. Such vertical and horizontal characteristics should optimize the public relations function within organizations.

These normative prescriptions of open-systems theory are unlikely to describe how organizations actually structure the public relations function. That is because the environmental imperative implicit in open-systems theory accounts only for a small amount of the variance in organizational structures. Other factors not considered by open-systems theory involve the divergent interests of members of the dominant coalition and the complex power-control relations that connect an organization together.

Open systems would have more power as a positive theory if consensus existed within dominant coalitions that organizations should seek optimum structures to control or adapt to environments. Such consensus does not exist. Rather, members of the dominant coalition seek first to maintain and enhance their control (Robbins, 1987). In so doing, the overall interests of the organization—such as optimum structure for controlling or adapting to organizational environments—are subordinated to the self-serving and divergent interests of members of the dominant coalition. The existing structure is successful, because the organization survives. Thus, the structure satisfies. Optimizing structures through change can proceed only through an understanding of power and control in organizations.

What Practitioners Can Do

How can practitioners gain the power required to change the vertical and horizontal structure of public relations in organizations? Astley and Sachdeva (1984) indicated that individuals or departments within organizations acquire the power through three mechanisms: hierarchical authority, control of resources, and network centrality. If public relations units are scattered throughout the organization, performing low-level technical functions, the public relations function has little hierarchical authority. If the public relations function is to acquire power needed to make structural changes, practitioners must seek power elsewhere, through control of scarce and valuable resources. Further, practitioners need to solve problems of importance to the organization.

Scanning Intelligence as a Scarce Resource.   What scarce and valuable resources can public relations practitioners control? Research by Dozier (1981, 1984, 1986, 1987) indicates that practitioners who engage in *environmental scanning* are more likely to participate in management decision making than practitioners who do not. Environmental scanning consists of both formal (scientific) and informal information gathering about changes and trends in the organization's environment. Practitioners use qualitative and quantitative research techniques—as well as informal, journalistic information gathering—to make their participation valuable to organizational decision makers. By collecting and controlling intelligence about the environment, practitioners become useful—even necessary—participants in strategic planning and decision making. This is one source of power that practitioners can use to redefine the public relations function and alter its vertical and horizontal structure.

Network Centrality.   Another source of power is *network centrality.* Network centrality means being in the "right" place in the organization, dealing with problems of critical importance to the organization. Some organizational units are perceived as more important than others, because they perform a function more critical to the organization's survival and growth. Changing environmental conditions may affect the network centrality of an organizational unit. Robbins (1987, p. 192) noted an increase in the power of the accounting and financial staff at Chrysler in the late 1970s as the corporation encountered major financial problems. Once those problems were reduced in the mid-1980s, the power of those staff declined.

Public relations practitioners have some discretion in the problems they select to correct. By working with publics to solve problems central to the organization's survival and growth, practitioners gain power and influence. Such strategies are risky. Failing to solve an important problem has more negative consequences than failing to solve an unimportant problem. Problem solving in general is more risky than simply generating communication at the orders of others higher in the organization. Good public relations planning—where significant and recognized problems with publics are corrected through goal-directed activities—assures the public relations unit of network centrality.

Pseudoplanning.   However, as Dozier (1985) argued, much of public relations planning is really pseudoplanning. *Process* goals, such as placing a specified number of news releases within a specified time frame, are substituted for *impact* goals, such as changing negative attitudes toward the organization among a priority public. Psuedoplanning is technician behavior masquerading as a management function. Such planning is "safe," because process goals like placing news releases are relatively easy to achieve.

Being an organized technician, as pseudoplanning implies, does not assure network centrality. Rather, such behavior simply reinforces the perception of others in the organization that public relations is a low-level output function. The strategic, problem-solving component of public relations is considered too important to be relegated to such technicians. As practitioners frequently lament, top jobs in public relations often go to people from outside public relations. The reason may be that the dominant coalition does not find management candidates among the public relations technicians in the public relations unit.

What Researchers Can Do

The environmental imperative has dominated much of our research in the 1980s. Such a paradigm seemed promising. As a positive theory, open systems seemed an ideal, high-level theory with applications to every organization and organizational setting. Indeed, research by Acharya (1981, 1983) and Johnson and Acharya (1982), among others, provides some evidence that the environmental imperative had some empirical foundation.

In 1986, however, J. Grunig and L. Grunig concluded that the particular application of open-systems theory to public relations structure, through the Hage–Hull (1981) typology, had little predictive power. The findings of J. Grunig and L. Grunig are consistent with more general research on organizations that indicate that the environmental imperative, along with other factors such as size, technology, and strategy, provides only moderate predictive power in explaining organizational structures. Clearly, more is going on in the formation and change of organizational structures than the influence of environment, technology, size, and strategy.

Building on Prior Research The power-control perspective provides a provocative and promising avenue for further research. First, the power-control perspective builds upon the theoretical and empirical work already completed. The power-control perspective argues that the organizational environment, along with other factors, constrain strategic choices of organizational structure available to the dominant coalition. Thus, open-systems theory does provide a partial explanation of organizational structure, contingent upon environmental conditions. But, within these constraints, the dominant coalition can select structural options that satisfice but do not optimize the organization's ability to control or adapt to its environment.

Researchers seeking to understand the seemingly idiosyncratic structures of public relations units should turn to factors suggested as important by the power-control perspective. Such researchers need to incorporate the power-control perspective in their theoretical thinking. That is, researchers must examine the ability of public relations units to control scarce and valuable resources. Researchers also must study ways public relations units establish network centrality through program planning that links public relations programs to the solution of significant, recognized organizational problems.

Methodology. Regarding methodology, the intensive approach followed by L. Grunig (1987; Schneider [aka L. Grunig], 1985a) seems most promising. In her study of 48 organizations in the Washington, DC, area, she collected information through face-to-face interviews and self-administered questionnaires. In addition, she collected annual reports, newsletters, memoranda, organization charts, news releases, and public service announcements from the organizations studied. She used purposive sampling techniques, seeking out organizations that typified key characteristics she was trying to measure. The combination of qualitative and quantitative data collection seems appropriate, for we are attempting to construct rather than test theory. An intensive, grounded theoretic approach is indicated.

The power-control perspective suggests methods appropriate for the constructs we need to measure. Regarding vertical structure, purposive sampling can be used to sample organizations with unified public relations units and organizations with the function scattered among several departments. Organizations where the public relations unit answers to the CEO can be sampled along with organizations where the public relations unit is low in the organizational hierarchy. Regarding horizontal structure, organizations with flexible, decentralized public relations departments can be sampled along with organizations with rigid, centralized structures. Within organizations sampled, information should be collected from several sources. The top public relations practitioner and the person to whom that top practitioner reports are obvious sources, but others may be involved as well. Formal and informal structures should be measured.

Studying History. Perhaps most important, the history of public relations within that organization should be detailed. The power-control perspective, along with Stinchcombe's (1968) historicist causal model, suggests that the present structure was formed in response to specific historical conditions. What were the critical conditions that led to the formation of the public relations department? Who were the members of the dominant coalition that brought that formation about? This implies that retired as well as active practitioners may need to be interviewed.

Multiple Observation Techniques. Finally, a variety of qualitative and quantitative techniques should be used to assess the degree to which public relations units control scarce and valued resources. In addition, a variety of techniques should be used to assess the degree to which public relations activities are addressing significant, recognized organizational problems.

Given the intensive nature of data collected from each organization, a long-range research strategy should start with case studies. Case studies lead to the refinement of measures of key constructs and the tentative testing of relations between those constructs. As measures are refined, and as the relations between constructs are discovered, the research strategy should move from intensive to extensive methods. Fewer data are collected from each organization, but more organizations are studied. Finally, panel designs should be used to observe the change in organizational structures (both overall and within the public relations unit) over time. This permits the testing of causal models that link environmental factors, the control of scarce resources, and network centrality to emergent vertical locations and horizontal structures of public relations units.

REFERENCES

Acharya, L. (1981, August). *Effects of perceived environmental uncertainty on public relations roles.* Paper presented at the meeting of the Public Relations Division, Association for Education in Journalism, East Lansing, MI.

Acharya, L. (1983, August). *Practitioner representations of environmental uncertainty: An application of discriminant analysis.* Paper presented at the meeting of the Public Relations Division, Association for Education in Journalism and Mass Communication, Corvallis, OR.

Argyris, C. (1964). *Integrating the individual and the organization.* New York: Wiley.

Astley, W. G., & Sachdeva, P. S. (1984). Structural sources of intraorganizational power: A theoretical synthesis. *Academy of Management Review, 9*(1), 104–113.

Bell, S. E., & Bell, E. C. (1976). Public relations: Functional or functionary? *Public Relations Review, 2*(3), 51–52.

Blumer, H. (1948). Public opinion and public opinion polling. *American Sociological Review, 13,* 542–554.

Blumer, H. (1966). The mass, the public, and public opinion. In B. Berelson & M. Janowitz (Eds.), *Reader in public opinion and communication* (2nd ed., pp. 43–50). New York: Free Press.

Bourgeois, L. J. (1981). On the measurement of organizational slack. *Academy of Management Review, 6,* 30.

Bourgeois, L. J., McAllister, D. W., & Mitchell, T. R. (1978). The effects of different organizational environments upon decisions about organizational structure. *Academy of Management Journal, 21,* 508–514.

Broom, G. M. (1986, May). *Public relations roles and systems theory: Functional and historicist causal models.* Paper presented at the meeting of the Public Relations Interest Group, International Communication Association, Chicago.

Child, J. (1972). Organizational structure, environment and performance: The role of strategic choice. *Sociology, 6*(1), 1–22.

Cutlip, S. M., Center, A. H., & Broom, G. M. (1985). *Effective public relations* (6th ed.). Englewood Cliffs, NJ: Prentice-Hall.

Dewey, J. (1927). *The public and its problems.* Chicago: Swallow.

Dozier, D. M. (1981, August). *The diffusion of evaluation methods among public relations practitioners.* Paper presented at the meeting of the Public Relations Division, Association for Education in Journalism, East Lansing, MI.

Dozier, D. M. (1984). Program evaluation and roles of practitioners. *Public Relations Review, 10*(3), 13-21.

Dozier, D. M. (1985). Planning and evaluation in public relations practice. *Public Relations Review, 11*(3), 17-25.

Dozier, D. M. (1986, August). *The environmental scanning function of public relations practitioners and participation in management decision making.* Paper presented at the meeting of the Public Relations Division, Association for Education in Journalism and Mass Communication, Norman, OK.

Dozier, D. M. (1987, May). *Gender, environmental scanning and participation in management decision making.* Paper presented at the meeting of the International Communication Association, Montreal, Canada.

Dozier, D. M. (1988, May). *The vertical location of the public relations function in organizations.* Paper presented at the meeting of the Public Relations Interest Group, International Communication Association, New Orleans.

Esman, M. J. (1972). The elements of institution building. In J. W. Eaton (Ed.), *Institution building and development* (pp. 19–40). Beverly Hills, CA: Sage.

Fabiszak, D. L. (1985). *Public relations in hospitals: Testing the Grunig theory of organizations, environments and models of public relations.* Unpublished master's thesis, University of Maryland, College Park.

Ford, J. D. & Slocum, J. W. (1977). Size, technology, environment and the structure of organizations. *Academy of Management Review, 2,* 561–575.

Grunig, J. E. (1978). Describing publics in public relations: The case of a suburban hospital. *Journalism Quarterly, 55*(2), 109–118.

Grunig, J. E. (1984). Organizations, environments, and models of public relations. *Public Relations Research and Education, 1*(1), 6–29.

Grunig, J. E., & Grunig, L. S. (1986, May). *Application of open systems theory to public relations: Review of a program of research.* Paper presented at the meeting of the Public Relations Interest Group, International Communication Association, Chicago.

Grunig, J. E., & Hunt, T. (1984). *Managing public relations.* New York: Holt, Rinehart & Winston.

Grunig, L. (1987, August). *Horizontal structure in public relations: An exploratory study of departmental differentiation.* Paper presented at the meeting of the Public Relations Division, Association for Education in Journalism and Mass Communication, San Antonio.

Hage, J. & Hull, F. (1981). *A typology of environmental niches based on knowledge, technology and scale: The implications for innovation and productivity.* Working Paper No. 1, University of Maryland, Center for the Study of Innovation, Entrepreneurship, and Organizational Strategy, College Park.

Johnson, D., & Acharya, L. (1982, July). *Organizational decision making and public relations roles.* Paper presented at the meeting of the Public Relations Division, Association for Education in Journalism, Athens, OH.

Katz, D., & Kahn, R. L. (1978). *The social psychology of organizations* (2nd ed.). New York: Wiley.

McMillan, S. J. (1984). *Public relations in trade and professional associations: Location, model, structure, environment and values.* Unpublished master's thesis, University of Maryland, College Park.

Pfeffer, J. (1978). *Organizational design.* Arlington Heights, IL: AHM Publishing.

Pfeffer, J. (1979). Power and resource allocation in organizations. In B. M. Staw & G. R.

Salancik (Eds.), *New directions in organizational behavior* (pp. 235–265). Chicago: St. Clair.

Pfeffer, J. (1981). *Power in organizations.* Marshfield, MA: Pitman.

Pollack, E. J. (1984). *An organizational analysis of four public relations models in the federal government.* Unpublished master's thesis, University of Maryland, College Park.

Pollack, R. A. (1986). *Testing the Grunig organizational theory in scientific organizations: Public relations and the values of the dominant coalition.* Unpublished master's thesis, University of Maryland, College Park.

Robbins, S. P. (1987). *Organization theory* (2nd ed.). Englewood Cliffs, NJ: Prentice-Hall.

Schneider (aka Grunig), L. A. (1985a). *Organizational structure, environmental niches, and public relations: The Hage–Hull typology of organizations as predictor of communication behavior.* Unpublished doctoral dissertation, University of Maryland, College Park.

Schneider (aka Grunig), L. A. (1985b). The role of public relations in four organizational types. *Journalism Quarterly, 62*(3), 567–576.

Simon, H. A. (1976). *Administrative behavior* (3rd ed.). New York: Free Press.

Stinchcombe, A. L. (1968). *Constructing social theories.* New York: Harcourt, Brace & World.

15 Women in Public Relations: Problems and Opportunities

Linda Childers Hon
Florida Institute of Technology

Larissa A. Grunig
University of Maryland

David M. Dozier
San Diego State University

ABSTRACT

y

Our theory of excellence in communication management has shown logically that the senior public relations person must be a strategic manager, have power in the organization, and have a symmetrical worldview for public relations to make organizations more effective. What would happen to this logic, however, if the majority of public relations practitioners who are most qualified for the role of a strategic manager and a two-way symmetrical communicator are systemically excluded from that role? Such a scenario seems to be unfolding in public relations—a scenario that could diminish the excellence of public relations, to the detriment of both women and men. Women now are the majority in the field. Most public relations students are women. Education in public relations, as chapter 16 shows, enhances the likelihood that practitioners will practice excellent public relations. Yet, as this chapter shows, discrimination keeps women out of the manager role. This chapter documents the discrimination against women and argues that "making women more like men" will not solve the problem. It reviews feminist theories that show that organizations must change fundamentally to empower women. As chapter 9 showed, excellent organizations foster the careers of women, including those in public relations. Excellence in public relations, therefore, may depend on changing the way organizations and society treat women.

Both educators and practitioners have recognized that public relations has experienced an influx of women. Feminization has been at the fore of discussions about the future of the field with regard to professionalism, prestige, and salaries.

The most common theme of these discussion has been the future of the field given the "problems" feminization seems to bring (Bates, 1983; Bernstein, 1986; "Could Be Woman's Field," 1982; Lesly, 1988; "PR People Deplore," 1984; Thaler, 1986). A less common, but growing, theme has been the opportunity afforded to communications by women's emergence (Creedon, 1989, in press; L. Grunig, 1988a, 1988b, 1989b; Rakow, 1987, 1989; Toth, 1989a, 1989b, 1990).

We address feminization here by documenting gender-based inequities in salary and status within public relations. Attention is given then to problems some women encounter with advancement in organizations. A discussion of practitioner roles and issues surrounding organizational power highlight these difficulties. Next, we examine the shortcomings of some of the proposed solutions put forth by scholars and practitioners for women's achieving equity in pay and rank. As an alternative approach, we pose a feminist perspective for understanding women's repression in organizations. We conclude by outlining variants of feminist thought and discussing how feminist theory informs our understanding of women in public relations.

INEQUITIES IN SALARY AND STATUS

A flurry of recent scholarship has focused on describing the inequities in salary and organizational status that female practitioners confront. The most important strain probably is Broom's investigation of organizational roles. Also notable are the International Association of Business Communicator's (IABC) 1986 *Velvet Ghetto* project and the 1989 follow-up study, *Beyond the Velvet Ghetto*. These three ventures are reviewed next. Related research also is discussed. To conclude, current findings about women's salary and status in public relations are presented.

Research on Public Relations Roles

Probably no program of research has stimulated so much discussion about gender issues in public relations as Broom's work on organizational roles. In 1982, he discovered that men outnumber women in managerial roles, whereas women tend to cluster in technical roles (Broom, 1982). This initial finding paved the way for Broom's discovering statistically significant salary differences between male and female members of the Public Relations Society of America (Broom & Dozier, 1986). By 1986, Broom and Dozier had concluded that "professional growth in public relations is a function of the practitioner's gender and role" (p. 55).

Related Research

Broom's (1982; Broom & Dozier, 1986) seminal work set off a flurry of speculation and research about the relationship between gender, roles, and salaries within public relations. Some attempted to offer alternative explanations to the gender–salary connection. For example, Winkleman and Pollock (1987) reasoned that the median salaries of men who responded to their 1987 survey in *Public Relations Journal (PRJ)* was higher than that of women because of age and experience. That is, men have been in the field longer than women and thus are positioned in the higher paying, top jobs. Jacobson and Tortorello (1990) reported, however, that *PRJ*'s latest salary survey found the earnings gap is largest among women and men with less than 5 years of experience. And, men are more likely than women to earn $45,000 or more despite level of experience.

Along these lines, Dozier, Chapo, and Sullivan (1983) documented that salary differences between men and women in public relations could not be explained by women's lower levels of education, fewer years of experience, and a shorter tenure with their present employer. Similarly, Childers (1986) provided evidence that among practitioners in PRSA, a statistically significant relationship remained between gender and salary even after controlling for the effect of role, years in public relations, tenure in present job, participation in organizational decision making, participation in evaluation research, and type of organization.

Turk (1986) found a definitive gender–salary link among practitioners involved primarily in university relations and development. Her survey of members of the Council for Advancement and Support of Education showed that "being male adds $3,686 to annual salary—all by itself, a difference of 12 percent" (p. 20).

Theus (1985) studied University of Maryland journalism graduates and discovered that men make up 95% of those earning $45,000 or more, 70% of those earning $35,000–$45,000, and 61% of those earning $25,000–$34,000. Women, however, comprise 64% of those earning $15,000–$24,000 and 77% of those earning $10,000–$14,000.

Despite these convincing findings of an unmitigated gender–salary connection, speculation about confounding variables continues. Recently, *Public Relations Reporter* ("Data Still Don't Show," 1989) reasoned that women in public relations make less than men because paychecks reflect experience. *PR Reporter* made this argument based on findings from its annual survey that show about three fourths of the practitioners with 5 or fewer years of experience are women, whereas three fourths or more of the practitioners with 20 or more years of experience are men. *PR Reporter* maintained its position about a salary–experience link despite finding that among practitioners who have 15–19 years of experience, women still receive an average of $8,200 less than men.

Looking at the international scene, Scrimger (1985) profiled women in Canadian public relations and concluded that the status of female practitioners is inferior to that of males. She found that although women outnumber men, fewer women function as managers; and very few hold the top management positions that lead to high salaries and stature.

More recently, however, Scrimger (1989) professed guarded optimism about the future of public relations in Canada. Her interviews with female practitioners and focus groups with female and male students showed that women are being promoted and students' aspirations are uniformly high. These practitioners and students also value critical managerial skills such as financial management and environmental scanning. And, Scrimger found that the male employers whom she interviewed consider women highly skilled.

The Velvet Ghetto Project

In 1986, IABC sponsored the *Velvet Ghetto* study to assess the impact of the feminization of communications. The results of this project showed that women are more likely to perceive themselves as technicians than managers, women are paid substantially less than men — even when other variables are controlled for — and other professions have diminished in salary and status as they moved from male to female dominance (Cline et al., 1986).

The authors of the *Velvet Ghetto* (Cline et al., 1986) put forth two conclusions. First, they argued that there is little overt bias toward women on the part of management, although some institutionalized salary bias may stem from the perceived value of public relations to the organization. Second, the authors suggested that a subtle socialization process operates on women and causes them to self-select the technician role. Linked to this socialization process are women's difficulty in negotiating a higher salary, their undervaluing of their own worth as a worker, and a strong conflict over their role as professionals and their roles as wives or mothers (or both).

Commenting on the findings of the *Velvet Ghetto, The Washington Post* (Oldenburg, 1986) noted that the difference in salary between men and women over a 40-year career in public relations can surpass $1 million. *The Post* also highlighted the report's finding that although the percentage of women in the U.S. work force has reached 44% more than 70% of those in business communication careers like public relations are women; and this figure soon will reach 80%. The consequences of this "gender switch" have been lower salaries and organizational status for some public relations practitioners (p. D5).

Gersh (1986) also expounded on the results of the *Velvet Ghetto*. She showcased the project's bottom-line finding that being female was the strongest predictor of low salary. Gersh also stressed the study's finding that women are assumed to be ineffective managers either because of nature or nurture (or both). That is, women are viewed as caring nurturers who may be skillful at sympathizing with clients but are not tough enough for the business world.

Current Findings

Recent salary figures from IABC show little has changed since the 1986 *Velvet Ghetto* project. In "Profile '89," IABC reported that gender alone explains why women earn about $5,600 less than men (IABC, 1989). Furthermore, although the salary gap found in 1989 is smaller than the discrepancy IABC documented in "Profile '85" ($6,000), the 1989 figure is larger than the disparity cited in "Profile '87" ($5,500; IABC, 1985, 1987). As Toth (1990) noted, "This indicates a 'leveling off' of the gains women seem to be making in achieving equitable salaries" (p. 9).

Concurrently, *PR Reporter*'s 1989 salary survey showed that the median salary difference between men and women was $16,000 ("25th Annual Survey," 1989). And, Jacobson and Tortorello (1990) reported that female respondents to *PRJ*'s latest survey had a median salary of $35,933, compared to a median salary of $53,637 for male respondents.

Beyond the Velvet Ghetto

Unresolved issues raised in the *Velvet Ghetto* prompted IABC's 1989 follow-up study, *Beyond the Velvet Ghetto*. Summarizing the findings of this project, Toth (1989b) reported that unmitigated gender differences in median and mean salaries persist. Further, information gleaned from management theory, government data, and expert opinion continues to suggest that the barriers women face are rooted more in nuances of socialization than overt discrimination. She pointed out, however, that this assertion has not been validated by systematic research specific to public relations.

Focus-group interviews with female and male practitioners conducted for *Beyond the Velvet Ghetto* revealed another concern—the lack of men in the field. Subjects expressed some apprehension about the impact male flight might have on salaries (Toth, 1989b).

The concerns of these practitioners underscore the importance of understanding and vanquishing gender-based inequities. Because women make up the majority of students and practitioners, all practitioners may suffer to the extent that the business world devalues women and women's work. We can better understand this devaluation through an examination of gender-specific problems some women face within organizations. A discussion of practitioner roles and issues surrounding organizational power addresses these difficulties.

GENDER-SPECIFIC PROBLEMS WOMEN MAY ENCOUNTER

Roles

Practitioner roles are important because they provide a partial theoretical explanation for women's subjugation. About two thirds of all American working women are clustered in about 20 occupational categories—the "pink collar ghetto" (Bryant, 1984). Dozier et al. (1983) argued that the technician role is a ghetto for some women in public relations. For them, the technician role serves the same function in public relations that occupational segregation performs in the larger labor force. The technician role provides a place to put female practitioners, appropriately classified so that they can be paid less than men of equal professional experience, education, and tenure with their current employer.

The mechanisms of role segregation are complex. Dozier et al. (1983) argued that constructs explaining role segregation can be classified as biological issues, social issues, labor force issues, and public relations professional issues. Biological issues include the finding that male children are more aggressive than female children, even when a wide range of social factors are controlled (Maccoby & Jacklin, 1974).

Important to note, though, higher levels of aggressiveness do not make men intrinsically better suited for management and leadership positions than women. Male traits are more congruent with high-level posts because most organizations have been and continue to be ruled by men ("A Double Edge," 1990). Thus, the workplace has tended to esteem masculine attributes while devaluing feminine qualities (Levine, 1990).

Biological distinctions like differences in levels of aggressiveness sometimes are coupled with differential socialization for women and men. Current research shows that both women and men aspire to top positions in public relations (Creedon, 1989; DeRosa & Wilcox, 1989). But, other research has found that women exhibit lower levels of job involvement, or the degree to which one's work is considered an important part of one's life (Lodahl & Kejner, 1965; Reitz & Jewell, 1979; Ruh, White, & Wood, 1975).

Some women also may consider contextual factors more important, whereas many of their male counterparts may consider task issues more important (Centers & Bugental, 1966; Goodale & Hall, 1976; Taylor & Thompson, 1976; Wheeler, 1981). Contextual factors are rewards gained from work but external to the work itself such as interpersonal relations and working conditions. Task issues are rewards gained directly from the work itself like responsibility and challenge, which are more common to high-level occupations (Gomez-Mejia, 1983).

Another issue is risk taking. Some women may avoid jeopardizing their security (Slovik, 1966). Antecedent to this risk avoidance is an "ambivalence many women feel regarding their careers" (Cline et al., 1986, pp. 1–7). Some women do not view themselves as primary wage earners but see work as a "temporary haven before marriage" (Simpson & Simpson, 1969, pp. 196–197). Thus, these women may seek secure, undemanding jobs in the semiprofessions where such contextual factors as "working with people" and "being of service" are prevalent (Cline et al., 1986; Simpson & Simpson, 1969). The inherently risky task-oriented rewards of "challenge" and "responsibility" may be avoided.

Still other research, however, has found that socialization differences between women and men favor women as managers and are contrary to gender stereotypes (Powell, 1988). For example, Chusmir (1985) found that women managers have a higher need for achievement than male managers. Similarly, Donnell and Hall (1980) found that compared with men, women are more concerned with opportunities for growth, autonomy, and challenge and less concerned with work environment. Powell (1988) argued that findings like these "support the notion that women managers possess traits superior to those of their male counterparts" (p. 157). He contended that because women have had to overcome stereotypical attitudes about their unsuitability for management, women who secure management positions are actually more motivated toward achievement and self-actualization than are men.

Despite findings like these, most public relations literature suggests that the biological and socialization attributes men bring to the labor force cause many of them to be predisposed to or self-select the inherently risky manager role. The argument goes that women, on the other hand, often choose the technician role because of its safety, its positive contextual attributes, and the low level of involvement that technical work demands.

This latter stance, however, is not without critics. For example, Ryan (quoted in Lukovitz, 1989) argued: "Contending that women aspire to be technicians is horrendously akin to blaming the victim. All the women I know perceive themselves as far transcending the roles they are obliged to occupy" (p. 20). For her, women's lower status in public relations is not of their own doing. Instead, women's subjugation is a result of the "corporate, male-dominated world that continues not to pay or promote women as it does men" (p. 20).

An example of this discrimination may be found in the passage of practitioners out of the technician role into the manager role. Druck and

Hiebert (1979) argued that the technical role is a transitory role—an initial step in the professional growth of the practitioner leading to managerial roles. This professional growth process is facilitated when managers select "informal assistants" (Graen, 1973) from the ranks of technicians to groom for management. These technicians are fed managerial problems in small pieces that the technician can solve. The process builds the future manager's competency at management functions and enhances the practitioner's self-esteem and self-confidence in taking risks associated with the management role.

Broom and Dozier (1986) provided evidence, however, that women face more difficulty advancing from the technician role than men with similar years of experience. The selection of male informal assistants by male public relations managers may be one cause. Male managers who hold stereotypes about women ("women don't take their careers seriously") are unlikely to groom such technicians for the manager role. Rather, women may be handed routine jobs isolated from decision making. Evidence supports the existence of such discrimination in other occupations (Terborg & Ilgen, 1975). The logic of stereotyping implies that these routine, technical jobs are more "fitting" for women because women exhibit low involvement, seek positive contextual attributes ("work with people" or "be of service"), and avoid risk.

A complex "push–pull" causal loop is set in motion. The predispositions of some women are stereotyped as attributes of all women. This, in turn, results in many women being sent the role expectations of technicians. Their routine tasks reinforce any predispositions of low involvement. This is reinforced further by the clearly perceived lower status and pay of technicians.

On this point, Sullivan, Dozier, and Hellweg (1985) provided evidence that practitioners perceive a clear hierarchy in public relations roles. At the low end, paid the lowest salary, is the public relations technician. A step above is the media relations specialist, then the communication liaison. At the top, paid the most, are public relations managers. In this study, practitioners were asked to respond to Broom's 24 role measures as they actually applied to the practitioner's daily work. Practitioners then were asked how often they would engage in each activity in their ideal job. As hypothesized, both female and male practitioners aspired to ideal roles higher in the hierarchy than their actual roles.

Thus, women are channeled through a complex set of antecedent socialization and organizational variables that often leads to the technician role. Although the technician role is relatively transitory for many male practitioners, the technician role is relatively permanent for many female practitioners.

Organizational Power

Beyond roles, issues of power lie at the heart of women's repression in organizations. Women's blocked advancement may result in part from not being automatically part of an organization's informational and decisional networks, especially when that organization's culture has been determined by men. Not fitting in with the organizational culture, women are excluded from key information and decision-making alliances. And, with few women as part of top management, the atmosphere may be unreceptive to other women's applying. As Moore (1986) reported, women perceive a more progressive climate in organizations that already employ a reasonable number of women.

Some approaches to advancement within organizations involve networking and coalition building where several people are relied on to form a support system. As Kanter (1986) stressed, having a "whole set of backers and supporters" lends the power to get activities done, especially innovative ventures (p. 108). Sandler and Hall (1986) pointed out, however, that tapping into departments' informal networks may be hard for some women because they often are excluded from the sharing of information and professional advice.

Another problem women may encounter has to do with the process of deciding who rises to the top. Those in power are often willing to share their special privileges only with those they perceive to be similar to themselves. And, as Moore (1986) noted, many of the older men who make these choices still do not feel comfortable with women. These men, however, do not consider themselves to be discriminating against women overtly; they are simply following their customary way of choosing people.

Another barrier faced by women has to do with greater difficulty in creating a persona, or public image, that is congruent with that of high power positions (Conrad, 1985). Because this persona was defined by men and continues to be enacted for the most part by men, it reflects male values—values that often differ from women's. And, if others in the organization perceive women to be lacking in the traditional characteristics that suggest power, then they are. On this point, Kasten (1986) noted: "Power is a funny thing—it's primarily a matter of perception. If you have power but I don't think so, then you don't really have it. If you don't really have power but I think you do, then you do" (p. 132).

Women's lack of organizational power also may stem from a shortage of support from home and society in general. Family concerns may impede some women because women continue to do more than their share of home maintenance activities in addition to pursuing careers (Heins, Smock, Jacobs, & Stein, 1976; Hochschild, 1989). And, as Kahn-Hut, Daniels, and

Coward (1982) pointed out, "Professional ideologies depict work as 'a calling' that requires round-the-clock devotion to work. This devotion is a primary allegiance that conflicts with the cultural mandate of women's primary responsibility to family" (p. 38).

One last issue is power itself. Women's difficulty in attaining organizational prowess may stem from the masculinism associated with power. Many women seem to thrive, however, when the feminine alternative to power, *empowerment,* is prized within an organization (Helgesen, 1990). Unlike power, which usually operates as a zero-sum game (the more power one has, the less others have), empowerment involves building up one's own strength by building up others (Helgesen, 1990).

Interestingly, this feminine leadership style has been hailed as more compatible with organizational changes that are underway in the 1990s than the traditional male model of "command and control" (Levine, 1990, p. 10c; see also Doyle, 1990). These changes include participatory management, high-involvement workplaces, and fast-changing environments (Wysmuller, quoted in "Employees Expect," 1991; American Society for Quality Control, quoted in Swoboda, 1990).

FAULTY SOLUTIONS

The problems many women face in advancing within organizations have led some public relations scholars and practitioners to prescribe various "remedies" for women who wish to enhance their salary and organizational status (Anderson, 1975; Ford, 1986; Mathews, 1988; Post, 1987; Rappaport, 1986; Stewart, 1988; Turk, 1986). Most often, these remedies focus on some deficiency that women possess when compared to men although this comparison is usually implicit. Proponents of this position have suggested that as soon as women correct or overcompensate for their deficiencies, they will be more likely to enjoy the salaries and status many men in public relations enjoy.

Although the attention given by these scholars and practitioners to women's issues should be applauded, we believe many of their proposed solutions are flawed on at least three points. First, these prescriptions are usually based on women's assuming masculine characteristics such as assertiveness, risk taking, toughness, power, ambition, and political savvy. This scheme may be ineffective because women who possess these characteristics often are not perceived the same way as men bearing these traits (Conrad, 1990). That is, men who exhibit masculine characteristics usually are judged positively because their persona fits proper male roles. Women who possess or adopt masculine characteristics, however, may be evaluated negatively because a masculine persona does not mesh with roles considered appropriate for women (Morrison, White, & Van Velsor, 1987). Thus, the assertive man may be viewed as "on his way up," although the assertive woman often is considered "pushy."

Second, the psychological and personal costs to the women these prescriptions do work for are often too high. The psychological price of "making it" in the business world often entails women's suffering from the imposter syndrome—doubting one's competence and feeling like a fake in a workplace dominated by men and designed by men according to their values (L. Grunig, 1989a). The personal cost often involves choosing between a career and family—a choice few men are forced to make.

Most important, though, these remedies miss the fundamental issue— society's devaluation of women and women's work. Women's work, whether it is technical or managerial, will be denigrated because it is associated with women. This assertion is substantiated primarily by salary data in public relations that show female managers are paid less than male managers despite comparable education, experience, and tenure with their present employer (Childers, 1986; Dozier et al., 1983; Turk, 1986).

A NEW PERSPECTIVE

To counter this devaluation, scholars and practitioners need a better understanding of and appreciation for the positive aspects female practitioners bring to their organizations. On this point, Creedon (in press) charged that the condition of female practitioners could be improved by revisioning the value of women's work in public relations. Important to note, though, she argued that this metamorphosis would be accomplished not by changing women's place in the current system, but by changes in the system itself. That is, attempts simply to assimilate women into management ranks as management is defined now do not represent the solution. Instead, the value system in organizations that champions masculinism while denigrating feminine values must be transformed. In its place would be a wholly new structure in which female-centered principles are not only legitimate, but esteemed.

Creedon's (in press) contention is particularly striking within the context of public relations. Feminine values have been linked (see Wetherell, 1989) to two-way symmetrical communication, the public relations model scholars and practitioners usually tout as the most ethical and effective (J. Grunig & Hunt, 1984). Two-way symmetrical communication invokes cooperation, collaboration, and relationship building—principles that "may be defined as female because they have been nurtured in the private, domestic sphere to which women have been restricted for so long" (Helgesen, 1990, p. xxi). Individual men may hold these values, but the general social (but not biological) domain to which these concerns are assigned is female.

Given this feminine propensity for fostering interdependence and mutuality, perhaps women's styles of communicating and managing should be heralded rather than forsaken. In support of this position, some public relations scholars have begun to point out that feminine values and women's contributions to organizations are legitimate and important (Creedon, 1989, in press; L. Grunig, 1988a, 1988b, 1989b; Rakow, 1987, 1989; Toth, 1989a, 1989b, 1990).

From this perspective, feminism emerges as a particularly useful framework for understanding women in public relations and empowering both female practitioners and the public relations function. As Rakow (1989) argued, "Feminism and its academic counterpart, feminist theory, is the lens through which we can see the [gender] issue in a different light by *valuing* the feminine and those characteristics traditionally relegated to women" (p. 288).

The feminist perspective, however, has not been called on often in public relations research or practice. Moreover, Rakow (1987) characterized most of our knowledge under the more general category of gender and communication as unhelpful to women. For her, this research has left assumptions about gender, public relations, organizations, and society unquestioned. And, too often, this scholarship has investigated " 'sex differences' in a way that assumes women are deficient" (p. 79).

Because women outnumber men in public relations classrooms and practice, a logical, if not moral, mandate suggests that research and discussion about women be carried out in a way that benefits women and, thus, public relations. Beyond logic and moral responsibility, practical concerns demand a fresh way of looking at gender issues. *Public Relations Reporter* ("Communicating to a Diverse Workforce," 1989) argued that passing "beyond obligatory requirements of Affirmative Action to valuing the positive strengths of a diverse workforce" is not merely a legal or moral concern for organizations now and in the future; extolling diversity is a pragmatic issue as well (p. 4).

On this point, Castro (1990) noted that in the 21st century work force taking shape now, White, U.S.-born men will be a minority. And, although the labor force will grow slowly over the next decade, two thirds of its increase will be women starting or returning to work (Castro, 1990). Given this shift, organizations will have to nurture and champion the talents of women if they are to survive (Helgesen, 1990). As Naisbitt and Aburdene (quoted in Helgesen, 1990) contended, the most successful companies in the future will be those that assertively hire and promote women.

This optimistic perspective, however, needs to be tempered with realism. As Koprowski (1983) contended, men have the upper hand in terms of power and probably will not relinquish it without plenty of "conscious or unconscious footdragging" (p. 43). However, despite this resistance, philosophical and practical arguments underscore the relevance of exploring a feminist perspective for public relations. This exploration is carried out here by outlining the variants of feminist thought. Through this examination, we can see how feminist theory provides deeper insights for understanding gender issues than does a nonfeminist approach.

VARIANTS OF FEMINIST THOUGHT

Developing a neat typology into which feminist theory can be compressed is not possible. Feminists tend to reject divisions and categories because they tend to be "limiting and distorting" (Tong, 1989, p. 8). That is, they believe science's preoccupation with tidy classification often causes the experiences of those outside the mainstream such as women to be omitted or misrepresented. For the purpose of explication, however, a forced distinction between *liberal, socialist/Marxist,* and *radical* feminism is made here.

Liberal Feminism

The main thrust of liberal feminism lies in the belief that sexism is rooted in socialization and discrimination (Toth, 1989a). In other words, the inequality women face is a result of "women's deprivation of equal rights" and "their learned reluctance to exercise them" (Anderson, 1988, p. 302). Toth explained that liberal feminists, therefore, focus equalizing access to education and employment opportunities and relearning traditional sex role attitudes and behaviors. Important to note, liberals disavow any need to restructure society. Instead, they believe that women should be assimilated into the existing system through an accumulation of reforms designed to produce egalitarianism (Toth, 1989a).

Some feminists, however, have pointed out the limitations of the liberal perspective. Namely, they have criticized the focus on equality that might put some women on par with men but ignores the need to transform the conditions of oppression that produce gender relations (Anderson, 1988). For them, liberalism places too much of the burden of change on women while failing to recognize that society also must change. Given these flaws, alternative points of view have developed. These include socialist/Marxist feminism and radical feminism.

Socialist/Marxist Feminism

Socialist/Marxist feminists believe that class oppression under capitalism is the fundamental factor in women's subjugation (Steeves, 1987). Socialist feminists go beyond Marxists, however, by contending that an interplay between capitalism and male-centered gender relations contributes to women's oppression above and beyond capitalism.

For socialist/Marxist feminists, women's repression originated in the introduction of private property. Tong (1989) explained that private ownership of the means of production by a few persons, originally all men, resulted in a class system that has manifested itself as corporate capitalism and imperialism. If women are to be liberated, capitalism must be replaced by a socialist system whereby the means of production belong to all.

Radical Feminism

Radical feminists go even further than their liberal or socialist/Marxist sisters (Tong, 1989). Radicals believe that the agglomeration of male-dominated institutions forms a "patriarchal system of oppression" (Beck, quoted in "Feminists to Bring," 1988; see also Anderson, 1988). Patriarchy — characterized by power, dominance, hierarchy, and competition — cannot be reformed but only "ripped out root and branch" (Tong, 1989, p. 3).

Some radical feminists believe that patriarchy stems from biology. For them, sexual relations and men's dominance over women are the central causes of women's oppression (Anderson, 1988). Other radicals concentrate on the ways in which sexuality and gender have been used to subordinate women to men (Tong, 1989). For them, women's inferiority is explained vis-a-vis a sex/gender system (MacKinnon, 1982) that assigns low value to feminine qualities and construes the definition of femininity for patriarchal purposes (Tong, 1989). Thus, some believe women's liberation will be achieved only when female qualities are valued in their own right. Others contend that liberation requires women's giving new female-centered meanings to femininity. The objective of both of these strategies, however, is the elimination of patriarchal forms of social organization. In their place would be new cultural forms based on the "non-hierarchal, other-oriented, and supportive values of women-centered culture" (Anderson, 1988, p. 323).

The important distinction to keep in mind among all these perspectives is whether they argue that women's oppression will be overcome by women's assimilation into the existing system through reform or by rejecting assimilation and demanding a restructuring of society and its institutions. Liberalism is the only approach that exclusively prescribes reform, whereas socialist/Marxist and radical feminism suggest restructuring.

FEMINIST THEORY AND RESEARCH ABOUT WOMEN IN PUBLIC RELATIONS

An appraisal of research about women in public relations reveals that the liberalism inherent in much of this scholarship provides an important, but incomplete, framework for understanding gender issues. This research may be classified as liberal because it usually assumes that the inequities female practitioners face result from their being denied access to managerial roles (Toth, 1989a). The implication is that women or people with feminine traits are poorly prepared to "play the game" because of biological or, more often, learned female attributes. Given this, solutions are offered for women who want to overcome their deficiencies and achieve parity with their male colleagues. Calls for restructuring rarely are put forth.

Researchers such as Rakow (1989) have challenged the liberal position that female students and practitioners need to change so they may integrate more effectively into the existing system. Taking a radical stance, she argued that the system of male-centered values that define worth in organizations and public relations classrooms should change.

Tong (1989) contended, however, that no feminist perspective is the answer to the "woman question(s)" (p. 1). Instead, each approach provides "a unique perspective with its own . . . strengths and weaknesses" (p. 1). For her, feminism's contribution is found in the way different viewpoints intersect and join together to lament women's oppression and provide at least partial formulas for their liberation.

Not all feminists would concur with Tong (1989), but her point seems fitting for public relations theory and practice. That is, although liberalism's explanation for women's oppression and prescriptions have some merit, they are clearly inadequate. The inequities female practitioners face are not exclusively the result of sexist discrimination and sexist socialization. Nor will equity be achieved completely through equalizing access and women's rising above traditional sex-role attitudes and behaviors. As socialist/Marxist and radical feminists have argued, societal and institutional changes are needed to eliminate sexism and its consequences.

Some of the macrolevel solutions these feminists offer, however, do not seem very helpful (at least in the immediate future) because female practitioners currently do not have the option of doing away with capitalism or ripping out patriarchal organizations where they work "root and branch" (Tong, 1989, p. 3). Nevertheless, an adaptation of the position underlying these alternatives—that women's oppression will be overcome only by restructuring institutions or creating new forms of organizations based on female values—suggests alternatives that are working for some women. Examples of the latter include public relations firms and businesses headed by women who have rejected the corporate "male cloning" that suppressed their communication and management styles and stifled their abilities (Rudolph, 1990, p. 53; see also Humphrey, 1990).

We believe evidence of restructuring will be found in the organizations characterized as "excellent" for this study. This evidence includes organizational policies that help nurture the careers of women. Some of these policies are mentoring, networking, flextime, reasonable paternity/

maternity leave, mandating the use of nonsexist language, and specific and effective guidelines for dealing with sexual harassment. We also believe that excellent organizations will have an equitable number of female practitioners in management roles and promote female technicians rather than hiring men with little or no public relations experience to manage the function.

TOWARD A FEMININE PUBLIC RELATIONS?

In summary, gender research and discussion in public relations too often have failed to recognize that if feminization brings deflating salaries and status, the real problem lies in societal devaluation of women and the feminine—not in women themselves. Thus, suggestions for retaining or salvaging public relations' stature merely by training women to more effectively ascend to a male-defined management structure miss the point. And, worse, these recommendations further exacerbate the underlying problem—gender-based evaluations that privilege men and penalize women.

An alternative perspective would call into question this position, not just for the degradation of women that it implies but also for its logical rigor. Many scholars and practitioners have argued that the increased efficacy and professionalism of public relations are linked to practicing two-way symmetrical communication. Given this, will the continuation of a masculine mind set lead to the "feminine qualities of consensus-building and listening" (Rudolph, 1990, p. 53) characteristic of this communication model?

The obvious answer is no. A strategy more consistent in its logic involves garnering the positive effects on the field, organizations, and society that public relations' swing to the feminine can bring (Rakow, 1989). These effects, however, will be realized only after societal and organizational changes occur. The most imperative is eradicating sexual discrimination in pay and promotion. Further, the degradation of the communications function because of its association with women must be turned around.

Efforts that might facilitate this shift include research and discussion that uncover and validate female-centered definitions of public relations. Recording and showcasing women's experiences and contributions as communicators and managers could be other ventures. In doing so, we could identify alternatives to communicating and managing that women use or would use if they could (Rakow, 1987). These challenges are the first steps toward assembling "a collection of women's eloquence" (Condit, 1988, p. 7) that should provide an empowering alternative for understanding the feminization of public relations.

REFERENCES

Anderson, J. H. (1975). Thoughts on being a woman in public relations. *Public Relations Journal, 31*(6), 25.

Anderson, M. L. (1988). *Thinking about women: Sociological perspectives on sex and gender.* New York: Macmillan.

Bates, D. (1983). A concern: Will women inherit the profession? *Public Relations Journal, 39*(7), 6–7.

Bernstein, J. (1986, January 27). Is pr field being hurt by too many women? *Advertising Age,* pp. 6–67.

Broom, G. M. (1982). A comparison of sex roles in public relations. *Public Relations Review, 8,* 17–22.

Broom, G. M., & Dozier, D. M. (1986). Advancement for public relations role models. *Public Relations Review, 12,* 37–56.

Bryant, G. (Ed.). (1984). *The working woman report: Succeeding in business in the 80s.* New York: Simon & Schuster.

Castro, J. (1990, Fall) Get set: Here they come. *Time,* pp. 50–52.

Centers, R., & Bugental, D. E. (1966). Intrinsic and extrinsic job motivators among different segments of the working population. *Journal of Applied Psychology, 50,* 193–197.

Childers, L. L. (1986). *Gender and salary: A panel study of public relations practitioners.* Unpublished master's thesis, University of Florida, Gainesville.

Chusmir, L. H. (1985). Motivation of managers: Is gender a factor? *Psychology of Women Quarterly, 9,* 153–159.

Cline, C. G., Masel-Walters, L., Toth, E. L., Turk, J. V., Smith, H. T., & Johnson, N. (1986). *The velvet ghetto: The impact of the increasing percentage of women in public relations and organizational communication.* San Francisco: IABC Foundation.

Communicating to a diverse workforce—do we know how? (1989, November). *Public relations reporter,* p. 4.

Condit, C. M. (1988). What makes our scholarship feminist? A radical/liberal view. *Women's Studies in Communication, 11,* 6–8.

Conrad, C. (1985). *Strategic organizational communication: Cultures, situations, and adaptation.* New York: CBS College.

Conrad, C. (1990). *Strategic organizational communication: An integrated perspective.* Fort Worth: Holt, Rinehart & Winston.

Could be woman's field. (1982, September). *O'Dwyer's newsletter,* quoted in *Ms.,* p. 125.

Creedon, P. J. (1989, August). *"Just a technician": Let's take another look at how we're trivializing the communications function in public relations.* Paper presented at the Seminar on Gender Issues and Public Relations, Public Relations Division, Association for Education in Journalism and Mass Communication, Washington, DC.

Creedon, P. J. (in press). Public relations and "women's work": Toward a feminist analysis of public relations roles. *Public Relations Research Annual.*

Data still don't show. (1989, December). *Public relations reporter,* p. 4.

DeRosa, D., & Wilcox, D. L. (1989). Gaps are narrowing between female and male students. *Public Relations Review, 15*(1), 80–90.

Donnell, S. M., & Hall, J. (1980). Men and women as managers: A significant case of no significant difference. *Organizational Dynamics, 8,* 60–77.

A double edge. (1990, November). *The Orlando Sentinel,* p. E-15.

Doyle, J. M. (1990, October 14). Men rule—but how much longer? *The Orlando Sentinel,* p. E-15.

Dozier, D. M., Chapo, S., & Sullivan, B. (1983, August). *Sex and the bottom line: Income differences among women and men in public relations.* Paper presented at the meeting of the Public Relations Division, Association for Education in Journalism and Mass Communication, Corvallis, OR.

Druck, K. B., & Hiebert, R. E. (1979). *Your personal guidebook to help you chart a more successful career in public relations.* New York: Public Relations Society of America.

Employees expect to work less by 2000. (1991, January). *The Orlando Sentinel,* p. E-15.

Feminists to bring broader perspective to disciplines. (1988, September). *Outlook,* p. 2.

Ford, K. B. (1986). *Women in public relations: Barriers and bridges.* Unpublished manuscript. University of Maryland, College Park.

Gersh, D. (1986, April 19). There are more women in public relations, but inequality still exists. *Editor and Publisher,* p. 78.

Gomez-Mejia, L. R. (1983). Sex differences during occupational socialization. *Academy of Management Journal, 26,* 492–499.

Goodale, J. G., & Hall, D. T. (1976). Inheriting a career: The influence of sex, values, and parents. *Journal of Vocational Behavior, 8,* 19–30.

Graen, G. (1973, August). *Role making processes and administration.* Paper presented at the meeting of the American Psychological Association, Montreal.

Grunig, J. E., & Hunt, T. (1984). *Managing public relations.* New York: Holt, Rinehart & Winston.

Grunig, L. A. (1988a). Journalism students and the glass ceiling in academia: Problems and progress. In P. J. Creedon (Ed.), *A gender perspective on issues in mass communication* (pp. 125–147). Newbury Park, CA: Sage.

Grunig, L. A. (1988b). A research agenda for women in public relations, *Public Relations Review, 14*(3), 48–57.

Grunig, L. A. (1989a). Sex discrimination in promotion and tenure in journalism education. *Journalism Quarterly, 66*(1), 93–100, 229.

Grunig, L. A. (1989b, August). *Toward a feminist transformation of public relations education and practice.* Paper presented at the Seminar on Gender Issues and Public Relations, Public Relations Division, Association for Education in Journalism and Mass Communication, Washington, DC.

Heins, M., Smock, S., Jacobs, J., & Stein, M. (1976). Productivity of women physicians. *Journal of the American Medical Association, 236,* 1961–1964.

Helqesen, S. (1990). *The female advantage: Women's ways of leadership.* New York: Doubleday.

Hochschild, A. (1989, September-October). Second shift. *New Age Journal,* pp. 60–64.

Humphrey, K. (1990). *Entrepreneurial women in public relations: Why open collars?* Unpublished master's thesis, University of Maryland, College Park.

International Association of Business Communicators. (1985). *Profile '85.* San Francisco: Author.

International Association of Business Communicators. (1987). *Profile '87.* San Francisco: Author.

International Association of Business Communicators. (1989). *Profile '89.* San Francisco, CA: Author.

Jacobson, D. V., & Tortorello, N. J. (1990, June). Salary survey. *Public Relations Journal,* pp. 18–25.

Kahn-Hut, R., Daniels, A. K., & Coward, R. (1982). *Women and work: Problems and perspectives.* New York: Oxford University Press.

Kanter, R. M. (1986). Mastering change: The skills we need. In L. L. Moore (Ed.), *Not as far as you think* (pp. 181–194). Lexington, MA: Lexington.

Kasten, B. R. (1986). Separate strengths: How men and women manage conflict and competition. In L. L. Moore (Ed.), *Not as far as you think* (pp. 121–134). Lexington, MA: Lexington.

Koprowski, E. J. (1983). Cultural myths: Clues to effective management. *Organizational Dynamics, 12,* 39–51.

Lesly, P. (1988). Public relations numbers are up but stature down. *Public Relations Review, 14,*(4), 3–7.

Levine, B. (1990, October 28). Female bosses' non-traditional approach may set leadership style of future. *The Sun,* p. 10C.

Lodahl, T., & Kejner, M. (1965). The definition and measurement of job involvement. *Journal of Applied Psychology, 49,* 361–368.

Lukovitz, K. (1989). Women practitioners: How far, how fast? *Public Relations Journal, 45*(5), 15–22, 34.

Maccoby, E. E., & Jacklin, C. N. (1974). *The psychology of sex differences.* Stanford, CA: Stanford University.

MacKinnon, C. A. (1982). Feminism, Marxism, method and the state: An agenda for theory. *Signs: Journal of Women in Culture and Society, 7*(3), 515–544.

Mathews, W. (1988). Women in public relations: Progression or retrogression? *Public Relations Review, 14*(3), 24–28.

Moore, L. L. (1986). Introduction. In L. L. Moore (Ed.), *Not as far as you think* (pp. 1–12). Lexington, MA: Lexington.

Morrison, A. M., White, R. P., & Van Velsor, E. (1987). Executive women: Substance plus style. *Psychology Today, 21,* 18–26.

Oldenburg, D. (1986, November 12). Women's pay penalty. *The Washington Post,* p. D5.

Post, L. C. (1987, February). View from the top: Women executives in communication. *IABC Communication World,* pp. 17–19.

Powell, G. N. (1988). *Women and men in management.* Newbury Park, CA: Sage.

PR people deplore encroachment by marketers and "feminization" of the field. (1984, December). *Marketing News,* p. 12.

Rakow, L. F. (1987). Looking to the future: Five questions for gender research. *Women's Studies in Communication, 10,* 79–86.

Rakow, L. F. (1989). From the feminization of public relations to the promise of feminism. In E. L. Toth & C. G. Cline (Eds.), *Beyond the velvet ghetto* (pp. 287–298). San Francisco: IABC Research Foundation.

Rappaport, F. L. (1986). Women in public relations. *The Counselor, 22*(3), 6,8.

Reitz, H. T., Jewell, L. N. (1979). Sex, focus of control, and job involvement: A six country investigation. *Academy of Management Journal, 8,* 300–312.

Rudolph, B. (1990, Fall). Why can't a woman manage more like . . . a woman? *Time,* p. 53.

Ruh, R. A., White, K., & Wood, R. R. (1975). Job involvement, values, personal background, participation in decision making, and job attitudes. *Academy of Management Journal, 8,* 300–312.

Sandler, B. R., & Hall, R. (1986). *The campus climate revisited: Chilly for women faculty, administrators, and graduate students.* Washington, DC: Project on the Status and Education of Women.

Scrimger, J. (1985). Profile: Women in Canadian public relations. *Public Relations Review, 11,* 38–47.

Scrimger, J. (1989). Women communicators in Canada: A case for optimism. In E. L. Toth & C. G. Cline (Eds.), *Beyond the velvet ghetto* (pp. 219–240). San Francisco: IABC Research Foundation.

Simpson, R. L., & Simpson, I. H. (1969). *Women and bureaucracy in the semi-professions and their organizations: Teachers, nurses, and social workers.* New York: Free Press.

Slovik, P. (1966). Risk-taking in children: Age and sex differences. *Child Development, 37,* 169–176.

Steeves, H. L. (1987). Feminist theories and media studies. *Critical Studies in Mass Communication, 4*(2), 95–135.

Stewart, L. J. (1988). Women in foundation and corporate public relations. *Public Relations Review, 14*(3), 20–23.

Sullivan, B. S., Dozier, D. M., Hellweg, S. A. (1985). Practitioner pursuit of the ideal role. *IPRA Review, 9,* 14–18.

Swoboda, F. (1990, September 30). Empowering the rank and file. *The Washington Post,* p. H3.

Taylor, R. N., & Thompson, M. (1976). Work value systems of young workers. *Academy of Management Journal, 9,* 522–535.

Terborg, J. R., & Ilgen, D. R. (1975). A theoretical approach to sex discrimination in traditionally masculine occupations. *Organizational Behavior and Human Performance, 13,* 352–376.

Thaler, R. E. (1986, December). The cutting edge: Where's the beef? *IABC Communication World,* pp. 14–17.

Theus, K. T. (1985). Gender shifts in journalism and public relations. *Public Relations Review, 11,* 42–50.

Tong, R. (1989). *Feminist thought. A comprehensive introduction.* Boulder, CO: Westview.

Toth, E. L. (1989a). Gender issues from the speech communication perspective. In E. L. Toth & C. G. Cline (Eds.), *Beyond the velvet ghetto* (pp. 59–70). San Francisco: IABC Research Foundation.

Toth, E. L. (1989b). Summary issues from the velvet ghetto: The impact of the increasing percentage of women in public relations and business communication. In E. L. Toth & C. G. Cline (Eds.), *Beyond the velvet ghetto* (pp. 7–24). San Francisco: IABC Research Foundation.

Toth, E. L. (1989c). Trends from focus group interviews. In E. L. Toth & C. G. Cline (Eds.), *Beyond the velvet ghetto* (pp. 71–95). San Francisco: IABC Research Foundation, pp. 71–95.

Toth, E. L. (1990, August). *Feminist communication perspectives for beyond the velvet ghetto: A review essay.* Paper presented at the meeting of the Committee on the Status of Women in Journalism Education, Association for Education in Journalism and Mass Communication, Minneapolis.

Turk, J. V. (1986). The changing face of CASE. *CASE Currents, 12*(6), 8–20.

25th annual survey. (1989, October). *Public relations reporter,* pp. 1–6.

Wetherell, B. L. (1989). *The effect of gender, masculinity, and femininity on the practice of and preference for the models of public relations.* Unpublished master's thesis, University of Maryland, College Park.

Wheeler, K. G. (1981). Sex differences in perceptions of desired rewards, availability of rewards and abilities in relation to occupational selection. *Journal of Occupational Psychology, 54,* 141–148.

Winkleman, M., & Pollock, J. C. (1987). Salary survey. *Public Relations Journal, 43*(6), 15–17.

16 Public Relations Education and Professionalism

William P. Ehling
Syracuse University

ABSTRACT

In chapter 1, a flow chart described the factors explaining why organizations practice public relations as they do—one of which was the "potential of the public relations department." Potential depends in large part on the body of knowledge and the professionalism that practitioners bring to bear on public relations problems. Chapter 11 reviewed research showing that practitioners with more education in and knowledge of public relations are more likely to be in the dominant coalition, to be in the manager role, and to practice the two-way symmetrical model of communication—all attributes of excellent public relations. This chapter, then, discusses the quality of training and knowledge available in public relations and the obstacles to increasing the knowledge and professionalism of practitioners. Education for and research on public relations have improved dramatically, providing the opportunity for excellence in communication practice. Often, however, practitioners resist the knowledge that can increase their stature in the organizations that employ them.

PROFESSIONAL CRITERIA

The relationship between public relations education and public relations professionalism appears simple and straightforward, at first glance. This relationship, it may be argued, is manifested through education, which should be viewed as a primary means for providing the necessary knowledge and skills needed to fulfill the tasks and responsibilities of any public

439

relations activity. This certainly seems commonsensical enough. Unhappily, common sense here, as is so often the case, does not have the last word.

The problem is that the meaning of several key terms such as *professionalism, education,* and *knowledge* are not self-evident. Take the term professionalism, for example. The various connotations associated with this word are spread over a continuum. At one end we have the notion of professionalism as a kind of activity or work for which one gets paid, as in the case of an amateur athlete turning professional, meaning that he or she is now engaged in sports for pay. At the other end, we have a concept of a professional as a person occupying a particular kind of position obtained through extensive education and test taking to attain a sanctioned status, as in the case of a person becoming a lawyer or doctor after completing a certain level of education and passing qualification examinations.

There are many—some would say too many—public relations practitioners and educators who, without too much reflection, simply assume that a public relations professional is anyone who gets payment for doing something loosely called public relations. There are others, however, who adopt a narrower and more demanding view of professionalism, who point to the fulfillment of certain standards as a necessary condition for the attainment of a professional status.

For example, Cutlip and Center (1978) in the fifth edition of their widely used textbook, *Effective Public Relations,* cited the standards put forth by John Marston (1968) as the key characteristics that distinguish a profession from a skilled occupation. These include:

1. A defined area of competence.
2. An organized body of knowledge of some consequence.
3. Self-consciousness.
4. Competence of entrants determined by controlled access.
5. Continuing education.
6. Support of research.
7. Aid in education of competent replacement.
8. Independence.

To this list Cutlip and Center (1978) added the following commentary:

Overall, there must be professional competence, recognition of obligations to others in the profession, and a dedication to serve, not injure, the public welfare.

Even though practitioners continue to be beset with all sorts of complexes and doubts as to their own worthiness, movement in these professional directions is apparent. (p. 581)

In the sixth edition of *Effective Public Relations,* however, Cutlip Center, and Broom (1985) gave more attention to the subject of professionalism; they noted among other things that:

> Among practitioners, many discussions focus on the extent to which public relations is a profession and its practitioners are professionals. The topic of professionalism dominates many conferences and other meetings. Almost every issue of the many publications and newsletters serving the field addresses some aspect of professionalism. (p. 72)

Cutlip et al. (1985) also revised the standards of professionalism as set forth in their earlier edition by pointing out that there is "general consensus" that a profession meets at least the following five criteria:

1. Acquisition of specialized educational preparation in the attainment of knowledge and skills that are based on a body of theory developed through research, with an emphasis on knowledge over skill.
2. Production of a unique and essential service that is recognized as such by the community.
3. Emphasis is placed on public service and social responsibility, making private economic gain and special interests subordinate to the public good.
4. Practitioners are granted autonomy as well as personal responsibility, meaning that the freedom to decide and act carries with it individual accountability.
5. Enforceable codes of ethics and standards of performance which are made manifest by a self-governing association of colleagues, including the disciplining of those who deviate from accepted behavior.

Grunig and Hunt (1984), in turn, pointed out that a substantial body of knowledge on professionalism developed in sociology in the 1950s and 1960s; what emerged from these studies was that professionalism was a certain set of attributes associated with the individual rather than with an occupation. This means that some individuals in a specified occupation area may be regarded as professionals whereas others may not, depending on the level and nature of the individual's performance. Applying this principle to public relations, this means that only some but not all who claim to be engaged in public relations qualify as professionals. Grunig and Hunt continued by noting that "we can say that an occupation becomes a profession when a majority of its practitioners qualify as professionals" (p. 66).

More specifically, Grunig and Hunt (1984) cited and elaborated five major characteristics of a professional:

1. A set of professional values. Such values include a commitment to serve others as being more important than attaining personal economic gain and a need for autonomy (namely, to do what is right rather than to do what others want).
2. Membership in a strong professional organization.
3. Adherence to professional norms.
4. An intellectual tradition associated with an established body of knowledge.
5. Technical skills acquired through long periods of prescribed professional education.

These criteria, along with those cited by Cutlip et al. (1985), find their justification in social research and scholarly inquiry by public relations scholars; they also make clear the close association between professionalism, on the one hand, and a well-defined body of knowledge and the role of education in transmitting that body of knowledge, on the other.

The views and activities of public relations practitioners also appear to corroborate the criteria used in defining professionalism. Practitioners have for years worked not only to build and strengthen such professional organizations as the Public Relations Society of America (PRSA) and the International Association of Business Communicators (IABC), but also to establish a code of ethics, formulate professional objectives and norms, and devise procedures for attaining accreditation through written examinations. The successful passage of such examinations allows one to place a letter designation after one's name; in the case of PRSA members, the designation is "APR" (Accredited Public Relations) and in the case of IABC members the designation is "ABC" (Accredited Business Communicator).

Hence, to be able to attain individual accreditation, a study guide must be followed, books about public relations must be consulted, and time must be devoted to studying for the examination. Professionalism, then, in part is contingent on education, even when education is pursued informally.

In an article entitled "Demonstrating Professionalism" (Jackson, 1988), a list of dates are cited to mark the important milestones along the road toward professionalism beginning as far back as 1922 with the founding of the first professional public relations society. The article was written by Patrick Jackson, APR, senior counsel of Jackson, Jackson, and Wagner, Exeter, NH. Jackson and Ann Barkelew are cochairpersons of PRSA's Committee on the Future of Public Relations, a committee established for the primary purpose of advancing the status of professionalism, especially among members of PRSA; Ms. Barkelew is vice president of corporate public relations, Dayton Hudson Corp., Minneapolis, MN.

Included among the milestone dates are:

1947 - The founding of PRSA
1950 - Adoption by PRSA of a Code of Ethics
1962 - Accreditation program started offering "APR" designation.
1980 - North American Public Relations Council established.
1986 - The first Symposium on Demonstrating Professionalism; starting the process of increasing professional standards among public relations practitioners.
1988 - A committee of scholars and practitioners completes its work in publishing an outline of a codified Public Relations Body of Knowledge. The cochairpersons of this Body of Knowledge Task Force were Dr. James Van Leuven of Colorado, and George M. Fowler of Mountain Bell, Denver, Colorado.

The Jackson (1988) article, in turn, was written in anticipation of the November 1988 PRSA convention at which time the PRSA Assembly was to take up the issue of professionalism by discussing and voting on the proposed professional progression model developed by PRSA's Committee on the Future of Public Relations. The Assembly at this time passed an enabling by-law that required those PRSA members who wished to retain their accreditation status to do something to demonstrate their professional growth. The Assembly at the 1989 convention would act on proposals of how such professional growth was to be achieved.

Although public relations practitioners, through such organizations as PRSA, were focusing on accreditation as one of the primary means to advance professionalism, public relations educators were coming together to examine the kind of curricular requirements needed to fulfill public relations education offered by colleges and universities in the United States.

COMMISSIONS ON PUBLIC RELATIONS EDUCATION

The first formal move was made in August 1973 when a Commission on Public Relations Education was established by official sanction of the Public Relations Division of the Association of Education in Journalism (later to be called the Association of Education in Journalism and Mass Communication [AEJMC]). This Commission of seven members was headed by cochairpersons, the late Carroll Bateman of the Insurance Information Institute and Professor Scott Cutlip of then University of

Wisconsin.[1] The work of the commission ended in 1975 with a report entitled "A Design for Public Relations Education" (Commission on Public Relations Education, 1975), setting forth, among other things, recom- mended curricula for public relations at the undergraduate and graduate levels. The report was acted upon by the AEJ Public Relations Division with a strong endorsement of the recommended curricula.

This was just the beginning. Within the next 12 years, two more commissions were established to review changes affecting public relations education and to update the curricula. These changes included the expan- sion of the public relations field itself, the increased number of master's degree programs in public relations, the rapid increase in enrollments in both undergraduate and graduate public relations sequences of study, the increasing concern of practitioners about the status of public relations professionalism, and the many new advances in communication technol- ogy, including among others computer utilization, cable television, satellite transmission, video recorders, and the like.

The Commission on Graduate Study in Public Relations was established by the Public Relations Division of AEJMC in August 1982, with the mission to update and provide a more detailed recommended curriculum for graduate education in public relations; the commission was headed by cochairpersons, Dr. Michael B. Hessee, University of Alabama, and Paul Alvarez, then president of Ketchum Communication.[2] It finished its work in 1985 with the endorsement of AEJMC's Public Relations Division; the report with its recommended graduate curriculum was published with a grant from the Foundation for Public Relations Research and Education for free distribution through PRSA's New York City headquarter office (Commission on Graduate Study in Public Relations, 1985).

The third commission came into existence in 1983. It, in turn, was called the Commission on Undergraduate Public Relations, and, as its name indicates, it confined its work to studying and recommending an updated version of a model undergraduate curriculum. The commission was estab- lished as a joint venture by the Public Relations Division of AEJMC, PRSA, and the Educators Section of PRSA. It completed its work in 1987

---

[1]Other members besides Bateman and Cutlip included Milton Fairman, public relations consultant; Dr. James Grunig, University of Maryland; Dr. Otto Lerbinger, Boston Univer- sity; Betsy Ann Plank, Illinois Bell Telephone Co.; and Prof. Alan Scott, University of Texas.

[2]Serving on the 12-member commission, in addition to Hessee and Alvarez, were John Bailey, International Association of Business Communicators; Dr. William P. Ehling, Syracuse University; Dr. William Faith, University of Southern California; Dr. James Grunig, University of Maryland; Dr. Frank Kalupa, University of Georgia; Elizabeth Ann Kovacs, PRSA; Betsy Ann Plank, Illinois Bell Telephone Co.; Ronald E. Rhody, Bank of America; Dr. Frederick H. Teahan, PRSA; and Prof. Frank W. Wylie, California State University, Los Angeles.

with a 40-page report made available, as with the other reports, through PRSA's New York City office (Commission on Undergraduate Public Relations Education, 1987).

The commission was headed by cochairpersons, Betsy Ann Plank, Illinois Bell Telephone, and Dr. William P. Ehling, Syracuse University. There were a number of similarities and differences between the 1983–1987 commission and its predecessor, the 1973–1975 commission. With reference to similarities, the 1983–1987 commission, at its initial meeting, reaffirmed the recommendations made by the first commission; it also retained the "design" designation used by the first commission in its final report. The pattern of membership for both commissions was the same with commissioners representing both education and practice.

However, the 1983–1987 commission differed from its predecessor by focusing attention exclusively on undergraduate public relations education; it did not list recommended courses to be included in a sequence of study, but, instead, identified intellectual and conceptual content areas that undergraduate public relations programs should cover in course work. Moreover, the 1983–1987 commission consisted of 26 members in comparison to only seven members of the 1973–1975 commission, and not all educators came exclusively from the ranks of the Public Relations Division of AEJMC.

To seek as broad a base as possible, the 1983–1987 commission included representatives from the IABC and its Educators Academy; the Foundation for Public Relations Research and Education; the American Marketing Association; the International Communication Association; the American Management Association, and the Speech Communication Association. All these organizations were identified as having an interest in and a concern for public relations education.

To understand something about the contributions that these commissions made to public relations education in little over a decade, it is necessary to return to the establishment of the first commission. In its 1975 report, the first commission stated that its establishment was the result of a "paper commenting on the unsatisfactory and disparate state of public relations education in U.S. colleges and universities" (see commission on Public Relations Education, 1975, p. 1). This paper was authored by the late J. Carroll Bateman and Prof. Scott M. Cutlip and presented to the Public Relations Division of the then Association of Education in Journalism (AEJ) at its annual 1973 meeting. The content of this paper was reprinted in part in the commission's 1975 report to provide the rationale and justification of the commission's establishment.

In this paper, Bateman and Cutlip (Commission on Public Relations Education, 1975) were critical of both public relations education and the practice. Among other things, they observed that:

The need for qualified, competent, professional assistance in this field was never greater than it is today. Yet the heavy hand of the past—its publicity genesis—still dominates public relations practice today when our divided society cries out for communication, conciliation and community. Call it "public relations," "public affairs," "corporation communications," or whatever you will, the need for trained persons in this area is likely to increase in coming decades, as our society becomes even more complex.

Yet, we have already witnessed and are witnessing today a dearth of professional public relations practitioners capable of operating at the higher executive levels in all institutions—public and private—where their counsel is needed. The number of qualified people in public relations is incapable of meeting the demand for competent practitioners. Generally speaking, most of those in public relations work today were not specifically educated for this type of career. They are "retreads" from other fields of communication.

In the last quarter-century, more and more institutions of higher learning have turned their attention to public relations as a field of study. To a very considerable extent, courses in public relations are offered on an elective basis at the undergraduate level. Many of the courses, however, are taught by instructors who themselves are not fully qualified in the theory and practice of public relations. Comparatively few colleges and universities offer degree programs in public relations at the undergraduate level, and fewer still an opportunity to study public relations at the graduate level. Generally, these degree programs are taught by, or under the direction of, well qualified faculty members.

But, overall, the quality of public relations education is spotty. There are few if any common standards to be met; only a handful of programs have been accredited by the American Council on Education in Journalism.

After some 30 years of public relations education, there is urgent need for a thorough examination and review of the educational process in respect to preparing people for the practice of public relations, and for managerial and administrative positions so that they will have an appropriate understanding of public relations practice and its values. (pp. 1–2)

The authors (Commission on Public Relations Education, 1975) were clear about the relationship of education and professionalism, noting that the latter was contingent on the former; they also were critical of the low state at which public relations was being practiced:

If the needs for public relations leaders for tomorrow are to be met, if public relations practice is to move further in the direction of professionalization, the educational process must be strengthened and standardized within flexible limits . . .

If public relations practice has not yet succeeded in becoming a profession —
and regrettably but understandably it has not — a portion of the causes may be
attributed both to the contemporary practitioners of the art and to the
educators who prepare young people for careers in this field . . . (p. 3)

But as the authors (Commission on Public Relations Education, 1975)
pointed out, the practice of public relations is still young, dating back to early
years of this century. Hence, there is a matter of time to allow public relations
practice to mature. However, there is more at stake than time alone:

But the passage of time alone will not assure the attainment of professional
status for public relations practitioners. Unless educators and practitioners in
the field of public relations act together to guide the art into the direction of
professionalism, the present practice of public relations may very well level
off at a point where the public relations practitioner is hardly more than a
messenger boy in the total communications system — a level of operation that
presently and unfortunately is all too common. (p. 3)

The 1973–1975 Commission on Public Relations Education was the
authors' answer to taking the first step in strengthening and standardizing
public relations education at both the undergraduate and graduate levels
through the joint action of educators and practitioners; serving on this
commission were four educators and three practitioners.

The commissioners saw the undergraduate curriculum for the education
of students preparing to enter the practice of public relations as "a series of
concentric circles" (Commission on Public Relations Education, 1975).

The smallest, central circle, would enclose those subjects specifically concerned with public relations practice. The second circle, somewhat larger,
would encompass related subjects in the general field of communications. The
third and largest circle would represent the general liberal arts and humanities
background expected of all students. (p. 8)

The commission spelled out in specific terms the kind of courses falling
into the three circles of liberal arts (or general studies), communication
studies, and public relations studies. The effort at standardizing the
undergraduate curriculum, then, took place in the areas of communication
and public relations. It was expected that a student majoring in public
relations would complete courses in Theory and Process of Communication, Writing for the Mass Media, Copy Editing, and Graphics of Communication in the communication studies area, and Introduction to Public
Relations, Publicity Media and Campaigns, Public Relations Case Problems, and Internship or Practicum in the public relations studies area. If
each of these courses were treated in terms of 3 credit hours, the public

relations major would be required to successfully complete 24 credit hours—12 credit hours in communications and 12 credit hours in public relations. To bring the public relations major to the conventional 30-hour level, several additional courses could be taken from communications or management.

Turning to the master's level of education, the commission noted that there existed only a few programs of study at this level and, in a critical note, pointed out that the few that did exist were "little more than glorified undergraduate programs" (Commission on Public Relations Education, 1975, p. 12). Hence, the commission called for a graduate curriculum that should focus the student's attention on research methods and existing research data, and, at the same time, require the student to engage in original research. Moreover, a master's degree program should be more flexible than an undergraduate program to permit the student to develop a program of study to fit such areas as corporate public relations, government public relations, and the like.

In keeping with this orientation, the commission recommended a set of courses from which a master's degree student would be able to "select a balanced program" (Commission on Public Relations Education, 1975, p. 13) of study from courses falling into two areas: (a) media studies which included courses in Mass Media and Society and Advanced Communication Theory, and (b) general public relations studies which included courses in Public Relations Law and Ethics, Contemporary Public Relations Problems, Organization and Management of Public Relations Organizations and Departments, and an advanced course in Public Opinion Research and Analysis of Social Trends. To this list, the student could add additional courses to fit his or her future plans, including a thesis to allow for original research.

The commission, recognizing that only a few doctoral-level programs permitted or encouraged specialization in public relations, gave only a limited amount of attention to this area of education, pointing out that it was:

> . . . desirable that doctoral level programs with a specialization in public relations be encouraged not only in schools of journalism and/or communications, but also in schools of business administration and public administration, and probably even in other specialized schools (international relations and school administration, to name a few). (Commission on Public Relations Education, 1975, p. 15).

Increasing the number of doctoral students in public relations, from the perspective of the commission, would increase the number entering the teaching field thereby increasing the number of public relations instructors with research competence to add to the body of knowledge of the field.

By hindsight, what was being advocated for undergraduate and graduate public relations curricula appears today to be fairly conventional. But it needs to be remembered that in the mid-1970s, public relations education hardly went beyond a one-course offering; the sequence of study was essentially a journalistic one with an introductory public relations course added usually as an elective. Hence, what the commission was proposing, in comparison to what actually was being done on the college campus, was indeed an important step forward in the effort to strengthen and standardize public relations education, especially at the undergraduate level. The commission's final report clearly emphasized the necessity of having a minimum of at least four clearly identifiable public relations courses to form the core of a public relations sequence of study.

In the early 1980s, Dr. Albert Walker of Northern Illinois University conducted a study of public relations education in the United States under a grant from the Foundation for Public Relations Research and Education, resulting in a report, "Status and Trends in Public Relations Education in U.S. Senior Colleges and Universities, 1981" (Walker, 1981). What he found, among other things, was a substantial growth in full-time undergraduate and graduate study and part-time study primarily on the graduate level, and a close partnership between public relations educators and practitioners in the teaching of public relations courses. He also found that, although some graduate public relations programs emphasized problem-solving and management skills, most of these programs contained only one or two identifiable public relations courses; the rest were courses imported from other areas and/or departments such as journalism and mass media, advertising and marketing, research in mass communication, and political science and public administration.

THE COMMISSION ON GRADUATE STUDIES IN PUBLIC RELATIONS

Nonetheless, in a brief period of 10 years since the first commission report, the public relations scene in higher education and the workplace had undergone a number of significant changes, calling for a reevaluation of graduate public relations education. These changes included the rapid growth in employment opportunities in public relations and an accompanying growth in graduate public relations education; by the early 1980s, more than 51 institutions indicated they were providing graduate-level programs in public relations. These changes were dramatic enough to bring educators and practitioners together in 1982 in the form of a 12-member commission, this one concerned exclusively with graduate public relations education; the commission was divided equally between educators and practitioners.

As with the first commission, this commission was concerned with the relationship between educators and practitioners and between education and professionalism.

In its final report, the Commission on Graduate Study in Public Relations (1985) wrote:

> As the public relations discipline reached toward maturity, legitimate concerns arose regarding the academic preparation of people entering the field. A trend aimed more at formalizing the practice of public relations stressed standards regarding qualifications, background and professionalism.
>
> The outgrowth has been the drive toward professionalism through new emphasis on graduate study in public relations. Practitioners and educators must act in concert to guide public relations in the direction of professionalism.
>
> Without this necessary partnership, the practice of public relations will never attain the professional status it needs and deserves to perform the communication and management tasks it has been assigned in the United States. (p. 5)

Hence, the Commission on Graduate Study in Public Relations (1985) had as one of its primary goals that of designing a model curriculum, while at the same time making recommendations concerning the "manner in which graduate-level education in public relations can meet the needs of the profession as well as bring about the improvement of practice itself" (p. 5).

To that end, the commission specifically recommended that at a minimum a student working toward a graduate degree in public relations should complete successfully courses in five areas including a thesis or a comprehensive examination so that a minimum total of 30 credit hours would be attained. The courses of study would fall into the areas of:

1. research and theory, including at least two required courses in research methodology and communication theory;
2. communication processes as applied to public relations including concepts and techniques relating to interorganizational theory, issue identification and analysis, conflict-cooperation assessment, and public opinion survey and analysis;
3. public relations management, including three required courses (i.e., Public Relations Principles, Practices, and Theory; Public Relations Management; and Public Relations Programming and Production) and one public relations specialty option;
4. a minor specialty of 6–9 credit hours, allowing students to specialize in such fields as corporate public relations, governmental public relations, and the like; and
5. a thesis worth 3 semester credit hours.

At the doctoral level, the commission, like its predecessor, noted that the purpose of a PhD degree program in public relations is to help students "develop the theoretical and research skills they will need to add to the body of public relations knowledge" (Commission on Graduate Study, 1985, p. 10). Clearly, then, it will be doctoral students and those continuing their research endeavors after obtaining a doctoral degree who will make the primary contributions to the growing body of public relations knowledge. In short, the body of public relations knowledge is heavily dependent on those who are the product of doctoral programs focusing on public relations activities and problems. More specifically, the commission pointed out that the core curriculum of a public relations-oriented doctoral program will be one emphasizing research methodology and research data analysis. In addition, such doctoral programs should include specialized seminars in public relations on topics of public relations management, organizational structure, interorganizational relations, public relations roles, public relations law, and the like. Finally, the public relations doctoral candidate should conduct dissertation research in which theory is applied to attain solutions to important public relations problems.

These recommendations, in contrast to those made by the first commission with respect to graduate education, were more explicit, more detailed, and more structured, even though the general rationale for graduate education was largely the same for both commissions. The Commission on Graduate Study in Public Relations, however, was mindful that more master's degree public relations programs were coming into existence, that many of these programs might be weak, and that a more specific graduate curricular model was needed to strengthen and standardize public relations graduate education.

THE COMMISSION ON UNDERGRADUATE STUDIES IN PUBLIC RELATIONS

Ten years after the first commission on public relations education was established and a year after the second commission on graduate education finished its work, members of the Public Relations Division of AEJMC again met; this time these educators examined the state of public relations education at the undergraduate level; they reviewed the changes that altered the production and management skills being utilized in public relations practice, the needs and uses of new evaluative research techniques, and the adoption of the rapidly expanding computer-based communication technologies. The outcome was the establishment in August 1983 of a 27-member Commission on Undergraduate Public Relations Education, jointly sponsored by AEJMC's Public Relations Division, PRSA, and PRSA's Educators Section.

At this time, as the commission's final report indicated, more than 150 colleges and universities said they had public relations sequences and degree programs; 60% of the public relations sequences now ranked first or second in student enrollment. In the mid 1980s, public relations majors constituted 13% of 82,760 students enrolled in schools or departments of journalism or communications. Accompanying this growth in student enrollment was the expansion of the field itself. The Department of Labor reported in 1985 that 143,000 people were engaged in public relations, a 24% increase since 1975.

The commission began its work by conducting formal research to determine what educators and practitioners believed should be the content of undergraduate public relations education.[3] It had been widely assumed before the research was undertaken that educators and practitioners differed substantially with regard to what should or should not be taught. This assumption turned out to be without substance. Instead, the research results indicated clearly that there was virtual unanimity of opinion held by educators and practitioners.

The research findings also laid the conceptual basis and provided the curricular guidelines in the discussions that took place during the next 3 years.

In its final report, the commission made a number of (Commission on Undergraduate Public Relations Education, 1987); recommendations of these there was the recommendation that of the credit hours required for a baccalaureate degree, a minimum of 54% should be secured in liberal arts, no more than 25% of the total number required for graduation should be obtained through professionally oriented courses. And of this 25%, a minimum of half of the credit hours should be in courses clearly identifiable as public relations courses.

Hence, the recommended undergraduate public relations curriculum, aside from required liberal arts (arts and sciences) courses, was divided into (a) "professional education" (25% of the total) with the content emphasis on technical/production, historical/institutional, and communication processes/structure, and (b) "public relations studies" (a minimum of half of

---

[3]The research project was coordinated by Prof. James W. Anderson, a commission member, and his associate, Dr. Robert L. Kendall, both of the University of Florida. In May 1985, 1,500 questionnaires were mailed to a sample of practitioners and to all educators listed as members of PRSA, the International Communication Association, and the IABC. Without follow-up reminders, 544 questionnaires (36.29% return) were sent back to be analyzed. Each respondent had been asked to give a value rating to 124 items, identified as courses, parts of courses, or topics considered to cover the scope of present-day undergraduate public relations education. The results are reported in full in the commission's final report, "Design for Undergraduate Public Relations Education," Commission on Undergraduate Public Relations Education, 1987.

the professional education area) with the content emphasis on public relations principles and theory (including ethics), communication principles as applicable to public relations activity, strategic planning and evaluative research, management principles involving goal setting and program implementation, and supervised internship program.

The commission made it a special point to provide, in considerable detail, the rationale for the various concepts employed in defining the content areas. It also made it clear that although undergraduate students were to attain a high level of writing and production skills, these skills and their use had to be understood within the framework of public relations management; it was at the management level where public relations executives engaged in accessing the social environment in which their organization had to function, formulating public relations objectives and communication strategies, conducting evaluative research on program performance, and doing benefit-cost analysis to justify the public relations effort. Hence, a clear understanding of the tasks and responsibilities of public relations management was regarded as prerequisite to grasping when, how, and why to apply production skills at the lower tactical level.

The ends of public relations education, then, are those emphasizing problem identification and problem solving, not publicity for publicity's sake. In this regard, the commission endorsed the "Official Statement of Public Relations," adopted by the PRSA Assembly, November 6, 1982; this statement defined public relations activity in management terms performed at the strategic level of operation to make it an activity far different and more inclusive than publicity narrowly confined to copy production and media placement.

FIVE-COURSE REQUIREMENT

The main plank in the commission's model curriculum was the so-called "five-course requirement," that is, five identifiable public relations courses. Some educators opposed this requirement in that it would require educational resources that some schools or departments did not have or were unwilling to allocate to public relations education; the counterargument was that in such cases public relations had not reached a level of academic maturity to be called a public relations sequence or a degree-granting program and, hence, ought not pretend to be something it was not.

To make the five-course requirement recommendation something more than just wishful thinking, several people who had served on the commission turned to the PRSA Assembly for legislative support. In 1987, the PRSA Assembly approved a resolution directed at conditions for establishing or maintaining a Public Relations Student Society of America

(PRSSA) chapter on college or university campuses. The resolution required as a condition for PRSSA chapter's existence that there be a program of undergraduate public relations study and such a program must have at least five courses with public relations in the title or catalog description. The PRSA Education Affairs Committee, in turn, contacted 158 schools with PRSSA chapters to provide data on the number of courses offered; by April 1988, 129 had responded, of which only 13% failed to meet minimum standards. The responses also showed that 112 schools met the five-course standard of which 59% offered five courses and 20 schools offered seven or more courses in public relations; the highest number was 12 courses. In short, what had been largely a state yet to be attained in 1975 when the first commission announced its recommended undergraduate public relations curriculum had become reality in 1988 when 87% of schools offering public relations programs had programs containing five or more public relations designated courses.

TWO NEW TASK FORCES

As the commission was nearing the end of its work, two other groups came into existence — the Task Force on Demonstrating Professionalism appointed by PRSA in 1986[4] and the Body of Knowledge Task Force appointed by PRSA in the same year. With respect to the latter task force, 20 leading scholars and practitioners labored for more than a year to define and categorize the subject matter of public relations and to take the first step in codifying the material making up this subject matter.[5]

After designating the main categories (e.g., Foundation of Public Relations, Organizational and Management Context, Communication and Relationship Context, etc.), task force members were assigned to each of these categories to refine and divide them into still smaller subcategories. Over 600 articles and books were identified by the task force members and

---

[4]This task force, chaired by Patrick Jackson, APR, senior counsel of Jackson, Jackson and Wagner, and Ann Barkelew, APR, Vice President, Corporate Public Relations, Dayton Hudson Corp., conducted in the spring of 1987 a symposium for 80 PRSA leaders and invitees of sister societies; this led to a list of suggestions on how to advance public relations professionalism, which, in turn, were brought before the PRSA Assembly for review. The task force, in turn, was re-formed as the Future of Public Relations Committee. An additional symposium was held; this in turn resulted in the presentation to the PRSA Assembly a model for professional progression in November 1988. This proposal is now under study.

[5]The first stage of a four-stage project was completed in a report published in the Winter 1987 issue of *Public Relations Review,* explaining the Body of Knowledge endeavor and the agreed upon subject matter categories. The final stages, begun in 1988, involves getting educators to write abstracts of all the identified articles and books and making these abstracts available on request at PRSA headquarters through computer retrieval.

assigned to their proper category and subcategory. This list, covering 16 pages, was published in the Winter 1988 issue of the *Public Relations Review.*

In a special issue on "Education in Public Relations," Catherine A. Pratt and Terry Lynn Rentner (1989) wrote about the Body of Knowledge project, noting the importance of "PRSA's Herculean efforts in gathering and organizing the diverse threats of research and information pertinent to the study and practice of public relations" which they regarded as "a seminal document of critical importance to public relations" (p. 57). In addition, the authors pointed out that such a body of knowledge does two things: (a) it provides "the foundation for a legitimate claim for the criterion of professionalism that requires an acceptable body of knowledge" and (b) it "should help current scholars to focus their efforts on areas where there is a decided lack of definitive research" (p. 57).

With the work of the Body of Knowledge well underway, it would appear that as the public relations enterprise moved into the 1990s all the criteria of professionalism finally had been met. The belief that public relations was more than an occupation, that it, indeed, was a true profession was forcibly presented by Jackson (1988) when he wrote: Public relations practitioners have been talking about professionalism, in one way or the other, for at least a half century. First, came the underlying question: can public relations be a true profession? The answer to that one is hardly debatable any longer (p. 27).

Jackson (1988) went on to say that "to qualify as a profession" a field of endeavor "must be endemic to the human condition" (p. 28); short, it must be an essential part of human existence. For Jackson, "public relations fits this criterion of professionalism: it is devoted to the essential function of "building and improving human relationships" (p.). Moreover, public relations is, like other professions, an "art applied to science" (p.); and most important, public relations qualifies as a profession "because it is an endeavor in which the public interest must be served" (p. 28):

Still, as every practitioner will recognize, there is a problem in all this. We may know we can qualify as a profession, but does the rest of the world know this? The resounding answer is no. What is needed, then, are strategic methods of demonstrating our professionalism.

The first one, obviously, is that each of us use the Public Relations Body of Knowledge, subscribe to the Code of Professional Standards, and exemplify the behavior of true professionals in all we do.

Second, many programs have been advanced through public relations organizations to help demonstrate the professionalism of public relations practice. (p. 30)

All this has led, according to Jackson's (1988) view, to the majority of practitioners agreeing that "professional development and training activities are the key" (p.) for completing the final requirement of professionalism. It was for this reason that Jackson strongly defended the *professional progression model* developed by his committee, the Committee on the Future of Public Relations of PRSA, and appealed to the PRSA Assembly to adopt it.[6]

Even earlier, Cutlip et al. (1985), stated that public relations already had met a number of conditions in its movement toward professionalism. Specifically, the assets that currently support professionalism include:

(1) large national societies (PRSA and IABC), supplemented by several strong specialized associations; (2) codes of ethics clearly spelled out; (3) association peer review judicial committee, created to enforce their standards upon member; (4) fairly stiff eligibility standards for full-fledged membership in PRSA and IABC; (5) training, education, and research in many universities and colleges, a small part of which is supported by PRSA and IABC; (6) a large and growing body of scholarly books, papers, and journals, in addition to professional technical publication; (7) greater status for practitioners within their organizations; and (8) increasing public service contributions by practitioners. (p. 454)

PRESENT LOW STATE OF PUBLIC RELATIONS

Although the picture of public relations professionalism has brightened over the years and public relations educational programs have grown and strengthened, all is not well. The need for either education or accreditation in public relations is still much in doubt. Entry into the public relations field does not require specialized educational preparation. Grunig (1989) pointed out that at least half of the active public relations practitioners do not have a formal education in public relations; Ferguson (1987) found even fewer with a public relations education.

Only a small fraction of those who claim to be engaged in public relations work belong to one or both of the two major public relations organizations or to any of smaller specialized public relations groups, and only a minority of practitioners seek to be accredited by either PRSA or IABC, which is regarded as a status of professionalism attained by meeting established standards and passing a series of examination (Cutlip et al., 1985, p. 73). Jackson (1988), in turn, admitted that "only a quarter of PRSA members are accredited" and that many within the PRSA ranks "still strongly resist"

[6]The professional progression model was present to the PRSA Assembly at its annual meeting in November 1988; further action was to take place at the 1989 meeting.

accreditation (p. 28). Although there has been much talk about mandated accreditation through licensing, no state requires those entering the field to be licensed. And at the point of employment, employers have shown no indication to make a public relations education or accreditation by one of the major public relations organizations prerequisite for obtaining a job.

Similar problems are encountered in public relations education itself. Although three commissions on public relations education have recommended model curricula for both undergraduate and graduate public relations education, institutions of higher education do not feel compelled to adhere to such recommended models; there still is widespread evidence that various schools and departments, cashing in on the popularity of public relations among students, have added a course or two to existing sequences in journalism and advertise them as bona fide programs in public relations. Even where public relations programs are in place, problems of inadequate support are encountered; as Grunig (1989) reported, the needed education resources for strengthening existing public relations educational programs are not forthcoming, even under circumstances where enrollments are rising. In schools of journalism or communication, where most public relations sequences of study are found, one finds tension and in-fighting between journalism-oriented faculty members and those who teach public relations courses; in the words of Cutlip et al. (1985), public relations still is seen as an unsavory activity committed to cluttering the mass media with the "debris of pseudoevents and phony phrases" leading to channels of communication being corroded "with cynicism and 'credibility gaps' " (p. 451). This issue again emerged when David Weaver of Indiana University, then president of the Association for Education in Journalism and Mass Communication, was quoted in the *Chronicle of Higher Education* as saying that public relations and advertising should not be taught in schools of journalism or mass communication — instead, they should be taught in such places as schools of business administration.[7]

To compound the difficulties confronting the public relations field, little agreement is found among either public relations educators or practitioners as to what constitutes public relations. Unhappily the term is widely equated with publicity, and viewed as the simple effort of writing news releases for placement in the mass media. To members of the lay public and to the majority of practicing public relations workers, public relations still means getting attention for a person, organization, or cause in the mass media by

---

[7]Grunig (1989) reported the reaction to Weaver's comments by noting that "Public relations educators were incensed because they had fought for years to gain resources for their programs from reluctant deans of journalism schools and higher administrators. Although they have had only limited success in getting resources, a statement such as Weaver's could only make the fight for resources more difficult" (p. 12).

whatever means available. This activity is anathema to representatives of the news media; it is called the "hype" and those doing it, "flacks."[8]

The news media representatives never tire in their use of the term in news stories to describe people, especially high-ranking politicians and government officials including the president of the United States, who are engaged, from the reporters' point of view, in deception of one kind or another, in dealing with appearances rather than substance, and in misleading the public through misinformation or what is now called *disinformation*. The term allows news representatives to editorialize in their news stories under the guise of reporting facts. Hence, for them anything that appears questionable, unethical, misleading, or nefarious is instantly assigned the term public relations.

But even serious attempts to give public relations content that has intellectual substance, which can be defended ethically and made administratively viable, often have led to more difficulties than solutions. Efforts at defining public relations have not as yet fully succeeded. Attempts to conceptualize public relations as some kind of socially oriented function frequently have resulted only in producing an outpouring of simple definitions that hardly get beyond that of slogans; Rex Harlow (1976, p. 36) found 472 such "definitions" from which he then attempted to construct his own, somewhat lengthy, definition. Members of PRSA worked for years to develop an acceptable statement spelling out the rationale and responsibilities of public relations while at the same time tying it to the top level of an organization's management operation; at the November 6, 1982 meeting, the PRSA Assembly adopted what was identified as the "Official Statement on Public Relations."

PRSA DEFINES PUBLIC RELATIONS

In this statement public relations is specified as a "management function" that is responsible for a host of tasks including such management activities as "anticipating, analyzing and interpreting public opinion, attitudes and issues which might impact" on an organization, doing research on a "continuing basis," "planning and implementing the organization's effort to influence or change public policy," and "setting objectives, planning, budgeting, recruiting and training staff"—in short, to manage "the re-

---

[8]One finds by turning to the Associated Press Managing Editors' manual, the *APME Guidelines,* the following: "A flack is a person who makes all or part of his income by obtaining space in newspapers without cost to himself or his clients. Usually a professional . . . they are known formally as public relations men. The flack is the modern equivalent of the cavalier highwayman of old." See Cutlip et al. (1985, p. 430).

sources needed to perform all of the above." Although these responsibilities appear to make public relations a top managerial function, unhappily they also equate public relations with the whole of an organization's management activity, producing conceptual confusion and an administrative paradox. Given PRSA's concept of public relations, one is required either to view anyone in the position of a public relations director as being a super executive overseeing all of an organization's activities, including those of chief executive officer and the board of directors, or to view every manager in an organization as engaging in public relations by virtue of doing what managers are supposed to do, namely, anticipate attitudes and issues, do research, set objectives, plan, fix budgets, and the like. The first view obviously is administratively outlandish; the second, because it makes public relations as a specialized administrative function irrelevant, is counter productive.

It also should be noted that the three commissions on public relations education did not spell out specifically the nature of public relations for which curricula were being designed. Hence, it is not clear just what the recommended curricula regarded as central to public relations education — publicity with its emphasis on copy preparation, or management with its emphasis on problem solving. Given this ambiguity, many of today's public relations curricula are really programs of publicity techniques featuring the writing of press releases, graphic layout, and public relations (i.e., publicity) campaigns.

PUBLIC RELATIONS VERSUS PUBLICITY

Nonetheless, a number of public relations educators and scholars have struggled to lift public relations practice to a place higher than publicity. Interestingly enough, in the first commission report a plea was made to disengage public relations activity from "its publicity genesis," associating it, instead, with the need for "communication, conciliation, and community" to bring pieces of a divided society together (Commission on Public Relations Education, 1975, p. 2). Dr. Glen M. Broom of San Diego State University also has held to the view that public relations was something more demanding than publicity. When he joined Scott Cutlip and Allen Center as the third author in writing the sixth edition of *Effective Public Relations* (Cutlip et al., 1985), he altered the book's definition of public relations to one that makes it a management function with the primary task of identifying, establishing, and maintaining "mutual beneficial relationships between an organization and the various publics on whom its success or failure depends" (p. 4).

Grunig and Hunt (1984), in their textbook *Managing Public Relations,* talked about various public relations models used by different practitioners;

these, ranging from the simplest to the more sophisticated, include press agentry, public information, two-way asymmetrical, and two-way symmetrical. The latter model, in Grunig's (1989) view, is one that describes the "public relations efforts which are based on research and that use communication to manage conflict and to improve understanding with strategic publics" (p. 17). It also is the one to which public relations practitioners are slowly moving in their professional roles. Ehling (1975, 1981, 1984, 1985, 1987) has insisted since 1975 that public relations can be conceived only as a management function if it is sui generis, that is, in a class by itself and, hence, functionally different from such activities as marketing, personnel, and financing. Moreover, public relations management only can achieve this status by making its primary mission (end state) that of attaining and/or maintaining accord between its organization and other organizations or social groupings making up the organization's social environment; however, to attain accord requires that a continual effort must be made to mediate and mitigate conflict between an organization and its environment. The means to be used in attaining this end state is a unique kind of communication system — a two-staged operation that is bilaterally designed jointly by the conflicting parties and conducted in such a way as to promote the two-way flow of information. This system stands as the polar opposite from that of publicity or advertising, which are one-staged, unilaterally designed systems intended to produce only a one-way information flow.

This view also has been articulated by some public relations practitioners. Gossen and Sharp (1987), for example, saw the primary mission of public relations practice as one that focuses on "how to manage dispute resolution" (p. 35). This approach sees communication in terms of a negotiating process between adversarial groups or organizations in which the objective of such negotiational type communication is to come to a "win-win" solution in which both parties gain something:

> This "win-win" negotiation (also known as "integrative negotiation") is the key to lasting success in dispute resolution. Often called "creative problem solving," this win-win modality of creating mutual gains is radically different from the "win-lose" (called "zero-sum") bargaining situation . . . But in public-policy disputes zero-sum agreements that favor business interest over public interest are short-lived, or are overturned by lawsuits initiated by unsatisfied public stakeholders . . . Although the dispute resolution process is issues-based, it requires more two-way communications and program-structuring techniques than does traditional issue management . . . Somewhat unique within public relations, dispute resolution activities create and manage actual communication channels, rather than relying on existing channels such as mass media. (p. 35)

Such a view of public relations' primary mission, which emphasizes win-win negotiational communication in dispute resolution, is held by only a few educators and practitioners. Admittedly there is a growing number of public relations executives (usually identified as vice presidents of corporate communication) who occupy high-ranking positions and have as their primary responsibility that of maintaining accord by handling negotiations in dispute-resolving cases; however, they are few in number.

The overwhelming number of practitioners who claim the title of public relations falls into the category of publicists—people who confine their activities to message producing with the hope of getting these messages used by the mass media; and much of this kind of activity is restricted further to product in publicity, making public relations subservient to marketing and an addendum to product advertising.

Dilenscheider (1987), president and chief executive officer of Hill and Knowlton, Inc., has been highly critical of this kind of public-relations-as-product-publicity activity. He referred to such efforts as a "logistic support business" (p. 3) and viewed it as standing in contrast to a "strategic problem-solving" (p. 3) activity which he regarded as the primary concern of public relations management. Moreover, he stated that there is "too broad willingness in the public relations business in this country to go for the quick fix rather than something that's sustained and lasting" (p. 3). He also noted that public relations practitioners, by succumbing to the lure of product publicity, are too easily taken in "by color, and by sound and by light and by delivery systems and the glitz of the message" (p. 3). In short, he sees that both corporate and agency public relations practitioners are "given the job of carrying out a logistical support effort to get the message out—whether it's correct or incorrect" (p. 3).

If, indeed, public relations is to be reduced to a low-level copy production and placement activity and identified as essentially a press agentry/publicity function, then there is little or no foundation upon which to build a profession, no basis for developing curricula for undergraduate and graduate education, and no reason for erecting something called a body of knowledge. Publicity activity is virtually devoid of intellectual content, and those who practice it certainly have little need for either a body of knowledge or a profession.

Lesly (1988) was even more candid in this regard, for he observed that:

> We are faced with an anomaly. Public relations seems to be destined to go on growing in numbers and in universality of its use—while slipping in stature. There will be more people doing more things—except having a role in the top levels of our institutions . . .

> Most people in this field now use "public relations" and "publicity" interchangeably. And the only examples they cite of work done is *publicity* efforts—dealing with the media, getting space or time, running opinion campaigns.

The media in the field, PRSA and everyone else cite publicity efforts when they write about accomplishments. Even reference to a Tylenol success deal with how information was gotten out and misconceptions corrected, far more than about strategy and shaping policy. The Silver Anvils (of which I've received three for the only entries I've made) reward only campaigns and programs—emphasizing the misconception that doing publicity is what this field is all about . . .

There are still many internal public relations executives who want only specific functions from their outside sources—not top-level thinking and creativity. That way no one else who is able to impress management is ever seen. As a result, others in their companies see only technicians and specialists and have no inkling of what professional counsel can offer. Those internal people are likely to find they won't progress beyond the technical level.

So we have an anomaly. The field is growing; the demand for people who can perform is high. Yet there are probably fewer people who really have the respect and ear of management than at any time in the past 20 years. Unfortunately, only a small percentage of people can aspire to the top professional level. The self-interest of all others is to be happy with what there is for them and not to rock the boat by standing up for higher standards and better understanding. (pp. 3–4)

Lesly's (1988) views are depressing for the public relations educator and for the practitioners seeking to advance professionally. From his perspective, public relations as publicity is now the prevailing model accepted by people inside and outside of the public relations field. Worse still, public relations has been reduced to this low level of activity for several critical reasons—because chief executive officers see public relations in technical production terms that yield evidence that is immediate and concrete as manifested in media placement and because practitioners accept this form of public relations since it provides a safe haven for them as long as top management is caught up in the glitz that goes with publicity viewed as a quick fix.

This reality, however, undercuts virtually everything that has been done over the years to advance public relations professionalism and strengthen public relations education. If publicity is to be taken as the be-all and end-all of public relations, then there is no basis for professionalism and no reason for education.

Grunig (1989), however, adopted a more optimistic view. He believed that the future will see more and more academic units in colleges and universities adopting the kind of curricula put forward by the 1987 Commission on Undergraduate Public Relations Education and the 1983 Commission on Graduate Study in Public Relations. Moreover, as Grunig's own research has shown, education in public relations, more than education in journalism or in any other field, predicts whether public relations practitioners will practice a sophisticated kind of conflict-resolution management.[9]

Clearly professionalism is dependent on a high level of sophistication presented through formal education. Given such a growing sophistication, public relations yet may rid itself of the shackles of publicity. Is such a vision of public relations education too optimistic? Grunig (1989) thought not:

> To make the vision a reality, both [practitioners and educators] must make the decision that the profession of public relations requires specialized scholarship and education. Then they must back that decision with their support—both political and financial.

> Public relations needs such a commitment. So does society. (p. 23)

REFERENCES

Commission on Graduate Study in Public Relations. (1985). *Advancing public relations education.* New York: Foundation for Public Relations Research and Education.

Commission on Public Relations Education. (1975). *A design for public relations education.* New York: Foundation for Public Relations Research Education.

Commission on Undergraduate Public Relations Education. (1987). *Design for undergraduate public relations education.* Chicago: Illinois Bell Telephone.

Cutlip, S. M., & Center, A. H. (1978). *Effective public relations* (5th ed.). Englewood Cliffs, NJ: Prentice-Hall.

Cutlip, S. M., Center, A. H., & Broom, G. M. (1985). *Effective public relations* (6th ed.). Englewood Cliffs, NJ: Prentice-Hall.

Dilenschneider, R. L. (1987, November). *Corporate accountability with constituent publics.* Paper presented at the annual meeting of the Corporate Section of the Public Relations Society of America, Los Angeles.

Ehling, W. P. (1975). PR administration, management science, and purposive systems. *Public Relations Review, 1*(2), 15–43.

Ehling, W. P. (1981, August). *Toward a theory of public relations management: Application of purposive and conflict theory to communication.* Paper presented at the annual convention of the Association for Education in Journalism, East Lansing, MI.

Ehling, W. P. (1984). Application of decision theory in the construction of a theory of public relations management, I. *Public Relations Research & Education, 1*(Summer), 25–38.

Ehling, W. P. (1985). Application of decision theory in the construction of a theory of public relations management, II. *Public Relations Research & Education, 2*(Summer), 4–22.

Ehling, W. P. (1987, May). *Public relations functions and adversarial environments.* Paper presented at the annual conference of the International Communication Association, Montreal.

---

[9]Grunig (1989) also noted: "Practitioners without education in public relations usually are little more then press agents or journalists-in-residence, unless they are able to get equivalent knowledge through continuing education or self study" (p. 14).

Ferguson, D. (1987). *A practitioner looks at public relations education.* The 1987 Vern C. Schranz distinguished Lecture in Public Relations, Ball State University, Muncie, IN.

Gossen, R., & Sharp, K. (1987). Managing dispute resolution. *Public Relations Journal, 43*(12), 35–38.

Grunig, J. E. (1989). Teaching public relations in the future. *Public Relations Review, 15*(1), 12–24.

Grung, J. E., & Hunt, T. (1984). *Managing public relations.* New York: Holt, Rinehart & Winston.

Harlow, R. F. (1976). Building a public relations definition. *Public Relations Review, 2,* 36.

Jackson, P. (1988). Demonstrating professionalism. *Public Relations Journal, 44*(10) 27–31.

Lesly, P. (1988). Public relations numbers are up but stature down. *Public Relations Review, 14*(4), 3–7.

Marston, J. (1968). Hallmarks of a profession. *Public Relations Journal, 24,* 22–27.

Pratt, C. A., & Rentner, T. L. (1989). What's really being taught about ethical behavior. *Public Relations Review, 15*(1), 53–66.

Walker, A. (1981). *Status and trends in public relations in education in U.S. senior colleges and universities.* New York: Foundation for Public Relations Research and Education.

IV THE ORGANIZATIONAL LEVEL: THE CONDITIONS THAT MAKE EXCELLENCE IN PUBLIC RELATIONS POSSIBLE

Thus far, the general theory of public relations developed in this book has shown how individual communication programs must be conducted and how public relations departments must be organized if managed communication is to make organizations more effective. Public relations departments do not exist in isolation, however, and conditions in and around organizations affect the structure and practice of the public relations function. Part IV explores those conditions.

17
How Public Relations/ Communication Departments Should Adapt to the Structure and Environment of an Organization . . . And What They Actually Do

Larissa A. Grunig
University of Maryland

ABSTRACT

Early sociological theories of organizations maintained that behavior in organizations can be explained better by the structure of the organization— such variables as the extent to which decision making is centralized or that there are many formal rules— than by the characteristics of people in the organization. Writers on organizational excellence, whose work was reviewed in chapter 6, also describe what sociologists call an "organic" structure as a characteristic of an excellent organization. Sociologists theorized later that organizations develop structures that are most appropriate for their environments. Public relations scholars have followed these precedents and researched the extent to which the environment and structure determine the nature of public relations. This chapter shows that environment and structure do affect public relations but that they are not the only reasons why some organizations have excellent public relations and others do not. The chapter also maintains that activists make up the critical part of the environment that communication managers should monitor in practicing strategic management of public relations.

For more than 20 years, sociologists have chosen to focus their study on the organization—rather than the individual manager—largely as a revolt from the earlier psychological work done in administration. Building on the work of Max Weber and his notion of the bureaucracy as an ideal form of organization, scholars such as Burns and Stalker, Woodward, Thompson, Perrow, and Hage and Aiken looked at the impact of structure on organizational effectiveness. They looked first at technology and size as

467

causes of structure. Then, with the ensuing investigations of Lawrence and Lorsch (1967) and Thompson (1967), they added environmental factors into the equation. In fact, as early as the 1950s Parsons (1956a, 1956b) had studied organizational interchanges with the environment as a means by which the organization obtains its necessary resources. Along with other systems theorists, he emphasized the importance of an organization's equilibrium with its environment.

This chapter summarizes briefly this seminal research, first by defining key aspects of organizational structure and environments. It continues by explaining why the typical organization often fails to interact successfully with critical publics in the environment. It concludes by describing the groups within the environment that typically constrain organizations the most. Its overarching premise is that the environment affects the structure of the organization, which in turn has a mediating effect on its public relations activity. For an organization to maintain its equilibrium in any environment, it must depend in part on the boundary role of the public relations department—especially to communicate with activist groups.

ORGANIZATIONAL STRUCTURE

The basic question that structuralism addresses is the same one that Weber asked almost 40 years ago: What is the best form of organization and why? To answer, we begin by isolating key structural variables.

Structure, in this chapter, deals with more than a consideration of how tasks are to be carved up within a single department or on a horizontal plane—which was the emphasis of chapter 14. Instead, it emphasizes the vertical nature of structure or, in the words of Robbins (1987), "who reports to whom, and the formal coordinating mechanisms and interaction patterns that will be followed" (p. 4). Attending to the complexities of organizational structure is critical because as J. Grunig (1976) pointed out, "the behavior of the public relations practitioner is largely determined by the structure of the organization and the practitioner's role in that structure" (p. 1).

Hage (1980) developed the following set of four structural dimensions. These variables allow for comparisons between organizational types and for understanding the interdependencies of each structural variable with each other. J. Grunig and Hunt (1984, p. 100) pointed out that these variables also help predict the model of public relations an organization is likely to adopt. As a result, Hage's variables are especially appropriate for this study. They have been shown to provide a reliable way to study organizational behavior, including that of the public relations practitioner operating within the organization.

Centralization. Hage's notion of *centralization* as the hierarchy of authority is echoed in the works of J. Grunig (1976), who called it "the extent to which decision-making is concentrated in upper reaches of the organizational hierarchy" (p. 18) and Hall (1977), who considered it simply the distribution of power (p. 181). Hage (1980) defined centralization as "the level and variety of participation in strategic decisions by groups relative to the number of groups in the organization" (p. 65).

Hage (1980) considered centralization a characteristic of rigidly structured organizations, those that assign little decision-making power to groups in lower levels of the hierarchy. He also believed that centralization is associated with relatively little communication — and that the communication is primarily downward, from superiors to their subordinates (p. 365). Hage and his colleagues developed an index of hierarchy of authority that measures the extent to which workers may make their own work-related decisions without interference from supervisors. They also designed a measure of decision making that gauges the degree to which workers are allowed to participate in determining the policies and goals of the whole organization.

The dispersion of information and decision making throughout the organization is considered *decentralization*. Decentralization allows for organizations to respond quickly to changing environments and for more input into the decisions that result. Simon (1976) explained the importance of the centralization/decentralization issue as one that relates primarily to information, rather than to decision making: Because managers in an age of information technology are deluged with data, the capacity to attend to that information is critical (p. 294). The scarce resource here is not information itself but the organization's ability to process it.

Robbins (1987) considered centralization the most problematic of the structural variables. Decentralization, for example, has the advantages of reducing the probability of information overload, providing more voices in the decision-making process, responding rapidly to new information, instilling motivation, and helping train managers to make good decisions. Advantages of centralization, on the other hand, include a comprehensive perspective to decisions and efficiency.

Stratification. Hage (1965) defined *stratification* as the way in which rewards are distributed within an organization (p. 292). Aiken and he (Hage & Aiken, 1970) measured stratification with two indicators: the differences in income and prestige among jobs within an organization and the rate of mobility between low- and high-ranking positions.

The extent to which there are dividing lines between status levels and upward mobility indicates whether an organization is stratified or destratified. As with centralization, low levels of communication are associated with stratification. And, like centralization, stratification leads to a predominately downward flow of communication. Kanter (1982) hypothesized that what she called "creative collaboration" uninhibited by status differences would foster the interaction necessary for innovation in successful organizations.

Formalization.   *Formalization* represents the importance of rules and the degree to which they are enforced in an organization (Hage & Aiken, 1970, pp. 21–33). As they did with stratification, Hage and Aiken divided their measurement of formalization into two indices: job codification, which assesses how many rules define the workers' tasks, and rule observation, or the diligence used to enforce those rules.

J. Grunig and Hunt (1984) argued that highly formalized organizations discourage innovation because of the predominance of rules and regulations. They associated formalization with rigidly structured organizations. Hage (1980) compared formalization with communication and found that they tend to be opposite means of control and coordination (p. 365). Communication helps an organization coordinate its members, whereas formalization controls those workers.

However, more recent theorizing may have blurred this distinction. Robbins (1987) suggested "organizational culture" as a viable substitute for formalization. He reasoned that because it increases behavioral consistency and implies control without written documentation, culture may in fact be more effective because "culture controls the mind and soul as well as the body" (p. 362).

Complexity.   Hage (1965) initially defined *complexity* as the number of occupational specialties found in an organization and the level of training required for each specialty. Two years later, Aiken and he (Hage & Aiken, 1967a, 1967b) expanded this definition to include professionalism. Typical measures of complexity include the number of departments, the number of job titles, the level of training, the extent of professional activity, degrees held, and routineness of tasks performed.

Upward communication correlates with complexity far more than do the other three structural variables (Hage, 1980, p. 365). Organizational complexity also correlates with complexity in the environment (J. Grunig, 1976, p. 17) and the extent of communication (Hage, 1980, p. 365). Hage (1974) argued that organizations, which should try to maximize their collective rather than individual efforts, must coordinate the activities of specialists. Others have contended that complexity—along with the size of the organization—compounds the problems facing experts in communication (Blau & Schoenherr, 1971, p. 311; Farace, Monge, & Russell, 1977, p. 5; Foltz, 1973, p. 80).

TYPES OF ORGANIZATIONS

Hage (1980) showed that the size of the organization and measures of nonvariability—which he called "scale" and "task complexity"—both have important effects on organizational structure. Scale represents the repetitiveness of events that characterize an organization's operation rather than a raw number such as employees, number of sales dollars, or number of clients. Complexity refers to the technical sophistication or knowledge base inherent in that operation. He and his colleague Hull (Hage & Hull, 1981) used these two basic dimensions to construct the following structural typology of organizations wherein each organizational type develops within an environmental niche.

Traditional or *craft* organizations are small-scale operations with low complexity. *Mechanical* organizations, on the other hand, are large-scale, low-complexity structures that employ many people. *Organic* organizations are small scale but characterized by high complexity. The relatively few employees they do have tend to be highly skilled professionals. *Mixed mechanical/organic* organizations are large in scale, high in complexity.

Much recent research, including two major investigations by this author, has looked at the practice of public relations within each organizational type (Schneider, aka L. Grunig, 1985a, 1985b). Schneider, for example, found that structural components and model of public relations within the public relations department vary significantly by Hage–Hull (1981) organizational type. For example, all three persuasive models (but especially the two-way asymmetric) characterize the traditional organization. Practitioners rarely counsel management about public opinion toward their organization. Public relations activities and policy clearance are more centralized than in other kinds of organizations; levels of power and authority are significantly lower. Mechanical organizations, by contrast, emphasize public information. There is less centralization of the public relations function in this type of organization. Organic organizations tend to practice two-way symmetrical communication more than does any other Hage–Hull type. They also emphasize internal communication, although their public relations departments tend to be the smallest—which might account for their typical lack of power within the organization. Public relations practitioners in the mixed mechanical/organic type enjoy the greatest autonomy, support, and value by top management. Because they are characterized by mixed products and accompanying shifting numbers of competitors, they seem to have the greatest need for a large, comprehensive public relations program that reaches outside of the organization.

However, the publicity model of public relations predominates in all four organizational types. Thus Schneider (aka L. Grunig, 1985a, 1985b) and others determined that the commonalities outweigh the differences. For instance, centralized decision making characterized most public relations departments she studied. Most departments were highly formalized as well. The majority operates under an organization chart that nearly everyone in the department follows. Most also have written job descriptions to which they adhere to a lesser degree.

Findings related to stratification were less consistent across all organizations, with more than half of her respondents (Schneider, aka L. Grunig, 1985a, 1985b) perceiving some differences in status but only about a third considering those differences to be overly conspicuous. Dimensions of complexity also were somewhat mixed. Most practitioners surveyed had a high level of education and some degree of professionalism, although relatively few were trained in the field of public relations and few departments were highly specialized. Instead, generalists predominate — public relations practitioners who see their jobs as being almost evenly divided among responsibilities as different as media and government relations, who write for several channels, and who attend both to internal and to external audiences.

Thus a three-year program of research concluded that the Hage–Hull (1981) typology provides only a minimal explanation for vertical structure of the public relations department and for which model of public relations is practiced (J. Grunig & L. Grunig, 1989). The conclusion was that the relationship between the models and the environment of an organization functions more as a normative than a positive one: how organizations should decide what kind of public relations to practice, rather than what they actually tend to do.

The one possible exception lies within the mixed mechanical/organic type, where organizational type is the strongest predictor of public relations behavior. Practitioners there practice both two-way models of public relations: symmetrical and asymmetrical, with slightly more emphasis on the former. This combination of persuasive and cooperative communication helps them exist within their varied, constantly changing, and large-scale environment. They are least likely to rely on the one-way, publicity model of public relations. However, they engage in the most public relations activity of any of the four Hage–Hull (1981) organizational types (in spite of a somewhat smaller than average budget). Public relations staffs are expected to communicate with more, different outside audiences than in the other Hage–Hull types. The dynamic, large-scale market context dictates a need for this constant environmental scanning and interaction with target audiences that are narrowly defined. Thus we turn our attention to a consideration of the organization's environment.

THE ENVIRONMENT

The relationship between organizations and their environments has grown increasingly important to organizational sociologists in recent years (Aldrich & Pfeffer, 1976, p. 79). Most agree that organizations must adapt — at least to some degree — to their external context. Organizations must adapt to their environments if they are to increase their effectiveness or even to survive. That means developing monitoring and feedback methods to assess the environment continuously. Public relations practitioners can do just that.

Although a myriad of definitions exists for the concept of the environment, Robbins (1987) summed them up by calling their commonality a "consideration of factors outside the organization itself" (p. 149). He defined the environment as "those institutions or forces that affect the performance of the organization, but over which the organization has little control" (p. 150). He further differentiated between the general and the specific environment. The former, in his view, includes everything outside of the organization: the political arena, economic conditions, the legal and social system, and culture. Their impacts on the organization are potential rather than actual and their relevance in most cases is indirect rather than direct. The specific environment, on the other hand, is directly relevant to the organization and its survival, growth, or attainment of goals. Because the organization's external constituencies — which include customers, clients, suppliers, competitors, legislators, unions, activist groups, or associations — can affect the organization positively or negatively, managers must attend to their immediate concerns.

This concept of specificity is also important to the public relations practitioner, who must determine target audiences to reach in his or her programs. As early as 1948, sociologist Herbert Blumer had differentiated between what he called a "mass" and a "public." Similarly, J. Grunig and Hunt (1984) distinguished between a "public" and a "nonpublic." The latter, they said, has no immediate consequences on the organization and vice versa (p. 145). The public (which Dewey, 1927, categorized as a group of people facing a similar problem, recognizing that that problem exists, and organizing to do something about it) does have direct consequences on the organization or vice versa.

Important distinctions exist between specific and general environments and the notions of mass versus public and heterogeneous versus homogeneous influences. The actual versus perceived environment is another important consideration. Research has shown that correlations between the organization's actual environment and administrators' perceptions of that external setting are at times minimal (Downey, Hellriegel, & Slocum, 1975). Further, Robbins (1987) contended that managers' perceptions — rather than objective assessments of the environment — are the basis for their decisions regarding organizational design. In other words, the perceived environment dictates the resultant structure. (Weick, 1969, however, argued that environments are created to reflect the structures from which they are observed.)

Robbins (1987) also contended that the environment represents a significant contingency only when that environment is fraught with uncertainty. One important aspect of environmental uncertainty is dynamism. Thus, according to Robbins, structuring an organization dependent on its environment is more important within a dynamic than a static context. Given the rate of change in the environment for most organizations today, of course, dynamism is the assumption rather than the exception.

J. Grunig (1984) developed another important contingency inherent in the environment-structure relationship. He found that organizations deal with their environments in one of two major ways: control or adaptation. Rigidly structured organizations, in his view, try to control their environments. Relatively unstructured organizations, in contrast, try to adapt to their environments. These two organizational goals may provide the key to explaining why public relations is practiced as it is. When the goal is control, J. Grunig hypothesized, organizations would practice either press agentry or two-way asymmetric public relations. When organizations value adaptation, their public relations behavior is either two-way symmetrical or public information.

The effect of the environment on structure and public relations practice can be understood further by separating the goals of what J. Grunig (1984) called the *product/service* environment from those of the *political/regulatory* environment — thus adding the last contingency relevant here. He contended that the typology of organizations developed by Hage and Hull (1981) could explain how each type uses public relations to support the marketing of its products or services (pp. 21–22). Scale and task complexity dictate varying degrees of reliance on communication to disperse the organization's outputs.

Adapting to the complex, changing product/service environment of the organic organization, for example, requires two-way symmetrical communication. The large, stable market characteristic of mechanical organizations, on the other hand, demands little information from consumers. Traditional organizations, too, seek little information from consumers on how to change or improve their products; simply publicizing existing products is the extent of communication typically exhibited in these small, relatively simple organizations. Mixed mechanical/organic organizations, though, rely on both two-way models of public relations. Their marketing public relations is asymmetrical but they also seek information to keep abreast of needs of consumers in their complex, changing environment.

Considerations of constraints and uncertainty, rather than scale and complexity, become important primarily in the political/regulatory environment of an organization. Regulation and uncertainty change the practice of public relations in a different way than do scale and complexity: Environmental constraints affect the symmetry of public relations and environmental uncertainty explains whether communication is one- or two-way (J. Grunig, 1984, p. 23).

J. Grunig (1984) reasoned that almost complete autonomy from the environment would allow organizations to practice asymmetrical communication. They could dominate their environment. However, as organizations face increasing constraint, they are forced to practice symmetrical public relations in an attempt to show they can be socially responsible, even without threatened governmental intervention. With extremely high levels of constraint or regulation, J. Grunig expected organizations to revert to asymmetric communication—either to try to reduce that regulation or to preserve it. He explained that some organizations welcome governmental regulation because it can create economies of scale (see also Mintzberg, 1979, p. 579).

J. Grunig (1984) went on to predict a different kind of relationship between environmental uncertainty—which he characterized as heterogeneous, unstable, dispersed, and turbulent—and the extent to which the practice of public relations is one-way or two-way. High uncertainty forces organizations to seek information from their environments as well as disseminating information to them. This two-way communication can be either symmetrical or asymmetrical, either balanced or unbalanced. Low uncertainty reduces the need for a two-way flow of information. Public relations programs become one-way, as practiced in the publicity or public information models.

Figure 1.1 depicts the factors that influence an organization's choice of a model of public relations. It also illustrates the notion of environmental interdependencies—showing how the environment, broken down into its product/service and political/regulatory domains and accenting the importance of activist groups, both affects and is influenced by the organization's power holders. Figure 1.1 further suggests that together, the CEO and other members of the dominant coalition assess that environment and, based largely on their assessment, determine the strategic publics for their organization. Significantly, top managers in the public relations department contribute to that choice of key publics only if they are included in the dominant coalition.

THE RELATIONSHIP OF ENVIRONMENT TO STRUCTURE

As with much of organizational theory, the relationship between the environment and structure is complex. Some scholars rely on an environmental imperative—that environmental pressures dictate tasks that are accomplished by technologies that in turn affect organizational structures. They have found that dependence on the environment—especially one that is frequently heterogeneous, dynamic, and complex—creates uncertainty for managers. One effective way to reduce that uncertainty is to design an organizational structure flexible enough to adapt to external conditions that change rapidly. For example, Hage and Aiken (1970) found that hospitals hire more public relations personnel when they become more dynamic and complex.

Other theorists, such as Weick (1969) who emphasized the perceived or subjective rather than the actual or objective environment, disagree. Robbins (1987), for another example, called the environment relatively impotent in affecting structure. He contended that factors such as the environment, organizational size, and technology explain less than half of the variance in organizational structure. Although these factors all may constrain the amount of discretion that managers enjoy, their power allows them the necessary room to maneuver. Further, organizational politics— reflected in power—explains the lack of rationality inherent in much contemporary organizational structure. Robbins argued that decisions about structure result from struggles between internal coalitions each arguing for a structural arrangement that best meets their own needs. He further explained that members of the power elite select both technologies and environments that they figure will help them maintain control.

Perhaps the major dissenter from the environmental imperative is Child (1972), whose "strategic choice" approach to market strategies argues that the organization's dominant coalition can choose different kinds of structures irrespective of the environment. He believed that organizational form is determined more by managers' values and their knowledge of constraints imposed by external forces. His argument helps account for the different organizational structures that exist within a single industry, such as airlines, where both organic and mechanical structures are prominent.

Child's (1972) and Robbins's (1987) line of reasoning also helps explain why some organizations exploit publics and others do not. The dominant coalition selects a course of action that becomes the organization's objective because it knows it has the power. That remains the structure until a new dominant coalition corrects what might have been mistakes of the earlier one and restructures.

These power elites, of course, are teams of leaders rather than individuals (Hage, 1980). Restructuring through "revolutions" in coalitions is to be expected and even hoped for, though, because organizations need to build in change. The ideologies or general values systems of the power elite, as described by Perrow in 1967, 1968, and 1970, have been shaped by prior socialization; they help explain the liberal or conservative bent of organizational leaders. These leaders, in turn, determine the organization's metagoals: innovation versus minimizing costs, quality versus quantity, and material costs versus human costs. (Performance goals are determined more by scale and complexity.)

We also know that the dominant coalition has the power to choose the model of public relations practiced, even though public relations practitioners rarely are included in that elite group (J. Grunig & L. Grunig, 1989). At the very least, though, top managers should be aware of and value the role of public relations practitioners (or any boundary spanners) in observing, interpreting, and responding appropriately to the environment. According to Allen (1979) and Maples (1981), the trend wherein public relations practitioners act as an integral part of the management team—if not the dominant coalition—is encouraging. As Maples put it, practitioners have become "actively involved with the crucial decisions required of the organization in its interaction with the environment" (p. 3). Sharpe (1983) listed reasons for this growing importance of the boundary-spanning function, which he called "a necessity for organizational harmony with the environment in which the organization must operate": "World population growth, improved communications systems, the desire of all men to have a voice in decisions that affect their destiny, and the need for organizations to be able to adjust to changes in public attitudes with the rapidity necessary for continued survival in a complex environment" (p. 2).

Sharpe (1983) emphasized that harmony is important to all types of organizations, from profit-making corporations to the government. The SRI Business Intelligence Program (Staff, 1981) predicted that this need for cooperation will result in the appointment of top public relations executives to corporate boards and in chief executive officers operating in public relations capacities.

Other major research on power elites has been conducted by Zald (1970), Vernon (1971), and Zeitlin (1974) in the sociological conflict-critical perspective and by Cyert and March (1963) in the political-value perspective. Chapter 18 contains a more complete discussion of power in public relations.

THE ROLE OF PUBLIC RELATIONS

Whether one adopts an environmental or power-control perspective to help explain organizational structure, most scholars agree that organizations continuously interact with their environments. One important role of the professional public relations practitioner (versus the careerist type) is that of organizing the information or perceptions necessary for innovation or adaptation in an uncertain environment. As Lawrence and Lorsch's (1967) research suggests, the successful organization in such a context uses these integrating individuals to interpret the environment.

Wright (1983), in examining the implications of the 1982 International Public Relations Society's "Gold Paper" on public relations education, contended that maintaining open communication ensures "the feedback necessary for management decisions based on accurate and complete information and . . . the organization's ability to respond and adjust to change as required by societal and environmental conditions" (p. 3). Further, J. Grunig (1984) asserted that an environment's structure and public relations behavior both depend on the environment (p. 15).

As Kuhn (1975) said, the organization only can respond to the parts of the environment of which it is aware. Systematic monitoring of the relevant external constituencies, those that can affect or are affected by the organization, presents a challenge for public relations departments. The process is complicated by the number and changing nature of such external publics.

One recent study attempted to answer the question of how successful public relations practitioners are dealing with all of the publics that stand to affect their organizations. L. Grunig (1987) began with the assumption that practitioners deal with a myriad of external constituencies—stakeholders such as clients or customers, communities, the mass media, labor unions, stockholders and financial analysts, suppliers, and competitors. She reasoned, though, that certain groups must present more of a problem than others. Activists and governmental regulatory bodies, in particular, pose a threat to organizational autonomy. Her argument was that to successfully monitor and interact with all external publics, practitioners need to know which publics are most constraining and how that constraint varies by the type of organization and environment they work in. Therein lies the heart of the strategic management of public relations, or the understanding that not all publics are "created equal."

Surprisingly, across organizational types the most autonomous and cooperative relationship exists between the mass media and the organization. (Surprising, of course, given the reliance that many practitioners and their bosses put on media relations.) Other cooperative relationships were discovered between the typical organization and its clientele, the community, and government. Opposition comes largely from stockholders and activists and, to a somewhat lesser degree, labor unions.

Encouragingly, more relationships are considered highly positive than highly negative. In any event, these data support Stolz's (1983) argument that public opinion threatens organizational autonomy more than does the direct influence of government. Activism, the organization of diffused publics into a powerful body attempting to control the organization from outside, is perceived as a more constraining force than is government. Only

4 of the 48 organizations surveyed reported highly cooperative relationships with these key groups. Activism is discussed at greater length in chapter 19. Clearly, public relations professionals in all types of organizations must develop and evaluate programs to deal more effectively with activists.

This chapter concludes with one overarching proposition that encompasses our discussion of organizational structure and environment:

Proposition: Excellent departments practice public relations appropriately for their environment in part because the structure of their organizations places the head of public relations in a position both to monitor that environment and to interact with the dominant coalition internally.

REFERENCES

Aldrich, H. E., & Pfeffer, J. (1976). Environments of organizations. *Annual Review of Sociology, 2,* 79–105.

Allen, T. J. (1979). *Managing the flow of technology: Technology transfer and the dissemination of technological information within the research and development organization.* Cambridge, MA: MIT Press.

Blau, P. M., & Schoenherr, R. A. (1971). *The structure of organizations.* New York: Basic.

Blumer, H. (1948). Public opinion and public opinion polling. *American Sociological Review, 13,* 542–554.

Child, J. (1972). Organizational structure, environment, and performance: The role of strategic choice. *Sociology, 6*(1), 2–22.

Cyert, R. M., & March, J. G. (1963). *A behavioral theory of the firm.* Englewood Cliffs, NJ: Prentice-Hall.

Dewey, J. (1927). *The public and its problems.* Chicago: Swallow.

Downey, H. K., Hellriegel, D., & Slocum, J. W., Jr. (1975). Environmental uncertainty: The construct and its applications. *Administrative Science Quarterly, 20,* 613–629.

Farace, R. V., Monge, P. R., & Russell, H. M. (1977). *Communicating and organizing.* Reading, MA: Addison-Wesley.

Foltz, R. G. (1973). *Management by communication.* Philadelphia: Chilton.

Grunig, J. E. (1976). Organizations and public relations: Testing a communication theory. *Journalism Monographs, 46.*

Grunig, J. E. (1984). Organizations, environments, and models of public relations. *Public Relations Research and Education, 1*(1), 6–29.

Grunig, J. E., & Grunig, L. A. (1989). Toward a theory of the public relations behavior of organizations: Review of a program of research. In J. E. Grunig & L. A. Grunig (Eds.), *Public relations research annual* (Vol. 1, pp. 27–63). Hillsdale, NJ: Lawrence Erlbaum Associates.

Grunig, J. E., & Hunt, T. (1984). *Managing public relations.* New York: Holt, Rinehart & Winston.

Grunig, L. (1987). Variation in relations with environmental publics. *Public Relations Review, 13*(3), 46–58.

Hage, J. (1965). An axiomatic theory of organizations. *Administrative Science Quarterly, 10,* 289–320.

Hage, J. (1974). *Communication and organizational control: Cybernetics in health and welfare settings.* New York: Wiley.

Hage, J. (1980). *Theories of organizations: Form, process, and transformation.* New York: Wiley.

Hage, J., & Aiken, M. (1967a). Program change and organizational properties: A comparative analysis. *American Journal of Sociology, 72,* 503–519.

Hage, J., & Aiken, M. (1967b). Relationship of centralization to other structural properties. *Administrative Science Quarterly, 12,* 72–91.

Hage, J., & Aiken, M. (1970). *Social change in complex organizations.* New York: Random House.

Hage, J., & Hull, F. (1981). *A typology of environmental niches based on knowledge technology and scale: The implications for innovation and productivity.* Working Paper 1, University of Maryland, Center for the Study of Innovation, Entrepreneurship, and Organization Strategy, College Park.

Hall, R. H. (1977). *Organizations: Structure and process* (2nd ed.). Englewood Cliffs, NJ: Prentice-Hall.

Kanter, R. M. (1982). The middle manager as innovator. *Harvard Business Review, 60*(4), 95–105.

Kuhn, A. (1975). *Unified social science.* Homewood, IL: Dorsey.

Lawrence, P. R., & Lorsch, J. W. (1967). Differentiation and integration in complex organizations. *Administrative Science Quarterly, 12,* 1–47.

Maples, S. F. (1981). *Relationship of organizational structure to public relations decision-making.* Unpublished master's thesis, California State University, Fullerton.

Mintzberg, H. (1979). *The structuring of organizations.* Englewood Cliffs, NJ: Prentice-Hall.

Parsons, T. (1956a). Suggestions for a sociological approach to the theory of organizations, I. *Administrative Science Quarterly, 1,* 63–85.

Parsons, T. (1956b). Suggestions for a sociological approach to the theory of organizations, II. *Administrative Science Quarterly, 1,* 225–239.

Perrow, C. (1967). A framework for the comparative analysis of organizations. *American Sociological Review, 32,* 194–209.

Perrow, C. (1968). Organizational goals. In D. L. Sills (Ed.), *International encyclopedia of the social sciences* (rev. ed., pp. 365–383). New York: Macmillan.

Perrow, C. (1970). *Organizational analysis: A sociological view.* Belmont, CA: Wadsworth.

Robbins, S. P. (1987). *Organization theory: Structure, design, and applications* (2nd ed.). Englewood Cliffs, NJ: Prentice-Hall.

Schneider (aka Grunig), L. A. (1985a). *Organizational structure, environmental niches, and public relations: The Hage-Hull typology of organizations as predictor of communication behavior.* Unpublished doctoral dissertation, University of Maryland, College Park.

Schneider (aka Grunig), L. A. (1985b). The role of public relations in four organizational types. *Journalism Quarterly, 62*(3), 567–576, 594.

Sharpe, M. L. (1983, October). *A design for public relations graduate education based on the current and future needs of professionals.* Paper presented at the meeting of the Public Relations Society of America, New York.

Simon, H. A. (1976). *The new science of management* (rev. ed.). Englewood Cliffs, NJ: Prentice-Hall.

Staff. (1981, March 13). SRI business intelligence program predicts growing importance of PR. *PR News,* p. 1.

Stolz, V. (1983). "Conflict PR" in the formation of public opinion. *Public Relations Quarterly, 38*(2), 28–31.

Thompson, J. D. (1967). *Organizations in action.* New York: McGraw-Hill.

Vernon, R. (1971). *Sovereignty at bay*. New York: Basic.

Weick, K. E. (1969). *The social psychology of organizing*. Reading, MA: Addison-Wesley.

Wright, D. K. (1983). Implications of the IPRA "Gold Paper." *Public Relations Review, 9*(2), 3–6.

Zald, M. N. (Ed.). (1970). *Power in organizations*. Nashville, TN: Vanderbilt University Press.

Zeitlin, M. (1974). Corporate ownership and control: The large corporation and the capitalist class. *American Journal of Sociology, 79,* 1073–1119.

18 Power in the Public Relations Department

Larissa A. Grunig
University of Maryland

ABSTRACT

After learning that the environment and structure of an organization cannot explain fully why some organizations have excellent communication departments and others do not, public relations scholars have turned to another sociological theory, the power-control perspective, for an explanation. The power-control perspective says that organizations do what they do because the people with the most power in the organization—the dominant coalition—decide to do it that way. Organizations practice public relations as they do, therefore, because the dominant coalition decides to do it that way. Public relations has a better chance of being excellent, it follows, if the senior communication manager is a member of that coalition. This chapter discusses the nature of power and ways in which communication managers can gain the power necessary for excellence.

Professionalism, although the buzzword at many an association conference, remains an elusive goal for public relations practitioners. Most public relations practitioners, men and women alike, remain at the technical level. That is, they engage in typically journalistic activities but they tend to remain "outside the door" when those top-level decisions are being made. They rarely ascend to the managerial level that would make them part of the decisional process. Further, their one-way communicative efforts may be inadequate for coping with the turbulent environment described in the last couple of chapters. Relegation to a functionary role also inhibits the professional development of individual practitioners and of the entire field of public relations.

The exclusion of most public relations practitioners from managerial decision making seems counterproductive for them, for their field, for their organizations, and perhaps even for the broader society in which those organizations operate. This chapter addresses what we know as well as the gaps that remain in our understanding of the role power plays in the practice of public relations. It takes a structural approach, as described in chapter 17. That is, relationships are viewed in the context of Hage–Hull's (1981) typology of organizational structure: *traditional* (small scale, low knowledge complexity), *mechanical* (large scale, low knowledge complexity), *organic* (small scale, high knowledge complexity), and *mixed mechanical/ organic* (large scale, high knowledge complexity).

To grasp the complexities of a theoretical understanding of power, we begin with a simple definition. But is it really so simple? Public relations, typically part of the managerial subsystem of organizations, can be defined many ways. In a definition consistent with systems theory, however, J. Grunig and Hunt (1984) defined it best: the management of communication between an organization and its publics. The key term relevant to this study is *management,* because management implies a role for public relations practitioners that goes beyond the technical. (These major roles in public relations — the technician and the manager — were described in greater detail in chapter 12.)

Broom and Dozier (1985) agreed that involvement in managerial decision making is fundamental to any definition of public relations. Isolating the public relations department from top administration, in their view, limits its practice to the role of "explaining and justifying" others' decisions. They argued that as long as this technical role dominates, professional status is unlikely — despite an era of unprecedented growth in the field.

The inclusion of practitioners in the organization's dominant coalition is "perhaps more important to the profession of public relations than any other measure of professional growth," according to Broom and Dozier (1985, p. 8). J. Grunig and Hunt (1984) went even further in asserting that there is little justification for any practice of public relations unless practitioners are included in the dominant coalition. If the assertions of these and other scholars are well founded, then determining the nature of the relationship between the distribution of power in organizations and the practice of public relations seems crucial.

UNDERSTANDING POWER AND INFLUENCE

First, one must understand the concept of *power.* Just as communication scholars have sought to define public relations, organizational theorists have posited many definitions. Common elements include the force necessary to change others' behavior (Emerson, 1962), an imbalance in the relationship between those with power and those without power (Simon, 1953), and the control of some over others (Morgenthau, 1960). The underlying theme, according to Gaski (1984), is "the ability to evoke a change in another's behavior" (p. 10).

Considered in this context, power is a personal attribute. It also can be seen as departmental or organizational. Its relevance in this chapter is to the relative position the public relations department occupies within the organizational structure. It refers at least in part to the department's ability to mobilize what are typically scarce resources. A related basis for power is being situated in an environmentally critical function (Hambrick, 1981). Crozier (1964) called power the unit's ability to deal with environmental uncertainty (see also Hickson, Hinings, Lee, Schneck, & Pennings, 1971; Perrow, 1961).

Power comes to public relations practitioners from different sources. The value the dominant coalition attaches to the public relations function is one key way. Thus, this chapter proposes first that the dominant coalition be "educated" to appreciate the potential of public relations:

Proposition 1: Members of dominant coalitions in excellent organizations will come to value public relations as a critical managerial — rather than merely technical — organizational function.

The expertise of practitioners, leading to increased professionalism, is another. Aldrich and Herker (1977), in their work on boundary spanning, explained this factor as follows: "The power of boundary role incumbents will vary inversely with boundary role routinization, and directly with their own expertise in accomplishing role requirements and with the costliness and unpredictability of interorganizational transactions" (p. 227).

Proposition 2: To increase their access to the dominant coalition, public relations practitioners should increase their own expertise via education, experience, and professionalism.

A third important contingency, according to J. Grunig (1976), is the relationship between placement in the hierarchy and the organization's degree of centralization. He reasoned that public relations departments in centralized structures would lack power unless they were located at the top of the hierarchy because rigid structures preclude decision making at lower levels. In decentralized organizations, the unit's power would be determined less by its location in the hierarchy because there discretionary power is distributed throughout the organization.

Proposition 3: Public relations departments in centralized structures should be located at the top of the organizational hierarchy.

Too often, public relations practitioners (or any other boundary-spanning personnel) lack the formal authority for action. As a result, they rely on subtle means of influence such as expertise, friendship, ingratiation, and even derision of the organization (Organ, 1971). This occupational hazard, according to Bales (1984), goes with the public relations territory. However, scholars rarely have distinguished between power and *influence* (Provan, 1980). One notable exception is the work of Katz and Kahn (1966), who said ". . . influence is a transaction in which one person (or group) acts in such a way as to change the behavior of an individual (or group) in some intended fashion. Power is the *capacity* to exert influence. Power does not have to be enacted for it to exist, whereas influence does; it is the demonstrated use of power" (p. 550). Influence derives from the informal power of those whose personal attributes result in the ability to persuade others (Hage & Aiken, 1970). However, like power influence often derives as well from the control of resources others value (Blau, 1964).

Cobb (1984) went a long way toward integrating these related yet distinct conceptions of power and influence. He argued that power is "the ability or potential to influence others or to control a situation" (p. 483). Cobb further explained the role that power and influence play in decision making, in behavioral outcomes, and in situational outcomes. Power may figure in the dynamics of decision making, he believed, when the target consciously considers the wishes of the agent; in such an instance, power is more appropriately conceived of as influence. Power is manifest, on the other hand, when the agent gets the target to do something he or she would not do otherwise. Power also is manifest in situations when the agent is unilaterally in control.

UNDERSTANDING POWER IN COALITIONS

Coalition is a related yet conceptually and operationally distinct concept from power and influence. Because the focus of this chapter is on groups (whether organizations or departments) rather than on individuals, an understanding of coalitions seems vital.

Stevenson, Pearce, and Porter (1985) found fewer than a handful of previous studies on coalitions in organizations. The major explanation for this dearth of scholarly research is the difficulty both in defining the concept and in studying coalitions in the organizational setting. Coalitions typically rely more on informal interaction than formal rules to define their membership. As a result, according to Stevenson et al., their boundaries may be fuzzy and ill-defined. Further, membership often shifts and is considered "illegitimate" by others in the organization, making coalitions difficult for researchers to identify—let alone study. However, Hage (1980) contended that changes in coalition membership do not necessarily result in changes in the coalition's power structure. The coalition will remain stable until it no longer is effective. As he put it, "Leaders come and go but dominant coalitions remain" (p. 151).

Difficult as the coalition is to identify and to study, coalitions have been the subject of interest to organizational scholars for at least 25 years. Cyert and March (1963) were the first to focus on this aspect of organizational power. By 1973, they had gone so far as to propose that an organization's behavior is determined by the values of its dominant coalition.

Why? With J. Thompson (1967) in the vanguard and their own studies in sociology's political-value paradigm as confirmation, Cyert and March (1963, 1973) came to realize that no one person, even an extraordinarily powerful person, could control an organization operating within the context of today's complex technology and environment. Later, Hage (1980) summed up this understanding: "The team approach, the variety of specialists, the complexity of the environment, the need for joint decision-making make the stamp of one man or woman less and less likely. This is the era of the dominant coalition" (p. 158).

We move now to a definition, both operational and conceptual, of the term coalition. Such a definition had remained elusive until the recent work of Stevenson et al. (1985): ". . . an interacting group of individuals, deliberately constructed, independent of the formal structure, lacking its own internal formal structure, consisting of mutually perceived membership, issue oriented, focused on a goal or goals external to the coalition, and requiring concerted member action" (p. 251).

Mintzberg (1983) is one of many scholars who has studied the make-up of the coalition. He developed a typology of coalitions based on external versus internal influence. External coalitions include stockholders, suppliers, clients, labor unions, the community, and government. Internal coalitions are comprised of full-time employees—those who make decisions and take action on a permanent and regular basis.

Top management, of course, normally is included (Cyert & March, 1963). Axelrod (1970) and Rosenthal (1970) added the understanding that people with similar ideologies are most likely to form coalitions. (In 1978, however, Murnighan found only limited support for the contention that coalitions form among actors with compatible ideologies.) Pfeffer (1981), who has studied the concept extensively, determined that coalitions consist of those who agree on a desired organizational outcome. Stevenson et al. (1985) reasoned that those with more discretion in carrying out their job responsibilities would have more opportunity to become part of a coalition.

With this understanding that different coalitions represent different goals, different ideologies, and different expertise, Thompson's (1967) concept of the "dominant" coalition becomes important. He called it simply the "inner circle." He reasoned that one group of influentials or powerful people must prevail at any given time. Robbins (1987) explained that any coalition that can control the resources on which the organization depends can become dominant. Mintzberg (1983) concluded that members of the power elite stand ready to exploit discretion in terms of their own goals.

Other scholars have looked at structural characteristics affecting coalitions. Bacharach and Lawler (1980), for example, determined that increasing centralization and formalization decrease the likelihood of coalition formation. As explained in chapter 17, Schneider (aka L. Grunig, 1985) also looked specifically at the relationship among structure, communication, and power. She found that the managerial role for public relations dominates only in the mixed mechanical/organic type of organization. Power correlated negatively with small-scale, traditional-type organizations. Together these data suggest that the public relations professional sits closer to the top of the hierarchy in large-scale organizations than he or she does in the organization of simple machines, few employees, and relatively low productivity.

Coalitions are threatened by structural or environmental changes because change necessarily affects the organization's dependencies. As a result, according to Thompson (1967), coalitions by definition remain "in process." Pfeffer (1981) agreed. He held that the coalition's need for organizational power explains its attempts at maintaining control over the environment: If it can manage its environment, it can avoid making structural changes within the organization; such change would interrupt the balance of power. However, Broom and Dozier (1985) pointed out that the relationship between public relations roles, organizational structure, and what they called the "management core" remains unclear.

This review of relevant theoretical concepts from the literature of sociology, political science, public policy, psychology, public relations, and business management suggests that power is an important subject in the study of organizations, their boundary personnel, and their environments. In fact, Allen (1979) believed that the dominant coalition dictates organizational action to a far greater degree than does even the environment, a long-cherished predictor of organizational structure and decision making (see, e.g., J. Grunig & L. Grunig, 1989).

But why is the inclusion of public relations practitioners within the dominant coalition so critical? Before attempting to answer the question, this chapter addresses what is known about the relationship between public relations and organizational power.

We know from several previous studies that public relations practitioners typically are excluded from the dominant coalition — whether it is called the inner circle, the power elite, or simply an internal influencer (Anshen, 1974; Brown, 1980; Close, 1980; Greyser, 1981; Lesly, 1981; Lindenmann & Lapetina, 1981; Newman, 1980). Some of these studies and still others have suggested reasons for public relations' lack of representation in top management circles. Management itself is one important factor. Its perception of public relations as a "necessary evil" (Strenski, 1980) and its myopic, self-interested concentration on the free-enterprise system (Forrestal, 1980) both contribute to its lack of confidence in public relations. According to Burger (1983), CEOs tend to consider public relations as a marginal function at best. (Pennings and Goodman, 1977, found, though, that the values of any group depend on who is a member of the group. It stands to reason, then, that if public relations managers become part of the dominant group, other members of that coalition would come to understand and to support their function.)

Allen (1979) contended that managers value the organizational roles that are part of their management teams. When public relations is excluded from the decision-making process (largely through the dominant coalition), as it tends to be in the typical traditional organization, one would expect managers to devalue its role. Maples (1981) agreed. She found that managers value organizational roles that demand autonomous decision making. Thus, the greater the autonomy, the greater the value that managers should hold for public relations practitioners. Managers who advocate symmetrical communication between their organization and relevant external publics also should value the people responsible for such two-way, balanced public relations (J. Grunig, 1984). Such interaction is necessary for organizational adaptation to a dynamic, large-scale environment.

Of course, characteristics of practitioners themselves are a significant factor in their exclusion from the dominant coalition. Key variables include their lack of broad business expertise (Lesly, 1981; Lindenmann & Lapetina, 1981); their passivity (Anshen, 1974); their naivete about organizational politics (Nowlan & Shayon, 1984); and their inadequate education, experience, or organizational status (Anshen, 1972). Other determinants of public relations role in the organization relative to power include gender and longevity in the job (Johnson & Acharya, 1981).

For these and other, less well-documented reasons, public relations professionals rarely enjoy an influential position within their organization. As a result, we only can hypothesize about the effects of a powerful public relations department. The next part of this chapter deals with possible impacts of power on the individual practitioner, on the field of public relations, on the organizational system, and on society.

EFFECTS OF POWER

Effects on Public Relations Practitioners

Why is it important to emphasize the managerial role over the technical for practitioners of public relations? For starters, managers earn more than do technicians. Broom (1982), considered the father of public relations roles research, characterized the technical role as relatively underpaid and confined to the rank of lower staff. Communication managers, on the other hand, are more highly paid. More important is the understanding that they help make decisions, rather than simply implementing the decisions of others (Dozier, 1981). (On the negative side, of course, is the accompanying responsibility for the success or failure of decisions implemented.)

Also more relevant than salary is the level of job satisfaction that often accompanies a rise from technical to managerial level. Dozier (1981) found that satisfaction increases with increasing professionalism. This is an important understanding in light of the literature on job satisfaction of boundary spanners in general. We know that because boundary spanners in essence lead a double life (by representing the organization to the outside and vice versa), ensuing role conflict may lead to job dissatisfaction (Miles, 1977). Finally, staffs in public relations departments should experience increased job satisfaction as their superiors become increasingly influential (Jablin, 1980).

Effects on the Field of Public Relations

Newman (1980) contended that public relations has evolved from its roots in the technical aspects of the field to a second phase of professional development. From that initial beachhead, he wrote, "we are ready to move inland, toward the command posts of corporate management" (p. 11). One former president of the Public Relations Society of America argued that the field never would attain professional status, however, until its practitioners regard themselves as part of a managerial team rather than as craftspeople (Hawver, cited in Baxter, 1980). (This remains a challenge when teaching undergraduate students, who typically enroll in public relations courses with the career goal of becoming primo technicians.)

Effects on the Organization

Practicing public relations professionally, and more as a managerial than technical process, undoubtedly would have positive effects on the organizational system. As the chairman of the board at Spring Mills, Inc., put it to a group of public relations practitioners: "Let's face it, in a climate of special interests and over-regulation, inflated dollars here and deflated dollars there, . . . the chief executive can use your help—if management is convinced you *can* help" (Close, 1980, p. 11).

Given the broadening challenges facing corporate management—witness the environment Close (1980) just described and chapter 19 that deals specifically with activism—including public relations in the dominant coalition seems vital. Professional public relations practitioners can share in the decision-making process and in the responsibility for the public's orientation toward the organization. Enhancing the power base of public relations in the organization gives the department a greater capacity to influence events (Quinn, 1980). This becomes increasingly important in situations of great uncertainty or dissensus about choices (Pfeffer, 1981).

Professionals who want to influence strategic decisions have more effect when they are part of a group than when they act as organizational entrepreneurs. Thus the public relations practitioner with the potential to contribute to organizational goals would be more effective as a member of the dominant coalition than as an independent actor in the organizational system. Recall that the group, rather than any one leader, typically makes decisions. Hage and Dewar (1973) found that the values of the power elite largely set organizational policy. Public relations, in its boundary-spanning role between organization and environment, warrants input into that policy process of strategic choices.

Effects on Society

Strategic publics in the broader environment of the organization could be affected positively by a burgeoning managerial role for public relations practitioners. Anshen (1974) emphasized the corporation's social responsibility and the part that public relations plays in managing that obligation. More recently, J. Grunig and L. Grunig (1989) suggested that only as part of the dominant coalition could public relations professionals be influential enough to shape the organization's ideology. Presumably, these boundary spanners would appreciate the point of view both of their employers and of their relevant external publics.

Thus we arrive at the proposition that has been apparent since the first page of this chapter: the need for representation of public relations in the dominant coalition.

Proposition 4: To be an excellent department, public relations must be included within the dominant coalition.

EMPOWERMENT STRATEGIES

Because the effects of power for public relations described earlier are primarily beneficial for all dimensions involved, the next logical step in this chapter is a discussion of empowerment strategies. How can public relations practitioners enhance their power base? And given the power struggles within organizations and between powerful coalitions, why should any influentials share their power with others?

Kanter (1979), whose work is not related strictly to public relations, still provides the most insightful answers. She studied both powerfulness and powerlessness. The latter, she contended, breeds bossiness—one main reason for empowering any bosses in organizations, including the head of the public relations department. She also linked powerlessness with job dissatisfaction, explaining that accountability without power (responsibility for results without the resources to get them) creates frustration or failure or both.

Think instead of the advantages to sharing power Kanter (1979) cited. Her revelation is that organizational power can grow—rather than shrink—by being shared. In Kanter's words, delegation does not mean abdication. Why? People with information and support make more informed decisions, act more quickly, and often accomplish more than those who are powerless. Thus the leader who empowers others actually increases his or her own power via increased productivity. The true sign of power, in Kanter's view, is accomplishment. And, she believed that even the powerless would increase what little power they do have by sharing it with others. She recommended that organizations work toward team-oriented, participatory, power-sharing management.

Of course, feminists (whether they are women or men) practicing or teaching public relations may feel uncomfortable with any discussion of power. Hartsock (1981) and other feminists have rejected the notion of "power over" others. They would choose to focus, instead, on values that include cooperation, negotiation, nurturing, and so forth. Hartsock made an important distinction between power as domination and the feminist definition that embraces working together, energy, effective interaction, and—perhaps most important—empowerment.

CURRENT RESEARCH ON POWER AND PUBLIC RELATIONS

Most research on power as it relates directly to public relations has been conducted in the decade of the 1980s (with the notable exception of the work of Anshen, 1974). Predictably, many of the studies have taken the form of graduate theses or dissertations. Because of their recency, their focus specifically on public relations, and their empirical findings, these studies deserve special attention here.

Pollack (1986), for example, looked at the support of top management for public relations in scientific organizations. She found that the dominant coalition tends to support the public relations department at least moderately; the power elite considers the department's functions important. The department itself is located at the middle or top managerial level; about half of its major recommendations are implemented by the organization.

Pollack (1986) did not determine the influence the public relations director enjoys in the typical scientific organization, nor did she explain his or her involvement in major organizational decisions. She did discover, though, that when public relations practitioners are represented in the dominant coalition, they are likely to practice two-way symmetrical communication. They conduct more managerial and somewhat more liaison activities.

Further, Pollack (1986) found that practitioners included in the inner circle tend to have more training in public relations (greater percentage of graduate and bachelor's degrees in the field) as opposed to just a few courses or seminars or no formal education in public relations. This finding is consistent with that of Lawler and Hage (1973), who more than a decade earlier had established that professional training, along with professional activity, decreases at least felt powerlessness. (In their study of social workers, they also found a significant relationship between professionalism and work autonomy.)

Nelson (1986) attempted an in-depth study of the dominant coalition in two organizations. She found that top management's concept of public relations dictates what type of program (such as media relations, employee relations, and community relations) dominates within the organization. Because that program emphasis or the model of public relations practiced may be inappropriate for the organization, given its environment, she recommended including public relations practitioners in the dominant coalition.

J. Grunig and L. Grunig (1989) integrated these and other recent findings into a program of research that approaches a general systems theory of public relations. They found that, in general, managerial support for and understanding of public relations correlated with the most sophisticated, two-way models of public relations (both balanced and imbalanced). Based primarily on Pollack's (1986) study, the Grunigs posited two explanations for the inclusion of public relations practitioners in the dominant coalition: Either public relations departments represented in the power elite are empowered to practice a two-way model of communication or only those practitioners with the expertise to practice such a model would be included in that inner circle. Because of the significant correlations between inclusion in the dominant coalition and both education and experience in public relations, they favored the latter explanation.

Ossareh (1987) hypothesized that the values of the dominant coalition would be a more significant predictor of use of technology for public relations tasks than would be the orientation or professionalism of public relations practitioners themselves. Through a nationwide survey of almost 500 practitioners, her assumption was confirmed. Again, as with the Pollack (1986) and J. Grunig and L. Grunig (1989) studies, representation of the public relations department in the managerial elite seems appropriate. Otherwise, a technological advance with potential for enhancing the practice of public relations may be ignored; inappropriate yet expensive technologies may be adopted.

The most recent, extensive study of power in public relations (L. Grunig, 1990) found the perception of almost unilateral support for the public relations function across organizations. At least interviewees from the 48 organizations studied reported virtually no opposition from top management to their role in the organization. Management also seems to have a clear understanding of public relations. Executives often involve themselves integrally in activities of the public relations department, and this is perceived as a positive indication of understanding and support. The strongest backing comes from administrators of the two types of organizations that have high complexity: organic and mixed mechanical/organic.

Apparently, though, support and understanding do not go hand in hand with value. Most respondents indicated only moderate levels of value for their role on the part of the organization's power elite. One interviewee, an assistant vice president for corporate communication at a large rail company, explained the devaluation of her field by the conservative culture of her organization—one consisting of what she called "old railroad men" who need a lot of education. Another respondent, the director of information for a county school system, described a limited degree of value for public relations in his organization because top management there thinks of public relations only as a conduit for information to the public. As he put it, "They emphasize the publicist aspect of the task and don't appreciate the counseling and public relations aspects."

Perhaps this lack of managerial value helps explains the limited degree of authority that respondents reported. Their power within the organization was rarely unbridled. Only practitioners in the mixed mechanical/organic organization experienced more authority and were required to engage in less rigorous clearance procedures than their counterparts in the other three Hage–Hull (1981) organizational types. By contrast, most interviewees were subject to an extensive clearance process for virtually all written materials and—in fact—approval from higher-ups on most decisions. Even seemingly autonomous decisions by public relations executives actually were constrained. As one firm's public relations coordinator revealed, "We're all given an opportunity to say what we think, but in the end the decisions are made for us."

Determinants of autonomy included distance from headquarters, routineness of the activity in question, the amount of money involved, and—predictably—the values of the dominant coalition. As the senior director of employee communications and special events for a rail company put it: "Although we're a new company, I've served under four presidents. Each has been different in approach. Some have regarded our department highly, and others are stubborn as hell."

Explanations frequently cited for lack of autonomy include sexism, newness to the organization, being in a regional office rather than at the headquarters, and restrictive government policy. Most constraining, though, is the lack of education in public relations on the part of the dominant coalition. Many reportedly equate public relations with publicity or—a related problem—believe the organization does not "need" the media.

Even in the relatively rare instances of powerful public relations practitioners, some qualifications exist. Respondents indicated that their autonomy may be contingent on dealing with routine situations, small amounts of money, the traditional areas associated with public relations (such as media relations) and a busy CEO. Others who reported a high degree of power qualified their status by alluding to practices such as "keeping the higher-ups informed as a courtesy" and the constraints imposed by budget or an even more powerful board.

The study revealed surprisingly extensive involvement of public relations practitioners with the dominant coalition. Many respondents indicated that they participate in weekly sessions dealing with operating decisions and problems of top management. Such self-reports are suspect, of course, but more than 4 out of every 10 alluded to involvement they characterized as "intimate," "integral," "daily," and "close" with the dominant coalition. Public relations practitioners in traditional organizations are somewhat less likely to be included in their dominant coalitions. Even in the critical area of issues management, though, most practitioners' role is more advisory than actual policy making.

This exploratory study was as important for what it did not find as for what it was able to establish about power in public relations. For example, responses indicated little specialization in public relations, a low degree of professionalism, little education in the field on the part of top management, and only limited power in public relations departments across organizations. That power was limited further to the technical or typically journalistic activities of public relations, rather than to the managerial role of counseling, planning, evaluating, and decision making. Finally, responses in many key areas varied insignificantly if at all among different structural types of organizations.

PROFILES OF POWER IN THE FOUR
ORGANIZATIONAL TYPES

Respondents in traditional organizations implied a high degree of managerial understanding of their field. Understanding does not lead to support for the public relations function, though, at least in the case of the traditional organization. Practitioners in this type indicated little managerial advocacy. (Of course, public relations is considered a staff — rather than managerial — function in traditional organizations.) Low professionalism also characterizes this organizational type; and this finding is consistent with the organization whose knowledge complexity is low and thus needs less innovation than do other types to survive or to increase their market share.

Managerial support for public relations is weaker in the mechanical organization than in both organic and mixed organizations. One explanation might lie in the limited understanding and value that most managers in mechanical organizations have for public relations. Also, their executives have the least education in the field of public relations. However, a more reasonable explanation probably is that these operations tend to be market oriented. They need public relations to dispose of their products or services in their vast market. At the same time, because their market is relatively stable, they need to gather little information from their environment.

Beyond that, however, the potential of public relations rarely is realized in the typical mechanical organization. Even the fact that practitioners there are more professional than in the other three types of organizations does not preclude their doing little more than disseminating information. When the power elite does not value nor understand their capabilities, practitioners may violate their professional norms or standards — thus compromising their professional judgment and even ignoring the public interest.

Managers in organic organizations support the public relations effort to a significantly greater degree than in both types of organizations with low task complexity (traditional and mechanical). Although most survey respondents said their top executives have little or no education in public relations, organic organizations reported significantly more members of the dominant coalition with such specialized knowledge. Employees in the public relations department there have a relatively high level of education in general.

Members of the power elite in mixed mechanical/organic organizations involve themselves in public relations activity somewhat more than in the other three types. Perhaps because top management is so intimately involved, it strongly supports and values the public relations department. A second outgrowth may be the autonomy granted public relations practitioners in the typical mixed organization: significantly more independence than in any other type. A second factor accounting for the high degree of autonomy (in addition to managerial support and appreciation) may be the kind of person typically working in these public relations departments. Administrators might feel secure in giving them free rein because of their high educational level and—probably more important—their specialized training in public relations.

Thus we see that using the Hage–Hull (1981) typology turned out to be only moderately useful as a theoretical approach to studying power and public relations. The typology does explain about 10% of the variance. However, correlations are small and so, much remains to be explained. However, mediating influences affect both organizational structure and power in public relations. Two major forces are managerial values for the public relations function and professionalism of staff members in public relations. The two are related: If top executives of the corporation do not value the role that public relations can play there, even the professional employee may compromise his or her judgment to keep the job.

IMPLICATIONS

In spite of this limitation, the L. Grunig (1990) study has important implications for public relations practitioners. The management vacuum in public relations is what a 1984 lead article in *pr reporter* called the "opportunity of a century" (Staff, 1984, p. 1). Filling the vacuum would allow public relations professionals to add to their skills and to realize their aspirations for leadership roles in organizations. The same article in *pr reporter* pointed out that practitioners are more concerned over their role in the future of the field than any other topic. They note with anxiety that non-public-relations people are getting top spots in public relations.

A managerial (rather than technical) approach to the practice of public relations would add to practitioners' acceptance and respect within their organizations and with the public at large. The lack of credibility is often a problem with boundary spanners. By increasing the probability that public relations practitioners attain managerial status, the field moves from a practice toward a profession. At that point, the organization gets its money's worth from employees who allocate their public relations budgets—typically in the hundreds of thousands of dollars—based on scientific monitoring of relevant concerns in the environment. This sensitivity and resultant ability to innovate benefit the larger society.

Practitioners, too, would benefit through the predictable increase in job satisfaction that accompanies growing power. When those in the dominant coalition become willing to share their power, the productivity of the organization as a whole should increase as well. Certainly it would be in a better position to manage its environmental interdependencies, as illustrated in Fig. 1.1.

All of this implies delegating more authority to the department. Public relations practitioners can be more than journalists in residence, more than communication technicians. They can be managers or part of the power elite themselves. As it is, though, they need more autonomy—especially in organic and traditional organizations where public relations departments have the most stringent clearance processes and the least power. Finally, public relations practitioners themselves will not meet the challenge until they have more education specifically in their field, especially at the graduate level.

Decision making separates managers from nonmanagers. The ability to make valid decisions in public relations depends partly on the knowledge of communication theory and research methods that comes with a university education in the field—primarily as a master's or doctoral student. Advanced training also leads to professionalism: taking advantage of the theoretical body of knowledge to build a practice based not on isolated experiences but on generalizable findings that apply to organizations beyond the individual cases studied or experienced. Specialized training in public relations also leads to professionalism in the sense that it indoctrinates one in the culture of the field. This, in turn, lays the groundwork for involvement in professional associations such as the International Association of Business Communicators.

REFERENCES

Aldrich, H. E., & Herker, D. (1977). Boundary spanning roles and organization structure. *Academy of Management Review, 2,* 217–230.

Allen, T. J. (1979). *Managing the flow of technology; Technology transfer and the dissemination of technological information within the research and development organization.* Cambridge, MA: MIT Press.

Anshen, M. (Ed.). (1974). *Managing the socially responsible corporation.* New York: Macmillan.

Axelrod, R. (1970). *Conflict of interest.* Chicago: Markham.

Bacharach, S. B., & Lawler, E. J. (1980). *Power and politics in organizations.* San Francisco: Jossey-Bass.

Bales, R. W. (1984, May). *Organizational interface: An open systems, contingency approach to boundary-spanning activities.* Paper presented at the meeting of the International Communication Association, San Francisco.

Baxter, W. (1980). *Our progress and our potential.* Working paper, University of Oklahoma, School of Journalism, Norman.

Blau, P. M. (1964). *Exchange and power in social life.* New York: Wiley.

Broom, G. M. (1982). A comparison of sex roles in public relations. *Public Relations Review, 8*(3), 17–22.

Broom, G. M., & Dozier, D. M. (1985, August). *Determinants and consequences of public relations roles.* Paper presented at the meeting of the Association for Education in Journalism and Mass Communication, Memphis.

Brown, D. A. (1980, March). Public affairs/public relations. *Public Relations Journal, 36,* 11–14.

Burger, C. (1983). How management views public relations. *Public Relations Quarterly, 27*(4), 27–30.

Close, H. W. (1980, March). Public relations as a management function. *Public Relations Journal, 36,* 11–14.

Cobb, A. T. (1984). An episodic model of power: Toward an integration of theory and research. *Academy of Management Review, 9,* 482–493.

Crozier, M. (1964). *The bureaucratic phenomenon.* Chicago: University of Chicago Press.

Cyert, R. M., & March, J. G. (1963). *A behavioral theory of the firm.* Englewood Cliffs, NJ: Prentice-Hall.

Cyert, R. M., & March, J. G. (1973). *A behavioral theory of the firm* (2nd ed.). Englewood Cliffs, NJ: Prentice-Hall.

Dozier, D. M. (1981, August). *The diffusion of evaluation methods among public relations practitioners.* Paper presented at the meeting of the Association for Education in Journalism, East Lansing, MI.

Emerson, R. M. (1962). Power-dependence relations. *American Sociological Review, 27,* 31–43.

Forrestal, D. J. (1980). Cited in B. Baxter, *Our progress and our potential.* Working paper, University of Oklahoma, School of Journalism, Norman.

Gaski, J. F. (1984). The theory of power and conflict in channels of distribution. *Journal of Marketing, 48,* 9–29.

Greyser, S. A. (1981). Changing roles for public relations. *Public Relations Journal, 18,* 18–25.

Grunig, J. E. (1976). Organizations and public relations: Testing a communication theory. *Journalism Monographs, 46.*

Grunig, J. E. (1984). Organizations, environments, and models of public relations. *Public Relations Research and Education, 1*(1), 6–29.

Grunig, J. E., & Grunig, L. S. (1989). Toward a theory of the public relations behavior of organizations: Review of a program of research: In J. E. Grunig & L. A. Grunig (Eds.), *Public relations research annual* (Vol. 1, pp. 27–63). Hillsdale, NJ: Lawrence Erlbaum Associates.

Grunig, J. E., & Hunt, T. (1984). *Managing public relations.* New York: Holt, Rinehart & Winston.

Grunig, L. A. (1990). Power in the public relations department. In L. A. Grunig & J. E. Grunig (Eds.), *Public relations research annual* (Vol. 2, pp. 115–155). Hillsdale, NJ: Lawrence Erlbaum Associates.

Hage, J. (1980). *Theories of organizations: Form, process, and transformation.* New York: Wiley.

Hage, J., & Aiken, M. (1970). *Social change in complex organizations.* New York: Random House.

Hage, J., & Dewar, R. A. (1973). Elite values versus organizational structure in predicting innovation. *Administrative Science Quarterly, 18,* 279–290.

Hage, J., & Hull, F. (1981). *A typology of environmental niches based on knowledge technology and scale; The implications for innovation and productivity.* Working Paper 1, University of Maryland, Center for the Study of Innovation, Entrepreneurship, and Organization Strategy, College Park.

Hambrick, D. C. (1981). Environment, strategy, and power within top management teams. *Administrative Science Quarterly, 26,* 253–276.

Hartsock, N. (1981). Political change: Two perspective on power. In Quest Staff and Book Committee (Eds.), *Building feminist theory* (pp. 3-19). New York: Longman.

Hickson, D. J., Hinings, C. R., Lee, C. A., Schneck, R. E., & Pennings, J. M. (1971). A strategic contingencies theory of intraorganizational power. *Administrative Science Quarterly, 16,* 216-229.

Jablin, F. M. (1980). Superior's upward influence, satisfaction, and openness in superior-subordinate communication: A reexamination of the "Pelz" effect. *Human Communication Research, 6*(1), 210-220.

Johnson, D. J., & Acharya, L. (1981, August). *Organizational decision making and public relations roles.* Paper presented at the meeting of the Association for Education in Journalism, Athens, OH.

Kanter, R. M. (1979, July-August). Power failure in management circuits. *Harvard Business Review,* pp. 65-75.

Katz, D., & Kahn, R. L. (1966). *The social psychology of organizations.* New York: Wiley.

Lawler, B. J., & Hage, J. (1973). Professional-bureaucratic conflict and intraorganizational powerlessness among social workers. *Journal of Sociology and Social Welfare, 1*(3), 92-102.

Lesly, P. (1981). The stature and role of public relations. *Public Relations Journal, 37,* 14-17.

Lindenmann, W., & Lapetina, A. (1981). Management's view of the future of public relations. *Public Relations Review, 81*(3), 3-13.

Maples, S. F. (1981). *Relationship of organizational structure to public relations decision-making.* Unpublished master's thesis, California State University, Fullerton.

Miles, R. H. (1977, August). *Boundary relevance.* Paper presented at the meeting of the Academy of Management, Kissimmee, FL.

Mintzberg, H. (1983). *Power in and around organizations.* Englewood Cliffs, NJ: Prentice-Hall.

Morgenthau, H. (1960). *Politics among nations.* New York: Knopf.

Murnighan, J. K. (1978). Models of coalition behavior: Game theoretic, social psychological and political perspectives. *Psychological Bulletin, 85,* 1130-1153.

Nelson, D. (1986). *The effect of management values on the role and practice of public relations within organizations.* Unpublished master's thesis, University of Maryland, College Park.

Newman, L. (1980). Public relations phase II: Adviser becomes decision maker. *Public Relations Journal, 36,* 11-13.

Nowlan, S. E., & Shayon, D. R. (1984). Reviewing your relationship with executive management. *Public Relations Quarterly, 39*(1), 5-11.

Organ, D. W. (1971). Linking pins between organizations and environments. *Business Horizons, 14*(12), 73-80.

Ossareh, J. C. (1987). *Technology as a public relations tool: Theoretical perspectives, practical applications, and actual use.* Unpublished master's thesis, University of Maryland, College Park.

Pennings, J. M., & Goodman, P. S. (1977). Toward a workable framework. In P. S. Goodman & J. M. Pennings (Eds.), *New perspectives on organizational effectiveness* (pp. 146-184). San Francisco: Jossey-Bass.

Perrow, C. (1961). Organizational prestige: Some functions and dysfunctions. *American Journal of Sociology, 66,* 335-341.

Pfeffer, J. (1981). *Power in organizations.* Boston: Pitman.

Pollack, R. (1986). *Testing the Grunig organizational theory in scientific organizations: Public relations and the values of the dominant coalition.* Unpublished master's thesis, University of Maryland, College Park.

Provan, K. G. (1980). Recognizing, measuring, and interpreting the potential/enacted power distinction in organizational research. *Academy of Management Review, 5,* 549-559.

Quinn, J. B. (1980). *Strategy for change: Logical incrementalism.* Homewood, IL: Irwin.

Robbins, S. P. (1987). *Organization theory: Structure, design, and applications* (2nd ed.). Englewood Cliffs, NJ: Prentice-Hall.

Rosenthal, H. (1970). Size of coalition and electoral outcomes in the Fourth French Republic. In S. Groennings, E. W. Kelley, & M. Leiserson (Eds.), *The study of collective behavior* (pp. 165–193). New York: Holt, Rinehart & Winston.

Schneider, (aka Grunig), L. S. (1985). The role of public relations in four organizational types. *Journalism Quarterly, 62*(3), 567–576, 594.

Simon, H. (1953). Notes on the observation and measurement of political power. *Journal of Politics, 15,* 500–516.

Staff. (1984, December 3). Must busy professionals be concerned about education for the field while battling issues like achieving top management decision making? *pr reporter*, pp. 1–2.

Stevenson, W. B., Pearce, J. L., & Porter, L. W. (1985). The concept of "coalition" in organization theory and research. *Academy of Management Review, 10*(2), 256–268.

Strenski, J. B. (1980, March). The top 12 public relations challenges for 1980. *Public Relations Journal, 36,* 11–14.

Thompson, J. D. (1967). *Organizations in action.* New York: McGraw-Hill.

Activism: How It Limits the Effectiveness of Organizations and How Excellent Public Relations Departments Respond

19

Larissa A. Grunig
University of Maryland

ABSTRACT

The environment plays a critical role in a theory of excellent public relations. First, strategic communication managers define and scan the environment. Second, the environment affects the structure of the organization and the nature of the communication function. Organizational theories show that organizations with dynamic, turbulent environments develop more flexible structures and more symmetrical public relations than those with static environments. What makes the environment of organizations most turbulent today is the presence of activist groups. Although activist groups present threats for organizations, they provide an opportunity for public relations. Excellent public relations, that is, helps organizations deal with activists— thus increasing the need for and the power of the communication department. This chapter explains the nature of activism and provides guidelines for communication managers to help organizations interact with these most strategic publics.

This chapter represents an attempt to help public relations practitioners deal in more than an ad hoc way with the opposition their organizations often face from activist groups. It applies Olson's (1982) theory of collective action to special interest groups that pressure governmental and corporate bodies. Olson explained the power of even very small groups to affect organizational policy. In fact, according to Olson, small interest groups can be more effective than larger and more established groups.

Too often in the past, corporate management has been inclined to ignore the potential impact of small collectivities. Compounding this "snail-darter

503

fallacy" is the lack of legitimacy granted any activist group by too many organizations, whether profit making, not for profit, or governmental. However, the work of Mintzberg (1983) shows that all organizations at least occasionally face legitimate power struggles from within and from without.

Exploring the extensive literature of activism results in a number of key assumptions about these groups—whether they are called pressure groups, special interest groups, grassroots opposition, social movements, or issue groups. Although each term may bring with it subtle differences in meaning, they all allude to collections of individuals organized to exert pressure on an organization on behalf of a cause.

Mintzberg (1983) found that such groups may form around an issue or that existing groups may turn their attention to new organizations or issues. Their activity may be episodic or regular, general or focused, detached or personal. Processes may be formal or informal. They may try to initiate or to obstruct action. Regardless, their purpose is to exert control over the organization even as outsiders. Voicing an opinion typical of many activists, Moore (1974) explained: "Our role is to present options as forcefully and as articulately as possible. But if the public does not pick up on these options, and I think there is sufficient evidence to show that it will, the corporation will have no choice. It will change or be changed" (p. 50).

The group actively seeks to influence and change a condition through means that range from education to violence. Its members are committed and organized behind appropriate leadership to reach their goals—which could be political, economic, or social. Members often are characterized by their motivation, fervor, and enthusiasm; they will persevere until they achieve their goal.

Distilling all of these characteristics results in the following definition of activism: An activist public is a group of two or more individuals who organize in order to influence another public or publics through action that may include education, compromise, persuasion, pressure tactics, or force.

By imposing an organizational perspective on the study of activism, this chapter looks for critical ways in which businesses and even the smallest of groups can listen to each other and share responsibility for decisions that affect all of society. The self-interest of the organization, though, is in retaining or enhancing its autonomy from the pressure of the activist group. The chapter also suggests ways in which public relations practitioners may function more as managers than as technicians in dealing with these special interests, thus enhancing their own self-interest in professional development.

The activist group's intent is to improve the functioning of the organization from outside. Using one of the four models of public relations, public relations practitioners work to improve the functioning of their organization from within. In fact, learning to reconcile the competing forces of activists and the organizations they pressure is the challenge facing many corporate communicators today. As Jones and Chase (1979) said, "The overwhelming important challenge faced by professional senior management is how to develop and establish a systems approach to the management of public policy issues in order not to surrender corporate autonomy and efficiency to the whims of bureaucrats and activist groups" (p. 8).

Thus this chapter is prescriptive as well as descriptive. We draw our prescriptive principles for management in the focused area of public relations rather than the broader concern of management per se. This is an important distinction, because in our view the most valuable application for leaders of both activist groups and organizations is not in knowing that communication between the two is important but in knowing how, when, and what to communicate.

Meeting the challenge often entails constantly monitoring the organization's relevant publics, especially those that are active and antagonistic. Knowing how those publics perceive an organization and how to reach them, via different channels of communication, goes hand in hand with the proactive public relations that emphasizes issues management. This role for public relations professionals in dealing with activism may be a new phenomenon, according to Harold Burson (quoted in Parket, 1983): "Not until the recent era of environmental and consumer issues did CEOs really seek a public relations officer who understood their business. . . . The corporation must have built-in sensing devices that can detect changes in the social winds" (p. 13).

Public relations practitioners or those sensing devices who engage in issues management expand their role beyond publicity or press agentry to (a) identify and analyze emerging issues and (b) evaluate alternative organizational responses. Rather than trying to manage the issue or the activists, they end up helping manage the organization's efforts to contend with the problem. In so doing, the public relations manager becomes part of the reconciliation process as well as the accompanying communication effort. Without this forward-thinking and far-reaching involvement on the part of public relations, Jones and Chase (1979) contended, the corporation "may find itself unprepared to face issues that later invite adverse public policy decisions" (p. 11). As a result, the CEO may simply turn to "outworn and traditional public relations defense mechanisms" (p. 7).

An illustrative case of what happens when planning and environmental scanning are missing from a public relations program can be found in the adverse public reaction to nuclear energy after Three Mile Island. Plumb (1984) contended that communication officials in the nuclear and electrical-utilities industries had done little to nurture public understanding or goodwill—based, apparently, on the premise that the public understood what they considered to be the obvious benefits of nuclear power. As a result, the industries had to spend millions of dollars in a campaign aimed at rebuilding public confidence after the accident in March 1979. Plumb's advice to public relations practitioners faced with similar opposition from outside groups was to regard their field as "a constant process of studying what an organization, company, or industry is doing, researching the constantly changing public climate within which it is doing it, and shaping communications programs to make sure people understand what's going on" (p. 4).

Proactive programs such as these are vital in the 1990s, largely as a result of the environmental, consumer, and feminist movements of the last several decades. What *Business Week* ("A New Breed," 1984) called a "new breed of grass-roots activists" can be expected to form coalitions that wield enormous power with both business and government. The resurgence of environmentalism, in particular, has resulted in a congressional lobby that Harrison (1982) described as a "green giant." Allen (1979), who also acknowledged the growing impact of citizens' groups on even mammoth organizations, considered too much public relations the result of reactive, rather than proactive, management.

Instead, dealing with opposition requires what Stolz (1983) called "conflict PR," mobilizing public opinion or preventing its formation. The public relations department, he said, should be aware of public opinion before it becomes a major threat to the organization. He cited causes of this friction as the high rate of economic growth (resulting in dissention over distribution), social changes causing problems with common values, and increasing governmental regulation.

Gollner (1984), a professor of political science who lectured to the Foundation for Public Relations Research and Education, described the growing interdependence he saw between organizations and other societal groups. He explained what he considered a "profound transformation" as follows:

> The process of industrialization and the developments of technology are relentlessly reducing the capacity of organizations & nations to remain islands unto themselves. Whether it's a government trying to reduce inflation or generate jobs, whether it's a corporation trying to increase its profits or enter new markets, external hands seem to weigh heavily upon the steering mechanism of most of our major institutions. In this new environment, corporate or any other organizational decision making is more & more externally driven. (p. 1)

In short, Gollner (1984) described the technological influences that have led to the increasingly common interplay among organizations. Resisting this trend, he contended, only could hinder competitiveness and innovation. So rather than considering the influences of external groups a threat, he encouraged organizations to regard then as *"the energy of our rejuvenation. This philosophy will significantly change the way we manage our relations with our neighbors and groups within society"* (p. 1).

Gollner (1984) grouped together competitors and adversarial publics when he spoke of organizations "increasingly buffeted by the decisional waves of others" (p. 2). If external issues continue to impinge upon traditional domains of management, he argued, organizational leaders must become more knowledgeable about the decision-making processes of those other organizations and groups that affect them. He concluded that anticipating and controlling for the consequences of interdependence is the stuff of modern management and a special onus for the profession of public relations.

Figure 1.1, which depicts the factors influencing how public relations is practiced, also emphasizes the environmental interdependencies to which Gollner (1984) was alluding. That is, activist groups – in particular – have the power to affect the organization. Top management, in turn, may try to manage these external publics as well. As chapter 17 showed, however, the dominant coalition may ignore such vital constituencies if it does not consider them crucial – often a problem with the subjective, perceived environment. This is also likely to happen when public relations is not represented in the organization's dominant coalition.

UNDERSTANDING THE POWER OF LARGE AND SMALL PUBLICS

Overcoming anachronistic responses requires more of a public relations person than a P. T. Barnum. One major dictate is for a professional who can undertake preliminary research on publics – perhaps through opinion polling, focus groups, coorientational studies, or other survey techniques. Why? Without a thorough understanding of adversarial groups, the organization may be at their mercy. According to Jones (1978): "Activist groups make public policy issues out of problems through the careful organization and the adroit use of propaganda techniques. All levels of government are increasing activities which attempt to satisfy the special economic and *information* needs of diverse activist groups" (emphasis added; p. 19).

Government may be trying to meet these needs, but too few corporations are – according to the bestseller *In Search of Excellence* (Peters & Waterman, 1982). Its authors pointed out that too many managers fail to deal with consumers, environmentalists, minorities, women's groups, activist church groups, stockholder blocs, antiestablishment educators, no-growth advocates, adversarial unions, and government. Managers described there eagerly seek "answers" that pretend they can ignore external publics and still control both organizational and public policy.

More effective is to identify and characterize relevant publics. For example, public relations practitioners must understand why individuals join groups or form collectivities. One of the most basic, yet most helpful explanations, came from Dewey (1927). He characterized a public as a group whose members face a similar problem, recognize that the problem exists, and organize to do something about it. J. Grunig (Grunig & Hunt, 1984, p. 145) expanded that definition by describing a group for which none of Dewey's conditions apply as a "nonpublic," one that has no consequences on the organization and vice versa. He called a group facing problems created by organizational consequences but failing to recognize those problems a "latent public." Publics become aware, according to J. Grunig, when they recognize the problem. Active publics, he said, organize to discuss and to do something about their problems. Allen (1979) acknowledged the growing impact of these citizens' groups on organizations. He called the gathering of information about them "breath to sustain life" in the corporate body.

In the case of these activist groups, it is particularly important to examine the size of the collective and the incentives used to entice members or the sanctions imposed on those who do not join. Olson (1982) argued that small groups have certain advantages over larger groups. Although he refrained from citing numbers that differentiate "small" from "large," he did argue that smaller groups tend to perform more efficiently than larger groups and that they seem to have wider support than they actually enjoy. Because smaller groups often display more "action-taking" behavior than do larger ones, the outcome in struggles between small, activist factions and large, established organizations can be asymmetrical (James, 1951; see also Buchanen, 1965). Olson (1982) concluded that "small 'special interest' groups . . . have disproportionate power" (p. 127).

Olson's (1982) overriding explanation for this phenomenon lies in economic theory and resulted in his radical theory of pressure groups. He began by rejecting the notion of traditional theorists, dating back to Aristotle, who believed that humans experience a "universal joining tendency." Olson also discounted the related concept of instinct as predictor of individuals joining groups. He cited extensive empirical evidence that establishes instinct or propensities as an insufficient explanation for why people join groups. In short, he said, "The allegation that the typical American is a 'joiner' is largely a myth" (p. 20).

Instead, Olson (1982) developed a theory that helps explain both why people join groups and why small groups can be more potent than large ones. His theory answers the questions of why small groups are more efficient and more viable than large groups and why even rational, self-interested individuals fail to act to achieve their common or group interests. He described the essence of an organization as providing an "inseparable, generalized benefit" (p. 15). He went on to explain: "Though all of the members of the group . . . have a common interest in obtaining this collective benefit, they have no common interest in paying the cost of providing the collective good. Each would prefer that the others pay the entire cost, and ordinarily would get any benefit provided whether he had borne part of the cost or not" (p. 21). Further, the larger the group, the more it must fall short of providing an optimal amount of the collective good. The more individuals in the group, the more serious the suboptimality; as a result, larger groups generally perform less efficiently than smaller ones.

Members of large groups know that their individual efforts rarely make much difference to the outcome; they often feel that the situation will turn out the same regardless of how much or how little they contribute (Olson, 1982, p. 53). How, then, did Olson explain the large number of participants in many well-known interest groups, such as the Sierra Club? He said that although people may join very small groups voluntarily, large-group membership depends on either rewards or sanctions. J. Grunig (1989), who studied members of the Sierra Club, found that some joined out of their desire to "delegate activism"—affecting policy even though they themselves do not benefit.

Because rational members of large groups typically try to maximize their individual welfare, they do not try to maximize the group goal—unless they are forced to do so or unless they receive a separate incentive. Thus, according to Olson (1982), successful large groups have the authority to coerce or to induce. Membership either is compulsory, as in the case of labor unions, or provides benefits—such as special publications—only to those who participate in the group.

UNDERSTANDING POWER
IN THE ORGANIZATION

Special interest groups operating outside the organization increasingly try to control it, according to management theorist Mintzberg (1983). His definitive text *Power in and Around Organizations* helps answer the question of who should control the corporation. Mintzberg defined power as "the capacity to effect (or affect) organizational outcomes" (p. 4). He explained that organizations are affected by four types of powerful groups: owners, associates (suppliers, clients, partners, or competitors—all of whom have a purely economic relationship with the organization), employee associations, and external publics.

Mintzberg (1983) went on to describe three categories of powerful external publics: the mass media, government, and special interest groups. The next part of this chapter deals briefly with each one, going beyond the work of Mintzberg to include relevant research from other scholars in communication, organizational sociology, economics, and political science. It delineates the interrelationship among these three kinds of publics. It concludes with an explanation of the conflict that often arises between the organization and its external influencers.

UNDERSTANDING THE POWER OF THE MASS MEDIA

Browne (1985) found that members of many interest groups consider their "target" organizations corrupt, inept, or unresponsive. They further contend that they "gain little cooperation except through threats and exposure" (p. 463). When this is the case, contact with the mass media becomes critically important. Media coverage conveys legitimacy. Agenda-setting theory holds that the media provide a form of legitimation and confer status on the individuals involved in activism. As Olien, Donohue, and Tichenor (1984) said, "Investigators in 'agenda-setting' research have frequently concluded that media coverage of events creates citizen definition of the importance of those events" (p. 2). Harris (1982) found that groups also use the media to build a favorable image, to educate the public, or to use the ensuing public opinion as a court of appeal.

However, media coverage of activism is not unilaterally favorable to the activist group at the expense of the organization being pressured. For one thing, the mass media are designed to cover events, not issues (Wolfsfeld, 1984). As a result, it is difficult—if not impossible—to convey ideological messages via the press. Second, media portrayal of conflict may not mirror reality. According to Wolfsfeld, "The media often tend to exaggerate the weird and the unusual about social movements in order to make them more newsworthy" (p. 555).

Nevertheless, activist groups often experience advantages over the organizations they oppose. Once again, size is a factor. Newsom (1983) pointed out that "small pressure groups have more flexibility in dealing with news media and are likely to approach them in the best possible problem-facing behavior" (p. 38). Fraser (1979) regarded the grassroots activist group as a "sleeping giant" because of its efficiency in supplying information to the media with resultant (favorable) public opinion. Further, Mazur (cited in Staff, 1986) found that the more the media cover an issue, the more negative the public's opinion of the organization being pressured. Historically, protest groups even have established their own media (Olien et al.,

1984). To summarize, Olien et al. argued the somewhat obvious point that "coverage of protest movements by the media, at different stages, may be vital to the level of public awareness and possible success or failure of a movement" (p. 1).

UNDERSTANDING THE ROLE OF GOVERNMENT

Haney (1983) found that consumer activists often work with government to affect the internal operations of organizations. She cited a Louis Harris survey that showed limited progress in decreasing public skepticism about the willingness of business to cooperate with consumers. Instead, many survey respondents considered the government a necessary watchdog.

Of course, the target of much activism in this country is the government itself — public agencies such as departments of transportation, education, or energy. Often, however, the pressure group tries to enlist the support of a governmental body in its crusade against an offending organization. At that point, the organization faces opposition from more than a single source and — with governmental intervention — real threats to its autonomy. As Mintzberg (1983) said, "Governments have special power over all organizations because, first, they represent the ultimate legitimate authority of the society, and second, they establish the rules — the laws and regulations — within which every organization must function" (p. 44).

The first phase of government intervention often is "moral suasion" followed by, if unsuccessful, legislation to control organizations Mintzberg (1983) termed "affected with the public interest" (p. 45). Fisse and Braithwaite (1983) devoted a major portion of their book *The Impact of Publicity on Corporate Offenders* to these effects of adverse publicity: the passage of new laws and the strengthening of regulatory agencies. Jones (1978) considered this the "institutionalization of activism." He cited as key examples the California state program that places lay members on regulatory boards and programs that make government funds available to consumer groups to help them present their point of view before hearings in federal agencies.

How legitimate is this claim of activists to control organizations they neither own, work for, supply, nor perhaps even patronize? Should organizations become, in essence, their instrument? Can a responsible organization maintain a closed system, remaining responsible primarily to its stockholders even in the face of governmental threats and negative coverage in the media? Perhaps an explanation of why such conflicts occur will make the answers to the aforementioned questions obvious. Such understanding also implies a systematic course of action for public relations practitioners involved in issues management.

Mintzberg (1983) explained the growing hostility between organizations and activist groups in four ways. First, he argued that economic power has become highly concentrated. The public worries about the enormous influence that rests in the hands of relatively few corporations. Second, this economic power of the private sector in general (and of individual, giant corporations in particular) has led to increasingly significant social consequences. Again, this has caused the public to question the role of business in society—looking hard at cultural, technical, environmental, and political ramifications of corporate policy as well as the social consequences mentioned earlier. Third, and as a result, the public's expectations of the economic and social responsibilities of business have risen. Finally, the corporation typically is controlled by its own administrators—despite what Mintzberg considered a fundamentally illegitimate basis for their power alone. Were the corporation controlled by those upon whom it had an impact, in Mintzberg's opinion there would be no issue of who should control it.

UNDERSTANDING THE ROLE OF PUBLIC RELATIONS

Public relations practitioners can play a significant part in resolving the fundamental conflicts previously described. Depending on their approach to the field, they can exacerbate or reduce the problem facing organizations pressured by outside constituencies. The four models of public relations described by J. Grunig (1984) provide options.

Public relations practitioners who follow the press agentry/publicity model often are regarded as "flacks," mere publicists not overly concerned with the truth. Instead, they promote their organizations at all costs—rarely bothering to research the nature of their publics or the effects of their efforts. The public information model is exemplified by "journalists in residence," practitioners who emphasize press relations by churning out news releases. Their voluminous output is primarily one-way, from organization to the publics, but they value accuracy and disclosure. Like press agents, they seldom conduct research—only occasionally surveying readership or readability.

Practitioners relying on the two-way asymmetrical model both gather and disseminate information. Because their goal is to persuade or to control their audiences, they acknowledge the need to know as much about those publics as possible. Then, armed with the results of opinion surveys or focus-group studies, they construct messages designed to appeal to the informational needs or attitudes of those publics. Two-way symmetrical, the newest approach to the practice of public relations, also involves both gathering and disseminating information—but with a radically different motive than that of its asymmetrical counterpart. Instead of trying to dominate their environment, practitioners of this model want to understand and to cooperate with their relevant external publics. Research is conducted more on level of information than on attitudes. Managers recognize that the organization may need to change as much as its publics in response to the intelligence gathered.

Although J. Grunig (1984) initially contended that all models may be appropriate for certain organizations in certain environments under certain circumstances, some may be more effective for organizations pressured by activist groups. The next section of this chapter makes assumptions about which model should predominate, given the important contingencies of media and governmental involvement and both activist and organizational stances on the issue.

ASSUMPTIONS ABOUT ACTIVISM

Distilling the literature on activism drawn primarily from the fields of political science, organizational sociology, business, and economics leads to the following assumptions about activist-organizational interaction. In the field of public relations, these assumptions had remained largely untested until a major series of case studies conducted during the mid-1980s. Those cases are described in detail later in this chapter. Then, findings from the cases are juxtaposed with these assumptions and implications from that analysis are expressed in the form of propositions for practicing excellent public relations:

1. Activist pressure is an extensive problem for organizations. As Mintzberg (1983) pointed out, most have experienced opposition from external forces in the form of special interest groups. Controversies escalate when the media become involved. Consequences are more serious when the government becomes involved.

2. Activist groups vary in size, range of issue involvement, tactics, and effectiveness—but all (especially the smallest, most active ones) are potentially damaging to the target organization.

3. Public relations practitioners are integrally involved in dealing with hostilities between organizations and activist groups. Both the organization and the group may employ these managers of communication.

4. Some organizations try to ignore all evidence of opposition from activist groups.

5. Among the organizations that do rely on public relations departments to respond to activist pressure, all of J. Grunig's (1984) models of public relations can be found.

6. However, the two two-way models of public relations (asymmetrical and symmetrical) are more effective than either of the one-way models (publicity or public information) in helping resolve conflict between an organization and its external publics. As J. Grunig (1982) said, "The best public relations program—in general—should be a two-way program in which the corporation attempts to learn from the public what adverse consequences it is having on the public and tells the public what the corporation is doing about those consequences" (p. 45).

7. The two-way asymmetrical model of public relations predominates among practitioners engaged in issues management. J. Grunig (J. Grunig & Hunt, 1984) said that although symmetrical communication would seem "essential" in this instance, such has not been shown to be the case.

8. The two-way symmetrical model of public relations is rarest but most effective in contending with activist pressure. The research inherent in this model allows for the crucial proactive, rather than reactive, public relations. The compromises it works for should eliminate any sustained, bitter social divisiveness. Unfortunately, because so little public relations practice follows this model, it remains largely untested as a strategy for coping with activism.

RESEARCH ON ORGANIZATIONAL RESPONSES TO ACTIVISM

A series of 34 in-depth case studies compiled in the last 5 years represents the first major step toward developing theoretical propositions about public relations behavior during conflict with activist groups (L. Grunig, 1986). Instances of activism came from throughout the country. Pressure groups opposed business (and even governmental) practices on a number of fronts (real estate development, schools, public transportation, logging, mining, nuclear waste, entertainment, communication, tobacco, bottling, and so forth).

The activist groups studied ranged from the well known, such as Greenpeace and the Humane Society, to the obscure, such as the local citizens' councils and students opposed to campus keg policies. The size and make-up of their membership, their goals, and their tactics were equally diverse. Their common thread was their ability to damage organizations with considerably larger reputations and resources. Although many of them relied on public relations themselves (either from staff members, volunteers, or counseling firms), in most cases the group's leader was the liaison with media, government, and the target organization.

Few charismatic or well-known leaders were interviewed. Only a few were seasoned political activists—including one who called himself "an old warrior who knows how to shake things up." Instead, most mirrored their members in terms of experience, age, education, income, occupation, and gender. Their major difference was the amount of activity in which they engaged. Twenty-five of the 34 activist groups studied had two kinds of members. The first, typified in either the leader of the group or a steering committee, made the decisions and initiated the action. The second, or general membership, contributed financially but only rarely became involved in decision making and action.

However, few generalizations can be made about the demographics or psychographics of those members. Often, their banding together seemed more a matter of proximity than of common age, salary, sex, or even ideology. Members of a no-growth committee in a resort community, for example, ranged from retired long-time property owners to summer residents with recently acquired lots. Although the newcomers tend to have high incomes and levels of education, the oldtimers (as retirees) get along on less. Another small group of activists, neighbors opposing a basalt-mining plant, range in age from 19 to 69 years; their occupations range from grocery-store clerk to university professor; and their education ranges from high-school graduate to PhD.

Small groups relied on sporadic contributions and volunteer efforts, especially in public relations and legal counsel. Of course, much pressuring activity can be accomplished with little financial investment; access to the media and to the government at least theoretically is free in the United States. Still, many groups characterized their impetus for joining coalitions as financial. A large civic association, for example, is an umbrella group of 13 smaller civic and homeowners' associations. The federation was formed to afford litigation against an area builder.

Two out of every three activist groups were concerned with a single issue. Issues, though, ranged from the very narrow to the very broad. An example of the former was opposition to destroying an historic tavern. One of the most all-embracing is the Humane Society's effort to eliminate cruelty toward animals—whether that brutality takes the form of hunting and trapping, exhibiting animals in zoos, or experimenting on them in university labs.

Whether the issue was circumscribed or inclusive, however, it—not the organization—remained the target in almost all cases (in spite of contentions on the part of a few public relations practitioners that activists are, on the whole, malcontents or are "out to get" their organization). For example, in a letter to a development company's board of directors, an activist leader said:

None of the land owners I know on the Bay bought property here expecting to fight anybody. That's not what living or recreating at [the] Port . . . is all about. I can tell you that we would much rather be leading the cheering section for [the company] than feeling compelled to organize a well-publicized continuous fight against the company on the battlefield of public opinion.

When it does come to a fight, the weapons in each activist's arsenal might vary. And as the battle drags on, the weapons might become more lethal. In a typical progression from the innocuous to the grim, one civic association studied went from informal dialogue to formal communication to political pressure to legal remedy in its successful action against a local contractor. Among the mildest protests encountered was a letter from a preservationist association to the local department of transportation, asking it to reconsider the alternatives it had proposed and recognize the "appropriateness of more modest and better solutions" to the traffic problem. The most violent were middle-of-the-night death threats against owners of a basalt-mining plant.

Between these isolated and extreme examples of activist tactics were the following (in approximate order of frequency): contact with the media (either informally or through news releases and press conferences), letter or telephone campaigns directed toward legislators or members of the public, lobbying, public forums, petition drives, litigation, pseudoevents (such as a massive Citizens' Lobby Day), public education (through tours of historic sites, publishing maps, developing slide presentations, and so forth), picketing, boycotts, and sit-ins.

Fourteen activist groups advocated regulation of the offending organization by asking the government to impose formal constraints. This was most often the case when activists believed that management could not be trusted or even pressured into behaving responsibly; so, they reasoned, management would have to be forced to be socially responsible. (Mintzberg, 1983, Drucker, 1973, and others have noted that organizations sometimes welcome regulation as a way of equalizing competition. However, none of the organizations cooperating in this study indicated such a position.)

One particularly interesting finding about activists is that unlike organizational stances, which were constant, their positions shifted. During a conflict, protest groups often fluctuated between pressuring directly and seeking regulation of their targets. Perhaps most significant for public relations practitioners, the activist stance tended to go from direct pressure or calls for regulation to a more trusting, cooperative attitude at the first sign of the organization's willingness to negotiate. For example, homeowners in suburban Maryland moved from their original stances of pressure and regulation of a developer to trust as soon as they reached a tentative compromise.

Mintzberg (1983) suggested that special interest groups shift stances in the following pattern: pressure, followed by regulation (if organizations fail to respond to initial protests), followed by trust (because the organization had been regulated into a less autonomous mode). However, evidence from this study refutes Mintzberg's progression. About a dozen activist groups began by wanting to regulate their target organizations but shifted to direct pressure. Why? The case of a national coalition for women in a highly publicized law suit against a college illustrates the reason so many groups consider pressure more effective than regulation.

The coalition's purpose is to monitor the enforcement of Title IX, a formal constraint to eliminate discriminatory practices in education. The problems Mintzberg (1983) cited regarding regulation are the reasons the coalition moved from that position to one of direct pressure against the liberal arts school. First, governmental regulation only sets minimal standards of acceptable behavior. Although Title IX constrains unacceptable behavior, it does not guarantee a substitute of desirable behavior. Second, regulation tends to be a slow, conservative process. Activists often become impatient. Third, regulation may be difficult to enforce. If a college signs an assurance-of-compliance form, how can the Department of Education be made aware of violations? Only through public protest, according to the coalition.

Most activist groups were willing for the organization to regain control over its operation—but with oversight from either the government or the group itself. Organizations, though, wanted to be left alone entirely, claiming that economic incentives would dictate their social responsibility. Most felt deserving of the public's trust. One encouraging finding, then, is that neither activists nor organizations typically espouse an extreme—or an extremely opposed—ideology. In other words, they might not be so far apart as they think. And their positions are rarely as radical as each might assume.

The typical organization's philosophical stance on the activist opposition was considerably more fixed than was the model of public relations it followed. The telephone company, for example, tends to practice two-way symmetrical public relations with its myriad stakeholders. This approach is consistent with most regulated utilities, trying to demonstrate their social responsibility to governmental watchdogs. When confronted by the citizens' coalition, however, it reverted to imbalanced communication—asymmetrical, rather than symmetrical—in an effort to dominate (rather than cooperate with) its environment.

This "closing-the-ranks" approach was echoed in several organizations that historically emphasized two-way asymmetrical communication. When pressured, they adopted a one-way pattern of public relations to deal with activists they considered "unreasonable." The newly adopted model would be either press agentry or public information, depending on the value management attached to honesty.

In fact, most (22 of 34) of the organizations studied operated more as a closed than open system with their influencers, both external and internal. That is, owners tended to discount any legitimate basis for input from activists and even from their own associates and employees. Given the extent of activism so many reported, this was surprising. Even organizations that had come up against powerful pressure groups with access to sympathetic media or governmental agencies (or both) often denied the risk of trying to ignore the demands of such activists.

Little cooptation via the board of directors or other decision-making bodies within the organization was evident. However, when this was tried (as in the case of a development corporation in its dealings with a preservationist group), it was effective.

Instead, CEOs or — in the case of government — department heads tried to maintain their goal of autonomy from the environment. They relied most often on public relations practitioners to help them cope with external demands. The corporate or department head, though, often was involved as well. Others typically assisting in cases of activism included lawyers, industrial relations staffs, and public affairs or governmental relations experts (in the case of the five largest organizations). About half of all organizations surveyed sought assistance from outside counsel as well — either public relations firms or attorneys. Two organizations relied on their own social responsibility committees to deal with the activists. Five received help from their industry associations.

Interviewees typically described the conflict in question in the most negative terms possible: intense rather than moderate or slight and enduring rather than brief. However, most of the issues under investigation were characterized as confined or discrete rather than pervasive. It seems, then, that although organizations often fight long, intense battles with activists — the battlefields have clear boundaries. (In fact, one beleaguered public relations professional referred to the situation as a "battle" and to his strategy for approaching the activists his "battle plan.")

Less than half of the organizations took action as a direct result of activist pressure in the cases investigated. Even an urban telephone company, with its large and sophisticated public relations operation, refused to deal directly with its state's Citizen Action Coalition when it opposed the company's plan for local measured service. Instead, the company stepped up its ongoing communication program that includes town meetings, a speakers' bureau, bill stuffers, radio talk shows, press "discussions" (informal q-and-a sessions), and "phone issues" conferences held at strategic locations around the state.

Other organizations took steps as a direct result of activism but restricted their communicative efforts to members of the public apart from the activist group. One example of deliberately disregarding the grassroots pressure came from a developer who said: "Let them rant and rave. We'll ignore them and keep up our own communication efforts [tabloid distributed to all citizens of the county, public forums, publicity on the environmental impact statement, etc.]."

Organizations that considered their opposition to be little or no threat rarely responded at all. Others pleaded lack of time or the resources necessary to respond. As an information specialist in a department of transportation said, because so many groups oppose its operation, "We can't hit all of the cylinders out there." Another respondent complained of recent budget cuts and said it was "handcuffed" by being reduced to few employees in the department.

Many of the organizations that responded did so in a cursory way. One answered with position papers. (A spokesman for the association acknowledged that this was largely reactive—but deliberately so. He explained that his association wanted the issue to be perceived as a nonissue.) Another only responded when forced to, as when a local education action league pressured the city into requesting that the state's Department of Energy (DOE) hold a hearing to discuss its proposed nuclear-waste depository. The hearing request was denied until the state's governor intervened with the DOE on the league's behalf.

Several others engaged in at least one-way communication when previously they had been silent. For example, when a preservationist association questioned the Department of Transportation's (DOT) plans to reroute traffic closer to the historical site, the DOT did initiate public hearings—but just to announce, in essence, "Here's what we're going to do." Another government agency responded in similar fashion when Greenpeace opposed its leasing of oil and gas drilling tracts in offshore Washington and Oregon. Its public affairs officer explained that releases distributed from the agency were generic in form, with the same message delivered to all members of the public; he said that because the sole function of the public affairs department is to distribute information, there was no need to meet with activists or engage in any other two-way communication.

The most frequent direct response to activist pressure was to gather intelligence. Hiring clipping services, contacting leaders of the activist group informally, querying reporters who covered the conflict, and even picking the brains of researchers involved in this study were commonplace. One typical public information officer described his mission as simply finding the facts, not debating the issues.

Less typical was compromise. When tried, however, results were deemed positive—at least to this researcher. For example, when a land-use dispute erupted, the construction company involved quickly chose to cooperate with the civic association opposing it. The company modified its plan by reducing the density and restricting the number of back-to-back units, with the following resolution (as described in the local newspaper): "The rift between the . . . Association and the . . . Organization was patched over Monday, when the developer submitted a new site plan for [the] Town Center, and the association withdrew its opposition to the original plan." In a second case of proposed compromise, the organization actually prevailed unilaterally because the activist group forfeited its voice in the decision process when it failed to accept the compromise.

The most dramatic instance of cooperative response came from a vice president for a development, construction, and management company: "Nearly every decision we make from planning to actual development involves publics and some type of regulatory agency." Response—or lack thereof—seemed to hinge partly on the organization's perception of the size and the strength of the group pressuring it. One large conglomerate, which virtually dismissed the activist group opposing it, characterized the group's leader as "nuts" and members of its steering committee as "crazies." Using this ad hominem argument (attacking the source of a statement rather than the statement itself) might obscure the issue or the activists' arguments.

Because few organizations took significant action to counter activist opposition, there was little subsequent evaluation of the effectiveness of their response. The telephone company conducted public opinion surveys in conjunction with the local measured service issue, the conglomerate commissioned a poll to determine the effects of its response to activist opposition, and officials of a beleaguered city college chatted informally with alumni and journalists about the college's reaction to an activist coalition for female students and their Title IX suit. These minimal evaluative efforts, however, were the exception.

In spite of this evidence, most public relations practitioners interviewed characterized their programs as "proactive" and "responsive." For instance, the public relations counselor handling relations with activists for a developer described his elaborate, five-part plan as including media relations, direct communication with the public via newsletters and tours of the facility, involving the public in the decision process through hearings, a comprehensive slide show, and publication of a critical water-quality study. However, he added that "in most environmental issues, 99 out of 100 times the developer is right but ends up spending thousands of dollars to prove it."

This less than open attitude was expressed by at least a dozen other interviewees. Paying lip-service to the importance of active, two-way communication with all of the organization's stakeholders was common. In actuality, few public relations staffs were willing or able to practice the kind of public relations they advocated. An alternative explanation might be that they lacked the support from the dominant coalition to do what they knew should be done.

Lack of training in public relations often was a problem. Most of the practitioners interviewed had neither the education nor the experience necessary to conduct the kind of program they espoused. In fact, only 5 of the 34 had formal training in public relations. And as Nanni (1980) found, training and professionalism are key predictors of public relations practice—second only to management's opinion of the value of public relations.

Perhaps this lack of in-house expertise accounts for the extensive reliance on outsiders for help—whether it comes from public relations or law firms—in coping with activism. One construction company that routinely hired attorneys with a background in public relations and land-use law was consistently successful in its dealings with grassroots activists. The company considered counselors who lived in the community as especially beneficial. Their unique qualifications enabled them to act as boundary personnel geographically, philosophically, and technically. As Burson (quoted in Parker, 1983) said, "Today's senior public relations officer has to be experienced not only in communication but also in the business that he or she represents" (p. 12).

Lack of skill in research seemed to be the greatest deficiency among practitioners interviewed. Without the ability to monitor issues and publics, many practitioners were caught off-guard. Typical was the public relations director of the college, who only learned of the threat posed by the national educational coalition when a local television station called for a statement. Even the telephone company, with its mammoth public relations operation and emphasis on stakeholder relations, was "surprised" at the pressure it received from the state's citizen action coalition because company officials had considered local measured service "one of the least confusing things to come out of the break-up of AT&T."

Research that was conducted typically was done for-hire rather than in-house. Gallup, Roper, and Harris polls were popular, as were the major clipping services. This monitoring of media coverage, though, usually was undertaken to review events rather than to plan for the future.

Organizations may consider activist pressure such as the scenarios described previously a monumental problem, but apparently the mass media do not. Coverage, in most cases studied, was minimal. Stories typically appeared on inside pages with little, if any, accompanying art. Reporters were, without exception, obscure. Television spots appeared toward the end of the broadcast and rarely lasted more than 30 s.

Such balanced—albeit minimal—coverage seemed to apply to organization and activists alike. This finding may come as a surprise to both sides. In a comment representative of many practitioners, the public relations counselor for a real estate developer said: "The media has had an unconscious bias over the years to question anything [the company] says. No matter how many press releases with data on water quality studies and bacteria count we give to the newspapers, the story always comes out against us." Activists in that same case complained of "the usual press 'genuflection' " toward the county's largest corporation. About one in four activist groups studied expected bias in reporting because their target organizations were major advertisers.

Organizations often do enjoy one advantage over the smaller groups that may pressure them: financial resources for rebuttal. As a spokesman for a tobacco company explained: "If you can't get a fair hearing in the press, sometimes you have to buy the ads. In the past, the Surgeon General gets the front page, and we'll be back in the classifieds."

One other obvious difference in media coverage emerged in this study. Local newspapers covered activist-organization conflict more extensively than did larger urban or regional papers. And, their reporting seemed to favor the activist group at least in terms of column inches devoted to expressing the activists' side of the controversy.

ANALYSIS OF THE RESEARCH

Findings led to the following analysis of the assumptions stated earlier in this chapter:

1. Activism, indeed, represents a major problem for organizations. Hostilities between organizations and pressure groups are commonplace. They may lead to a marshalling of public opinion against the organization that may, in turn, result in governmental regulation.

Both sides involved in the typical controversy feared that the other had the advantage in news coverage; both claimed bias on the part of the media. Activists considered the press favorably disposed toward the organizations that often happen to be advertisers. Organizations, on the other hand, thought that the media favor the underdog, represented in small activist groups, and that activists often stage dramatic pseudoevents for the sole purpose of media exposure. Although this study uncovered few instances of violent or even dramatic protest, it did expose a pattern of activist appeal to both the media and the government: If organizations failed to respond to initial overtures from activists, then the interest groups would contact the press or some regulatory body.

2. As expected, a variety of types of activist groups pressured the organizations included in this study. Issues tended to be discrete; only a few escalated beyond the initial concern. These collectives used a myriad

techniques to try their target organizations in the court of public opinion. Tactics ranged along a continuum from polite letters to protest rallies to death threats. Groups were as small as a handful of island homeowners or as large Greenpeace, with its hundreds of thousands of members worldwide.

More of the disputes studied were enduring than short term but again, difference was more the rule than the exception. One of the longest lasting controversies raged on a peninsula, where an association of oyster growers fought a developer for 7 years. (Ultimately, the development company lost its battle to build a resort on the wetlands there.)

Regardless of the length of the dispute, the intensity of the conflict or the media coverage involved, however, all activist groups studied had disrupted the target organization. This study cannot analyze the effects of activist pressure in direct relation to the outcome of each case, though, for several reasons. Many controversies are on-going, with no settlement in sight. In other instances, both sides claim the outcome as a victory—as in the case of the builder who managed to complete his convention complex on schedule—but 500 ft from the original site. Even in clear instances of compromise, the extent to which each side had to concede might not be equal.

In still other situations, a short-term triumph for the organization might lead to long-term problems with disgruntled activists. One likely example is a deposit coalition, licking its wounds over defeat of the deposit law fought by a major bottling company. The company's director of public relations acknowledged that the issue of returnable bottles undoubtedly will come up again and again, until the conservationists are successful in implementing the deposit legislation.

No case represented a clear victory for the organization. The half-dozen compromises were "as good as it got." In all other situations (and even in some settlements), the organization suffered. For example, a moratorium on building a sewage treatment plant led to the layoffs of 115 employees and higher interest rates at the time of the actual construction. A resort was forced to spend $300,000 to improve its sewage system. A proposed basalt-mining operation never got off the ground after its small-town neighbors complained. (As one of its owners said, "We hadn't even started and we already had opposition.")

These instances are relatively easy to document; the costs of governmental regulation and negative public opinion were often concomitant but harder to measure. As Stolz (1983) said, the organization that believes it is only threatened by government is wrong; he concluded that public opinion is the bigger foe.

3. Activists and organizations alike relied on public relations practitioners to help communicate with each other. As the literature had predicted,

the involvement of public relations personnel was considerably more pronounced in organizations than in pressure groups. Also, organizational executives typically involved themselves in the controversies investigated. Surprisingly few organizations described social responsibility committees set up to monitor issues or to deal with activists.

Small and medium-size organizations often did a better of job of communicating with activists than did the largest organizations. Small organizations, whose very existence could be threatened by protestors, tended to hire the help they knew they needed. Because they had few employees, and fewer still with expertise in public relations, they were quick to pay for professional assistance in the form of public relations or legal counsel. Organizations of moderate size, those with a correspondingly medium-size public relations department, relied on their own staffs to develop a plan for dealing with the activists. Large organizations commonly continued their established programs in public relations, rarely redesigning communication strategies as a result of outside pressure. Instead, they tended to brush aside the concerns of activist groups—especially if the group was small and relatively unknown. If they did acknowledge the threat of activism, they might call on their industry association—rather than a law or public relations firm—for help.

4. More than a few organizations did try to ignore all evidence of pressure from outside publics. Managers of public relations explained their inaction in a variety of ways: They had too little money, the threat was not great enough to bother about, they did not want to legitimize the activists' complaint, their efforts were spread too thin by facing many different pressure groups, they could rely on their association to handle the problem, or the media were prejudiced anyway.

5. As foreseen, all of J. Grunig's (1984) models of public relations were found among the organizations studied.

6. The sixth assumption suggested that two-way communication would prove more effective than one-way efforts at dealing with activism. Perhaps that is so, but too few instances of two-way symmetrical communication were found to establish the validity of this assumption. Instead, most organizations practiced either two-way asymmetrical public relations or one of the one-way models—either press agentry or public information. None of the three prevalent models, though, seemed even moderately successful in coping with activism (including the two-way but imbalanced, asymmetrical model).

7. Many interviewees described their involvement in issues management. These practitioners were more likely to practice two-way asymmetrical public relations than were the communication technicians who responded to the study. However, even communication managers were more apt to

practice one-way public relations than the more sophisticated two-way approach that the literature suggested.

8. The final assumption held that two-way symmetrical public relations would be the least practiced yet most effective organizational response to activist pressure. Once again, too little evidence of balanced communication emerged to support or to invalidate this claim.

IMPLICATIONS OF THE RESEARCH

Few organizations were successful in their dealings with pressure groups. The three most typical models of public relations used — press agentry, public information, and two-way asymmetrical — seemed ineffective. Because so few practitioners relied on the fourth model of public relations, two-way symmetrical, we cannot establish yet that this approach would have been more efficacious. However, the theories described at the beginning of this chapter suggest that practitioners should try this approach. The following propositions all deal with aspects of two-way, balanced communication as viable ways to overcome bitter social divisiveness.

> *Proposition 1:* Excellent organizations use two-way communication to learn the consequences of what they are doing on all of their relevant publics — not just their owners, their employees, and their associates.

Negative consequences mentioned in these 34 cases include reducing available prime farm acreage and open space; polluting the air and water; damaging fragile wetlands; increasing traffic, litter, and noise; dumping hazardous waste; raising the costs of necessary products and services; eliminating jobs; lowering property values; and discriminating against women.

> *Proposition 2:* Excellent organizations use two-way communication to tell the publics what they are doing about any negative consequences.

The study showed that the adage "what they don't know won't hurt them" no longer works — if it ever did. As Sullivan (1976) said, "The most common response from a technology's developer to citizens seeking information is that they don't need it" (p. 440).

Instead, the complexity of the environment of the 1990s dictates an equally comprehensive and dynamic public relations plan. Rather than feeling wed to the speakers' bureau, ad campaign, or press conferences they have relied on in the past, public relations practitioners should be flexible.

They should consider adopting new strategies or new messages, depending on the needs and predispositions of the activists opposing their organizations. For example, rather than releasing position papers to the media or hosting an open house at the new plant, organizations might develop task forces with members of community groups during the decision process on building a new facility.

Establishing such a "public issues committee" would involve outsiders early on, before their opposition may crystallize. It would offer managers more information on which to base their ultimate decisions. It also would remove some power from the position of the chief executive officer or the board of directors. After all, if real communication is to occur, there has to be the possibility of mutual influence. Otherwise, as Parson and Linkugel (1970) said, "Communication between the powerful and the powerless becomes only a monologue with the powerless simply listening and receiving instructions" (p. 13).

Involving the public relations staff in a joint organization-activist committee also would help transform the perception of public relations from corporate mouthpiece to advocate for understanding. Public relations personnel, no longer yes-people for management playing a zero-sum game with their opponents, could become mediators in a win-win situation. This, in turn, would have two major benefits. First, it would enhance the professional status of the field. Second, it would enhance the careers of individuals.

Proposition 3: Continuous efforts at communicating with activists are necessary to contend with their shifting stances.

The two-way symmetrical approach to public relations is inherently an on-going process. The study showed that at times, interest groups are willing to trust organizations but that at other times, they appeal either to the government or to the media for satisfaction. Rather than writing off efforts to communicate with activists as "chasing butterflies" when they lobby or hold press conferences, organizations should realize that this push for regulation or the pressure of public opinion may not last. Keeping channels of communication open may encourage interest groups to adopt the "trust it" stance—especially if that communication emphasizes the possibility of compromise.

Creating those channels before the controversy erupts makes sense. Plumb (1984), a veteran of disputes between environmentalists and the forest-products industry, explained that the time to start "spewing out facts" to support the company is not when it is in big trouble but when things are going well. Being proactive and establishing long-term relationships with consumer groups were major components of Texaco's model program of constituency relations. The oil company realized that trust in big business (especially the oil business) is not born overnight; it takes time, commitment, on-going personal contact, and accessibility (Pires, 1983).

Proposition 4: An on-going, balanced and proactive program of constituency relations must acknowledge the legitimacy of all constituent groups — regardless of their size.

Even the concerns of the smallest collectivities should be taken into consideration during any organization's decision process. Dewey (1927) contended that an organized public of many groups is the path toward what he called the "Great Community." Zisk (1969) called the very existence of interest groups a "major link" between citizens and their government. He considered pressure a legitimate method of communication between activists and legislators or organizational decision makers. J. Grunig and Hunt (1984) also considered the concerns of activists legitimate: "Generally, the arguments of both the activists and the organizations that resist them have merit — it just depends on who is suffering which consequences. Environmentalists want clean air and the beauty of pristine areas preserved. Businessmen want to mine coal, produce electricity, and make more profit. Both cannot have all of what they want" (p. 313).

Proposition 5: Conducting a two-way symmetrical communication program hinges on employing people with the necessary background and education.

In other words, public relations practitioners not only must appreciate the value of monitoring their external publics and devising programs to meet their needs — they have to know how to do all of that. The study showed that often, outside help augmented or replaced the efforts of in-house public relations departments during conflict with activists. If lawyers, in particular, are not to supplant public relations personnel, then public relations practitioners must learn the vital skills of negotiation and research.

Public relations managers with such expertise can expect senior management to grant them the autonomy to move about in the community, gathering information whether pro or con without fear of recrimination when reporting back to the organization (Ryan & Martinson, 1983). Finally, an experienced, highly trained public relations practitioner with input into organizational decision making should be less susceptible to influence of the company's dominant coalition on just how public relations is practiced. As it is, the values of the power elite seem to account for the often-inappropriate model of public relations practiced in many organizations (Nanni, 1980).

> *Proposition 6:* Excellent organizations learn to measure their effectiveness in terms of more than simplistic, short-term gains or losses — such as whether a returnable-bottle bill is defeated.

Research is an important variable in the two-way symmetrical model of public relations. The study demonstrated that issues endure. Environmentalism, for example, was a growing trend in this country during the 1960s and 1970s; it persists, as the focus on environmentalism in the cases investigated here shows.

As a result, public relations practitioners should institute a continuous program of evaluation. Organizations need more than piggyback questions to Roper polls to define and describe their publics. Counting clips gives minimal evidence of effectiveness. Any one-shot measures of the outcome of clashes between organization and activists are inadequate for program planning, proactive communication, and issues management.

CONCLUSION

Nothing in the aforementioned propositions suggests a radical departure from what textbooks already recommend for the effective practice of public relations. Instead, the findings of the study described in this chapter add support for what educators, scholars, and astute practitioners have advocated for decades: Organizations need to look ahead. Nothing fails like success, and what worked in the past no longer may. Issues resurface. Publics change.

Perhaps most important, the study lends the strongest endorsement to date for the need for two-way symmetrical communication between organizations and activists. Support comes not from success stories, but from glaring lack of success on the part of the 34 cases explored. Even if the two-way balanced model of public relations turns out to be no panacea, it should help to balance the demands of all the organization's constituencies — even the smallest (but not necessarily the least powerful). It also holds the promise for greater organizational autonomy within a dynamic and at times antagonistic environment.

In an increasingly pluralistic society (Drucker, 1984), we can expect a correspondingly growing number of moral disputes. Their congenial resolution rests at least in part on the shoulders of public relations practitioners. Even if satisfactory resolution eludes the organization, the value of participation in deliberating over the common good cannot be overstated.

REFERENCES

Allen, T. J. (1979). *Managing the flow of technology: Technology transfer and the dissemination of technological information within the research and development organization.* Cambridge, MA: MIT Press.

Browne, W. P. (1985). Variations in the behavior and style of state lobbyists and interest groups. *Journal of Politics, 47,* 450–68.

Buchanen, J. (1965). An economic theory of clubs. *Economica, 76,* 1–15.

Dewey, J. (1927). *The public and its problems.* Chicago: Swallow.

Drucker, P. F. (1973). *Management: Tasks, responsibilities, practices.* New York: Harper & Row.

Drucker, P. F. (1984). The new meaning of corporate social responsibility. *California Management Review, 26,* 53–63.

Fisse, F., & Braithwaite, J. (1983). *The impact of publicity on corporate offenders.* Albany: State University of New York Press.

Fraser, E. (1979). Marketing public policy through grass roots action. *Public Relations Quarterly, 24,* 14–17.

Gollner, A. (1984). Interdependence and its impact on public relations/public affairs. *Tips & Tactics* (Suppl. of *pr reporter*), *22*(14), 1–2.

Grunig, J. E. (1982, Fall). Developing economic education programs for the press. *Public Relations Review, 8,* 43–62.

Grunig, J. E. (1984). Organizations, environments, and models of public relations. *Public Relations Research and Education, 1,* 6–29.

Grunig, J. E. (1989). Sierra Club study shows who become activists. *Public Relations Review, 15*(3), 3–24.

Grunig, J. E., & Hunt, T. (1984). *Managing public relations.* New York: Holt, Rinehart & Winston.

Grunig, L. A. (1986, August). *Activism and organizational response: Contemporary cases of collective behavior.* Paper presented to the Association for Education in Journalism and Mass Communication, Norman, OK.

Haney, C. (1983). Consumer concern: Another explosion? *Public Relations Journal, 39,* 28.

Harris, P. (1982). Pressure groups and protest. *Politics, 17,* 111–20.

Harrison, E. B. (1982). In the grip of the "Green Giant." *Public Relations Journal, 38*(12), 19–20.

James, J. (1951). A preliminary study of the size determinant in small group interaction. *American Sociological Review, 16,* 474–477.

Jones, B. L. (1978). Issue management by objective: The new frontier for business. *Enterprise 23,* 19–21.

Jones, B. L., & Chase, W. H. (1979, Summer). Managing public policy issues. *Public Relations Review, 5,* 3–23.

Mintzberg, H. (1983). *Power in and around organizations.* Englewood Cliffs, NJ: Prentice-Hall.

Moore, P. W. (1974). Corporate social reform: An activist's viewpoint. In S. P. Sethi (Ed.), *The unstable ground: Corporate social policy in a dynamic society* (pp. 47–66). Los Angeles: Melville.

Nanni, E. (1980). *Case studies of organization management and public relations practices.* Unpublished master's thesis, University of Maryland, College Park.

A new breed of environmentalists puts the heat on industry. (1984, March 19). *Business Week,* pp. 86B–86N.

Newsom, D. A. (1983, Fall). Conflict: Who gets media attention—And why. *Public Relations Review, 9,* 35–39.

Olien, C. N., Donohue, G. A., & Tichenor, P. T. (1984). Media and stages of social conflict. *Journalism Monographs, 90.*

Olson, M. (1982). *The logic of collective action: Public goods and the theory of groups.* Cambridge, MA: Harvard University Press.

Parker, R. A. (1983, November). Potholes lurking on the PR path: An interview with Harold Burson, Burson-Marsteller CEO. *Communication World,* pp. 12–13.

Parson, D. W., & Linkugel, W. A. (1970). *Militancy and anti-communication.* Lawrence, KS: House of Usher.

Peters, T. J., & Waterman, R. H. (1982). *In search of excellence: Lessons from America's best-run companies.* New York: Harper & Row.

Pires, M. A. (1983, April). TEXACO: Working with public interest groups. *Public Relations Journal, 39,* 16–19.

Plumb, J. W. (1984). Hostile journalists aren't the issue; Need ongoing PR before crises hit. *Media Institute Forum, 1,* 2–4.

Ryan, M., & Martinson, D. L. (1983). The pr officer as corporate conscience. *Public Relations Quarterly, 34,* 20–23.

Staff. (1986, January 6). Too much media coverage backfires. *pr reporter,* p. 4.

Stolz, V. (1983). "Conflict PR" in the formation of public opinion. *Public Relations Quarterly, 34,* 28–31.

Sullivan, J. B. (1976). A public interest laundry list for technology assessment: Two dozen eternal truths about people and technology. *Technological Forecasting and Change, 8,* 439–440.

Wolfsfeld, G. (1984). Symbiosis of press and protest: An exchange analysis. *Journalism Quarterly, 61,* 550–55, 742.

Zisk, B. H. (1969). *American political interest groups.* Belmont, CA: Wadsworth.

20 Symmetrical Systems of Internal Communication

James E. Grunig
University of Maryland

ABSTRACT

The internal communication system of an organization functions both as a necessary condition for excellent public relations and as a part of an excellent public relations program. Chapter 9 identified symmetrical communication as 1 of 12 characteristics of excellent organizations — as well as human resources, leadership, and culture that are related to communication. This chapter reviews the theories of internal communication developed in the field of organizational communication — *the name used for internal communication in academic departments of speech communication. It reviews the relationship of organizational communication to job satisfaction and other* organizational outcomes *that are indicators of organizational effectiveness. Communication systems do increase job satisfaction, the chapter concludes, as long as that system is based on the principles of symmetrical communication. Organizations seldom develop symmetrical systems of communication, however, unless they also have organic structures and participative cultures. The chapter concludes with advice to communication professionals on how to make the internal communication system symmetrical and how that system can make the structure and culture of the organization more excellent.*

Two-way information sharing can improve decision making and work performance by facilitating the making of decisions at the lowest possible levels by employees who know the most about getting the job done right. In turn, this increased participation can contribute to higher levels of employee satisfaction and quality of work life.

> —General Motors Policy Statement on Employee Communication,
> as quoted in Smith (1991, p. 24)

Internal communication is so entwined with the process of organizing and with organizational structure, environment, power, and culture that many theorists of organizational communication argue that organizations could not exist without communication.

This chapter could have been placed in any of the first four parts of this book. Internal communication could have been placed in Part I because it is one of the most important contributors to organizational effectiveness — it helps organizations define their goals, values, and strategic constituencies. It also could have been placed in Part II because employees almost always are a strategic public for organizations, and most organizations have formal programs to communicate with employees. Organizational communication could have been placed at the managerial level of Part III because symmetrical communication is 1 of 12 components of an excellent organization, and excellent public relations departments have a system to manage it. Finally, internal communication is linked logically with the conditions that make excellent public relations possible — structure, environment, power, and culture — which are discussed in Part IV of the book.

This chapter on internal communication appears in Part IV, however, because of its integral relationship with the conditions that make excellent public relations possible. Excellent communication helps to make organizations excellent, and excellent organizations foster excellent communication — both are part of a holistic system. Systems of internal communication are part of organizational structure and culture; yet they also create structure and culture. The environment affects how the people with power in an organization construct its structure, culture, and communication. Structure, culture, and communication, however, also affect who has power and how an organization perceives (or enacts) its environment and how it responds to the environment.

This chapter reviews research that shows that excellent organizations have a symmetrical system of internal communication — a characteristic of excellent organizations identified in chapter 9. As the opening quote of this chapter suggests, the chapter also reviews evidence that symmetrical communication increases the job satisfaction of employees — an effect of communication that allows organizations to build long-term relationships of trust and credibility with strategic employee publics. The chapter shows that symmetrical communication can foster other attributes of excellent organizations — organic structure, shared power, and participative culture. But it shows also that changes in communication alone — without changes in structure, power, and culture — cannot make an organization effective.

We begin this examination of internal communication systems, then, by reviewing the history of programs on internal communication in organizations and the domain of research that commonly is called *organizational communication* in universities.

THE PRACTICE OF EMPLOYEE
COMMUNICATION

In the world of communication practice, most organizations have some program of internal communication. Usually this program features a publication or other formal system of mediated communication. Usually, the program is staffed by communication technicians with journalistic training (Shatshat, 1980), although more and more organizations now have managed programs of employee communication rather than simply having an employee publication or publications for their own sake (D'Aprix, 1982; Emanuel & York, 1988; Lewton, 1991, chapter 15; Smith, 1991; Troy 1989). In general, though, technique still dominates management and theory in the world of practice.

Redding and Tompkins (1988) pointed out that the training of journalists and their dominance in employee communication has affected the practice of internal communication in organizations:

> ... by its very nature, journalism has always encouraged a one-way, downward-oriented approach to corporate communication practices; and this fact, we believe, has had a profound impact upon the way in which most managers view communication.

> It is still true, in the late 1980s, that the most appropriate "entry jobs" for organizational communication graduates are likely to be in the area of employee publications, an area where journalists occupy a majority of the positions (according to annual surveys conducted by the International Association of Business Communicators). In the light of all these circumstances, one can readily understand some of the reasons why organizational communication has yet to solve its identify problem. (pp. 14–15)

Specialists in employee communication once were known as industrial editors or business journalists. The International Association of Business Communicators (IABC) was formed in 1970 from a merger of the American Association of Industrial Editors and the International Council of Industrial Editors. Although the association's focus at first remained internal communication, it enlarged its mission to a larger focus on public relations and communication management when research showed that many of its members left the association as they advanced out of their entry-level positions in internal communication to the broader public relations function to which internal communication usually reported (Charlton, 1990):

> For beginning communicators, the traditional route to success was to be hired into the Public Relations Department as a newsletter editor. He/she would serve an apprenticeship, learn the company and its business, and join IABC.

> When job responsibilities switched to external communication, the IABC membership was often dropped.
>
> In fact there was a desire on the part of some IABC members to differentiate themselves from public relations practitioners. Intramural bad blood sometimes existed between internal and external communicators, and the PR name was acquiring tarnish in the media. . . .
>
> As IABC began to examine its members' ultimate development needs, however, it became obvious that (a) for the great majority of members, the name of advancement was in fact Public Relations, and (b) if IABC would not provide appropriate programs and services for advanced PR practitioners, senior members would indeed seek professional support elsewhere. (p. 33)

Shatshat (1980) also found that internal communication activities generally are part of the larger public relations function of an organization. He studied the role of "communication directors" in 106 companies and expressed surprise that most had responsibility for external as well as internal communication. In addition, he found that most of these communication directors had responsibility only for journalistic/technician activities, although the respondents reported that they also would have responsibility for communication management in an ideal role.

In this book, we have maintained that employees are a strategic public for nearly all organizations (chapter 6) and that programs to communicate with them should be part of an integrated and managed communication program—that is, public relations. In many organizations, a debate rages over whether employee communication should report to human resources departments or public relations departments. The *Wyatt Communicator* ("Results of the 1989 Wyatt Communication Survey," 1989) reported that a survey conducted by that management consulting company showed a trend toward housing the internal communication function in human resources/personnel departments rather than in public relations or corporate communication departments:

> An increasing number of organizations are recognizing that objectives of internal communication are very different from those of corporate communication or public relations. While those areas of the organization are charged with "selling" the company and its products or services to the public, the objectives of internal communication are to inform employees about key job-related and business issues and, through that process, gain their commitment to their work and the organization. (p. 6)

In contrast, Smith (1991) pointed out that the Wyatt survey ("Results of the 1989 Wyatt Communication Survey," 1989) was weighted heavily toward small companies and that in the majority of companies with more than 10,000 employees internal communication programs were housed in public relations departments. He added that a 1989 survey of public relations practitioners reported in *pr reporter* "Will Public Relations & Human Resources Clash," 1989) showed that 70% of employee communication programs reported to public relations: "It appears obvious that in the larger companies, the trend is to retain employee communication as a part of corporate communications. Many smaller companies are paying more attention to employee communication. But—and this is true in plant locations of large corporations, too—the function is being handled by a personnel professional, often as a lower-level priority on a part-time basis" (p. 59). Smith then described how General Motors "tried it both ways" and settled on public relations as the home for employee communication—in large part because human resources executives did not understand communication, especially what we have called symmetrical communication throughout this book.

A study by the Conference Board (Troy, 1989) showed that far more executives responsible for employee relations report to a department of communication, public relations, or public affairs than to human resources but that they work "hand-in-glove" with human resources departments. Human resources executives also take charge of specialized messages, "such as employee-orientation and compensation and benefit materials, and run bulletin board programs" (p. 29).

Although this chapter attempts to show that excellent internal communication is symmetrical communication, the previous quote from the *Wyatt Communicator* ("Results of the 1989 Wyatt Communication Survey," 1989) about the role of public relations in selling the organization reveals that other models of communication often prevail. Several reviews of the history of organizational communication (e.g., J. Grunig & Hunt, 1984, p. 241; Richetto, 1977) have cited Dover's (1964) article on three eras of employee communication. J. Grunig and Hunt equated the first three eras to the press agentry, public information, and two-way asymmetrical models of public relations described in chapters 2 and 11.

Dover's (1964) era of "entertaining employees" (press agentry) prevailed in the 1940s, his era of "informing employees" (public information) prevailed in the 1950s, and his era of "persuading employees" (two-way asymmetrical) prevailed in the 1960s. J. Grunig and Hunt (1984) added that a new era of open (symmetrical) communication developed in employee communication in the 1970s and 1980s. Richetto (1977) concurred: ". . . there appears to be a trend toward examining relational consequences such as trust, credibility, or satisfaction in terms of specific antecedent conditions, as with studies of the effects of homophily on perceived trust or credibility or the effects of perceived openness in communication on overall supervisor satisfaction" (p. 337).

This brief review of the practice of employee communication suggests that, like other programs to communicate with stakeholders of an organization, excellent programs of employee communication are based on the concepts of strategic management, an integrated communication function, the managerial role, and the two-way symmetrical model of public relations. In less excellent organizations, in contrast, the literature suggests that the technician role dominates, that these technicians produce publications or other media with no strategic purpose in mind, that communicators report to human resources managers rather than to communication managers, and that the programs resemble the press agentry, public information, or two-way asymmetrical models of public relations.

ORGANIZATIONAL COMMUNICATION
AS AN ACADEMIC DISCIPLINE

Organizational communication as a subject of research and teaching can be found in a number of academic disciplines, including organizational psychology, organizational sociology, business and management, journalism, and speech communication. Organizational communication, is, as J. Grunig (1975) described it, "like an oasis in the middle of the desert through which many travelers pass, but in which few linger long enough to meet one another" (p. 99). Redding (1985) described the oasis as follows:

> With very few exceptions truly scientific work in our field — until well after 1950 — was completed by researchers identified with various "*non*communication" areas of interest. These include such academic fiefdoms as social psychology, industrial (later "organizational") psychology, sociology, applied anthropology, "human relations" (an amalgam of several social sciences), business administration, management, economics, and industrial (or labor) relations. The fact is that the typical *scholarly* study of industrial communication in the 1940s and early 1950s treated "communication" not as a focal object of inquiry, but as a *by-product* of investigating some other topic. Indeed, this statement can still be made of a substantial portion of our literature in the 1980s. (p. 31)

Organizational psychologists have taken an interest in communication because of its relationship to phenomena of concern to them, such as human relations, job satisfaction, productivity, leadership, or superior–subordinate relationships. Organizational sociologists often have missed the oasis completely, as recent textbooks such as those by Daft (1983), Hodge and Anthony (1988), and Jackson, Morgan, and Paolillo (1986) not only do not have chapters on communication but have no references to communication in their indices. Others, such as Robbins (1990), mention the relationship of communication to conflict. Some sociologists such as Hage (1974, 1980) and Hall (1987) have discussed how organizational structure affects communication—a relationship to which this chapter devotes special attention later.

A few researchers and theorists in public relations such as J. Grunig (1975, 1985), J. Grunig and Hunt (1984), J. Grunig and Theus (1986), Pincus (1986), Pincus and Rayfield (1989), and Pincus, Knipp, and Rayfield (1990) have examined organizational (internal) communication as a component of public relations. Most public relations scholars, however, have abandoned internal communication to their technical colleagues who teach courses in the production of house organs or the teaching of "business and industrial journalism."

Speech Communication as an Academic Home

As the result of a secondary interest in internal communication in other disciplines, scholars in speech communication have been given the almost exclusive privilege of colonizing the oasis of organizational communication. For the field of public relations/communication management, delegating research on internal communication to speech communication has had profound consequences. On the one hand, the amount and quality of research and theory have improved dramatically in recent years as the discipline of speech communication has grown and prospered. On the other hand, the research and theories of speech have been oriented heavily toward the rhetorical, interpersonal, and persuasion emphases of that discipline in ways that have limited the value of the theories to public relations practitioners who specialize in internal communication.

Putnam and Cheney (1985), Redding (1985), and Redding and Tompkins (1988) traced the origin of organizational communication in speech departments to programs in the 1920s to train corporate executives to speak. Many of these programs were motivated by or came in competition with simplistic popularizers such as Dale Carnegie and his 1930s book, *How to Win Friends and Influence People*. Redding and Tompkins identified three conceptual roots of the academic field of organizational communication: "(a) *traditional rhetorical theory* (as modified and truncated in business writing and business speaking texts, (b) *human relations models* (actually, mini-theories and prototheories rather than full-blown theories), and (c) *early versions of management-organization theories* (again, prototheories would be a more accurate designation" (p. 11).[1]

---

[1]Most textbooks on organizational communication discuss such management theories as scientific or classical management, human relations, human resources, and systems theories.

Redding (1985) emphasized the effect that the human relations movement had on organizational communication, a movement that originated at the Harvard Business School and that was typified by the Hawthorne studies of Roethlisberger and Dickson (1939). The essential assumption of the human relations movement was that management was rational, that workers were irrational, and that communication – especially simplistic and asymmetrical techniques – could be used to persuade employees to "cooperate" with management. "There can be little doubt," Redding said, "that the 'conventional' literature of industrial communication in the 1940s and 1950s reflected various (sometimes puzzling) combinations of Dale Carnegie, Harvard, and public speaking concepts – a sort of mushy melange, if you will. For better or for worse, neither the Carnegie nor the Harvard versions of human relations can be excluded from the history of our field" (p. 30).

By about 1970, according to most scholars of organizational communication, these traditions had produced a large body of research and prescriptive advice but very little integrating theory. In the words of Richetto (1977): "Thus, when one views organizational communication in 1976–77, one finds, not surprisingly, far more research than theory. In less academic terms, organizational communication, like the teary-eyed little girl in party dress, appears to be 'all dressed up with no place to go' " (p. 331). In addition, scholars also generally agree that research until about the 1980s had a management bias. That is, it was conducted to learn how managers could use communication to influence and secure cooperation from employees in meeting the goals of management and not to change the organization or to increase the satisfaction and quality of work life of employees. Redding (1985) described the management bias as "the ideology of rational, omniscient management versus nonrational, uninformed employees" (p. 28) and that "management knows best" (p. 29).

In short, whereas education for internal communication in journalism schools emphasized the technician role and the public information model of public relations, speech departments emphasized the equivalent of the press agentry model in the Dale Carnegie approach and the two-way asymmetrical model in the Harvard model of human relations. Redding (1985) described the two-way asymmetrical model perfectly when he said that a burgeoning interest in two-way communication still reflected a management bias: "The benefits of 'tapping employee thinking' were primarily to be found in providing information about the employee audience, which in turn would enhance the probability that *management's message* would be more effective" (p. 31).

Recent research in organizational communication has departed from this asymmetrical bias to examine "interaction, or the social creation of message and meaning" (Putnam & Cheney, 1985, pp. 130–131) – that is, symmetrical communication. To understand this development in the field, we look next at some categories that describe scholarship in organizational communication.

Research Traditions

The major purpose of this chapter is to integrate relevant concepts from theories and research on communication internal to an organization into an integrated theory of excellence in public relations and communication management. The chapter asks, that is, what characteristics of communication inside an organization correlate with the other attributes of excellence isolated throughout this book to produce a system of communication that helps to make an organization more effective.

The literature in organizational communication, however, is broad, diverse, and disintegrated. In the preface to a recent *Handbook of Organizational Communication,* Jablin, Putnam, Roberts, and Porter (1987) put a boundary around what they called an "empirical dust bowl" or "something even worse—an empirical swamp" by pointing out that organizational communication is concerned with "the nature, types, and outcomes of communication that take place in organizational settings" (p. 8). They added that scholars have looked at organizational communication from four levels of analysis: dyadic, group, organizational, and extraorganizational. As Redding and Tompkins (1988) pointed out, however, "external communication [the fourth category] has received no more than cursory attention from specialists in organizational communication" (p. 13). That aspect of organizational communication has been the province of public relations scholars (see, e.g., J. Grunig, 1975).

In short, scholars of organizational communication have examined almost every conceivable aspect of communication that takes place inside an organization. The majority of scholars have been concerned with interpersonal (dyadic) communication within organizations, but others have examined channels, flows, and networks of communication throughout the organization. Recently, scholars have examined how communication defines the organization as a whole, including its culture. Several authors of review articles have developed classifications of the most frequent problems and phenomena studied in organizational communication. Others have classified the theoretical and methodological perspectives applied within those research traditions.

In one of the first of these reviews, Goldhaber, Yates, Porter, and Lesniak (1978) identified two traditions of research: information flows and perceptual/attitudinal research. Putnam and Cheney (1983) expanded this classification into four traditions. In a later article, Putnam and Cheney (1985) added four, recent traditions to the older four. These eight traditions, therefore, provide an overview of what researchers have studied in organizational communication.

Communication Channels. Researchers in this tradition (who were most active in the 1950s and 1960s) examined the flow of information throughout the organization—upward, downward, and horizontal. They have studied different types of distortions in these channels, the "grapevine," information overload, and the link between adequacy of information and communication *outcomes* such as job satisfaction, job performance, and organizational effectiveness. In part, this research reflected the managerial bias of early theories of organizational communication as well as the influence of industrial journalism, because it tracked the flow of information in official and unofficial channels and assumed that communication consists primarily of the dissemination of information.

Communication Climate. The concept of climate originated in organizational psychology where it reflected the tradition of gestalt psychology. Organizational climate refers to a psychological atmosphere in an organization that is warm, tolerant, and participative and where quality of work life, innovation, and organizational development are valued (Schneider, 1985). Communication climate was similar: A positive climate features trust, openness, credibility, accuracy, and frequent communication. Although climate studies expanded beyond the simplistic ideas of the human relations movement, most of the theories originated from the simplistic notions that leaders of that movement developed about how to make people happy and work hard.

Research on communication climate flourished in the 1960s and 1970s. Researchers measured both types of climate by aggregating responses to questionnaires completed by individual employees. Thus, it was a *perceptual, attitudinal* tradition of research. Researchers believed that climate was a characteristic of the organization, however, not of individuals—an "atmospheric condition" in the organization. Climate researchers, like channels researchers, linked the concept to communication outcomes such as job satisfaction and performance.

Network Analysis. Network analysis originated from experimental studies of communication in small groups in social psychology and from research on the diffusion of information in sociology. The basic assumptions about communication were similar to those found in the research on communication channels, but the methodology was more complex.

Network research, which flourished in the 1970s, traced linkages among dyads of employees throughout the organization (for a review, see Wigand, 1988). Computer programs identified clusters of communicating employees and key communication roles in the network, such as those of *liaisons, linking pins,* or *key communicators.* Researchers also identified different attributes of networks such as symmetry, centrality, and connectedness. In contrast to the first two traditions, however, network researchers looked more at the causes of different kinds of networks—such as the task and maintenance functions of systems—than at the effects of networks on outcomes such as job satisfaction.

Superior–Subordinate Communication. Researchers working in this tradition, also to a large extent in the 1960s and 1970s, borrowed concepts from theories of information flow and communication climate and applied them to the dyadic relationship between superiors and subordinates—a relationship that reflected the central interest in interpersonal communication in speech communication. Researchers in this tradition devoted most of their attention to seven areas: "(1) perceptions of the amount, frequency, and mode of interaction; (2) upward distortion; (3) upward influence; (4) openness; (5) feedback; (6) communicator style; and (7) effectiveness of superior–subordinate relationships" (Putnam & Cheney, 1985, p. 141).

Later research in this tradition centered on the relationships between superiors and subordinates (a symmetrical concept), rather than on the flow of task-related messages between them (more of an asymmetrical concept). In general, research suggested that symmetrical relationships (employee-centered style, tolerance for disagreement, innovativeness, open, and trusting) resulted in greater employee satisfaction that did more asymmetrical relationships. Some researchers (Dansereau & Markham, 1987; Jablin, 1979, 1987; Kelly, 1982), however, pointed out that superior–subordinate relationships are affected by variables of the larger organizational system and that the two levels of theory should be linked—a key point to which this chapter returns later.

One or more of these four traditions have appeared in most reviews of research on organizational communication published before and into the 1980s. Putnam and Cheney (1985) concluded that research over four decades in these traditions reflected four characteristics: the human relations approach, a preoccupation with effective management (the management bias), simple measures of communication as information flows or perceptions of climate or relationships, and positivistic methodologies.

In the 1980s, they (Putnam & Cheney, 1985) added, researchers added additional theoretical perspectives and more interpretive and humanistic methodologies. They identified four new research traditions, each of which bears a "family resemblance" to the others:

The Information-Processing Perspective. Although this approach originated outside the field of communication, communication scholars have begun to reflect it in their work in large part because of the influence of psychologist Karl Weick (e.g, 1979). Putnam and Cheney (1985) said that organizational scholars with this perspective view organizations as information-processing systems: "The essence of organizing, in this perspective, is the gathering, transmitting, storing, and using of information" (p. 144).

Organizational sociologists most often have used the information-processing approach to research the effects of structural variables on communication networks, channels, and amount of communication. Others have examined the processing of information from the environment. Public relations scholars have made use of both types of research to analyze external communication (e.g., J. Grunig, 1976). In addition, J. Grunig (1975, 1976, 1985; see also chapters 17 and 18 of this book) frequently has pointed out the need to incorporate structure and environment into theories of internal communication.

Most of the organizational scholars outside communication took what Putnam and Cheney (1985) called a mechanistic view of communication, "emphasizing the amount, direction, structure, and type of information flow while ignoring message reception and interpretation" (p. 145)." They added that Weick (1979) addressed the same problems from more of an interpretive perspective. Organizational structures and environments, according to that perspective, exist in the minds of people in the organization. Members of organizations, for example, enact their environments — select relevant portions of it to which they pay attention — rather than react to a neutral environment that is the same for everyone in the organization. Information, too, is symbolic — constructed differently by different people.

The Rhetorical Perspective.   An increasing number of scholars in speech communication have returned to the roots of their field in classical rhetoric and have applied those concepts to organizations. These scholars examine how people use communication to organize (i.e., create organizations) (e.g., Eisenberg & Riley, 1988), make decisions (e.g., Tompkins & Cheney, 1983), and control people in organizations (e.g., Tompkins & Cheney, 1985). In addition, rhetorical scholars have analyzed the rhetorical strategies that organizations use for corporate advocacy and issues management (e.g., Cheney & Vibbert, 1987) — both traditional concerns in public relations — and in the speeches of corporate executives.

The Cultural Perspective.   In the last decade, culture has become one of the most popular concepts in most fields of organizational studies. Organizational communication quickly adopted this new perspective, because communication creates culture and culture shapes communication. Cultural theories borrow from anthropology, but one approach is more empirical and the other more interpretive. The first approach, therefore, treats culture as a variable in organizations—something that organizations have and that affects other organizational processes. The second approach treats culture as something that an organization is. (See Barnett, 1988; O'Donnell-Trujillo & Pacanowsky, 1983; Smircich & Calas, 1987; and chapters 21 and 22 for detailed reviews of the literature on culture.)

The Political Perspective. As chapters 3 and 18 have documented, the power-control or political perspective has become one of the most important areas of research on organizations; and it occupies a central role in our theory of excellence in public relations and communication management. Scholars of internal communication, too, have realized its importance. In particular, they have studied the role of communication in dealing with the by-products of power: conflict, influence, politics, autonomy, control, bargaining, negotiation, and issues management (e.g., Frost, 1987; Putnam & Poole, 1987). Most of this research has produced relational theories of communication (see chapter 11 for a review), which essentially are symmetrical theories of communication.

Each of these eight research traditions has value in itself, although the latter four traditions rapidly are replacing the earlier four. If we are to develop a theory of excellence in communication management for the organization as a whole, however, we must extract attributes from these perspectives that can be integrated into a systemic theory of internal communication. Researchers in each tradition, no doubt, will continue to study the elements of an integrated theory, but we must have a general theory to be able to set up a system of internal communication that will make an organization excellent and therefore more effective. Although communication occurs in dyads and groups in an organization, communication at those levels generally reflects the characteristics of an organization-wide system of communication that affects, is affected by, or is part of the structure and culture of an organization. Structure and culture, in turn, are affected by the environment. Structure and culture, in addition, affect the way an organization perceives, or enacts, its environment.

The first four research traditions, among other things, seem to have identified the importance of a symmetrical system of communication in making an organization more effective—effective as defined by outcomes of communication such as job satisfaction. For example, research on channels of communication has identified the importance of horizontal and upward communication, which are more symmetrical than downward communication. The climate tradition, next, identified the importance of such concepts as openness, trust, credibility, and warmth in communication—all of which are primarily symmetrical in nature. The network tradition, third, identified such symmetrical concepts as symmetry and connectedness in networks. Research on superior–subordinate communication defined such symmetrical concepts as employee-centered communication, trust, and feedback in this dyadic relationship—which is a critical interpersonal link in a larger system of internal communication.

The four newer traditions have added four concepts, in addition to symmetrical communication, to a theory of excellent internal communication. The information-processing approach identified the effect of structure and environment on the communication system and the effect of the communication system on structure and environment (see chapter 17 for a discussion of their effect on public relations and chapter 9 for a discussion of the importance of organic structures in defining excellent organizations). The rhetorical approach provided a method of understanding and criticizing the use of communication to organize, to structure organizations, and to enact and shape their environments. The cultural perspective identified the key role of that concept in defining an organization and in shaping its system of organizational communication—as well as the role of communication in shaping culture. Finally, the political perspective helps us to understand why structures, cultures, and communication systems take on the form they do—they are shaped by the people in power in an organization—and the role of communication in resolving conflict in an organization. The political perspective, in addition, has provided concepts of symmetrical communication that are valuable in constructing a theory of a symmetrical system of internal communication.

We look at the role of each of these concepts in more detail later. First, however, we examine research in organizational communication from one additional perspective: the epistemological approach taken to the philosophy of science.

Philosophical Approaches

According to Redding and Tompkins (1988), the earliest theories of organizational communication were neither scientific nor scholarly. Instead, they were "formulary-prescriptive"—that is, based on the simple prescriptions of traditional rhetoric, corporate speech, Dale Carnegie, or human relations. The theories became more scholarly in the 1940s, but they were based almost entirely on empirical, positivist methods of research. As we have seen, these methods produced many studies but few integrated theories.

In recent years, scholars of organizational communication have examined the nature and quality of the theories in the field and have written extensively about different theoretical approaches. Because of the effort devoted to theory, it is useful here to describe the approaches in order to understand current research in organizational communication.

As a result of these theoretical discussions, many—if not the majority—

of organizational communication scholars have turned to an interpretive approach—one that has a central concern with "the centrality of meaning in social action" (Putnam, 1983, p. 32)—that is, with how people actually understand and interpret the meaning of what they do. Interpretive scholars (e.g., Putnam, 1983) criticize researchers who use traditional methods of social science for a naive belief in the objectivity of science and in the regularity and predictability of the behaviors they observe. Interpretive scholars prefer qualitative and humanistic methods to empirical methods. Most of these critics fail to realize, however, that a large number—if not the majority—of empirical social scientists have moved away from positivist views of science to what could be called an interpretive empirical approach (see chapter 2 for an example of such thinking).

Thus, we can identify four epistemological approaches in the literature on organizational communication—the first of which was common in the first four research traditions and the last three in the more recent traditions.

Positivist Social Science. Logical positivism dominated scientific thinking until it came under challenge in the 1950s and 1960s. For logical positivists, science is objective and reality is ordered and deterministic. Thus, in this view a scientist who can construct a theory (the "logical" in logical positivism) that corresponds to objective, empirical measures of reality (the "positivism") should be able to predict and control future events. For example, early theorists of organizational communication would have assumed that communication channels, networks, climates, and the like exist in objective reality and that they and the variables they influence can be measured and controlled. They would have assumed, to continue the example, that creation of a positive communication climate would lead, almost automatically, to greater job satisfaction.

Putnam (1983) called the positivist approach to organizations "functionalism"; Putnam and Cheney (1983) called it "empirical/analytic"; Krone, Jablin, and Putnam (1987) called it "mechanistic"; and Redding and Tompkins (1988) called it "modernist." Although the assumptions of logical positivists have been abandoned by most philosophers of science (although not by many practicing scientists), the research based on the approach still has value. It simply needs to be interpreted differently.

The Rhetorical/Hermeneutic Approach. A new generation of scholars in organizational communication considers this approach to be the opposite of logical positivism (e.g., Putnam, 1983; Tompkins, 1987). Theorists call the approach interpretive (Tompkins, 1987), which is the meaning of the term *hermeneutic,* or interpretive/symbolic (Krone et al., 1987). Interpretive scholars argue that reality is not objective, that it is symbolic and created by people. Thus, to interpretists, organizations are not "containers" that determine or channel communication or the behavior of individuals in them (Putnam, 1983, p. 35). Rather, organizations are symbolic in nature. They are created by people, largely through communication, and can be changed by people through symbolic, rhetorical actions. Whereas positivists invent names of terms in their theories, interpretists use the actual language of people in organizations in their interpretations—people are allowed to interpret their own reality. Thus, Redding and Tompkins (1988) called this approach "naturalistic." The interpretive approach is more humanistic than scientific, although it is guided by theories and produces theories in the same way as social science.

Interpretive Social Science.   Although interpretive theorists typically describe their approach as a stark contrast to empirical social science, they overlook the fact that many social scientists and most philosophers of science have abandoned the positivist approach. Philosophers such as Laudan (1977), Shapere (1984), and Suppe (1989) have developed a more subjective or semantic concept of theories. These philosophers believe that scientists construct theories and, in doing so, supply meaning to (make sense of) the reality they observe and measure. In contrast, logical positivists believed that reality provided meaning for theories and that the scientific method would keep subjectivity out of observation. Whereas logical positivists saw research as an active attempt to falsify theories with evidence, contemporary philosophers see research more as the process of building theories from vague, general hunches into broad, integrated theories.[2] Thus, this current view of social science can be called interpretive. In contrast to the rhetorical/hermeneutic approach, however, interpretive social scientists interpret the behavior of the people they observe whereas interpretists in the hermeneutic/symbolic approach ask people to interpret their own behavior.

Interpretive social scientists, such as Weick (1983, 1987) and the "rules theorists" in speech communication (e.g., Cushman, King, & Smith, 1988), often merge the two approaches by looking at how people they study interpret reality as they build theories to explain the behavior of the people they observe. Thus, the approach also is naturalistic (Redding & Tompkins, 1988). The difference between the two approaches, then, is that the social scientist uses concepts to describe reality that generally do not correspond to the interpretations of the people they observe. In organizational communication, the approach that Krone et al. (1987) called the "systems-interaction" perspective is typical of interpretive social science. That

---

[2]Weick (1983) expressed the same idea as follows: ". . . instead of stating a hypothesis and attempting to falsify it, we should commit ourselves to a belief and in our research see if we can muster the evidence to support it" (p. 22).

approach looks at the overall patterns of behavior that develop over time in an organization rather than reducing behavior to a few variables as positivists do.

The Critical Approach.   Although researchers using each of the first three approaches to epistemology can and do criticize organizations and organizational processes, they strive more to develop theoretical understanding than to expose negative conditions in organizations. The mission of critical researchers, in contrast, is to expose oppression, alienation, or injustice in organizations (Putnam & Cheney, 1983). Critical theorists also interpret reality in organizations, but they do it with a mission in mind—to improve the situation of workers (Redding & Tompkins, 1988). Putnam and Cheney said that few organizational theorists take the critical perspective but that such criticism can be seen in studies of power, ideology, and conflict in organizations.

Organizational scholars, then, have approached each of the eight research traditions through these four philosophical approaches.[3] However, most of the research on channels, climates, networks, and superior–subordinate communication has been based on the positivist approach. Increasingly, however, theorists have reinterpreted those results with interpretive theories—such as in the information-processing and political traditions and, to some extent, the cultural tradition. Rhetoricians seldom venture outside the rhetorical/hermeneutic tradition, but their theories have stimulated social scientists to use more qualitative methods and interpretive theories. Similarly, about half of the research in the cultural tradition is rhetorical and half interpretive social science; and the interaction between the two approaches has enriched both kinds of theories.

The theory of an excellent communication system being developed in this chapter is predominantly a theory based on the approach of interpretive social science, although it shares common elements with rhetorical and critical theories. Next, then, we examine research on each of the major concepts of the theory.

COMMUNICATION AND ORGANIZATIONAL OUTCOMES

In the past, scholars of organizational communication often have acted like religious fanatics: They took an item of faith—the value of communication—and religiously promoted it as the solution to all problems (the early

---

[3]For a hypothetical discussion among a pluralist (interpretive social scientist), interpretist, and critic, see Hawes, Pacanowsky, and Faules (1988).

prescriptive theories of communication) or diligently searched for evidence that their faith was indeed true. Weick (1983) explained this passion as follows:

> Communication scholars seem to push an undifferentiated view that communication is the source of all problems interpersonal, organizational, and societal. Obviously, communication has both functions and dysfunctions. These vary among organizational settings, yet documentation of these contingencies is not common. . . . Only in some organizations at some times is it the case that more communication is better. (pp. 15–16)

Goldhaber, Dennis, Richetto, and Wiio (1984), for example, defined organizational communication in a way that suggests its great power is axiomatic—that is, always true. They said that many theorists treat communication in organizations "on the same level with such behavioral variables as motivation, leadership, and job satisfaction" (p. 334). Communication, however, is more important: "We suggest that organizational communication cannot be compared with other organizational variables: it makes all the other variables possible. Without communication there can be no motivation, no leadership, no productivity, and no organization" (p. 335).

On the one hand, Goldhaber et al.'s (1984) statement reflects the assumption of the rhetorical/hermeneutic approach to communication (that organizations are symbolic and that communication makes them possible), which is a logical position to take. On the other hand, one easily could maintain that the opposite causal relationship is true—that such variables as motivation, leadership, and productivity affect the way people communicate in organizations. In general, though, the statement represents the typical unbridled acceptance that scholars of organizational communication have had for the value of communication.

Two reviews of organizational communication completed nearly 20 years ago paraphrased a statement by Roberts, O'Reilly, Bretton, and Porter (1973) and Roberts and O'Reilly (1974) that "if communication is bad, an organization is likely to have problems, and it is good, an organization's performance and overall effectiveness will also be good" (Brooks, Callicoat, & Siegerdt, 1979, p. 131; Goldhaber et al., 1978, p. 83). Both reviews went on to show that research both has supported and failed to support this assumption. Nevertheless, the statement does reflect an axiom in organizational communication that has motivated extensive research to determine whether communication makes organizations more effective. Because the evidence has provided mixed support for this assumption, researchers recently have tried to isolate the characteristics of communication that make organizations effective and the different ways in which communication makes organizations effective.

Both bodies of research are relevant to our purposes in this book and this chapter. First, we want to show that managed communication (including internal communication) makes organizations more effective (the purpose of chapter 3). Second, we want to isolate the attributes of internal communication that contribute most to organizational effectiveness—the characteristics of an excellent system of internal communication (our purpose in this chapter).

Dependent Variables: Job Satisfaction and Others

Because scholars of organizational communication seem to have had the axiomatic belief that communication makes organizations more effective, the study of the relationships between communication and organizational outcomes has been perhaps the most active area of research in organizational communication—at least into the 1980s (for reviews, see Downs, Clampitt, & Pfeiffer, 1988; Downs & Hain, 1982; Pincus & Rayfield, 1989). Researchers have examined the effect of communication on two organizational outcomes in particular—job satisfaction and job performance. They also have examined its effects on other outcomes, such as absenteeism, turnover, safety records, and health indices (Downs et al., 1988, p. 197), or role stress, organizational commitment, and socialization (Schneider, 1985).

All of these outcomes reflect the individualistic view of organizations of psychologists. Indeed, many organizational psychologists have defined organizational effectiveness as the extent to which internal participants are satisfied with the organization (Daft, 1983, p. 99; Hall, 1987, p. 278). Chapter 3 did not include the satisfaction of participants as a principal component of organizational effectiveness because of the obvious fact that the organization as a whole could be ineffective even though participants are happy (Hall, 1987, p. 279). Nevertheless, as Hall added, internal participants are among the strategic constituencies that could constrain the ability of an organization to meet its goals (p. 282)—an approach to effectiveness that occupies a central role in chapter 3. Measures of job satisfaction and the other individual outcomes of organizational behavior and communication, therefore, provide valuable indicators of the extent to which employees are likely to support or constrain the mission of the organization.

Organizational psychologists have studied job satisfaction extensively. Locke (1976) estimated that over 3,000 articles and dissertations had been published on job satisfaction at the time he wrote the article; and Downs et al. (1988) estimated that the number would have grown to at least 5,000 articles 12 years later. As such a volume of research might suggest, there are many definitions and theories of the nature and causes of job satisfaction.

Locke's definition perhaps is cited most often. He stated that job satisfaction is "a pleasurable or positive emotional state resulting from the appraisal of one's job experiences" (p. 1297). Similarly, Schneider (1985) defined it as "the congruence or fit of the person to the setting" (p. 580). Pincus and Rayfield (1989) concluded: "Common to the different definitions of job satisfaction is that each appears to focus on an individual's perceptual or emotional response to certain aspects of his or her work environment" (p. 187).

Researchers also have debated whether job satisfaction has different facets, such as satisfaction with pay, hours, supervisor, or co-workers[4] or whether it is a summary evaluation of an individual's experience with an organization (Downs et al., 1988, pp. 197–198; Falcione, McCroskey, & Daly, 1977, p. 364; Pincus & Rayfield, 1989, pp. 186–187; Schneider, 1985, p. 580). The debate seems to have produced the consensus that there is a difference between the satisfaction of individuals with their work and their satisfaction with the organization as a whole (Pincus & Rayfield, 1989; Zeitz, 1983). For example, Hage (1980) distinguished between morale (satisfaction with the organization) and the satisfaction of individuals with their job or role within the organization. He argued, however, that morale is collective and job satisfaction individual (p. 297). That is, job satisfaction may vary widely among individuals in an organization; but morale will be high or low among most participants in the organization. Morale, in a sense, pervades the organization. J. Grunig (1985, 1987), in three studies of the communication systems of educational organizations, factor analyzed several indicators of job satisfaction and identified these same two levels of satisfaction—with the job and with the organization. He called them individual and organizational job satisfaction—concepts used in the employee portion of the IABC excellence study for which this book provides the theory.

Research, therefore, shows that some characteristics of organizations correlate better with individual satisfaction and others better with organizational satisfaction. For example, J. Grunig (1985) found complexity of the job to be the best predictor of individual satisfaction and organic organizational structure and a symmetrical communication system to be the best predictors of satisfaction with the organization (Hage, 1980, p. 319, cited similar findings). Organizational satisfaction, therefore, seems to be the best indicator of the extent to which organizational communication contributes to organizational effectiveness (see, e.g., Downs et al., 1988, p. 204). It also could explain why measures of communication explain job satisfaction better than job performance (Downs et al., 1988; Falcione,

---

[4]Such facets are measured, for example, by the widely used Job Description Index developed by Smith, Kendall, and Hulin (1969).

Sussman, & Herden, 1987; Fisher, 1980; Hellweg & Phillips, 1981; Pincus, 1984, 1986). Individuals may perform their jobs well, that is, even though they are unhappy with the organization to such a degree that they constrain the ability of the organization to achieve its mission.[5]

Given these definitions of job satisfaction, communication researchers next asked what characteristics of organizations affect job satisfaction and what is the relative importance of communication among those characteristics.

Independent Variables: Communication, Climate, Superior-Subordinate Communication, and Satisfaction with Communication

After extensive reviews of research on the relationship between organizational communication and job satisfaction, both Downs et al. (1988) and Pincus and Rayfield (1989) concluded that there is clear evidence that communication increases job satisfaction. Many researchers, especially the early ones, referred to communication in a general sense—as though communication is always the same. When they operationalized communication for an actual study, however, these researchers developed several concepts of what communication is. The most popular concepts have been communication climate; satisfaction with communication; perceptions of the amount, sources, and flows of communication; and the amount and type of supervisor-subordinate communication. These concepts reflect the emphases of the first four research traditions in organizational communication described earlier.

Communication Climate. *Communication climate* owes its heritage to the broader concept of organizational climate. Schneider and Snyder (1975) defined organizational climate "as a summary perception which people have of (or about) an organization. It is, then, a global impression of what the organization is" (p. 318). Such a definition sounds like a global definition of job satisfaction, a conceptual overlap that has produced a debate over whether organizational climate and job satisfaction are really the same thing (e.g., Johannesson, 1973; LaFollette & Sims, 1975; Muchinsky, 1977; Payne, Fineman, & Wall, 1976). The debate seems to have produced the consensus that there is a difference: Climate consists of employee perceptions of what an organization is like; satisfaction consists of the evaluations or affective responses of employees of the organization.

---

[5]For examples, employees who perform their jobs well still could have high rates of absenteeism and turnover or communicate their unhappiness to strategic constituencies in the environment (see, e.g., Schneider, 1985, p. 579).

Nevertheless, researchers generally have limited their definitions of climate to the social climate in an organization: "When used this way it refers to both formal and informal policies and activities that are typical of the way peers relate to each other ('open') and/or the 'style' that characterizes superior-subordinate relationships ('trusting')." (Schneider, 1985, p. 595). Schneider added that climate also has been used to refer to other sets of formal and informal policies and activities. According to Pincus and Rayfield (1989), "Frequently cited dimensions of organizational climate are organizational structure, individual responsibility, warmth or support, rewards and punishments, conflict resolution, performance standards, and organizational identity" (p. 187).

Schneider (1985) went on to say that "climate research seems to have died from acceptance" (p. 595). Researchers now generally accept its importance, that is, but instead of measuring climate as a global concept they have measured and examined the effects of one or more of the many concepts that climate disguises.

Communication scholars, following this tradition, have developed various concepts and measures of communication climate—the second research tradition in organizational communication discussed earlier. Falcione et al. (1987) reviewed the extensive literature on climate and acknowledged that many concepts of communication climate, such as openness and trust, overlap those of organizational climate. They added that there may be different communication climates at the levels of dyads, groups, and the overall organization. After reviewing the research on the relationship between *climate subsystems* and organizational outcomes, they concluded that climate accounts for only a small part of the variance in outcomes such as job satisfaction: "This suggests that communication climate is *necessary* for member satisfaction but not *sufficient*" (p. 222).

Like organizational psychologists, scholars of organizational communication have broken the concept of communication climate into several dimensions, some of which affect organizational outcomes more than others (Falcione et al., 1987)—dimensions to which we return in discussing symmetrical communication systems and organizational structure.

Superior-Subordinate Relations.   Falcione et al. (1977) correlated several characteristics of organizational communication and of individuals with the facets of job satisfaction measured by the Job Description Index (JDI). Although they hoped to find characteristics of communication and of individuals that would predict most facets of job satisfaction, they could not find such a pattern. The different facets of satisfaction correlated with different communication and individual characteristics in diverse types of organizations. They did find a consistent relationship with the way employees perceived the communication behavior of their supervisor and their satisfaction with the supervisor: "Supervisor satisfaction appears to be most closely associated with perceived communication behavior (perceived listening, understandingness, quality), credibility, attractiveness, and attitude homophily . . ." (p. 373).

However, Falcione et al. (1977) also found that some kinds of employees are likely to be dissatisfied regardless of how their supervisor communicates with them — "those with high oral communication apprehension and/or low self esteem" (p. 373). This study, therefore, represents a second common operationalization of communication in the relationship with job satisfaction — emphasizing superior–subordinate communication — which also is the fourth research tradition discussed previously (for additional reviews, see Dansereau & Markham, 1987; Jablin, 1979; Pincus, 1986).

Communication Satisfaction. Downs and Hazen (1976) consolidated most of these operationalizations of communication into eight dimensions of *communication satisfaction* — a concept with roots in two classic books on organizational communication (Redding, 1972; Thayer, 1968). Downs and Hazen factor analyzed 88 items measuring the satisfaction of employees with different aspects of communication and developed what has become a widely used measure of communication satisfaction (Downs et al., 1988). The dimensions of satisfaction are communication climate (with items like those used by others to measure climate), communication with supervisors (also with items like those used in previous research), organizational integration (satisfaction with information about how an employee's job fits into the overall organization), media quality (satisfaction with media, publications, meetings, etc.), horizontal communication (interpersonal, informal communication with peers), organizational perspective (satisfaction with information about the overall organization and its relationship with its environment), subordinate communication (upward and downward communication and extent of overload), and personal feedback (information on performance and role).

After reviewing the research using this instrument, Downs et al. (1988) concluded:

(a) Employees were most satisfied with Subordinate Communication and Supervisory Communication, while they were least satisfied with Personal Feedback. (b) Job satisfaction is related to a number of the communication satisfaction dimensions. The Communication Climate, Personal Feedback, and Supervisory Communication dimensions seem to be most strongly related to job satisfaction. (c) Communication satisfaction is related to the satisfaction and fulfillment of certain needs. (d) The communication satisfaction instrument is a useful tool in a wide variety of industries, cultures, and with various job classifications. Yet little theoretical work has been done to show if, how, and why there are differences between companies, cultures, and job types. (p. 203)

Pincus (1984, 1986) revised the Downs–Hazen instrument into three dimensions of communication satisfaction: relational dimensions (subordinate communication, horizontal communication, and top management communication), informational/relational dimensions (personal feedback, communication climate, and supervisor communication), and informational dimensions (media quality, organizational integration, and organizational perspective). Pincus's major addition to the instrument was top management communication—the extent to which top management communicates openly with employees.

Pincus (1986) concluded that these employee perceptions of organizational communication are related to job satisfaction and performance but not strongly related to performance. Next, he found the information/relationship characteristics to be most strongly related to job satisfaction. He also concluded that his research confirmed the importance of supervisor–subordinate communication but also that top management communication is strongly related to satisfaction.

In a later study, Pincus et al. (1990) found that a factor they called "trust and influence" explained job satisfaction more than supervisor–subordinate communication. They also found the same correlation with top management communication that Pincus (1986) had found. They concluded, ". . . as individuals rise in the organizational hierarchy and get closer to the top, their desire for communication with top management may increase. Concomitantly, the importance that supervisors attach to communication with their immediate supervisors may drop off accordingly" (p. 185). Later, Pincus, Rayfield, and Cozzens (1991) reviewed research on the role of the CEO in both internal and external communication and concluded that the role was central. In internal communication, communication with the CEO and others in top management seems to be an integral component of the symmetrical communication system that this chapter maintains is a key attribute of an excellent organization.

Few of these studies found as strong a relationship between communication media and satisfaction as they did between the interpersonal variables and communication—a finding that should be disillusioning for the internal communication professionals whose major concern is with the techniques of internal media and publications. Smith (1991), in an applied book on internal communication, recognized the importance of these findings when, in a chapter on media in organizations, he said that "the most fundamental and most important medium is face-to-face communication—one-on-one or in groups" (p. 129). He then went on to discuss how formal media can supplement interpersonal communication. D'Aprix (1982), also in a practical handbook, pointed out that employees want to "identify and relate to some flesh-and-blood representative of the organization. The first choice is always the boss" (p. 12). Finally, the Conference Board study reported by Troy (1989) documented "a preference among employees for a two-way communication process and a face-to-face delivery system" (p. 30).

L. Grunig (1985) found, however, that the most active of three employee publics—which she called the information-seeking public—preferred oral communication to written media. The least involved—and least active—publics were content to process information passively from printed media. Because the most active publics are most likely to be strategic to an organization, face-to-face communication is particularly important for them. L. Grunig also found that the most active employee publics wanted information about the overall management of the organization and reports on the research being done in the university-based research organization she studied.

The Downs–Hazen and Pincus research, likewise, showed the importance of providing employees information about the organization as a whole, its relationship with outside groups, its plans and policies, and the employees' role in the broader organization. It also shows the importance of open communication between top management and other employees. These findings, too, confirm the advice of D'Aprix (1982) in his practical handbook:

> The evidence from the research done on the subject indicates that employees generally have three communication needs. They want to know where the organization is heading and how it will get there and—most important—what all that means to them. The logic of the employees' needs is clear. Employees understand that their individual well-being and their very futures are tied closely to the overall success of the work organization. As members of the enterprise, they want to know generally what the battle plan is, what strategy has been worked out to make that plan work, and how hard they will have to fight to do what actually has been charted for the organization. (p. 11)

Communication Audits. In addition to the climate, superior–subordinate, and satisfaction operationalizations of communication in studies of communication and organizational outcomes, a number of researchers have developed standardized instruments for use as audits of communication in an organization. Two of these were developed in Finland by Osmo Wiio and colleagues in response to requests for help in auditing communication from industry (Goldhaber et al., 1984; Greenbaum, Hellweg, & Falcione, 1988). The two Finnish instruments are known as the LTT Audit (after the Finnish name for the Helsinki Research Institute for Business Economics) and the OCD (Organization Communication Development) Procedure, which is a refinement of the LTT Audit.

The Finnish instruments are similar to a third instrument developed by a team of researchers from the Organizational Communication Division of the International Communication Association from 1971 to 1973. These researchers wanted an instrument that would overcome deficiencies in previous measures of communication and that would provide data that could be aggregated and compared across organizations. The ICA Audit incorporated aspects of most of the previous operationalizations of communication and reflected parts of each of the first four research traditions in the field. The ICA Audit, which is reproduced and described in detail in Goldhaber and Rogers (1979), contains information on information flows (amount received and sent), sources of information, timeliness of information, communication relationships, organizational outcomes, channels and media of communication, and demographics. After each of these sections of fixed-response questions, the audit asks respondents in open-end questions to describe communication experiences they have had that are related to the fixed-response questions.

In 1978, the ICA dropped its affiliation with the audit, and the instrument passed into the public domain, where it has been accepted by a large number of independent researchers (Greenbaum et al., 1988, p. 311). In addition, several reviewers have developed generalizations from the many applications of the Finnish and ICA procedures (Brooks et al., 1979; Goldhaber et al., 1978; Goldhaber et al., 1984). Many of the conclusions are atheoretical (such as the demographic categories describing people who need more or less information) or situational (not consistent across organizations).

All three reviews, however, generally found support for the relationship between satisfaction with communication and job satisfaction. However, Brooks et al. (1979) could find no clear improvements in the outcomes of communication—such as morale and turnover—after organizations made changes recommended by communication auditors even though they did find that managers had implemented recommended improvements in communication. Goldhaber et al. (1978) concluded that "organizational communication relationships," particularly superior–subordinate relationships, and "involvement within a worker's system" are the most important predictors of job satisfaction.

In addition, Goldhaber et al. (1984) concluded that increased amounts of communication do not necessarily lead to greater satisfaction with communication (p. 344). For example, a study of miners in Finland showed that improvements in the communication system after an audit reduced job satisfaction as measured in a follow-up study because the changes in communication led the miners to believe that they would participate more in decision making, which did not happen. This conclusion and Goldhaber et al.'s (1978) finding of a relationship between "involvement in the system" and satisfaction suggest that changes in the communication system will not make employees more satisfied or an organization more effective unless concomitant changes are made in organizational structure (J. Grunig, 1985)—of which participation in decision making is an indicator.

Finally, Goldhaber et al. (1984) concluded that content of communication relates strongly to the organizational and communication climates. Employees who received information about their own jobs and on organizational and external situations (the same findings as in the Downs–Hazen and Pincus research) perceived the climate as more trusting, open, and supportive. Similarly, when Spiker and Daniels (1981) operationalized "amount of information received" from the employees' perspective as "information adequacy," they found a consistent positive relationship between that variable and satisfaction with the supervisor and with top management.

Goldhaber et al. (1984) provided a fitting summary for the extensive research on the relationship between the various operationalizations of communication and job satisfaction: "A practitioner often asks the researcher in organizational communication: will my workers be more satisfied if I improve communication in my organization? Our answer is: not necessarily, but your organization may function better" (p. 345). This statement, in other words, supports the aforementioned conclusion that satisfaction is not a direct measure of organizational effectiveness. Rather, it is an indicator that strategic employee publics will not constrain the mission of the organization—that is, communication will allow the organization to function better, to be excellent.

In spite of all of this research, however, we emerge from this section with little theoretical understanding of how internal communication makes organizations more effective. In the earlier quote on their conclusions about research using the Downs–Hazen measure of communication satisfaction, Downs et al. (1988) said that "little theoretical work has been done to show if, how, and why there are differences between companies, cultures, and job types" (p. 203). The thesis of this chapter is that the answer lies in the nature of the communication system, organizational structure, and organizational culture—the topics to which we turn next.

SYMMETRICAL COMMUNICATION SYSTEMS

As we worked through the operationalizations of organizational communication and their relationship to job satisfaction in the previous section, we saw that researchers moved from a generic concept of communication to conceptualizations of more specialized communication variables. Yet researchers examined those variables and their relationships to various facets of job satisfaction one at a time and have not developed an integrating theory of why some facets affect satisfaction and others do not. Goldhaber et al. (1984) even concluded that scholars should give up the quest for a "grand theory" in organizational communication, "at least if the theory is expected to manifest universally predictive power" (p. 354).

The integrating thread that seems to weave throughout these studies is the concept of symmetrical communication, as it was conceptualized in chapters 2 and 11. J. Grunig (1985, 1987; J. Grunig & Theus, 1986) included questions about symmetrical and asymmetrical communication in an audit instrument that he developed for studies of a state department of education, a county educational system, and a major state university. J. Grunig's instrument analyzes an organization's communication system, structure, and individual and organizational job satisfaction simultaneously.

To describe the communication system, J. Grunig (1985, 1987; J. Grunig & Theus, 1986) combined several items that he wrote to measure symmetrical and asymmetrical communication with several indicators of communication satisfaction from the ICA Audit. Factor analysis produced symmetrical and asymmetrical factors in two of the studies and a single factor in the third on which the symmetrical and asymmetrical items had opposite signs. Most of the communication satisfaction items loaded on the symmetrical factor, suggesting that symmetrical communication underlies most of the measures of communication climate and satisfaction discussed in the previous section. In addition, J. Grunig found strong positive correlations between symmetrical communication and job satisfaction, but stronger correlations with organizational satisfaction than with individual satisfaction. In contrast, he found negative correlations between the index of asymmetrical communication and job satisfaction.

As this chapter has shown, symmetrical concepts run throughout the literature on organizational communication, especially in the eight research traditions discussed earlier. Symmetrical concepts such as trust, credibility, openness, relationships, reciprocity, network symmetry, horizontal communication, feedback, adequacy of information, employee-centered style, tolerance for disagreement, and negotiation pervade the literature. Similarly, communication audits of the content of communication suggest the presence of symmetrical communication. In particular, audit studies show that employees are most satisfied with information that helps them make sense of their situation—in essence, a reflection of the rhetorical/ hermeneutic approach—by telling them how their job fits into the organizational mission, about organizational policies and plans, and about relationships with key constituencies in the organization's environment.

Finally, the desire that employees have, especially those in managerial ranks, to communicate openly with top management also suggests symmetrical communication. Both symmetrical content and open communication with top management marks a complete turnaround from the managerial bias of early research on organizational communication—which reflected the press agentry, public information, or two-way asymmetrical models of public relations.

Even research that shows the importance of interpersonal communication in job satisfaction provides evidence of the value of symmetry in communication. Face-to-face communication makes symmetrical communication easier, although mediated communication also can be symmetrical if its content meets the employee's need to know rather than management's need to tell.

Although the symmetry of communication can vary at the interpersonal, group, and organizational levels, it seems likely that organizations have communication systems that pervade the three levels. As we see next, the symmetry of the system reflects the structure and culture of the organization.

In summary, then, the first principles of an integrated theory of internal communication can be stated:

Proposition 1: Excellent systems of internal communication reflect the principles of symmetrical communication.

Proposition 2: Symmetrical systems of communication make organizations more effective by building open, trusting, and credible relationships with strategic employee constituencies.

Proposition 3: Good relationships with employee constituencies are indicated by high levels of job satisfaction, especially organizational job satisfaction.

ORGANIZATIONAL STRUCTURE

Research on organizational communication, especially in academic departments of speech communication, had its roots more in organizational psychology than sociology. As a result, scholars looked at communication more often from the level of individuals, dyads, and small groups than from the level of the total organization. Organizational sociologists, in contrast, study organizations from a macro, total organizational level. The concept of structure dominated organizational sociology for many years, although concepts of environment, power, and culture now have assumed equal importance in the field (see chapter 17; see also Hage, 1980; Hage & Aiken, 1970; Hall, 1987; Mintzburg, 1983; Robbins, 1990).

Although J. Grunig (1975, 1976) studied the impact of structure on organizational communication 15 years ago, scholars in speech communication only recently have begun to look at its effect both on job satisfaction and communication in organizations (Jablin, 1987; McPhee, 1985). Others, in addition, have begun to examine the effect of communication on structure—how individuals use communication to build structure (Conrad & Ryan, 1985; Poole, 1985; Poole & McPhee, 1983). Nevertheless, scholars of organizational communication generally have failed to recognize that the structure and the communication system of an organization are closely entwined and that the job satisfaction attributed to communication could occur as much from the nature of structure as from the nature of communication.

Organizational sociologists have found that job satisfaction—especially morale or organizational job satisfaction—increases when an organization has a structure that is appropriate for its employees (Hage, 1980, pp. 293–320). In particular, complex organizations with complex environments generally employ specialists who require autonomy to do their work. Without autonomy they become dissatisfied with their work. Although sociologists have theorized that autonomy is more important for specialists than for workers whose positions require less education and specialized training, J. Grunig (1985, 1987) found autonomy to be equally important in explaining the satisfaction of nonspecialists as specialists. Indeed, the early experimental studies of the structure of small groups in the network tradition of research described earlier found the autonomy of subjects in the experiments to be correlated with their satisfaction with the experience (Shaw, 1964).

Autonomy, therefore, provides a key to job satisfaction. The amount of autonomy an employee has depends on an organization's system of constraints, which makes up the structure of an organization (Thayer, 1968, pp. 95–97). The structural framework connects employees and restricts their behavior so that the organization functions as a single system. Rigid structures can be used to coordinate employee behaviors with relatively little need for communication, except for commands and instructions and positive messages designed to make people feel good about their role—the press agentry and human relations approaches to internal communication described earlier in this chapter.

Organizational sociologists have identified four structural variables that have the greatest effect on job satisfaction and communication (see, e.g., Hage, 1980; Hage & Aiken, 1970; Hall, 1987; Robbins, 1990). These variables also are discussed in greater detail in chapter 17. *Centralization* describes the extent to which decision making is concentrated at the top of the organizational hierarchy. The more an organization is centralized, the greater the constraints on employees outside top management and the less autonomy they have to make their own decisions. *Stratification* describes the extent to which an organization makes it clear who are its higher level employees and who are its lower level employees. Stratified organizations limit interaction between employees at different ranks and make it difficult for them to move from lower to higher ranks. Stratified organizations give clear preference in prestige and pay to higher level employees and provide the higher employees such perquisites as private offices, executive dining rooms, and wooden desks to set them apart.

Formalization is the extent to which an organization follows rules and regulations. Rules, charts, and procedures discourage autonomy, innovation, and morale in an organization (Hage, 1980, pp. 40–42), although formalized procedures have been found to increase employee satisfaction when they clarify what is expected of employees without reducing autonomy (Hage, 1980, p. 311; J. Grunig, 1985, 1987). *Complexity,* the fourth variable, describes the extent to which an organization has educated, professionalized employees who fill specialist roles as well as the extent to which jobs in the organization are routine and unchanging or require changing, flexible behavior.

A fifth structural variable that is particularly relevant to communication, *participation in decision making,* does not appear in sociological theories but is included in most audits of organizational communication and appears in psychological theories of leadership (e.g., Vroom & Jago, 1988) and management (e.g., Lawler, 1986). Although scholars of organizational communication generally consider participation in decision making to be a communication variable, it seems to be more of a structural variable. It is a structural variable because participation strategies – such as participative management, quality circles, teams, or delegation of responsibility – increase the autonomy of individuals and reduce their constraints. Participation is particularly relevant to communication because it increases the amount and symmetry of communication and increases the likelihood of organizational outcomes associated with communication – involvement, innovation, and job satisfaction.[6]

Participation has strong positive effects on job satisfaction in particular (Lawler, 1986; Monge & Miller, 1988), as do other structural variables that increase autonomy. Thus, it is likely that some of the effects of communication on job satisfaction occur not because of communication but because participation – a structural variable that affects communication – was included in the audit instrument as a characteristic of communication.

Structural variables do not occur independently of each other but interact in a pattern that produces types of organizations (Hage, 1965, Hage, 1980;

---

[6]See Monge and Miller (1988) for a discussion of the implications of participation for communication.

Hage & Aiken, 1970; Hall, 1987; Robbins, 1990). One type of organization is centralized, formalized, stratified, less complex, and does not allow most employees to participate in decision making. That organization generally is called *mechanical,* following Burns and Stalker (1961). Another type, generally called *organic,* is decentralized, less formalized, less stratified, and more complex; and it facilitates participation in decision making. Hull and Hage (1982) have shown that organizations, especially large ones, can be a mixture of these two types (see also chapter 17); thus, the two types of organizations could instead be two structural dimensions that characterize most organizations to varying degrees. To understand the impact of structure, however, we can treat organic and mechanical structures as though they are mutually exclusive.

Structure, as we have seen, affects morale and job satisfaction as well as the amount, direction, and symmetry of communication. Although most organizational sociologists ignore communication, a few have examined the effect of structure on communication (e.g., Bacharach & Aiken, 1977; Hage, 1974; Hall, 1987, chapter 7). Structure channels communication, or in the words of Hall (1987): "The very establishment of an organizational structure is a sign that communications are supposed to follow a particular path" (p. 176). In addition, more communication takes place in organic than in mechanical organizations. People also communicate downward more often in mechanical organizations; whereas they communicate in horizontal, upward, and crisscross directions more often in organic organizations (Hage, 1974, 1980).

Most important, perhaps, is that the communication system is symmetrical in organic organizations and asymmetrical in mechanical organizations (J. Grunig, 1985, 1987; J. Grunig & Theus, 1986). J. Grunig (in preparation) had difficulty determining, in a LISREL path analysis, whether organizational structure determines the nature of an organization's communication system or is a part of that structure. He also has had difficulty determining whether the structural variables and the communication system have independent effects on individual and organizational job satisfaction. Thus, he concluded that the communication system actually is part of the structure that defines the nature of an organizational system.

Communication professionals, those findings imply, probably cannot implement a system of symmetrical communication without a simultaneous change in organizational structure. In Jablin's (1987) words, the relationship between the structure and communication system of an organization is "complex and reciprocal" (p. 413). In addition, the effects of communication and structure on job satisfaction are linked; and a change in one without a change in the other will not improve job satisfaction and may even reduce it—a conclusion supported by Goldhaber Dennis et al.'s (1984) review (p. 344).

Scholars in the rhetorical/hermeneutic tradition in speech communication, however, feel uncomfortable with the conclusion that communication is a product of or is constrained by organizational structure. Tompkins (1987) argued, for example, that without communication there would be no organization. Poole and McPhee (1983), Poole (1985), McPhee (1985), and Conrad and Ryan (1985) developed theories of how people use communication in the *structuration* of organizations. Structuration means that people create structure as they organize, and they must communicate to do so. The theoretical dilemma, then, is that communication helps to produce structure but that structure shapes and limits communication. How, then, can people change the structure when that structure shapes the communication system to make change difficult? The answer lies in the forces that shape structure, to which the next section is devoted.

The next principles of an integrated theory of internal communication, then, can be stated:

Proposition 4: Organizations with organic structures have symmetrical communication systems, and organizations with mechanical structures have asymmetrical communication systems.

Proposition 5: Job satisfaction, especially organizational job satisfaction, is higher in organizations with organic structures than in organizations with mechanical structures.

Proposition 6: Symmetrical communication can help to create organic structures in organizations.

WHAT CAUSES STRUCTURE? ENVIRONMENT, CULTURE, AND POWER

In his book on organizational sociology, Robbins (1990) devoted five chapters to a discussion of the extent to which organizations choose a structure with a rational strategy or whether structure occurs because of the size, technology, or environment of an organization. He found that each factor explains structure to some extent but that a fifth factor, power and politics, has emerged as the key explanation of structure. Power helps us to connect theories of organizational communication with theories of structure because of the central role of power and politics in the theory of organizational effectiveness in chapter 3 and the relationship of power with communication in the interpretive and critical approaches to organizational communication. Robbins (1990) summarized the research on the causes of structure as follows: "No more than 50 to 60 percent of the variability in structure can be explained by strategy, size, technology, and environment. A substantial portion of the residual variance may be explained by the power-control view of structure, which states that an organization's structure, at any given time, is largely the result of those in power selecting a structure that will, to the maximum degree possible, maintain and enhance their control" (pp. 270–271).

Although the concept of power has a negative connotation for most people, it is important to recognize that power can be used asymmetrically or symmetrically. People in organizations use power asymmetrically when they try to control and make others dependent on them. Robbins (1988) described the asymmetrical use of power vividly:

> As a manager who wants to maximize your power, you will want to increase others' dependence on you. You can, for instance, increase your power in relation to your boss by developing knowledge or a skill that he *[sic]* needs and for which he *[sic]* has no ready substitute. But power is a two-way street. You will not be alone in attempting to build your power sources. Others, particularly subordinates, will be seeking to make you dependent on them. The result is a continual battle. While you seek to maximize others' dependence on you, you will be seeking to minimize your dependence on others. And, of course, others you work with will be trying to do the same. (p. 151)

The symmetrical concept of power, in contrast, can be described as *empowerment*— of collaborating to increase the power of everyone in the organization, to the benefit of everyone in the organization. According to Frost (1987): "Current writings and research on empowerment . . . treat . . . empowerment as the use of power to create opportunities and conditions through which other actors can gain power, can make decisions, can use and expand their abilities and skills, can create and accomplish organizational work in ways that are meaningful to them . . ." (p. 539). Organic structures and symmetrical systems of communication make organizations excellent and effective precisely because they empower people. Politics in the organization then becomes constructive because it embodies negotiation and compromise. In organizations with mechanical structures, in contrast, power holders use asymmetrical communication in a continual battle of independence and dependence. As chapter 9 showed, *empowered* organizations are excellent, *battlefield* organizations are not.

In addition to these explanations of structure, organizational psychologists and communication scholars recently have devoted much of their energy to studying the extent to which organizations are cultures and the effect of culture on behaviors in organizations (e.g., Barnett, 1988; O'Donnell-Trujillo & Pacanowskyi, 1983; Smircich & Calas, 1987). Schneider (1985) pointed out that culture is a "deeper construct than climate" (p. 596), and Putnam and Cheney (1983) argued that culture could resolve what they called the conceptual confusion about climate (p. 217). Although sociologists have not identified culture as a cause of structure, Robbins (1988, 1990) pointed out that culture can serve as a substitute for formalization, a structural variable.

Like power, however, culture can enhance organizational and communication excellence, or it can be a liability (Robbins, 1988). According to Robbins, "Culture is a liability where the shared values are not in agreement with those that will further the organization's effectiveness" (p. 210). Chapters 9 and 21 identify two types of organizational culture—*authoritarian* and *participative*. Participative cultures foster organic structures, symmetrical communication systems, and organizational excellence and effectiveness. Authoritarian cultures, in contrast, foster mechanical structures, asymmetrical systems of communication, and mediocrity and ineffectiveness.

From the literature reviewed in this chapter, the literature on structure and the environment in chapter 17, the literature on power in chapter 18, and the literature on organizational culture in chapter 21, we can conclude that the power holders in an organization—the dominant coalition—choose a structure and concomitant communication system for an organization. Who comes to power in an organization and the extent to which power is shared throughout the organization, however, reflect to a large extent the environment and culture of the organization.[7]

Weick (1979) has been cited widely by scholars of organizational communication for his idea that people in organizations define—or enact—their environments. That is, environments are, at least in part, a product of communication as well as a cause of communication. That rhetorical/hermeneutic concept is a close analogue of culture defined by that same perspective. Communication, therefore, both creates and is shaped by culture.

As a result of these final insights, we can use the concepts of culture, environment, power, structure, internal communication systems, job satisfaction, and organizational effectiveness to explain the causes and effects of the system of organic structure and symmetrical communication described by six propositions stated earlier in this chapter. That integrated theory is depicted in Fig. 20.1. The central concepts of the communication system and structure are enclosed within a dotted line and connected with reciprocal arrows to show that they are integrated into a central structure of the organization. Power holders in the organization choose that central

---

[7]Euske and Roberts (1987) wrote one of the few articles relating sociological theories of organizational-environment relationships to internal communication. They acknowledged that few communication scholars have looked at the impact of the environment on internal communication processes and pointed out that sociological theories of resource dependency, population ecology, and institutionalization open up new avenues for the study of organizational communication.

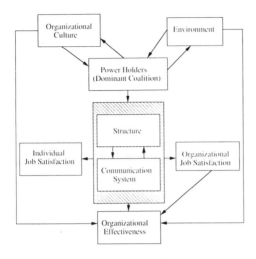

FIGURE   20.1   Power-Control model of organizational Communication and Structure.

structure. Who holds power is affected by the culture and environment of the organization, but the power holders in turn enact the culture and environment.

Organizations are effective—the organizational effectiveness variable increases—when their structure, culture, and environment are in harmony. This, essentially, is the theory of organizational effectiveness developed in chapter 3. The environment is important because the strategic constituencies in it constrain or enhance the mission of the organization. Employees, a key constituency in the internal environment of an organization, can have a similar impact. That is why satisfaction with the organization is a critical outcome of the structure-communication system of the organization and a critical link to organizational effectiveness.

The theory modeled in Fig. 20.1 shows, therefore, how the internal communication system fits into the pattern of an excellent organization that provides the context for excellent public relations and communication management. A symmetrical communication system was one of the components of an excellent organization identified in chapter 9, as were the other components of the model. A symmetrical system of communication, therefore, is necessary for excellence; but it also is a product of excellence. That conclusion leads to implications for practical communication strategy—the last section of this chapter.

IMPLICATIONS FOR COMMUNICATION PROFESSIONALS

This chapter stated earlier that housing the academic study of internal organizational communication in departments of speech communication has limited the value of the theory and research in the field to public relations, primarily because of a preoccupation in speech with individuals and with interpersonal and group communication in organizations. Communication professionals specializing in internal communication generally are found in public relations departments. In contrast to the research done in organizational communication, the professionals manage systems of communication—which function at the organizational level but which influence and incorporate the communication of groups, dyads, and individuals.

In this chapter, we have found that the work in speech departments has great value for public relations but that it must be integrated into a theory of communication systems—as this chapter has done—for that value to be apparent. The theory of communication systems, in turn, must be integrated into a larger organizational theory of structure, environment, culture, and power—which this chapter also has done. This chapter has shown that a symmetrical communication system is a characteristic of excellent and effective organizations. Someone has to design and manage such a symmetrical system, however, and that is the role of internal communication managers.

Although organizational excellence fosters a symmetrical system of communication, senior managers cannot assume that a symmetrical system will develop without planning and without professional guidance. D'Aprix (1988), a veteran consultant on internal communication, recognized the interlocking role of organic structure and symmetrical communication when he said that research (like that reviewed in chapter 9) shows that organizations "will become 'flatter' and more entrepreneurial as time goes on" and that "because we are dealing with human complexity, the communication system will have to be designed to accommodate humans" (p. 270). Emanuel and York (1988), also senior communication consultants, recognized the same components of excellence when they maintained in a handbook on "human resources communication" that communication must replace authority as a way to manage (organic structure and participative culture) and that communication must be two-way from management to employees and employees to management.

D'Aprix (1988) added that a communication system must be planned. Planning requires a well thought out communication strategy, managers who are accountable for the success of the strategy, and training to prepare communication managers for their new accountability. Smith (1991) also emphasized the importance of the strategic management of employee communication (p. 49), and L. Grunig (1985) demonstrated how research can isolate the active, most strategic publics in an organization. In short, internal communication must be an integral part of the strategic management of an organization just as communication programs for other strategic publics must be.[8] Communication managers must be accountable for the function, however, "so that communicators are no longer regarded as narrow technicians, but as part of the management team"—to use the words of Troy (1989, p. 31). Third, according to D'Aprix (1988), communication professionals must be trained in the new behaviors expected of them as managers.

One of the new behaviors that will be expected of them will be formative and evaluative research. Emanuel (1985) emphasized research to audit the effectiveness of employee communication. As this chapter has shown, scholars of organizational communication have developed such audit instruments. Most of these instruments, however, do not include organizational characteristics, especially structure and culture, that influence and are influenced by communication in their audits. Thus, communication professionals should audit structure and culture as well as communication and job satisfaction. The research team for the IABC study of excellence, for which this book was the first stage, developed an audit that measures communication, structure, culture, and job satisfaction in the same instrument, an instrument that is available for use by practitioners.

Audits can show whether these four aspects of organizations must be changed to make them excellent. Communication managers cannot change structure and culture by themselves but they can alert senior managers— through communication—to structures and cultures that limit organizational excellence. Managers can plan symmetrical systems of communication but those systems cannot be fully effective without changes in culture and structure. Symmetrical communication, as rhetorical scholars argue, can be the catalyst that initiates overall organizational excellence and effectiveness. Symmetrical communication probably will fail to change the organization, however, unless it produces structural and cultural change before a mechanical structure and an authoritarian culture kill off the new system of communication.

A symmetrical system of communication is an abstract concept, but several practical books discuss what essentially are symmetrical techniques of internal communication (D'Aprix, 1982; Emanuel & York, 1988; J. Grunig & Hunt, 1984, chapter 12; Smith, 1991). A symmetrical system of communication functions throughout an organization, but it operates at the interpersonal and group level as well as at the mediated, organizational level. The research cited in this chapter emphasizes that interpersonal

---

[8]Researchers at the University of Maryland have conducted several studies using a situational theory of publics to identify strategic employee publics of organizations, research that is not reviewed in this chapter. That research is reviewed in chapter 6 and in J. Grunig and Hunt (1984, chapter 12). The research reported in J. Grunig (1985, 1987), which is reviewed in this chapter, provides an example of how employee publics relate to the organizational structure and communication system of an organization.

communication is key, and both D'Aprix (1982) and Smith (1991) provided professional communicators with advice on how to make interpersonal communication symmetrical. Many textbooks on organizational communication (e.g., Conrad, 1985; Daniels & Spiker, 1987; Goldhaber, 1990) also provide practical advice on how communication managers can train employees throughout the organization to communicate more symmetrically — thus using the work from speech communication in public relations.

Although D'Aprix (1988) emphasized the importance of training for communication managers, his advice also could be applied to training of employees throughout the organization — especially middle managers — on how to communicate more effectively (Troy, 1989, p. 31). Shatshat (1980) asked communication directors in 106 corporations to rate the extent to which they practiced 19 communication roles. As reported earlier in this chapter, most respondents reported that they filled mostly technical roles. Although few said that they conduct formal training for employees in communication, respondents reported that training should be included in the ideal communication program.

In academic circles, scholars and educators in organizational communication and public relations seldom interact. Scholars in organizational communication have provided valuable research and theories on face-to-face communication, but the communication practitioners generally are trained only in the techniques of media in journalism schools. Professionals in internal communication need both kinds of knowledge to manage both face-to-face and mediated communication. If professionals learn the knowledge of interpersonal and group communication from speech scholars, they could help to manage face-to-face communication in their organizations by formally training individuals throughout the organization in communication.

As Smith (1991) pointed out, however, mediated communication backs up and complements interpersonal communication. Or, as Troy (1989) added, "The printed word remains a communication staple" (p. 30). Emanuel and York's (1988) handbook provides practical advice on how to make written communication more symmetrical, as do several of the chapters in the Reuss and Silvis (1985) handbook published by IABC. These handbooks and this chapter show clearly that mediated communication can be symmetrical as long as it addresses the needs of employees to make sense of how they fit into the organization, to communicate openly with top management about plans and policies, and to understand the activities of the organization in the outside environment.

Internal communication, then, is the catalyst if not the key to organizational excellence and effectiveness. Communication managers, in turn, are essential to organizations, as long as they are, to use D'Aprix's (1988) terms, strategic, accountable, and trained.

REFERENCES

Bacharach, S. B., & Aiken, M. (1977). Communication in administrative bureaucracies. *Academy of Management Journal, 20,* 365-377.

Barnett, G.A. (1988). Communication and organizational culture. In G. M. Goldhaber & G. A. Barnett (Eds.), *Handbook of organizational communication* (pp. 101-130). Norwood, NJ: Ablex.

Brooks, K., Callicoat, J., & Siegerdt, G. (1979). The ICA communication audit and perceived communication effectiveness changes in 16 audited organizations. *Human Communication Research, 5,* 130-137.

Burns, T., & Stalker, G. M. (1961). *The management of innovation.* London: Tavistock.

Charlton, R. G. (1990, May-June). Whatever happened to the fruit-hat ladies? A tale of two surveys 1970 vs. 1989. *Communication World,* pp. 32-34.

Cheney, G., & Vibbert, S. L. (1987). Corporate discourse: Public relations and issue management. In F. M. Jablin, L. L. Putnam, K. H. Roberts, & L. W. Porter (Eds.), *Handbook of organizational communication: An interdisciplinary perspective* (pp. 165-194). Newbury Park, CA: Sage.

Conrad, C. (1985). *Strategic organizational communication.* Fort Worth: Holt, Rinehart & Winston.

Conrad, C., & Ryan, M. (1985). Power, praxis, and self in organizational communication theory. In R. D. McPhee & P. K. Tompkins (Eds.), *Organizational communication: Traditional themes and new directions* (pp. 235-258). Newbury Park, CA: Sage.

Cushman, D. P., King, S. S., & Smith, T., III (1988). The rules perspective on organizational communication research. In G. M. Goldhaber & G. A. Barnett (Eds.), *Handbook of organizational communication* (pp. 55-94). Norwood, NJ: Ablex.

Daft, R. L. (1983). *Organization theory and design.* St. Paul, MN: West.

Daniels, T. D., & Spiker, B. K. (1987). *Perspectives on organizational communication.* Dubuque, IA: Brown.

Dansereau, F., & Markham, S. E. (1987). Superior–subordinate communication: Multiple levels of analysis. In F. M. Jablin, L. L. Putnam, K. H. Roberts, & L. W. Porter (Eds.), *Handbook of organizational communication: An interdisciplinary perspective* (pp. 343-388). Newbury Park, CA: Sage.

D'Aprix, R. (1982). *Communicating for productivity.* New York: Harper & Row.

D'Aprix, R. (1988). Communication as process: The manager's view. In G. M. Goldhaber & G. A. Barnett (Eds.), *Handbook of organizational communication* (pp. 265-272). Norwood, NJ: Ablex.

Dover, C. J. (1964). Three eras of management communication. In W. C. Redding (Ed.), *Business and industrial communication: A source book* (pp. 61-65). New York: Harper & Row.

Downs, C. W., Clampitt, G. G., & Pfeiffer, A. L. (1988). Communication and organizational outcomes. In G. M. Goldhaber & G. A. Barnett (Eds.), *Handbook of organizational communication* (pp. 171-211). Norwood, NJ: Ablex.

Downs, C. W., & Hain, T. (1982). Productivity and communication. In M. Burgoon (Ed.), *Communication yearbook 5* (pp. 435-453). Newbury Park, CA: Sage.

Downs, C. W., & Hazen, M. D. (1976). A factor analytic study of communication satisfaction. *Journal of Business Communication, 14,* 63-73.

Eisenberg, E. M., & Riley, P. (1988). Organizational symbols and sense-making. In G. M. Goldhaber & G. A. Barnett (Eds.), *Handbook of organizational communication* (pp. 131-150). Norwood, NJ: Ablex.

Emanuel, M. (1985). Auditing communication practices. In C. Reuss & D. Silvis (Eds.), *Inside organizational communication* (pp. 45-58). New York: Longman.

Emanuel, M., & York, A. M. (1988). *Handbook of human resources communications.* Greenvale, NY: Panel Publishers.

Euske, N. A., & Roberts, K. H. (1987). Evolving perspectives in organization theory: Communication implications. In F. M. Jablin, L. L. Putnam, K. H. Roberts, & L. W. Porter (Eds.), *Handbook of organizational communication: An interdisciplinary perspective* (pp. 41–69). Newbury Park, CA: Sage.

Falcione, R. L., McCroskey, J. C., & Daly, J. A. (1977). Job satisfaction as a function of employee's communication apprehension, self-esteem, and perceptions of their immediate superiors. In B. D. Ruben (Ed.), *Communication yearbook I* (pp. 363–375). New Brunswick, NJ: Transaction.

Falcione, R. L., Sussman, L., & Herden, R. P. (1987). Communication climate in organizations. In F. M. Jablin, L. L. Putnam, K. H. Roberts, & L. W. Porter (Eds.), *Handbook of organizational communication: An interdisciplinary perspective* (pp. 195–227). Newbury Park, CA: Sage.

Fisher, C. D. (1980). On the dubious wisdom of expecting job satisfaction to correlate with performance. *Academy of Management Review, 5,* 607–612.

Frost, P. J. (1987). Power, politics, and influence. In F. M. Jablin, L. L. Putnam, K. H. Roberts, & L. W. Porter (Eds.), *Handbook of organizational communication: An interdisciplinary perspective* (pp. 503–548). Newbury Park, CA: Sage.

Goldhaber, G. M. (1990). *Organizational communication* (5th ed.). Dubuque, IA: Brown.

Goldhaber, G. M., Dennis, H. S., III, Richetto, G. M., & Wiio, O. A. (1984). *Information strategies: New pathways to management productivity* (rev. ed.). Norwood, NJ: Ablex.

Goldhaber, R. M., & Rogers, D. P. (1979). *Auditing organizational communication systems: The ICA communication audit.* Dubuque, IA: Kendall/Hunt.

Goldhaber, G. M., Yates, M. P., Porter, D. T., & Lesniak, R. (1978). Organizational communication: 1978. *Human Communication Research, 5,* 76–96.

Greenbaum, H. H., Hellweg, S. A., & Falcione, R. L. (1988). Organizational communication evaluation: An overview, 1950–1981. In G. M. Goldhaber & G. A. Barnett (Eds.), *Handbook of organizational communication* (pp. 275–317). Norwood, NJ: Ablex.

Grunig, J. E. (1975). A multi-systems theory of organizational communication. *Communication Research, 2,* 99–136.

Grunig, J. E. (1976). Organizations and public relations: Testing a communication theory. *Journalism Monographs, 46.*

Grunig, J. E. (1985, May). *A structural reconceptualization of the organizational communication audit, with application to a state department of education.* Paper presented at the meeting of the International Communication Association, Honolulu.

Grunig, J. E. (1987, July). *An audit of organizational structure, job satisfaction, and the communication system in the Allegany County School System.* Cumberland, MD: Allegany County Board of Education.

Grunig, J. E. (in preparation). *Employee communication systems and organizational effectiveness: A public relations perspective.*

Grunig, J. E., & Hunt, T. (1984). *Managing public relations.* Fort Worth: Holt, Rinehart & Winston.

Grunig, J. E., & Theus, K. T. (1986, August). *Internal communication systems and employee satisfaction.* Paper presented at the meeting of the Association for Education in Journalism and Mass Communication, Norman, OK.

Grunig, L. A. (1985). Meeting the communication needs of employees. *Public Relations Review, 11*(2), 43–53.

Hage, J. (1965). An axiomatic theory of organizations. *Administrative Science Quarterly, 10,* 289–320.

Hage, J. (1974). *Communication and organizational control: Cybernetics in health and welfare settings.* New York: Wiley-Interscience.

Hage, J. (1980). *Theories of organizations: Form, process, & transformation.* New York: Wiley-Interscience.

Hage, J., & Aiken, M. (1970). *Social change in complex organizations.* New York: Random House.

Hall, R. H. (1987). *Organizations: Structures, processes, and outcomes* (3rd ed.). Englewood Cliffs, NJ: Prentice-Hall.

Hawes, L., Pacanowsky, M., & Faules, D. (1988). Approaches to the study of organization: A conversation among three schools of thought. In G. M. Goldhaber & G. A. Barnett (Eds.), *Handbook of organizational communication* (pp. 41–54). Norwood, NJ: Ablex.

Hellweg, S. A., & Phillips, S. L. (1981). Communication and productivity in organizations: A state of the art review. In K. H. Chung (Ed.), *Academy of Management 1981: Proceedings* (pp. 188–192). Wichita, KS: Academy of Management.

Hodge, B. J., & Anthony, W. P. (1988). *Organization theory* (3rd ed.). Boston: Allyn & Bacon.

Hull, F., & Hage, J. (1982). Organizing for innovation: Beyond Burns and Stalker's organic type. *Sociology, 16,* 564–577.

Jablin, F. M. (1979). Superior–subordinate communication: The state of the art. *Psychological Bulletin, 86,* 1201–122.

Jablin, F. M. (1987). Formal organization structure. In F. M. Jablin, L. L. Putnam, K. H. Roberts, & L. W. Porter (Eds.), *Handbook of organizational communication: An interdisciplinary perspective* (pp. 389–419). Newbury Park, CA: Sage.

Jablin, F. M., Putnam, L. L., Roberts, K. H., & Porter, L. W. (Eds.). (1987). *Handbook of organizational communication: An interdisciplinary perspective.* Newbury Park, CA: Sage.

Jackson, J. H., Morgan, C. P., & Paolillo, J. G. P. (1986). *Organization theory: A macro perspective for management* (3rd ed.). Englewood Cliffs, NJ: Prentice Hall.

Johannesson, R. E. (1973). Some problems in the measurement of organizational climate. *Organizational Behavior and Human Performance, 10,* 118–144.

Kelly, L. (1982, May). *A critical review of the literature on superior–subordinate communication.* Paper presented at the meeting of the International Communication Association, Boston.

Krone, K. J., Jablin, F. M., & Putnam, L. L. (1987). Communication theory and organizational communication: Multiple perspectives. In F. M. Jablin, L. L. Putnam, K. H. Roberts, & L. W. Porter (Eds.), *Handbook of organizational communication: An interdisciplinary perspective* (pp. 18–40). Newbury Park, CA: Sage.

LaFollette, W. R., & Sims, H. P., Jr. (1975). Is satisfaction redundant with organizational climate? *Organizational Behavior and Human Performance, 13,* 257–278.

Laudan, L. (1977). *Progress and its problems.* Berkeley: University of California Press.

Lawler, E. E., III (1986). *High-involvement management.* San Francisco: Jossey-Bass.

Lewton, K. L. (1991). *Public relations in health care: A guide for professionals.* Chicago: American Hospital Publishing.

Locke, E. A. (1976). The nature and causes of job satisfaction. In M. D. Dunnettee (Ed.), *Handbook of industrial and organizational psychology* (pp. 1297–1349). Chicago: Rand McNally.

McPhee, R. D. (1985). Formal structure and organizational communication. In R. D. McPhee & P. K. Tompkins (Eds.), *Organizational communication: Traditional themes and new directions* (pp. 149–178). Newbury Park, CA: Sage.

Mintzberg, H. (1983). *Structures in fives: Designing effective organizations.* Englewood Cliffs, NJ: Prentice-Hall.

Monge, P. R., & Miller, K. I. (1988). Participative processes in organizations. In G. M. Goldhaber & G. A. Barnett (Eds.), *Handbook of organizational communication* (pp. 213–229). Norwood, NJ: Ablex.

Muchinsky, P. M. (1977). Organizational communication: Relationships to organizational climate and job satisfaction. *Academy of Management Journal, 20,* 592–607.

O'Donnell-Trujillo, N., & Pacanowsky, M. E. (1983). The interpretation of organizational cultures. In M. S. Mander (Ed.), *Communications in transition* (pp. 225–241). New York: Praeger.

Payne, R. L., Fineman, S., & Wall, T. D. (1976). Organizational climate and job satisfaction: A conceptual synthesis. *Organizational Behavior and Human Performance, 16,* 45–62.

Pincus, J. D. (1984). *The impact of communication satisfaction on job satisfaction and job performance: A field study of hospital nurses.* Unpublished doctoral dissertation, University of Maryland, College Park.

Pincus, J. D. (1986). Communication satisfaction, job satisfaction, and job performance. *Human Communication Research, 12,* 395–419.

Pincus, J. D., Knipp, J. E., & Rayfield, R. E. (1990). Internal communication and job satisfaction revisited: The impact of organizational trust and influence on commercial bank supervisors. In L. A. Grunig & J. E. Grunig (Eds.), *Public relations research annual* (Vol. 2, pp. 173–191). Hillsdale, NJ: Lawrence Erlbaum Associates.

Pincus, J. D., & Rayfield, R. (1989). Organizational communication and job satisfaction: A metaresearch perspective. In B. Dervin & M. J. Voigt (Eds.), *Progress in communication sciences* (Vol. 9, pp. 183–208). Norwood, NJ: Ablex.

Pincus, J. D., Rayfield, R. E., & Cozzens, M. D. (1991). The chief executive officer's internal communication role: A benchmark program of research. In L. A. Grunig & J. E. Grunig (Eds.), *Public relations research annual* (Vol. 3, pp. 1–36). Hillsdale, NJ: Lawrence Erlbaum Associates.

Poole, M. S. (1985). Communication and organizational climates: Review, critique, and a new perspective. In R. D. McPhee & P. K. Tompkins (Eds.), *Organizational communication: Traditional themes and new directions* (pp. 79–108). Newbury Park, CA: Sage.

Poole, M. S., & McPhee, R. D. (1983). A structurational analysis of organizational climate. In L. L. Putnam & M. E. Pacanowsky (Eds.), *Communication and organizations: An interpretive approach* (pp. 1951–220). Newbury Park, CA: Sage.

Putnam, L. L. (1983). The interpretive perspective: An alternative to functionalism. In L. L. Putnam & M. E. Pacanowsky (Eds.), *Communication and organizations: An interpretive approach* (pp. 31–54). Newbury Park, CA: Sage.

Putnam, L. L., & Cheney, G. (1983). A critical review of research traditions in organizational communication. In M. S. Mander (Ed.), *Communications in transition* (pp. 206–224). New York: Praeger.

Putnam, L. L., & Cheney, G. (1985). Organizational communication: Historical development and future directions. In T. W. Benson (Ed.), *Speech communication in the 20th century* (pp. 130–156). Carbondale: Southern Illinois University Press.

Putnam, L. L., & Poole, M. S. (1987). Conflict and negotiation. In F. M. Jablin, L. L. Putnam, K. H. Roberts, & L. W. Porter (Eds.), *Handbook of organizational communication: An interdisciplinary perspective* (pp. 549–599). Newbury Park, CA: Sage.

Redding, W. C. (1972). *Communication within the organization: An interpretative review of theory and research.* New York: Industrial Communication Council.

Redding, W. C. (1985). Stumbling toward identity: The emergence of organizational communication as a field of study. In R. D. McPhee & P. K. Tompkins (Eds.), *Organizational communication: Traditional themes and new directions* (pp. 15–54). Newbury Park, CA: Sage.

Redding, W. C., & Tompkins, P. K. (1988). Organizational communication—past and present tenses. In G. M. Goldhaber & G. A. Barnett (Eds.), *Handbook of organizational communication* (pp. 5–33). Norwood, NJ: Ablex.

Results of the 1989 Wyatt communication survey: Breaking down the barriers. (1989, June Special Issue). *Wyatt Communicator,* pp. 3–27.

Reuss, C., & Silvis, D. (Eds.). (1985). *Inside organizational communication*. New York: Longman.

Richetto, G. M. (1977). Organizational communication theory and research: An overview. In B.D. Ruben (Ed.), *Communication yearbook I* (pp. 331–346). New Brunswick, NJ: Transaction.

Robbins, S. P. (1988). *Essentials of organizational behavior (2nd ed.)*. Englewood Cliffs, NJ: Prentice-Hall.

Robbins, S. P. (1990). *Organizational theory: Structure, design, and applications* (3rd ed.). Englewood Cliffs, NJ: Prentice-Hall.

Roberts, K., & O'Reilly, C. (1974). Measuring organizational communication. *Journal of Applied Psychology, 59,* 321–326.

Roberts, K., O'Reilly, C., Bretton, G., & Porter, L. (1973, May). *Organizational theory and organizational communication: A communication failure?* (Tech. Rep. No. 2). Washington, DC: Office of Naval Research.

Roethlisberger, F. J., & Dickson, W. J. (1939). *Management and the worker*. Cambridge, MA: Harvard University Press.

Schneider, B. (1985). Organizational behavior. *Annual Review of Psychology, 36,* 573–611.

Schneider, B., & Snyder, R. A. (1975). Some relationships between job satisfaction and organizational climate. *Journal of Applied Psychology, 60,* 318–328.

Shapere, D. (1984). *Reason and the search for knowledge*. Dordrecht, Netherlands: Reidel.

Shatshat, H. M. (1980). A comparative study of the present and ideal roles of communication directors in selected business organizations. *Journal of Business Communication, 17*(3), 51–63.

Shaw, M. E. (1964). Communication networks. In L. Berkowitz (Ed.), *Advances in experimental social psychology* (Vol. 1, pp. 111–149). New York: Academic.

Smircich, L., & Calas, M. B. (1987). Organizational culture: A critical assessment. In F. M. Jablin, L. L. Putnam, K. H. Roberts, & L. W. Porter (Eds), *Handbook of organizational communication: An interdisciplinary perspective* (pp. 228–263). Newbury Park, CA: Sage.

Smith, A. L. (1991). *Innovative employee communication*. Englewood Cliffs, NJ: Prentice-Hall.

Smith, P. C., Kendall, L. M., & Hulin, C. L. (1969). *The measurement of satisfaction in work and retirement*. Chicago: Rand-McNally.

Spiker, B. K., & Daniels, T. D. (1981). Information adequacy and communication relationships: An empirical examination of 18 organizations. *Western Journal of Speech Communication, 45,* 342–354.

Suppe, F. (1989). *The semantic conception of theories and scientific realism*. Urbana: University of Illinois Press.

Thayer, L. (1968). *Communication and communication systems*. Homewood, IL: Irwin.

Tompkins, P. K. (1987). Translating organizational theory: Symbolism over substance. In F. M. Jablin, L. L. Putnam, K. H. Roberts, & L. W. Porter (Eds.), *Handbook of organizational communication: An interdisciplinary perspective* (pp. 70–96). Newbury Park, CA: Sage.

Tompkins, P. K., & Cheney, G. (1983). Account analysis of organizations: Decision making and identification. In L. L. Putnam & M.E. Pacanowsky (Eds.), *Communication and organizations: An interpretive approach* (pp. 123–146). Newbury Park, CA: Sage.

Tompkins, P. K., & Cheney, G. (1985). Communication and unobtrusive control in contemporary organizations. In R. D. McPhee & P. K. Tompkins (Eds.), *Organizational communication: Traditional themes and new directions* (pp. 179–234). Newbury Park, CA: Sage.

Troy, K. (1989, February). Internal communication restructures for the '90s. *Communication World,* pp. 28–31.

Vroom, V. H., & Jago, A. G. (1988). *The new leadership: Managing participation in organizations*. Englewood Cliffs, NJ: Prentice-Hall.

Weick, K. E. (1979). *The social psychology of organizing* (2nd ed.). Reading, MA: Addison-Wesley.

Weick, K. E. (1983). Organizational communication: Toward a research agenda. In L. L. Putnam & M. E. Pacanowsky (Eds.), *Communication and organizations: An interpretive approach* (pp. 13–30). Newbury Park, CA: Sage.

Weick, K. E. (1987). Theorizing about organizational communication. In F. M. Jablin, L. L. Putnam, K. H. Roberts, & L. W. Porter (Eds.), *Handbook of organizational communication: An interdisciplinary perspective* (pp. 97–122). Newbury Park, CA: Sage.

Wigand, R. T. (1988). Communication network analysis: History and overview. In G. M. Goldhaber & G. A. Barnett (Eds.), *Handbook of organizational communication* (pp. 319–360). Norwood, NJ: Ablex.

Will public relations & human resources clash in the 90s? Survey finds trust in management translates into quality; Whose job—or both—is it to build trust in management? (1989, August 28). *pr reporter, 32,* pp. 1–3.

Zeitz, G. (1983). Structural and individual determinants of organization morale and satisfaction. *Social Forces, 61,* 1088–1108.

21 Corporate Culture and Public Relations

K. Sriramesh
Purdue University

James E. Grunig
University of Maryland

Jody Buffington
Blue Cross and Blue Shield of Maryland

ABSTRACT

Chapter 9 identified a "strong, participative culture" as one of 12 character-istics of an excellent organization. Chapter 20 showed why and how organi-zational culture is entwined with the communication system and structure of an organization. Culture is the glue that holds excellent organizations together and keeps mediocre organizations mediocre. Some theorists would say that an organization is a culture. In that sense, managers must develop an excellent culture to have an excellent organization. This chapter traces the development of the concept of organizational culture and develops theoretical propositions of its effect on public relations. Culture produces the worldview for public relations in an organization that chapter 2 described as a key determinant of an excellent public relations function. However, this chapter concludes that public relations departments can become countercultures that change the larger culture of the organization to make it more excellent.

"Culture is an idea whose time has come" wrote Smircich (1983, p. 339). Although the culture concept itself is not new, having been studied by ethnographers since the 17th century, what is new is its popularity as a key variable that affects organizational processes (Smircich & Calas, 1987, p. 229). Academicians have used the concept in their attempt to address the many facets of organizations going beyond the "merely logical or econom-ic" (Jelinek, Smircich, & Hirsch, 1983, p. 331). As is highlighted in chapter 22, the need for getting a cultural perspective of organizations was felt to be essential when traditional theories such as the contingency theory failed to resolve several problems in understanding organizational processes.

Another factor that acted as a catalyst in hastening the popularity of viewing organizations as cultural entities was the turbulence and eventual shift in the balance of global economy. The meteoric rise of Japan as an industrial and economic power spawned a plethora of books and journal articles and theories about Japanese industry and management style (Ouchi, 1981; Pascale & Athos, 1981). The mushrooming of multinational and transnational business enterprises has induced managers to see themselves as members of a global economy (Smircich & Calas, 1987). Interest in Japanese management and multinational business, in turn, spurred interest in the concept of organizational culture.

Scholars have attempted to identify cultures in organizations singly or through a combination of multiple dimensions. Although strongly agreeing with the myriad researchers who view culture—both internal and external to an organization—as a determinant of organizational processes, we have found few studies that have made a conceptual link between organizational culture and the practice of public relations. Yet, culture should have a strong effect on public relations, and our purpose in this chapter is to review the literature on organizational culture (corporate culture) to identify its direct and indirect effects on public relations.

Figure 1.1 in chapter 1 summarized the effect of a number of factors on the choice of a model of public relations by an organization. In doing so, Fig. 1.1 identified several conceptual links between culture, public relations, and other organizational processes that affect public relations. This chapter supports the linkage between culture internal to the organization (corporate culture) and the public relations practice of organizations. Chapter 22 conceptualizes the impact that societal culture (external to the organization) has on the way organizations conduct public relations. Our distinction between corporate culture and societal culture is similar to the differentiation posited by Smircich (1983) that is reviewed in chapter 22.

Figure 1.1 showed that organizations exist in and have an interdependent relationship with elements in the environment whose goals and interests often are inconsistent with those of the organization (Burns & Stalker, 1961; Lawrence & Lorsch, 1967). Expressed in systems terms, this means that the environment supplies inputs to an organization (by providing raw materials for the labor force, e.g.) and provides demand for outputs that are vital for sustaining the organization. But, as Child and Tayeb (1983) observed, contingency and systems theories disregarded the impact of culture, a key element of the environment, on organizational processes. In the last two decades, several scholars have tried to rectify this anomaly. The literature on corporate culture is a significant outcome of these attempts.

Further, the symbiotic interdependence conceptualized by contingency theorists is not always simple and clearly defined. Elements in the environment such as activist and special interest groups frequently cause the imposition of political or governmental regulations that restrict organizational processes and constrain organizational autonomy. As boundary spanners, public relations practitioners have one foot in the organization and the other in the environment, constantly interacting with constituencies within and outside the organization. They, therefore, play a crucial role in managing an organization's interdependence with its environment.

Public relations practitioners, however, seldom are free from organizational constraints when they deal with external constituencies. The power holders in an organization, the CEO and the key managers in a dominant coalition, scan the environment for strategic publics that provide threats or opportunities for an organization. Ideally, they would scan the environment (for environmental scanning, see Dozier, 1986, and chapter 12) and communicate with crucial yet variant constituencies in the environment through public relations practitioners.

The nature of that communication depends on the model of public relations chosen by the power holders. The model chosen is a product of choices made by the dominant coalition, choices that are influenced by the organization's schema for public relations (its conceptual understanding of public relations), the potential of the public relations department to practice different models, and the culture of the organization. Corporate culture thus influences public relations by providing a broad base of worldview, meaning, and values that affect all decisions in the organization—including the choice of a model of public relations and the development of a schema that defines public relations and its purpose.

Public relations practitioners have the greatest impact on decisions made about public relations when one or more of them are included in the organization's dominant coalition. If a public relations practitioner is not part of the dominant coalition, which is frequently the case, public relations practitioners function more in the implementation of decisions about public relations than in their formulation. Corporate culture also has indirect effects on public relations. Corporate culture is affected by the power holders in the dominant coalition, and it affects which key managers gain enough power to be in the dominant coalition.

Finally, public relations can affect corporate culture in addition to corporate culture affecting public relations. In particular, internal communication affects organizational culture and, in turn, is affected by it—a relationship that was explored in chapter 20. Externally, both public relations practitioners and power holders must know the prevailing culture or cultures in the organization's environment so that they can make appropriate strategic choices of constituencies as well as communication strategies for interacting with these key constituencies. Such an understanding also will help them improve their capabilities for communicating successfully across cultural boundaries—a relationship that is explored in chapter 22.

Culture, although largely ignored in most research on public relations, seems to be vitally important as a component of both the normative and positive theories of public relations developed in this book. Before developing those theories, therefore, we turn to a review of the theories and research on organizational culture. In our review, we first allude to literature that defines corporate culture and describes its nature. We then allude to scholars who developed a rationale for studying the concept of corporate culture—in their effort to answer the question why is it important to study corporate culture? We then focus attention on the studies that describe when corporate culture becomes most apparent. Scholars also have made prescriptions about changing (managing) an organization's culture, which are reviewed next. Next, we review studies linking culture with communication to set up the context for our efforts to study the impact of corporate culture on the public relations activity of organizations. Finally, we make conceptual links between public relations and corporate culture as a prelude to an assessment of the relationship between the two notions.

FROM CULTURE TO CORPORATE CULTURE

The buzzword *culture* does not have a unanimously accepted definition in the field of anthropology, the field in which it originated. Anthropologists have given hundreds of interpretations regarding what the term means and what it encompasses (Kroeber & Kluckhohn, 1952). Tylor's (1871) definition of the culture concept is acknowledged by most as the first comprehensive definition of the term (Rohner, 1984). Kluckhohn (1951), a noted anthropologist, attempted to define culture thus: "Culture consists in patterned ways of thinking, feeling and reacting, acquired and transmitted mainly by symbols, constituting the distinctive achievements of human groups, including their embodiments in artifacts; the essential core of culture consists of traditional (i.e., historically derived and selected) ideas and especially their attached values" (p. 86).

Hofstede (1980) posited that values are among the building blocks of culture. He saw it as a "system of values," elaborating that it is "the collective programming of the mind which distinguishes the members of one human group from another" (p. 25). It is crucial to note here that Hofstede conceded that his definition was not comprehensive but that it covered what he could measure. This is another example of the malleable nature of the concept. Culture is viewed universally as a construct that reduces ambiguity and facilitates interaction in social settings. One often becomes unconscious of the existence of cultural idiosyncracies, taking them for granted. In turn, these traits control one's perception of the world. Crucial elements of culture, latently embedded in individuals and groups, are projected in the form of shared meanings or symbols (Mitroff, 1983).

When a concept that is so diversely defined is compounded with another used equally frequently in various contexts — organization — the complexity and semantic confusion are bound to multiply (Schein, 1985). Scholars constantly have tried to define organizational culture, thus providing an array of concepts. Deal and Kennedy (1982) saw it as the set of dominant values espoused by an organization. They posited that these "core values" determine "what products get manufactured to how workers are treated" (p. 31). Peters and Waterman (1982) saw corporate culture as the set of values that help "in unifying the social dimensions of the organization" facilitating financial stability (p. 106). In the course of their intense analysis of various American corporations, the authors found that corporate excellence does not result from organizational structure alone. They prescribed what they called the "7-S Framework," consisting of seven variables (each starting with the letter S and hence the name) as their formula for organizational success (p. 10). "Shared Values," one of those variables, was accorded pivotal place in their framework.

Organizational culture also has been referred to as the *rules* of the game for getting along in the organization, the *ropes* that a newcomer must learn in order to become an accepted member. Wallach (1983) saw corporate culture as "the shared understanding of an organization's employees — how we do things around here (p. 29)." Schein (1984, 1985) addressed it as the synthesis of "basic assumptions" (p. 3) that members of an organization share. He saw these beliefs as "learned" responses to a group's problems of survival in its external environment and its problems of internal integration. These beliefs operate unconsciously and help members define their view of the organization and its relationship with its environment. These beliefs come to be taken for granted because they solve problems repeatedly and reliably and so corporate culture, a learned product of such group experiences, evolves only when there is a definable group with a significant history.

Ouchi (1981) and Pascale and Athos (1981) saw organizational culture as the "philosophy" that guides an organization's policy toward employees and customers. Like Schein (1985), they contended that these philosophies would be passed on and cemented over generations as a result of long-time membership. Barley (1983) viewed organizational culture as a system of meaning and proposed semeiotics — the investigation of the use of signs that help interpret communication — as an approach in identifying and analyzing cultures in organizations. Martin, Feldman, Hatch, and Sitkin (1983) saw organizational stories as an integral component of the corporate culture of an institution.

Wilkins and Ouchi (1983) gave culture a different nomenclature — clan — and posited that only under certain circumstances does corporate culture improve organizational efficiency. The authors specified key conditions that encourage the development of "thick" social understandings unique to each organization which in turn lead to the formation of clans. They placed long history and stable membership as observed in Japanese firms at the top of their list. A longer membership facilitates sharing of the corporate rituals, myths, and stories that Deal and Kennedy (1982) found so vital to the existence of a strong organizational culture. Older members can share elements of corporate culture with newer employees and keep the flow of culture learning perennial, similar to the acculturation of members of a society.

Giving the analogy of first generation immigrant parents who try to infuse their "home" cultures to young children who are inundated with an alternate way of living, Wilkins and Ouchi (1983) presented a key condition for the birth and subsistence of a clan: the absence of institutional alternatives. They argued that organizational culture is more likely to develop when conflicting social institutions are either missing or discredited. Another prerequisite the authors proposed for the formation of a clan is interaction among members, which facilitates unification of the worldview rather than disjointed idiosyncratic opinions.

KINDS OF CORPORATE CULTURE

Scholars have differentiated between different kinds of corporate culture and have advocated using these distinctions to analyze organizations. Buono, Bowditch, and Lewis (1985) distinguished between *subjective* and *objective* cultures in organizations. They saw subjective culture as a "shared pattern of beliefs, assumptions, and expectations held by organizational members and the group's characteristic way of perceiving the organization's environment and its norms" (p. 480). Objective culture, the authors posited, consists of organizational artifacts such as physical settings, office decor, and executive privileges. The authors contended that the discerning eye could draw many inferences merely by observing an organization's objective artifacts.

Martin and Siehl (1983) viewed organizational culture as a complex and multifaceted phenomenon comprising *subcultures* and *countercultures,* expounding the notion that the same organizations may have more than one culture, often in the form of one dominant culture and many subcultures.

According to the authors, the dominant culture consists of core values shared by a majority of the organization's members. In addition, the authors contrived at least three types of subcultures: *enhancing, orthogonal,* and *countercultural.* They believed that enhancing subcultures exist in an "organizational enclave" advocating loyalty to the core values or the dominant culture of the organization. The orthogonal subculture embodies members who, while being deferent to the core values, also nurture a separate unconflicting value system unique to their subgroup. Finally, counterculture, as the name suggests, runs converse to some or all significant values of the dominant culture. The authors referred to the simultaneous existence of organizational culture and counterculture as an "uneasy symbiosis." Countercultures are most likely to arise in a distinctly centralized organization that has permitted significant decentralization in a few of its segments, which are generally characterized by a structural boundary and a charismatic leader. It is important to note here that countercultures need not always be counterproductive. In countercultures, Martin and Siehl saw "some useful functions for the dominant culture, such as articulating the foundations between appropriate and inappropriate behavior and providing a safe haven for the development of innovative ideas" (p. 52).

Although the concept of a distinctive organizational subculture within a larger societal culture prevails in most current literature on organizational culture, differences in opinion are neither absent nor muted. Wilkins and Ouchi (1983) observed that the cultures of some organizations are considerably less unique than others. These authors also argued that because the communities that anthropologists study differ profoundly from organizational settings, the two should not be seen as being analogous. We have termed the culture of different societies as *societal culture.* Wilkins and Ouchi argued that societal culture is acquired gradually through intimate contact, a situation not easily replicated in most organizations.

Schein (1984) took a view similar to that of Wilkins and Ouchi (1983) when he asserted that the "strength" of culture in an organization is dependent on the "homogeneity and stability" of group membership and the "length and intensity" of shared experiences of the group (p. 7). We are of the opinion that societal culture does have an impact on organizational culture but the two are not always parallel. Therefore, corporate culture and societal culture have been linked to public relations in two separate chapters in this book.

HOW IMPORTANT IS ORGANIZATIONAL CULTURE?

Achieving organizational effectiveness is the ultimate aim of any aspiring manager (see Sathe, 1983, for a brief distinction between efficiency and effectiveness). Organizational theorists have proposed many methods that help managers fulfill this objective. Scientific management, stakeholder management (Freeman, 1984), organizational structure (Mintzberg, 1979; Robbins, 1983, 1987), and corporate strategy are some of the perspectives that scholars have suggested. Although at various times these propositions looked sound, managers soon found them to be inadequate and looked beyond strategy for their success. Organizational culture perhaps may be the most intricate and elusive, yet most pervasive influence on organizational effectiveness (Tichy, 1982, p. 62). According to Smircich (1983), understanding and managing corporate culture may be a key to managing an effective organization.

Just as culture is the central factor that influences the way people in a society behave, cultures specific to an organization seem to evolve over time and influence the way in which individuals in the organization interact and react to the challenges posed by the environment. This makes it vital for practitioners to understand their organizational culture. Deal and Kennedy (1982) underscored the importance of comprehending organizational culture by affirming that corporations have "values and beliefs to pass along—not just products. They have stories to tell—not just profits to make" (p. 15). They argued that organizations with strong cultures have precedents that employees use as referents when they act in a given situation or attempt to solve problems. In weak cultures that do not record organizational precedents, time is wasted in determining appropriate responses to challenges, thus drastically reducing efficiency. In a study of several corporations, Deal and Kennedy found that employees of organizations with stronger cultures feel secure about what they are doing and therefore, try harder to do it.

Tichy (1982) stressed the significance of corporate culture metaphorically. He used the analogy of a rope to do this, referring to an organization as "the strategic rope" with three intertwined strands. The three strands of this rope correspond to three key elements (environments) of an organization—technical, political, and cultural. Tichy contended that just as the individual strands of a rope are not discernible from a distance, a casual observer is most likely to miss the tenuous distinctions among the three corresponding components of organizations. And, just as each major strand in a rope is made up of many substrands, each organizational environment has many subsystems (subcultures). The author argued that just as the separation of strands weakens a rope, so also an organization with clashing subcultures becomes highly vulnerable. Strategic managers should aim to maintain harmony among the three subcultures in order to prevent threats from a turbulent environment. Therefore, the author argued, it is important to know and understand corporate culture.

Schein (1985) listed three reasons for studying culture in organizations.

First, organizational culture is highly "visible" and "feelable." It is real and has an impact on a society, occupation, or organization. Second, by understanding culture one can evaluate organizational performance and gain knowledge of how people in it behave and perceive the organization. Finally, knowing the nature and dimensions of the concept facilitates the formulation of a "common frame of reference," which is vital for analyzing the notion. The author contended that the concept of organizational culture often has been misinterpreted because of attempts to equate it with such terms as "climate," "philosophy," "ideology," "style," or "how people are managed" (p. 24). These meanings, according to the author, are not the essence of the term culture. He argued that the term corporate culture "should be reserved for the deeper level of basic assumptions and beliefs that are shared by members of an organization, that operate unconsciously, and that define in a basic 'taken-for-granted' fashion an organization's view of itself and its environment" (p. 6).

Koprowski (1983) viewed the "myths" of culture as clues to effective management. He saw a need to evaluate corporate culture because of what he called the three contemporary management challenges: the changing role of women in the work force, the attribution of Japanese success to their management philosophy, and the manager's role as a hero. As social entities, organizations are held together by what Tichy (1982) called a "normative glue" typified by the sharing of certain important beliefs by organizational members. Consequently, organizations must analyze and determine what norms and values members should share and, more critically, what groups within the organizational system should share which values.

In his analysis of why culture has so much influence on organizational life, Sathe (1983) asserted that culture is an asset that begets efficiency when shared beliefs facilitate and economize communications and shared values induce higher levels of participation and dedication. It becomes a liability, however, when these beliefs are not consonant with the needs of the organization, its members, and its constituencies. In attempting to study the impact of culture on behavior, Sathe examined five basic organizational processes: communication, cooperation, commitment, decision making, and implementation. He concluded that a better understanding of organizational culture is key to the understanding and proper handling of managerial situations.

Because culture constrains strategy, a company must analyze its culture and learn to manage within its boundaries or, if necessary, change it (Peters & Waterman, 1982; Schwartz & Davis, 1981). Jelinek et al. (1983) perceived an evolution in organizational analysis toward "more complex, paradoxical, and even contradictory modes of understanding" (p. 331). The authors argued that we need to understand the multidimensional nature of organizations—the macro and the micro, organizational and individual, conservative and dynamic—leading us to perceive the "machine-like, organism-like, and culture-like aspects" (p. 331) of organizations. They believed that key elements as yet unidentified possibly could exist in organizations and determine their function. Thus, although different scholars have used different terminologies and different approaches, they are united in the importance they attach to the significant impact that corporate culture has on organizational processes.

WHEN IS CORPORATE CULTURE MOST APPARENT?

Studies have also alluded to the specific instances when corporate culture becomes apparent. Wilkins (1983) listed three periods when organizational culture becomes most apparent: when employees change roles after a transfer or promotion, when subcultures conflict or assign stereotypical characteristics to one another, and when the dominant coalition makes and executes key decisions about company direction and style. When new employees are infused into an organization (a role change for them), they are very receptive to learning the ropes of the organization. In addition to trying to understand what is expected of them, employees are keen to know factors such as what the potential rewards are for excelling in their work, the potential for rising in organizational hierarchy, and discipline procedures. Acculturated employees, on the other hand, respond to new employees in a variety of ways, Wilkins posited. Some tell stories and offer advice on "proper" behavior, whereas others may ridicule, lecture, or shun these new entrants. Wilkins cautioned researchers to be wary about the "organization's official pronouncements to newcomers," which are usually idealistic. New employees, the authors noted, learn more by listening to the stories they hear and the experiences they encounter. An organization's corporate culture, then, is very discernible when new employees are induced into it.

We have alluded to the work of Martin and Siehl (1983), who contended that organizations frequently have subcultures and countercultures and that countercultures sometimes can be helpful. Wilkins (1983) extended the notion of subcultures into determining an organization's culture when he suggested that a second occasion when an organization's culture becomes most apparent is when subcultures collide:

> The conflict between cultures provides a clear picture of the dominant subculture (A) because subculture B adherents are much more aware of differences than are those of subculture A. As a minority group, they feel as if they are sort of mutual protection society that must assert its differences

with the majority clearly and defend its members from being overwhelmed. Further, each group seems to characterize the other as representing the dark side of its own most cherished values . . . Thus one group's descriptions of the other and their conflicts can produce rich information about the culture and its subcultures. (p. 35)

Wilkins (1983) identified the behavior of top management as the third indicator of an organization's culture. Because these senior decision makers control such desired rewards as promotions, budget allocations, and work assignments, they are in a position to espouse their value systems on the employees, at least within the confines of the organization. Specifically, the author identified two ways by which top management could assert its assumption on the organization: (a) through their personal behavior, seen in actions such as what they say, who they reward, and what kinds of actions they encourage, and (b) through the formal systems they create such as incentives, reporting mechanisms, and evaluation programs. Wilkins suggested a "culture audit" as a tool for understanding and managing organizations.

Buono et al. (1985) emphasized that corporate culture plays a critical role when organizations merge. Based on a study of culture before and after the merger of two mutual savings banks, the authors argued that in addition to differences in organizational culture that exist between industries, organizations develop distinct cultures even within the same industry. They studied the perplexity of the employees not only before and during the merger, but also its accentuation after the merger when the new entity sought to establish its own culture. They further studied the two medium-size savings banks before and after merger also to understand the influence of organizational culture on aspects such as job satisfaction, individual behavior, and the process underlying organizational mergers. Their study concluded that although culture change and adaptation during mergers is difficult and often resisted, employees eventually will support the change if they can understand the need for it (p. 497). The authors argued that the onus is on managers to facilitate this understanding aimed at garnering employee support.

MANAGING CULTURE

What happens when an organization with a weak culture decides to have the strong corporate culture that Deal and Kennedy (1982) recommended? Can managers tailor corporate culture at will? Summing up the two schools of thought that hold quite contradictory beliefs in the matter, Martin, Sitkin, and Boehm (1985) observed that cultural "pragmatists" answer "yes" whereas "purists" find it asinine to talk of changing or managing culture. The pragmatists view culture as a key to productivity and profitability and argue that culture in organizations can be molded to suit goals. On the contrary, the purists find it unethical to view the concept in terms of dollars and cents and believe the phenomenon cannot be managed. For purists culture develops, not with the conscious effort of a CEO or the dominant coalition, but by the majority of members in an organization. Martin et al. further contended that the goals of the CEO or the dominant coalition often are incongruent with those on lower rungs of the hierarchical ladder.

The literature seems to reveal that scholars can be placed on a wide spectrum ranging from Martin et al.'s (1985) pragmatists (like Deal & Kennedy, 1982; Lundberg, 1985; Ouchi, 1981; Peters & Waterman, 1982; Tichy, 1982) to her purists (like Gregory, 1983; Martin et al., 1985) although the former seem to outnumber the latter. Their inclination to either ideology seems to be determined by how they conceptualize culture — as an epitomy of deeply rooted unconscious beliefs or a manifestation of more trite characteristics such as reward structures or dress codes (Martin et al., 1985). Purists (like Gregory, 1983) argue that it is not the founder alone who creates a culture in an organization; members at various levels contribute equally toward the formation of institutional subcultures. Although we agree with purists on the creation of cultures, like the pragmatists we feel that cultures can be changed and molded to suit organizational goals.

Ouchi (1981) was convinced that organizational culture could be managed strategically. His extensive study of American corporations led him to believe that American organizations are prone to have "authoritarian" cultures where decisions are made at the top of the organizational hierarchy. He called these Type A organizations. His study of similar companies in Japan revealed that Japanese organizations practice consensual participation getting input from all levels of the organizational hierarchy leading to internal democratization. He called organizations with these cultures Type J institutions. He prescribed worker participation as a principal key to organizational success and developed a step-by-step formula for turning Type A organizations to Type Z (American corporations with Type J characteristics).

Siehl (1985) analyzed how the corporate culture of an organization changes when its founder resigns and is replaced by a new CEO who has a value system quite different from that of the values of the outgoing CEO. She found that her analysis did not explain, with any degree of certainty, whether culture could be managed. Her study did suggest, however, that during the time of transition, the expression of cultural values possibly could be managed (p. 139). Although some scholars view managing culture and changing culture as diverse phenomena, she viewed them synonymously.

Deal and Kennedy (1982) also can be categorized as Martin et al.'s (1985) pragmatists as they believed that corporate culture can be changed. Noting that even strong cultures may sometimes find themselves in "poor alignment" with a changing environment, they listed situations in which managers should consider managing culture. First, managers must contemplate seriously management of culture when an industry with traditional values (e.g., the American car industry) finds itself in an environment that is undergoing fundamental changes.

Lundberg (1985) took a similar view positing that "external enabling conditions" make culture change either easy or difficult (p. 176). Second, managers must consider strategies for cultural change when their industry is highly competitive and the environment changes quickly. They argued that companies that build cultures capable of responding to changes in customer needs will be highly successful. They asserted that "building a responsive and adaptive culture may be the only way to institutionalize a real capability to adapt" (p. 160). Lundberg's third situation warranting culture management has to do with self-assessment of corporate performance. He said that when the company is "mediocre or worse" and going downhill, managers must seek solutions through management of culture.

Deal and Kennedy (1982) did not advocate management of culture only during times of poor organizational performance. Their fourth and fifth situations in which managers should contemplate management of culture seriously are: when a corporation is on the verge of expansion and when a company finds itself growing rapidly. On a similar note, Tunstall (1983) advocated managing cultural change during the divestiture of a large corporation. Viewing the process as a metamorphosis, he observed that "changing the corporate culture is the most difficult task facing management" (p. 25).

COMMUNICATION AND ORGANIZATIONAL CULTURE

As a prelude to conceptualizing a link between public relations and organizational culture, we find it relevant to link organizational culture with communication. Many scholars have taken a communication perspective to organizational culture (Bormann, 1985; Broms & Gahmberg, 1983; Edelstein, 1983; Packanowsky & O'Donnell-Trujillo, 1983; Schall, 1983). Packanowsky and O'Donnell-Trujillo (1983) viewed organizational communication as a cultural performance. They viewed organizations as theaters in which the same member performs various roles based on the situation, his or her status, and responsibilities. For example, the CEO treats the secretary as well as the general manager politely but both players know their places in the stratified relationship. The authors observed that although the notion of organizations as theaters implies a parting of ways from the established practice of viewing them as machines or organisms, it also suggests that organizational communication is "situationally relative and variable." They further contended that organizational performances were dialogues staged by multiple actors and organizational communication is a cultural performance that leads to ritual, sociality, politics, and passion. They equated their analysis of organizational culture to the way an anthropologist studies "folk tales and ritual practices of a culture" (p. 122). They preferred to view culture as a process rather than an artifact.

Bormann (1985) took a similar view defining communication as "the human social processes by which people create, raise, and sustain group consciousness" (p. 100). He saw public consciousness as a significant constituent in the culture of a group or organization. In the communicative framework, he added, culture is "the sum total ways of living, organizing, and communing built up in a group of human beings and transmitted to newcomers by means of verbal and nonverbal communication" (p. 100). He saw communication as an inevitable cause of the development of organizational culture and noted that without components like stories, rites, rituals, artifacts, and technology, culture cannot develop in the organizational context. Schall (1983) viewed cultures as "being created, sustained, transmitted and changed through social interaction—through modelling and imitation, instruction, correction, negotiation, story-telling, gossip, remediation, confrontation, and observation" all of which are based on communication (p. 560).

Broms and Gahmberg (1983) defined two modes of communication that differentiated between cultural groups. They identified the first as the traditional sender–receiver technique that is outwardly directed and adds quantitatively to a person's level of information and knowledge. The second mode, *autocommunication,* is the phenomenon through which one repeatedly communicates inwardly to oneself. Often autocommunication does not add to knowledge or information but serves the important function of enhancing the ego. Such internal communication as writing a diary or reading a religious text helps the communicator clarify thoughts by self-cuing. Even communication that is directed to external recipients (a memo, e.g.) facilitates autocommunication as the sender also is cuing internally when he or she writes the memo. The authors recalled Lotman's reference to these two forms of communication as representing two divergent cultures—Eastern and Western.

CORPORATE CULTURE AND PUBLIC RELATIONS

At the beginning of this chapter, we discussed the relationship between culture and public relations that was articulated in Fig. 1.1 of chapter 1 — a positive, descriptive theory of how the power holders in an organization choose a model of public relations. Now we can return to that model to see how the literature on organizational culture supports that conceptualization.

Although there are many definitions and descriptions of culture in the literature, we found something of a consensus that organizational culture consists of the sum total of shared values, symbols, meanings, beliefs, assumptions, and expectations that organize and integrate a group of people who work together. As such, corporate culture essentially consists of the set of presuppositions that make up a worldview — as it was defined in chapter 2 on assumptions about public relations — and the products of that worldview such as values, stories, myths, artifacts, or rituals.

Chapter 2 argued that presuppositions strongly influence the way an individual or an organization defines public relations, what organizational members expect to be its effect, and what they believe to be its social purpose. In the model in Fig. 1.1, the presuppositions of a culture influence the choice of a model of public relations directly or indirectly by influencing the organization's schema for public relations or by affecting the people or types of people who come to power in an organization.

The link from the environment to culture in Fig. 1.1 shows that culture external to an organization (societal culture) can impose a paradigm or a worldview upon the organization. A national, regional, or local culture can affect an organization directly because employees are enculturated outside the organization as well as inside.

External culture also affects the environmental interdependencies of an organization. On a continuum, external culture may vary from an open, pluralistic, or democratic system to a closed, authoritarian, or autocratic one. Organizational culture need not be consonant with a society's culture but it cannot help but be affected by it. Thus, as mentioned at the beginning of this chapter, chapter 22 explores the differences in public relations across external cultures and the implications for a normative theory of cross-cultural public relations for multinational or other organizations dispersed geographically.

Chapter 2 argued that worldviews about public relations range on a continuum from asymmetrical to symmetrical and that these worldviews of public relations covary with broader presuppositions that we now see to be essentially cultural presuppositions — ranging from pluralistic to authoritarian. Research on organizations, likewise, has been filled with theories of centralized versus decentralized structures and authoritarian and segmented versus integrated and participatory management styles and organizational climates — essentially the same continuum that is found in the cultures of larger societies.

Several theorists have constructed typologies of organizational cultures that approximate the continuum from participatory to authoritarian (e.g., Ernest, 1985; Kanter, 1983; Schein, 1985; Wallach, 1983). Thus, when we take a broad view both of public relations and culture, we cannot escape the conclusion that presuppositions about public relations are embedded in broader presuppositions of both organizational culture and external culture:

Proposition 1: The presuppositions about public relations in an organization will reflect that organization's internal and external culture.

Thus, a public relations manager or external counselor would have an extremely difficult job implementing a normative theory of how public relations should be practiced in order to contribute most to the effectiveness of an organization when the way public relations is being practiced cannot be changed without changing organizational culture.

That conclusion takes us to the literature on the management of cultural change. If we take the purist view, that organizations are cultures that are the product of everyone in the organization over a long period of time, we would have to conclude that changing a culture and its presuppositions about public relations will be extremely difficult if not impossible. Although we reject the absolutism of this view, we do acknowledge the difficulty of changing public relations that it articulates.

The pragmatic view, in contrast, has identified the strategic opportunities that open a window for changes in culture and in presuppositions about public relations: when a founder passes from the scene, when an organization's culture is misaligned with its environment, when the environment changes, when the organization performs poorly, or when the organization expands, grows rapidly, or is divested. The public relations manager, therefore, who wants to gain power in the organization or who is waiting for a strategic opportunity to suggest a new, more effective model of public relations should be aware of these windows of opportunity to make a political move in the organization or to suggest changes in public relations policy.

Our second presupposition, then, is:

Proposition 2: Public relations managers will be most likely to change the model of public relations practiced in an organization when organizational culture is changing.

The literature we have reviewed also suggests the crucial role that internal communication plays in the development, continuation, and revision of organizational culture. As the model in Fig. 1.1 shows, internal public relations can affect culture and a communication manager charged with developing an internal communication system to bring about a change in culture or a communication system for a new culture must be aware of the close relationship between communication and culture. That relationship is explored in more depth in Chapter 20 on internal communication.

Finally, the literature on subcultures and countercultures in organizations offers two intriguing ideas for practicing and understanding public relations. First, countercultures create conflicts in organizations, conflicts that require internal communication to manage. Thus, identifying countercultures with cultural audits should be an important component of internal communication audits.

Second, public relations departments may develop their own countercultures, especially when a public relations manager is not part of the dominant coalition. If that is the case, we must ask how the public relations counterculture can maintain itself while waiting for an opportunity to make changes in the dominant culture. We hypothesize that education in public relations and its subsequent effect on professionalism holds the answer (see chapter 14 on education in public relations) and propose a final proposition:

Proposition 3: A public relations department that is high in potential (because of managerial roles, education in public relations, and professionalism) will develop a counterculture when the organization's culture and worldview for public relations do not reflect the presuppositions and worldview for public relations of the department.

REFERENCES

Barley, S. R. (1983). Semiotics and the study of occupational and organizational cultures. *Administrative Science Quarterly, 28,* 393–413.

Bormann, E. G. (1985). Symbolic convergence: Organizational communication and culture. In L. L. Putnam & M. E. Pacanowsky (Eds.), *Communication and organizations: An interpretive approach* (pp. 99–122). Beverly Hills, CA: Sage.

Broms, H., & Gahmberg, H. (1983). Communication to self in organizations and cultures. *Administrative Science Quarterly, 28,* 482–495.

Buono, A. F., Bowditch, J. L., & Lewis, J. W. (1985). When cultures collide: The anatomy of a merger. *Human Relations, 38* (5), 477–500.

Burns, T., & Stalker, G. M. (1961). *The management of innovation.* London: Tavistock.

Child, J., & Tayeb, M. (1983). Theoretical perspectives in cross-national organizational research. *International Studies of Management & Organization, 12*(4), 23–70.

Deal, T. E., & Kennedy, A. E. (1982). *Corporate culture: The rites and rituals of corporate life.* Reading, MA: Addison-Wesley.

Dozier, D. M. (1986, August). *The environmental scanning function of public relations practitioners and participation in management decision making.* Paper presented at the meeting of the Public Relations Division, Association for Education in Journalism and Mass Communication Annual Convention, University of Oklahoma, Norman.

Edelstein, A. S. (1983). Communication and culture: The value of comparative studies. *Journal of Communication, 33*(3), 302–310.

Ernest, R. C. (1985). Corporate cultures and effective planning. *Personnel Administrator, 30,* 49–60.

Freeman, R. E. (1984). *Strategic management.* Boston: Pitman.

Gregory, K. L. (1983). Native-view paradigms: Multiple cultures and culture conflicts in organizations. *Administrative Science Quarterly, 28,* 359–376.

Hofstede, G. (1980). *Culture's consequences.* Beverly Hills, CA: Sage.

Jelinek, M., Smircich, L., & Hirsch, P. (1983). Introduction: A code of many colors. *Administrative Science Quarterly, 28,* 331–338.

Kanter, R. M. (1983). *The change master: Innovation and entrepreneurship in the American corporation.* New York: Simon & Schuster.

Kluckhohn, C. (1951). The study of culture. In D. Lerner & H. Lasswell (Eds.), *The policy sciences: Recent developments in scope and method* (pp. 86–101). Stanford, CA: Stanford University Press.

Koprowski, E. J. (1983, Autumn). Cultural myths: Clues to effective management. *Organizational Dynamics,* 39–51.

Kroeber, A. L., & Kluckhohn, C. (1952). Culture, a critical review of concepts and definition. *Papers of the Peabody Museum of American Archaeology and Ethnology* (Vol. 47, No. 1). Cambridge, MA: Harvard University.

Lawrence, P., & Lorsch, J. W. (1967). *Organization and environment: Managing differentiation and integration.* Boston: Harvard Business School Press.

Lundberg, C. C. (1985). On the feasibility of cultural intervention in organizations. In P. J. Frost, L. F. Moore, M. R. Louis, C. C. Lundberg, & J. Martin (Eds.), *Organizational culture* (pp. 197–200). Beverly Hills, CA: Sage.

Martin, J., Feldman, M. S., Hatch, M. J., & Sitkin, S. B. (1983). The uniqueness paradox in organizational stories. *Administrative Science Quarterly, 28,* 438–453.

Martin, J., & Siehl, C. (1983, Autumn). Organizational culture and counterculture: An uneasy symbiosis. *Organizational Dynamics,* 52–63.

Martin, J., Sitkin, S. B., & Boehm, M. (1985). After the founder: An opportunity to manage culture. In P. J. Frost, L. F. Moore, M. R. Louis, C. C. Lundberg, & J. Martin (Eds.), *Organizational culture* (pp. 99–124). Beverly Hills, CA: Sage.

Mintzberg, H. (1979). *The structuring of organizations.* Englewood Cliffs, NJ: Prentice-Hall.

Mitroff, I. I. (1983). *Stakeholders of the organizational mind.* San Francisco: Jossey-Bass.

Ouchi, W. G. (1981). *Theory Z: How American business can meet the Japanese challenge.* Reading, MA: Addison-Wesley.

Pacanowsky, M. E., & O'Donnell-Trujillo, N. (1983). Organizational communication as organizational performance. *Communication Monographs, 50,* 126–147.

Pascale, R. T., & Athos, A. G. (1981). *The art of Japanese management.* New York: Simon & Schuster.

Peters, T. J., & Waterman, R. H., Jr. (1982). *In search of excellence.* New York: Harper & Row.

Robbins, S. (1983). *Organization theory: The structure & design of organizations.* Englewood Cliffs, NJ: Prentice-Hall.

Robbins, S. P. (1987). *Organization theory: Structure, design, and applications.* Englewood Cliffs, NJ: Prentice-Hall.

Rohner, R. P. (1984). Conception of culture. *Journal of Cross-Cultural Psychology, 15*(1), 111–137.

Sathe, V. (1983, Autumn). Implications of corporate culture: A manager's guide to action. *Organizational Dynamics,* 5-23.

Schall, M. S. (1983). A communication-rules approach to organizational culture. *Administrative Science Quarterly, 28,* 557-581.

Schein, E. H. (1984). Coming to a new awareness of organizational culture. *Sloan Management Review, 25,* 3-16.

Schein, E. H. (1985). *Organizational culture and leadership.* San Francisco, CA: Jossey-Bass.

Schwartz, H. M., & Davis, S. M. (1981). Matching corporate culture and business strategy. *Organizational Dynamics,* Summer, 30-48.

Siehl, C. (1985). After the founder: An opportunity to manage culture. In P. J. Frost, L. F. Moore, M. R. Louis, C. C. Lundberg, & J. M. Martin (Eds.), *Organizational culture* (pp. 125-140). Beverly Hills, CA: Sage.

Smircich, L. (1983). Concepts of culture and organizational analysis. *Administrative Science Quarterly, 28,* 339-358.

Smircich, L., & Calas, M. B. (1987). Organizational culture. In F. M. Jablin, L. L. Putnam, K. H. Roberts, & L. W. Porter (Eds.), *Handbook of organizational communication* (pp. 228-263). Newbury Park, CA: Sage.

Tichy, N. M. (1982). Managing change strategically: The technical, political, and cultural keys. *Organizational Dynamics, 11*(2), 59-80.

Tunstall, W. B. (1983). Cultural transition at AT&T. *Sloan Management Review, 25*(1), 15-26.

Tylor, E. B. (1871). *Primitive culture.* London: Murray.

Wallach, E. J. (1983). Individuals and organizations: The cultural match. *Training and Development Journal, 37*(2), 29-36.

Wilkins, A. L. (1983). The culture audit: A tool for understanding organizations. *Organizational Dynamics, 12*(2), 24-38.

Wilkins, A. L., & Ouchi, W. G. (1983). Efficient cultures: Exploring the relationship between culture and organizational performance. *Administrative Science Quarterly, 28,* 468-481.

22

Societal Culture and Public Relations

K. Sriramesh
Purdue University

Jon White
Management Consultant,
Bedford, United Kingdom

ABSTRACT

Just as the communication system of an organization does not exist in isolation from its culture, so organizational culture does not exist apart from the culture of the society in which it is found. Chapter 9 identified a "collaborative societal culture" as a characteristic of an excellent organization. This chapter pursues the question of the extent to which societal culture ultimately determines the nature of public relations in an organization. The cultural framework makes it possible to expand our general theory of public relations to other cultures, to explain how public relations might be practiced differently as culture changes. It closes by proposing that public relations could be excellent in spite of authoritarian societal cultures if the dominant coalition of the organization develops a participative organizational culture with a symmetrical system of communication and public relations.

One unifying theme highlighted by contributors to this volume is that the theory of public relations conceptualized in this book is still evolving. In the opening chapter, J. Grunig stated that in building this theory, relevant concepts and theories have been borrowed from various disciplines and an attempt has been made to link them logically with the existing body of public relations knowledge. This chapter continues this borrowing process by attempting to identify the relevance of the culture concept to public relations activities. In addition to urging greater sensitivity to the fact that our world is a cultural kaleidoscope, we argue that the cultural differences among societies must affect the way public relations is practiced by peoples of different societies.

Public relations theorizing had been virtually nonexistent until over a decade ago because it has been, and continues to be, regarded as a profession where technicians do the same image-building chores. Most of the theorizing that has been attempted thus far has been done in the United States. This is probably because public relations activity is widely regarded as a quintessentially American invention. Carlson (1968), writing in the *International Encyclopedia of the Social Sciences,* suggested that public relations is a child of 20th-century United States. He contended that public relations is an outgrowth of the respected democratic belief that facts and issues that influence public policy should be available to all sections of the population in a society. The author also saw public relations at its most developed state in the private industrial sector in the United States.

Tedlow (1979) also viewed public relations as an outgrowth of U.S. political and commercial developments. He saw the United States as a land where salesmanship permeated all sections and levels of the society. The author contended that public relations was one pillar of American salesmanship. He believed that public relations has broad cultural implications and that its practice was initiated primarily as a political device. Tedlow viewed corporate public relations as a method of protection against the political consequences of hostile public opinion. At the same time, he saw public relations as an indication of the health of American democracy because it is built on a faith in the power of communication, and of discussion of issues, rather than on violent confrontation.

Pimlott (1951), who visited the United States in the late 1940s to study U.S. public relations practice, saw the dominant social and political role it played in U.S. society. He perceived public relations as one of the weapons used by businesses in meeting the challenge to the survival of capitalism, and as a means by which U.S. society adjusts to changing circumstances.

Introductory textbooks such as Wilcox, Ault, and Agee (1989) echo the sentiments of these authors, agreeing that public relations is a U.S. phenomenon. The authors also alluded to the fact that American techniques have been adapted to national and regional practices throughout the world, including many totalitarian nations. J. Grunig and Hunt (1984) charted the history of public relations in the United States and identified various practitioners who used different techniques (models) of public relations.

Consequently, the belief that most other nations replicate the public relations techniques from the United States continues to be popular. This also might seem logical given the fact that most managers and executives from almost all nations are trained predominantly in the United States or the United Kingdom. Therefore, they carry back similar management philosophies to their native countries. Others not making these "pilgrimages" are acculturated into the management creed of the West through textbooks published there. Although making assumptions that Western public relations practices are copied in other parts of the world may seem logical, these assumptions become mere speculations if they are not substantiated by empirical data emanating from comparative research in this area. The move to make western Europe a single market in 1992 is raising doubts about the appropriateness of U.S. models for training the European manager of the future. Therefore, we see a need for studies that should seek not only to identify the public relations practices of organizations in different nations (cultures) but also to identify whether the theories conceptualized in the United States adequately explain these practices.

Public relations scholars should seek answers to questions such as what kinds of problems do managers in other cultures face when they attempt to replicate the techniques practiced in the West? Are they forced to make changes to suit the sociocultural environments of their organizations, say, by dropping some techniques and only concentrating on a few? Most important, academicians should question whether Western theories are comprehensive enough to explain public relations activities around the world. It behooves scholars to highlight not only the inconsistencies of Western theories and techniques but also to assess the applicability or limitations of these theories in cross-cultural settings. Having thus stressed the need for greater sensitivity to cross-cultural issues in public relations, we attempt to conceptually link societal culture with public relations by reviewing literature in the areas of cultural anthropology and organizational dynamics.

In addition to its youth as a body of knowledge, most public relations theorizing has taken place only in the United States, although some commentary has originated in countries such as the United Kingdom and Canada. Public relations writings are also available in French, German, Spanish, and other languages but have not been extensively translated. The European public relations association, CERP, only now is beginning to gather European literature on public relations practice. Almost all the empirical evidence for the elements of the theory conceptualized in this book is based on the work of scholars who have analyzed only U.S. organizations. To achieve credence as elements of a good theory, these concepts must be comprehensive as abstractions of reality in different organizational environments. That is, they should be tested in different cultural environments.

When Schneider's (aka L. Grunig, 1985) study of 48 organizations failed to find a strong link between J. Grunig's models of public relations and environmental variables (such as scale and complexity) and organizational structural variables (based on the Hage–Hull typology propounded by Hage & Hull, 1981), she concluded that J. Grunig's models of public relations (explaining different techniques employed by organizations) are normative theories vis-a-vis their relationship with the environment. After reviewing

L. Grunig's work and 13 other studies, J. Grunig and L. Grunig (1989) concluded that culture could be a key determinant of the public relations activity of organizations. Our effort as part of the *Excellence Project* is breaking fresh ground by attempting to cross at least some national and cultural boundaries and evaluating public relations practices in the United States and two other countries (the United Kingdom and Canada). Therefore, this chapter reviews literature to support the main thesis that societal culture can play a significant role in the way organizations in different societies practice public relations.

Following the pattern that Smircich (1983, p. 342ff) explained, we see a distinction between corporate culture and societal culture although it seems fair to assume that the latter has a great influence in the formation of the former. Smircich distinguished between organizational studies that viewed culture in different contexts. The first form of research Smircich posited sees culture as an independent variable mainly for comparative management studies. In these approaches, culture is almost synonymous with country imported into the organization through its employees (e.g., Hofstede, 1980; Tayeb, 1988). Scholars conducting these studies typically chart the similarities and differences among nations (societal cultures) and try to compare management practices cross-nationally (cross-culturally). Smircich noted that such studies would be especially helpful to multinational organizations, as evidenced by the popularity of *Theory Z* (Ouchi, 1981) and *The Art of Japanese Management* (Pascale & Athos, 1981). This chapter advocates the relevance of this first kind of comparison to the evolving theory of public relations.

A second linkage between culture and organizations that Smircich (1983) identified is the one conceived by those researchers who view culture as a variable internal to an organization. Referring to this internal culture as *corporate culture,* these scholars viewed organizations as culture-producing phenomena (e.g., Deal & Kennedy, 1982; Tichy, 1982). They agree that organizations exist in a wider cultural context (which we refer to as societal culture), but focus on the cultural artifacts that organizations produce such as legends and stories (Martin, Feldman, Hatch, & Sitkin, 1983; Wilkins, 1983), heroes, rites, and rituals (Deal & Kennedy, 1982), and shared assumptions and meanings (Schein, 1985). Chapter 21 reviewed studies belonging to this category and argued that corporate culture also determines the nature of public relations practiced by an organization.

The previous two perspectives linked the concepts of culture and organization by viewing organizations as organisms. Culture, for them, is something an organization has. The next three perspectives that Smircich (1983, p. 347) posited view culture not as a variable but as a "root metaphor"—as something an organization is. They each respectively take cognitive, symbolic, and structural perspectives of organizations. We contend in this chapter that although corporate culture (culture internal to an organization) is a factor that affects public relations, societal culture (external to an organization) is equally important because it has a significant impact on an organization's human resources as well as its corporate culture.

ARE ORGANIZATIONAL PROCESSES CULTURE-BOUND?

It is important to note that the idea that culture, both societal and corporate, has an impact on organizations is not accepted by all researchers. Smith and Tayeb (1988, pp. 154–156), drawing distinctions somewhat similar to those posited by Smircich (1983), identified two kinds of organizational researchers. The first category of *macroresearchers* study the organization as a whole unit and analyze formally prescribed structures such as departments and decision procedures (e.g., Hickson, Hinings, McMillan, & Schwitter, 1974; Hofstede, 1980; Pascale & Athos, 1981; Shenoy, 1981; Tayeb, 1988). The second category of *microresearchers,* Smith and Tayeb posited, study the work group of the organization — an organization's human resources. These researchers focus on the nature of superior–subordinate relationships through an analysis of leadership and participation (e.g. Misumi, 1985; Sinha, 1981).

Tayeb (1988) identified two opposing schools of thought: those proposing what she called a *culture-free* thesis and those advocating the *culture-specific* approach. Most macroresearchers have advocated the culture-free thesis, arguing that the link between organizational characteristics such as organizational structure and their contextual factors are stable across societies. Microresearchers, on the contrary, have leaned heavily in favor of a culture-specific approach. Smith and Tayeb (1988) observed that microresearchers may have favored the culture-specific approach "because a more microscopic focus upon the behavior of particular leaders within an organization makes it increasingly difficult to formulate measures that are truly culture-free" (pp. 161–162). The logic of the culture-free thesis was stated by Hickson et al. (1974):

> [Our] hypothesis rests on the theory that there are imperatives, or "causal" relationships, from the resources of "customers," of employees, of materials and finance etc., and of operating technology of an organization to its structure, which take effect whatever the surrounding social differences . . . Whether the culture is Asian or European or North American, a large organisation with many employees improves efficiency by specialising their

activities but also by increasing, controlling and coordinating specialities. (pp. 63–64)

Tayeb (1988) found conceptual and methodological flaws in studies adopting the culture-free approach. Drawing from Maurice (1976), she argued that proponents of this approach tried solely to "test the stability of relationships between organizational structure and its environmental variables, rather than to examine their underlying rationale" (p. 21). These studies looked only for similarities, Tayeb argued, and therefore found similarities. The author criticized the approach for totally ignoring the differences that are so vital to obtaining a total understanding of organizations.

Tayeb (1988) also attacked Haire, Ghiselli, and Porter (1966) for proposing a culture-free approach. Haire et al. implied that cultural differences do not affect managerial thinking when they stated that "being a manager is a way of life and . . . a French manager might be expected to be more similar to an Indian manager, say, than to a French non-manager" (p. 9). Tayeb contended that in making such inferences from their study, Haire et al. completely overlooked the fact that most of their respondents had been undergoing management training courses during the time they participated in the study. They were being exposed to similar Western management philosophies when they were asked to respond to the survey questionnaire, which may have caused them to give similar responses. Tayeb also pointed out that Haire et al. neither studied the structure of the organizations supervised by these managers, nor did they gather data on the perceptions of the subordinates of these managers on how the organization was being run, both of which are vital indicators of managerial practice. Tayeb observed: "To agree with statements favoring, say, a participative management style is one thing; actually to behave like a participative manager is another" (p. 21).

In her own comparative analysis of English and Indian organizations, Tayeb (1988) found that organizations in these diverse cultures responded identically to similar contextual demands but that, the "means" of arriving at these responses were significantly different. She found, for example, that although the structures of organizations in both these countries tended to be centralized, the processes that lay behind this similarity were different. In her English sample, she found a greater degree of consultation between senior managers and subordinates before a decision was made, a process she did not see in her Indian sample. She showed conclusively that these different means of achieving the same end could be explained by the cultural characteristics of the two samples. Her conclusions were consistent with an earlier study of organizations in Taiwan conducted by Negandhi (1973), which inferred that when size and market were held constant, there were significant differences between the structures of Taiwanese-owned, Japanese-owned, and American-owned firms.

In evaluating the work-related attitudes of organizational employees, most scholars have borrowed concepts from other disciplines. Hofstede (1980, p. 14) linked thought and behavior by using the term *mental programs* to explain how human beings try to predict one another's behavior. He stated that the closer the mental programs of two people are, the more accurately they can predict one another's behavior. Stating that every person's mental programs are partly unique and partly shared with fellow beings, Hofstede identified three levels of mental programs. At the *universal* level are elements of mental programming common to all human beings that are transferred genetically. At the *collective* level only people belonging to the same societal group share the same elements of mental programs. The *subjective* human culture (as opposed to the *objective* material cultural artifacts) identified by Triandis (1972, p. 4) belong in this level of mental programs. Subjective culture is most visible in cultural tendencies such as showing deference to elders or maintaining a certain distance from other people in social settings. At the third and most unique *individual* level of mental programs identified by Hofstede, no two people are alike in their thought and behavior. The second and third levels of mental programming, anthropologists agree, are transmitted societally through the process of *acculturation*.

Hofstede (1980) used the terms *values* and *culture* to describe *mental programs*. Whereas he saw values as attributes of individuals and collectivities, he saw culture as a property of collective human groups. He acknowledged that the term value has several connotations in the social sciences. Anthropologically, the term has come to mean the conventional codes of conduct of a social unit. Hofstede observed that values are non rational because they are imbued into individuals very early in their lives. This explains why what is perfectly normal behavior in one society may often be considered abnormal in another. Unless one is sensitized to the differences in the value systems of different cultures, there is a tendency to regard one's own values as being rational. Anthropologists belonging to the relativistic school have strongly criticized such ethnocentricity (Kaplan & Manners, 1972).

Hofstede (1980, p. 25) equated culture with human personality when he remarked that culture is to a human collectivity what personality is to an individual. Just as individuals have a distinct personality, human collectivities have a distinct culture. He noted that it is not just nations that have cultures; any collectivity of individuals that comes together for an extended period of time is likely to form its own cultural idiosyncrasies. Organizations fit very well into this scenario. In his evaluation of the work-related attitudes of employees of a multinational corporation (named HERMES to retain the anonymity of the corporation) in 39 countries, Hofstede found many cultural similarities and stark differences as well. It is important to ask, then, what factors influence the cultural idiosyncracies of a society?

DETERMINANTS OF CULTURE

We found answers to this question in what Kaplan and Manners (1972) called the *subsystems* of culture. Because of the nature of these subsystems and their definitive impact in shaping a society's culture, we prefer to refer to them as the *determinants* of culture. Kaplan and Manners argued that these determinants help explain a majority of the cultural traits of an individual. The authors called these determinants the "variables or aspects of institutionalized behavior that can be analytically isolated for purposes of explaining, at least in part, how a society both maintains itself and undergoes change" (p. 89). Anthropologists have used one or more of these determinants to explain cultural variations in societies.

Cultural materialists like Harris (1968, 1979) have viewed a society's culture from an economic perspective. The first cultural determinant that Kaplan and Manners (1972) identified, *technoeconomics,* has its underpinnings in cultural-materialism. The authors saw the first part of the term, techno, as the technical material, equipment, and knowledge available to a society, and the second part, economics, as the arrangements employed by a given society in applying its technical equipment and knowledge to the "production, distribution, and consumption of goods and services" (p. 93). Technology also can be viewed as the opportunities available to a society and economics as the way in which that opportunity is exploited to the benefit of the society. Kaplan and Manners speculated that Karl Marx may have had these two phenomena in mind when he distinguished between "means of production" and "mode of production."

The impact of a society's technical equipment on the rest of the cultural system is channeled through socioeconomic arrangements. Nimkoff and Middleton (1968) studied a sample of 549 cultures to underscore the impact of technoeconomic factors on a society's culture. They found that family types varied with technoeconomic arrangements. Hunting-and-gathering and industrial societies predominantly had conjugal, independent families whereas horticultural or agricultural societies tended to favor the joint or extended family. Hofstede (1980) coined the terms *individualism* and *collectivism* (to be reviewed presently) respectively to refer to these family patterns. Typically, an individual's personality is largely determined by the individual's experiences within the family.

After his ethnographic analysis of the Polynesian culture, Sahlins (1958) demonstrated that higher levels of productivity will generate increased levels of sociopolitical complexity. Sociopolitical complexity, another term for modernization, in turn affects the worldviews of individuals. Modernization is an ongoing phenomenon in most parts of the world and its components, industrialization and urbanization, have been known to cause qualitative and quantitative changes in peoples' lifestyles.

Williamson (1982) contended that "a study of attitudes — such as the extent of social interaction, sense of mobility, and secularism and related values . . . will reveal varying degrees of acceptance of modernism" (p. 232). Basically this is a move from *Gemeinschaft* (sacred) rules to *Gesels-chaft* (secular) norms. Williamson used rationality to measure modernism. He recorded the presence of low kinship orientation, preference for an urban rather than an agrarian lifestyle, belief in the mutability of "human nature," low stratification of life chances, universalistic norms for mobility, and related aspects of the urban-industrial value structure. In Williamson's study, although in general the difference between the developing and developed nations held, interestingly, the United States came out to be more traditionalistic than the author initially had hypothesized.

Social structure was the second cultural determinant identified by Kaplan and Manners (1972). The authors, highlighted the myriad definitions that scholars have attributed to this term. Kaplan and Manners noted that the noted British anthropologist Radcliffe-Brown defined social structure as "the continuing arrangement of persons in relationships defined or con-trolled by institutions." Other theorists have defined the concept differ-ently. Regardless of the differences in definitions, the social structural theory attempts to study how we can distinguish most usefully between the parts of a social system and the relationships among them. For example, factors such as the stipulation of societal roles or differences between egalitarian lineage and ranked lineage in a given society, are determined by that society's social structure. The significance of social structure is that one can observe social interactions and analyze them. In fact, some social-structural theorists have gone so far as to reject the culture concept calling it too broad and amorphous to serve as an analytic tool. They have tried to interpret a society's ideologies, technoeconomic state, and range of person-ality types based on aspects of role behavior and role relationships in a society's institutions such as the family, church, school, or factory. However, Kaplan and Manners (p. 102) observed that even socio-structural theorists ultimately have to make use of one of the other three "subsystems" to explain role behavior.

Referring to their third cultural determinant, *ideology,* as the "ideational realm" of culture, Kaplan and Manners (1972) found ideology to be representative of the values, norms, knowledge, themes, philosophies and religious principles, worldviews, and ethos held by people of a society. Human beings are basically conceptualizing and symbolizing animals. This implies that the same ideologies and symbols that humans use to order their social and natural environments will be utilized to set up, maintain, and change social and cultural structures. There is a great deal of disagreement among anthropologists concerning how much of a determinative role ideological factors play in the maintenance and change of culture. The debate on this issue is based mainly on the fact that the elements of a society's ideology are subjective in nature and hence involve a great deal of interpretation on the part of an ethnographer studying a culture.

Highlighting the methodological difficulties in analyzing ideology as a concept, Agar (1980) cited the case of two ethnographers (Lewis and Redfield) who visited the same village in Mexico but gave totally contradictory reports of the culture of the people of the village. The ideological domain of any culture is extremely difficult to decipher, let alone quantify. In most cases, the people of a culture themselves may not be able to verbalize some of their ideologies and worldviews. Ideological entities such as values, themes, and ethos are identified largely by the subjective perception of the ethnographer based on observed patterns of behaviors. With an increase in the extent of personal interpretation, there is a corresponding decrease in empirical controls. This is the biggest methodological problem that an anthropologist faces and one that theorists applying these concepts to organizational settings should be wary about.

Although it is beyond doubt that ideas affect human behavior, it is difficult to identify to what extent ideological components have causal effects on cultural behavior. This is because we often do not know to what extent individuals of a culture have learned or internalized the cultural worldviews prevalent in their society. Spiro (1966) listed five "levels" of ideological learning that may help explain the impact of ideological elements on a given culture:

1. Individuals learn cultural idiosyncracies through formal or informal instruction.
2. They also learn (understand) to use such ideological constructs in the appropriate social context.
3. They believe these constructs to be true and valid.
4. These constructs have some *cognitive salience*—individuals use them as guides in structuring their social and natural worlds.
5. In addition to cognitive salience, constructs also have been internalized by individuals so that, in addition to serving as guides, they initiate behavior.

The author inferred that even when we observe an ideological concept or set of concepts in action, we cannot determine correctly either the level of cognitive salience or the level to which ideological concepts have been internalized. Hence, attaching causal efficacy to ideological concepts like worldview, values, and norms is often difficult and controversial.

The fourth cultural determinant that Kaplan and Manners (1972) identified, *personality,* has its roots in the psychological state of individuals. The study of mental processes is not new to the field of anthropology. However, the popularity of Freudian psychology in the 1920s and 1930s gave an enormous impetus to anthropological theorizing about personality. American anthropologists (members of the "old school" of personality), in particular, began systematic studies of child-rearing practices in various cultures in accordance with the Freudian theory that held that human personality is greatly affected by these initial experiences in life. The child-rearing practices of a society, therefore, give rise to the personality traits (basic personality structure), which are shared by members of a society. These personality traits, anthropologists argued, have an impact on the primary or secondary institutions of a society. The family unit is the primary institution and establishments such as art, religion, mythology, or folklore are secondary institutions.

DIMENSIONS OF CULTURE

The concerted work of several scholars has yielded dimensions of culture that researchers can use to place a particular society on the cultural continuum (Crozier & Thoening, 1976; Hofstede, 1980; Kluckhohn & Strodtbeck, 1961; Tayeb, 1988). We can use these dimensions to chart out similarities and differences among societies. Studies by these and other scholars also have shown conclusively that cultural dimensions are reflected in management styles across different cultures (nations).

Hofstede's (1980) study is among the more popular works in this domain. From the data gathered in his HERMES study in 39 nations, Hofstede was able to factor out four principal dimensions of culture. The first cultural continuum, *individualism-collectivism,* has been recognized and studied by many theorists as a dimension affecting intergroup processes. Individualistic cultures stress individual goals and expect individuals to care for themselves and the immediate members of their family. Collectivist cultures, in contrast, stress group goals and individual good is superseded by the welfare of the community. In collectivist cultures, the community takes care of individuals in exchange for their loyalty to the group. One can hypothesize, then that workers in collective cultures may be more attached to the organization they work for.

Triandis et al. (1986) extended the individualism/collectivism dimension to the psychological level, which is similar to the personality dimension that Kaplan and Manners (1982) saw as a cultural subsystem. Triandis et al.

equated individualism with what they called *idiocentrism* and collectivism with *allocentrism*. In general they found that individuals with idiocentric qualities tend to be the traditional "Type A" people who perceive themselves as loners and emphasize achievement. Allocentrics, in contrast, rely on social support. Triandis et al's data also indicated that although a society may have one or the other characteristic predominantly, it is quite normal to find allocentrics in individualistic cultures and idiocentrists in collectivistic societies. Employees in collectivist societies have been shown to have a greater degree of emotional dependence on organizations. They expect the organization to assume responsibilities for them (Tayeb, 1988).

The second dimension that Hofstede (1980) identified based on his HERMES study is related conceptually to the organizational structural variables of centralization and stratification. *Power distance* indicates the extent to which power is distributed unequally among people belonging to different strata. In other words, power distance indicates to what extent a society is class oriented and has different value systems and expectations for members of different classes. In class-oriented cultures, power is concentrated in a few elite members. Organizations in such cultures have been shown to have tall, hierarchical structures and restricted upward communication.

Hofstede's (1980) third dimension, *uncertainty avoidance,* is more akin to the formalization or standardization that many organizational theorists have defined. It refers to a society's lack of tolerance for ambiguity, which leads to increased levels of anxiety. Anxiety leads to a greater need for formal rules and low tolerance for people with deviant views. Consequently, organizations existing in cultures with low tolerance for ambiguity emphasize greater formal codes of conduct to ensure uniformity among members and avoid risky and untested ideas.

Hofstede (1980) identified a fourth dimension, *masculinity/femininity,* as a measure of the nature of society's culture. Traditionally, almost all societies have assigned societal roles based on gender, identifying men as being assertive and women as being nurturant. This trend continues although the value systems of some Western societies are changing. Repeated studies have shown men to value advancement in job levels and earnings whereas women place greater importance on quality of life and relationships with people.

Tayeb (1988) studied a fifth dimension of culture, *interpersonal trust.* In her sample of employees in organizations in England, Tayeb found hostility and mistrust between managers and lower level workers. She attributed this to the class struggle in English society. Managers had a tendency to feel that they were members of the middle class that shared the ownership of these organizations whereas workers saw themselves as members of the working class who were being exploited by owners identified with the middle class (p.

136). This variance in the perception of roles often leads to mistrust between members of the two classes. Tayeb saw a similar class conflict in the sample of Indian organizations she studied, which was compounded further by caste differentiations. Tayeb also found a related sixth dimension, *commitment*. Managers in both countries felt more committed to their organizations than workers. She observed that commitment was directly proportional to the benefits employees got from the organization.

SOCIETAL CULTURE AND PUBLIC RELATIONS

Having thus reviewed the notion of culture, as well as some of its key determinants and dimensions, we now can link it conceptually to public relations. We are in strong agreement with the advocates of the culture-specific approach and contend that organizations are affected by culture. We draw a relationship between culture and public relations by first linking culture with communication. We argue that the linkages between culture and communication and culture and public relations are parallel because public relations is primarily a communication activity.

Many scholars have seen a link between the culture of a society and the nature of communication prevalent in it. Hall (1959) saw such a strong interconnection between the two concepts that he remarked that "culture is communication and communication is culture" (p. 191). Pacanowsky and O'Donnell-Trujillo (1983) saw culture as "the residue of the communication process" (p. 123). According to Spradley (1980), culture is "learned revised, maintained, and defined in the context of people interacting" (p. 6). The list of scholars who have found a definitive link between culture and communication is long. We contend that because a society's culture affects the pattern of communication among members of a society, it also should have a direct impact on the public relations practice of organizations because public relations is first and foremost a communication activity. J. Grunig and Hunt (1984) saw this relationship when they defined public relations as "the management of communication between an organization and its publics" (p. 8). As boundary spanners linking key publics with the organization, public relations practitioners primarily use communication techniques. Whether their purpose is to act as liaisons between the organizations and its internal publics such employees or its external stakeholders such as investors, consumers, and activist groups, public relations practitioners must use communication.

We also see a conceptual link between culture and public relations through the *presuppositions* (worldviews held by public relations practitioners) that J. Grunig (1989) identified (see chapter 3). He logically linked presuppositions to public relations practice. J. Grunig contended that practitioners who hold *asymmetrical* presuppositions see public relations as a tool used in a war among opposing social groups with the organization on one side and the public on the other. Organizational members holding asymmetrical presuppositions, J. Grunig (pp. 32–33) argued, feel that they know what is good for their stakeholders and therefore try to manipulate their audience to the viewpoint of the organization. He called this elitism. These members see organizations as closed systems and consequently try mostly to disseminate information out from the organization and not to assimilate any into it. This asymmetrical worldview, J. Grunig argued, also breeds "internal orientation" among organizational members preventing them from looking "into" the organization to assess it as outsiders see it. Smith and Tayeb (1988) have synthesized the same phenomenon as the *emic* (internal view) versus *etic* (view from the outside) dilemma. Practitioners with asymmetrical presuppositions are also more likely to have authoritarian tendencies, holding the view that power should be concentrated in the hands of a few top managers and that employees should have little autonomy because they do not have the necessary knowledge base to make independent decisions about how to perform their own jobs.

Going back to our review of the dimensions of culture, it is safe to hypothesize that societies with greater power distance in relationships also will tend to be more elitist and therefore harbor asymmetrical worldviews. Consequently, public relations practitioners operating in these societies will tend to practice the one-way press agentry model of public relations that J. Grunig identified in chapter 11. Managers in these cultures also may be more prone to viewing the organization as a closed system that should only disseminate information without assimilating any from its environment. The traditional cultures that Williamson (1982) alluded to also may be more prone to having another asymmetrical worldview, which J. Grunig called *conservatism.* Managers in these cultures see a need to maintain the status quo because they are in a privileged position. For them change is undesirable and any external pressures intended to change the organization should be considered subversive and hence resisted.

A lack of trust between managers and employees, a cultural dimension that Tayeb (1988) studied, can result in the asymmetrical presupposition of central authority that further leads to the centralization of power. Managers may be reluctant to delegate responsibility because of their inherent mistrust in the ability of subordinates to carry out their responsibilities effectively. This leads to high centralization as organizations begin to operate as autocracies. Several scholars have found that cultures in which tolerance for ambiguity is lower will tend to have more formal rules (e.g., Tayeb, 1988). Robbins (1987) argued that culture could be a substitute for organizational formalization. We hold a similar view and contend that in many societies, cultural codes such as deference to seniors may substitute for the need to lay strict codes of conduct regarding seniority in the organizational hierarchy.

J. Grunig (1989, pp. 37–40) listed an opposing set of worldviews and referred to them as *symmetrical* presuppositions. Practitioners with symmetrical presuppositions see organizations as open systems that can benefit from input of information from outside the organization. These managers are also more egalitarian in their approach to managing human resources because they believe that every employee, regardless of status in the organization, has the potential to make suggestions that can benefit the organization as a whole. Management in these organizations tends to be collective and as many decisions as possible are made by consensus or at least after due consultation. Such organizations also tend to resolve conflicts through negotiation.

In conclusion, we contend that public relations has been primarily a U.S. practice, tempered by some lessons from its practice in the "Anglo" countries such as the United Kingdom, Australia, and Canada. White's studies of practitioner groups in the United States, Canada, and the United Kingdom suggest few differences between these groups in terms of their preparation for the practice of public relations (White, 1987; White, Hammonds, & Kalupa, 1987; White & Trask, 1982).

However, we foresee an era in which public relations will undergo fundamental changes and become enriched as a profession. The growth of Asian nations like Japan and Korea as industrial powers, the recent political changes in Europe opening new markets, and the forthcoming formation of a single market in western Europe are all key developments that will affect the way public relations practitioners conduct their activities. To succeed in their effort to communicate to their publics in a global marketplace, public relations practitioners will have to sensitize themselves to the cultural heterogeneity of their audiences. In the process, they not only will be called upon to tailor their activities to the cultural idiosyncracies of their publics, but may also have to change certain techniques to suit different cultures. The result will be the growth of a culturally richer profession.

PROPOSITIONS LINKING SOCIETAL CULTURE WITH PUBLIC RELATIONS

We sum up our conceptualization linking societal culture and public relations by making the following propositions:

Proposition 1: Societal cultures that display lower levels of power distance, authoritarianism, and individualism, but have higher levels of interpersonal trust among workers, are most likely to develop the excellent public relations practices identified in this book.

Proposition 2: Although such occurrences are rare, organizations that exist in societal cultures that do not display these characteristics conducive to the spawning of excellent public relations programs also may have excellent public relations programs if the few power holders of the organization have individual personalities that foster participative organizational culture even if this culture is atypical to mainstream societal culture.

REFERENCES

Agar, M. H. (1980). *The professional stranger: An informal introduction to ethnography.* Orlando, FL: Academic.

Carlson, R. (1968). Public relations. In D. L. Sills (Ed.), *International encyclopedia of the social sciences* (pp. 208–216). London: Macmillan.

Crozier, M., & Thoening, J. C. (1976). The regulation of complex organized systems. *Administrative Science Quarterly, 21,* 547–570.

Deal, T. E., & Kennedy, A. E. (1982). *Corporate culture: The rites and rituals of corporate life.* Reading, MA: Addison-Wesley.

Grunig, J. E. (1989). Presuppositions as a framework for public relations theory. In C. H. Botan & V. Hazleton, Jr. (Eds.), *Public relations theory* (pp. 17–44). Hillsdale, NJ: Lawrence Earlbaum Associates.

Grunig, J. E., & Grunig, L. S. (1989). Toward a theory of the public relations behavior of organizations: Review of a program of research. In J. E. Grunig & L. S. Grunig (Eds.), *Public Relations Research Annual 1* (pp. 27–63). Hillsdale, NJ: Lawrence Earlbaum Associates.

Grunig, J. E., & Hunt, T. (1984). *Managing public relations.* New York: Holt, Rinehart & Winston.

Hage, J., & Hull, F. (1981). *A typology of environmental niches based on knowledge technology and scale: The implications for innovation and productivity* (Working Paper No. 1). College Park: University of Maryland:, Center for the Study of Innovation, Entrepreneurship, and Organization Strategy.

Haire, M., Ghiselli, E. E., & Porter, R. W. (1966). *Managerial thinking: An international study.* New York: Wiley.

Hall, E. T. (1959). *The silent language.* Garden City, NY: Doubleday.

Harris, M. (1968). *The rise of anthropological theory.* New York: Crowell.

Harris, M. (1979). *Cultural materialism: The struggle for a science of culture.* New York: Vintage.

Hickson, D. J., Hinings, C. R., McMillan, C. J., & Schwitter, J. P. (1974). The culture-free context of organization structure: A tri-national comparison. *Sociology, 8,* 59–80.

Hofstede, G. (1980). *Culture's consequences.* Beverly Hills, CA: Sage.

Kaplan, D., & Manners, R. A. (1972). *Culture theory.* Englewood Cliffs, NJ: Prentice-Hall.

Kluckhohn, F., & Strodtbeck, F. (1961). *Variations in value orientations.* Evanston, IL: Row, Peterson.

Martin, J., Feldman, M. S., Hatch, M. J., & Sitkin, S. B. (1983). The uniqueness paradox in organizational stories. *Administrative Science Quarterly, 28,* 438–453.

Maurice, M. (1976). Introduction: Theoretical and ideological aspects of the universalistic approach to the study of organizations. *International Studies of Management and Organization, 6,* 3–10.

Misumi, J. (1985). *The behavioral science of leadership.* Ann Arbor: University of Michigan Press.

Negandhi, A. R. (1973). *Management and economic development: The case of Taiwan.* The Hague, Netherlands: Nijhoff.

Nimkoff, M. F., & Middleton, R. (1968). Types of family and types of economy. In Y. A. Cohen (Ed.), *Man in adaptation: The cultural present.* Chicago: Aldine.

Ouchi, W. G. (1981). *Theory Z: How American business can meet the Japanese challenge.* Reading, MA: Addison-Wesley.

Pacanowsky, M. E., & O'Donnell-Trujillo, N. (1983). Organizational communication as organizational performance. *Communication Monographs, 50,* 126–147.

Pascale, R. T., & Athos, A. G. (1981). *The art of Japanese management.* New York: Simon & Schuster.

Pimlott, J. A. R. (1951). *Public relations and American democracy.* Princeton, NJ: Princeton University Press.

Robbins, S. P. (1987). *Organization theory: Structure, design, and application of organizations.* Englewood Cliffs, NJ: Prentice-Hall.

Sahlins, M. D. (1958). *Social stratification in Polynesia.* Seattle: University of Washington Press.

Schein, E. H. (1985). *Organizational culture and leadership.* San Francisco: Jossey-Bass.

Schneider [aka Grunig], L. A. (1985). *Organizational structure, environmental niches, and public relations: The Hage-Hull typology of organizations as predictor of communication behavior.* Unpublished doctoral dissertation, University of Maryland, College Park.

Shenoy, S. (1981). Organization structure and context: A replication of the Aston study in India. In D. J. Hickson & C. J. McMillan (Eds.), *Organisation and nation: The Aston programme IV* (pp. 113–154). Farnborough, Hampshire, England: Gower.

Sinha, J. B. P. (1981). *The nurturant task manager: A model of the effective executive.* Atlantic Highlands, NJ: Humanities Press.

Smircich, L. (1983). Concepts of culture and organizational analysis. *Administrative Science Quarterly, 28,* 339–358.

Smith, P. B., & Tayeb, M. (1988). Organizational structure and processes. In M. H. Bond (Ed.), *Cross-cultural challenge to social psychology.* Newbury Park, CA: Sage.

Spiro, M. E. (1966). Buddhism and economic action in Burma. *American Anthropologist, 68,* 1163.

Spradley, J. P. (1980). *Participant observation.* New York: Holt, Rinehart & Winston.

Tayeb, M. H. (1988). *Organizations and national culture: A comparative analysis.* London: Sage.

Tedlow, R. S. (1979). *Keeping the corporate image: Public relations and business 1900–1950.* Greenwich, CT: JAI.

Tichy, N. M. (1982). Managing change strategically: The technical, political, and cultural keys. *Organizational Dynamics, 11*(2), 59–80.

Triandis, H. C. (1972). *The analysis of subjective culture.* New York: Wiley.

Triandis, H. C., Bontempo, R., Villareal, M., Asai, M., Lucca, N., Betancourt, H., Bond, M. H., Leung, K., Brenes, A., Georgas, J., Hui, H., Marin, G., Setiadi, B., Sinha, J., Verma, J., Spangenberg, J., Touzard, H., & de Montmollin, G. (1986). *Individualism and collectivism: Cross-cultural perspectives on self-group relationships.* Unpublished manuscript, University of Illinois, Urbana.

White, J. (1987). *Professional development needs of UK public relations practitioners.* Institute of Public Relations.

White, J., Hammonds, L., & Kalupa, F. (1987, August). *Professional development needs of U.S. public practitioners.* Paper presented at the meeting of the Association of Education in Journalism and Mass Communication, San Antonio, TX.

White, J., & Trask, G. (1982). *Professional developmental needs of Canadian public practitioners.* Halifax, Nova Scotia. Dalhousie University, Canadian Public Relations Society and Advanced Management Centre.

Wilcox, D. L., Ault, P. H., & Agee, W. K. (1989). *Public relations: Strategies and tactics.* New York: Harper & Row.

Wilkins, A. L. (1983). The culture audit: A tool for understanding organizations. *Organizational Dynamics, 12*(2), 24–38.

Williamson, R. C. (1982). Attitudes accompanying modernization in advanced and developing societies. In L. L. Adler (Ed.), *Cross-cultural research at issue.* New York: Academic.

V

THE ECONOMIC LEVEL: WHAT PUBLIC RELATIONS AND COMMUNICATION CONTRIBUTE TO THE BOTTOM LINE

If excellence in communication management makes organizations more effective by building stable, trusting relationships with strategic publics, there should be a payoff for the organization. Part V concludes the book by discussing that payoff.

23 Estimating the Value of Public Relations and Communication to an Organization

William P. Ehling
Syracuse University

ABSTRACT

The research project for which this book was written began with the "bottom-line question": How much is excellent public relations worth to an organization? This chapter shows that few if any theorists have discussed the economic contribution that communication makes to an organization, even though many have discussed its social value. The chapter reviews theories of benefit-cost analysis to derive procedures that can be used to estimate the economic value of excellent public relations. Communication managers can use benefit-cost analysis to estimate the value of individual communication programs for strategic publics. Researchers can use benefit-cost analysis to estimate the overall value of these programs to the organization.

The logic underlying the economics of public relations focuses on the relationship between benefits and costs associated with the implementation of a public relations program. Implicit in such a benefit-cost relationship is the managerial imperative that benefits attained through a public relations program should exceed, or at least equal, its cost. Conversely, if costs exceed benefits, then the program should be either altered (to make benefits exceed costs) or discontinued.

Given this logic, the economic component of public relations management should loom large in determining the worth (specified in monetary terms) of not only a specific public relations program but also of the public relations department and its function in an organization. However, when one examines the public relations literature, including textbooks, nothing is said specifically about economic benefits or how to achieve them via public relations.

An important exception is Grunig and Hunt (1984), who review a number of economic decision-making procedures that should be employed by public relations managers. These include conventional budgeting techniques and network analysis, including the use of Gantt charts, Program Evaluation and Review Techniques (PERT), and Critical Path method (CPM), as well as benefit-cost analysis, expected-value analysis, and simplified programming.

On the whole, however, the worth of public relations frequently is discussed in terms of the *social* worth of public relations. Attempts are made to tie the social component of public relations to the so-called social responsibilities of an organization specifically and the public interest in general. (For views on this subject by Edward L. Bernays and Harwood Childs, see Simon, 1980, pp. 53–56. See also comments made about public relations as a "social philosophy" in Moore & Kalupa, 1985, pp. 7–11. See further Cutlip, Center, & Broom, 1985, p. 452; Newsom & Scott, 1981, p. 54; Reilly, 1981, pp. 6–7.)

Harwood Childs, better than most even today, saw in 1940 that public relations was "simply a name for activities that [sic] have a social significance." Childs saw that the problem in each corporation or industry is to find out what these activities are, find out what social effects they have, and if they are contrary to the public interest, find ways and means for modifying them so that they will serve the public interest.

To enunciate the social worth of public relations is one thing. To demonstrate the economic worth of these activities is another matter. The former has to lay the basis for legitimization of public relations; the latter has to provide the managerial basis for the departmentalization of these endeavors. Social and economic worth are closely bound at the organizational level, but they can be separated analytically and operationally at the managerial level. Scant attention, unfortunately, has been paid the economic side of public relations management in literature identified as "public relations body of knowledge." This literature, organized by dozens of categories and published in the spring 1988 issue of *Public Relations Review,* provides no category or listing under "economics."

Turning to public relations practitioners, silence on the subject is even more conspicuous and paradoxical. After all, in-house public relations departments operate with budgets, sometimes impressively large budgets, and public relations agencies charge sizable fees for services rendered to clients.

Such outlays for public relations activities beg an obvious managerial question: What is being accomplished in monetary terms? Answers to this question are generally muted, murky, and often misleading. In short, a review of the literature and of the practice finds no specific method in use today that relates in measurable terms the resources used (computed in costs) and economic benefits realized from public relations expenditures.

Turning to other functional areas in organizations, one finds generally that benefit-cost analysis is key to evaluating programs or projects in production, finance, marketing, and even personnel (or human resources). Paradoxically, public relations appears excluded or exempt from such economic assessment. Why should this be the case?

PUBLIC RELATIONS AND OPERATIONAL CONDITIONS

Several concepts are helpful in understanding the seeming exemption of public relations from rigorous benefits-cost analysis. The first of these, *operational reducibility,* occurs when the operational commitment to public relations is reduced from a strategically directed management endeavor to a technically driven production activity. Instead of regarding commitment to public relations as a primary function of an organization, such activities are largely reduced and confined to low-level technical production such as copy preparation and distribution.

Debit affordability refers to the inclination of chief executive officers and fiscal executives to treat money budgeted for public relations as "administrative overhead" along with other costs associated with running an organization. Such budgetary items are treated as financial "losses" and are placed on the debit side of the ledger. Under the circumstances, little or no pressure exists to deal with these debit-side expenditures in terms of return-on-investment or some kind of benefit-cost ratio principle.

Outcome intangibility is the belief that the full, long-term outcomes or benefits of public relations cannot be quantified, making it impossible to assign dollar amounts to such outcomes. Some practitioners even go so far as to maintain that public relations outcomes cannot be qualified, and, hence, are not specifically "knowable." This argument says that "doing public relations" will produce something good, but no attempt is made to clarify what this good might be, because public relations is concerned with long-term ends that are "intangibles."

Goal displacement and functional subserviency accept operational reductionism of public relations but go further. Public relations is regarded as a journalistically oriented, publicity-driven activity organized as a service unit to perform logistically defined duties for other functional areas such as marketing, finance, or personnel (human resources). As a result, public relations activity is made subservient to other functional units and ordered to pursue goals or objectives from these other units. These include sales promotion, increasing stock purchases, improving workers' morale, or increasing productivity of the labor force. The most common form of this functional subservience is the operationalization of public relations as *product publicity*. In one stroke, public relations is reduced operationally to publicity, and at the same time, it is assigned implicitly a marketing goal of increasing sales (sales promotion).

In summary, public relations is not subjected to rigorous benefits-cost analysis because management reduces public relations to low-level communication production activities which are treated simply as a "cost of doing business." Communication and public relations activities are viewed as generating no direct tangible benefits to the organization as a whole; instead they are treated as technical activities designed to support other organizational functions such as marketing, personnel, or finance. Such management conceptualizations of public relations (specifically, of the tasks and responsibilities assigned this activity) reflect a lack of sustained organizational commitment to public relations as a strategic management function. This lack of commitment, coupled with conceptual flaws, deflect both public relations practitioners and top-level executives from focusing serious attention on the economic importance of public relations and on its benefit-cost relationship.

MEETING ANTECEDENT CRITERIA AND SPECIFYING PUBLIC RELATIONS' PURPOSE

Given these four conceptualizations of public relations, several observations can be made. One observation is that the development and use of benefit-cost analysis in the evaluation of public relations programs cannot proceed until the four conditions identified earlier are confronted and the problems they pose solved. Another observation is that the question before practitioners and executives is not whether benefit-cost analysis can or cannot be applied in public relations program analysis, but whether public relations generally pursues end-states (goals, objectives) to which benefit-cost analysis cannot apply. (See the discussion of public relations without purpose in chapter 7.) If, indeed, cost-benefit analysis is to be used, then public relations end states must be appropriate, attainable, measurable, and economically worthwhile. The economic factor of worth cannot be given serious consideration until conditions of appropriateness, attainability, and measurability have been met.

Ambiguity about end states is rooted in uncertainty about the appropriate mission of public relations. With little or no agreement about the appropriate mission or purpose of public relations as a discrete management function, then almost anything can be (and usually is) substituted for public relations goals or objectives—sales, workers' morale, productivity, image, trust, consent, and attitude or opinion change.

As detailed in chapter 6, public relations technicians attempt to get around this by treating public relations as both a means and an end at the same time. For these practitioners, the business of doing public relations (treated as a means) leads to good public relations (an end). Here, the doing is the equivalent of having accomplished something, namely, the activity of doing.

Some public relations textbooks also have succumbed to confusing means with ends. By stressing the centrality of communication in public relations, textbook writers make communication the principle defining characteristic of public relations, and in the process, make communication (a means) the very end state for which one is communicating in the first place. This logic, however, leads to an interesting result. If the purpose of communication (means) is to communicate (end), then communicating (e.g., publicizing something) becomes its own reward that needs no further analysis, especially by something as sophisticated as cost-benefit analysis. Such logic can postpone dealing with what constitutes the purpose of public relations or some public relations-driven communication system. However, it cannot eliminate the question of what should one seek to attain by means of communication.

When the question of mission and end states (goals) finally is raised and confronted, the popular response is that the purpose of public relations is to persuade people to adopt the communicator's point of view. Here the practitioner seeks to change attitudes, opinions, images, impressions, or some other mental state. Communication researchers and theorists, however, repeatedly have cautioned communication practitioners not to believe that the relationship between communication (and its many configurations) and various changes in mental states is simple, direct, and powerful. To the contrary, research has shown that such mental states are not easy to change, measure, or predict. (See chapter 7 of this book. See also Galtung, 1967; Grunig & Hunt, 1984; Littlejohn, 1983; McQuail, 1983; Rice & Paisley, 1981; Severin & Tankard, 1988, Shimanoff, 1980; Smith, 1982; Tan, 1981c.)

Despite research findings to the contrary, many public relations practitioners continue to define the practice as producing communication they believe to be persuasive, to be capable of shaping, molding, influencing, altering, or changing opinions, attitudes, images, impressions, and beliefs. Such grand claims of sweeping power often are made with no effort to show how these states can be measured.

To paraphrase Berelson (1959), even if some kinds of messages may on some occasions change some kinds of mental states of some people some of the time, the question remains: Why expend so much time and energy in the name of public relations to bring about such precarious, limited, and generally unmeasured changes in attitudes, opinions, or other outcomes?

The popular answer, arising more from prevailing ideology than from facts, is that some desired behavior (e.g., the purchase of goods or the casting of votes) flows always and exactly from such mental states. Yet, the correlation between mental states and behavioral states has ranged from 0 to .3. This weak association makes one wonder why an effort is made to change these mental states in the first place (see DeFleur & Ball-Rokeach, 1982; Katz, 1987; Severin & Tankard, 1988, pp. 183–185). Nonetheless, popular practitioner ideology defines the purpose of public relations as modifying people's attitudes, opinions, or images to create desired end states.

The economics of benefit-cost analysis requires a different definition of purpose. Recent thinking about the primary mission or overall purpose of public relations has shifted. Public relations activity, according to recent thought, is treated implicitly or explicitly as a managerial and, hence, a decision-making responsibility. In the first five editions of *Effective Public Relations* by Scott M. Cutlip and Allen H. Center, public relations activity was defined as "a planned effort to influence opinion." In the sixth edition, however, Cutlip, Center, and now Glen M. Broom (1985) specified public relations as a "management function that identifies, establishes, and maintains mutually beneficial relationships between an organization and the various publics on which its success or failure depends." This shift from influencing "opinion" to establishment of "mutually beneficial relation-ships" indicates an important change in the conceptualization of the primary mission of public relations management. (The term *relationship,* however, may be far too open-ended to be helpful in giving needed specificity to this kind of end state.)

Cutlip et al.'s (1985) definition also makes no reference to communica-tion as the appropriate means for achieving mutually beneficial relation-ships. On the other hand, Grunig and Hunt (1984) are more explicit, making communication central to public relations. They also note that, historically, four kinds of public relations models have emerged—press agentry/publicity, public information, two-way asymmetrical, and two-way symmetrical. The latter model is the most recent and also the one that holds the best promise for allowing an organization to deal successfully with threats in its environment.

Communication, conceived as a two-way, dialogical message-exchange system, differs sharply in form, content, and purpose from the rather simplistic one-way press agentry/publicity effort. Hence, both the ends sought by public relations and the means used in attaining such ends have been reassessed and reformulated. Such reformulation gives public relations a different definition of purpose and a more defensible rationale for money and effort invested.

Some practitioners (Gossen & Sharp, 1987) see the primary mission of public relations as "how to manage the dispute resolution." This approach recognizes a number of important facets of relationships between the organization and its environment that are variants of public relations. Namely, a public relations setting is an interorganizational one.

This interorganizational environment is characterized by negotiation between conflicting parties, and negotiation requires extensive and extended reciprocal communications. Gossen and Sharp (1987) observed:

> Disputes involving many stakeholders and multiple issues are becoming a way of life in the business and public policy world. More importantly for public relations, a demand for "cutting edge" communications requires both more communications and expanded communication techniques. Designing and implementing processes to prevent or resolve disputes in the business/public policy arena are services beginning to be widely demanded of practitioners.

> "Dispute resolution" processes help enhance the client's ability to function successfully in a volatile environment. Designed to prevent stakeholders' interest from becoming hardened, irreconcilably positioned; the process seeks to determine and dissect the interest of divergent groups and ultimately to forge options to satisfy all interests.

> This "win-win" negotiation (also known as "integrative negotiation") is the key to lasting success in dispute resolution. Often called "creative problem-solving," this win-win modality of creating mutual gains is radically different from the "win-lose" (called "zero-sum") bargaining situation, a common negotiation mode in business-to-business transactions. (It simply means "one for me is one less for you." Such bargaining is power- or persuasion-based, with little attention paid to the other parties' wants, needs, or desires.)

> But in public policy disputes, zero-sum agreements that favor business interests over the public interest are often short-lived or are overturned by lawsuits initiated by unsatisfied public stakeholders. Win-win communication is analysis-based via its identification of, and outreach to, stakeholders by seeking to satisfy their underlying interests. The philosophies between the two bargaining positions vary as much as the process a marriage counselor employees does from that of a used car salesman unloading a lemon.

> Although the dispute resolution process is issue-based, it requires more two-way communications and program structuring techniques than does traditional issue management. It generally consists of identifying all stakeholders to the issue, gathering information and research, strategizing, conveying and facilitating any of various forums to gather direct input from stakeholders, structuring and implementing multiparty two-way communica-

tion, creative problem-solving, and negotiation to resolve the disputes surrounding the issue. (pp. 35–36)

Unlike "journalist-in-residence" public relations, dispute resolution activities create and manage the actual communication channels rather than relying on existing mass media channels. This view stands in sharp contrast to the prevailing ideology among many public relations practitioners who see themselves as especially gifted in bringing about mass persuasion of the public by cleverly crafted messages that are given wide distribution by the mass media.

Ehling (1975, 1983, 1984, 1985, 1987) argued that the primary purpose of public relations management is the "resolution of conflict" between a specific organization (called a "focal unit") and other organizations or social groupings (stakeholders) on which the focal unit depends to carry out its objectives. Hence, to have a "public relations situation," an organization must be placed in a situation that manifests actual or potential conflict. This condition constitutes one of the critical components of the situation. The other condition is that primacy is given to two-way (bilateral) institutional (interorganizational) communication as the principal and appropriate means to mediate and mitigate interparty conflict, disagreement, or dispute.

Central to the establishment of a theory of public relations management are concepts and measures derived from *purposive* systems, a critical concept in any decision-making scheme (see Ackoff & Emery, 1972; Foerster, White, Peterson, & Russell, 1968). As Ackoff and Emery showed, once the defining attributes of purposive have been identified, a quantifiable model of choice behavior, a purposeful state, can be established. Such a model allows additional measures to be developed, such as measures of information, communication, and conflict, as well as two derivatives of conflict: cooperation and exploitation (see also Ackoff, 1961; Ackoff & Sasieni, 1968).

Can this quantifiable approach be expanded further to formulate measures of utility (worthiness) in public relations? Can cost-benefit analysis be applied to the evaluation of public relations? In the next section, conflict and cooperation are quantified. The final section addresses benefit cost analysis.

Conflict and Cooperation

In Appendix A, the formal quantification of a purposeful state is provided. If you are not comfortable with mathematical notation, skip Appendix A. The explanation in the next paragraph is sufficient to continue with this chapter.

A *purposeful state* or *choice condition* is one in which there is a decision maker, several courses of action from which the decision maker may choose, several outcomes that will result from these courses of action, and a setting (milieu) in which the decision maker and the courses of action exist. To achieve the most desired outcome, we must consider the likelihood of the decision maker selecting each of the courses of action available. We also must consider the likelihood of each course of action being successfully executed. Finally, we must consider the value of each outcome. The most desired outcome is the one that is the best combination of value, likelihood of successful execution, and likelihood of being selected by the decision maker. Appendix A provides a more precise description.

Quantification of Conflict and Cooperation

In any social environment, such as an organizational environment, there are many ways to describe the effects of interaction occurring between, for example, two parties (individuals or organizations), which we call A and B. One meaningful way to talk about such interaction is in terms of the *effect* one has on the other. Such effects can be described through measures of cooperation or conflict.

Cooperation and conflict may be thought of as states located at the opposite ends of a single continuum. Cooperation and conflict are opposites and can be expressed in degrees. That is, as one moves away from the cooperation end point, the movement is toward conflict. The degree of cooperation decreases as the degree of conflict increases and vice versa. The generic meanings found in cooperation and conflict also are found in accord and discord, consensus and dissensus, agreement and disagreement, and concordance and discordance.

Appendix B provides a mathematical description of how cooperation and conflict can be quantified. If you are not comfortable with mathematical explanations, skip Appendix B. The following paragraph is sufficient to continue with this chapter.

Organization A and Public B can make choices about each other. The relationship that Organization A desires to have with Public B (and Public B with Organization A) can be called expected relative value. What is the relationship's value to the organization (or the public)? The nature of the relationship can be understood and described by considering what the situation would be like without the other party. If the expected relative value is greater to the organization if Public B is present than if Public B is absent, then Public B cooperates with Organization A. If the expected relative value is less to the organization if Public B is present than if Public B is absent, then public B conflicts with Organization A (from the organization's perspective). If the expected relative value is the same whether Public B is present or absent, then Organization A and Public B are independent of each other. We can assign numbers to states of complete cooperation ($+1$), complete conflict (-1), and complete independence (0). We can use the range of numbers between -1 and $+1$ to describe the degree of cooperation/conflict between Organization A and Public B, from the organization's perspective. Looking at the same relationship from Public B's perspective, the same range of number (-1 to $+1$) can be used to describe the degree of cooperation/conflict. The degree of cooperation may shift, depending on perspective. From Organization A's perspective, Public B may be seen as somewhat cooperative (e.g., $+5$). From Public B's perspective, Organization A may be seen as conflicting with Public B (e.g., -5). This describes a situation of mixed or unequal exploitation. If the relationship yields negative numbers from both perspectives (organization and public), then the relationship can be described as exploitive. If both are positive, the relationship is cooperative.

In public relations, a course of action may be a communication program. For example, we find a well-specified communication activity—a course of action—among many that are available to the decision maker, the public relations manager. Communication, of course, may produce a variety of outcomes, some of which have little to do with public relations (e.g., product advertising). An important set of outcomes that uniquely define a public relations *situation* are interrelationship states. These states or conditions can be expressed as degrees of conflict or cooperation between an organization and other organizations or social groupings.

Given these differing degrees of conflict or cooperations, the decision maker (public relations manager), reflecting the general aims of the organization, can place value on these outcome states, using a utility–disutility scale whose measures are percentages of preferences. Efficiencies may be measured on a number of different scales, including—ideally—various monetary scales.

Frequently, however, the nature of the problem precludes using a monetary scale. When this is the case, a more general scale may be used: a probability scale. In such an event, efficiencies are specified in probability terms. That is, efficiency of a course of action is the probability or likelihood that the course of action will achieve a designated outcome. When all these numerical values are multiplied together, the expected relative value of a choice situation is stated as a probability.

These measures may be employed over time to measure the degree of escalation (or de-escalation) of conflict or cooperation. One generally hears of an escalation (or de-escalation) of conflict but rarely about the escalation (or de-escalation) of cooperation. The latter condition, however, prevails just as often as the former.

Let us now take a situation in which actual or potential conflict exists between Organization A and Public B. The question arises as to how serious such a conflict may be. Will such conflict (actual or potential) be disruptive? If so, will the disruption be costly?

To answer these questions we must determine the disutility or negative value such conflict brings in the short or long run. We also need a transformation function, a formula that can change the negative value to a natural measure of dollar costs (or benefits). This can be done in three steps.

Appendix C provides a detailed explanation of steps required to convert negative values or disutility into dollar measures. However, this explanation involves mathematical notations and symbols. If you are not comfortable with such material, skip Appendix C. The paragraph that follows provides you with sufficient information to continue with the chapter.

To determine dollar costs or benefits, conflict between an organization and a public must be quantified as outlined previously. Degrees of conflict can be converted to corresponding values of disunity or dissatisfaction. See Appendix C for references useful in making such conversions. Because episodes of conflict occur over time, and the disunity they cause accumulate over time, a rough measure is required of the instances of conflict over a period of time (e.g., 1 year). Finally, a mathematical transformation (a formula) is needed to change a given subjective state of dissatisfaction into a dollar figure. In order to transform feelings of dissatisfaction into dollars, a method known as *compensating variation* is used. The concept and methods are set forth in detail in Hicks (1943), Huber (1980), and Thompson (1980). In addition, conditions that justify measuring program attributes based on willingness to pay are set forth by Keeney and Raiffa (1976). General introductions to benefit cost analysis are found in Pliskin and Taylor (1977) and Sugden and Williams (1978). Additional sources on evaluation research are found in Patton (1978), Rutman (1984), Morris and Fitz-Gibbon (1978), and Alkin and Solomon (1983).

Compensating Variation and Cost-Benefit Analysis

Compensating variation may be used with both future and past situations. When the decision maker plans a communication program, he or she tries to select the best alternative course of action or program for future implementation. When the decision maker evaluates program impact, he or she attempts to determine whether a previously executed program of action achieved its goals and objectives. The technique of compensating variation may be used as part of future-oriented research that Ackoff (1962) called "development" and Grunig and Hunt (1984) called "formative." It also may be used as part of conventional fact-gathering and assessment research that both Ackoff (1962) and Grunig and Hunt (1984) called "evaluative."

As Thompson (1980, p. 39) noted, a *benefit* in general terms occurs whenever a party is favorably affected by a program. A party in this case may be a single individual or a group of individuals, such as several executives or leaders working together. *Cost* (or *disbenefit*) occurs whenever a party is unfavorably affected.

Monetary effects, in turn, easily are set as the amount of money gained or lost by those affected. However, monetary valuation, although often a good approximation, is not the same as — nor can it be directly substituted for — a decision maker's utility or subjective valuation. In short, monetary valuation is limited as a direct measure of subjective valuation, which is usually the basis for individual decision making. Nonetheless, conversion to a monetary scale is desired whenever possible, because dollar values allow for ease of manipulation and calculation. In many instances, as with investments in the stock or bond market, both benefits and costs are specified in monetary terms, making evaluation straightforward.

In the case of nonmonetary effects, on the other hand, the problem is finding a method to convert such nonmonetary effect (sometimes termed intangibles) into monetary terms. Once so converted, various nonmonetary effects can be compared directly to monetary effects, as well as to each other. Such transformation allows appropriate comparisons to be made among many types of effects, giving each its proper importance in decision making.

This transformation is not always easy. At the same time, the transformation is neither impossible nor impractical. Difficulty, unfortunately encourages analysts to avoid even attempting such a transformation. The drawback to such avoidance, Thompson (1980) noted, is that "nonmonetary effects are often critical, and failure to quantify them even crudely may lead in decision-making either to overlooking them or to haphazardly allowing them too great or too small an influence" (p. 40).

Compensating variations (CV) theoretically provides an optimal solution to placing dollar value on communication program effects. Mishan (1976) provided the following specification:

> A compensating variation (CV) is 1) for a program beneficiary, the amount of money he could pay so that, with the program and having paid this money, he would be just as well off as without the program and without payment, and 2) for a person made worse off by a program, the amount of money he would have to be paid so that, with the program and the payment, he would be just as well off as without the program and the payment. CVs are taken to be positive for gainers and negative for losers. (p. 41)

For example, a communication manager at Organization A spends considerable time and energy maintaining a program of service directed at Public B in order to sustain a harmonious (nonconflict, nonadversarial) relationship. The annual benefit to the top decision maker of Organization A would be equal to the money that could be taken from Organization A each year and leave the decision maker indifferent about continuing or discontinuing efforts toward a harmonious relationship. This dollar figure is the top decision maker's *break-even* point, where the cost of communication is equal to the subjective benefits of cooperation and harmony with Public A. If the communication program were to cost more, the decision maker may decide that disharmony and conflict are less costly than a communication program that reduces such conflict. If serious disagreement and conflict break out between Organization A and Public B, the concern is cost. The compensating variation method states that such cost is the amount of money a top decision maker in Organization A would be willing to pay to implement a communication program to achieve the same subjective break-even point, the point where the decision maker would be indifferent to executing or not executing the communication program.

Although the logic underlying CV is relatively easy to grasp, dollar valuation is not always easy to estimate or assign. Hence, one drawback of CV is the difficulty of measurement. Thompson (1980) pointed out that difficulty arises because "people have not thought through how much they would pay for nonmonetary effects, and if questioned, give haphazard, inconsistent answers" (p. 41). Another drawback is the insensitivity of CVs to what is called the "distribution" problem, or the problem of distributional equity, a condition whereby all parties affected by the program are fairly treated or compensated.

The alternatives of CV, however, are even more unsatisfactory. We have discussed the drawback of a nonmonetary (or, more generally, a nonquantification) approach in decision making. Another option is a valuing technique called *shadow prices,* the direct assignment of value to a good not traded in the market. The drawback here is the unwarranted assumption that true value can be estimated from actual prices paid for similar goods in different situations. For example, the value of water when it is available is assumed equal to the value of water when it is not available, according to shadow pricing. The rationale for CV, on the other hand, is that there should be, in most cases, certain amounts of money that actual gainers would pay for their benefits or that would compensate actual losers for their disbenefits.

We proceed on the assumption that most communication and public relations program effects can be quantified by using compensating variations techniques. Programs are projects or courses of action that, from the public relations management perspective, could be grouped under the heading communication, or more specifically, identified as an interparty negotiational effort directed at producing accord, cooperation, or agreement.

The concept of compensating variations leads to an eight-step method to conduct cost-benefit analysis, based on the best methodologies currently available (Thompson, 1980, p. 47):

1. Identify the decision-makers and their basic concerns.
2. Identify alternative programs of action available to the decision-makers.
3. Identify costs, including program expenses and all unwelcome disbenefits.
4. Identify benefits, including both direct and indirect benefits.
5. Assign monetary values to the program's effects.
6. Discount if effects occur at different times (if all effects occur at the same time, discounting is not needed).
7. Take into account, when appropriate, the distributional equity effects.
8. Aggregate and interpret the resultant valued effects.

Steps 1 and 2 establish the conditions under which CV is to be determined. Core to the method are Steps 3 through 6. Steps 7 and 8 introduce the distributional concerns that often, for practical reasons, cannot be handled numerically. Frequently, the methodology is divided into two parts. The first part, Steps 1 through 6, is dealt with separately, and the results are examined for their importance. The second part, Steps 7 and 8, then is examined to determine how to handle the problem of equity or fairness. This separation reflects the general distinction made between program *efficiency* and program *fairness* and the frequent necessity to balance the two in the final decision.

The first six steps, however, allow one to calculate present-valued net benefits (PVNB). These benefits equal the total of all program effects, positive or negative, summed over all parties affected by the program and over all *categories* of program effects. This is expressed algebraically in Appendix D.

Several objections may be raised to the formulation in Appendix D. First, compensating variation may not be additive. Second, there is no consensus appropriate discount rate. Although both objections may be raised in some cases, Thompson (1980, p. 51) argued that, for most cost-benefit analyses, these objections are not serious considerations.

More important than these objections is the need for overall accuracy in the identification and valuation of individual effects. If such accuracy is achieved, then the formulation in Appendix D is both appropriate and adequate to evaluate the efficiency of public relations programs.

Interpreting Cost-Benefit Calculations

Once costs and benefits of a communication program have been calculated, one still must interpret the figures, If we let the positive compensating variations denote benefits, B, and the sum of all the negative CVs as costs, C, then the relationship between benefits and costs can be expressed in two ways. One is called simply *net benefit,* determined by subtracting costs from benefits, that is, B − C. The other expression is a *benefit-cost ratio,* computed by dividing the cost into the benefits, that is, B/C.

Communication and public relations decision makers usually face three different situations. The first situation involves deciding between spending resources on a public relations program and not doing so, a "go/no-go" decision. A second situation is one where a decision must be made among mutually exclusive, competing public relations programs, a decision as to which is "best" to implement. Finally, decision makers might select from a large set of programs the best subset that will stay within a fixed budget allocation.

In each case, which of the two — net benefits or benefit-cost ratio — ought to be used? Sometimes differences are good decision guides, sometimes quotients are, and sometimes neither is. What general rules help interpret cost and benefit figures for decision-making purposes? If the situation involves a go/no-go decision, the decision maker may use either the net benefit or the benefit-cost ratio. If managers must pick one of several mutually exclusive alternative programs (or projects), decision makers ought to use net benefit. If managers must decide about programs to complete a roster of a fixed total budget, the decision maker ought to use the benefit-cost ratio.

For example, a communication budget allocation has been set at $500,000. The department has identified a number of communication programs or projects that ought to be implemented over the next year, but implementation costs of all programs far exceed the fixed budget allocation. Which programs, then, should the department implement? Benefit-cost ratios of each program suggest a solution. First choose the program with the highest ratio, then the one with the next highest, and so on until the fixed budget allocation is fully used.

Neither the net benefits nor the benefit-cost ratio work adequately in some situations. These situations are ones in which a decision must be made about alternative projects where all unspent money can go to other, underfunded projects. In such situations "opportunity costs" are manifest. Such situations are not well understood nor widely recognized. Such decisions require an alternative strategy to net benefit or benefit-cost ratios.

Another aspect of benefit-cost analysis in program evaluation involves the number of issues and the number of parties involved in a dispute or conflict. Raiffa (1982) dealt with negotiations in conflict situations, classifying them into three general categories: (a) two parties and one issue (about which there is disagreement), (b) two parties and many issues, and (c) many parties and many issues. Raiffa reviewed the various strategies that may be employed in these differing situations. For more information about multiparty, multiissue evaluation, see Raiffa.

In addition, decisions must be made under varying informational conditions. These conditions specify four kinds of decision making: (a) decision making under certainty, (b) decision making under risk, (c) decision making under uncertainty, and (d) decision making under conflict. For information about dealing with these varying conditions, see Miller and Starr (1960), Luce and Raiffa (1957), and Kaufmann (1963, 1968). Finally, within the framework of traditional benefit-cost analysis, attention needs to be directed at the Kaldor–Hicks criterion for public decision making.

Kaldor–Hicks Criterion for Public Decision Making

Using the CV technique, we sum all CVs — both positive and negative. Such calculation may show that (a) the sum is positive; this generally means that gainers from the program could fully compensate all losers from the program (so that no party feels worse off with the program than without it), and some gainers would remain better off with the program. Or, (b) the sum may be negative; this means that payments could not be arranged without having at least one party worse off with the program.

The Kaldor–Hicks criterion for a public (or interparty) decision simply states that a positive sum of the CVs is a necessary and sufficient condition for executing such programs. This criterion specifically applies to a program designed to attain, maintain, or enhance cooperation or agreement in a public relations situation. This is a technical way of describing the rationale to implement a program to bring about a "win-win" condition. All programs meeting the Kaldor–Hicks criterion are also *potential Pareto improvements* (pPis). Such programs are an extension of the economic concept of Pareto improvement, defined as any change that makes at least one person better off and no one worse off (see Thompson, 1980, pp. 42-43). In more technical terms, a potential Pareto improvement (pPi) is any change that, with suitable hypothetical redistributions, makes at least one person or party better off and no one worse off. Such a pPi is obtained whenever the net sum of the CVs is positive.

CONCLUSION

To summarize, we note that little serious effort has been made in public relations and communication management to establish accountability in economic terms. Several factors block such accountability, even though many practitioners have called for such accountability. To achieve economic accountability, expressed in terms of benefit-cost analysis of public relations programs, several steps first must be taken to reformulate and institutionalize the primary mission of public relations management and offset current emphasis on technical tasks (e.g., marketing support). Such reformulation requires a socially defensible mission as well as one that is organizationally relevant and capable of being quantified. This primary mission can be established by drawing on four theoretical systems—interorganizational theory, decision-management theory, conflict resolution theory, and communication theory.

With quantification of public relations' primary end state—the maximization through communication of the difference between cooperation and conflict such that cooperation becomes the prime benefit—the methods and techniques of benefit-cost analysis can be brought to the evaluation of all public relations programs. To be public relations programs, their principal aim must be to attain, maintain, or enhance accord (cooperation, agreement, consensus) between an organization and its environment.

These end states (attaining, maintaining, or enhancing accord) can be valuated by assigning utilities to the various degrees of achievement and by converting these utilities to monetary equivalents. Compensating variations CVs provide a methodology that establishes and measures such equivalents. These CVs, when positive and summed, meet the Kaldor–Hicks criterion for making public relations decisions—an economically and socially justifiable criterion for enacting or continuing public relations interparty negotiational communication programs.

APPENDIX A:
QUANTIFICATION OF A PURPOSEFUL STATE

What is developed here is derived primarily from Ackoff and Emery (1972) whose conceptualization rests on a decision-making paradigm, or more specifically, on the nature of a "purposeful system." Such a system is specified by several components and parameters.

A *purposeful state* is a state of a potential decision maker, who may be a single person or a group of persons, such as the dominant coalition of an organization. This state consists of four parts (components) and three boundaries (parameters) (see Ackoff & Emery, pp. 39–42). A purposeful state also may be called a *choice situation* in which a potential decision maker meets all the conditions to be able to make a choice.

The four components are a potential decision maker, D, available courses of action, C_j, possible outcomes, O_j, and the environment or social milieu,

M, in which choices can be made. The three parameters are the *probabilities* of D selecting each of the available courses of action, P, the *efficiencies* of the courses of action for each outcome, E_{ij}, and the *utility* or value (preference) of the outcomes for the decision maker, U_j.

These components and parameters now may be combined to yield an argument of a decision maker's purposeful state, PS, that must be some function, f, of P_j, E_{ij}, and U_j. That is,

$$PS = f(P_i, E_{ij}, U_j) \tag{1}$$

As Ackoff and Emery (1972, p. 143) noted, the nature of the function, f, depends on the specification of the state's value. This value may be designated as expected return, expected gain, or expected loss. One meaningful way, however, to express the PS in numerical terms is to make PS equal to the expected relative numerical value, EV, which, in turns, is equal to the double sum of the product of the three parameters. This is,

$$PS = EV = \sum_{i=1}^{m} \sum_{j=1}^{n} P_i E_{ij} U_j \tag{2}$$

APPENDIX B:
QUANTIFYING COOPERATION AND CONFLICT

Equation 2 in Appendix A allows us to express a purposeful state, PS, in terms of an expected relative value, EV. This terminology and measure can be used now to develop additional measures of cooperation and conflict and other derivatives.

Consider now two individuals or units, A and B, in a potentially choice-making situation, M. Using the conceptualization set forth by Ackoff and Emery (1972, pp. 197–207), let (EV_A/B) represent the expected relative value of A in A's choice situation when B is present in it. Let (EV_A/B') represent this value when B is not present. By the same token, (EV_B/A) and (EV_B/A') are the corresponding expected relative values for B.

As Ackoff and Emery (1972) noted, we now can operationalize cooperation, conflict, and independence as follows:

In a particular milieu, M, if:

1. $(EV_A/B) > (EV_A/B')$, then it can be said that B cooperates with A.
2. $(EV_A/B) < (EV_A/B')$, then it can be said that B conflicts with A.
3. $(EV_A/B) = (EV_A/B')$, then A is independent of B.

We now can turn to the specification of the *degree* of cooperation or conflict. The degree of cooperation of B with A can be expressed as

$$DC_{BA} = (EV_A/B) - (EV_A/B') \tag{3}$$

In turn, the degree of conflict of B with A is expressed as

$$DC_{BA} = -DC_{BA} \tag{4}$$

These measurements can take on values from -1 to $+1$. Negative values of the degree of cooperation represent conflict and vice versa. Cooperation and conflict exhaust the ways one party can affect the expective relative values (EVs) of another.

The relationship of cooperation or conflict between two parties need not be equal. That is, the two parties may affect each other differently. The measure of this difference is a measure of exploitation. Hence, the degree to which one party (B) exploits another (A) is

$$DX_{BA} = DC_{AB} - DC_{AB} \tag{5}$$

and the degree to which A exploits B is

$$DX_{AB} = 1 - DX_{BA} = DC_{BA} - DC_{AB} \tag{6}$$

This measure can range from -2 to $+2$. It allows one to distinguish three kinds of exploitation. If DC_{AB} and DC_{BA} are both positive but unequal, then the two parties cooperate but unequally. If DC_{AB} and DC_{BA} are both negative but unequal, then A and B are in conflict with each other but unequally. And if one party cooperates with the other, but the other is in conflict with the first party, then we have a case of mixed and unequal exploitation.

The degree of exploitation, then, is the *difference* between the degree of conflict of A with B and B with A. The *sum* of these degrees also has significance because these degrees measure the *intensity* of cooperation (or conflict). Hence, the intensity of cooperation (conflict) between two parties who cooperate or conflict with each other is the sum of the degree of cooperation or conflict between them.

The intensity of cooperation (IC) between two parties is

$$IC = DC_{BA} + DC_{AB} \tag{7}$$

and the intensity of conflict between two parties who conflict with each other is

$$IC' = (-DC_{BA}) + (-DC_{AB}) \tag{8}$$

The sum has meaning if and only if A and B are in cooperation or conflict with each other. Negative values stand for intensity of conflict, and positive values stand for intensity of cooperation. Minimum and maximum values are -2 and $+2$, respectively.

We can have a condition where $DC_{AB} = DC_{BA}$, but when this equality is different from zero, meaning that there is no exploitation, there may be an intensity of cooperation or conflict. In other words, intensity can increase as exploitation decreases, and exploitation can increase as intensity decreases. On the other hand, they may increase or decrease together, the measures make this explicit.

APPENDIX C:
QUANTIFYING DISUTILITY IN MONETARY FORM

By utilizing the scheme of a purposeful state as specified in Appendix B, values are assigned to the various degrees of conflict, that is,

$$U_j(DC'_j) \tag{9}$$

For every degree of conflict, DC'_j, there is a matching value of disutility (dissatisfaction or negative preference), U_j.

A number of ways of measuring or approximating utility (including disutility) exists. Ackoff (1962) listed the von Neuman–Morgenstern measure of utility, the Davidson–Siegel–Suppes measure of utility, the Churchman–Ackoff approximate measure of value, and the Case measure of relative value.

The value set, U, may be decomposed into two subsets, one including positive values and one including negative values. All negatively signed values, U'_j, are associated with the various degrees of conflict, DC'_j. All positively signed values, U_j, are assigned to various degrees of cooperation, C_i.

Second, a time period is specified that has relevance to the decision maker. This time period may be weeks, months, or years. During such a period, instances of conflict (in contrast to instances of cooperation or independence) need to be determined.

Third, a transformation function like f^* must be designated to allow a subjective state of disutility (dissatisfaction, negative preference) to be converted into monetary value, that is,

$$\text{Dollars} = f^*(U) \tag{10}$$

Thus, dollar costs can be matched with the values of disutility (dissatisfaction, negative preference), that is,

$$\text{Dollar costs} = f^*(U'_j) \tag{11}$$

See Patton (1978), Rutman (1984), Morris and Fitz-Gibbon (1978), and Alkin and Solomon (1983) for further information.

APPENDIX D:
QUANTIFYING PRESENT-VALUED NET BENEFITS

$$PVNBs = \sum_{i=1}^{n} \sum_{j=1}^{m} \frac{CV_{ij}}{(1 + d)^{l_{ij}}} \tag{12}$$

where:

PVNBs = the present-valued net benefits,

CV_{ij} = the compensating variation of the jth category of effect on the ith party,

d = the discount rate (when applicable),

l_{ij} = the number of years until the ith person is affected by the j^h kind of effect,

m = the number of different categories of effect (e.g., effects on a party as manufacturer,

taxpayer, community "citizen," contributor to the performing arts, etc.),

n = the number of parties affected by the program.

REFERENCES

Ackoff, R. L. (1962). *Scientific method.* New York: Wiley.

Ackoff, R. L. (Ed.). (1961). *Progress in operations research* (Vol. 1). New York: Wiley.

Ackoff, R. L., & Emery, F. E. (1972). *On purposeful systems.* Chicago: Aldine-Atherton.

Ackoff, R. L., & Sasieni, M. W. (1968). *Fundamentals of operations research.* New York: Wiley.

Alkin, M. C., & Solomon L. C. (Eds.). (1983). *The cost of evaluation.* Beverly Hills, CA: Sage.

Berelson, B. (1959). The state of communication research. *Public Opinion Quarterly, 23,* 1–6.

Childs, H. (1940). *An introduction to public opinion.* New York: Wiley.

Cutlip, S. H., Center, A. H., & Broom, G. M. (1985). *Effective public relations* (6th ed.). Englewood Cliffs, NJ: Prentice-Hall.

DeFleur, M. L., & Ball-Rokeach, S. (1982). *Theories of mass communication* (4th ed.). New York: Longman.

Ehling, W. P. (1975). PR administration, management science, and purposive systems. *Public Relations Review, 1*(2), 15–42.

Ehling, W. P. (1983, August). *Application of decision theory in the construction of a theory of public relations management.* Paper presented at the meeting of the Association for Education in Journalism and Mass Communication, Corvallis, OR.

Ehling, W. P. (1984). Applications of decision theory in the construction of a theory of public relations management, I. *Public Relations Research and Education, 1,* 25–38.

Ehling, W. P. (1985). Applications of decision theory in the construction of a theory of public relations management, II. *Public Relations Research and Education, 2,* 4–22.

Ehling, W. P. (1987, May). *Public relations function and adversarial environments.* Paper presented at the meeting of the International Communication Association, Montreal.

Foerster, V. H., White, H. D., Peterson, L. J., & Russell, J. K. (1968). *Purposive systems.* New York: Spartan.

Galtung, J. (1967). *Theory and methods of social research.* New York: Columbia University Press.

Gossen, R., & Sharp, K. (1987). How to manage dispute resolution. *Public Relations Journal, 43,* 35–38.

Grunig, J. E., & Hunt, T. (1984). *Managing public relations.* New York: Holt, Rinehart & Winston.

Hicks, J. R. (1943). The four consumer surpluses. *Review of Economic Studies, 9,* 31–41.

Huber, G. P. (1980). *Managerial decision making.* Glenview, IL: Scott, Foresman.

Katz, E. (1987). Communication research since Lazarsfeld. *Public Opinion Quarterly, 51*(4), 25–45.

Kaufmann, A. (1963). *Methods and models of operations research.* Englewood Cliffs, NJ: Prentice-Hall.

Kaufmann, A. (1968). *The science of decision making.* New York: McGraw-Hill.

Keeney, R. L., & Raiffa, H. (1976). *Decision with multiple objectives: Preferences and value trade-offs.* New York: Wiley.

Littlejohn, S. W. (1983). *Theories of human communication* (2nd ed.). Belmont, CA: Wadsworth.

Luce, R. D., & Raiffa, H. (1957). *Games and decisions: Introduction and critical survey.* New York: Wiley.

McQuail, D. (1983). *Mass communication theory.* Beverly Hills, CA: Sage.

Miller, D. W., & Starr, M. K. (1960). *Executive decision and operations research.* Englewood Cliffs, NJ: Prentice-Hall.

Mishan, E. J. (1976). *Cost-benefit analysis.* New York: Praeger.

Moore, H. F., & Kalupa, F. B. (1985). *Public relations, principles, cases and problems.* Homewood, IL: Irwin.

Morris, L. L., & Fitz-Gibbon, C. T. (1978). *How to measure program implementation.* Beverly Hills, CA: Sage.

Newsom, D., & Scott, A. (1981). *This is PR: The realities of public relations* (2nd ed.). Belmont, CA: Wadsworth.

Patton, M. Q. (1978). *Utilization-focused evaluation,* Beverly Hills, CA: Sage.

Pliskin, N., & Taylor, A. K. (1977). General principles: Cost-benefits and decision analysis. In J. P. Buner, B. A. Barnes, & F. Mosteller (Eds.), *Cost, risks, and benefits of surgery* (pp. 5–27). New York: Oxford University Press.

Raiffa, H. (1982). *The art and science of negotiation.* Cambridge, MA: Harvard University Press.

Reilly, R. (1981). *Public relations in action.* Englewood Cliffs, NJ: Prentice-Hall.

Rice, R. E., & Paisley, W. J. (1981). *Public communication campaigns.* Beverly Hills, CA: Sage.

Rutman, L. (Ed.). (1984). *Evaluation research methods: A basic guide* (2nd ed.). Beverly Hills CA: Sage.

Severin, W. J., & Tankard, J. W., Jr. (1988). *Communication theories* (2nd ed.). New York: Longman.

Shimanoff, S. B. (1980). *Communication rules: Theory and research.* Beverly Hills, CA: Sage.

Simon, R. (1980). *Public relations concepts and practices* (2nd ed.). Columbus, OH: Grid.

Smith, M. J. (1982). *Persuasion and human action.* Belmont, CA: Wadsworth.

Sugden, R., & Williams, A. (1978). *The principles of practical benefit-cost analysis.* London: Oxford University Press.

Tan, A. S. (1981). *Mass communication theories and research.* Columbus, OH: Grid.

Thompson, M. S. (1980). *Benefit-cost analysis for program evaluation.* Beverly Hills, CA: Sage.

Author Index

639

469, 470, 473, 474, 476, 480, 488, 501,
537, 559, 560, 562, 563, 564, 565, 574,
584, 594, 610, 613
Roberts, K. H., 539, 548, 565, 571, 572,
574
Robertson, T. S., 141, 155
Robinson, E. J., 162, 184, 336, 337, 354
Robinson, R. B., Jr., 119, 120, 121, 155
Roethlisberger, F. J., 538, 574
Rogers, D., 74, 88
Rogers, D. P., 556, 571
Rogers, E. M., 141, 142, 155, 279, 284
Rohner, R. P., 580, 594
Roloff, M. E., 384, 393
Roos, L. L., Jr., 77, 89
Rosenblum, J. W., 117, 119, 122, 156
Rosengren, K. E., 165, 184, 384, 393
Rosenthal, H., 487, 501
Roser, C., 136, 151
Rothe, J. T., 360, 391
Rothschild, M. L., 136, 156
Rudolph, B., 433, 434, 437
Ruh, R. A., 424, 437
Ruhl, M., 51, 64
Russell, H. M., 70, 87, 470, 479
Russell, J. K., 624, 638
Rutman, L., 627, 637, 638
Ryan, M., 209, 215, 295, 323, 527, 530,
560, 563, 570
Sachdeva, P. S., 411, 415
Sahlins, M. D., 604, 613
Salancik, G. R., 67, 68, 69, 77, 78, 80, 81,
89, 93, 104, 107, 126, 155
Salmon, C. T., 136, 156
Sandler, B. R., 427, 437
Sandman, P. M., 315, 317, 318, 320, 322,
324
Sasieni, M. W., 252, 253, 257, 260, 267,
282, 284, 384, 390, 393, 624, 637
Sathe, V., 583, 585, 595
Scanlan, T. J., 101, 108
Schaffer, R. H., 330, 352
Schall, M. S., 589, 590, 595
Schein, E. H., 330, 354, 581, 583, 584, 592,
595, 600, 613
Schelling, T. C., 278, 284
Schneck, R. E., 78, 88, 485, 500
Schneider, B., 540, 549, 550, 551, 552, 564,
574
Schneider (aka Grunig), L. A., 34, 62, 64,
72, 73, 74, 76, 89, 139, 156, 287, 293,
294, 298, 304, 305, 324, 403, 404, 405,

406, 414, 417, 471, 472, 480, 488, 501,
599, 613
Schnelling, T. C., 384, 393
Schramm, W., 256, 284
Schroenherr, R. A., 470, 479
Schwartz, D. F., 148, 156
Schwartz, G., 377, 386, 393
Schwartz, H. M., 585, 595
Schwitter, J. P., 601, 612
Scott, A., 329, 330, 354, 618, 638
Scott, W. R., 71, 74, 78, 86, 89, 260, 283,
384, 386, 391, 392
Scrimger, J., 422, 437
Seashore, S. E., 72, 90
Seitel, F. P., 256, 284
Sereno, K. K., 384, 393
Sethi, P., 383, 393
Setiadi, B., 607, 613
Severin, W. J., 384, 393, 621, 622, 638
Shapere, D., 34, 37, 64, 546, 574
Shapiro, B. P., 128, 129, 132, 134, 151
Sharp, K., 178, 180, 183, 267, 283, 313,
322, 373, 389, 391, 460, 464, 623, 638
Sharpe, M. L., 477, 480
Shatshat, H. M., 533, 534, 569, 574
Shaw, D., 164, 184
Shaw, M. E., 560, 574
Shayon, D. R., 489, 500
Shenoy, S., 601, 613
Sherif, C. W., 136, 156, 174, 184
Sherif, M., 136, 156, 174, 184
Shimanoff, S. B., 621, 638
Shocker, A. D., 134, 156
Shrimp, T. A., 376, 377, 393
Siegerdt, G., 548, 556, 570
Siehl, C., 582, 586, 588, 594, 595
Siemens, N., 259, 260, 267, 284, 384, 393
Silva, M. A., 222, 223, 232, 234, 237, 238,
249
Silverman, D., 99, 107
Silvis, D., 569, 574
Simon, H. A., 73, 89, 99, 105, 106, 107,
342, 354, 406, 417, 469, 480, 485, 501
Simon, R., 618, 638
Simpson, I. H., 328, 354, 425, 437
Simpson, R. L., 328, 354, 425, 437
Sims, D., 94, 104, 106
Sims, H. P., Jr., 551, 572
Sinha, J. B. P., 601, 607, 613
Sitkin, S. B., 582, 587, 588, 589, 594, 600,
612
Slama, M. E., 136, 156

Subject Index